Advanced PowerBuilder 4® Techniques

D. Derrik Deyhimi

David Scott Heath

David Mosley

A Wiley—QED Publicaiton

John Wiley & Sons, Inc.

New York • Chichester • Brisbane • Toronto • Singapore

Publisher: Katherine Schowalter
Editor: Robert Elliot
Managing Editor: Micheline Frederick
Text Design & Composition: Publishers' Design and Production Services

Designations used by companies to distinguish their products are often claimed as trademarks. In all instances where John Wiley & Sons, Inc. is aware of a claim, the product names appear in initial capital or all capital letters. Readers, however, should contact the appropriate companies for more complete information regarding trademarks and registration.

The contents of the disk included with this book are solely for use by the owner of the book and are not for resale or commercial distribution. In addition, the tools and utilities provided with the book are to be used at the discretion of the book owner, with no expressed or implied warranty from the publisher or the authors.

Screen shots reprinted with premission from Microsoft Corporation.
All Oracle documentation reproduced herein are Copyright © Oracle Corporation 1992. All rights reserved.
This text is printed on acid-free paper.

Library of Congress Cataloging-in-Publication Data:

ISBN (pbk) 0471-04989-1

Printed in the United States of America
10 9 8 7 6 5 4 3 2 1

The authors would like to dedicate this book
to their family and friends.

Derrik Deyhimi would like to offer a special dedication
to his grandfather Bijan Gillanshah.

Trademark Acknowledgments

PowerBuilder, PowerMaker, and PowerView are trademarks of Powersoft Corporation. IBM PC DOS, IBM PCs, and IBM OS/2 are trademarks of IBM Corporation.

Windows NT, MS-DOS, MS-Word, MS-Excel, OLE, MAPI, MS-Mail, and MS Windows are trademarks of Microsoft Corporation.

cc:Mail and Lotus Notes are trademarks of Lotus Development Corporation.

Oracle and Oracle7 are trademarks of Oracle Corporation.

Macintosh is a trademark of Apple Computer, Incorporated.

Other trademarked names appear throughout this book. Rather than list the names and entities that own the additional trademarks or insert a trademark symbol with each mention of the trademarked name, the publisher states that it is using the names only for editorial purposes and to the benefit of the trademark owner, with no intention of infringing upon that trademark. In all instances where John Wiley and Sons, Inc. is aware of a claim, product names appear in initial capital or all capital letters. Readers, however, should contact the appropriate companies for more complete information regarding trademarks and registration.

Acknowledgments

The authors would like to thank a number of people who provided understanding and assistance in the preparation of this book. First and foremost, we thank our family and friends for putting up with us during the writing effort. We also thank the management of BSG for supporting us throughout the entire process, especially David Debbs for helping to get the book kicked off and Steve Guengerich for his work to make the book a reality.

Special thanks also go to Ginny Green, Cydney Berry, and Tod Knight for their invaluable assistance in editing the manuscript. We thank them for their time and hard work, as we thank Kathleen Saux for her dedicated service in coordinating the complex effort of a team who never seemed to be in the same city at the same time.

We particularly thank Cyrus Deyhimi for testing the tools, Ray Letulle and Keith Meurer for providing sample code and Eric Reed for providing his white paper on the subject of PowerBuilder inheritance. We also thank Bob Cave for his work in the design and development of the tab-folder modules.

Bob Zurek of Powersoft has been especially helpful to us. In addition to reviewing the manuscript, Bob served as a key contact regarding PowerBuilder 4, and made the PowerBuilder 4 beta version available to us. We are extremely appreciative to Bob for his help and to Powersoft in general.

About the Authors

D. Derrik Deyhimi

Derrik Deyhimi is a Senior Technical Manager with Business Solutions, Inc. in Houston, TX. Derrik has over seven years of experience in the design and implementation of departmental and enterprise wide applications and architectures using distributed technologies. Derrik has been designing and developing PowerBuilder applications and architectures since the beta release of PowerBuilder 1.0. Derrik's specialty is in the design of client/server application architectures. Derrik is in the process of writing another book on ODBC for C/C++ developers. During his career he has worked with companies in a variety of industries, including manufacturing, financial services, transportation, healthcare, and petrochemical. Derrik received his BA from the University of Texas in Austin and his MBA from the University of Houston. Derrik has also done studies in computer science at the University of Houston and Columbia University.

David Scott Heath

Scott Heath is a Technical Manager with Business Solutions, Inc. in Austin, TX. Scott has over seven years of experience in the design and implementation of departmental and enterprise wide applications using client/server technologies. Scott has not only been involved in the design and development of PowerBuilder applications, he has also managed a number of successful PowerBuilder projects and has served as president of the Houston PowerBuilder User Group. Scott's industry experience includes oil & gas, aerospace, healthcare, and manufacturing. Scott received his BS in Electrical Engineering from Texas A&M University.

David Mosley

David Mosley is a Technical Manager with BSG, Inc. in Houston, TX. David has over eight years of experience in the design and implementation of departmental and enterprise wide client/server systems using distributed technologies. David's specialty is in relational databases and data access mechanisms such as gateways, TP Monitors, and RPC architectures. David has also been working with PowerBuilder since version 1.0. His industry experience includes manufacturing, aerospace, healthcare, and petrochemical. David received his BS in computer science from Texas A&M University.

Table of Contents

Foreword

Make no mistake, this book was written to help you better use a particular piece of software: Powersoft's PowerBuilder. However, new and advanced PowerBuilder users alike, take a few moments to consider the world of applications development changing around you.

Information technology is awash in change. Not only are new products literally introduced every week, whole new computing concepts are introduced regularly. What is fueling this change? We believe it is the constant pursuit by companies to use technology as an enabler—often *the* enabler—for creating new markets, finding new customers, and creating value within their organizations.

Notice the emphasis on creating, as opposed to the more traditional view of the information technology payback coming from cost reductions and containment. Sure, companies are taking advantage of the scalability of client/server networks and installing applications in workgroups where it was previously too costly or the lead time too long to get new systems developed. However, most studies today are concluding that the pure costs of migrating to, and then managing client/server systems are roughly on par with those of older, traditional systems. Traditional ROI (return on investment) is no longer good enough.

The real advantage with client/server systems is in the system flexibility and scalability, the intense involvement of users in the development and deployment cycle, and the overall improvement in quality of decision-making and responsiveness of the ultimate users of these systems. ROI^3 (return on investment, imagination, and innovation) is a new standard that business people and applications developers should use together in measuring the gain from new information technology products.

BSG has been working with Powersoft since "before the beginning." In

1990, we met with Powersoft to understand and discuss their PowerBuilder product plans and attended their very first PowerBuilder training courses. In 1991, when PowerBuilder v1.0 was released, BSG had already designed our first custom application for a corporate customer, using a beta release of PowerBuilder. Later that year, after PowerBuilder was commercially available, BSG introduced BSG's BluePrint v1.0 Object Development Environment for PowerBuilder. Today, in its fourth release, the BluePrint ODE still sets the standard by which other development environments for PowerBuilder must be measured for functionality and support of large-scale applications development.

The knowledge gained from this close relationship between BSG and Powersoft and the PowerBuilder product line is embedded throughout this book, delivering ROI[3] from the first chapter to the code samples on the disk. In addition to the fine work Derrik, David, and Scott have done writing this book, special thanks go to BSG's Eric Reed, the "godfather" of BSG's BluePrint and an early liaison to Powersoft, and to BSG's Tod Knight, BluePrint's current product manager "dad."

At BSG, through the efforts of folks like these, we've earned the reputation as the leading Next Generation IT Services Company. We hope that you find this book an invaluable source in building your own applications for the next generation of computing.

STEVEN G. PAPERMASTER
Chairman, CEO, and President
BSG Corporation

April 1995

PART I

Overview

CHAPTER 1

Introduction

Since corporations have begun migrating their applications from traditional mainframe-based systems to a LAN-based client/server environment, the need for powerful yet easy-to-use application development tools has grown rapidly. PowerBuilder has, in a relatively short time, become one of the leading client/server development tools in the market today. PowerBuilder's object-based development environment, its ability to handle large-scale, multi-developer projects, and its open systems approach set it apart from other products. Version 4.0, which in this text we will refer to as PowerBuilder 4, will strengthen PowerBuilder's position as an industry-leading development tool by adding support for other operating platforms (Macintosh, Windows NT, and UNIX Motif), supporting OLE 2.0, and improving performance over version 3.0, among the many other enhancements.

Client/server technology has been advancing at an increasing rate and will continue to do so in the years to come. This rate of advancement has moved us away from the single-vendor solution of the past into a more open environment. In the client/server arena, there are a number of technologies and vendors, each providing a solution for different parts of a system. When developing mission-critical applications or products in this environment, one must insist on an open and scalable architecture. It is important that applications and development tools be interoperable with other vendors' products and be open enough to take advantage of emerging technologies. Powersoft has positioned PowerBuilder as an "open" development environment, capable of tightly integrating with third-party software products such as project management tools, transaction processing monitors, version control software, CASE tools, and others. This enables an organization to put together a "best of breed" client/server software solution.

ABOUT THIS BOOK

This book provides developers, designers, and administrators of Power-Builder projects a resource to use when dealing with some of the issues encountered when building client/server applications. It is not meant to replace the PowerBuilder documentation, but rather to serve as an extension of it. In some cases, this extension relates not only to Power-Builder itself, but also to an extension in scope to include other areas of a client/server system.

This book is written for the novice as well as for the advanced user. The authors assume that the reader has, at a minimum, a basic knowledge of PowerBuilder. This level may be achieved by taking an introductory PowerBuilder class or doing some design and development of a PowerBuilder application. Although not required, the reader will also benefit by having a working knowledge of Windows programming and SQL. While this book provides numerous examples of working source code for some intermediate to advanced PowerBuilder topics, the authors hope that the reader learns as much about "why" to do certain things as "how" to do them.

Part I of the book includes Chapters 1 and 2. Chapter 1 serves as an introduction, providing an overview of the book. Chapter 2 addresses the topic of an application architecture and discusses the various options and design concepts that should be considered when building a client/server system. This chapter includes a discussion of object orientation and how it is implemented in PowerBuilder. Chapter 2 also discusses the use of shared objects and how to set up a development architecture to maximize their use.

Part II of the book discusses various development concepts, focusing specifically on the PowerBuilder development environment. This section includes Chapter 3 DataWindows, Chapter 4 Multiple Document Interface (MDI), Chapter 5 Menus, Chapter 6 Windows, Chapter 7 User Objects, Chapter 8 Functions, Chapter 9 Graphs and Reporting, Chapter 10 Printing and File I/O, and Chapter 11 Debugging. This section is intended mainly for application developers and designers and includes many code examples and valuable tips and techniques.

Part III of the book covers advanced development concepts, focusing on the interfaces between PowerBuilder and external tools and resources. This section includes Chapter 12 eMail Interfaces, Chapter 13 PowerBuilder's Open Repository Case (ORCA) API, Chapter 14 Interfacing with the Operating System, and Chapter 15 Network Considerations. This section, which also includes many code examples and techniques, includes a discussion on how to write dynamic linked libraries. With Powersoft strategically positioning their development tools as open systems, the need to understand these interfaces is critical. This section is intended for both application developers and designers.

Part IV addresses database connectivity. This section includes Chapter 16 ODBC, Chapter 17 Watcom SQL, and Chapter 18 Other Databases. Some of the issues related to connecting from a PowerBuilder application to a database, including a brief description of the architecture of some of the more popular RBDMSs, are discussed. This section is intended for the developer, designer, and administrator.

Part V covers administration. It includes Chapter 19 Project Standards and Naming Conventions, Chapter 20 Creating an Executable, Chapter 21 Testing PowerBuilder Applications, Chapter 22 PowerBuilder Software Migration, Chapter 23 Performance Considerations, and Chapter 24 The Data Pipeline.

This book also includes a set of Windows tools and utilities that can be used in conjunction with PowerBuilder to enhance applications. These tools can be used to assist both a PowerBuilder developer and an end user of a PowerBuilder application. The tools are discussed in greater detail in Appendix D.

We hope you enjoy using PowerBuilder as much as we do. It's a powerful tool that has far-reaching capabilities in the world of emerging technologies.

CHAPTER 2

Application Architectures

This chapter will focus on the different ways an application architect can develop an application. Some of the high-level concepts will be discussed in this chapter, while other concepts relevant to building applications in PowerBuilder are discussed throughout the book.

Developing applications is like building a house and an application architect is like the architect of a house. An architect who is hired to build a house delivers the blueprint of the house to be constructed after many hours of work. This is very similar to the case of the application architect. The blueprint delivered by the application architect is called the system architecture. The building blueprint can be for a one-, two-, or three-story building. Similarly, the system architecture can be for a one-, two-, or three-tier system. A building architect, when designing the blueprint, can take advantage of many industry standards and accepted methods related to the different aspects of the building or house about to be constructed. The application architect can and should also take advantage of many standards when designing an architecture for an application. Some of the system standards include: MAPI, CORBA, X.500, OOP, IDAPI, OOD, RPC, DCE, VIM, X.400, ODBC, and many others. These standards can be complementary or competing with each other, but each in its own way can assist the application architect when designing the system architecture. The most important thing that architects have to base the entire architecture or blueprint on is the requirements of the client or user. Based on the customer's requirements, the framework or the direction of the architecture can be determined. A client's requirements for building a house can include the geographic location; for example, if the house will be constructed on the west coast of the United States, then the structure of the house has to comply with the earthquake standards set by the region. Another requirement is the location of the house; for example, if the house will be built on a hill, near the ocean, or on flat ground. Similarly, when developing an application there are requirements that can affect a system's architecture. Performance, maintenance, data distribution, and scalability are some of the many customer requirements that can affect a system's architecture.

When implemented correctly, an application architecture can bring many benefits to the application developer, the customer, and the user. These benefits include reduced development time, reuse of major application components across other applications, scalability of applications, ease of maintenance, and better application performance. However, developing an application architecture for the first time requires much more initial planning and investment than simply developing the first application. But without this investment, the customer or user will have duplicate work, produce high maintenance applications that do not comply with common standards set by an architecture, duplicate testing and documentation, and the developer will have a very difficult time of satisfying the customer's ever-changing business needs. In short, if an organization or customer is planning on only developing one application, then the investment in an application architecture may not be justified. But, as each additional application gets developed, the organization or customer and the developers will quickly enjoy the rewards of their investment in an application architecture.

This chapter will cover the following application architecture issues:

- Tiered Architecture
- Services Architecture
- PowerBuilder Object Orientation
- PowerBuilder Class Libraries

TIERED ARCHITECTURE

When developing a PowerBuilder client/server application based on the application or enterprise requirements, different types of architectures would make sense. This section will discuss two types of tiered architectures. A tiered architecture is when a logical section of an application can be divided into categories or tiers. The two types of tiered architectures that will be discussed in this section are two-tiered and three-tiered architectures.

Two-tiered Architecture

A two-tiered architecture is the traditional client/server environment that divides the application into the graphical user interface (GUI) (cli-

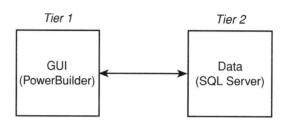

Figure 2.1   A two-tiered architecture.

ent) and the Data (server). The GUI can be developed using a product like PowerBuilder and the Data can be setup using a database management system (DBMS), as shown in Figure 2.1.

The GUI is often referred to as the presentation layer. In the two-tiered environment all the pieces of the application are either on tier one (client) or tier two (server). For example, if the application has a number of business rules that it needs to process, then the business rules either reside on the client or the server. If the business rules are on the client, then the code is either written as part of the DataWindow, as a window level function, or as user objects (see Figure 2.2).

The other alternative is to write the business rules on the server tied to the DBMS, as shown in Figure 2.3. In this case, the business rules can be written in the form of stored procedures, functions, triggers, or any other DBMS vendor-specific method.

For the most part in a two-tiered environment, all the components of the application are either written on the client (tier one) or the server (tier two) pieces of the application. This method has some advantages and disadvantages.

Some of the advantages of a two-tiered approach include: There are

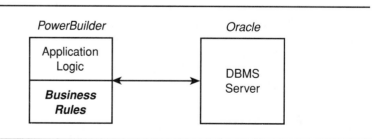

Figure 2.2   Business rules residing on the client side of a two-tiered architecture.

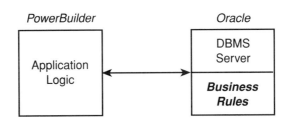

Figure 2.3   Business rules residing on the server side of a two-tiered architecture. (DBMS Server)

only two pieces to deal with. In most cases only two vendors, the GUI tool vendor (e.g., Powersoft) and the DBMS vendor (e.g., Powersoft, Microsoft, Sybase, Oracle). Developers do not have to learn multiple products. Development time is faster.

Some of the disadvantages include: All the rules are written either on the client tool or on the DBMS. The problem is, if the business rules are written on the DBMS, when the DBMS is changed from SQL Server to Oracle then all of the rules that were written on the DBMS have to be rewritten for Oracle. This may not be a serious issue if there are a few business rules, but in most cases a large investment is made in the development of the business rules.

The same issue is true for the client tool. If all the business rules were written using a third-party 4GL development tool other than Power-Builder, then when deciding to switch to PowerBuilder the code would, most likely, have to be rewritten.

Also, if other nonPowerBuilder-based applications want to share the business rules, they couldn't. So, reuse across multiple applications would be limited to PowerBuilder applications.

Another main disadvantage of a two-tiered application/architecture is the scalability of the application. There are many other advantages and disadvantages, but only a few are mentioned here.

Three-tiered Architecture

A three-tiered architecture is when an application is divided into three logical categories or tiers. The three tiers are the presentation or GUI, the business rules, and the data server tiers. Figure 2.4 shows a three-tiered architecture.

With a three-tiered architecture, by separating the business rules of an enterprise, the investment in the business rules will not be lost as

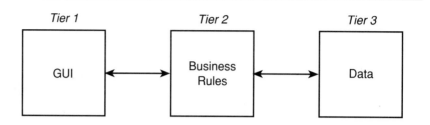

Figure 2.4   A three-tiered architecture.

applications and the application development tools are changed or if the DBMS is changed. The three-tiered architecture will also solve the problem of reuse and scalability. In the three-tiered architecture the business rules are designed as a separate tier such that any application(s) or any DBMS can be used, as shown in Figure 2.5.

It does not always make sense to jump into a three-tiered architecture, because there are some disadvantages. The first is setup costs. It would take more investment in time and resources to put in place a three-tiered architecture. Second, the administration of a three-tiered architecture can be more complex than that of a two-tiered. Third, the technologies used are newer and the skill set in the industry is often not available, but when it is, it is more expensive. Fourth, in most cases at least, an additional vendor has been introduced; therefore,

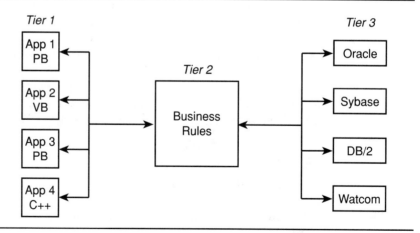

Figure 2.5   A three-tiered architecture with the business rules as a separate tier (shared by any Tier 1 client and Tier 3 DBMS).

another mechanism is in the architecture that could break. But, for enterprise-wide applications a three-tiered versus a two-tiered architecture is most often recommended to deliver a truly successful system.

Both architectures have advantages and disadvantages. Neither architecture should be selected until the goals of the users, application, department, and the enterprise have been carefully examined. Once the overall requirements, extending beyond just one application, have been gathered, a more calculated architecture can be selected. Many developers fall into the trap of quickly building an application and not considering the objectives of the entire department or even the enterprise; then, issues such as scalability and reuse arise. The classic example of this is a prototype/small departmental application turning into an enterprise application. After the small departmental application gains popularity and the demand for it extends beyond the department and spans the enterprise, scalability issues arise. Again, this can be avoided by gaining an understanding of the goals of the enterprise before quickly building an application to satisfy the short-term needs of a user or department.

SERVICES ARCHITECTURE

A services architecture is a very critical piece of a system. In most cases applications perform services such as printing, eMail, fax, data access, error handling, DDE, OLE, and many others. These services should be decoupled from a particular application such that they could be reused by many applications or potentially the entire corporation. When designing these services, in addition to decoupling the services from an application, one needs to make a decision to build all or some of these services using a distributed architecture. This can be achieved by having a server(s) that contains the different distributed services. This can be much more involved than creating reusable modules in the form of DLLs, but it should be a consideration based on the requirements of the architecture.

This section will discuss some of the many services that could be included as part of a services architecture. Figure 2.6 shows how some services are separate from the application, via a generic services interface. The service modules shown in the figure, such as eMail, I/O, pager, and error services, can be accessed via a common interface.

Separating the services from the application permits more reuse throughout the organization. In addition to the reuse there are many other advantages, such as ease of maintenance. Assume the following architecture has been developed and some services, such as eMail, have been integrated with 20 different applications across the company. The huge advantage gained here—in regards to maintenance—is if the eMail service is switched from cc:Mail to MS Mail; then, changes need

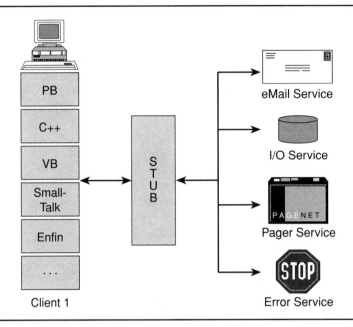

Figure 2.6   Services separate from the application via a generic services interface.

only be made in the eMail service module and the 20 or more applications that interfaced the eMail service remain untouched. Traditionally, each of the 20 applications had to be recompiled to incorporate changes in its modules. This advantage is achieved not only by building the services separate from the application but also by enabling some object-oriented concepts and hiding the complexities of the individual services by incorporating stub layers throughout the architecture. Additional object-oriented components can be incorporated into a services-based architecture such as broker agents, authentication, and object repositories. What follows is a discussion of a simple approach to building some service modules.

eMail

Integration with an eMail service has been very popular in the client/server environment. This integration has included sending someone mail from within an application by invoking the eMail software, to providing full integration by being able to send and receive reports from within an application. There are many different methods for implementing an eMail service. In the sections to follow, a simple and practi-

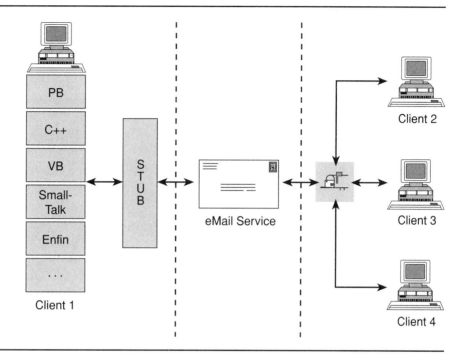

Figure 2.7   Separation of the eMail service from the application.

cal solution will be discussed. Figure 2.7 shows the separation of the eMail service from the application.

An eMail Service Architecture Figure 2.8 shows the three logical layers of the eMail service. The first layer is the application and a generic service stub (stub 1). The second layer contains a generic eMail stub (stub 2) and the different messaging APIs. The third layer is the actual eMail service, such as Lotus Notes, Lotus cc:Mail, Microsoft Mail, or any other mail package.

Stub 1 is used to provide a common interface to the different services, eMail being one of the services. From the PowerBuilder application a generic **DoService( )** function is called specifying the particular service (e.g., eMail), the specific subservice (SendMail) within the service, and a structure as the third parameter for the **DoService( )** function. The structure will pass the data that needs to be sent. This common interface can be used for any service. The **DoService( )** function can map the service and subservice request to the appropriate service agent and send across the appropriate data.

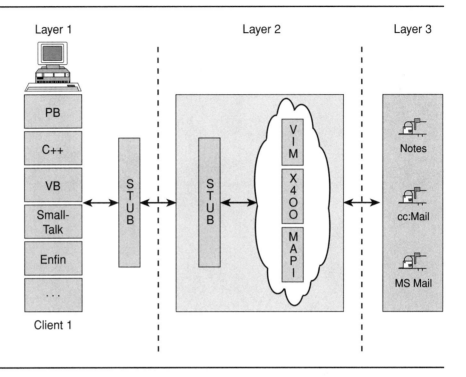

Figure 2.8   The three layers of eMail service.

Note: The first and second layers can exist on the same PC or on a network in the form of a DLL. In a distributed service environment, the second layer would exist on a separate server not known to the first layer. In a distributed approach, remote procedure calls (RPC) or messaging architectures can be implemented. The architect can design the stub 1 layer to interface with a broker to determine the location of the service requested. At runtime, this location can be a distributed server that needs to be invoked via an RPC call or the location can be a DLL on the network that could be invoked via a normal function call.

The next step is within the second layer. Once service and the subfunction have been invoked, the stub 2 functionality will determine which mail service is active and map the subfunction to the appropriate messaging API. For example if the mail product used is MS Mail the stub 2 functionality is smart enough to interface with the Microsoft Messaging Application Programming Interface (MAPI). This method is useful because the applications and the general services stub do not care about the details of the vendor API or even which API is going to be used. This approach will provide a very maintainable interface not only from the applications that interface with the service, but also from within the service itself.

Within the eMail service any of the specific vendor APIs can be swapped with no changes to the applications, no changes to the services architecture, and with minimal changes within the eMail service itself. The functionality can be built within the eMail service to determine which vendor API to use. If that functionality is built in, switching between the different vendor APIs will also result in no changes to the eMail service.

The final step is for the vendor API to interface with the third layer, which is the vendor mail engine, and send the mail.

The next section will briefly define some other services that can be developed using the same architecture.

Other Services

There are many different services that can be implemented using a general services architecture. This section will discuss some of the services with an explanation of each.

Data Access The data access object can contain any and all data access mechanisms for any and all PowerBuilder applications. All data access methods can be located in a data access library shared by all applications. The individual applications do not interact with the data directly, but rather call generic functions in the data access layer that, in turn, interface with the data sources. One of the many advantages of doing this is that when the data source is changed or when data attributes are changed, only the data access layer is affected. None of the applications have to be modified.

The previous description is for a PowerBuilder-based data access layer. There are different ways of implementing a data access solution that is not PowerBuilder-based and supports distribution. There are messaging or RPC-based mechanisms that provide for a more open data access service. In fact, since PowerBuilder has been very committed in working with vendors to provide extensions to PowerBuilder, many new interfaces have been introduced in the market. For example, companies like Open Environment Corporation are selling three-tiered DCE-based data access solutions that provide native language support for products like PowerBuilder, Visual Basic, and others. Though one of

PowerBuilder's strengths is its data access capabilities, one has to keep in mind ways to reuse an architecture to its full potential.

Print This service includes print functionality for all applications.

OLE This service includes OLE functionality for all applications.

DDE This service includes DDE functionality for all applications.

Clipboard This service includes clipboard functionality for all applications.

Security This service includes security for applications. All the methods and attribute structures for application security are developed and put in the nonvisual architecture object. Security can be developed at either the macro application level or down to the micro level of objects. A security mechanism can be developed within PowerBuilder as a nonvisual PowerBuilder object that is used across PowerBuilder applications. This security user object can interface with an external security service that is used across other applications. For distributed applications the security service should be able to interface with the Kerberos Authentication Security Service.

Modem This service includes modem communication functionality for all applications. Applications do not need to be concerned with functionality specific to different modems. Instead they call generic functions that provide an interface to a modem.

Drag-and-Drop This service includes drag-and-drop functionality for all applications.

Fax This service includes fax functionality for all applications.

DOS/File I/O This service includes DOS/File I/O functionality for all applications. If an application needs access to an environment variable, the application developer would make a simple call to a generic environment variable function.

Multimedia This service includes sound and image functionality for all applications. The multimedia API, in the Windows environment, is mmsystem.dll.

EDI This service includes electronic data interchange (EDI) functionality for all applications.

POWERBUILDER OBJECT ORIENTATION

It is often considered that the most important stage in building applications is the design stage. This section discusses some important design concepts of object-oriented systems. Other design concepts relevant to building applications in PowerBuilder are discussed throughout the book.

Object orientation is becoming a relatively popular approach to application design and development. It is based on breaking an application down into a set of objects, each object having a defined set of attributes and behaviors.

In an object-oriented system, each object is designed to accomplish a specific application task. Objects communicate with each other by passing messages. Objects react to messages passed to them by doing something.

When implemented correctly, object-oriented design and development can bring many benefits to both the application developer and the end user. These benefits include reduced development time and better application performance. However, using object orientation requires much more initial planning and investment than does a traditional approach. Without this investment, developing in an object-oriented environment can be difficult and result in a slower, less efficient application.

The four major topics presented in this section are:

- Inheritance
- Encapsulation
- Polymorphism
- Binding

Inheritance

Inheritance is a mechanism that allows an object to obtain its attributes and behaviors from another object. This allows development of a basic set of objects, known as base classes or superclasses, that contain a set of attributes reusable by "descendant" objects (i.e., those that inherit attributes and/or behaviors from other objects).

Inheritance is established in the form of an object hierarchy. This hierarchy is generally in the form of an inverted tree, with the more generic functionality defined in objects at the top of the hierarchy and more specific functionality defined in objects at the bottom of the hierarchy (see Figure 2.9).

True inheritance allows descendant objects to both extend and override the properties of its ancestor. Because the code is passed to the descendant objects instead of being merely copied, a descendant class can change some of the attributes or behavior of its ancestor while

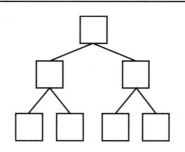

Figure 2.9   Inheritance tree structure.

maintaining the core set of functionality built into the ancestor. A well designed object hierarchy makes use of virtual classes of objects. A virtual class is an object class that is not intended to be directly used, but rather to serve as an object from which other objects are inherited. For example, in the inheritance structure just described, the top and middle layers of objects could serve as virtual classes. All objects would then be inherited from one of these classes and the descendants would extend or override the functionality built into these classes.

Advantages of Inheritance

Code Reusability Because code inherited from another object class does not have to be rewritten in the descendant class, inheritance provides a method of code reusability. This also reduces the amount of code needed in the descendant classes.

Code Sharing Code sharing is one of the major benefits of object-oriented development. Building a common set of functionality into a class library provides all developers of a given application the ability to inherit from these classes, extending or overriding the code of the ancestors as needed. Code sharing is increased when multiple classes are inherited from a single base class. For example, an architecture could define a ReportWin class and a QueryWin class, each inherited from StdWindow (see Figure 2.10).

Inheritance provides the code of StdWindow to ReportWin and QueryWin in this situation.

Code Reliability Using inheritance makes code more reliable because code contained in ancestor objects is defined in a single place and doesn't have to be duplicated in different objects. Eliminating duplicate code reduces the chance for error and provides an easier way to track and

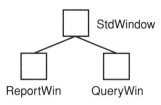

Figure 2.10   Sample inheritance tree.

correct bugs. When an error has been corrected in an ancestor object, it is corrected throughout the entire application.

For example, suppose that for every window in an application, a message box is to be displayed asking the user to save any changes in the window. With inheritance, this code can be part of a virtual class, eliminating the need to have it in every window in the application. Any errors in this functionality encountered during development or testing can be traced to its single location and corrected there for all windows in the application.

Interface Consistency Providing a consistent interface throughout an application can be difficult for large applications being developed by many people. Inheritance ensures interface consistency by guaranteeing that all objects inherited from a base class provide a common interface. Interface standards should be established and built into the virtual classes.

Code Maintenance One of the biggest advantages of inheritance is the increased maintainability of code. Sharing code throughout an application obviously reduces the maintenance effort. Eliminating duplicate code also makes error tracing much simpler, thus reducing the time to find and correct bugs.

Disadvantages of Inheritance

Execution Speed Some people mistakenly believe that inheritance alone hampers performance. This is simply not true. (See Appendix D.) While a poorly designed object hierarchy can hurt performance, a well designed object hierarchy can actually improve both performance and memory efficiency.

Program Size The use of object libraries obviously adds to the size of an application. Although this is true, it is becoming less of an issue as the price of memory decreases. Most people are willing to put up with this disadvantage to gain the many benefits of inheritance.

Program Complexity Applications using inheritance may be more complicated than traditional, structured applications because code can be in different locations throughout an object hierarchy. The ability to extend and override ancestor events and functions adds complexity to the flow of an application. The ease of maintenance resulting from the use of inheritance, however, often outweighs the disadvantage of increased complexity.

Inheritance in PowerBuilder In its ability to inherit windows, menus, and user objects, PowerBuilder provides full inheritance capabilities. Other tools offer the capability to copy or reuse code but do not allow the code to be passed on to descendant objects. With such tools, the benefit of ease of maintenance is lost. As stated previously, when a PowerBuilder descendant object has been created, the events and functions associated with the ancestor object can be extended or overridden, but all the benefits of inheritance survive.

PowerBuilder allows the user to create an unlimited number of descendants for an object, each of which can, in turn, be an ancestor. Extending an ancestor event or function results in execution of the ancestor code plus the execution of any code defined for the event in the descendant object. Overriding an ancestor event or function results in execution of only the code defined in the descendant object. Taken together, the true inheritance provided in PowerBuilder provides maximum code reusability and ease of code maintainability.

Design Considerations When designed correctly, an object hierarchy can provide many benefits, including improved performance. It is important that only the appropriate levels of inheritance be defined and that as much code as possible be inherited from the set of virtual classes.

Interface standards such as screen layout, colors, fonts, and menus should be defined in virtual classes, along with the basic functionality necessary at each level. Examples of common functionality that can be included in ancestor scripts include: standard error trapping routines, exit functionality, window initialization, database connectivity, and many others.

An example of a type of function that should be included into a virtual class inheritance structure is the use of a common exit from a window. Such basic functionality should be defined only once and inherited for lower windows. This is a basic example of the type of code that could be used. (Further working examples of inheritance are shown in later chapters.)

```
/* if changes were made, allow to save */
if hasChanged( ) then
```

```
        if not askSave("Exit") then
                        return false
        end if
end if
```

This is a generic close function that should be defined in the base ancestor class. All normal shutdown would be funneled through this function. This function calls another function, **hasChanged( )**, to determine if changes have been made. If a change has been made, the function **askSave( )** can be called to save the changes before exiting. Because it is defined in the base ancestor class, it can be implemented for the entire application.

Object hierarchies should be defined for all possible objects, not only for windows. The higher-level objects should perform a broad range of general functionality with the descendant objects performing the specific tasks. To provide a method of inheriting DataWindow controls (or other window controls), the developer can define a user object virtual class that has a DataWindow control within it. Events and functions that pertain to the DataWindow control can also be encapsulated in this user object (see the next section). The user object can then be included within one of the virtual window classes or within an application window. This allows more complex items to be defined and tested at the ancestor level so that all descendants can utilize them without the developer reinventing them each time they are required. The example in Figure 2.11 illustrates the use of user objects at different levels in the inheritance structure.

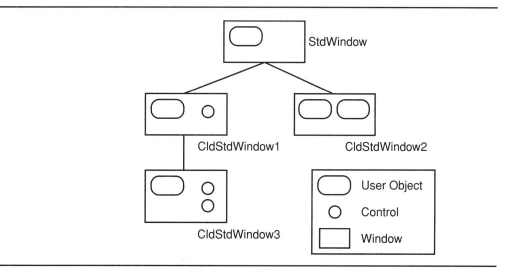

Figure 2.11   Virtual class window with user object.

For further discussion of this topic, see the Design Considerations section of Chapter 7.

Encapsulation

Encapsulation is the concept of packaging a set of attributes and behaviors into an object. This allows the definition of data, functions, and variables at the object level, meaning that all the functionality of an object is grouped into a single integrated package.

A major benefit of encapsulation is the ability to hide information and shield complexity from users of the object. Information-hiding is achieved because a developer only needs to know how to interface with a particular object and not the specific details of how that object accomplishes its tasks.

For example, the code to enable or disable menu options based on a user's security privileges to a particular object can be developed as a window function of a virtual window class. A descendant window only has to know how to call this function and what it returns. It does not need to know how the function determines whether the menu option should be enabled or disabled.

Encapsulation in PowerBuilder PowerBuilder supports the encapsulation of variables, events, and functions at the object level for windows, menus, and user objects. Through the use of instance variables, standard and user-defined events, and object-level functions, all the data and behaviors of the object can be encapsulated into a single package.

Design Considerations All interaction with the attributes of an object should be done through interface functions, rather than referencing the attribute directly. For example, to check the value of an instance variable, a call to a function that returns the value of the variable should be done rather than referencing the variable directly. This method of encapsulation achieves the hiding of information and thus simplifies application maintenance.

As mentioned previously, the functionality of a DataWindow control (or any other window control) can be encapsulated within a user object. For example, suppose we want to develop a master-detail maintenance conversation. Within this conversation, we need a master DataWindow control and a detail DataWindow control. These two types of DataWindow controls have some common functionality, but also contain functionality specific to each DataWindow control. The functionality for each type of DataWindow control can be encapsulated in a separate virtual user object class; these then can be used as ancestors to any master-detail maintenance conversations in the application(s).

Within the DataWindow user object, the developer will want to include all the different types of functionality that will be needed. Types of DataWindow functionality might include functions to enable or disable the fields in the DataWindow, validate text entries, and trap errors. An example of functionality that should be included in an encapsulated DataWindow is initialization of the DataWindow using the PowerBuilder function **setTransObject( )**.

```
/*
Initialize the DataWindow. Fill in our parent reference so we can
call functions and trigger events, and set the transaction.
*/
i_dwParent = aParent
if useTransObj then
        setTransObject(this,aTransaction)
else
        setTrans(this,aTransaction)
end if
return true
```

Polymorphism

Polymorphism is the ability of a function to behave differently, depending on the context in which it is called. This allows the definition of functions at a high level, with the details of the function handled by each individual object at the lower levels. To create a drawing application using traditional programming techniques, for example, one would need to define functions to draw each type of object (rectangle, circle, line, etc.). The main function would then need to know which type of object is to be drawn so it could call the appropriate function.

With polymorphism, a class could be defined for each object type; each class would contain a draw function. The draw function would be defined at a higher level of detail, making it more functional. Because the main program would not need to know the type of object to be drawn, it could simply tell the object to "draw." The details would then be handled by the object receiving the request. This approach also allows the addition of new objects to the draw function with no impact on the main program. This is the case because the interface to draw the new objects would be the same as the existing interface. One could add a triangle object with its own function, for example, and with no other changes, the application would be able to draw triangles.

Overloading Polymorphism provides the ability to overload both functions and operators. A function is said to be overloaded if two or more function bodies contain the same name. In the previous example, the draw function would be considered an overloaded function.

Overloaded functions may be defined with different argument lists and different argument types. The argument list and argument types are used to determine which version of an overloaded function is executed. For example, assume an application needs to display messages containing both integer and string data. A function named **displayMessage** could be defined to accept a single string argument. This function could then be overloaded to accept a single integer argument. Within the application, a call to **displayMessage** with either a string or integer argument would execute the correct function.

Overloading is not restricted to functions; operators can also be overloaded. Overloaded operators work in a fashion similar to overloaded functions. For example, the "+" operator can be defined to behave differently depending on the operands with which it is being used. With two string operands, the "+" operator could be defined to concatenate the two strings, while with two integer operands it would perform an addition operation.

Overriding   Much of the power of object orientation lies in the ability to override the attributes or behaviors of an ancestor object in the descendant objects. Without the ability to override the functionality of ancestor objects, much of the flexibility and power of object orientation is lost.

Polymorphism in PowerBuilder   PowerBuilder supports polymorphism in the form of overloaded functions and the capability to override ancestor functions and events. Polymorphism allows the developer to define generic types of functionality in virtual class windows. This, in turn, provides the flexibility of having different routines at specific object levels to handle generic functionality such as printing, enabling, and disabling windows.

A good example of polymorphism would be the following razor object. If the razor object were used by a male, it would be primarily for grooming facial hair. The same razor object, when used by a female, however, would be used to groom leg hair. Even though both people are told by the ancestor object to perform the function shave, the function actually does different things.

Design Considerations   When building different applications, it is a good idea to create windows that have generic references that can use the aspects of polymorphism. These references allow the objects to be reused again and again by other coding with generic references. An example of this would be a function that can be included within the "DataWindow user object" to disable a DataWindow. The ancestor object calls a function to disable the DataWindow. If there are two different descendant objects, each of these might logically carry out the same type of functionality, but the code might be different.

One of the descendant objects might handle disabling the DataWindow with this code:

```
dwModify(this,colname+".color=~""+DISABLED_COLOR+&
    "~""+colname"+.pointer=~"Arrow!~""+&
    colname+".TabSequence=0")

return true
```

while the other object might handle the disabling of the DataWindow in the following manner:

```
this.enabled = false
return FALSE
```

Thus, the two descendant objects achieve the disabling of a Data-Window in different ways.

Binding

Binding is the association of an object attribute and its meaning. This can be broken down into:

1. The binding of an identifier with its type
2. The binding of a message to an object method

One issue in object-oriented programming concerns the time at which binding occurs. Binding can occur at compile time, linkage time, or execution time. Binding at compile or linkage time is known as static binding; binding at execution time is known as dynamic binding.

With static binding, the meaning and types of all attributes must be known at compile time. Programming languages that require binding at compile time are said to be "strongly typed." PowerScript falls into this category.

Dynamic binding, on the other hand, binds all attributes at execution time. This provides greater flexibility because, for example, a single identifier can be used differently throughout an application.

Design Considerations There is one basic trade-off between static and dynamic binding: performance versus flexibility. Static binding results in better performance than dynamic binding because dynamic binding requires the extra step of matching an identifier with its type or a message with its method.

Error detection is also much simpler when using static binding. This is so because any errors are found at compile time, making it easier to know the location of an error. With dynamic binding, errors often go undetected and are much more difficult to locate when they do occur.

POWERBUILDER CLASS LIBRARIES

So far, many different concepts have been discussed, from tiered architectures to inheritance. Many of these concepts are the foundation of an application architecture. One additional component of an application architecture, that has not been discussed in detail, is the presentation layer or the PowerBuilder GUI architecture. With PowerBuilder, an architecture can be developed to complement the development of PowerBuilder applications at the presentation layer. PowerBuilder is a graphical, partially object-oriented application development environment. As such, it provides the developer with many tools and facilities to enable the rapid development of client/server applications. However, in an ever-changing business environment PowerBuilder needs to be extended such that some reusable class libraries can be used in order to react in a timely manner to the request of the customers. The PowerBuilder class libraries should be the PowerBuilder version of the presentation/GUI layer in the tiered architectures previously explained. These class libraries can be either purchased or developed. An example of a class library that can be purchased is the PowerBuilder Library for Lotus Notes. There are also different consulting firms and vendors that provide class libraries. These class libraries should be studied closely and matched up against the specific business needs. The other option is to develop a custom set of class libraries. Throughout this book are suggestions on developing different modules of the class libraries. In Appendix D a detailed discussion of a tab-folder class library takes place.

An overall application architecture can extend PowerBuilder to create an environment suited to building corporate application systems. Such an architecture consists of a PowerBuilder application, class hierarchies of reusable system objects, common functions, and object construction tools that support both the development and execution environments.

The overall PowerBuilder class library in Figure 2.12 shows the basic structure of a suitable application architecture in the PowerBuilder environment. This figure shows the dependence of applications on the architecture. If an application architecture did not exist, all the code and logic

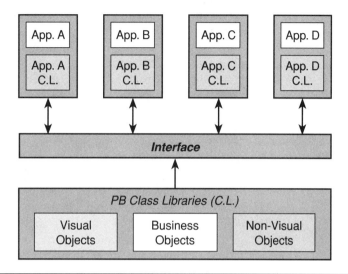

Figure 2.12   Corporate application structure in support of multiple PowerBuilder applications.

would have to be developed for each application, reducing productivity and increasing application delivery time. After the initial investment is made in an application architecture, all applications can take advantage of much of the functionality built into the architecture. Each application can take advantage of the architecture's visual, business, and service objects. All the components of the architecture can be shared between applications.

When developing PowerBuilder class libraries, the architect must have an understanding of the overall application development vision for the corporation. The architect must have established and frequent communication with each application's project manager, lead designers, and analysts in order to understand the common modules in each application. These common modules could be either visual, business, or service objects/modules. Through a series of ongoing meetings/sessions, the architect determines the level of commonality between applications.

Developers can also determine which unique pieces of an application should be built into the corporate application architecture for future flexibility, reusability, and modularity. There is often functionality that is unique to an application, but common to all the different pieces of the application. Each application can also have its own individual architecture that is built using the objects in the application architecture. An individual application's architecture should be developed to minimize/eliminate duplicate design and development.

All conversations in a medium- to large-scale application system have similar features and functionality. In addition, the architecture specification requires that conversations follow a certain protocol (e.g., a tab folder protocol) in order to take advantage of it. This situation presents a two-fold problem. First, the requirement of architecture-support code and common functions in every conversation creates a very repetitive recoding task for each conversation. Second, it is extremely important in large-scale applications that common functionality, errors, and other standard operations are handled consistently from both a code maintenance and user interface standpoint. A good application architecture addresses both of these issues by defining common code in class hierarchies from which all system components inherit. This structure produces a system of reusable component objects that take full advantage of such object-oriented programming concepts as inheritance, encapsulation, and polymorphism. In addition, the architecture's object construction facility should create reusable open boxes, search boxes, and lookup dialogs as well as almost-functional standard maintenance conversation—all within a tab folder (or any other) interface.

Figure 2.13 shows examples of visual objects, business objects, and service/nonvisual objects. Visual objects and service objects are, in most cases, technology/interface-based. Business objects are defined specifically to address the business requirements of the corporation. Using object-oriented analysis and design, the business is broken down into business objects with attributes and methods that can be built into the application architecture.

The visual objects of an architecture are technology-based objects that are visible to the user. These objects can include windows, menus, toolbars, tabs, DataWindows, and other objects. These high-level objects can be broken down into more detail/specific objects by taking advantage of inheritance.

Unlike visual objects, service/nonvisual objects cannot be seen by the user. These are objects that add service-level functionality to an application. Some examples of service objects are data access objects, OLE objects, print objects, and many more. An application or a window is given access to a print object so it can print windows or a specific window. A print object can be developed once and added to the application architecture, allowing each application that needs some level of print functionality to simply add the print object to the window(s) of the application. Details about visual, business, and service/nonvisual objects follow.

A corporate PowerBuilder class library should also provide tools

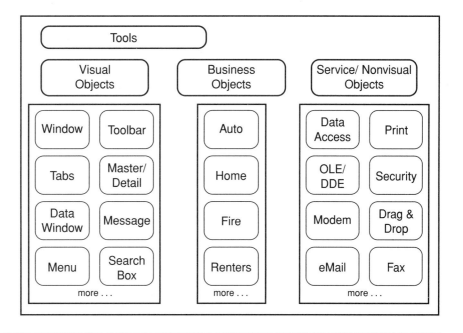

Figure 2.13   Example of a PowerBuilder class library breakdown.

that facilitate the building of screens and interfaces. In Visual C++, Wizards, a standard object constructor empowers the developer with an easy interface to the architecture. Wizards automatically constructs screens and code by simply requiring the developer to input some specific information about the screen being developed. Such automatic construction of application code becomes more imperative as the underlying architecture increases in its complexity and functionality. In addition to a standard object constructor, application architecture should include a security maintenance application for building the security module and a workstation painter for creating icon-based, workstation-style menu screens. There should also be a configuration utility that permits developers/administrators to create DLLs, INI files, EXEs, and PBDs and provides the capability to modify global parameters, such as color and font, on demand throughout the application objects.

In any environment in which multiple PowerBuilder applications are going to be built, the investment in a PowerBuilder class library is imperative.

Sharing PowerBuilder Objects

As previously described, an application architecture should include a .PBL (or set of .PBLs) to store shared objects. All types of PowerBuilder objects can and should be shared among developers of one or many applications. Object-sharing begins with the definition of an object class hierarchy. As previously mentioned, a class hierarchy can be defined for windows, user objects, and menus. However, object-sharing extends beyond these objects to other objects such as DataWindows, functions, structures, and SQL.

For windows, user objects and menus, functionality should be built into a set of virtual classes from which application objects can be derived. DataWindows can be shared by encapsulating them within a user object. Using user objects allows the virtual classes of DataWindow controls to be defined and implemented in the same way as other object hierarchies.

Through the course of application design and development, it usually becomes clear that different functions in an application will have some overlapping components. For example, a query conversation and a reporting conversation both require a connection to a database. The code to set up the PowerBuilder transaction object and handle communication with a database can be shared by both functions. Another example of code that can be shared is a function to generate sequential numbers. This generic type of code can provide functionality common to many application functions.

SQL can be shared by storing common queries in files. These files can then be used as a data source for any other application DataWindow.

One of the most valuable benefits of object-oriented development is this ability to share objects. A correctly built PowerBuilder application uses the power of inheritance to minimize coding and to maximize efficiency. Sharing objects then increases code reliability and interface consistency and eases the task of code maintenance by reducing or eliminating the need for duplicate code.

PART II

Development Concepts

CHAPTER 3

DataWindows

The DataWindow object provides developers a simple way of retrieving, displaying, and updating data from a specified data source. Although the data source is usually a database, it can be other things such as a text file or data structure. The DataWindow object allows the developer to define not only the data source, but also the presentation style, edit masks, and validation criteria of a data set.

The DataWindow control, on the other hand, is a window control that allows the incorporation of DataWindow objects within a Power-Builder window object. The DataWindow control has a set of events encapsulated within it that provides a great deal of flexibility to developers, including the ability to dynamically bind to different DataWindow objects at runtime.

This chapter discusses the following topics related to DataWindow objects, DataWindow controls, and related design considerations:

- DataWindow Objects
  - Data Sources
  - Presentation Styles
  - Groups
  - Filters
  - Sorting
  - Sliding Columns
  - Data Validation
  - Display Formats and Edit Masks
  - Computed Columns and Fields
  - Update Characteristics
  - Child DataWindows

- DataWindow Controls
  - DataWindow Buffers
  - Drag-and-Drop
  - Transaction Processing
  - Dynamic DataWindows
  - Query Mode and Prompt for Criteria
- Design Considerations
  - Embedded SQL
  - Handling Large Result Sets
  - Shared Result Sets
  - Retrieve as Needed
  - DataWindows as Buffers
  - Code Tables
  - Using a DDDW vs. filling a DDLB
  - Using Bitmaps in DataWindows
  - OLE Columns
  - Stop Light Reports
  - Creating a DataWindow Architecture

DataWindow objects and controls work together to provide the developer a much simpler and more efficient database interface than writing the data access code from scratch. Because a great deal of functionality is encapsulated within both the DataWindow object and DataWindow control, developers are saved from having to write a large amount of database access code.

DATAWINDOW OBJECTS

Data Sources

The DataWindow data source options are Quick Select, SQL Select, Query, External, and Stored Procedure. This section provides a brief overview of each option.

Quick Select The Quick Select option provides a fast method for choosing the tables and columns that provide the data source of a DataWindow object. The Quick Select window allows selection from the available tables in the current database. In version 3.0 of PowerBuilder, only a single table could be selected using the Quick Select option. However, version 4.0 has added the ability to select data from more than one table if the tables share a key relationship. When the initial table is selected, the Tables box lists all tables with a primary or foreign key relationship with the initial table. For example, when selecting the employee table of the

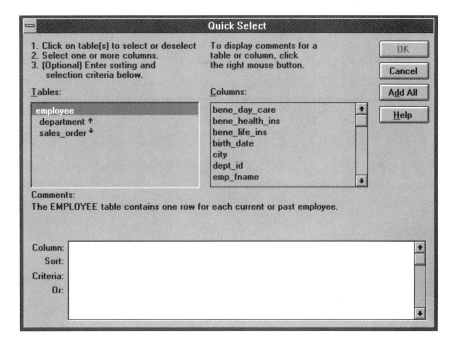

Figure 3.1   Selecting the employee table of the Powersoft sample database from the Quick Select dialog.

Powersoft sample database from the Quick Select dialog, the screen shown in Figure 3.1 is displayed.

Notice that the columns of the employee table are displayed in the Columns box and that all tables in the database having a key relationship with the employee table are shown indented under the employee table in the Tables box. If one of the indented tables is then selected, the list of columns from that table is added to the Columns box. For example, if the department table is selected from the dialog shown in Figure 3.1, the dialog would change to that shown in Figure 3.2.

Note: Table comments are displayed when the table is selected from the Tables box. To view the comments of a column, hold the right mouse button down while positioning the cursor on the column name. The comments will disappear when the right mouse button is released.

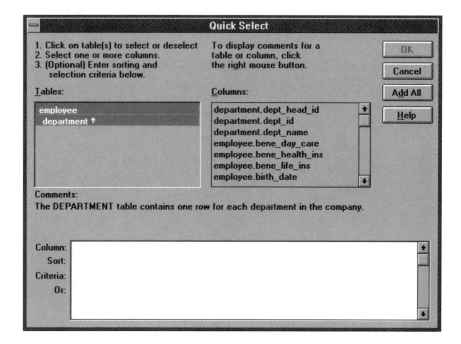

Figure 3.2   Selecting the department table of the Powersoft sample database from the Quick Select dialog.

Once the tables and columns of the query have been selected, selection and sorting criteria can be specified in the Quick Select window by entering the criteria in the grid at the bottom of the window. For example, selection of employee records for all department numbers over 200 sorted in descending order by the employee's last name would be done on a Quick Select window that looks like Figure 3.3.

The SQL syntax for the above query is:

```
SELECT "department"."dept_id", "employee"."emp_lname",
      "employee"."emp_fname"
 FROM "employee", "department"
 WHERE ( "employee"."dept_id" = "department"."dept_id" ) and
      ((("department"."dept_id" > 200)))
ORDER BY "employee"."emp_lname" DESC
```

Notice that the join between the employee and department table is automatically added to the query by PowerBuilder. PowerBuilder adds

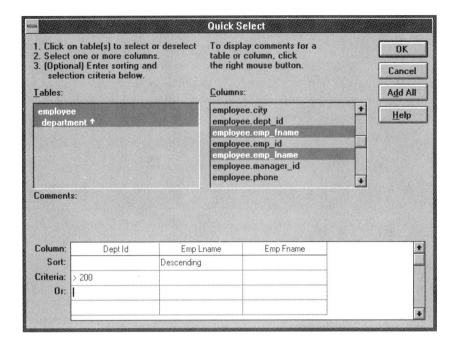

Figure 3.3   Selecting employee records on a Quick Select window.

the join to the Where clause based on the defined key relationship between the two tables.

Note: When selecting from more than one table using Quick Select, PowerBuilder will add only one set of join criteria to the Where clause of the resulting Select statement for each pair of tables. If more than one primary or foreign key relationship exists between two tables, verify that the correct join criteria has been specified by looking at the syntax of the Select statement in the Select painter.

The Quick Select data source is good to use for relatively simple queries. It does not allow specification of retrieve arguments or a table join (other than the join specified by a key relationship), but these can be added later through the Select painter, at which point the query generated with a Quick Select data source is no different than a query generated with a SQL Select data source.

SQL Select The SQL Select data source is the most common data source of a DataWindow object. Like the Quick Select, the SQL Select involves the selection of tables and columns to construct the query. The SQL Select allows all aspects of the query to be defined, however, rather than just the selection columns, sort order, and limited selection criteria. The SQL Select data source is generally used for more complex queries, including those containing joins, Group By clauses, and Having clauses.

PowerBuilder 4 has enhanced the Select painter to use a tab interface combined with drag-and-drop to define each element of the query. For example, to sort a list of employees by last name, click the Sort tab and drag the emp_lname column from the list of columns on the left to the box on the right as shown in Figure 3.4.

Query PowerBuilder query objects can also be used as the data source of a DataWindow object. To use this type of data source, the developer simply chooses the query object from the appropriate .PBL. Queries are

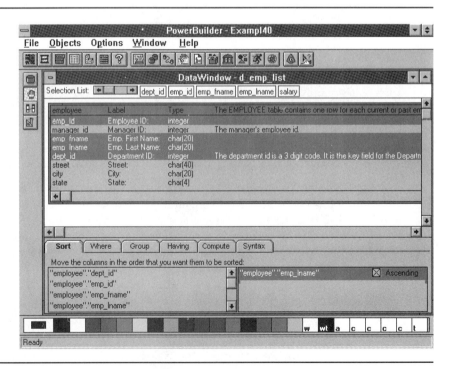

Figure 3.4   Sorting a list of employees by last name using Select painter.

good to use when there is a query that is used often in an application and thus has been saved to a file.

External External data sources represent data that is not retrieved from an application database. When creating a DataWindow with an external data source, a result set must be defined. This result set is a listing of columns and their datatypes. One reason for using DataWindow objects with external data sources is to enable the validation and editing capabilities built into the DataWindow object. External data sources can also be used when the data is stored with the DataWindow object instead of retrieved from a database. For example, to store a list of states within a DataWindow, the developer would define an external data source with a code and description element and store the state information within the DataWindow as shown in Figure 3.5.

Stored Procedures If an application DBMS supports stored procedures, they can be used as a data source for a DataWindow object. To use a stored procedure as a data source, the stored procedure must have the ability to return result sets to PowerBuilder. While most DBMSs that support stored procedures have this capability, Oracle7 does not. For this reason, PowerBuilder 3.0 did not allow Oracle stored procedures to be used as a data source. However, PowerBuilder 4 has solved this problem

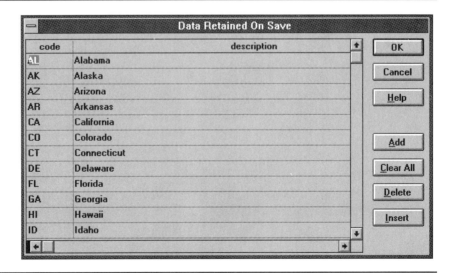

Figure 3.5   Storing a list of states within a DataWindow.

by creating a customized Oracle package, PBDBMS, that provides this capability—with some help from the developer. To allow Oracle-stored procedures to be used as a data source, the developer must:

- Install the PBDBMS package on the Oracle 7 server.
- Set the new DBParm variable PBDBMS to 1.
- Modify the stored procedure by replacing the SQL Select statement with calls to the PBDBMS function **Put_Line( )**.

Calling **Put_Line( )** will put the syntax of the Select statement into a buffer that PowerBuilder will later use to retrieve and execute the Select statement and return the data to the DataWindow.

PowerBuilder 4 has also added a new preference variable named *stored_procedure_build* that allows the automatic building of the result set when using a stored procedure data source. To enable this feature, set *stored_procedure_build* to 1. When *stored_procedure_build* is not set to 1, the developer is prompted for the result set description (as in PowerBuilder 3.0).

Presentation Styles

This section provides a brief description of the different DataWindow object presentation styles supported by PowerBuilder. For a more detailed description of each presentation style, refer to PowerBuilder documentation.

Composite PowerBuilder 4 has added the capability to place multiple DataWindows or reports within a DataWindow. This feature, referred to as nested or composite reports, allows existing DataWindows or reports to be added to any band of a DataWindow of any presentation style. Multiple reports can be included in a single DataWindow and composite reports will print on the same page as the DataWindow when it is printed.

A composite report may or may not be related to the DataWindow to which it is added. Composite reports that are not related to the DataWindow are used as a method of placing multiple reports on the same page. For example, it may be desirable to have three DataWindows that display a single data set using different presentation styles on a single page. Composite reports provide a simple method of doing this. To create a set of nonrelated reports, select Composite as the presentation style of the new DataWindow. This will then display a dialog of all available DataWindows. From this list select all of the DataWindows that will be included in the base DataWindow.

If a composite report is related to the DataWindow, the data in the composite report is in some way dependent on the data in the Data-Window. The relationship between the composite report and the Data-Window is specified using the Specify Retrieval Criteria dialog of the DataWindow painter. For example, assume we want to list the department id and name in one DataWindow and include a DataWindow listing all employees of the department as a composite report within the department DataWindow. To do this, first create the department Data-Window as shown in Figure 3.6.

Next, click the report icon from the DataWindow PainterBar (📖). This will display a dialog of all available DataWindows. From this list choose the employee list DataWindow (d_emp_list) and place it below the department name, as shown in Figure 3.7.

To define the relationship between the nested report and the Data-Window, select the report, press the right mouse button, and select the Criteria... option, as shown in Figure 3.8.

This will display the Specify Retrieval Criteria dialog. This dialog

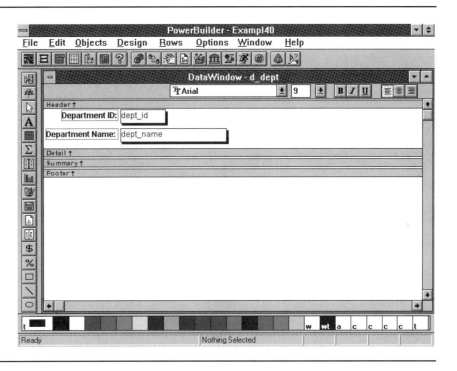

Figure 3.6   Creating the department DataWindow.

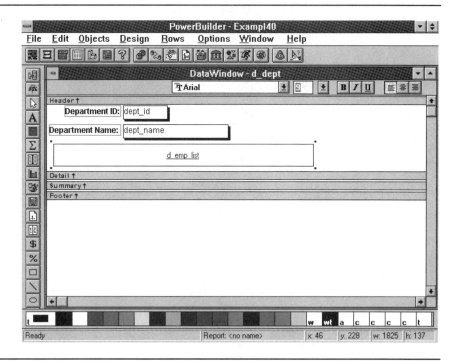

Figure 3.7   Choosing the employee list DataWindow and placing it below the department name.

displays each column of the nested DataWindow and allows the entry of selection criteria for the nested report. Values in this dialog may either be constants or names of columns from the base DataWindow. For this example, retrieve all employees whose department id is the same as the department id of the base DataWindow, as shown in Figure 3.9.

If the nested report contains retrieval arguments, they may be specified using the Retrieval Arguments dialog. To display this dialog, select the report, press the right mouse button, and select the Retrieval Arguments... option, as shown in Figure 3.10.

This will display the Retrieval Arguments dialog. This dialog displays each retrieval argument defined for the nested DataWindow and allows the selection of columns from the base DataWindow or the definition of an expression. For this example, select the dept_id column. This will use the dept_id value of the base DataWindow when retrieving data into the nested DataWindow, as shown in Figure 3.11.

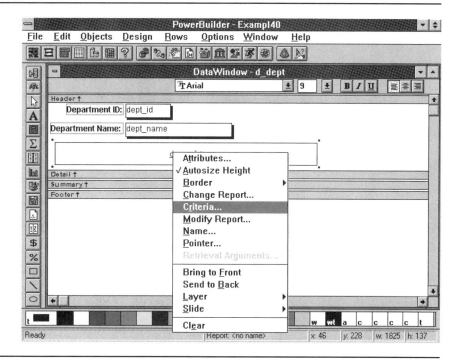

Figure 3.8   Defining the relationship between the nested report and the DataWindow.

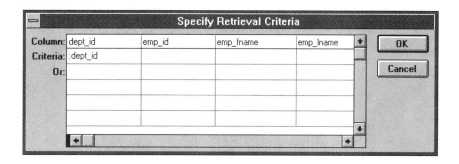

Figure 3.9   The Specify Retrieval Criteria dialog window.

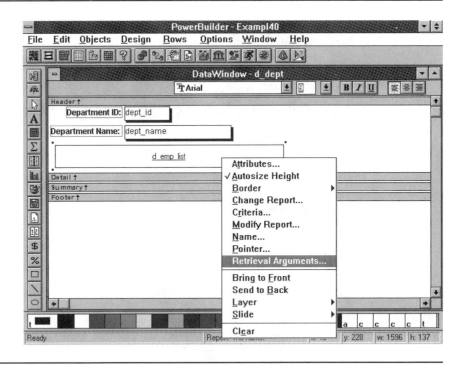

Figure 3.10   Obtaining the Retrieval Arguments dialog.

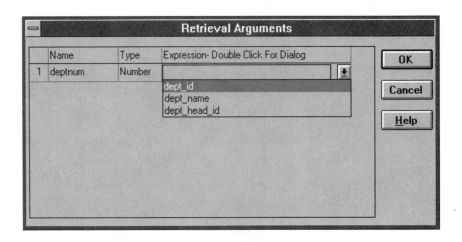

Figure 3.11   Selecting the dept_id value from the Retrieval Arguments dialog.

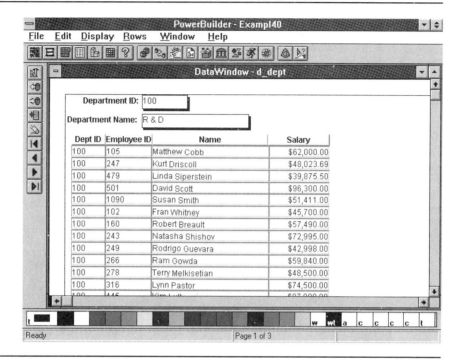

Figure 3.12   Retrieval of all employees for current department.

This will then retrieve all employees for the current department, as shown in Figure 3.12.

Composite reports simplify the development of DataWindows with a master/detail relationship. Instead of having two (or more) separate DataWindow controls for the master and detail DataWindows—each of which must have code written to set the DataWindow's transaction object, retrieve, update, and so on—composite reports allow for a single DataWindow control and are more efficient because only one transaction is required.

Crosstab   The crosstab presentation style presents data in a matrix format, as shown in Figure 3.13.

PowerBuilder 4 has enhanced the Crosstab Definition dialog, adding a drag/drop capability for defining the various elements of the crosstab. Figure 3.14 shows the Crosstab Definition dialog for the previous example.

PowerBuilder 4 has also changed the default style of a crosstab DataWindow to display headers for rows, columns, and values. In addi-

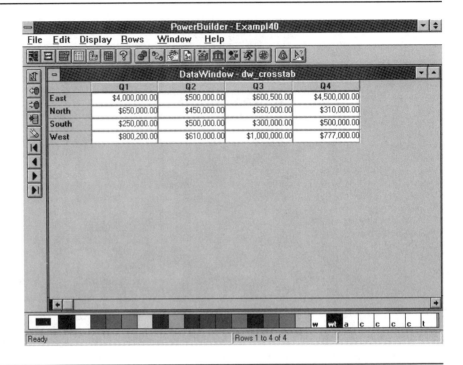

Figure 3.13   Matrix format of the crosstab presentation style.

tion, the default crosstab includes computed fields to display a grand total for each column and row as well as a grand total for the entire crosstab. PowerBuilder 4 also allows source column names to be changed. This is done by double-clicking on the column in the Source Data list of the Crosstab Definition dialog. To do this at runtime, call **dwModify( )** using the DataWindow.Crosstab.Sourcenames parameter. To display the Crosstab Defintion dialog at runtime, call the DataWindow function **datawindow.CrosstabDialog( )**.

PowerBuilder 4 has added three new options for crosstab and grid DataWindows. They are:

- Column Moving—Allows the user to reorder columns by dragging/ dropping (default True).
- Mouse Selection—Allows the user to select multiple columns and rows (default True).
- Row Resize—Allows the user to resize rows (default False).

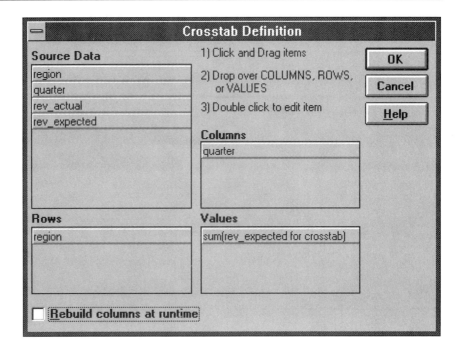

Figure 3.14   Crosstab Definition dialog window.

These options are set by clicking the right mouse button while positioned in an unused area of the DataWindow and selecting the <u>G</u>rid option.

Freeform The freeform presentation style, generally used for data entry forms, places fields down the page, with labels next to each data column. In PowerBuilder 3.0, all fields were placed in a single column along the far left side of the detail band of the DataWindow. In freeform DataWindows with a large number of fields, this method of placement usually required a great deal of modification of the field positions by the developer.

PowerBuilder 4 has modified the default field placement of freeform DataWindows by allowing the specification of a wrap height. The wrap height, measured in inches, specifies the default height of the detail band of the DataWindow. This allows fields to be placed in multiple columns of the detail band. For example, to specify a wrap height of one inch, select the freeform presentation style and click the **Options...** button on the

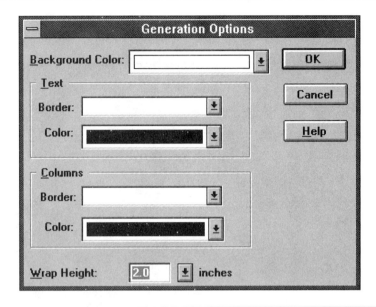

Figure 3.15   Selecting wrap height in the Options dialog.

new DataWindow dialog. In the Options dialog, enter (or select) the desired wrap height as shown in Figure 3.15.

The default DataWindow will then create multiple columns of fields, if necessary. An example default freeform DataWindow with a wrap height of one inch is shown in Figure 3.16.

Note: While the previous example shows only one row, additional rows are displayed by scrolling down the page. If the developer wants to show only one row, the DataWindow control can be sized to show only a single row and set up to not allow scrolling.

Graph The graph presentation style allows the developer to choose from a wide range of graph types in which to present DataWindow data. Graphs are discussed further in Chapter 9.

Grid The grid presentation style presents data in a row-column format. Rows and columns are separated by a grid line. A further discussion of grids can be found in Chapter 9.

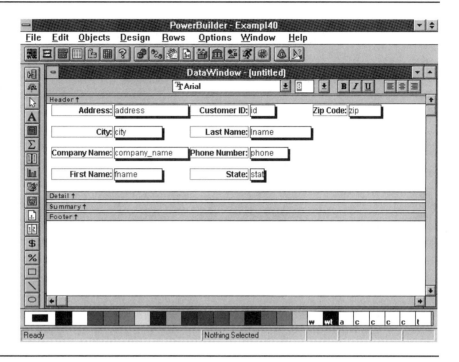

Figure 3.16   Example of a default freeform DataWindow with a wrap height of one inch.

Group The group presentation style allows groups to be defined when the DataWindow is created. Groups are discussed in more detail in the next section of this chapter.

Label The label presentation style is a customized report style used to print mailing labels. The developer can define the size of the label, the printing sequence, and other attributes using the label specification window, as shown in Figure 3.17.

N-Up The N-Up presentation style allows rows to be displayed side-by-side in the DataWindow. The developer can define the number of rows to display in the detail band of the DataWindow.

Tabular The tabular presentation style presents data in the format of columns across the page with a header above each column. The tabular format is often used to display many rows of data at once. For example, Figure 3.18 shows a list of customers in a tabular format.

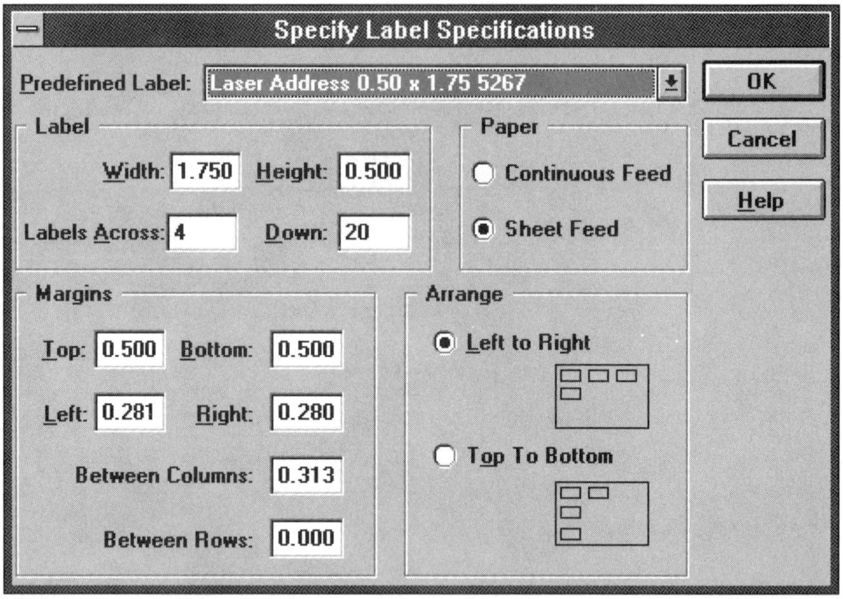

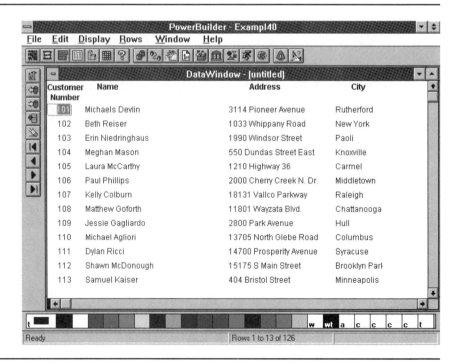

Figure 3.17   Label Specifications window.

Figure 3.18   List of customers in a tabular format.

Groups

PowerBuilder allows related rows to be grouped together for the purposes of formatting or performing group-related functions such as group sums, averages, and the like. Using a PowerBuilder group is different from adding a Group By clause to a Select statement because the grouping is done on the client rather than the server.

Groups are created either by specifying a group presentation style when creating a new DataWindow or by selecting the Create Group... option from the Rows menu of the DataWindow painter. PowerBuilder assigns a sequential number (beginning with 1) as the group name. For example, to show an average salary for all employees by manager within a department, the developer goes through a number of steps. First, the developer creates a group break on the dept_id and manager_id columns in the employee table, by completing the Group Specification dialog as shown in Figure 3.19.

Notice that the Group Definition dialog has been changed in Power-Builder 4 to use a drag/drop interface. Next, a computed field with the expression shown in Figure 3.20 must be created.

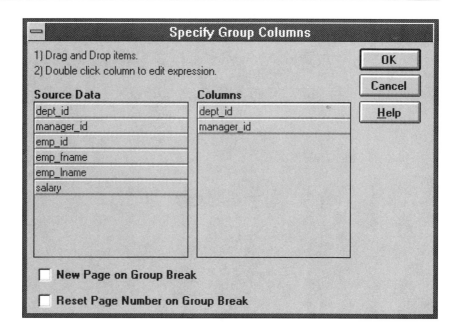

Figure 3.19   The Group Specification dialog window.

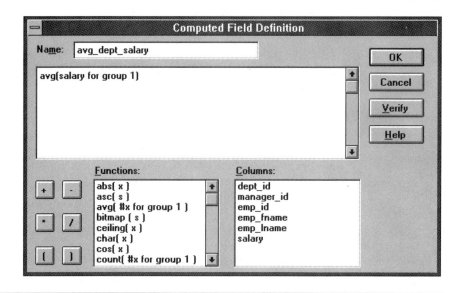

Figure 3.20 Computed Field definition.

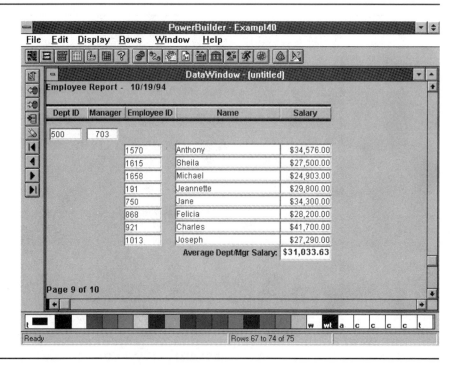

Figure 3.21 Employee data display.

This displays the employee data as shown in Figure 3.21.

Group calculations are performed after the data has been retrieved from the database. Should rows be inserted, deleted, or modified during a user session, it may be necessary to repeat the group calculation on the new set of rows. Rather than retrieving the data again, the calculation can be performed by calling the PowerBuilder **dwGroupCalc( )** function.

Note: It is important to make sure data is sorted before being used in a group. Sorting can be done either on the server, by adding an Order By clause to the Select statement, or on the client, by specifying sort criteria when creating the DataWindow or using the **Sort( )** function.

Filters

Filters provide a way of limiting the part of a result set a user interacts with. A filter is different from a Where clause in the DataWindow's Select statement in that it is done on the client instead of the server. With a filter, all data from a Select is returned to the client and then filtered by PowerBuilder. A filter is a Boolean expression defined using PowerBuilder functions. The filter shown in Figure 3.22 could be defined for the previous example, to limit what is displayed in the DataWindow to those rows in which dept_id = 100.

Filters can be modified dynamically using the **SetFilter( )** and **Filter( )** functions. **SetFilter( )** allows a new filter to be defined for a DataWindow, while **Filter( )** actually applies the filter to the DataWindow. For example, to change the filter in the previous example from dept_id = 100 to dept_id = 200, the following script would be executed:

```
dw_emp.SetFilter("dept_id = 200")
dw_emp.Filter( )
```

To determine how many rows have been filtered out by a filter, use the **FilteredCount( )** function. For example, the following script uses **FilteredCount( )** to tell how many employees work in departments other than 200:

```
dw_emp.Retrieve( )

dw_emp.SetFilter("dept_id = 200")
dw_emp.Filter( )
If dw_emp.FilteredCount( ) > 0 then
```

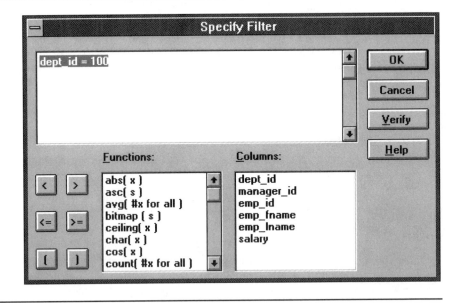

Figure 3.22   Specifying the filter.

```
    // Processing for non dept. 200 employees
End if
```

Using filters provides some flexibility with regard to what data is displayed in a DataWindow. Filters can also improve performance by limiting the number of required database retrievals. They do, however, add some overhead on the client. In addition, instead of retrieving a large result set and using filters, it is generally better to use a Where clause to restrict the amount of data returned from the server.

Sorting

Like filters, sorting can be done on the client as well as the server. Sorting on the server is accomplished using an Order By clause in an SQL Select statement. When sorting on the client, all data from a Select is returned to the client and then sorted by PowerBuilder. This provides a method of off-loading the sorting process from the server to the client.

A DataWindow sort order can be changed dynamically using the **SetSort( )** and **Sort( )** functions. **SetSort( )** defines the sort order of a DataWindow, while **Sort( )** actually performs the sort operation on the data. For example, the following script changes the sort order of a Data-Window to sort on the manager_id field. Then it sorts the data:

```
dw_emp.SetSort("manager_id A")
dw_emp.Sort( )
```

Whether to sort on the client or the server depends on the size of the result set, the resources available on the server and client, and how often the sorting criteria are to be changed. If server resources are not limited, sorting can usually be done more quickly on the server, but if the data must be sorted multiple times in an application, sorting on the client will usually result in better overall performance than executing the query multiple times on the server. In addition, PowerBuilder 4 has increased the performance of sorting operations that do not involve expressions. According to Powersoft, tests show approximately five times better performance of sorts in PowerBuilder 4 compared to PowerBuilder 3.0.

Sliding Columns

PowerBuilder 4 has added a new option for DataWindow and Report columns that provides a way to remove the excess space between columns. There are three options available for sliding columns:

- Left—Slides the selected column to the left, removing excess space between the selected column and the column to its left. One popular use of sliding columns to the left is the removal of space between a first and last name. Without this capability, presenting a first and last name with a single space between the two usually required the creation of a computed field or included the concatenation within the Select statement of the DataWindow. This feature makes it easier for the developer to present data in this fashion.
- Up-All Above—Slides all columns positioned above the selected column up, removing excess vertical space between columns. This can be used for such things as mailing labels.
- Up-Directly Above—Slides only columns positioned directly above the selected column up, removing excess vertical space between columns.

Note: To use sliding columns, the AutoSize Height attribute of the column must be set to True. This is because blank columns still have a height that must be able to be changed in order to slide the column.

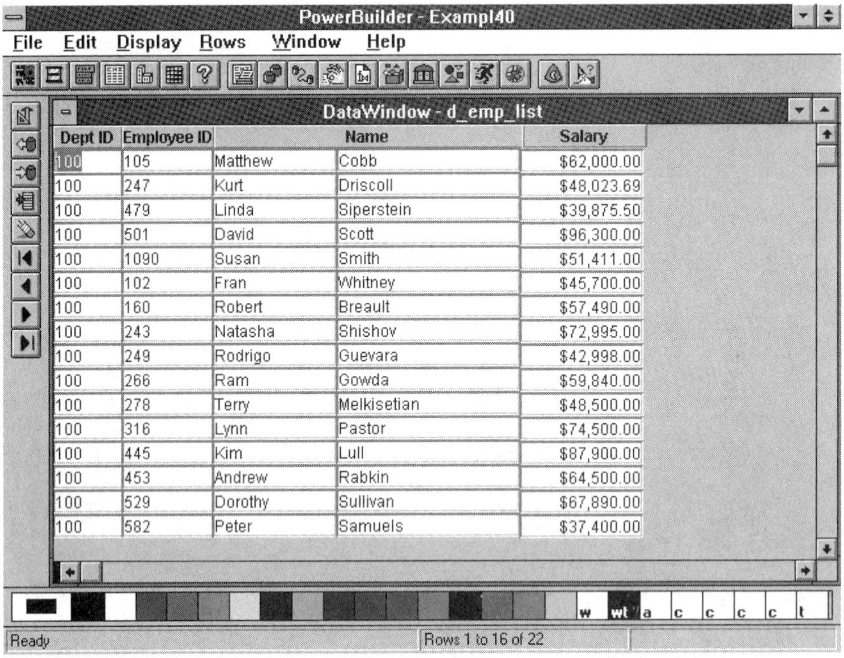

Figure 3.23   List of employees displaying first and last names.

For example, suppose we want to retrieve a list of employees and display the first and last name with a single space between them. By default, the data is presented as shown in Figure 3.23.

To slide the last name column to the left, select the last name column and set the Slide attribute as shown in Figure 3.24.

This will display the list with a single space between the first and last name, as shown in Figure 3.25.

Data Validation

One of the benefits of using DataWindows is the built-in validation capabilities. To better understand how validation works, it is necessary to look at how a DataWindow is actually represented to the user. A DataWindow consists of two logical pieces—a presentation layer (consisting of a floating "edit control") and the underlying DataWindow buffer. Data is entered by the user into the edit control. This data must then be validated before being passed to the DataWindow buffer, as shown in Figure 3.26.

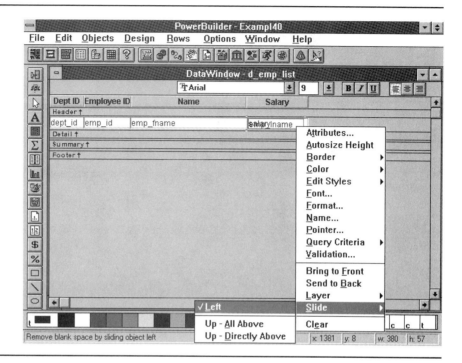

Figure 3.24   Sliding the last name column to the left.

In this example, the salary retrieved from the database for the first employee is 41023.69. After retrieval, this value is in both the edit control and the DataWindow buffer. When the user changes this value to 50000.00, the change is only recognized in the edit control. The Data-Window buffer does not receive the new value until the data is validated.

Note: Changes can be made to the DataWindow buffer directly using the **SetItem( )** function. This function bypasses all validation other than data type validation.

Validation is triggered by any of the following:

- The user attempting to leave the column
- The user pressing the Enter key
- The **AcceptText( )** function being executed

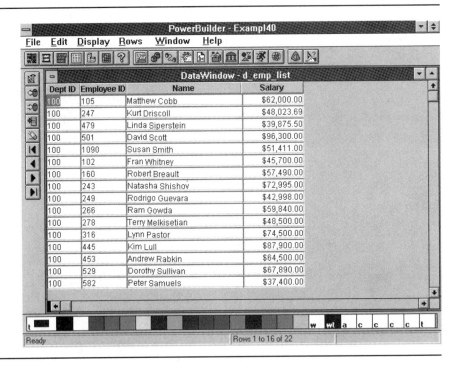

Figure 3.25 Employee list with single space between first and last name.

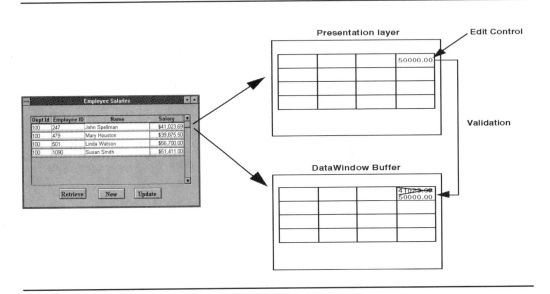

Figure 3.26 Validation of data entered by user into the edit control.

These events cause PowerBuilder to begin its three-step validation process. The steps are:

- Data Type validation
- Validation Rules validation
- ItemChanged Event validation

These steps are discussed in the following sections.

Data Type Validation In the data type validation step, PowerBuilder makes sure that the data type entered by the user is the same as the data type of the column. For example, if a user enters "ABC" into a numeric field, an error occurs.

Validation Rules PowerBuilder allows developers to create custom validation rules. These rules consist of PowerScript Boolean expressions that are defined using either the Database painter or the DataWindow painter. Rules defined using the Database painter, which are stored in the PowerBuilder system tables as extended attributes, are available for reuse with any DataWindow column. Within the DataWindow painter, a default validation rule can be used or a new rule can be created for the current column only. When creating validation rules, therefore, it is important to know if the rule should be shared among multiple columns in any application.

From the Database painter, rules can be defined in two ways. The first method is to position the cursor over the desired column and click the right mouse button to display the column's popup attribute menu. For example, to create a validation rule for the dept_id column in the employee table, select the Validation option from the column's popup menu, as shown in Figure 3.27.

This displays a list of all the rules defined for the same data type as the selected column. In our example, when selecting the validation attribute for the dept_id column, all rules for integer type columns in the current database would be listed. The column validation window allows the creation and modification of rules, along with the setting of an initial value for the column, as shown in Figure 3.28.

The second method is to select the Validation Maintenance... option from the Objects menu of the Database painter, as shown in Figure 3.29.

This lists **all** defined rules for the current database, as shown in Figure 3.30.

When a rule is defined for a column using the Database painter, it is used whenever the column is included as part of a DataWindow. When

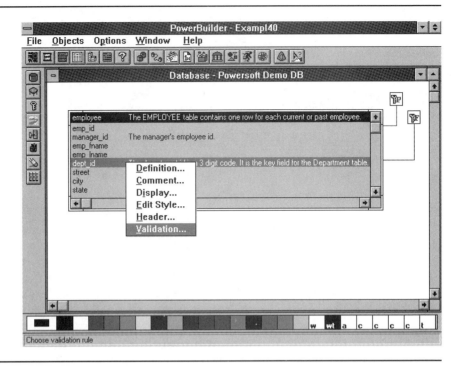

Figure 3.27   Selecting the Validation option.

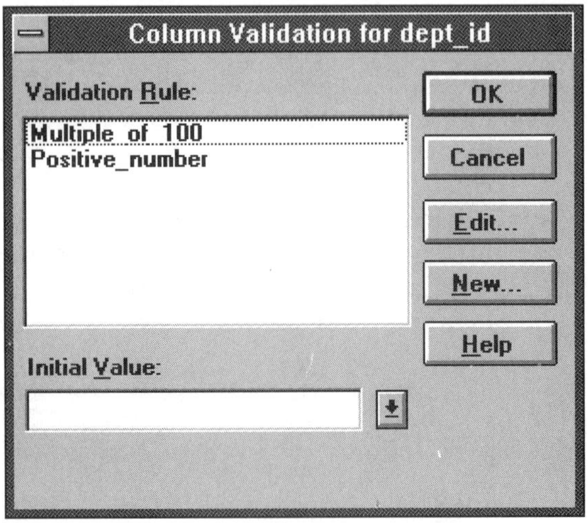

Figure 3.28   Column Validation window.

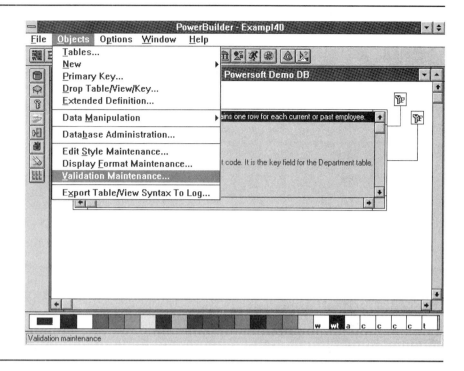

Figure 3.29   Selecting the <u>V</u>alidation maintenance... option.

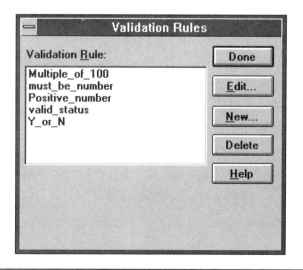

Figure 3.30   Listing of all defined Validation rules.

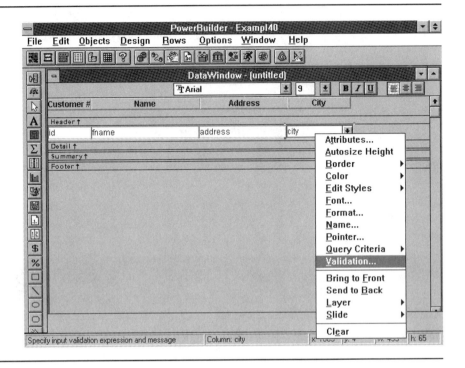

Figure 3.31   Selecting the Validation... option.

the column is placed onto a DataWindow, any changes made to the rule subsequently are **not** reflected in the column on the DataWindow.

To define a rule from the DataWindow painter, select the Validation... option from the Column Attribute menu (obtained by selecting the column and holding down the right mouse button), as shown in Figure 3.31.

This displays the column validation definition screen, on which the validation rule and default validation error message are defined, as shown in Figure 3.32.

For information on the set of PowerBuilder functions available for use in rule expressions, see the PowerBuilder Function Reference.

The developer should realize that any rules defined from the Data-Window painter are not stored in the system tables and thus cannot be used by other columns.

Changing Rules Dynamically Rules can be changed at runtime using the **GetValidate( )** and **SetValidate( )** functions. **GetValidate( )** re-

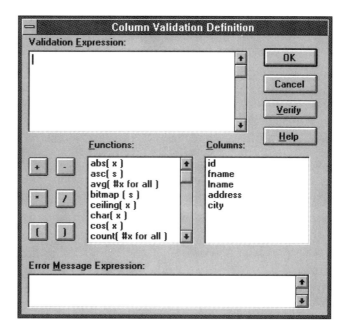

Figure 3.32   Column Validation Definition screen.

trieves the current rule of a DataWindow column into a string variable; **SetValidate( )** redefines the rule of a column. These functions are generally used to temporarily change a rule during execution and later reset it to its original value. This same functionality can also be accomplished through **dwDescribe( )** and **dwModify( )** using the columnName.validation attribute. **DwModify( )** can also be used to change the validation error message—using the columnName.validationMsg attribute.

Note: For performance reasons, the developer should try to minimize the number of times a rule is changed.

ItemChanged Event The ItemChanged event is triggered whenever data in a column has been changed and the column loses focus. In columns with a DropDownListBox edit style, the ItemChanged event is triggered when a user selects an item in the list, but before the column loses focus. In either case, the ItemChanged event is usually used to validate any business rules pertaining to the column. This is the final step in the validation process.

It is important that code in the ItemChanged event not cause another ItemChanged event to be triggered, resulting in an endless loop. To keep this from occurring, **AcceptText( )**, **SetColumn( )**, and **SetRow( )** function calls should not be put into the ItemChanged script. In addition, because the **Update( )** function does an **AcceptText( )** by default, the **Update( )** function should only be called with the first parameter set to False—to keep **AcceptText( )** from being executed.

The ItemChanged event has a set of action codes associated with it that allow the developer to specify the action that is taken when the event occurs. Action codes are set using the **SetActionCode( )** function, which behaves differently depending on the context in which it is called. For the ItemChanged event, the valid action codes are:

0—Accept the data value (default).

1—Reject the data value.

2—Reject the data value but allow the focus to change.

When validation passes through the ItemChanged event, it is passed from the edit control to the DataWindow buffer.

Process Flow The validation process flow is shown in the diagram in Figure 3.33. It is important to note that the validation process occurs only if data has changed. Whether data has changed is determined by comparing the value in the edit control to the item in the DataWindow buffer. Because this comparison is not made until the column loses focus, situations in which a user makes a change and re-enters the original value before leaving the column are not considered changes.

As each level of validation is passed, PowerBuilder performs the test at the next level (if available). If any of the steps fail, PowerBuilder triggers the ItemError event. If there is no error-handling code in the ItemError event, PowerBuilder handles the error by displaying a message box similar to the one in Figure 3.34.

At this point, the cursor returns to the field in question and the user must re-enter the value.

Note: To restore the original value from the DataWindow buffer into the edit control, press the **Escape** key.

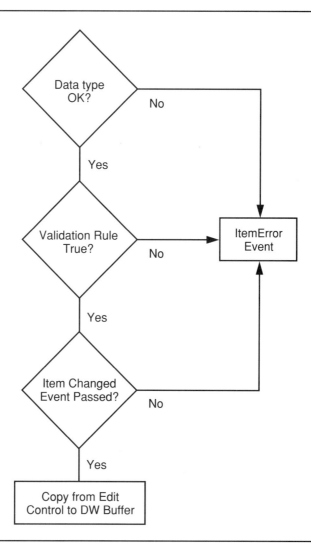

Figure 3.33   Diagram of the validation process flow.

ItemError Event The ItemError event can be used to code such customized error handling as writing to an error log when an error occurs or changing the message displayed to the user. The following code can be placed in the ItemError event of a DataWindow control to change the error message displayed to the user:

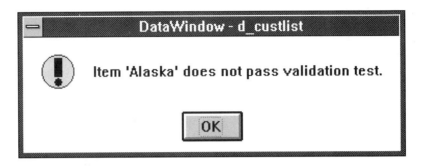

Figure 3.34   Message box for handling errors.

```
string sColValue, sColName

// Get the current column name and the text in the column
sColName = this.GetColumnName( )
sColValue = this.GetText( )

// Call the function to display the custom error message
DisplayMsg("Validation Error", &
    "'" + sColValue + "' is not valid for column '" + sColName + "'")

// Set action code to not display system message
this.SetActionCode(1)
```

Notice the last line of this code calls the **SetActionCode( )** function. For the ItemError event, the value passed to **SetActionCode( )** determines how to handle the error. The valid action code values for the ItemError event are:

0—Reject the data value and show a system error screen (default).

1—Reject the data value but do not show a system error screen.

2—Accept the data value.

3—Reject the data value but allow the focus to change.

Note: Include a call to **AcceptText( )** in the LoseFocus event of the DataWindow control to make sure the data at the current position within the DataWindow has been validated.

Protecting Columns Prior to PowerBuilder 4, the only way to keep a user from entering a column in a DataWindow was by either setting the tab order of the column to 0 or programmatically preventing user access to the column. PowerBuilder 4 has added the Protect column attribute to prevent users from entering a column without having to set the tab order to 0. The Protect attribute can be a constant or expression and is set using the Attribute Expressions dialog, as shown in Figure 3.35.

If the expression defined for a column's Protect attribute evaluates to True, the column is protected and the user cannot enter the column. If the expression evaluates to False, the column is not protected and the user is able to enter the column. The Protect attribute provides a simple way of conditionally protecting a column, using such things as row or column status and the value of other columns to determine if a column should be protected. For example, if a column should be protected for existing rows and unprotected for new rows, the protect expression could be defined as shown in Figure 3.36.

The Protect attribute provides a way of protecting a column without requiring additional code to set the tab order of the column.

Code Tables Code tables provide a method of validation by ensuring that the data entered by the user is in a predefined table of codes. Code tables are discussed in further detail in the Design Considerations section of this chapter.

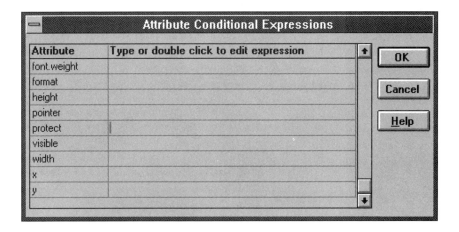

Figure 3.35   Attributes Expressions dialog box.

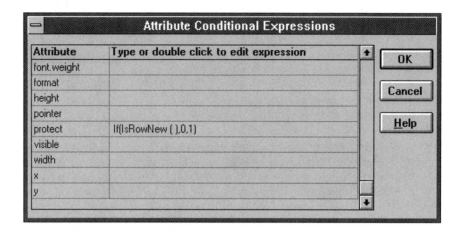

Figure 3.36   Example of defining the Protect expression.

Finding Required Columns Use the **dwFindRequired( )** DataWindow function to find all required DataWindow columns that contain Null. The syntax of this function is shown below:

```
datawindowname.dwFindRequired ( dwbuffer, row, colnbr, colname, &
      updateonly )
```

where:

datawindowname—the name of the DataWindow control in which to find the required columns that have Null values.

dwbuffer—a dwBuffer enumerated data type indicating the Data-Window buffer to search for required columns (Primary!, Filtered!)

row—the row at which to begin searching (1 to search all rows). **dwFindRequired** increments the row number automatically after it validates the row in all the columns. When it finds a row with a required column with a Null value, its row number is stored in row. After **dwFindRequired** validates the last column in the last row, it sets row to 0.

colnbr—the number of the column at which to begin searching (1 to search all columns). After validating the last column **dwFind Required** sets colnbr to 1 and increments row. When it finds a required column without a Null value, the column number is stored in colnbr.

colname—string variable in which to store the name of the required column containing a Null value (the name of colnbr).

updateonly—indicates whether to validate all rows and columns or only rows that have been inserted or modified. (True—Validate only those that have changed. Setting updateonly to True enhances performance in large DataWindows. False—Validate all rows and columns.)

Starting at row, colnbr in datawindowname, **dwFindRequired( )** finds the row and column location of a required column that contains a Null value and stores the row number in row, the column number in colnbr, and the column name in colname. If updateonly is True, **dwFind Required** checks only rows that have been inserted or modified.

This function should be called before updating a DataWindow in order to prevent the sending of an Insert or Update statement that is known to cause an error. The following code illustrates the use of **dwFindRequired( )**:

```
long    lRowNum
int     iColNum
string iColName

lRowNum = 1
iColNum = 1

// Loop to find all instances
DO WHILE row <> 0
// Exit if an error occurs
  if dw_1.dwFindRequired(primary!,row,colnbr,colname,TRUE) < 0 then
      exit
  end if

// If row is not 0, a required row,column was found without a value.
// Display a message indicating the row and column in error
  if row <> 0 then
      MessageBox("Required Value Missing","Enter a value in " &
        + colname +"Row " + string (row) )
      // Go to the row and column in error
      dw_1.SetColumn(colnbr)
      dw_1.ScrollToRow(row)
      exit
  end if
```

```
// This row and column was ok, continue
LOOP
```

Display Formats and Edit Masks

Display formats control how data is displayed to the user; an edit mask defines the way the data must be entered by the user. While these two things have a great deal in common, they can be different for a given column. For example, a phone number may have an edit mask of ########## and a display format of (###) ### - ####.

PowerBuilder allows developers to create custom display formats and edit masks, using either the Database painter or the DataWindow painter. Formats and edit masks defined using the Database painter are stored in the PowerBuilder system tables as extended attributes and are available for reuse with any DataWindow column. Within the DataWindow painter, a default format or edit mask can be used or a new edit mask can be created for the current column only. When creating a display format or edit mask, therefore, it is important to know if it will be shared among multiple columns in any application.

From the Database painter, display formats can be defined in two ways. The first method is to position the cursor over the desired column and click the right mouse button to display the column's Popup attribute menu. For example, to create a display format for the dept_id column in the employee table, select the **Display** option from the column's popup menu, as shown in Figure 3.37.

This displays a list of all the formats defined for the same data type as the selected column. In this example, when selecting the display attribute for the dept_id column, all display formats for integer type columns in the current database would be listed. The column display format window allows the creation and modification of formats, along with the setting of the display height and width and the justification of the column, as shown in Figure 3.38.

For edit masks, select the Edit Style... option from the column's popup menu, as shown in Figure 3.39.

This displays the Edit Style window. This window lists all edit styles defined for the current database, as shown in Figure 3.40.

To modify an existing edit mask, select the edit style and press the **Edit...** button. To create a new edit mask for a dept_id column that only allows three numbers, the developer would click the edit mask icon in the New group box and complete the edit mask window as shown, in Figure 3.41.

The second method used to define display formats and edit masks

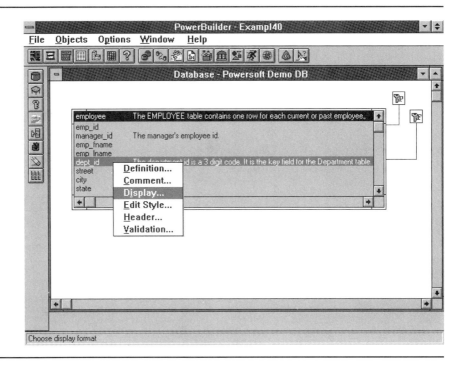

Figure 3.37   Selecting the Display option.

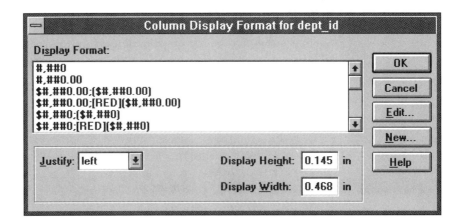

Figure 3.38   Column Display Format window.

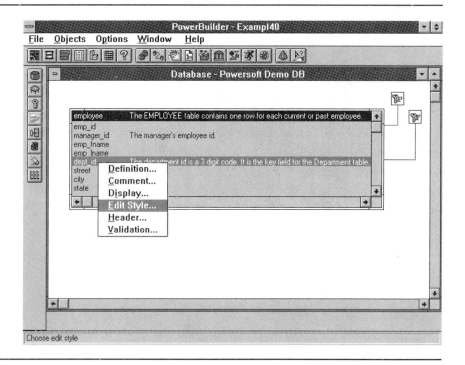

Figure 3.39   Selecting the Edit Style... option.

from the Database painter is to select the Edit Style Maintenance and Display Format Maintenance options from the Objects menu, respectively, as shown in Figure 3.42.

When a display format or edit mask is defined for a column using the Database painter, it is used whenever the column is included as part of a DataWindow. When the column is placed onto a DataWindow, changes made to the format or edit mask subsequently are **not** reflected in the column on the DataWindow.

To define a display format from the DataWindow painter, the developer selects the Format... option from the Column attribute menu (obtained by selecting the column and holding down the right mouse button), as shown in Figure 3.43.

This displays all the formats defined for the data type of the column. In our example, with the id column, the display format window displays all defined formats for an integer data type, as shown in Figure 3.44.

To define an edit mask from the DataWindow painter, the developer selects the Edit Mask option from the Edit Styles menu of the

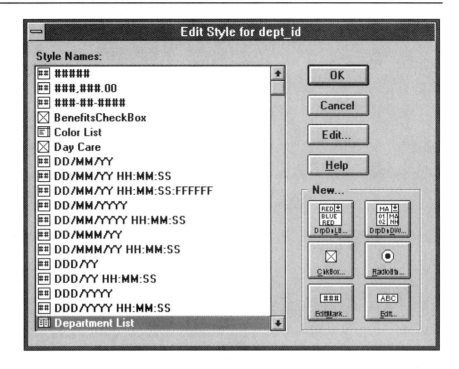

Figure 3.40   The Edit Style window.

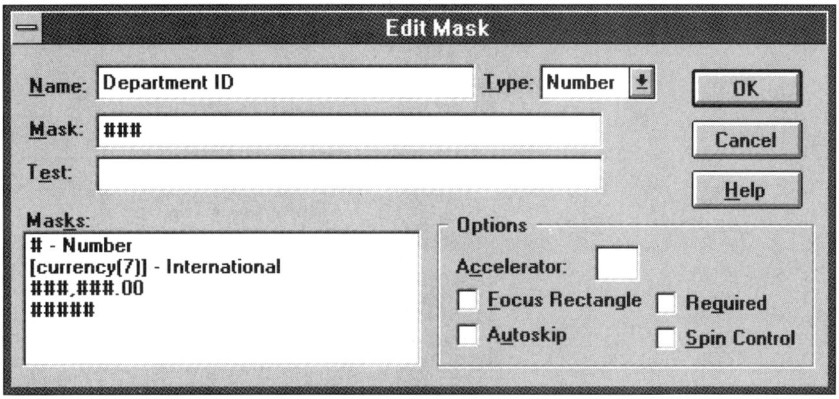

Figure 3.41   The Edit Mask window.

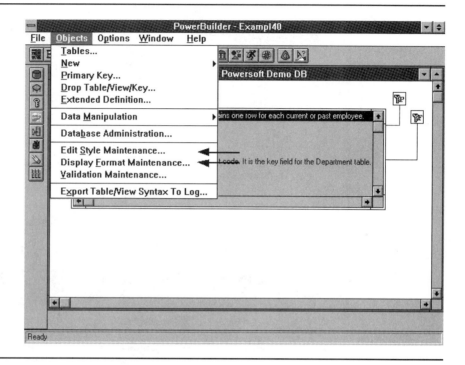

Figure 3.42   The second method for defining display formats and edit masks.

column attribute list (obtained by selecting the column and holding down the right mouse button), as shown in Figure 3.45.

This displays all the edit masks defined for the data type of the column. In our example, with the id column, the Edit mask dialog displays all defined edit masks for an integer data type, as shown in Figure 3.46.

Changing Display Formats Dynamically Display formats can be changed at runtime using the **GetFormat( )** and **SetFormat( )** functions. **GetFormat( )** retrieves the current display format of a DataWindow column into a string variable; **SetFormat( )** redefines the display format of a column. These functions are generally used to temporarily change a display format during execution and later reset it to its original value. To illustrate the changing of display formats, suppose the format of a string DataWindow column will change depending on the value retrieved from the database. For example, if the value is a phone number, the display format will be (@@@) @@@—@@@@, but if the value

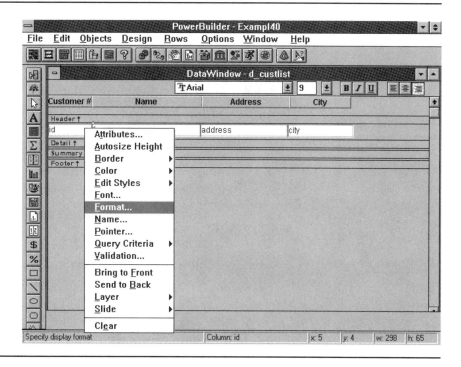

Figure 3.43 Selecting the Format... option from the Column attribute menu.

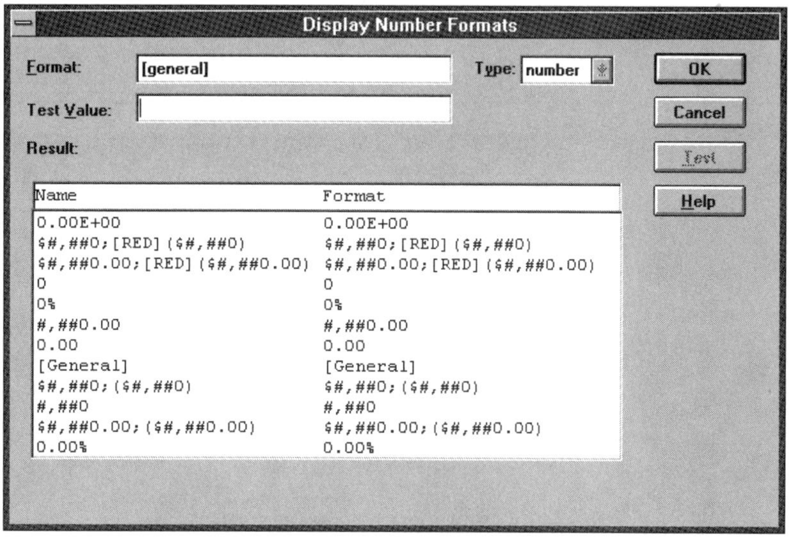

Figure 3.44 The Display Format window.

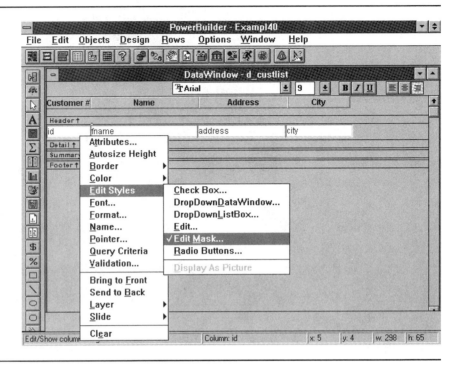

Figure 3.45   Selecting the Edit Mask... option.

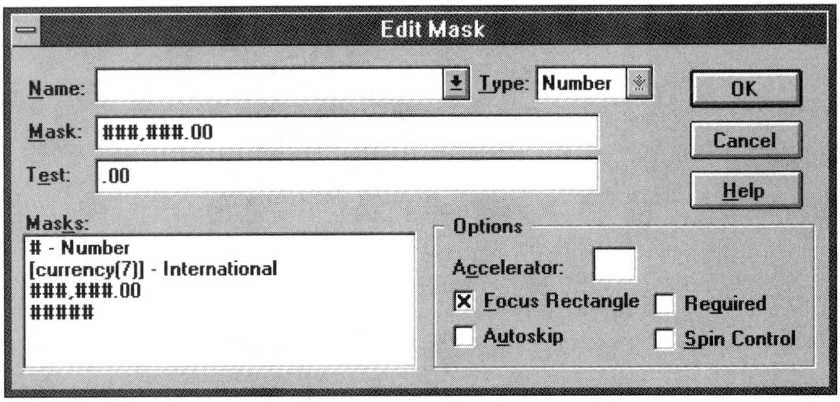

Figure 3.46   The Edit Mask dialog box.

is a social security number, the format will be @@@-@@-@@@@. To do this, the developer puts the following code in the clicked event of the **Retrieve** command button (assume the instance variable *i_sNumType* has previously been set):

```
int     iRetCode
string sOldFormat

sOldFormat = dw_main.GetFormat("num_col")

CHOOSE CASE i_sNumType
    CASE "PHONE"
        dw_main.SetFormat("num_col","(@@@) @@@-@@@@")
    CASE "SOCIAL_SEC"
        dw_main.SetFormat("num_col","@@@-@@-@@@@")
END CHOOSE

iRetCode = dw_main.retrieve()
if (iRetCode = -1) then
    MessageBox("Select Error", sqlca.sqlerrtext)
end if
```

This same functionality can also be accomplished through **dwDescribe( )** and **dwModify( )** using the ColumnName.Format attribute for the display format and the ColumnName.EditMask.Mask attribute for the edit mask. **dwDescribe( )** and **dwModify( )** are discussed later in this chapter.

Spin Controls A spin control is a type of edit mask that allows users to increment and decrement a value by clicking an up or down arrow on the control. To define a spin control, the developer checks the spin control checkbox in the edit mask definition window. This displays the data shown in Figure 3.47.

Spin controls can be defined for numbers, dates, and strings. For numbers, a spin control uses the values entered in the Spin Range group box and increments/decrements the value by the number in the Spin Increment column.

The same is true for dates, except that the values entered in the Spin Range group box must be valid dates. When changing date values with a spin control, the day, month, and year must be changed individually. For example, to change 01/28/93 to 02/01/93 requires using the spin control to change both the day (from 28 to 01) and the month (from 01 to 02). The change cannot be made by selecting the entire date and clicking the up arrow four times.

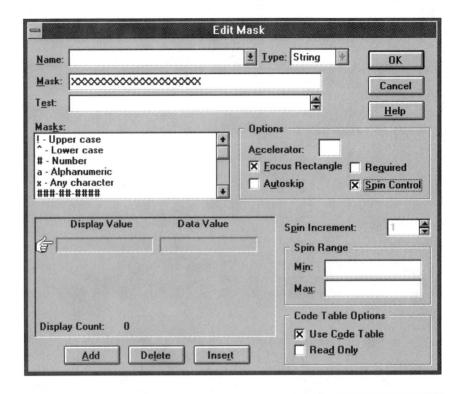

Figure 3.47 The Edit <u>M</u>ask definition window with the spin control checkbox checked.

For strings, the range of values is determined by what is in the code table display. For example, to use a spin control to choose between a set of cities, the developer would define the edit mask as shown in Figure 3.48.

This would display the city column in a customer list as shown in Figure 3.49.

The user could then scroll through the list of cities using the spin control.

Computed Columns and Fields

DataWindows can greatly be enhanced through the use of computed columns and fields. Computed columns are additional columns that can be added to a DataWindow as part of the SQL Select statement used to

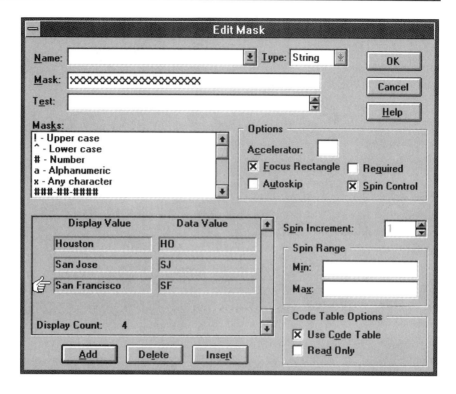

Figure 3.48   Defining the edit mask.

retrieve the DataWindow's data. Computed columns can consist of columns, DBMS functions (not PowerScript functions), operators, and retrieval arguments. Because they are in the Select statement, computed columns are only calculated when the DataWindow's **Retrieve( )** function is executed. The two important things to remember about computed columns are that they are an extension of the DBMS language (not PowerScript) and, because they are part of the Select statement, they can only be used within the detail band of a DataWindow.

For example, the following SQL statement creates a computed column with the total price of each product, calculated as the unit price of the product multiplied by the number of products ordered:

```
SELECT prod_num, prod_price, prod_qty, product_price * qty
FROM Products;
```

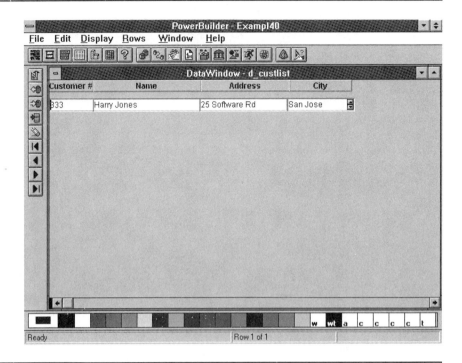

Figure 3.49 The city column displayed in a customer list.

Computed fields, on the other hand, are fields created dynamically by PowerBuilder **after** the DataWindow's **Retrieve( )** function has been executed. Computed fields, which can be used within all DataWindow bands (header, group headers, detail, group trailers, summary, and footer), can be changed based on the contents of the DataWindow object. Unlike computed columns, computed fields are not restricted to DBMS functions. They can contain both built-in and user-defined PowerScript functions, columns, operators, retrieval arguments, and references to other computed fields (new in PowerBuilder 4).

Computed fields are commonly used to provide summary information (both overall and by group), concatenated data ("Average salary for Dept." + dept_id + ":"), and system information (date, userid, etc.).

For example, assume the DataWindow shown in Figure 3.50 is used to track employee salary information and suppose the developer wants to enhance this DataWindow to do the following:

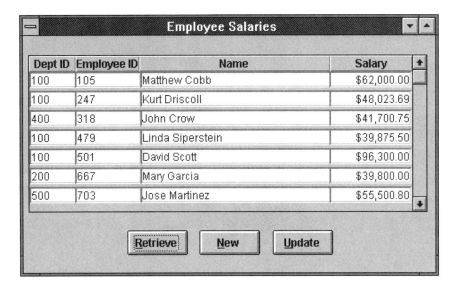

Figure 3.50   DataWindow for tracking employee salary information.

1. Show the average monthly salary for each employee.
2. Group the list by department and show the average monthly salary for employees in the department.
3. Add a page number to the bottom of each page.

To show the average monthly salary for each employee, create the computed field as shown in Figure 3.51.

Place the new computed field at the end of the DataWindow's detail band, as shown in Figure 3.52.

Next, group the list by department by selecting the Create Group... option from the Rows menu, as shown in Figure 3.53.

There are two ways to create the calculated field to compute the average monthly salary in each department. The first way is by clicking the icon to create a computed field and placing the field onto the DataWindow. Doing this displays the Computed Field Definition window. When completed, this window looks like the one in Figure 3.54.

The second way of creating the computed field is using the Objects menu of the DataWindow painter. This menu provides a quick method of creating the more commonly used computed fields, including column

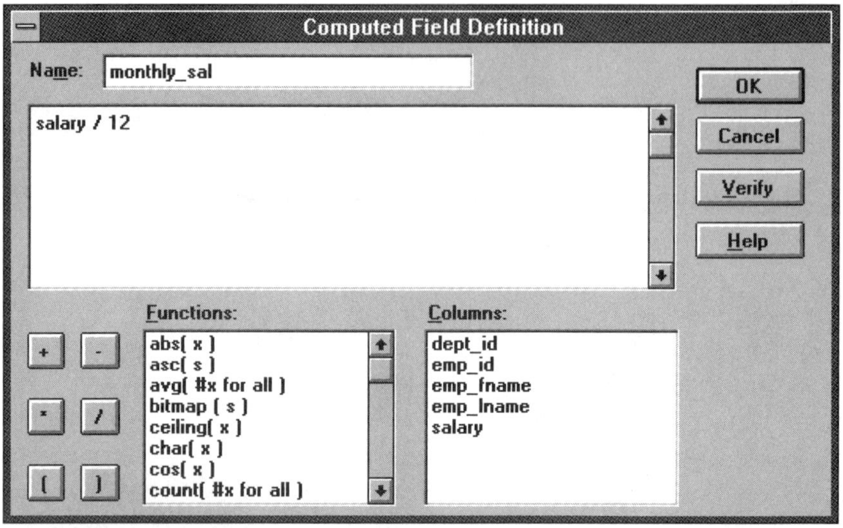

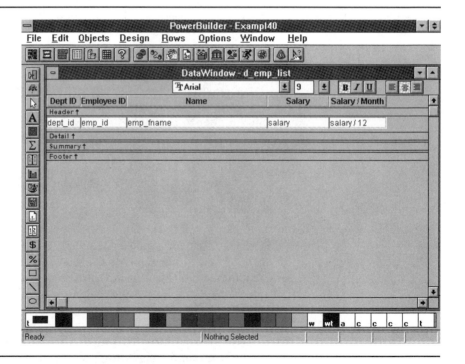

Figure 3.51   The Computed Field window.

Figure 3.52   Placement of the new computed field.

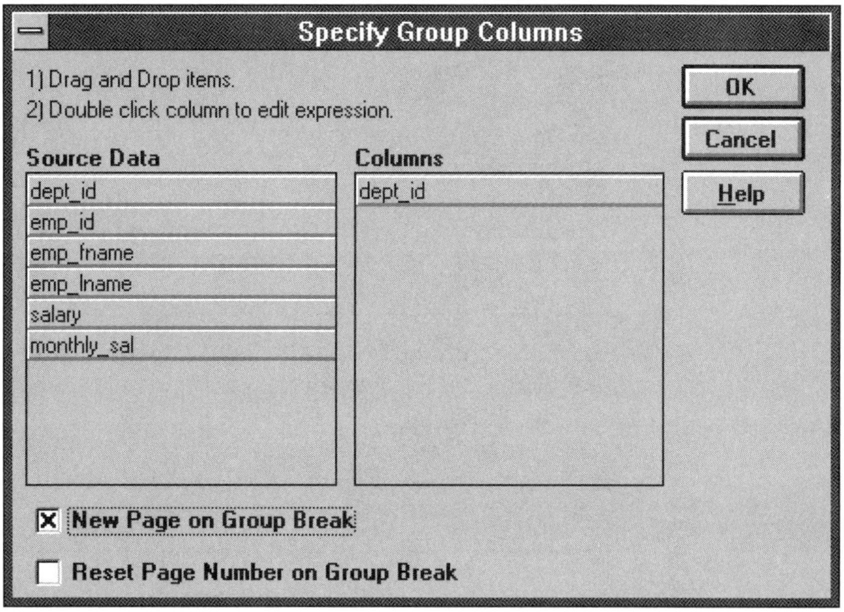

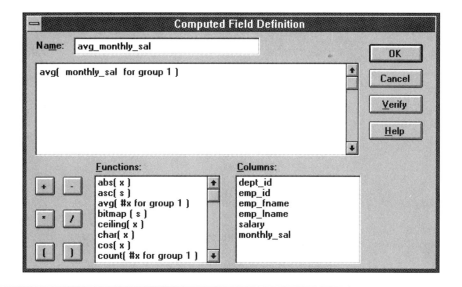

Figure 3.53   Grouping the list by department.

Figure 3.54   The completed Computed Field Definition window.

averages, column counts, page numbers, column summations, and the current date.

For this example, select the monthly salary computed field and choose the Average-Computed Field option from the Objects menu, as shown in Figure 3.55.

This automatically creates the computed field, using the expression of the selected computed field (monthly_sal) within its definition.

Note: The computed field (avg_monthly_sal) just created references another computed field (monthly_sal) in its expression. This feature is new to PowerBuilder 4. PowerBuilder 4 also allows DataWindow retrieval arguments to be referenced in a computed field expression. This capability is true of other PowerBuilder expressions as well (Sort, Filter, and Group).

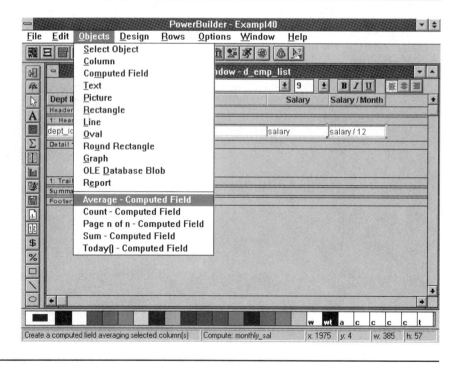

Figure 3.55   Selecting the Average-Computed Field option.

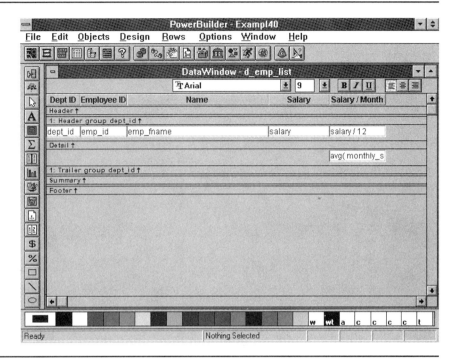

Figure 3.56   DataWindow showing the new group and computed field.

Both methods result in the same definition for the new computed field. After adding the new group and creating the computed field, the DataWindow looks like the one in Figure 3.56.

As previously mentioned, adding the page number can be done using the Objects menu and clicking somewhere in the footer band to place the computed field onto the DataWindow. With a few other cosmetic modifications, the new DataWindow looks like the one in Figure 3.57.

At runtime, the DataWindow looks like that in Figure 3.58.

In deciding whether to use computed columns or computed fields, the developer should consider the following:

- If it is best to perform the calculations on the database server, use a computed column.
- If the value is to appear on any DataWindow band other than the detail band, a computed field must be used.
- If the value cannot be computed using only the syntax of the DBMS language, a computed field must be used.

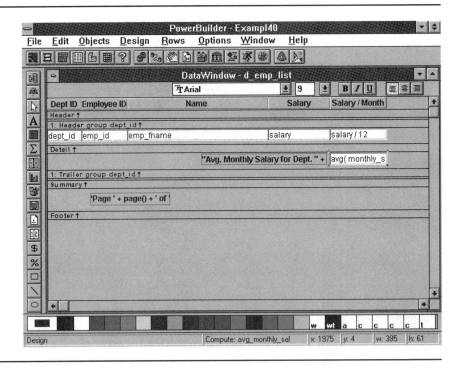

Figure 3.57   The new DataWindow.

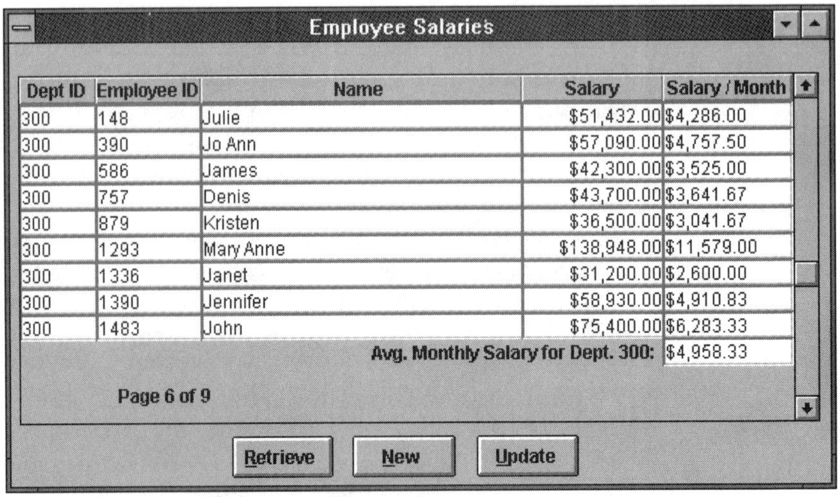

Figure 3.58   The DataWindow at runtime.

Update Characteristics

The Update SQL statement that PowerBuilder sends to the database can be specified by selecting the Update... option from the Rows menu in the DataWindow painter, as shown in Figure 3.59.

This window is very important because its contents determine how PowerBuilder builds the default SQL statement it uses when the Data-Window **Update( )** function is executed. This window allows the developer to specify the:

- Table to update
- Where clause for updates and deletes
- Key modification
- Updateable columns
- Key columns

Each of these options is discussed in the following section.

Table to Update PowerBuilder allows the update of only one table through a DataWindow. This table is selected from the DropDownListBox at the top of the window. Any other updates that need to be performed

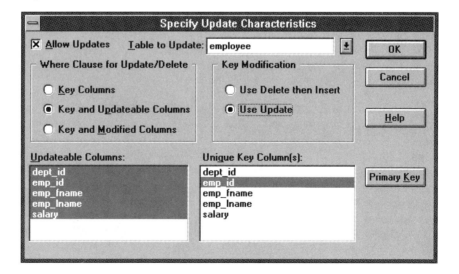

Figure 3.59   Specifying update characteristics.

when the **Update( )** function is executed must be coded by the developer, either by using the **dwModify( )** function or through embedded SQL.

Where Clause for Updates and Deletes PowerBuilder provides three ways of structuring the Where clause of an Update or Delete statement:

- Key Columns—This option builds a Where clause consisting of only the key values of the selected table. The Where clause compares the value originally retrieved for the key value(s) against the key column(s) in the database. For example, if the key column for a table of customers is custnum, the Where clause generated by PowerBuilder would be like the one shown in Figure 3.60.
- Key and Updateable Columns—This option builds a Where clause consisting of the key values and original values of any column identified as updateable for the selected table. The Where clause compares the values originally retrieved for these columns against the columns in the database. In the previous example, if address and city are updateable and the address column has been modified, the SQL statement generated by PowerBuilder would be like that shown in Figure 3.61.

  Using this method, an error occurs if any of the updateable columns are modified and saved to the database by another user, between the time the user retrieves the row and performs the **Update( )** function. In this example, if a second user updated either

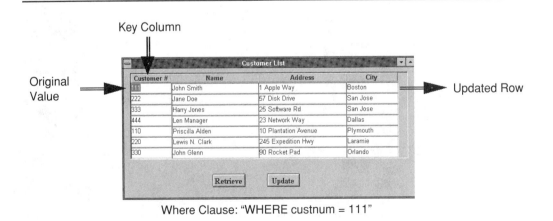

Figure 3.60   The Where clause.

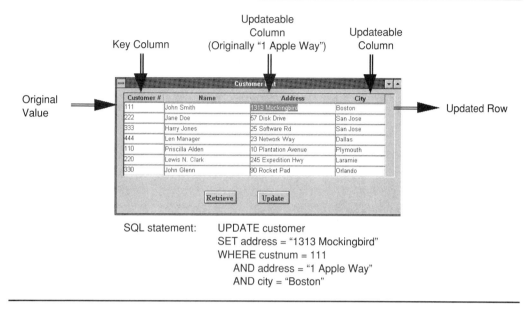

Figure 3.61 is illustrated with:

- Key Column
- Updateable Column (Originally "1 Apple Way")
- Updateable Column
- Original Value
- Updated Row

Customer #	Name	Address	City
111	John Smith	1313 Mockingbird	Boston
222	Jane Doe	57 Disk Drive	San Jose
333	Harry Jones	25 Software Rd	San Jose
444	Len Manager	23 Network Way	Dallas
110	Priscilla Alden	10 Plantation Avenue	Plymouth
220	Lewis N. Clark	245 Expedition Hwy	Laramie
330	John Glenn	90 Rocket Pad	Orlando

Retrieve   Update

SQL statement: UPDATE customer
SET address = "1313 Mockingbird"
WHERE custnum = 111
  AND address = "1 Apple Way"
  AND city = "Boston"

Figure 3.61   The generated SQL statement for updateable columns.

the address column or the city column of this row between the time the first user selects it and updates it, an error would occur.

- Key and Modified Columns—This option builds a Where clause consisting of the key values and original values of any column that has been modified for the selected table. The Where clause compares the values originally retrieved for these columns against the columns in the database. In the previous example, if address and city are updateable and the address column has been modified, the SQL statement generated by PowerBuilder would be like that shown in Figure 3.62.

The only difference between this Update statement and the previous one is that it does not contain the portion of the Where clause that checks the city. This is because only the address column has been modified.

Using this method, an error occurs if the modified column is modified and saved to the database by another user between the time the user retrieves the row and performs the **Update( )** function. In this example, if a second user updated the address column of this row between the time the first user selects it and updates it, an error would occur.

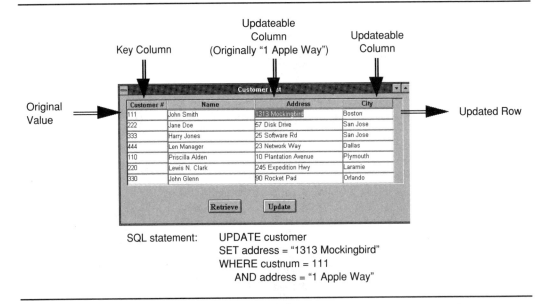

SQL statement: UPDATE customer
                   SET address = "1313 Mockingbird"
                   WHERE custnum = 111
                       AND address = "1 Apple Way"

Figure 3.62   The generated SQL statement with a column modification.

Key Modification PowerBuilder generates one of two SQL statements whenever a key column (specified in the Unique Key Column(s) box) is modified. These two statements are:

- Issuing a Delete then Insert—This is the default method. This method deletes the row with the modified key and inserts a new row with the new key value. Using this method ensures that any Delete or Insert triggers are performed and provides a reliable method of handling multiple rows with modified keys.
- Issuing an Update—This method updates the row with the modified key by replacing the value in the key column with the new key value. This method ensures that any Update triggers are fired, but does not fire any Delete or Insert triggers. With this method, there may also be problems updating multiple rows in which the key value has changed.

The decision of which of the two methods to use should be based on the extent to which triggers and referential integrity constraints are used in the application. In general, however, key columns should not be modifiable.

Updateable Columns This option allows the developer to specify which columns are updateable. As previously mentioned, because this is used in building the SQL Update statement, it can have performance implications. Only columns that the user can modify should be included in this list. If a column is disabled or has a tab order of 0, and thus cannot be modified by the user, it should not be included in this list.

Key Columns This option allows the developer to specify which columns are included as part of the key for the selected table used in the DataWindow **Update( )** function. Columns specified as key columns are included in the Where clause for all Update statements generated by PowerBuilder. Consequently, they also can have performance implications. Only true key columns for the selected table should be included in this list. Automatic selection of key columns can be done by clicking the **Primary Key** command button on the window.

Child DataWindows

A child DataWindow, implemented in version 3.0 of PowerBuilder, is defined as a DropDownDataWindow (DDDW) in a DataWindow object. This can be thought of as a DataWindow within a DataWindow.

For example, assume the DataWindow d_cities retrieves a list of cities from the database. This DataWindow can be used as a child DataWindow to any other DataWindow that needs a list of cities. In the previous customer list example, the city column can be defined as a DDDW with the definition as shown in Figure 3.63.

The data in the child DataWindow d_cities is retrieved when either the **Retrieve( )** or **InsertRow( )** function is called for the parent DataWindow d_custlist. The user can then select from the list of cities retrieved using d_cities, as shown in Figure 3.64.

When the child DataWindow is defined to accept retrieval arguments, the **Retrieve( )** function for the child DataWindow (with the retrieval arguments) must be called before the **Retrieve( )** function for the parent DataWindow. This is necessary to keep the Specify Retrieval Arguments dialog from displaying to prompt the user to enter retrieval arguments.

Note: The child DataWindow must also be retrieved after executing a **dwModify( )** against the DDDW. This is because PowerBuilder automatically performs a **Retrieve( )** after a **dwModify( )** is performed against a DDDW. Retrieving the child DataWindow can be done as described in the next section.

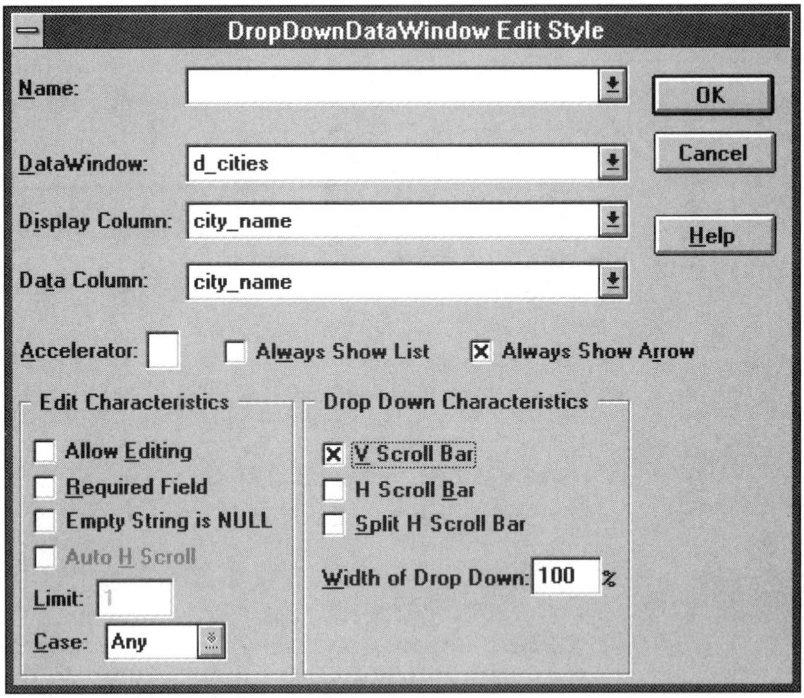

Figure 3.63   The DropDownDataWindow edit style.

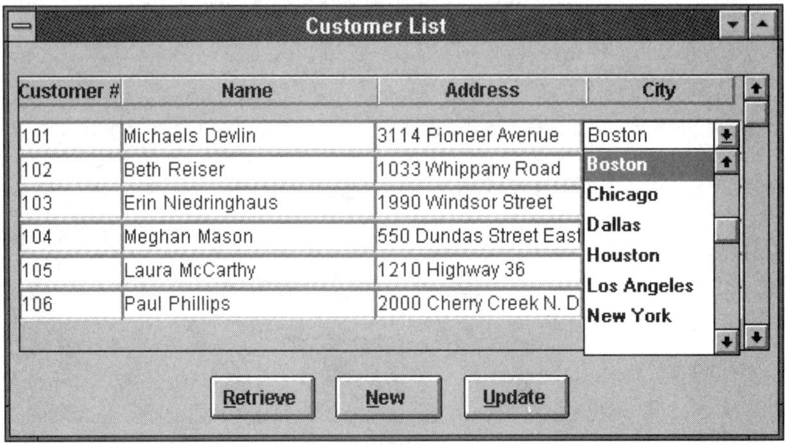

Figure 3.64   The parent DataWindow customer list.

Calling the **Retrieve( )** function for the child DataWindow requires the use of the **dwGetChild( )** function to obtain a handle to the child DataWindow. After the handle has been obtained, it can be used in all of the DataWindow-related functions.

To illustrate, assume that in the previous example a clerk is only allowed to enter customer records for customers in his/her home state. This value could be stored in an application .INI file and retrieved into the instance variable *i _sMyState*. This value could then be passed to the **Retrieve( )** function for the DDDW d_cities. Assume that the state code is TX and this value already exists in *i_sMyState*. To pass this value to the **Retrieve( )** function of the DDDW d_cities, the following code could be put in the constructor event of the main DataWindow:

```
// Declare the child DataWindow variable dw_child
DataWindowChild      dw_child
int          iRtn

// Get the handle of the child DataWindow into dw_child
iRtn = dw_2.dwGetChild("city",dw_child)

//Check for errors
if iRtn = -1 then
      DisplayMsg("Error","Error obtaining child DataWindow handle")
else
      // Set the transaction object for dw_child and retrieve
      dw_child.SetTransObject(SQLCA)
      dw_child.Retrieve(i_sMyState)
end if
```

In this example, since the value passed to the **Retrieve( )** function of the DDDW d_cities is static (it will always be TX), it is more efficient to put the code in the constructor event of the main DataWindow, where it is only executed once. Putting this code into an event such as the clicked event of the **Retrieve** command button would result in the same code being executed needlessly if the command button is clicked more than once.

If the argument passed to the **Retrieve( )** function is dynamic, however, the code would need to be put in a place where it is executed before the **Retrieve( )** or **InsertRow( )** functions of the main DataWindow. For example, in a master/detail conversation, to only display valid cities in a DDDW of a detail DataWindow for a state listed in the master DataWindow, the **Retrieve( )** function of the DDDW should be called before the **Retrieve( )** function of the detail DataWindow:

```
// Declare the child DataWindow variable dw_child
DataWindowChild        dw_child
int    iRtn

// Get the handle of the child DataWindow into dw_child
iRtn = dw_detail.dwGetChild("city",dw_child)

//Check for errors
if iRtn = -1 then
        DisplayMsg("Error","Error obtaining child DataWindow handle")
else
        // Set the transaction object for dw_child and retrieve
        dw_child.SetTransObject(SQLCA)
        dw_child.Retrieve(dw_master.GetItemString(1,"state"))
end if
```

Exclusive DDDWs There may be instances when a developer wants to create a DataWindow containing only DDDWs. In such cases, there would be no data source for the main DataWindow and therefore no **Retrieve** is required. Although it may not seem necessary to have another DataWindow, a main DataWindow is always required in order to use a DDDW. This situation is handled by specifying an external data source for the main DataWindow and performing an **InsertRow( )** on this DataWindow instead of a **Retrieve( )**. Because the main DataWindow does not retrieve data, the **InsertRow( )** must be called in order to display the single row used by any child DataWindows. For example, to view a list of customers for a particular city, the developer would create another DataWindow that only contains the DDDW d_cities. The user would use this DataWindow to choose a city, as shown in Figure 3.65.

When the user selects a city, data is retrieved into the customer list, as shown in Figure 3.66.

To perform the **Retrieve** of the child DataWindow, the following code is put into the constructor event of the top DataWindow (this assumes the use of *i_sMyState* to select only the cities from the clerk's state):

```
// Declare the child DataWindow variable dw_child
DataWindowChild        dw_child
int    iRtn

// Get the handle of the child DataWindow into dw_child
iRtn = dw_city_select.dwGetChild("city",dw_child)
```

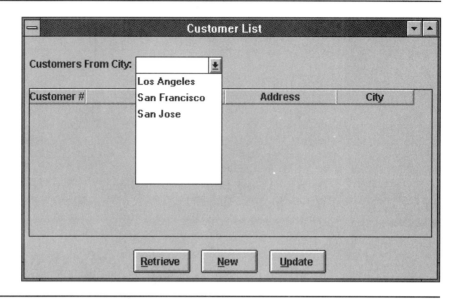

Figure 3.65   DataWindow containing the DDDW d_cities.

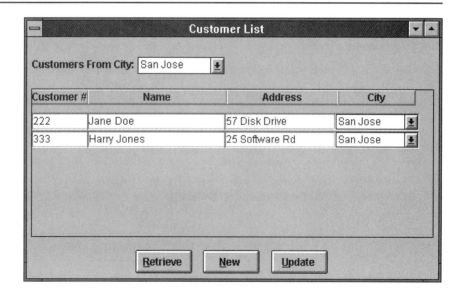

Figure 3.66   Retrieval of data into customer list.

```
//Check for errors
if iRtn = -1 then
        MessageBox("Error","Error obtaining child DataWindow handle")
else
        // Set the transaction object for dw_child and  retrieve
        dw_child.SetTransObject(SQLCA)
        dw_child.Retrieve(i_sMyState)
end if

// Perform insertrow( ) to have a row displayed in dw
dw_city_select.insertrow(0)
```

To retrieve the data into the customer list DataWindow, the following code is put into the clicked event of the **Retrieve** command button:

```
int     iRtn

// Retrieve the data for the customer list. Use getItemString( ) to
// get the data from the DDDW in dw_city_select
iRtn = dw_custlist.retrieve(dw_city_select.getItemString(1,1))
if (iRtn = -1) then
    MessageBox("Select Error", sqlca.sqlerrtext)
end if
```

DATAWINDOW CONTROLS

DataWindow Buffers

PowerBuilder provides four different DataWindow buffers:

- **Primary!** The primary DataWindow buffer contains all the data visible to the user. This includes any rows retrieved using the **Retrieve( )** function plus any new rows added using the **InsertRow( )** function.
- **Filter!** The filtered buffer contains any rows filtered from the primary buffer using the **Filter( )** function.
- **Delete!** The delete buffer contains any rows deleted using the **DeleteRow( )** function that have not yet been deleted from the database.
- **Original!** The original buffer contains data used to generate the Where clause used in the DataWindow **Update( )** function.

PowerBuilder uses these filters to create the SQL statements used in the execution of the DataWindow **Update( )** function. The data deleted when executing the **Update( )** function is the data in the Delete! buffer. If a DataWindow does not allow updates, the Delete! and Original! buffers are not maintained.

Data can be retrieved from any of the buffers using the **GetItemxxxx( )** functions (where xxxx corresponds to the data type of the column being retrieved). For example:

```
int iFilterVal
iFilterVal = dw_1.getItemNumber(1, 1, Filter!, FALSE)
```

In this code, the **GetItemNumber( )** function retrieves the integer value located in the first column of the first row of the Filter! buffer.

PowerBuilder has added the following DataWindow control functions to manipulate data in the different DataWindow buffers:

* **RowsCopy( )**—Allows rows to be copied from one DataWindow buffer to another. This function can be used to copy rows between different buffers of the same DataWindow control or between buffers of different DataWindow controls. The syntax of the **RowsCopy( )** function is:

```
datawindow.RowsCopy ( startrow, endrow, copybuffer, targetdw,
beforerow, targetbuffer )
```

where,

> datawindow—the name of the source DataWindow control.
>
> startrow—the number of the first row to copy (Long).
>
> endrow—the number of the last row to copy (Long).
>
> copybuffer—the buffer from which to copy the rows (Primary!, Delete!, Filter!).
>
> targetdw—the name of the DataWindow control where the rows are to be copied. This can be different than the source DataWindow control.
>
> beforerow—the number of the row before which to insert the copied rows (Long). To insert after the last existing row, use any value that is greater than the number of existing rows.
>
> targetbuffer—the buffer to which the rows are copied (Primary!, Delete!, Filter!).

RowsCopy( ) copies the rows in the copybuffer of datawindow beginning with startrow and ending with endrow and inserts them in targetdw before beforerow in the targetbuffer.

For example, to copy all the rows from the Delete! buffer of dw_1 to the Primary! buffer of dw_2, call **RowsCopy( )**:

```
dw_1.RowsCopy(1, dw_1.DeletedCount( ), Delete!, dw_2, 1, Primary!)
```

The **RowsCopy( )** function gives developers the ability to quickly move data between different DataWindows and their respective buffers. Prior to PowerBuilder 4, this function was a much more manual process, often requiring the developer to use PowerScript to loop through the source buffer and insert new rows into the target buffer.

- **RowsMove( )**—Allows rows to be moved from one DataWindow buffer to another. This function is basically the same as **RowsCopy( )**; the only exception is that the rows are removed from the source buffer once they are copied to the target buffer. **RowsMove( )** provides a simple way of "undeleting" rows deleted from the Primary! buffer. To do this, call **RowsMove( )** as shown:

```
dw_1.RowsMove(1, dw_1.DeletedCount( ), Delete!, dw_1, 1, Primary!)
```

- **RowsDiscard( )**—Allows rows to be permanently removed from a DataWindow buffer. The syntax of the **RowsDiscard( )** function is:

```
datawindow.RowsDiscard ( startrow, endrow, buffer)
```

where,

datawindow—the name of the DataWindow control.

startrow—the number of the first row to discard (Long).

endrow—the number of the last row to discard (Long).

buffer—the buffer from which to discard the rows (Primary!, Delete!, Filter!).

RowsDiscard( ) permanently deletes the rows in datawindow beginning with startrow and ending with endrow in the buffer DataWindow buffer.

For example, to permanently delete all the rows in the Delete! buffer of dw_1, call **RowsDiscard( )** as shown:

```
dw_1.RowsDiscard(1, dw_1.DeletedCount( ), Delete!)
```

Drag-and-Drop

Drag-and-drop is a type of graphical interface that can make an application intuitive and friendly to the user. Adding products to an order in an order entry system, for example, can be as simple as dragging a product from a list of products into an order (located somewhere else in the window). PowerBuilder provides drag-and-drop capabilities for all controls other than drawing objects. These controls have two attributes:

- **DragAuto**—A Boolean value to automatically place a control into drag mode when it is clicked.
- **DragIcon**—The icon to display when the control is being dragged.

In addition to these two attributes, each control has four events and two functions pertaining to drag-and-drop. The events are:

- **DragDrop**—When a dragged control is dropped on a target control.
- **DragEnter**—When a dragged control enters a target control.
- **DragWithin**—When a dragged control is within a target control.
- **DragLeave**—When a dragged control leaves a target control.

The drag-and-drop functions are:

- **Drag( )**—Starts or ends the dragging of a control based on the value of the argument passed to it. Valid arguments are:
  - **Begin!**—Begin dragging the control.
  - **Cancel!**—Stop dragging the control and do not trigger a DragDrop event.
  - **End!**—Stop dragging the control and trigger a DragDrop event if positioned over a target control.
- **DraggedObject( )**—Returns a reference to the control being dragged. This value can be accessed using the **TypeOf( )** function.

To illustrate a simple use of drag-and-drop, assume a list of customers as shown in Figure 3.67.

To enable deletion of a customer record using drag-and-drop, add a picture control to the window. This picture control, which has a bitmap of a trash can, is used as the target object. Records from the customer DataWindow will be deleted by dragging a row from the DataWindow and dropping it on the picture control.

Next, put the following code in the clicked event of the DataWindow control:

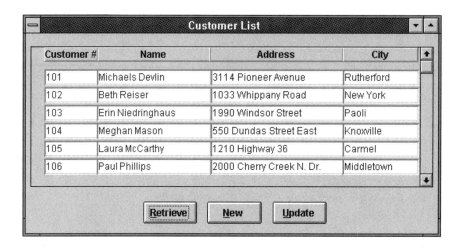

Figure 3.67   Customer list.

```
/*****************************************************
** If we haven't clicked within a column, start dragging this dw
** object. Because the DataWindow is editable, we don't want to
** drag if a column is clicked.
*****************************************************/
if this.getClickedColumn( ) < 1 and this.getClickedRow( ) > 0 then
     this.drag(begin!)
end if
```

After selecting the drag icon for the DataWindow (the Question! icon in this example), create the trash can picture control and add the following code to the dragdrop event:

```
DragObject     which_control

// determine which control type was dropped
which_control = DraggedObject( )

choose case    TypeOf(which_control)
case DataWindow! // If DW, delete the current row and invert the
// picture
    dw_custlist.DeleteRow(0)
    this.invert = false
```

```
case CommandButton!
   // Command button handling
case SingleLineEdit!
   // SingleLineEdit handling
End choose
```

Finally, to invert the picture object when the dragged control is within the picture control, add the following line to the dragenter event of the picture control:

```
this.invert = true
```

To restore the picture control to its original state after the dragged control leaves the picture control, add the following line to the dragleave event of the picture control:

```
this.invert = false
```

When the user clicks within the DataWindow (but not on a column), the drag icon appears as shown in Figure 3.68.

When the dragged icon enters the picture control, the control is disabled, as shown in Figure 3.69.

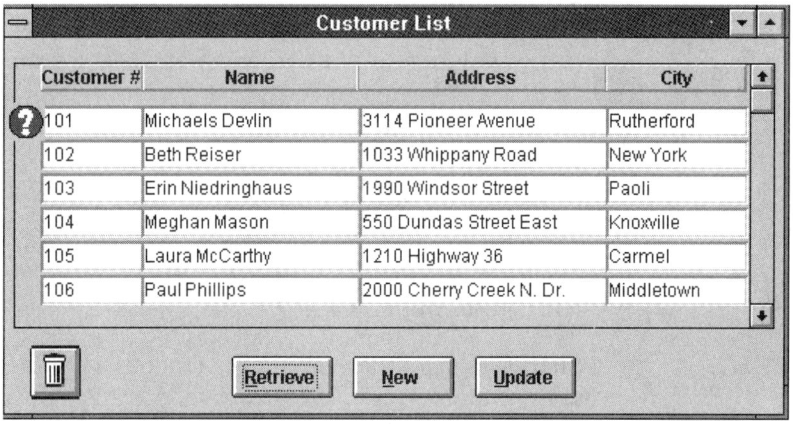

Figure 3.68   The drag icon.

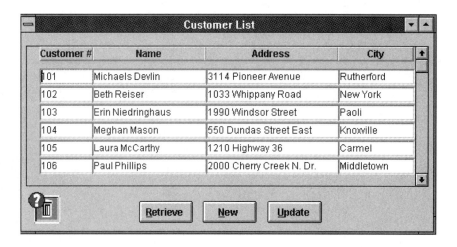

Figure 3.69 The dragged icon disabling the picture control.

When the icon is dropped, the current row in the DataWindow is deleted.

Transaction Processing

Transaction processing is a key element in most PowerBuilder applications. Any application that accesses a database must have the ability to create and manage a transaction. This includes creating a connection, sending commands to the database, and error handling. This section discusses the following topics related to transaction processing:

- Transaction objects
- Associating transaction objects with a DataWindow control
- The **Retrieve( )** and **Update( )** functions
- Error handling (embedded SQL)
- Error handling (DataWindows)
- The logical unit of work

Transaction Objects PowerBuilder manages its connection to a database through the use of a transaction object. A transaction object is a special, nonvisual, PowerBuilder object that contains the parameters necessary for establishing and maintaining a database connection. PowerBuilder provides the global transaction object, SQLCA. Additional transaction objects can be created using the following statements:

```
// Create transaction object mytran
transaction mytran
mytran = CREATE transaction
```

These statements first create a variable (mytran) of type transaction, and then create an instance of the transaction using the Create statement. The transaction object is nothing more than a structure that provides an interface from PowerBuilder to a database. The elements of the transaction object structure are:

Table 3.1   Elements of Transaction Object Structure

Attribute	Data Type	Description
DBMS	String	Name of the database vendor (e.g., Sybase, Oracle, ODBC)
Database	String	Name of the specific database to which you are connecting
UserID	String	User ID of the user connecting to the database
DBPass	String	Password of the user connecting to the database
LogID	String	Logon ID used to connect to the database server
LogPass	String	Password of the logon used to connect to the database server
ServerName	String	Name of the server where the database is located
DBParm	String	DBMS-specific
AutoCommit	Boolean	Used for automatically committing after each database activity (must be TRUE to create temporary tables)
Lock	String	Lock isolation level (DBMS-specific)
SQLCode	Long	Success code of a database operation: 0 — Success 100 — No result set returned -1 — Error
SQLNRows	Long	Number of rows affected by a database operation (DBMS-specific)
SQLDBCode	Long	DBMS vendor's specific error code
SQLErrText	String	DBMS vendor's specific error message
SQLReturnData	String	DBMS-specific

Before connecting to a database, the elements of the transaction object must be filled appropriately. The elements required for the transaction object may vary among the different databases. The following example shows the code for creating a transaction object and connecting to a WATCOM SQL database:

```
// Open script for myapp. Sets up transaction object mytran, reads
// parameters from myapp.ini, and connects to the database

transaction mytran

mytran = CREATE transaction

mytran.DBMS = ProfileString("myapp.ini","mytran","dbms","")
mytran.database = ProfileString("myapp.ini","mytran","database","")
mytran.userid = ProfileString("myapp.ini","mytran","userid","")
mytran.dbpass = ProfileString("myapp.ini","mytran","dbpass","")
mytran.logid = ProfileString("myapp.ini","mytran","logid","")
mytran.logpass = ProfileString("myapp.ini","mytran","logpass","")
mytran.servername = ProfileString("myapp.ini","mytran","servername","")
mytran.dbparm = ProfileString("myapp.ini","mytran","dbparm","")

connect;
if (mytran.sqldbcode) <> 0 or (mytran.sqlcode) <> 0 then
    MessageBox ("Sorry! Cannot Connect to Database", mytran.sqlerrtext)
end if

open(w_main)
```

This example obtains the values for the transaction object from the file myapp.ini. This method of storing the connection parameters provides some flexibility over hard-coding the values into the script. This flexibility comes from the fact that any changes in the parameters can be made in the .INI file and do not require changes to the application code. The mytran section of myapp.ini would then look something like:

```
[mytran]
dbms=ODBC
database=MYDB
userid=DBA
dbpass=SQL
logid=
logpass=
```

```
servername=
DbParm=DataSource='MYDB',Connectstring='DSN=MYDBL;UID=DBA ;PWD=SQL'
```

The details of creating a transaction object for each of the major DBMSs supported by PowerBuilder are discussed in Chapter 18.

Associating Transaction Objects with a DataWindow Control After a transaction object has been created, it can be associated with a Data-Window control, using either the **SetTrans( )** or **SetTransObject( )** function. **SetTrans( )** and **SetTransObject( )** differ in the way they manage the database connection. **SetTrans( )** connects and disconnects to the database for each database transaction; **SetTransObject( )** leaves it up to the developer to code the Connect, Disconnect, Commit, and Rollback statements.

While using **SetTransObject( )** may seem like more work for the developer, it provides more control over transaction management and generally yields better performance than using **SetTrans( )**. Figure 3.70 shows the difference between **SetTrans( )** and **SetTransObject( )**, for the retrieval and update of two DataWindows in a master/detail conversation. The example assumes that **SetTrans( )/SetTransObject( )** has been called for both DataWindows in the open event of the window.

As the figure shows, using **SetTrans( )** doubles the number of connections to the database. Because the Connect operation is generally an expensive one in terms of performance, its use should be minimized. Therefore, **SetTrans( )** should be used only for applications in which database access is minimal.

The Retrieve( ) and Update( ) Functions The **Retrieve( )** and **Update( )** functions are built-in PowerBuilder functions of the DataWindow control that generate SQL code and send it to the database for processing. The statement that is generated is dependent upon the status of each row in the DataWindow. Rows and columns in a DataWindow can have a status of:

New!
NewModified!
NotModified!
DataModified!

While rows can have any of these statuses, columns can only have a status of NotModified! and DataModified!

SetTrans(): Total of 4 CONNECTS to perform query and update

Data Retrieval:

```
dw_master.Retrieve() ——  CONNECT using mytran;
dw_detail.Retrieve()      dw_master.Retrieve()
                          DISCONNECT using mytran;

                          CONNECT using mytran;
                          dw_detail.Retrieve()
                          DISCONNECT using mytran;
```

Data Update:

```
                          CONNECT using mytran;
                          dw_detail.Update()
                          DISCONNECT using mytran;

                          CONNECT using mytran;
                          dw_master.Update()
                          DISCONNECT using mytran;

if dw_detail.Update(false,false) = 1 then
  if dw_master.Update(false,false) = 1 then
    return true
  else
    /* error updating dw_master -
       return false to calling function */
    return false
  end if
else
  /* error updating dw_detail -
     return false to calling function */
  return false
end if
```

SetTrans(): Total of 2 CONNECTS to perform query and update

Data Retrieval:

```
CONNECT uisng mytran;
if (mytran.SQLDBCode <>0) or (mytran.SWLCode <> 0) then
  DisplayMsg("Connect Error", mytran.SQLErrText)
  return
end if

if (dw_master.Retrieve() > 0) then
  dw_detail.Retrieve()
end if

DISCONNECT using mytran;
```

Data Update:

```
CONNECT using mytran;
if (mytran.SQLDBCode <>0) or (mytran.SQLCode <> 0) then
  DisplayMsg("Connect Error", mytran.SQLErrText)
  return
end if
if dw_detail.Update(false,false) = 1 then
  if dw_master.Update(false,false) = 1 then
    COMMIT using mytran;
    DISCONNECT using mytran;
    return true
  else
    /* error updating dw_master - return false to calling function */
    ROLLBACK using mytran;
    DISCONNECT using mytran;
    return false
  end if
else
  /* error updating dw_detail - return false to calling function*/
  DISCONNECT using mytran;
  return false
end if
```

Figure 3.70   Using SetTrans( ) vs. SetTransObject( ).

Immediately after a **Retrieve( )** is issued, each row and column has a status of NotModified!. When a column is changed, the status of both the row and column is changed from NotModified! to DataModified!

When a row is inserted into the DataWindow using the **InsertRow( )** function, the row has a status of New! and each column in the row has a status of NotModified! The column status changes from NotModified! to DataModified! after the value in the column is changed. When the status of any column in a new row changes to DataModified!, the status of the row changes from New! to NewModified!. See Figure 3.71 for examples of these functions.

When the **Update( )** function is then called, Update or Insert SQL statements are executed based on the status of each row in the Primary! or Filter! buffer, and Delete statements are generated for each row in the Delete! buffer. Each row with a DataModified! status causes the execution of an Update statement; each row with a NewModified! status causes the execution of an Insert statement.

The columns included in an Update statement depend on whether the column is on the list of updateable columns (see the previous section on specifying update characteristics) and whether it has a status of DataModified!. All columns displayed in the DataWindow are included in an Insert statement, with blank or empty columns represented as NULL.

The **dwGetItemStatus( )** and **dwSetItemStatus( )** functions can be used to modify row and column status programmatically. In addition to these functions, PowerBuilder 4 has added two new functions: **IsRowModified( )** and **IsRowNew( )**. **IsRowModified( )** returns True if the row number (passed as an argument) has been changed. **IsRowNew( )** returns True if the row number (passed as an argument) is new. A developer could use these functions to check the status of a row or column in order to, for example, force a particular SQL statement to be executed (in place of the one that PowerBuilder automatically generates).

Update Flags PowerBuilder uses update flags to determine if a Data-Window row has been modified. For each row in a DataWindow buffer, the update flag is set for each row inserted, updated, or deleted. When the DataWindow **Update( )** function is executed, PowerBuilder uses the row status of each row in the DataWindow with its update flag set to generate the appropriate SQL statement. By default, PowerBuilder will reset the update flags of each modfied row in the DataWindow if the **Update( )** function executes successfully.

There may be situations in which the update flags of a DataWindow should not be reset immediately after the execution of the **Update( )** function. For example, to update two DataWindows in a master/detail situation, the master DataWindow is updated first, followed by the de-

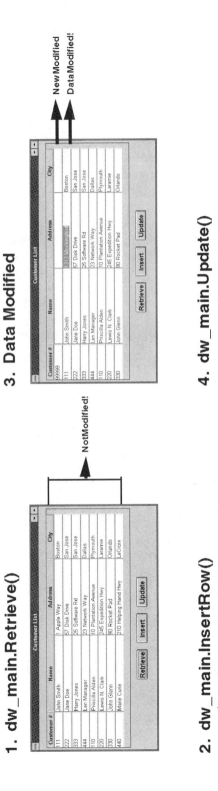

Figure 3.71   Using the Retrieve(), InsertRow(), and Update() functions.

tail DataWindow. Assume that if an error occurs in either DataWindow, the transaction is rolled back and no changes are made to the database.

In this case, if the update flags of the master DataWindow are reset and an error occurs in updating the detail window, the entire transaction will be rolled back, yet the update flags of the master DataWindow will be reset—indicating that no changes to the master DataWindow have been made. When the data in the detail DataWindow is corrected and the **Update( )** function is called again, the master DataWindow will not update the database because the update flags have been reset. To avoid this problem, execute the **Update( )** function with the Resetflags attribute set to False. Once the two **Updates( )** have executed successfully, reset the update flags manually by calling the **dwResetUpdate( )** function. An example of this is:

```
int iRtn

// Update the master DataWindow without resetting the update flags
iRtn = dw_master.Update(True, False)

// If the master update is successful, update the detail
// DataWindow without resetting its update flags
if iRtn = 1 then
        iRtn = dw_detail.Update(True, False)
        // If the detail update is successful, commit the transaction
        // and reset the update flags for both DataWindows
        if iRtn = 1 then
                COMMIT using SQLCA;
                dw_master.dwResetUpdate( )
                dw_detail.dwResetUpdate( )
        else
                // Detail update failed, so rollback the transaction
                ROLLBACK using SQLCA;
        end if
else
        // Master update failed, so rollback the transaction
        ROLLBACK using SQLCA;
end if
```

Note: This first parameter passed to the **Update( )** function determines whether to perform an **AcceptText( )** function before executing the **Update( )**. The default is True, but in order to specify the resetflag value, the accepttext value must also be included in the call to **Update( )**. **AcceptText( )** applies the contents of the current edit field to the current item in the DataWindow after the value passes validation.

Error Handling (Embedded SQL) The SQLCode, SQLDBCode, and SQLErrText elements of the transaction object provide a method of error handling when accessing a database by means other than a Data-Window. (When dealing with a DataWindow, the return codes of the DataWindow functions are used instead of these values.) These values should be checked when accessing a database using embedded or dynamic SQL and also when using the CONNECT, DISCONNECT, COMMIT, and ROLLBACK statements.

SQLCode is used to determine only whether the most recent database operation of a given transaction object was successful. There are only three possible values for SQLCode:

     0 — Operation successful

  100 — Operation successful, but no data returned

  -1 — Operation failed

SQLCode should be checked after every database interaction. The following example shows how SQLCode is checked after an embedded Select statement (using the transaction object mytran):

```
// Function to select employee information

SELECT emp_id, emp_fname, emp_lname
FROM employee
USING mytran;

if mytran.SQLCode <> 0 then
    DisplayMsg("Select Error",mytran.SQLErrText)
    return false
end if


return true
```

SQLDBCode provides vendor-specific information regarding a particular error. The information provided from SQLDBCode is more detailed than what is provided from SQLCode. Because there are times that SQLCode will return 0 even if no connection to the database is made, SQLDBCode should also be checked when connecting to a database. This was shown in the previous **SetTrans( )** example as follows:

```
CONNECT using mytran;

if (mytran.SQLDBCode <>0) or (mytran.SQLCode <> 0) then
    DisplayMsg("Connect Error", mytran.SQLErrText)
```

```
end if
...
...
```

SQLErrText contains the vendor-specific text of the error code contained in SQLDBCode. This value should be used to display the error in a more meaningful form.

Error Handling (DataWindows) Error handling for DataWindows is done differently from the way it is done for embedded SQL. Both the **Retrieve( )** and **Update( )** functions return values that should be checked for errors. The **Retrieve( )** function returns the following:

> > = 1 — Success
>
> > 0 — No data returned (no error)
>
> > -1 — Error

The following code calls the **Retrieve( )** function of DataWindow dw_main and displays a message if an error occurs:

```
int iRtn

iRtn = dw_main.Retrieve( )
if (iRtn = -1) then
    DisplayMsg("Select Error", "Error Selecting Data")
end if
```

Note: SQLCode, SQLDBCode, and SQLErrText should not be used when handling DataWindow errors. They should only be used when handling embedded SQL errors.

The **Update( )** function returns one of two values: 1 if successful or -1 if unsuccessful. A check similar to the one for the **Retrieve( )** function should also be done when performing an **Update( )**.

Another method of error handling for DataWindow retrieves and updates is provided by the DBError event. This event, which is part of the DataWindow control, is triggered by PowerBuilder each time an error occurs when retrieving or updating a DataWindow. This event can be used to trap error codes and messages and for customized error processing. To retrieve the error code and error message, use the

DBErrorCode( ) and **DBErrorMessage( )** functions, respectively. For example, the following code could be put into the DBError event of a DataWindow to display a different message when a user attempts to update a table that he or she does not have access to:

```
/* Trap any database errors. */

// If the user doesn't have update rights, display an informative
// message. NO_RIGHTS is set to the vendor-specific value for
// insufficient privilege at login time.

if DBErrorCode(this) = NO_RIGHTS then
    DisplayMsg("Insufficient Rights", &
      "You do not have rights to this table. Please check with the DBA.")
else
// Other errors
   DisplayMsg("Update Error", &
        string(this.DBErrorCode( ))+"~n"+this.DBErrorMessage( ))
end if

// Set Action code to avoid displaying default message
this.setActionCode(1)
```

The DBError event can also be used to determine which row in a multi-row DataWindow caused an error to occur. This is done using the **dwGetUpdateStatus( )** DataWindow function. This function returns the first row in which an error occurred. For example, the following code calls **dwGetUpdateStatus( )** in the DBError event to display which row in the DataWindow caused the error:

```
long lRowNum
dwBuffer buffer_type
string sMsgTxt

// Get the error message text.
sMsgTxt = DBErrorMessage( )

// Get the row in which the error occurred.
this.dwGetUpdateStatus(lRowNum, buffer_type)

// Display the location of the error and the error message.
MessageBox("Database Error in Row "+ String(lRowNum), sMsgTxt)

// Set the action code for the DBError event to 1 to prevent the
// DataWindow object from displaying its error message.
this.SetActionCode(1)
```

The DBError event provides a method of overriding PowerBuilder's default DataWindow error processing.

Note: When debugging DataWindow errors, use the SQLPreview Data-Window event to trap SQL statements sent to a database from the Retrieve( ), Update( ), and ReselectRow( ) functions. This event occurs after the function is called but before the statement is sent to the database for processing.

The Logical Unit of Work A logical unit of work (LUW) is a set of database transactions grouped together as a single transaction. All database transactions that are part of a LUW are accepted or rejected as a whole. Defining what goes into a LUW is extremely important and should be thought out carefully at design time. If transactions are not grouped into a LUW correctly, data integrity problems may result.

In PowerBuilder, a LUW begins with the Connect statement and ends with either a Disconnect, Commit, or Rollback statement. Issuing a Disconnect (which commits before disconnecting) or Commit causes all transactions sent to the database since the Connect was executed to either be committed to the database or rejected. Any single transaction that is not accepted causes **all** transactions in the LUW to not be accepted.

Issuing a Rollback causes the LUW to end without attempting to commit anything to the database. Both Commit and Rollback cause the closing of any open cursors or procedures and cause the release of any locks held against the database from the transactions in the LUW.

Using **SetTransObject( )** rather than **SetTrans( )** to bind a DataWindow control to a transaction object makes the developer responsible for managing a LUW. Each LUW should be as short as possible to minimize resource utilization and locking problems. Issuing a Commit ends the current LUW and starts a new one. It is recommended that Commits be done as often as possible, even after data retrieval, in order to release locks and free system resources.

Dynamic DataWindows

DataWindow objects, and all the controls within a DataWindow object, can be created and modified dynamically. Doing this provides a great deal of flexibility in situations in which it is impractical to develop a static set of objects to satisfy a wide range of requirements. Providing true ad hoc query capability, for example, is a situation that leans towards the use of dynamic DataWindows.

Dynamic DataWindows allow the user to modify all attributes of a DataWindow, including columns, colors, fonts, and the result set. Users can then save the DataWindow object in a library for later use.

Creating a DataWindow Dynamically To create a DataWindow dynamically, two things must be done:

1. The syntax of the DataWindow object must be built.
2. The DataWindow object must be bound to a DataWindow control.

Building the syntax of the DataWindow object can be done in one of three ways:

- Using the **dwSyntaxFromSQL( )** function—The syntax is:

```
transobj.dwSyntaxFromSQL(sqlselect, presentation, err)
```

where transobj is the transaction object associated with the function, sqlselect is the SQL Select statement used as the data source of the DataWindow, presentation is a string containing the presentation style of the DataWindow, and err is a string containing any error information.

The **dwSyntaxFromSQL( )** function returns a string containing the syntax necessary for creating the new DataWindow object. This is the most common way of creating a new DataWindow object.

- **Exporting an Existing DataWindow Object**—The syntax of an existing DataWindow object can be exported using the **LibraryExport( )** function. This function returns the syntax of the DataWindow object into a string that can then be modified to reflect the syntax of the new DataWindow object.

- **Manually**—DataWindow syntax can be created manually within a string variable. Although this option will not be used frequently, it is the only option available for some of the advanced DataWindow attributes, such as group breaks.

When the syntax of the DataWindow is known, it can be bound to a DataWindow control using the **dwCreate( )** function. Its syntax is:

```
dw_controlname.dwCreate(Syntax [, errorMsg])
```

where dw_controlname is the name of the DataWindow control that is to be bound to the new DataWindow object, Syntax is a string containing the source code of the new DataWindow, and errorMsg (optional) is a string containing any error messages encountered when creating the DataWindow.

The following PowerScript uses **dwSyntaxFromSQL( )** to create the syntax of a new DataWindow and **dwCreate( )** to bind the new DataWindow object to the DataWindow control:

```
string, sSQLSelect, sPresentation, sErrmsg

sSQLSelect = "SELECT name, address, city FROM customer ORDER BY name"

sPresentation = "style(type=grid)"

dw_2.dwCreate(SQLCA.dwSyntaxFromSQL(sSQLSelect, sPresentation,
sErrmsg))

dw_2.SetTransObject(SQLCA)
```

Notice that **SetTransObject( )** must be executed after the **dw Create( )** command in order to link a transaction object to the new DataWindow.

Modifying a DataWindow Dynamically DataWindows can be modified dynamically with the following two functions:

- **dwDescribe( )**—returns DataWindow attribute information
- **dwModify( )**—sets DataWindow attributes

dwDescribe( ) **dwDescribe( )** accepts an attribute or list of attributes (including DataWindow expressions) and returns a string value containing the value(s) of the attribute(s). For example, to retrieve the list of columns for the DataWindow shown in Figure 3.72, **dwDescribe( )** would be called as:

```
dw_custlist.dwDescribe("DataWindow.objects")
```

In this example, **dwDescribe( )** returns the following tab-separated string containing all the objects in the DataWindow:

```
id_t    fname_t    address_t   city_t     id    fname
  lname address    city
```

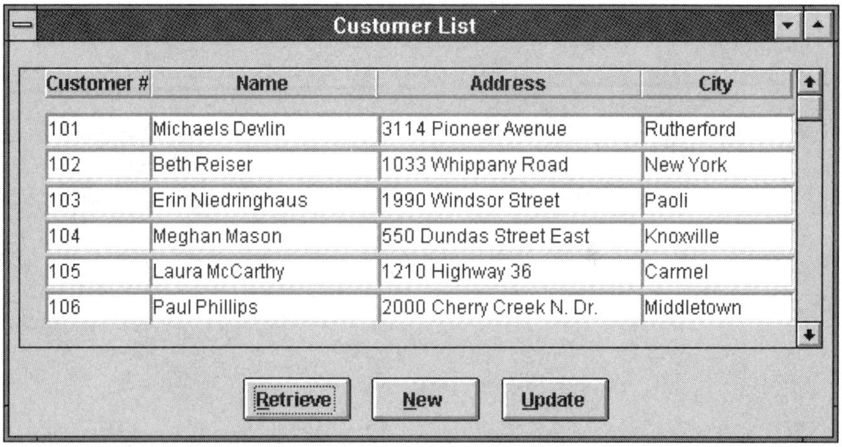
Customer List
Customer #
Name
Address
City
101
Michaels Devlin
3114 Pioneer Avenue
Rutherford
102
Beth Reiser
1033 Whippany Road
New York
103
Erin Niedringhaus
1990 Windsor Street
Paoli
104
Meghan Mason
550 Dundas Street East
Knoxville
105
Laura McCarthy
1210 Highway 36
Carmel
106
Paul Phillips
2000 Cherry Creek N. Dr.
Middletown
Retrieve
New
Update

Figure 3.72 DataWindow showing customer list.

The first four items in the list represent the names of the text column headers; the last five items represent the names of the columns.

In situations in which a name does not exist, PowerBuilder assigns a name beginning with "obj_" to the object. For example, if the "Customer ID" column header in the previous example had no name, **dwDescribe( )** would return the following:

```
obj_7699111  fname_t  address_t  city_t  id  fname
  lname address  city
```

If an error occurs, **dwDescribe( )** returns an !. If more than one attribute is contained in the function call and an error occurs, only the values up to the point at which the error occurs are displayed. If an attribute does not contain a value, **dwDescribe( )** returns a ?.

Continuing with the previous example, to return the color and (x,y) position of the ID column, **dwDescribe( )** would be called as:

```
dw_custlist.dwDescribe("id.color id.x id.y")
```

This would return the color, x position and y position separated by a tab character:

```
0  284  4
```

Another good use of **dwDescribe( )** is when something needs to occur based on the column type. For example, if an error occurs in a DataWindow, the data type of the column in error can be determined through a call to **dwDescribe( )** in the ItemError event of the DataWindow:

```
string sColType

sColType = this.dwDescribe(this.GetColumnName( )+".coltype")

CHOOSE CASE sColType
  CASE "number"
       // Number error-handling code
       This.SetActionCode(3)
  CASE "char"
       // Char error-handling code
       This.SetActionCode(3)
  CASE "date"
       // Date error-handling code
       This.SetActionCode(3)
  CASE "time"
       // Time error-handling code
       This.SetActionCode(3)
  CASE "datetime"
       // DateTime error-handling code
       This.SetActionCode(3)
END CHOOSE
```

For a list of valid attributes that can be retrieved with **dwDescribe( )**, refer to PowerBuilder documentation.

dwModify( ) **dwModify( )** is used to do three things with DataWindows:

- Create DataWindow objects—To dynamically add an object to a DataWindow, **dwModify( )** is called with the CREATE objdef parameter. For example, to add the bitmap named banner.bmp to the header band of a DataWindow, **dwModify( )** would be called as shown:

```
dw_custlist.dwModify("create bitmap(band=header.1 "&
+"x='1000' y='4' height='138' width='121' "&
+"filename='C:\RESOURCE\BANNER.BMP' name=banner "))
```

For the syntax required to create each type of object, refer to the PowerBuilder User Guide and online documentation.

- Destroy DataWindow objects—To dynamically remove an object from a DataWindow, **dwModify( )** is called with the DESTROY objname parameter. When removing a column, the word column must come before objname. For example, to destroy the banner column created previously:

```
dw_custlist.dwModify("destroy banner")
```

To destroy the city column:

```
dw_custlist.dwModify("destroy column city")
```

- Assign values to DataWindow attributes—This is the area in which **dwModify( )** is used most. Attributes of the DataWindow and any columns or objects within the DataWindow can be modified using **dwModify( )**.

To illustrate the use of **dwModify( )**, refer to Figure 3.73. In this example, only employees from one department at a time are displayed. That department is chosen by the user using a DropDownListBox, as shown in the figure.

Assume that the salary column should only be displayed if the user is in the "ADMIN" group (a global variable set at login time). For "ADMIN" users, the color of the salary column for employees making over $50,000 should be red with a black background, while the color for all other employees is to be green with a blue background. And finally, assume the salary column is not defined as updateable in the DataWindow, but must be updateable for "ADMIN" users.

The open event of the window checks the user type and either destroys the salary object and text or makes the salary column updateable by using **dwModify( )**:

```
/*******************************************************
** Employee window open event. Checks global variable for user
** type. If "ADMIN" user, make salary column updateable, else
** destroy the column and the header. Also, if the user is an
** "ADMIN" user, the color and background of the salary column are
** changed. Also, get the SELECT statement of the DataWindow
** and store it in an instance variable for later use.
*******************************************************/

if g_sUserType <> "ADMIN" then
  dw_emp.dwModify("destroy column salary ~t destroy salary_t")
else
```

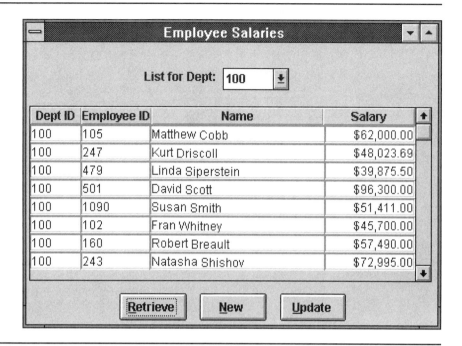

Figure 3.73   List of employees from one department chosen by using the DropDownList Box.

```
  dw_emp.dwModify("salary.Update=Yes ~t salary.color=' 0~t
if(salary>50000,255,65280)'" +&
    "~tsalary.background.color=' 0~t
if(salary>50000,0,16711680)'")
end if

// Get DataWindow's SELECT statement
i_sSQLStmt = dw_emp.dwDescribe("DataWindow.Table.Select")
```

The clicked event of cb_Retrieve calls the function **my_sql( )**, passing it the department id from the DropDownListBox:

```
// Call the function to update the SQL statement and retrieve
// the DataWindow
my_sql(ddlb_dept.text)
```

The function **my_sql( )** takes the department id parameter and uses **dwModify( )** to change the Where clause of the original SQL statement. To add the Where clause in this example, the original SQL statement must **not** contain any clauses (e.g., Where, Order By, Group By) after the From clause. This is because the Where clause is appended to the end of the original statement and is not necessarily placed in the correct position within the Select statement. In a production application, the string containing the Select statement could be parsed to find the appropriate place to put the Where clause. The code for **my_sql( )** is:

```
/******************************************************
** This function changes the Where clause of a DataWindow's
** SQL statement based on the passed department id and then
** retrieves the data.
******************************************************/

string sNewWhere, sRtn, sModTxt

sNewWhere = " WHERE dept_id = " + dept_id

sModTxt = "DataWindow.Table.Select = ~" " +
i_sSQLStmt+sNewWhere+"~""

sRtn = dw_emp.dwModify(sModTxt)

if sRtn = "" then
  dw_emp.retrieve( )
else
  DisplayMsg("Error", "dwModify failed: " + sRtn)
end if
```

Note: In order to add to a Select statement obtained using **dw Describe( )** in the manner just given, the DataWindow SQL statement must be converted from the graphical format to its SQL syntax. This is because the graphical format represents the query in a different way than the SQL syntax does.

For example, using **dwDescribe**(DataWindow.Table.Select) to obtain the statement "Select dept_id from department" returns the following if the query is defined in graphical mode:

```
PBSELECT(TABLE(NAME=~"department~" )
COLUMN(NAME=~"department.dept_id~") )
```

If defined in SQL syntax, the same call to **dwDescribe( )** returns the following:

```
SELECT ~"department~".~"dept_id~" FROM ~"department~"
```

For "ADMIN" users, the salary column is made updateable and the values in the salary column have different colors depending on the employee's salary, as shown in Figure 3.74.

For non-"ADMIN" users, the salary column is removed and the window looks like the one in Figure 3.75.

Although there are better ways to accomplish this functionality, the method used here is intended only to show how **dwModify( )** can be used to modify various aspects of a DataWindow. It is also important to note that PowerBuilder 4 has added the capability to conditionally set column attributes from the DataWindow painter instead of using **dwModify( )**. To do this, select the desired column, click the right mouse button, and select the Attributes... option, as shown in Figure 3.76.

This will display the Attribute Expressions dialog, shown in Figure 3.77.

Like other expressions, the Attribute Expressions dialog can contain constants or expressions. For example, to set the color of the salary column to red for all employees in department 100, add the following expression to the color attribute of the salary column, as shown in Figure 3.78.

Figure 3.74   Updateable, color-coded salary column for "Admin" users.

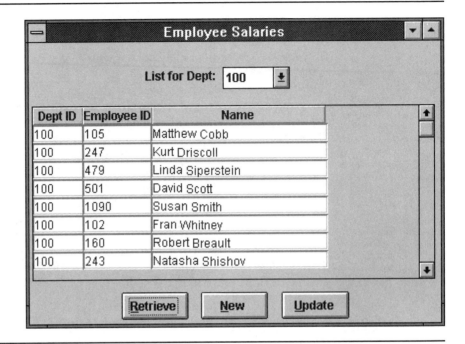

Figure 3.75   Employee window with salary column removal.

This new feature allows the conditional setting of column attributes without requiring a call to **dwModify( )**.

dwModify( ) can also be used to update more than one table when an **Update( )** is executed. By default, PowerBuilder allows only one table to be updated when executing the **Update( )** function. To update more than one table, use **dwModify( )** to change the update characteristics of the DataWindow. The following example shows how to update the department and employee tables using a single DataWindow (dw_dept):

```
int iRtn
// Update the department DataWindow without resetting the
// update flags in case an error occurs on the second update
iRtn = dw_dept.Update(TRUE,FALSE)

// If the update is successful, modify the update characteristics of
// the DataWindow object to point to the employee table.
If iRtn = 1 THEN
```

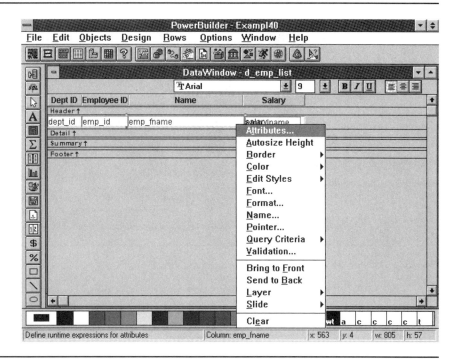

Figure 3.76   Conditional setting of column attributes from the DataWindow painter.

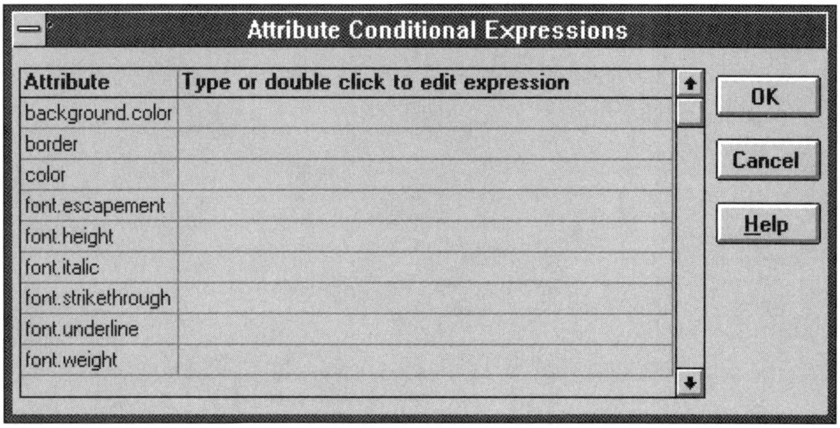

Figure 3.77   The Attributes Expression dialog box.

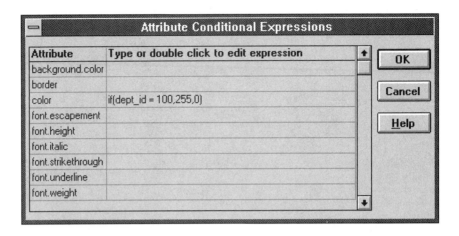

Figure 3.78   Setting the color of the salary column.

```
//Turn off update for department columns and set the table to employee
     dw_dept.dwModify("department_dept_name.Update = No" + &
          "department_dept_id.Update = No" + &
          "department_dept_id.Key = No" + &
          "DataWindow.Table.UpdateTable = ~"employee~"")

//Turn on update for desired employee columns.
     dw_1.dwModify("employee_emp_id.Update = Yes" + &
          "employee_emp_fname.Update = Yes" + &
          "employee_emp_lname.Update = Yes" + &
          "employee_emp_id.Key = Yes")
// Update the employee table, resetting the update flags.
     iRtn = dw_dept.Update( )
     IF iRtn = 1 THEN
         COMMIT USING SQLCA;
     ELSE
        MessageBox("Error","Update of employee table failed. "+ &
          +"Rolling back changes department and employee.")
          ROLLBACK USING SQLCA;
     END IF
ELSE
     MessageBox("Error","Update of department table failed. " + &
          +"Rolling back changes to department.")
      ROLLBACK USING SQLCA;
   //
```

```
// Use dwModify( ) to reset the update characteristics to the
// department table
END IF
```

Query Mode and Prompt for Criteria

In addition to the **dwModify( )** function, PowerBuilder provides two other methods of dynamically modifying the Where clause of a Select statement:

- Query Mode
- Prompt for Criteria

Either method can be used to add Query By Example (QBE) functionality to an application.

Query Mode A DataWindow can be put into query mode by modifying its Querymode attribute. To do this, call **dwModify( )** as follows:

```
dwname.dwModify("datawindow.querymode=yes")
```

When in query mode, the DataWindow allows the user to input selection and sort criteria. This information is then appended to the Select statement defined for the DataWindow.

When **dwModify( )** puts a DataWindow into query mode, the DataWindow is cleared (any existing data in the DataWindow is hidden) and the user is free to enter selection and sort criteria. For example, to select all customers from San Francisco, the query DataWindow would look like the one in Figure 3.79.

Notice that the equal sign does not have to be put in front of the value. Notice also that no quotation marks are required around string data types. When all criteria have been entered, the **Retrieve( )** function is executed with a modified Select statement. Assuming no Where clause exists for the DataWindow, the new Where clause would be:

```
WHERE (city = 'San Francisco')
```

AND operators are added when selection criteria is put on more than one column for the same row; OR operators are added when criteria are entered in more than one row for the same column. Consider the following extension to the previous example, as shown in Figure 3.80.

The Where clause for this Select would be:

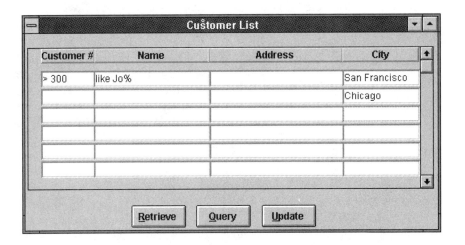

Figure 3.79   The query DataWindow after criteria selection.

```
WHERE (id > 300) AND (fname like 'Jo%') AND (city = 'San Francisco')
OR (city = 'Chicago')
```

Notice that it is not possible to add AND or OR operators between values in the same column. To do this requires the Where clause to be modified by using **dwModify( )** exclusively.

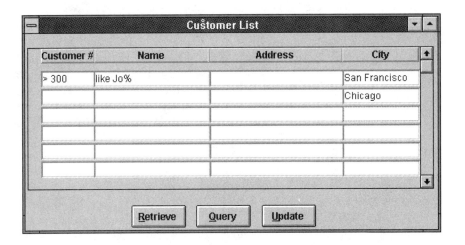

Figure 3.80   Using AND and OR operators in query mode.

Sort criteria can be added by using the Querysort DataWindow attribute. This attribute is set using the **dwModify( )** command:

```
dwname.dwModify("datawindow.querysort=yes")
```

This allows the first line of the query DataWindow to be used for entering sort criteria. When adding sort criteria, selection criteria are entered beginning on the second line. In the previous example, to sort by customer number in ascending order, the developer would complete the query DataWindow as shown in Figure 3.81.

The Where clause and Order By for this Select are:

```
WHERE (id > 300) AND (fname like 'Jo%') AND (city = 'San Francisco')
OR (city = 'Chicago')
ORDER BY 1 ASC
```

Note: Setting datawindow.querysort=yes puts a DataWindow into query mode, eliminating the need to explicitly set the datawindow. querymode attribute.

Data entered as either sort criteria or selection criteria does not take effect until the user leaves the field. In addition, the **Retrieve( )**

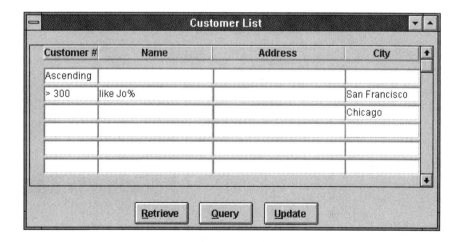

Figure 3.81   Query DataWindow indicating to sort by customer number in ascending order.

must be performed in order to execute the new Select statement. To retrieve the new SQL statement, the developer uses **dwModify( )**, passing it the datawindow.table.select parameter as shown:

```
dwname.dwModify("datawindow.table.select")
```

The value returned from this function can be stored in a local variable or displayed in a MessageBox for debugging purposes.

Before executing the **Retrieve( )**, the DataWindow should be reset to its normal state by setting the Querymode attribute to false. Again, this is done using **dwModify( )**:

```
dwname.dwModify("datawindow.querymode=no")
```

Prompt for Criteria Prompt for Criteria provides an interface similar to that used when defining a Quick Select data source. Prompt for Criteria is set on a column-by-column basis either by using **dwModify( )** or through the DataWindow painter using the Prompt for Criteria... option of the Rows... menu, as shown in Figure 3.82.

The window shown in Figure 3.82 designates the id and city col-

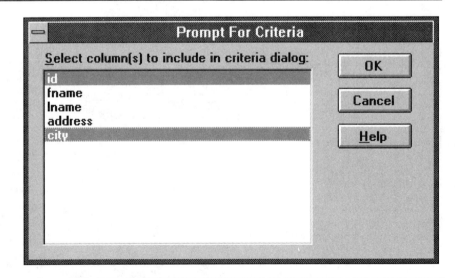

Figure 3.82   The Prompt for Criteria... option.

DATAWINDOWS **129**

umns to be prompted for selection criteria. The same thing can be done programmatically as follows:

```
dw_custlist.dwModify("id.criteria.dialog=yes")
dw_custlist.dwModify("city.criteria.dialog=yes")
```

Doing this causes the window in Figure 3.83 to be displayed when the **Retrieve( )** function is called.

This screen is completed just like the Quick Select criteria window. The same operators used when completing a query DataWindow (>, <, =, >=, <=, like, in) can be used to complete this window. One difference when using Prompt for Criteria is that no sorting criteria can be specified. If sorting criteria are required, Query Mode must be used instead of Prompt for Criteria.

Note: Query Mode and Prompt for Criteria should not be used together. Using them together can have mixed results. Generally, if sort criteria need to be entered, use Query Mode. If the number of columns for which the user may enter selection criteria must be limited, Prompt for Criteria must be used.

Override Edit and Equality Required When using either Query Mode or Prompt for Criteria, two other characteristics can be modified by the

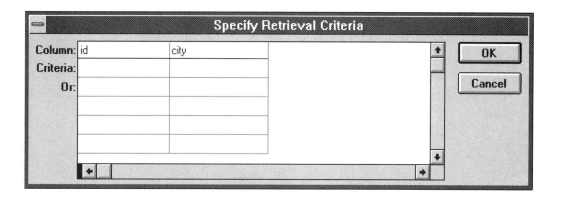

Figure 3.83   The Specify Retrieval Criteria window.

developer. These two characteristics are Override edit and Equality required.

Override Edit Override edit allows the edit characteristics of a column to be overridden only while in query mode (or being prompted for criteria). This changes the edit style of the column to the 'edit' style only while selection criteria are being entered.

When the selection criteria have been input and the data is retrieved, the column reverts to its defined edit style. This is generally used for columns that have an edit style of something other than the 'edit' style, such as a checkbox, radiobutton, or dropdownlistbox. This attribute can be set by selecting the Override Edit option of the Query Criteria menu for the column (by pressing the right mouse button within the column), as shown in Figure 3.84.

This can also be done programmatically through the **dwModify( )** function:

```
dw_custlist.dwModify("id.criteria.override_edit=yes")
```

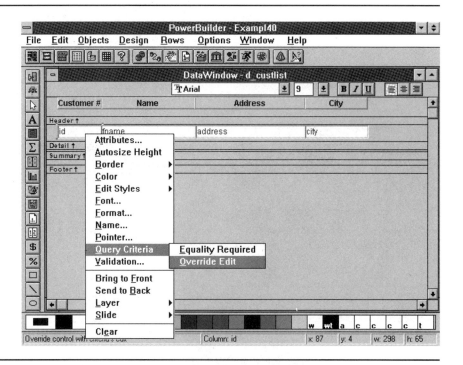

Figure 3.84   Setting the attribute using the Override Edit option.

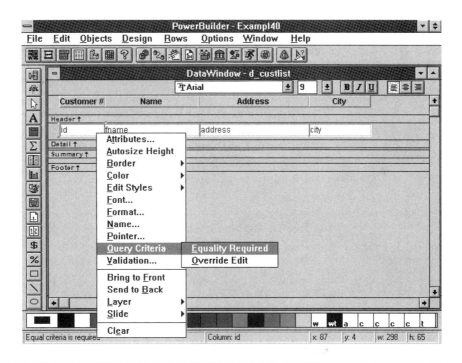

Figure 3.85   Selecting the Equality Required option.

Equality Required Equality required means that the user can only use the = operator when entering selection criteria. This attribute can be set by selecting the Equality Required option of the Query Criteria menu for the column (by pressing the right mouse button within the column), as shown in Figure 3.85.

This can also be done programmatically through the **dwModify( )** function:

```
dw_custlist.dwModify("id.criteria.equality=yes")
```

DESIGN CONSIDERATIONS

Embedded SQL

DataWindows vs. Embedded SQL Developers often face the question of when to use a DataWindow rather than embedded SQL. As a general rule, data displayed to the user should be accessed using a DataWindow whenever possible. The reason for this is that, in addition to better performance, the functionality built into the DataWindow saves development time and effort. However, most large development projects cannot rely on the DataWindow alone for data access. Embedded SQL may be required for performing such functions as data integrity validations, data definition language (DDL) statements, or any manipulation of non-displayed data.

In situations that require data to be processed in a row-by-row fashion, the options are to either use a cursor (discussed next) or to use a DataWindow and go through it row by row. Depending on the size of the data set, going through a DataWindow row by row can be slower than using a cursor because of all the **GetItemXXXX( )** function calls required to get the data from the DataWindow.

Static SQL Embedded SQL exists in either a static or dynamic mode. Static SQL is used for any data manipulation language (DML) statements in which the structure of the SQL does not change. While the SQL statement may be executed multiple times with different values in program variables used in the Where clause, the structure of the statement itself may not change. For example, the following statement is considered to be static SQL:

```
SELECT emp.dept_id, emp_id, emp_fname, emp_lname
FROM emp, dept
WHERE emp.dept_id = dept.dept_id
 AND dept_id = :dept_no
USING mytrans;
```

Although the value in the program variable *:dept_no* may change, this statement is static because the columns being selected and the structure of the Where clause are constant.

Static SQL also includes cursors. Cursors provide a row-by-row processing capability to what is normally a set-oriented processing model. In PowerScript, any embedded SQL Select statement that returns more than one row must use a cursor. Cursors are implemented by first declaring the cursor, then opening it and fetching one row at a time until the cursor is closed. For example, to go through customer records one by one, the developer would create a cursor and fetch each row until all rows have been processed:

```
integer iCustNum, iLocID
string sCustName, sAddress, sCity

iLocID = dw_master.GetItemNumber(dw_master.GetRow( ), "loc_id")
```

```
// Declare cursor to select customer data
DECLARE cust CURSOR FOR
SELECT "customer"."custnum",
    "customer"."name",
    "customer"."address",
    "customer"."city"
FROM "customer"
WHERE location_id = :iLocID
USING SQLCA;

OPEN cust;

// Fetch until all rows have been processed
DO WHILE SQLCA.SQLCode = 0
 FETCH cust
 INTO :iCustNum,
   :sCustName,
   :sAddress,
   :sCity ;

//
// Perform data manipulation (setItems, etc.)
//

LOOP

CLOSE cust;
```

Note: For databases that support updateable cursors, the row currently held by the cursor can be updated using the UPDATE ... WHERE CURRENT OF ... statement.

Stored procedures are another type of static SQL. Like a cursor, a stored procedure can be used to go through a result set in a row-by-row fashion. For example, the following script executes the previous example using the stored procedure process_cust_list, which accepts department id as an argument:

```
integer iCustNum, iLocID
string sCustName, sAddress, sCity

iLocID = dw_master.GetItemNumber(dw_master.GetRow( ), "loc_id")

// Declare procedure to select customer data
DECLARE cust_proc PROCEDURE FOR
```

```
    process_cust_list @location_id = :iLocID
USING SQLCA;

EXECUTE cust_proc;

// Fetch until all rows have been processed
DO WHILE SQLCA.SQLCode = 0
 FETCH cust_proc
 INTO :iCustNum,
   :sCustName,
   :sAddress,
   :sCity ;

//
// Perform data manipulation (setItems, etc.)
//

LOOP

CLOSE cust_proc;
```

PowerBuilder's support of stored procedures is DBMS-specific. This topic is discussed further in Chapter 18.

Dynamic SQL Dynamic SQL differs from static SQL in that it allows the structure of a SQL statement to change dynamically. Dynamic SQL is used when the format of a SQL statement cannot be determined until runtime, such as with ad hoc queries. There are four dynamic SQL statement formats (Formats 1–4):

Format 1 Format 1 is used when no input parameters are passed to the SQL statement and the statement does not return a result set. Format 1 SQL statements are executed through the **Execute Immediate** command. For example, the following script drops a table selected in dw_master:

```
string sTabName, sSQLStmt

sTabName = dw_master.GetItemString(dw_master.GetRow( ),"table_name")

sSQLStmt = "DROP TABLE " + sTabName

EXECUTE IMMEDIATE :sSQLStmt USING SQLCA;
```

Format 2 Format 2 is used when the input parameters passed to the SQL statement are known and the statement does not return a result set. To accomplish this, PowerBuilder uses a dynamic staging area (SQLSA, by default) to store information about a SQL statement before it is executed.

The dynamic staging area is used in formats 2, 3, and 4 to provide a connection between a SQL statement and a transaction object. Information about the SQL statement is placed in the dynamic staging area by using the Prepare statement.

The following example shows how data can be updated using a table and set of columns selected by the user at runtime:

```
string sSQLStmt, sUpdCol, sUpdVal, sID
int iID

sID = sle_id.text
sUpdCol = ddlb_cols.text

sSQLStmt = "UPDATE employee " + &
        "SET " + sUpdCol + " = ? " + &
        "WHERE emp_id = " + sID

PREPARE SQLSA FROM :sSQLStmt USING SQLCA;

sUpdVal = sle_updval.text

EXECUTE SQLSA USING :sUpdVal;
```

Notice that the question mark is used to designate an argument that is not known until runtime. For SQL statements that have multiple dynamic parameters, the developer must make sure the sequence of the question marks in the statement matches the sequence of arguments in the Execute statement.

Format 3 Format 3 is used when the input parameters and result set columns of the SQL statement are known and the statement returns a result set. Like Format 2, Format 3 uses a dynamic staging area to store information about the SQL statement before it is executed.

Format 3 differs from the previous two formats in that the SQL statement returns a result set. To handle the result set, PowerBuilder uses either a dynamic cursor or dynamic stored procedure. The following example uses a dynamic cursor to process a list of employees based on the job title, experience, and salary entered by a user:

```
string sSQLStmt, sTitle, sFname, sLname
int iMonths, iID
long lSalary

sSQLStmt = "SELECT emp_id, emp_fname, emp_lname " + &
         "FROM employee " + &
         "WHERE title = ? AND exp >= ? AND salary <= ? "

DECLARE placement_info DYNAMIC CURSOR FOR SQLSA;

PREPARE SQLSA FROM :sSQLStmt USING SQLCA;

sTitle = ddlb_title.text
iMonths = integer(sle_exp.text)
lSalary = long(sle_salary.text)

OPEN DYNAMIC placement_info USING :sTitle, :iMonths, :lSalary;

DO WHILE SQLCA.SQLCode = 0
 FETCH placement_info INTO :iID, :sFname, :sLname;
// Process row

LOOP

CLOSE placement_info;
```

Format 4 Format 4 is used when the input parameters and result set columns of the SQL statement are not known until runtime and the statement returns a result set. Like Format 3, Format 4 uses a dynamic staging area and either a dynamic cursor or dynamic procedure to process the result set.

   Because the input parameters and result set columns are not known until runtime, PowerBuilder uses a dynamic description area (SQLDA, by default) to store information about these variables. After information about the SQL statement has been placed into the dynamic staging area (SQLSA) using the Prepare statement, a Describe statement is used to place information from SQLSA into SQLDA. SQLDA is then used when opening a dynamic cursor or executing a dynamic stored procedure. SQLDA is also used with each Fetch statement to return data. The following SQLDA elements are made available to developers:

- **numinputs**—The number of input parameters. This is set when the Describe statement is executed.

- **inparmtype**—An array of input parameter types. This can be set when the Describe statement is executed.
- **numoutputs**—The number of output parameters. This is set either after the Describe statement or after the first Fetch statement.
- **outparmtype**—An array of output parameter types. This is set either after the Describe statement or after the first Fetch statement.

PowerBuilder uses the **SetDynamicParm( )** function to set the SQLDA elements pertaining to the input parameters. **SetDynamic Parm( )** is called before an Open or Execute statement to assign values to input parameters.

After the SQL statement has been executed, data can be retrieved using the following functions:

GetDynamicDate( )

GetDynamicDateTime( )

GetDynamicNumber( )

GetDynamicString( )

GetDynamicTime( )

The following example shows how Format 4 Dynamic SQL can be used to provide ad hoc query capability. This example queries employee information based on the department and columns selected by the user. For example, if the user chooses to display the employee id, first name and last name of employees in department 100, the screen looks like the one in Figure 3.86.

The script in the clicked event of the query button is shown below:

```
/*******************************************************
** The following example shows how Dynamic SQL Format 4 can be
** used to display employee information for a department selected by
** the user. The user also specifies the columns to be retrieved from
** the employee table.
*******************************************************/

string  sSQLStmt, sResults, sColList
int i, iTotCols, iColCount

// Get the list of columns from the listbox
iTotCols = lb_cols.TotalItems( )
FOR i = 1 to iTotCols
```

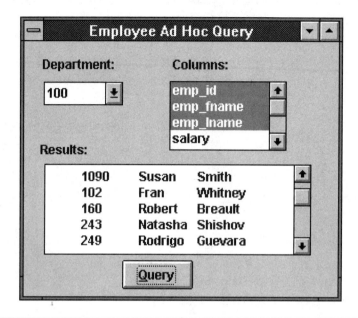

Figure 3.86   Employee ad hoc query.

```
  if lb_cols.state(i) = 1 then
   iColCount = iColCount + 1
   if iColCount > 1 then
     sColList = sColList + ", "
   end if
   sColList = sColList + lb_cols.text(i)
  end if
NEXT .

sSQLStmt = "SELECT " + sColList + " FROM employee " + &
          " WHERE dept_id = " + ddlb_dept.text

DECLARE emp_cur DYNAMIC CURSOR FOR SQLSA;

PREPARE SQLSA FROM :sSQLStmt USING SQLCA;
if sqlca.sqlcode <> 0 then
   MessageBox("Prepare Error", sqlca.sqlerrtext)
   return
end if
```

```
DESCRIBE SQLSA INTO SQLDA ;
if sqlca.sqlcode <> 0 then
   MessageBox("Describe Error", sqlca.sqlerrtext)
   return
end if

// Fill the one element of the input descriptor array
// with the value in the department DDLB

SetDynamicParm(SQLDA, 1, ddlb_dept.text)

OPEN DYNAMIC emp_cur USING DESCRIPTOR SQLDA ;

// The output descriptor array contains returned
// values from the result set

DO WHILE SQLCA.SQLCode = 0
 FETCH emp_cur USING DESCRIPTOR SQLDA ;

 FOR i = 1 to SQLDA.numoutputs
  CHOOSE CASE SQLDA.OutParmType[i]
      CASE TypeString!
           sResults = sResults + GetDynamicString(SQLDA, i) + ' '
      CASE TypeDate!
           sResults = sResults + &
          string(GetDynamicDate(SQLDA, i)) + ' '
      CASE TypeDateTime!
           sResults = sResults + &
          string(GetDynamicDateTime(SQLDA, i)) + ' '
      CASE TypeTime!
           sResults = sResults + &
          string(GetDynamicTime(SQLDA, i)) + ' '
      CASE TypeInteger!
           sResults = sResults + &
          string(GetDynamicNumber(SQLDA, i)) + ' '
       CASE TypeLong!
            sResults = sResults + &
           string(GetDynamicNumber(SQLDA, i)) + ' '
  END CHOOSE
 sResults = sResults + "~t"
 NEXT
 sResults = sResults + "~r~n"
LOOP

CLOSE emp_cur ;
mle_1.text = sResults
```

Note: Because DDL statements are not supported by PowerBuilder in static SQL, they must be executed through dynamic SQL Format 1 or 2.

Handling Large Result Sets

There may be times when you want to limit the amount of data retrieved from a database into a DataWindow. Reasons for doing this are to improve perceived performance or to keep a user from executing a long running query and tying up system resources. In order to control large result sets, it is best to either notify the user of a potentially time-consuming query or impose a limit on the number of rows retrieved. There are several ways of accomplishing this in PowerBuilder.

Retrieve As Needed Retrieve as needed allows a result set to be returned to the client in small groups instead of one large data set. This reduces the amount of data initially returned to the client and allows the client to cancel the query without returning the entire result set. Retrieve as needed is discussed in greater detail later in this section.

Cursors Cursors can be used to limit the data returned to the client by only allowing a certain number of rows to be fetched from the server. Using a cursor gives the developer the ability to control when data is sent to the client. For example, the following cursor fetches rows in groups of 100. When each 100th row is retrieved, the user is prompted to continue. If the user chooses not to continue, the cursor is closed. Otherwise another 100 rows are fetched:

```
integer iCustNum, iMore, iCurRow = 0
string sCustName, sAddress, sCity

// Declare cursor to select customer data

 DECLARE cust CURSOR FOR
 SELECT "customer"."custnum",
    "customer"."name",
    "customer"."address",
    "customer"."city"
  FROM "customer" ;

OPEN cust;

// Fetch until done or until user wants to quit
DO WHILE SQLCA.SQLCode = 0
```

```
FETCH cust
  INTO :iCustNum,
    :sCustName,
    :sAddress,
    :sCity ;

//
// Perform data manipulation (setItems, etc.)
//

  // Increment row count and check for 100th row
  // If multiple of 100th row found, prompt user to continue
  iCurRow = iCurRow + 1
  if(iCurRow = 100) then
      iCurRow = 0
      // OKorCancel is window function that calls MessageBox with the
      // OKCancel! button parameter
      iMore = OKorCancel("Data Retrieval","100 rows retrieved. Continue?")
      if (iMore <> 1) then
          // exit loop and close cursor
          EXIT
        end if
      end if
LOOP

CLOSE cust;
```

When using cursors, the developer should be careful not to allow them to remain open for a long period of time. Because opening a cursor locks the data being retrieved, holding a cursor can restrict access of the data to other users. Cursors also consume resources on both the client and server.

The COUNT(*) function The **Count**(*) function can be executed before a query to determine exactly how many rows will be returned. This approach is usually not desirable because of the inefficiency of having to do two queries—one to obtain the number of rows and one to perform the retrieve.

The RetrieveRow event The RetrieveRow event is a DataWindow control event that is triggered each time a row is retrieved from the server to the client. This event can be used to control the number of rows returned to the client, by using a row counter similar to the cursor example just discussed. In this case, an instance variable is created to keep a count of the number of rows retrieved. This variable would then be incremented in the RetrieveRow event, each time a row is returned to the client. To use the same example as previously, the variable *i_iCurRow* has been declared as an instance variable and is incremented in the RetrieveRow event:

```
integer iMore
i_iCurRow = i_iCurRow + 1

if(i_iCurRow = 100) then
  i_iCurRow = 0
  // OKorCancel is window function that calls MessageBox with the
  // OKCancel! button parameter
  iMore = OKorCancel("Data Retrieval","100 rows retrieved. Continue?")
  if (iMore <> 1) then
    // stop the retrieval
    this.SetActionCode(1)
  end if
end if
```

Using the RetrieveRow event can significantly slow performance because the code in the event is executed every time a row is retrieved. Consequently, it should be used sparingly.

Shared Result Sets

PowerBuilder allows the sharing of result sets between two or more DataWindow controls in a window. Taking advantage of this capability can reduce the number of queries against the database and thus improve application performance. To share data between two DataWindow controls, use the **dwShareData( )** function:

```
dwPrimary.dwShareData( dwSecondary )
```

where dwPrimary is the name of the primary DataWindow control. This DataWindow is considered the owner of the data and shares its data with one or more secondary DataWindow controls. dwSecondary is the name of the DataWindow control that dwPrimary shares its data with. To share data with more than one secondary DataWindow control, **dwShareData( )** must be called once for each secondary DataWindow control.

For example, to share the result set of dw_p1 with dw_s1, the following script would be executed in the open event of the window:

```
connect;
dw_p1.SetTransObject(SQLCA)
dw_p1.Retrieve( )
dw_p1.dwShareData(dw_s1)
```

dwShareData( ) allows the sharing of only data between two DataWindow controls. This includes the data in all three data buffers (Primary!, Filter!, and Delete!) and the sort order. Because formatting information is not shared, shared DataWindows can display the same data with a different appearance.

The Select statement of any DataWindows sharing data may be different, but the result set description must be the same. Note that although the result set description of a primary and secondary Data-Window must be the same, different columns may be displayed in each DataWindow. This provides additional flexibility in the appearance of DataWindows sharing a result set. If the result set description is not the same, an error occurs and no data is displayed in the secondary DataWindow. DataWindows using a script data source can also be used, as long as the columns defined match those of any DataWindow it will be sharing data with. For example, result sets can be shared among DataWindows with the following Select statements:

SELECT emp_id from employee

SELECT emp_id from employee where dept_id = 300

SELECT emp_id from employee_address

However, none of the three DataWindows with the following Select statements could share result sets because of a different result set description:

SELECT emp_id from employee

SELECT emp_id, first_name from employee

SELECT emp_id, ss_number from employee

Shared DataWindows are treated as independent DataWindow objects. This allows each DataWindow to have its own set of attributes that can be retrieved or modified using the **dwDescribe( )** and **dwModify( )** functions. However, because the data of the DataWindow is shared, any functions that change the data in a primary or secondary DataWindow result in changes in both DataWindows (and any other secondary DataWindows). In addition, the following functions are applied to the primary DataWindow control when called for a secondary DataWindow control:

Delete( )	**ImportString( )**	**SetFilter( )**
Filter( )	**Insert( )**	**SetSort( )**
ImportClipboard( )	**Retrieve( )**	**Sort( )**
ImportFile( )	**Reset( )**	**Update( )**

To disable data sharing between two DataWindows, the **dwShare DataOff( )** function is called:

```
datawindowname.dwShareDataOff( )
```

where datawindowname is the name of either the primary or secondary DataWindow control. If datawindowname is the name of the secondary DataWindow, sharing is only disabled between it and the primary Data-Window. If datawindowname is the name of the primary DataWindow, sharing is disabled between the primary DataWindow and all secondary DataWindows sharing its data. In either case, when sharing is disabled, all secondary DataWindows are cleared and no data appears in any of them.

Sharing data can provide performance gains in situations in which common data is used throughout an application. For example, a Data-Window containing employee information that is to appear throughout a set of application functions, such as the employee's name, can be retrieved into a single DataWindow and shared among multiple secondary DataWindows, as shown in Figure 3.87.

Instead of having to retrieve the employee name information once for each time it is used, the data from the top DataWindow used in the Employee Address window is shared with the top DataWindow in the Employee Dates window.

While PowerBuilder's implementation of shared DataWindows can reduce the number of database retrievals required and thus improve performance, it does have some limitations. Because all shared Data-Windows use the same data buffer, a secondary DataWindow cannot filter the data of the primary DataWindow without changing the data in both DataWindows. Therefore, it is not possible to retrieve a large set of data and apply different filters for different shared DataWindows.

However, with the new **RowsCopy( )** function, it is much easier to move data between DataWindows, allowing data from one DataWindow to be copied to another without having to query the database more than once. While this is not the same as sharing a DataWindow, **RowsCopy( )**

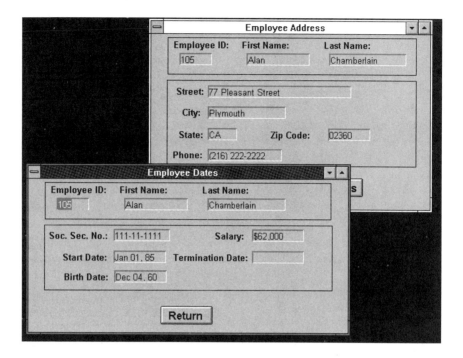

Figure 3.87   Shared data among secondary DataWindows.

does provide a method of taking a single result set and using it in more than one DataWindow.

Retrieve as Needed

Retrieve as needed, introduced in PowerBuilder 3.0, provides the capability to bring a result set from the server to the client only as the rows are needed for display in a DataWindow. For example, if a DataWindow control is sized to only show three rows at a time, retrieve as needed initially only brings back enough data from the server to show the first three rows. As the user pages down through the data, PowerBuilder continues to return data from the server to display in the DataWindow. The user can continue to page down until all the data in the result set has been returned to the client. Figures 3.88 and 3.89 illustrate how retrieve as needed differs from traditional data retrieval.

Retrieve as needed is implemented by selecting the Retrieve Only As

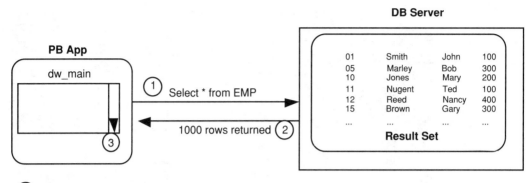

1 dw_main.Retrieve() sends the query to the server.

2 Server sends the entire result set to the client buffer.

Figure 3.88   Data retrieval without retrieve as needed.

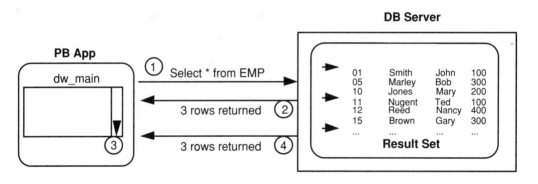

1 dw_main.Retrieve() opens a cursor and fetches
   the first three rows from the server.

2 The server only sends the first three rows to the
   client buffer.

3 The user pages down in dw_main causing the client
   to fetch the next three rows from the server.

4 The server sends the next three rows to the client.
   The new rows are added to the client buffer.

Figure 3.89   Data retrieval with retrieve as needed.

Needed option from the Rows menu of the DataWindow painter. PowerBuilder implements retrieve as needed by opening a cursor and maintaining it as rows are retrieved from the server. When data is needed on the client, PowerBuilder simply fetches enough rows from the server (in two-page increments) to update the display of the DataWindow.

Retrieve as needed is overridden if there are any sorting, filtering, or aggregate functions (e.g., sum, average) performed against the DataWindow. This is because PowerBuilder must bring back the entire result set in order to perform any of these functions. A developer can make sure retrieve as needed is not overridden by adding an Order By clause to the Select statement to handle sorting, adding a Where clause instead of using a filter, and putting any computed columns in the Select statement instead of in the DataWindow as computed fields.

Using retrieve as needed does not impact the execution of the retrievestart, retrieverow, and retrieveend events. Retrievestart is triggered when the retrieval begins and retrieverow is triggered for every row retrieved. Retrieveend is triggered only when the last row has been retrieved or when the **dbCancel( )** function is executed.

The **Retrieve( )** and **Rowcount( )** functions behave differently, however, when using retrieve as needed. **Retrieve( )** returns only the number of rows initially brought back to the client; **Rowcount( )** returns the total number of rows that have been returned to the client. Using the previous example, these functions work as illustrated in Figure 3.90.

To obtain the total number of rows that satisfy the query, the COUNT(*) SQL function can be used.

The printing of DataWindows is also impacted by retrieve as needed. When a DataWindow is printed, only the rows that have been returned to the client are printed. To print all the rows of a DataWindow, retrieve as needed must be disabled. This can be done programmatically using the **dwModify( )** function. Setting the RetrieveAsNeeded DataWindow attribute to False causes the remaining rows of the result set to be returned to the client:

```
dw_main.dwModify("datawindow.RetrieveAsNeeded=FALSE")
```

To reset retrieve as needed to True after all rows have been returned to the client for printing, **dwModify** is executed as follows:

```
dw_main.dwModify("datawindow.RetrieveAsNeeded=FALSE" &
              + "datawindow.RetrieveAsNeeded=TRUE")
```

This sets retrieve as needed to False, causing all remaining rows to be returned to the client. It is then immediately reset to True.

The performance benefits of retrieve as needed depend on the size

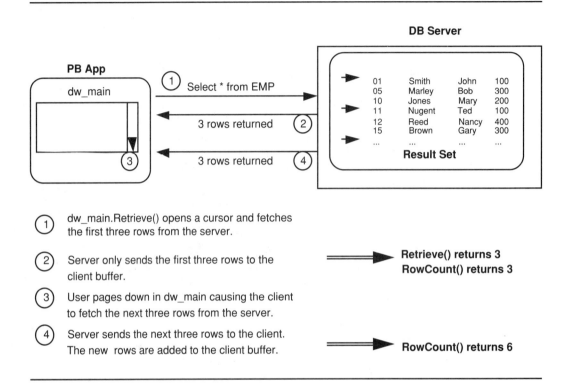

Figure 3.90   **Retrieve( )** and **RowCount( )** with retrieve as needed.

of the result set and the nature of user interaction with the data. If the user is going to page through a large percentage of the result set, retrieve as needed will decrease perceived performance because the data retrieval is being done each time the user scrolls. In this situation, retrieve as needed should probably not be used. However, if a large result set is being retrieved and the user will usually not page through the result set, retrieve as needed can provide a big perceived performance gain.

DataWindows as Buffers

In addition to using a DataWindow to present data to the user, a Data-Window can also be used as a data buffer. A developer can take advantage of the great deal of functionality encapsulated within a DataWindow to accomplish such things as storing application-specific security information, maintaining user configuration information, or storing data read from a file, among others.

One common use of a DataWindow as a buffer is to put data into a format for printing. For example, assume we have a data entry Data-Window designed to load data into an application database. For the sake of this example, assume that in order to expedite the data entry process, this DataWindow is designed with a very plain, straightforward presentation style. Also assume that there is a need to print reports to verify the data entered by the user and that the presentation style of this report differs from the data entry form.

One possible solution for this situation is to create a second Data-Window used for printing, create a hidden DataWindow control on the data entry window with the "print" DataWindow as its DataWindow object, and copy the desired data to the "print" DataWindow before printing. In this case, the "print" DataWindow is serving only as a data buffer—it is not being displayed to the user. The new **RowsCopy( )** and **RowsMove( )** DataWindow functions could also be used to simplify the transfer of data between the two DataWindows.

Code Tables

Code tables provide a method of reducing the amount of data stored in a database, by storing an encoded representation of a value. When used in DataWindows, code tables consist of a data value, which is the value retrieved from and stored in a database, and a display value, which is the value shown to the user. A list of states can be implemented as a code table, for example, with the state abbreviation being the data value and the state name the display value:

Data Value	Display Value
CA	California
FL	Florida
TX	Texas
WA	Washington
...	...

Code tables are defined through the edit style of a column. Code tables can be defined for the following edit styles:

- Checkbox
- DropDownDataWindow
- DropDownListBox

- Edit Style
- Edit Mask with Spin Control
- Radiobuttons

Each of these edit styles is discussed in the following section.

Checkbox Code Tables Although not widely used, code tables can have a checkbox edit style. The value stored is dependent on the state of the checkbox, therefore only three possible values (on, off, or other) can be stored for any one column. For example, a column containing employee status can be implemented as a checkbox by defining the On value to mean "Active" and the Off value to mean "Inactive." Active and Inactive are designated by the codes "AC" and "IN," respectively, as shown in Figure 3.91.

Because a user can only choose between the two states of the checkbox, no validation is required.

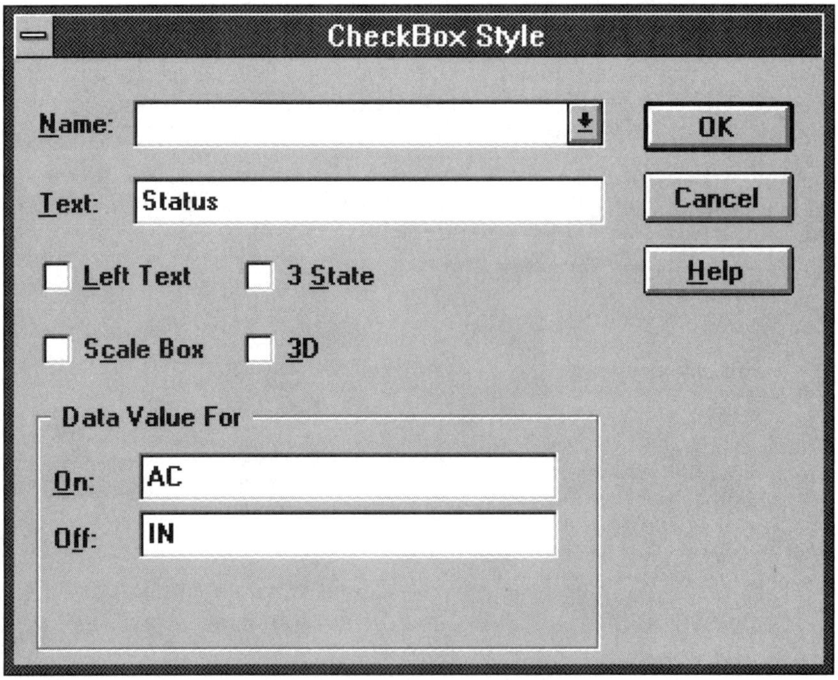

Figure 3.91   Checkbox edit style.

DropDownDataWindow Code Tables The DropDownDataWindow (DDDW) edit style can be used to define a child DataWindow as the code table for the column. This style is commonly used for code tables shared throughout an application. For example, the DataWindow state_dddw is defined with the following Select statement as its data source:

```
SELECT state_id, state_name
FROM states
```

This DataWindow only displays the state_name column, as shown in Figure 3.92. state_dddw can now be used as a DDDW in any other DataWindow that contains a state column, as shown in Figure 3.93.

If the data displayed using a DDDW is fairly static, storing the data with the DataWindow can improve performance by eliminating the need to retrieve the data from the database. In this example, because the data in state_dddw will most likely never change, the data should be

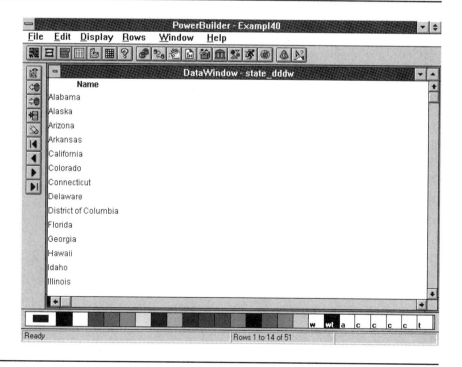

Figure 3.92   DataWindow displaying state_name column only.

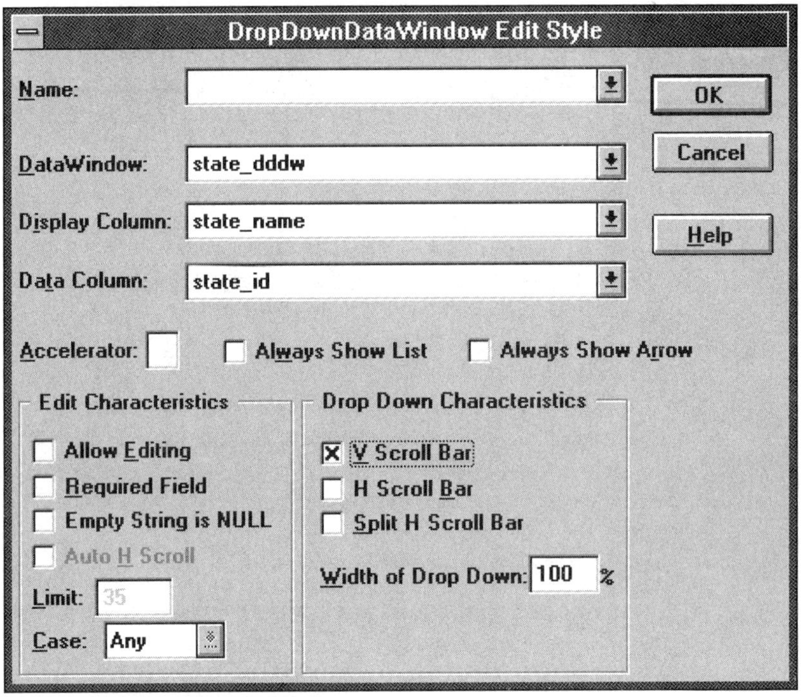

Figure 3.93 DropDownDataWindow edit style.

stored with the DataWindow object. To do this, the developer selects the Data option from the Rows menu in the DataWindow painter and completes it as shown in Figure 3.94.

Should this data change, the DataWindow object would need to be modified and the application redistributed.

DropDownListBox Code Tables A DropDownListBox (DDLB) edit style can be used to define code table data and display values. For a list of states, the DDLB style window is completed as shown in Figure 3.95.

The values in a DDLB can either be hard-coded, as shown in the figure or filled from a database programmatically. With DDDWs, filling a DDLB from the database is not necessary.

Edit Style Code Tables Code tables can be defined for edit-style columns by checking the Use code table checkbox in the edit style window. Checking this column allows the developer to enter the data and display values for the code table, as shown in Figure 3.96.

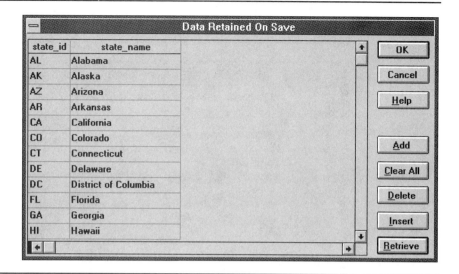

Figure 3.94   Data retained on save.

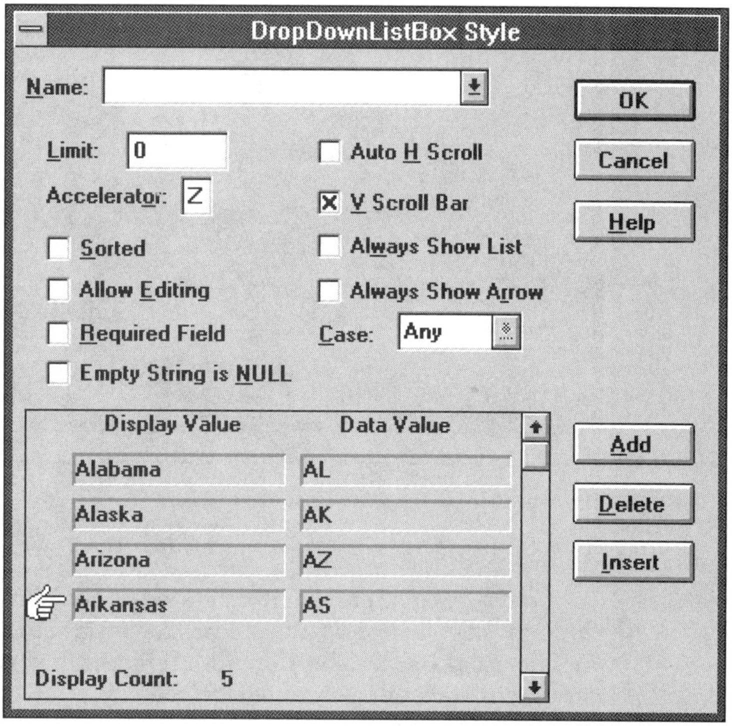

Figure 3.95   DropDownListBox style.

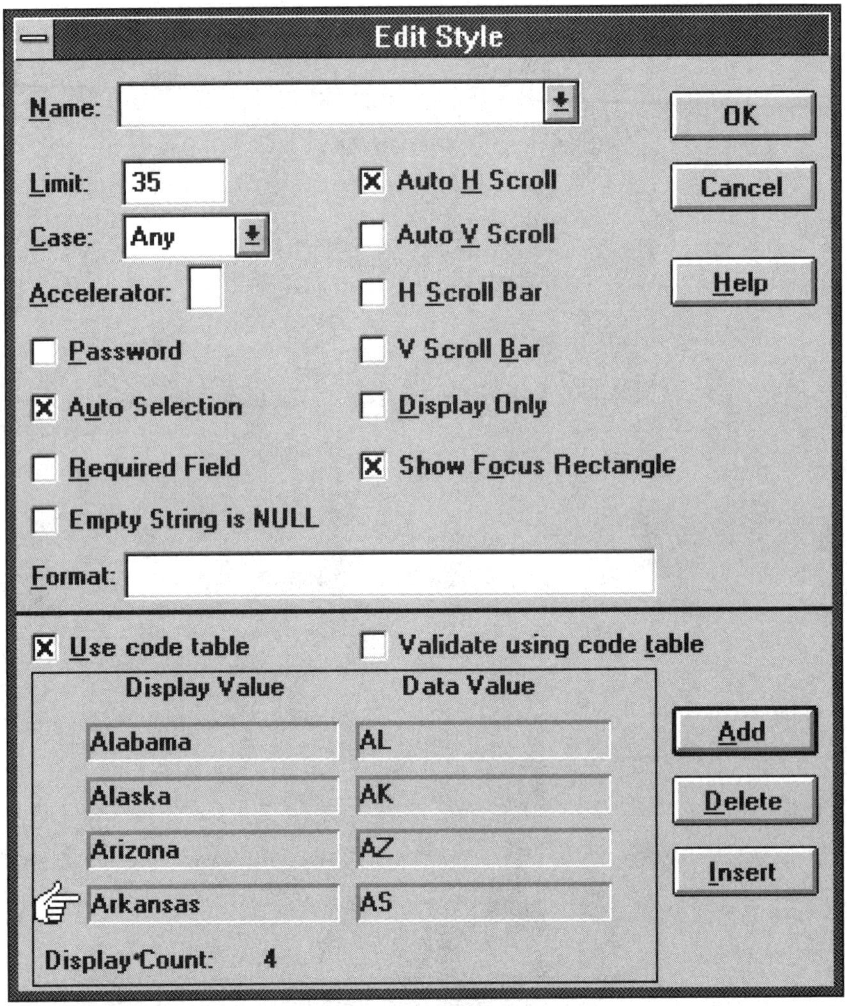

Figure 3.96 The edit style window.

Edit style columns can be validated either by using the code table or through code written in the ItemError event of the DataWindow control. To use the code table for validation, the developer checks the Validate using code table checkbox on the edit style window, and does not put any code in the ItemError event. If an error occurs, a message box is displayed with a generic message.

To customize the error processing, code should be put in the ItemError event. For example, to customize the error message if an invalid employee status code is entered into an edit style column, add the following code to the ItemError event of the DataWindow control:

```
string sColValue, sColName

// Get the current column name and the text in the column
sColName = this.GetColumnName( )
sColValue = this.GetText( )

// Display custom error message
DisplayMsg("Validation Error", &
    "'" + sColValue + "' is not valid for column '" + sColName + "'")

// Set action code to not display system message
this.SetActionCode(1)
```

Edit Mask with Spin Control Code tables can be used with spin controls to allow the user to scroll through the list of code table values. For the list of states example, the edit mask would be defined as shown in Figure 3.97.

Radiobuttons Code tables can be used with radiobutton edit styles by defining a fixed number of possible values for a given column. For example, if an employee's status can either be active, terminated, or on leave, radiobuttons can be used with a code table as shown here in Figure 3.98.

Radiobuttons are treated the same way as edit styles; the only difference is that the user must choose one of the possible options (there is no editing capability). Radiobuttons are good for small, static code tables.

Dynamically Changing Code Tables There may be times when the values for a code table need to be changed, such as when the value of a code table is dependent on the value of another column in the DataWindow. To do this, simply use **dwModify( )** to set the values attribute of the column to the new code table.

For example, the following code will set the codes table for the DropDownListBox column "city" to the cities for the state displayed in the state column:

```
string sStateVal

sStateVal = dw_1.GetItemString(1,"state")
```

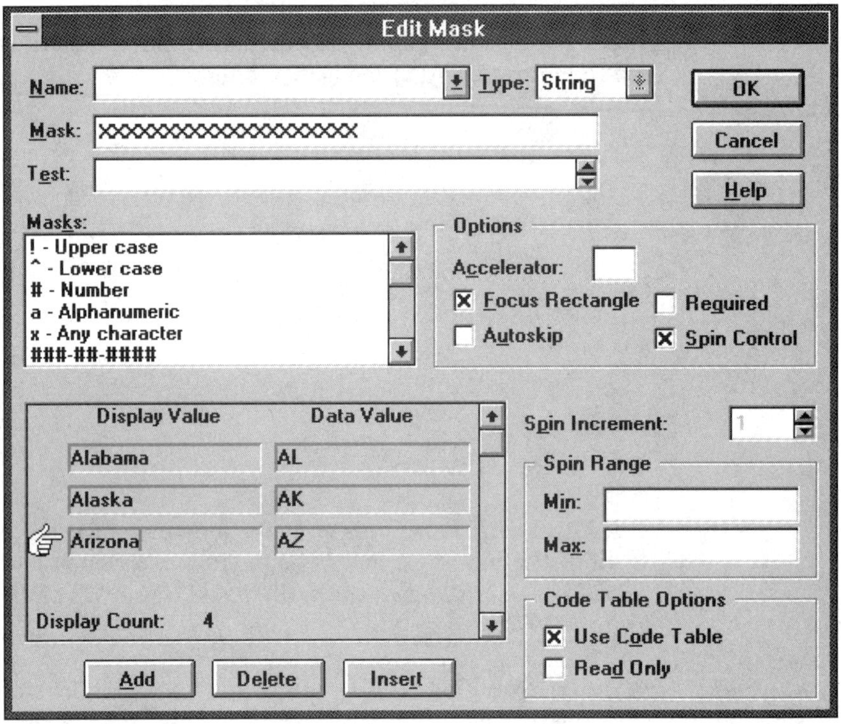

Figure 3.97 The edit mask.

```
CHOOSE CASE sStateVal
  CASE "TX"
    dw_1.dwModify("city.values = 'Houston~tHO/Dallas~tDA' ")
  CASE "CA"
    dw_1.dwModify("city.values = 'Los Angeles~tLA/San
Francisco~tSF' ")
...
...
END CHOOSE
```

While all of these code tables (other than the DropDownDataWindow) maintain the code table data within the client application, it is usually desirable to store code table information in an application database. In this case, the code table data must be retrieved from the database and any changes to a code table must be written back to the database.

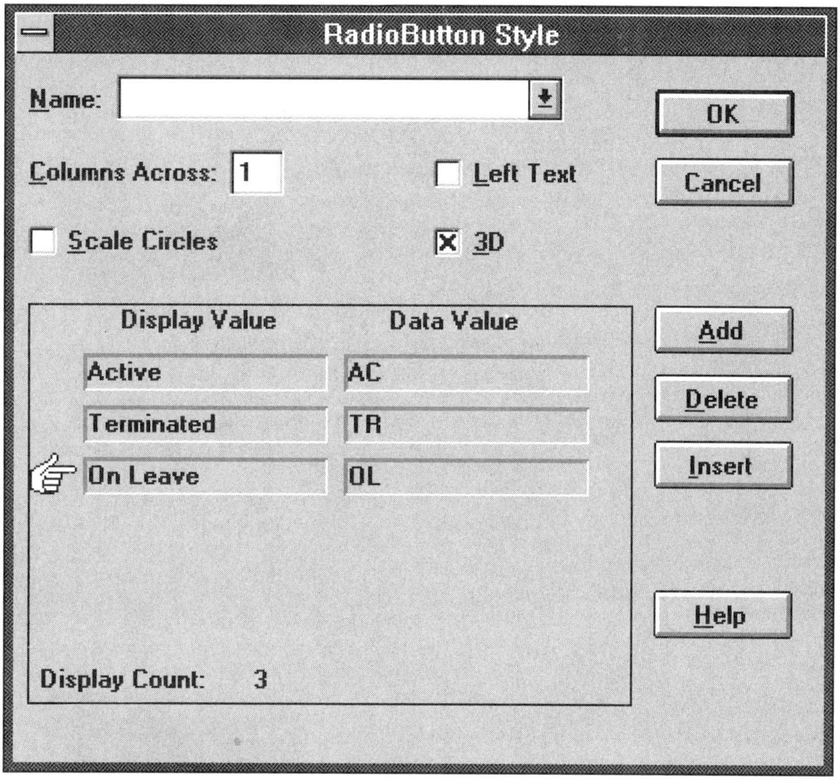

Figure 3.98 Radiobutton style.

There are two design approaches when storing code tables in a database. One approach is to store each individual code table as a separate database table. For example, if an application requires code tables to maintain a list of states, a list of company division names, and a list of employee titles, three tables would be created, each with the following columns:

```
code char(10) Not Null
description char(40) Not Null
```

Another approach is to store all code tables in a single database table. In this case, the table would need to have a column designating the type of code:

```
code_type char(10) Not Null
code char(10) Not Null
description char(40) Not Null
```

Deciding which method to use depends on the number of code tables and the frequency in which the code tables are queried and updated. For a larger number of code tables, maintenance will be simplified by using the one-table approach. However, depending upon such things as the nature of transactions against the code tables and the DBMS, it may be desirable to distribute code table data among separate database tables.

Using a DDDW vs. Filling a DDLB

Previous to PowerBuilder 3.0, developers were forced to explicitly fill any DropDownListBox (DDLB) window controls that contained data from the database. With the addition of the DropDownDataWindow (DDDW) to PowerBuilder 3.0, child DataWindows can be defined to accomplish this (see the section on Child DataWindows in this chapter). DDDWs should be used instead of filling DDLBs using embedded SQL. Using DDDWs usually results in better performance, in addition to allowing developers to take advantage of the functionality already built into the DataWindow object.

Using Bitmaps in DataWindows

Bitmaps can be used in different ways to enhance the look of a Data-Window. This can be done by:

- Setting the Display As Picture attribute
- Using a computed field
- Using **SetRowFocusIndicator( )**

These methods are discussed in the following sections.

Display As Picture The Display As Picture attribute can be used to display a bitmap file named in a database column. This method is usually used when the bitmap file name is stored in the database. For example, suppose the table part_image, which contains a set of part names and their corresponding bitmap file names, is defined as:

```
part_name char(10)    NOT NULL
bmp_file  char(15)    NOT NULL
```

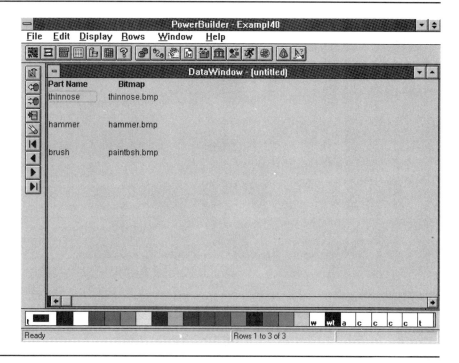

Figure 3.99   Retrieval of part name and bitmap file name only.

Without setting Display As Picture, retrieving this data would simply retrieve the part name and the name of the bitmap file, as shown in Figure 3.99.

To specify that the column should be displayed as a bitmap, the developer would select the Display As Picture option from the Edit style menu of a database column, as shown in Figure 3.100.

This displays the bitmap file itself, rather than just the name of the file, as shown in Figure 3.101.

As mentioned previously, this method is usually used when the name of the bitmap is being stored in the database. Depending on the nature of an application, this may or may not be desirable. When dealing with a large volume of image data, this method of image display may be preferable to storing the images in the database. While storing image data in a database has advantages, it can also significantly slow performance.

Another thing to remember regarding this method of image display

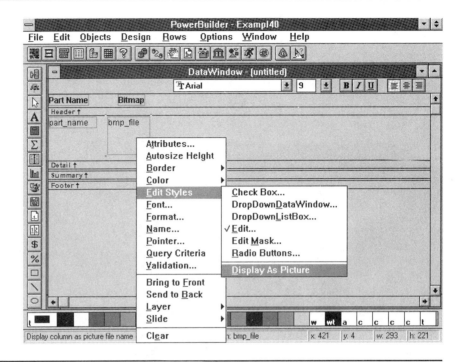

Figure 3.100   Selecting the Display As Picture option.

is that it does not allow any editing of the image. The file name can be changed, but the image itself cannot be modified. To allow image editing from within a PowerBuilder application, the developer would create an OLE column with the bitmap as the data source. OLE columns are discussed later.

A second example using Display As Picture is to use a bitmap to indicate that a row has been selected. For example, if multiple rows in a DataWindow can be selected, a column can be defined with the Display As Picture attribute set to use a bitmap to indicate that the row has been selected. To do this, first modify the DataWindow Select statement to add a computed column. This can be done by simply adding an empty string to the Select:

```
SELECT '', "cust_order"."ordnum", "cust_order"."custnum",
       "cust_order"."duedate", "cust_order"."balance"
FROM "cust_order"
```

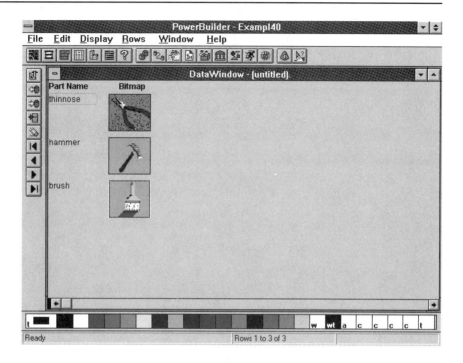

Figure 3.101   The bitmap file.

Next, this column is added to the DataWindow. It is placed at the leftmost part of the body and the Display As Picture attribute is selected, as shown in Figure 3.102.

From the Window painter, the following code is added to the clicked event of the DataWindow control:

```
/******************************************************
** If we click in the selection column, then select/deselect this
** row. Row selection is indicated by setting the selection column
** to the name of the bitmap file returned from the selectionBMP( )
** function.
******************************************************/

long lRow
int iSelCol
string sTemp
```

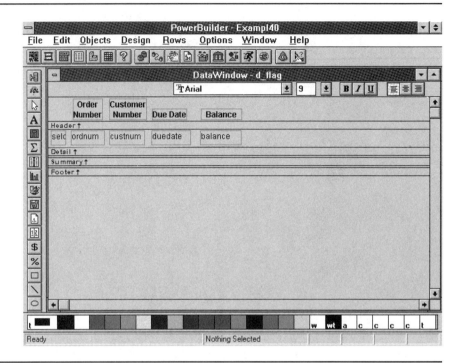

Figure 3.102   Selected column placed at leftmost part of window.

```
// Only do this if we clicked in our "selection column."
// The selection column is returned from the selectionColNo( ) function

iSelCol = selectionColNo( )
if (iSelCol > 0) and (getClickedColumn(this) = iSelCol) then
        // First - force to process any changes - only continue if no
        // errors
        if acceptText(this) < 0 then
                // Error - don't do rest of this event
                return
        end if
        lRow = getClickedRow(this)
        if lRow > 0 then
                // Set this to the current row and get the bitmap file
                // name
                setRow(this,lRow)
                sTemp = getItemString(this,lRow,iSelCol)
```

```
                  // If the column is empty, set it to the bitmap file name
                  // else, set it to empty string
                  if (sTemp = "") or isNull(sTemp) then
                      setItem(this,lRow,iSelCol,selectionBMP())
                  else
                      setItem(this,lRow,iSelCol,"")
                  end if
          end if
  end if
```

Notice that the above script calls two new functions, **selection ColNo( )** and **selectionBMP( )**. **selectionColNo( )** is a window function that returns the number of the selection column (1, in this example). **selectionBMP( )** is also a window function, returning a string containing the name of the bitmap file used to indicate row selection ("asterisk.bmp" in this example).

Note: If the same selection column or bitmap was going to be used by multiple DataWindows in an application, it would be better to create **selectionBMP( )** as a window function of an ancestor window.

When executed, clicking on the selection column toggles between the asterisk and an empty string to indicate whether a row is selected. So, if the second and third rows are selected, the window would look like that in Figure 3.103.

Code could also be added to perform some process against each of the selected rows.

Using a Computed Field Another method for displaying bitmaps in DataWindows is using a computed field. The computed field expression uses the **Bitmap( )** function, which takes a single argument that is either a DataWindow column or a string naming the bitmap file to be displayed. This function is used in the expression of the computed field to dynamically determine the bitmap to be displayed for each row in the DataWindow.

Using the previous example, assume we want to display a red flag if the balance is over $1,000 and over 90 days past due. To do this, a computed field is added to the DataWindow with the expression shown in Figure 3.104.

This uses the **Bitmap( )** function to display flag.bmp if the balance is > 1000 and the difference between today's data and the due date is more than 90 days. The results are shown in Figure 3.105.

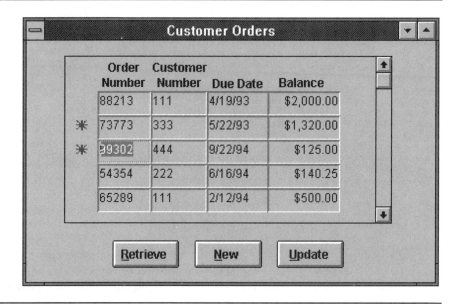

Figure 3.103   Selecting rows.

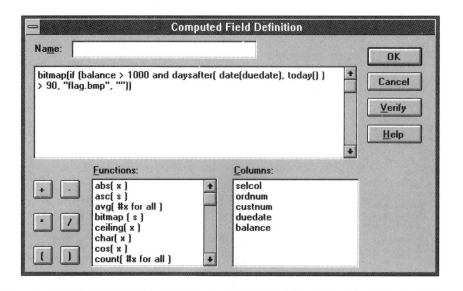

Figure 3.104   Adding a computed field.

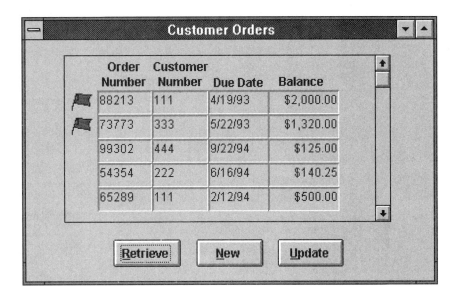

Figure 3.105   The results of using **Bitmap( )** function.

This method provides more flexibility than the previous method because the computed field can be defined so that the bitmap is determined dynamically based on the values of other columns in the DataWindow.

Using SetRowFocusIndicator( ) Bitmaps can be used to indicate the current row in a DataWindow by using the **SetRowFocusIndicator( )** function. This function takes either a picture control or a value of the RowFocusInd enumerated data type. To use a picture control as the row focus indicator, the developer places the picture control on the window containing the DataWindow. The picture control can either be hidden or placed under the DataWindow control, to keep it from being displayed on the window. For example, to set the row focus indicator to asterisk.bmp, the developer creates a picture control with asterisk.bmp as its picture and calls **SetRowFocusIndicator** before retrieving the DataWindow:

```
int    iRtn

dw_cust_order.SetRowFocusIndicator(p_1)
```

```
iRtn = dw_cust_order.retrieve( )
if (iRtn = -1) then
   MessageBox("Select Error", sqlca.sqlerrtext)
end if
```

As a result, the DataWindow uses the picture object as the row focus indicator, as shown in Figure 3.106.

The enumerated data type RowFocusInd contains a set of values that can be used as parameters for SetRowFocusIndicator. This data type is defined as:

Off!—No indicator

FocusRect!—Puts a rectangle around the current row

Hand!—Uses the hand bitmap to indicate the current row

The **SetRowFocusIndicator( )** also takes an X and Y value as parameters to indicate where within the DataWindow control the indicator will be displayed. These arguments are only used when using a picture control or the Hand! value as the indicator. The defaults for the

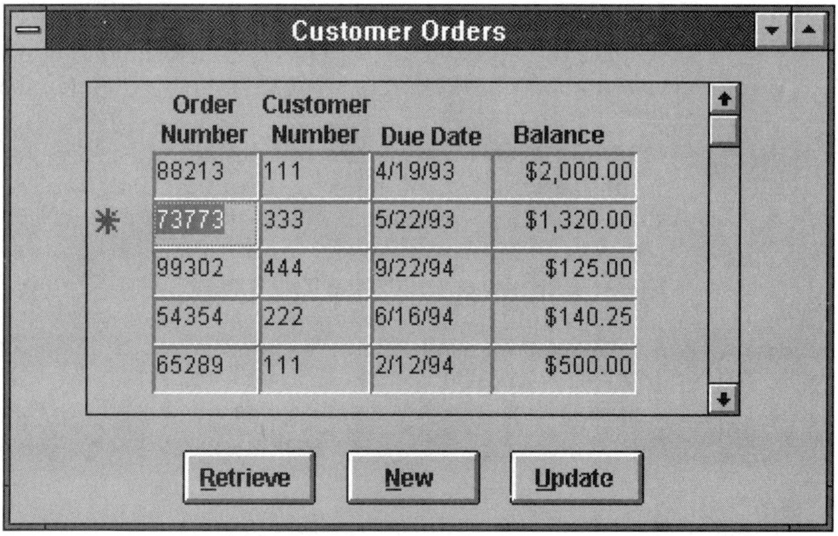

Figure 3.106   Using the picture object as the row focus indication.

X and Y position are 0; this displays the indicator at the leftmost side of the DataWindow body. To replace the asterisk previously used with the hand bitmap, the developer simply changes the parameter passed to SetRowFocusIndicator:

```
int    i_retcode

dw_cust_order.SetRowFocusIndicator(Hand!)

i_retcode = dw_cust_order.retrieve( )
if (i_retcode = -1) then
    MessageBox("Select Error", sqlca.sqlerrtext)
end if
```

This code displays the DataWindow as shown in Figure 3.107.

OLE Columns

Microsoft's object linking and embedding (OLE) provides a method of communicating between Windows applications. This method allows the integration of information from a variety of sources into a single docu-

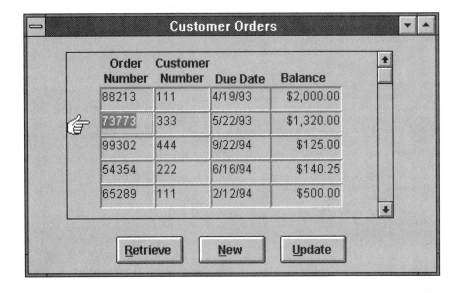

Figure 3.107   The final DataWindow.

ment. PowerBuilder supports OLE in the form of a window control as well as in the form of an OLE column in a DataWindow. This section discusses the OLE column of a DataWindow only. For a discussion of creating an OLE 2.0 window control, refer to Chapter 14.

OLE DataWindow columns can be used to store binary large objects (Blobs) such as bitmaps, Excel spreadsheets, and Microsoft Word documents in a database.

In order to better understand the concepts of OLE, common terms are defined here.

Client Application:	The application in which an OLE object is linked or embedded. If an Excel graph were embedded in a Word document, Word would be the client application.
Server Application:	The application from which an OLE object is linked or embedded. If an Excel graph were embedded in a Word document, Excel would be the server application.
OLE Client Library:	The client application uses this library, OLECLI.DLL, to interact with the OLE protocol. It contains functions used by client applications.
OLE Server Library:	The server application uses this library, OLESVR.DLL, to interact with the OLE protocol. It contains functions used by server applications.
Registration Database:	This database is found in the SHELL.DLL library. It contains information needed by clients and servers to determine what servers and objects are available.
Native Data:	This is data stored by the client only for embedded objects. It is the server document that is the embedded object. When a client needs an embedded object manipulated, it passes this data to the server. Because this data is "native" to the server, it produces a document from this data that can be manipulated just like any of the server's documents. When the user is finished with the server, the server passes

the updated native data back to the client for storage.

Presentation Format:	This is data stored by the client for both embedded and linked objects. It is passed to the client library from the client application so that the object can be displayed within the client's document. This data is needed so that the client can represent the server's document within its own document. Because the client does not understand the native data of the server and therefore cannot display it, the server must provide a format that can be used by the client to display the object. This data is the presentation format.
Owner Link:	This is data that a client stores for embedded objects to determine what application is the server. It is originally passed from the server.
Object Link:	This is data a client stores for linked objects to determine the server and the original file to which the link is made. It is originally passed from the server.

PowerBuilder uses Blobs to store the binary information required by OLE. Because the Blobs are in a database table, PowerBuilder requires at least two columns in a table containing a Blob—one for the Blob itself and one for a unique identifier of the Blob (e.g., a file name or an object number). This column is usually defined as the key of the table.

For example, create a DataWindow for maintaining a set of employee status and expense reports. This DataWindow is to contain the employee id, a week-ending date, and two Blob columns—one for the status report (an MS Word document) and one for the expense report (an Excel spreadsheet). The WATCOM table is defined as shown in Figure 3.108.

To create a DataWindow with a Blob column, first paint a Select statement including the identifier column in the select list, but not the Blob. Because PowerBuilder does not directly support the Blob data type, the Blob column cannot be included in the select list. In this example, the emp_id and week_ending columns will be selected. After the Select statement has been created, the Blob is placed on the DataWindow by selecting OLE Database Blob from the Objects menu. After choosing where to

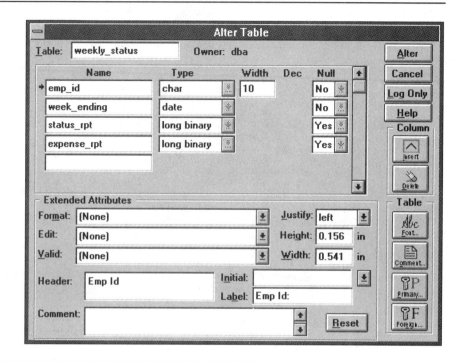

Figure 3.108   Definition of the WATCOM table.

place the Blob column, the Blob definition window appears. The window is completed to create the status report Blob as shown in Figure 3.109.

The Name field contains the name used by PowerBuilder to reference the object within the DataWindow. The Client Class, Client Name, and Client Name Expression fields are concatenated together to yield a string used by the server application as a title of the document. The Client Name Expression allows the title to be dynamically associated with runtime values within the client application. For example, this window displays the unique identifiers emp_id and week_ending from the current row in the DataWindow within the phrase "Status report for... " in the titlebar of the window of the server application.

The Table and Large Binary/Text Columns combo boxes are used to tell PowerBuilder which column the OLE Blob is referring to. In the window shown in Figure 3.109 the status report Blob is stored in weekly_status.status_rpt. The Key clause is used for retrieving and updating Blobs from the database. It defines the Where clause needed to identify

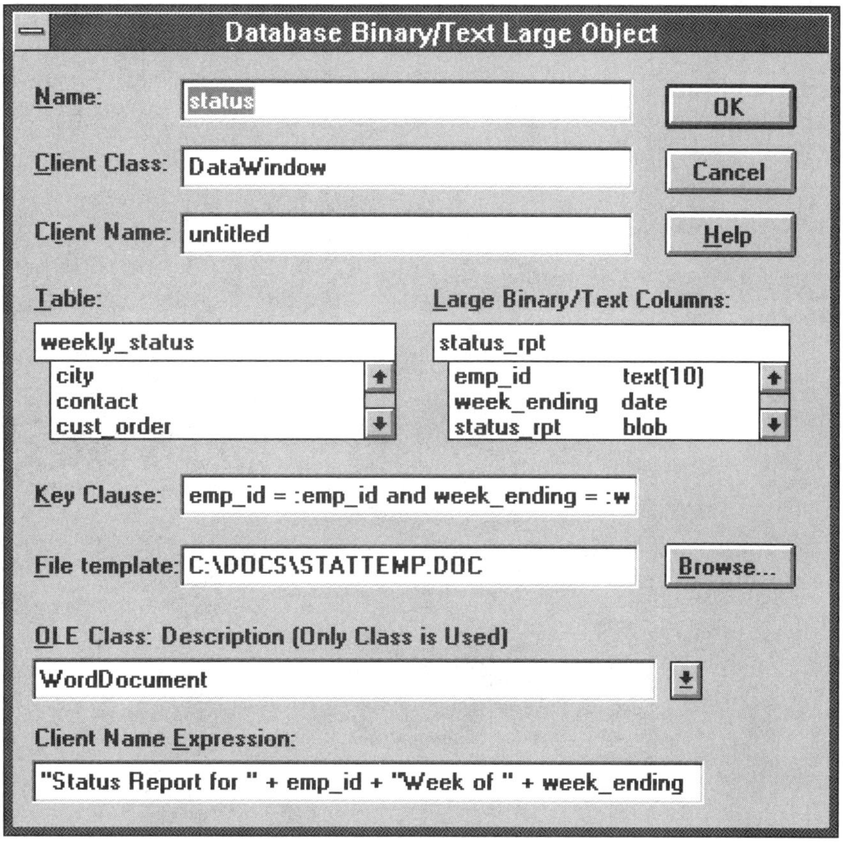

Figure 3.109   The status report Blob.

a specific Blob. In this example, the emp_id and week_ending columns are used in the Where clause to uniquely identify the Blob columns.

The File Template field is used by PowerBuilder when a new Blob is created. If an **InsertRow( )** is done in the DataWindow, PowerBuilder creates a new row with an empty Blob. By double-clicking on this Blob or calling **dwOLEActivate( )**, the server application defined by the OLE Class field is started. If there is a filename in the File Template field, the server application brings up this file as the default data for the new object. In our example, the file C:\DOCS\STATTEMP.DOC will be opened when creating a new status report.

The OLE Class field is not required if a File Template is entered that contains an extension that is registered in the OLE registration database. PowerBuilder searches the OLE registration database for the class associated with this extension and starts that class' application.

To define the Blob column used for expense reports, the previous steps are repeated and the Blob definition window is completed as shown in Figure 3.110.

After the Blob columns have been identified, the DataWindow should look something like that in Figure 3.111.

When this example is executed, existing rows have an icon representing the document in the Blob column, as shown in Figure 3.112.

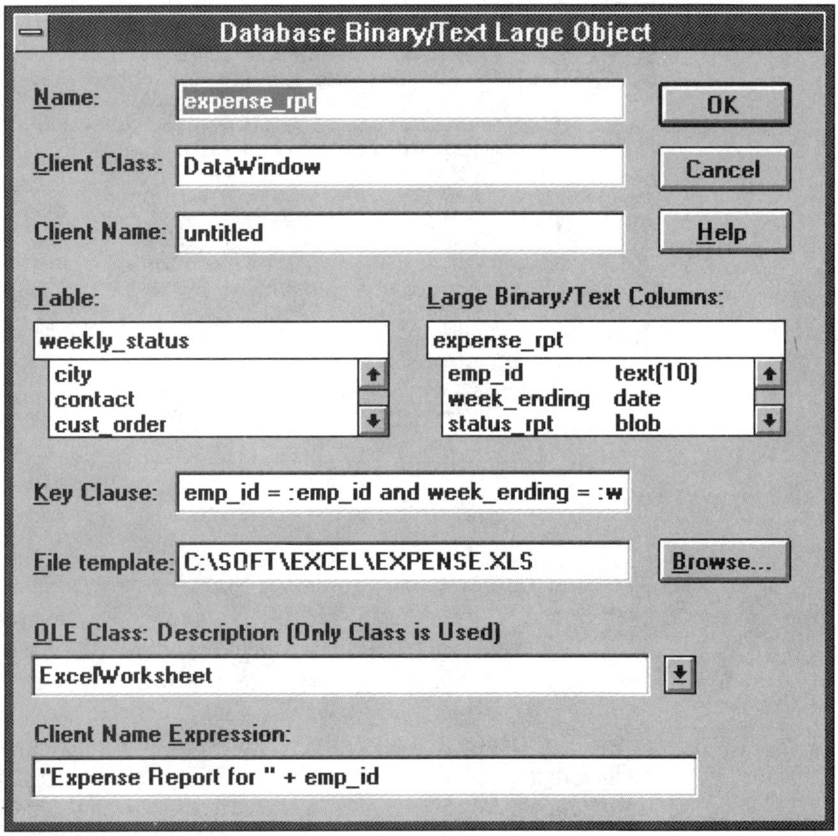

Figure 3.110   The Blob definition window.

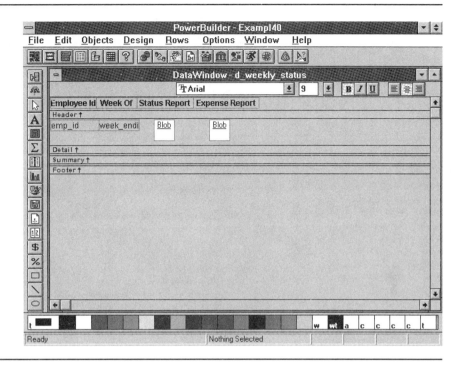

Figure 3.111   DataWindow after identification of Blob columns.

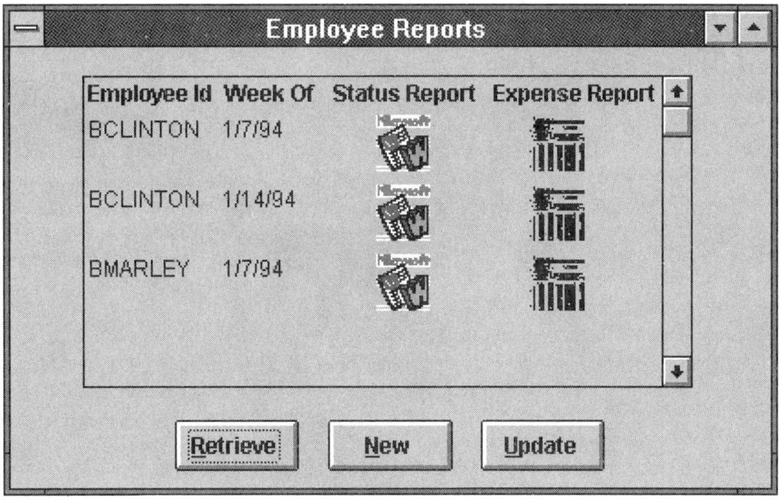

Figure 3.112   Icon representing the document in the Blob column.

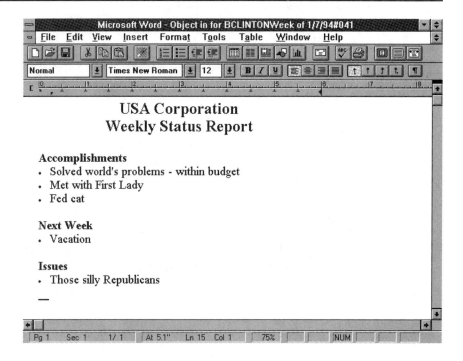

Figure 3.113 Document contained in the Blob column opened after double-clicking on Microsoft Word icon.

Double-clicking on the MS Word icon in the status report column invokes MS Word and opens the document contained in the Blob column, as shown in Figure 3.113.

Double-clicking on the Excel spreadsheet icon in the expense report column invokes Excel and opens the document contained in the Blob column, as shown in Figure 3.114.

When a new row is inserted, the Blob columns are initially blank. Double-clicking on either of the Blob columns brings up the OLE server application and opens the file specified by the file template defined in the Blob definition window, as shown in Figure 3.115.

Note: To show the users where to click to activate an OLE column, place an object or bitmap behind the Blob column.

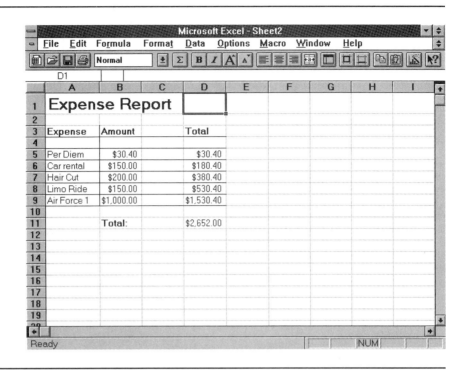

Figure 3.114 Document contained in the Blob column opened after double-clicking on Excel spreadsheet icon.

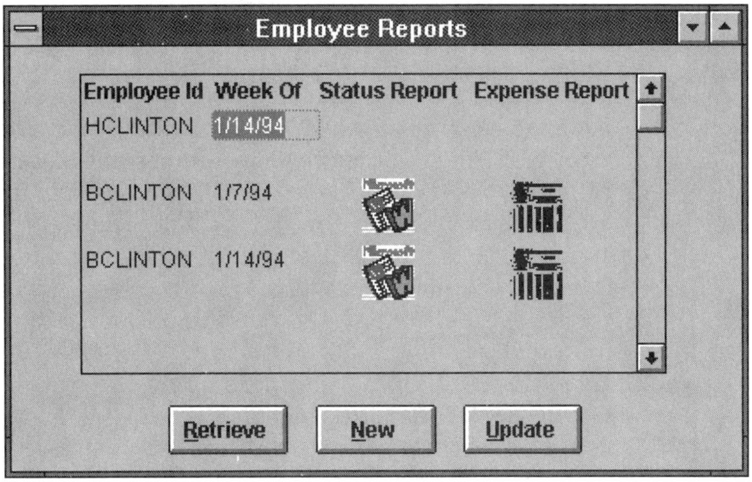

Figure 3.115 Specified file opened.

It is important to note that a Blob column does not require a database in order to start a server and view a specific file. Although this information is never actually embedded in the DataWindow because there is no place to store it, the Blob can be used to allow users to look at a specific file from a server application.

For example, to allow a user to view the Excel file EXPENSE.XLS from a PowerBuilder application, a DataWindow can be created using an external data source and a Blob column. In this instance, the only meaningful field in the Blob definition window is the File Template. The OLE Class can be left blank and the Client Class, Client Name, and Client Name Expression can be set to whatever values are appropriate. The Table, Large Binary/Text Columns, and the Key clause can contain anything because the value is not used, but it must contain some value. The File Template field should contain a fully qualified reference to EXPENSE.XLS.

To view the spreadsheet, the developer calls **InsertRow( )** to create a new row in the DataWindow and double-clicks on the Blob column (or calls **dwOLEActivate( )**). PowerBuilder then starts the OLE server application and opens EXPENSE.XLS because it was defined as the template file for that OLE column in the DataWindow. It is important to note that this is not the actual EXPENSE.XLS file. The sheet displayed by Excel is the OLE object belonging to PowerBuilder, and any changes made to it will not be reflected in EXPENSE.XLS. Exiting the server returns the presentation data from the server to the DataWindow.

Limitations According to Microsoft's OLE specifications, the difference between linking and embedding is usually a function of whether the user uses a **Paste** or a **Paste Link** command. Because the functionality of a DataWindow does not lend itself to either of these commands, there is no reason why a **Paste** or **Paste Link** command is required to perform OLE. There is, however, an important distinction between what the client application does to enable linking as opposed to embedding.

Embedding is performed if the native data is the first format on the clipboard that the client application can use; otherwise, the format is copied to the client as in a standard cut and paste. If the native data is the first useful format, the client application stores the native, owner link, and useful presentation data. This allows a client to represent server data by calling the client library to draw the object (using the **OleDraw( ) function**), but also allows the client to pass the native data back to the appropriate server to be edited (or used in some other manner). The important point to note is that once the data is copied from the server to the client, the client stores the information. There is no way to "link" back to an original source document owned by the server. This is PowerBuilder's current functionality. The native data is stored in the database Blob along with the owner link and presentation data. The **dwOLEActivate( )** function or double-clicking on the Blob brings up the server application with the native data stored in the database.

In the case of a link, the client application looks for the object link format on the clipboard and uses a presentation format (or a package icon) to display the object within its application. The advantage of a link is that any changes made to a file are reflected in the client's application document. In terms of a PowerBuilder application, the object link and presentation format would be stored in the database. When the DataWindow retrieves this information, the **dwOLEActivate( )** function or a similar function could be used to update the presentation data to reflect the current state of the original document.

Stop Light Reports

Computed columns and bitmaps can be combined in a DataWindow to produce what are called stop light reports. These reports, generally used in executive information system-type (EIS) applications, use a background of a specific color to represent a certain status of a given column. For example, to represent the urgency of past due account balances, a red background could be used in a balance column for values > 2000, yellow for values over 1000, and green for all other values. The DataWindow might look like the one in Figure 3.116.

To do this, create a computed field with the expression shown in Figure 3.117.

This column would then be placed behind the balance column in the DataWindow. Next, make the background of the balance column transparent to allow the bitmap to show.

Creating a DataWindow Architecture

Through user objects, a DataWindow architecture can be developed in the same manner as windows and menus are. Creating a user object hierarchy allows user-defined events, functions, and variables to be encapsulated into what is essentially a customized DataWindow. Functions such as error handling, setting the transaction object, and enabling or disabling the columns within a DataWindow can be built into an ancestor DataWindow class and inherited by all application DataWindows.

Because of the specific maintenance needs of list DataWindows (e.g.,

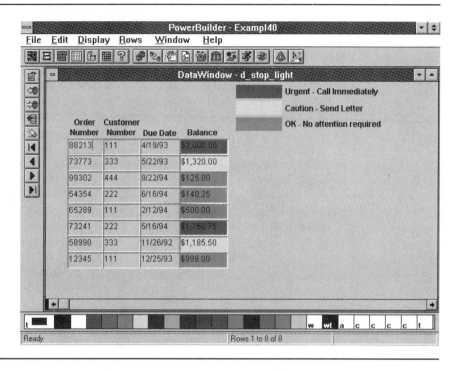

Figure 3.116   DataWindow with stop light reports.

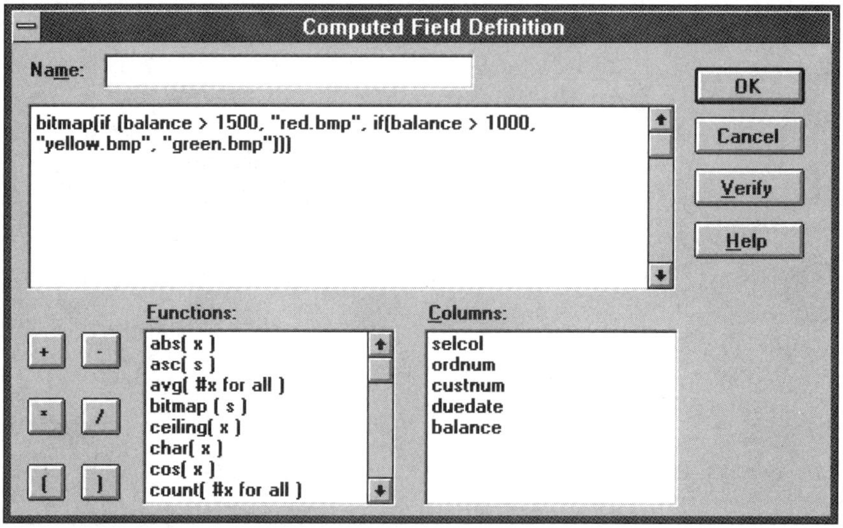

Figure 3.117   Computed field definition.

inserting and deleting rows), it may be a good idea to create a List DataWindow class. This class can be inherited from the base class and extend or override the functionality as needed. All application list DataWindows could then be inherited from this class, while all others are inherited from the base class directly.

Before designing a DataWindow architecture, the issue of data access in general needs to be addressed. A concern among application designers and developers is what to do if the data source(s) for an application change. For example, if the data source of an application changes from DB2 to Sybase, how would it affect the application code?

While ODBC attempts to solve this problem, it does not allow developers to take advantage of the various SQL extensions of the different DBMSs. These extensions, while not all accepted as standards, provide developers much more flexibility than standard ANSI SQL. Using these extensions, however, means that a change in DBMS will result in some modification of application code.

A good data access design can greatly simplify these changes. Abstracting the data access pieces of an application, or set of applications, into an overall data access layer can reduce the development time needed to make the changes required when data sources are changed.

Data access in a PowerBuilder application is accomplished using either a DataWindow or embedded SQL. The maintenance of DataWindow SQL is fairly straightforward. It is the embedded SQL maintenance that can be a problem. All embedded SQL should be abstracted into a set of functions that can be put into a data access .PBL. In an architecture like the one previously described, these functions can either be global functions or user object functions. Abstracting this code into a data access layer greatly simplifies the maintenance required when a data source changes.

CHAPTER 4

Multiple Document Interface (MDI)

The multiple document interface (MDI) is a Windows interface style used to create an application consisting of related subapplications or sheets containing similar information. An MDI application allows the user to interact with several different windows within an application at the same time.

This chapter covers:

- Types of MDI Applications
- Components of MDI
- Creating and Manipulating an MDI

When used for the right type of application and developed properly, an MDI application can provide a friendly and flexible user interface.

TYPES OF MDI APPLICATIONS

One of the main differences between an MDI application and a single document interface is that the MDI frame is considered to be the parent window for all of the different windows within the application. Even if a sheet window is a Main window type, it is subordinate to the MDI frame. In addition, each of the other types of windows can be subordinate to the Main window sheet, if needed. Another difference with the MDI application is that the MDI frame and an MDI sheet are activated at the same time.

Some examples of MDI applications are Microsoft Word, Excel, and even PowerBuilder. These applications use toolbars, sheets, and MicroHelp to guide their users. When the developer is considering creating an MDI application, there are two basic categories of MDI to consider:

- Single Task
- Multiple Task

Single Task

The Single Task MDI application consists of a frame window that allows many similar sheets or window instances to perform the same type of task within the application. An example of this type of MDI application is MS Word. This application can bring up many instances of the main type Document for simultaneous use (see Figure 4.1). Another use for this type of MDI would be in a contact management application that brings up many different types of contacts by business name.

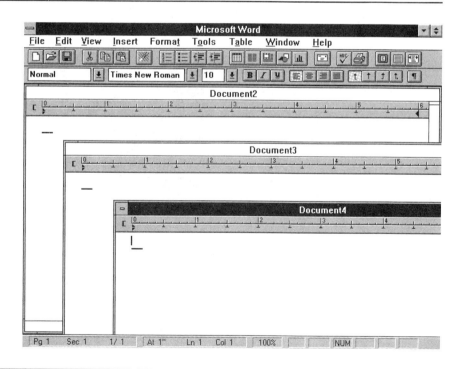

Figure 4.1　　The Single Task MDI application.

Multiple Task

The Multiple Task MDI application consists of a frame window that allows many different instances of windows to be opened for performing different tasks. The Multiple Task MDI typically consists of subapplications that may consist of nested windows. An example of this type of MDI application is the PowerBuilder development environment. A user can work in the Library painter and DataWindow painter within the PowerBuilder application frame simultaneously. Because both painters are considered to be different sheets or subapplications, the user can switch between the Library painter to the DataWindow painter within the same instance of the PowerBuilder development environment, as shown in Figure 4.2.

Unfortunately, many developers incorrectly use the MDI paradigm and create applications that probably should not be built using MDI. The application should be scrutinized to see if the system requirements actually fit the definition of MDI. MDI is intended for displaying mul-

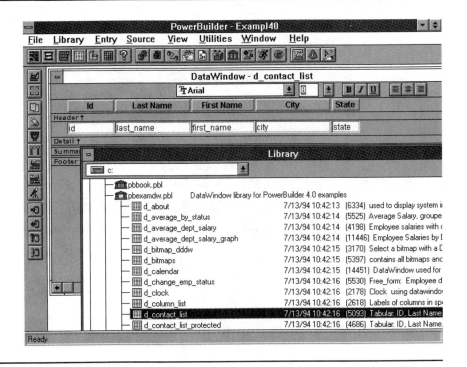

Figure 4.2   The Multiple Task MDI application.

tiple instances of documents or subapplications and not because the user would like to have MicroHelp and toolbars.

COMPONENTS OF MDI

Frame

The MDI frame is the application shell and contains the client area MDI_1, menu, MicroHelp, and all of the related sheets within it. Because the majority of the work is accomplished within the sheets, the MDI frame should be designed to have a minimum amount of controls.

When the developer creates a PowerBuilder MDI frame, a client area is automatically created. This area is the workspace for all of the application's sheets. The client area is space between the sides of the frame below the standard menu area and above the MicroHelp area. PowerBuilder automatically sizes this area when the developer creates a standard MDI. If any controls are added to the frame, the developer must resize the client area. PowerBuilder automatically names the client area MDI_1. When an MDI frame is saved, the object MDI_1 is created and can be seen when browsing the list of PowerBuilder objects. Unfortunately, MDI_1 cannot be selected and does not have any events associated with it, but it does have alterable attributes and functions. (See the PowerBuilder Objects and Controls manual for further explanation.)

There are two basic types of frames that can be used in an MDI application:

- Standard Frame
- Custom Frame

The standard frame is the basic frame generated by PowerBuilder that contains a border and menu bar with MicroHelp. Each sheet uses the main menu bar when it is activated. The second type of frame is the custom frame. This type of frame is basically a standard frame with user-created buttons or objects. Figure 4.3 shows an example of a custom MDI frame.

Standard MDI Frame Creating an MDI standard frame is done in the same way as a normal window. To make the window into an MDI frame, the developer chooses MDI or MDI with MicroHelp under the Window style menu. The MDI frame should include any functionality that is central to the application and the sheets within the conversation. This functionality might include the use of security for the sheets, loading and passing of variables, and error handling.

Figure 4.3 Example of a custom MDI frame.

Custom MDI Frame When the developer adds controls to a standard MDI frame, it becomes a custom MDI frame. When using a custom frame, the developer must resize the client area or the sheets will not fit properly on the frame.

Resizing the Client Area When creating a custom MDI frame, a developer must take note of the new controls that have been added to the frame in order to correctly size the MDI client area. The new items that have been added must be sized consistently with the client area in order to present a consistent look. In the initial creation of MDI_1, PowerBuilder automatically defaults the size of the window to a height and width of 0. If an application is designed to open more than one sheet, some of the sheets may not be visible if the client area is sized incorrectly.

If a custom user object, **uo_1**, were added to a frame to create a custom frame, the following code would resize the client area:

```
int      iWidth, iHeight
// Obtain the width and height of the workspace

iWidth = WorkSpaceWidth (w_mdi_frame)
iHeight = WorkSpaceHeight (w_mdi_frame)
// Calculate workspace between the User Object
// and the MicroHelp. uo_1 is the User Object
// nearest the top left-corner of the frame.

iHeight = iHeight - (uo_1.y + uo_1.height)
iHeight = iHeight - (mdi_1.microhelpheight)

// Move the upper-left corner of the client area (mdi_1)
// to the bottom-left corner of the User Object (uo_1).
Move (mdi_1, 0, uo_1.height)

// Resize the client area. The frame window has a line
// below the buttons at the top of the window so add 4
// to nHeight to allow for the line.
Resize (mdi_1, iWidth, iHeight + 4)
```

The frame now looks like what is shown in Figure 4.4.

Sheets

The most important part of the MDI application is the sheet. The sheet is where the majority of the work is done by the user. When the MDI is invoked, the application frame acts as the main window and each of the corresponding sheets is subservient to the frame window. Even though the sheets are main windows, they interact with the MDI frame like child windows in non-MDI applications. Each of the sheets may also have child windows, but the tracking and manipulation of nested sheets (i.e., sheets within sheets) is not a recommended practice.

An example of child windows that are subordinate to a main window sheet is the Database painter within the PowerBuilder development environment. Each of the separate table windows for a particular database are children to the Database painter sheet window.

Managing Sheets

Prior to PowerBuilder 4, one of hardest parts of developing an MDI application was the management of the associated sheets. Approaches to managing sheets in PowerBuilder 3.x include maintaining the logical name of

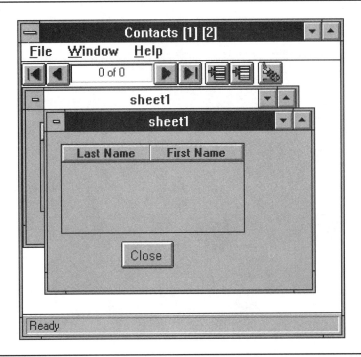

Figure 4.4   Custom frame with a resized client area.

each sheet in an array or using a reference variable. The addition of the **GetFirstSheet( )** and **GetNextSheet( )** functions to PowerBuilder 4 has greatly simplified the management of MDI sheets. These two functions provide a method of programmatically going through the list of open sheets in an MDI application, thus eliminating the need of arrays to maintain MDI sheets. Basically, PowerBuilder is now maintaining the array for the user. This section briefly discusses the use of arrays and reference variables to handle sheet maintenance and goes on to show examples using **GetFirstSheet( )** and **GetNextSheet( )**.

Arrays Prior to PowerBuilder 4, one of the most common ways to track MDI sheets was by using an array. Arrays can be used for creating and maintaining both multiple instances of a window sheet or multiple instances of separate kinds of window sheets. However, the use of arrays requires a nontrivial amount of code in the application. The use of a dynamic unbound array can work if implemented properly.

The benefits of using an array to keep track of sheets are:

- Because the developer is assigning each sheet a different variable name, accessing one sheet from another sheet is simplified.
- Because the developer is creating the array as an instance or global variable, debugging is a bit easier.

The drawbacks of using arrays for this purpose are:

- This technique is useful in situations in which the sheets need to be passing information from sheet to sheet, but the developer must maintain the empty slots in the array to avoid sheet management problems.
- There is a negative impact on Windows resources when sheets are allocated up front and not reused.

When using arrays to track open sheets, the developer can use either dynamic or static arrays. Dynamic arrays allocate memory for sheet instances as they are opened throughout an MDI application. While this provides some flexibility, it results in a performance hit whenever a new sheet is opened (see Chapter 23). Because PowerBuilder allocates memory for static arrays upon creation, there is no need to request more blocks of memory from Windows when another array element is added. In addition, the boundaries of the array are specified so there is no processing overhead while checking the validity of the array subscript.

Reusable Reference Variable The use of a reusable variable provides an easier solution than arrays for simple sheet management. The reusable variable allows the developer to declare a variable local to the instance of the sheet being opened. This allows the same variable to be used for all sheets and eliminates the need to use an array to maintain each sheet. Also, because each sheet is reusing the same variable, the memory used to store the window instance is returned when the sheet is closed.

When a variable is used to track open sheets, only one instance of that variable name can be opened. If the MDI application executes another **Open( )** or **OpenSheet( )** function with the same variable, only the first instance of the variable is shown—the other instances are not displayed in the active frame. If multiple instances of a window need to be opened, a different variable name must be defined for each new instance. In the following example, hard-coding the value "w_sheet1" instead of using the variable *WinInstance* would only allow one instance of the sheet to be opened.

The following code shows the use of the variable *WinInstance* to maintain an instance of window w_sheet1:

```
w_sheet1 WinInstance
OpenSheet(WinInstance,"w_sheet1",w_mdi_frame,2,Cascaded!)
```

The benefits of doing this are that using a local variable allows you to open as many instances as required of w_sheet1 and this method does not require tracking of the array variables, thus simplifying maintenance. The drawback of this method is the user's inability to access one sheet from another sheet. Reusable variables should be used when an application requires simple sheet management.

GetFirstSheet( ) and GetNextSheet( ) As mentioned previously, **GetFirstSheet( )** and **GetNextSheet( )** remove the need to add extra code for maintaining MDI sheets. The next example uses these two functions to get the title of all open sheets in Figure 4.5 and write them to the WIN.INI file:

```
// Save the title of all open sheets to WIN.INI

window currentsheet
string sText
int iSheetNum

currentsheet = this.GetFirstSheet( )

DO WHILE IsValid(currentsheet)
// There is an active sheet, so get its title.
        sText = currentsheet.title
        iSheetNum = iSheetNum + 1
        SetProfileString("win.ini","MyApp","Sheet"+&
              string(iSheetNum),sText)
        currentsheet = this.GetNextSheet(currentsheet)
LOOP

return true
```

The next example, from the PowerBuilder 4 sample application, uses **GetFirstSheet( )** and **GetNextSheet( )** to determine if a particular sheet is already open. This menu function accepts a string parameter open_title and goes through the list of open sheets to check for a matching title:

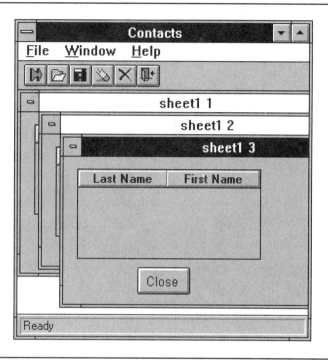

Figure 4.5   Titles of all open sheets.

```
window win
// get the first sheet
win = parentwindow.GetFirstSheet( )

do while isvalid(win) // if we got a valid sheet
        if win.title = open_title then return true // if the titles
// match then
return true
        win = parentwindow.GetNextSheet(win) // get the next sheet
loop
return false
```

CREATING AND MANIPULATING AN MDI

OpenSheet with Parameters Because PowerBuilder is built on top of the
Windows operating system, it is able to use many of Windows' underlying
structures. One of these is the Microsoft Messaging structure. If an event

occurs that is not a PowerBuilder-defined event, PowerBuilder uses the MS Message object.

MDI applications can take advantage of the Message object by calling the **OpenSheetWithParm( )** function. This function uses the Message object to store parameters when opening sheets. This allows the sheet being opened to retrieve the parameters from the Message object and perform processing based on their value. This is handy in situations such as passing database key values among MDI sheets.

OpenSheetWithParms( ) is used as follows:

```
OpenSheetWithParm (sheet_refvar, parameter{, window_name},
mdiframe &{, position {, arrangeopen} } )
```

The Message object allows the developer to pass different types of variables into a sheet for processing. A window function can store a set of variables in the Message object, allowing a sheet to be opened with the value, or the sheet can store a value in the Message object to be used by another sheet. These are a few of the Message attributes that can be used to retrieve arguments passed when opening an MDI sheet.

```
message.DoubleParm       Numeric
message.PowerObjectParm  PowerObject
message.StringParm       String
```

The Message object is discussed further in Chapters 8 and 14.

Minimize Sheets in MDI_1 When executing an MDI application, many different sheets can appear within the client area MDI_1. Many users will want to minimize the different sheets that are being used within the application area. This example shows how to minimize a sheet by double-clicking on the sheet's control menu.

First, create a global Boolean variable *g_bCloseFrame*. This variable will be used to determine whether to close the sheet or minimize it. Next, in the open event of the MDI frame, set *g_bCloseFrame* to False, meaning that the sheet will be minimized:

```
// Minimize sheet windows when double-clicking the Control Menu

g_bCloseFrame = False
```

In the closequery event of the MDI frame, the variable is reset to True.

```
// Close sheet windows

g_bCloseFrame= True
```

In the closequery event of the MDI sheet w_sheet1 or w_base_sheet, the following code is inserted:

```
// Check g_bCloseFrame to determine whether to close or minimize sheets

If not g_bCloseFrame then
    this.windowstate = minimized!
    message.returnvalue = 1
Else
    message.returnvalue = 0
end if
```

This enables the user to minimize MDI sheets via the Control menu.

Finding Active Sheets When maintaining different sheets within the MDI frame, a developer may want to determine which sheet is active. The PowerBuilder function **GetActiveSheet( )** can be used to return the active sheet in an MDI application. In the following example, the MDI frame window function **Save1( )** uses **GetActiveSheet( )** to get the title of the active window and write it to the WIN.INI file:

```
// Save the title of the active sheet to WIN.INI

window activesheet
string sText

activesheet = w_mdi_frame.GetActiveSheet( )
If IsValid(activesheet) then
// There is an active sheet, so get its title.
    sText = activesheet.title
end if

SetProfileString("win.ini","MyApp","ActiveSheet",sText)
return true
```

Preventing an MDI Sheet from Maximizing Developers may want to prevent a user from maximizing a sheet within an MDI application. This can be done by removing the maximize attribute from the sheet. To do this, add the following code to the open event of the sheet:

```
long var

var = SetWindowLong(Handle(this), -16, 1456340992)
```

This will keep the user from maximizing the window by dimming the Maximize menu item on the system menu.

Menus and Toolbars

Another aspect of creating an MDI application is the use of menus and toolbars. Although these items provide a simple method of navigating through a system, navigating can be cumbersome if they are not designed correctly.

Because MDI applications open multiple instances of a window, the menus associated with each sheet can sometimes point to the wrong menu instance. When multiple instances of a window are created, PowerBuilder automatically creates a global variable for the menu and an instance of the menu for each window instance. Because the global variable points to the last menu instance that was created, the pointer can sometimes point to the wrong menu. If the code for the menu uses hard-coded references, the menu choices end up referencing the last menu instance that was created, instead of the proper menu instance. This problem is similar to a sheet that does not have a menu and inherits the last opened menu.

If, for example, the last window in an MDI that is opened is sheet1[instance 4] and a user chooses a menu item on the menu for the associated window sheet1[instance 1], the wrong MenuItem appears. This is because the menu on window instance 1 is actually pointing to the menu on window instance 4. There are two ways to avoid this problem. The first method is to use correct pronoun references (see Chapter 19) and the other is to create an instance variable.

For example, in a menu of color choices, the pronoun "this" and the noun "parent" can be used instead of hard-coding the menu reference to check the selected color and uncheck the other color MenuItems. The script for the clicked event of the MenuItem m_red is:

```
This.Check( )
parent.m_blue.Uncheck( )
parent.m_green.Uncheck( )
```

Placing the pronoun/noun reference in the script ensures that the code references the current instance of the menu.

The second method is to create an instance variable, set the MenuID to the current menu, and point it to the appropriate window instance. This involves the following steps:

- Create an instance variable called *i_active_mnu* of type m_stdmnu (your menu name).
- In the open event of the window w_sheet1, set *i_active_mnu* = *this.menuid*. This now becomes a pointer to the menu instance associated with this instance of the window.
- Create a global variable called *g_active_sheet* of type w_sheet1.
- Set *g_active_sheet* = *this* in the activate event of w_sheet1. This now properly identifies the current instance of the window w_sheet1.

So now the code in the menu would be:

```
g_active_sheet.i_active_mnu.m_color.m_red.enable( )
g_active_sheet.i_active_mnu.m_color.m_blue.disable( )
g_active_sheet.i_active_mnu.m_color.m_green.disable( )
```

Obviously, the use of pronoun references is simpler to develop and maintain.

Menus The frame window in the MDI application is the controlling window. This allows the menus that are associated with the sheet windows to pass through it. Because the frame window is the central window in the application, it should always have a menu/toolbar associated with it.

Another item to consider when developing menus is the association of menus with sheets. If a currently active sheet window does not have a menu associated with it, it inherits the last opened menu and toolbar that were opened. This can become confusing to the user of the application if the application is not intended to operate in this manner. If any sheet window requires a menu, all of the sheets should have menus associated with them.

If the particular sheet has a corresponding menu, the sheet's menu becomes the frame's menu. Obviously, if the sheet does not have a menu, the menu remains as the frame's menu. If the designed MDI only has one menu in the main frame area, all of the sheets or subapplication's menus pass through the frame's menu.

Note: The developer can design an MDI that has one or more sheets with corresponding menus and one sheet without a menu. The sheet without a menu will take the last inherited menu. This inherited menu could be the frame's menu or one of the other sheet's menu, depending on the last activated object.

A function that can be integrated into an MDI application is the showing of the last n files that have been saved or opened. This functionality is not automatically handled by PowerBuilder, but can be added programmatically. This functionality is seen in many third-party products such as Microsoft Word and Microsoft Excel. Unfortunately, PowerBuilder does not allow the developer to dynamically add and subtract menu items like lower-level languages do, but this can be overcome by using functions that read and write information to an initialization file, such as WIN.INI.

The example in Figure 4.6 will open two sheets in the MDI frame: sheet1-Person and sheet2-Phone. When each of the sheets is saved, they will be written to the WIN.INI file and inserted into the MDI frame menu under the first set of menu items. In order to do this, the developer should first create the menus m_stdmnu for the MDI frame and m_stdmdi. The

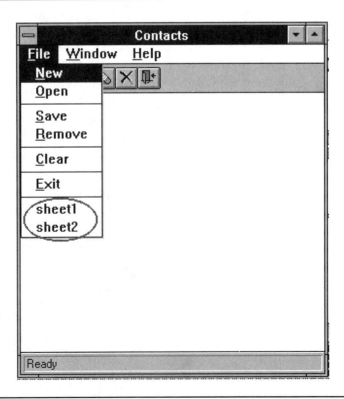

Figure 4.6   Saving previously opened sheets in the MDI frame.

menu m_stdmnu should have a MenuItem File with sub-MenuItems Open, Save, Exit, and two additional items placed at the end of the MenuItem list called File1 and File2. The menu m_stdmdi should have the same options as m_stdmnu under File but should also include the MDI functionality of Tile, Cascade, and Layer. The File1 and File2 items should be created as Invisible because they will be changed and made visible to show the two saved file names later.

The MDI frame window is w_mdi_frame, and it is created as an MDI frame with Microhelp. In addition, the menu m_stdmnu is associated with it. Each of the sheets, w_sheet1 and w_sheet2, are main windows that have m_stdmdi associated with them. The windows w_sheet1 and w_sheet2 retrieve information from the database about the Person and Phone information.

In addition, the Exit MenuItem should contain Close(parentwindow), to allow closure of each MDI sheet. In order to make this example work, two sheets can be opened by inserting the following into the Open MenuItem of m_stdmnu. For the purposes of this example, the values "w_sheet1" and "w_sheet2" are hard-coded into the sWinName[] array below:

```
//Open for 2 sheets
string sWinName[] = {"w_sheet1", "w_sheet2"}
Window WinArray[]

integer i

For i = 1 to 2

        OpenSheet (WinArray [i], sWinName[i],w_mdi_frame,2)
    Next
```

Because the sheets are now opened, the MDI frame window is controlled by the currently active sheet's menu m_stdmdi. Within m_stdmdi, the developer should create the following four menu functions of the Boolean type. The first function called lastsheet( ), and reads the value ItemCount from the WIN.INI file to see how many files have been saved for showing in the menu. Based on the number of items that have been saved, it will call the functions save1( )–save3( ).

```
//Function LastSheet( )
//Code for inserting last 2 files saved
string s_lastfile,s_lastfile2
int i_counter
i_counter=ProfileInt("win.ini", "LastSheet", "ItemCount", 0)
```

```
If i_counter = 0 then
      save1( )

elseif i_counter = 1 then
      save2( )

elseif i_counter = 2 then
     save3( )
else
    // can add more functions for more sheets
end if
return true
```

The second function, save1( ), gets the active sheet's title name and saves it to the WIN.INI file for the value of LastSheet1. This will be used later to add to the MDI frame menu m_stdmnu.

```
//Function Save1( )
// Declare active sheet (a window data type).
window         activesheet
string sheet_name, text
activesheet = w_mdi_frame.GetActiveSheet( )
If IsValid(activesheet) then
// There is an active sheet, so get its title.
    Text = activesheet.title
else
end if
SetProfileString("win.INI","LastSheet","ItemCount","1")
SetProfileString("win.INI","LastSheet","LastSheet1",Text)
return true
```

The third function, save2( ), gets the next active sheet's title name and saves it to the WIN.INI file for the value of LastSheet2.

The last menu function, **save3( )**, gets the last active sheet's title name, swaps the value of LastSheet1 with the value of LastSheet2, and inserts the new value into LastSheet1.

```
//Code for saving last sheet to INI file
string sLastFile1
window activesheet
string sText
activesheet = w_mdi_frame.GetActiveSheet( )
If IsValid(activesheet) then
// There is an active sheet, so get its title.
        sText = activesheet.title
```

```
else
end if

sLastFile1 = ProfileString("win.ini", "LastSheet", "LastSheet1", "")

SetProfileString("win.INI","LastSheet","LastSheet2",sLastFile1)
SetProfileString("win.INI","LastSheet","LastSheet1",sText)
return true
```

When all of the functions have been created, the Save option will call the **LastSheet( )** function.

Now that the menu functions have been created, the developer can create a function called **LastFile( )** of type Boolean in the window w_mdi_frame. This function references the MDI frame menu m_stdmnu and pulls the saved LastSheet values from the WIN.INI. Depending on the sheets, it will also **Show( )** the additional menu item and change the text to that of the sheet value.

```
//Function LastFile( )
//Code for inserting last 2 files saved
int iCounter
iCounter=ProfileInt("win.ini", "LastSheet", "ItemCount", 0)
string sLastFile,sLastFile2
If iCounter = 1 then
    sLastFile = ProfileString("win.ini", "LastSheet", "LastSheet1", "")
    m_stdmnu.m_file.m_file1.show( )
    m_stdmnu.m_file.m_file1.text=sLastFile
elseif iCounter = 2 then
    sLastFile = ProfileString("win.ini", "LastSheet", "LastSheet1", "")
    sLastFile2 =ProfileString("win.ini", "LastSheet", "LastSheet2", "")
    m_stdmnu.m_file.m_file1.show( )
    m_stdmnu.m_file.m_file2.show( )
    m_stdmnu.m_file.m_file1.text=sLastFile
    m_stdmnu.m_file.m_file2.text=sLastFile2
else
    //want default menu to not show file1 & file2
    m_stdmnu.m_file.m_file1.hide( )
    m_stdmnu.m_file.m_file2.hide( )
end if

return true
```

When the function **LastFile** has been coded, the developer should create a user-defined event called refreshmenu with the event id of pbm_custom01 (or the next available event id). When the event is created, the developer should place the function call to **LastFile( )**. This custom user event allows the developer to trigger the functionality of **LastFile( )** after all of the sheets have been closed. In addition, the developer should call **LastFile** from the open event of the window w_mdi_frame, to allow any previously saved files to be found when the window is opened. To refresh the list of files when the File menu item is clicked, add the following code to the clicked event of m_stdmnu.m_file:

```
//Code in Clicked event in m_stdmnu File
//Code for saving last sheet to INI file
w_mdi_frame i_parent
i_parent = parentwindow

i_parent.triggerevent("refreshmenu")
```

When all of the other functions are coded, the application can be run to open each sheet and then save it. When all of the sheets are closed and the frame menu is viewed, the last two files that were saved are listed in the menu. When a sheet is still active, the menu that is displayed is the sheet menu, so the saved files are not visible. If this functionality is required in the sheet menu, the same code can be used to create it.

In addition, a Clear MenuItem might be added to allow the user to clear the last two sheets. The code for the Clear MenuItem would be:

```
//Code for saving last sheet to INI file
w_mdi_frame i_parent
i_parent = parentwindow

SetProfileString("win.INI","LastSheet","ItemCount","0")
SetProfileString("win.INI","LastSheet","LastSheet1","")
SetProfileString("win.INI","LastSheet","LastSheet2","")
i_parent.postevent("refreshmenu")
```

When the Clear function is executed, the WIN.INI file looks like this:

```
[Lastsheet]
ItemCount=0
LastSheet1=
LastSheet2=
```

Toolbars Menu toolbars only work on the MDI frame and MDI sheet windows. If a non-MDI window opens a menu with a toolbar item associated with it, the toolbar does not appear. Again, needing an application with toolbars is not a reason to create an MDI application. A toolbar can be created as a user object and placed in the inheritance structure.

PowerBuilder allows the application designer to create a toolbar in the Menu painter and attach it to an MDI frame or sheet like a menu. The toolbar can allow the application to run other applications outside of PowerBuilder, create or print reports, and perform other user-defined functions.

The most common function of the toolbar is to allow the toolbar buttons to visually mimic the functionality of the current menu. Because the toolbar buttons are related directly to the menu items, if the menu item is disabled, the toolbar button is also disabled. The visible attribute of the toolbar will not change appearance, however. In addition, hiding a menu item does not cause the submenu item to disappear; it only disables the functionality of the toolbar button.

A more in-depth discussion of the menus and toolbars can be found in Chapter 5.

Creating a Clock on the Frame

A convenient feature for an MDI application is displaying the system time in the lower right MicroHelp area on the MDI frame. Unfortunately, PowerBuilder does not include this feature in the creation of the MDI frame. However, by creating a popup window that resizes itself in the MDI frame, the functionality can be added. The result looks like that shown in Figure 4.7.

The first step in doing this is to add the following code to the open event. This code takes the current size of the MDI frame and workspace (x, y, height, and width). Then it opens the popup window, w_clock, and moves the clock to the bottom right-hand corner. If the clock is desired elsewhere on the MDI frame, the move function coordinates can be changed accordingly.

```
// Open and show the clock on the MDI frame. The clock will be
// positioned in the resize event

open(w_clock)
show(w_clock)
```

The second step is to place the following code in the resize event of the MDI frame window, w_mdi_frame, to adjust the sizing and positioning of the popup window according to the frame and workspace.

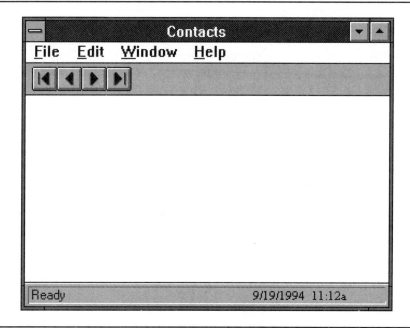

Figure 4.7   A popup window created in the MDI frame.

```
// Position the clock in the lower right corner of the MDI frame
integer wx, wy, wh, ww

wx=this.workspacex( )
wy=this.workspacey( )
wh=this.workspaceheight( )
ww=this.workspacewidth( )

if (handle (w_clock) > 0 ) then
 move(w_clock,wx+ww - w_clock.width, wy+wh -w_clock.height - 20)
end if

Setfocus(this)
```

The next step is to create a custom user event for the MDI frame w_mdi_frame window called Move and map it to the PowerBuilder event id pbm_move. The move event will trigger the resize event to repaint the clock when the MDI frame is moved within the Windows desktop.

Finally, a window w_clock is created with a single line edit (SLE) named sle_time. After the SLE has been created, the developer will want to adjust the size of the SLE and the window, to fit just the date and time and to look good in the corner of the application.

In order to get the clock to adjust the time within the frame, the developer places the code in the open event of the popup window. To update the clock, set the timer for 10 seconds. After 10 seconds, the timer event triggers to update the frame with the changed time:

```
sle_time.weight=300
timer(10)
triggerevent(this,"timer")
```

Within the timer event of w_clock, the developer calls a function called **settime( )** that gathers the system time and formats it correctly. The function **settime( )** is a type of Boolean and contains the following code:

```
// Get the date and time for clock
Time tCurrentTime
date dCurrentDate
string sRealTime, sClock, sAmPm

tCurrentTime=now( )

dCurrentDate=today( )

sle_time.hide( )
sle_time.text=space(len(sle_time.text))
// format 24-hour clock
if int(hour(tCurrentTime)) > 12 then
        sRealTime = string(int(hour(tCurrentTime)) - 12)
        sAmPm = "p"
else
        sRealTime = string(hour(tCurrentTime))
        sAmPm = "a"
end if
sClock = sRealTime + ":" + string(minute(tCurrentTime)) + sAmPm
sle_time.text= string(month(dCurrentDate))+ "/" + &
        string(day(dCurrentDate)) + "/" + &
        string(year(dCurrentDate)) + " " +sClock
sle_time.show( )
```

MICROHELP

The use of MicroHelp can enhance an MDI application by offering additional help text for key items within a menu frame. PowerBuilder creates this facility for the developer at the bottom left corner of the MDI frame.

This area can display a meaningful description about menu or toolbar items that might be cryptic or hard to define in one word. PowerBuilder allows the developer to include MicroHelp in the Menu painter. In order to include MicroHelp, the developer should enter the Menu painter and then enter the appropriate text in the MDI MicroHelp section.

MicroHelp with Objects

MicroHelp can also be used with controls or objects by using the Tag attribute in conjunction with the **SetMicroHelp** function. The Tag attribute allows the developer to tag values to columns, fields, graphic objects, and user objects. The use of MicroHelp can also be valuable for providing an explanation of error messages or invalid entries to the user. There are two ways of utilizing MicroHelp with objects:

- A getfocus event
- A mouse move with a custom event

Getfocus Event For example, to display MicroHelp for a CommandButton **cb_close** in the MDI sheet window w_sheet1, the developer would:

- Assign the desired string as the tag value for **cb_close**.
- In the script for the getfocus event in **cb_close**, include this statement:

```
SetMicroHelp(w_sheet1,this.tag)
```

Mouse Move To have MicroHelp text change when a user moves the mouse pointer over window controls, the developer puts PowerScript in the window controls to change the MicroHelp text. The developer would:

- Assign the desired string as the tag value for **cb_close**.
- Create a custom user event for the button **cb_close** called mousemove and map it to pbm_mousemove.
- In the script for the mousemove event in **cb_close**, include this statement:

```
SetMicroHelp(parent,this.tag)
```

- Then, to set the MicroHelp back to a value when the mouse leaves the button, the developer would place a similar script in the mousemove event for the window sheet1.

```
SetMicroHelp("Ready")
```

In conclusion, the creation of an MDI application can meet many project requirements, but it will create more problems than it solves if it is not designed properly. An MDI application should be created for an application that requires multiple instances of non-modal windows. These windows can be simple windows or subapplications that will be manipulated by the user simultaneously. The developer can use the PowerBuilder functions **GetActiveSheet( )**, **GetFirstSheet( )**, and **GetNextSheet( )** to maintain sheets within the application. Because of the complexity of MDI applications, if an application only needs toolbars and MicroHelp, another interface should be considered. If needed and done properly, however, an MDI application can provide a friendly and flexible interface to the user.

CHAPTER 5

Menus

Menus are the standard method for interfacing between the user and the application. Menus allow the user to navigate through the application and perform specific tasks with a minimum amount of previous experience. PowerBuilder allows the developer to create menus for an application using the Menu painter. The developer can also use inheritance, scripts, and functions to enhance the functionality of MenuItems.

This chapter discusses the following topics:

- Types of menus
- Inheritance
- Menu events, scripts, and funtions
- Menus in MDI applications
- Toolbars
- Intergrating with INI file
- Accelerator and ShortCut keys
- MenuItem attributes
- Design considerations

TYPES OF MENUS

Menus within PowerBuilder can be divided into two groups: menu bars and popups.

Menu Bar

The menu bar, the most common kind of menu, is a horizontal row of MenuItems that appears below the title bar. Each menu item displays either a cascading or a dropdown menu that offers the user further choices related to the MenuItem chosen. A dropdown menu displays the associated MenuItems below the MenuItem within the menu bar. A cascading menu is a submenu that is displayed to either side of a MenuItem below an item on the menu bar. The cascading menu is usually denoted by an arrowhead next to the associated choice in the menu bar. The cascading menu is used for multiple options (i.e., color choices). Any window created within an application should have a menu bar associated with it.

The only exception is a child or Response window. Because a child window is always opened from within the parent window and is never considered active, it cannot have a menu. Therefore, the parent window always has the menu for the child window. Response windows are also unable to have menus because they are always opened from the parent and are application modal.

Popup Menus

The other kind of menu is a popup. This type of menu can be invoked from a MenuItem in a menu bar or it can be invoked when a user chooses something within the work area and clicks with either the right or left mouse button. Because they are usually placed on the most frequently used areas or menu items, popup menus are sometimes referred as contextual menus.

The system menu or Control menu is an example of a popup menu. The Control menu is associated with the minus sign at the left end of the menu bar. This menu contains many of the standard system commands that are defaulted by PowerBuilder for the application. Most PowerBuilder applications do not require the developer to add any menu choices into the Control menu because the application-specific MenuItems should be created and placed in the application menus, not in the Control menu.

To allow the user to use the system commands throughout the application, it is a good idea to associate a Control menu with all of the PowerBuilder window types except the Response window because it is application modal. The Response window should allow the user to move the window but not to exit the window. An example of a window without a Control menu would be a Messagebox. A Messagebox does not allow the user to continue until a response is given. The default commands in a Control menu include the following: **Move**, **Size**, **Maximize**, **Minimize**, **Close**, and **Switch to**.

Unfortunately, PowerBuilder does not allow the developer to directly alter the Control menu from the Menu painter. Unlike PowerBuilder, however, the MS Windows SDK allows the application developer to use the **GetSystemMenu( )** function to copy the default window's system menu (Control menu) and add menu choices. The **AppendMenu( )**, **InsertMenu( )**, and **ModifyMenu( )** functions can be used to add the menu choices to the copy of the control menu. This copy of the control window can then be associated with a particular window. Because the commands in the Default control menu use identifier numbers greater than 0xF00, the developer should use identifier numbers less than 0xF000. Because the majority of applications do not require any changes or additions to the system menu, this is typically not a problem.

Even though PowerBuilder does not explicitly allow the developer to alter the Control menu, there are ways to trap Windows messages. This can be accomplished by creating a user-defined event ControlMenu. This event, which fires when the Control menu is clicked, allows the developer to trap the messages sent from the underlying Windows functions. A further discussion of trapping Windows messages is in Chapter 14.

To display a popup menu that is already associated with the window, the developer can simply call the menu item directly with the **PopMenu( )** function. To use the **PopMenu( )** function, the developer can either use the current cursor position or hard-code the X and Y coordinates. The example in Figure 5.1 illustrates the popup menu by placing the following code in the rbuttondown event to trigger the popup for the single line edit (SLE). The menu, m_stdmnu is inherited from m_basemnu.

This statement displays the popup menu m_file at the cursor position when the single line edit (SLE) is clicked with the right mouse button: (see Figure 5.1)

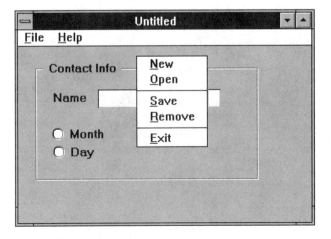

Figure 5.1   The popup menu.

```
m_stdmnu.m_file.PopMenu( PointerX( ), PointerY( ) )
```

Another way to show the popup menu is to hard-code the X and Y coordinates in the **PopMenu** function. These statements display the MenuItem m_file at location 100, 200:

```
m_stdmnu.m_file.PopMenu( 100,200 )
```

Note: If the Visible attribute of the MenuItem is False, you must make the MenuItem visible before you can display it as a popup menu.

INHERITANCE

The easiest method for implementing and maintaining menus within an application is using inheritance. Although inherited menus have some drawbacks, using them simplifies application maintenance.

In addition, creating menus that inherit base functionality allows the developer to extend the menu's functionality for specific needs at the window level. Note that within PowerBuilder scripts, ancestor menus are referenced the same as they are in the other painters:

```
ancestormenu::Menuitem
```

PowerBuilder's support of inheritance for menu objects is similar to that of other PowerBuilder objects, allowing the developer to do the following:

* Add new MenuItems to an inherited menu
* Modify existing MenuItems
* Build scripts
* Extend and Override ancestor scripts
* Declare functions, structures, and variables

PowerBuilder 4 has added the ShiftToRight attribute to MenuItems. ShiftToRight allows MenuItems to be inserted between inherited MenuItems. For example, assume the menu m_stdmnu is defined with the MenuItems File, Window, and Help and that the Window and File items have their ShiftToRight attributes set to True (see Figure 5.2).

Next, assume the menu m_editmnu is inherited from m_stdmnu and contains the Edit MenuItem. Prior to version 4.0, it would not have been possible to insert the Edit item between the File and Window items. But, because the Window and Help items have their ShiftToRight attributes set to True, any new MenuItems defined in m_editmnu will

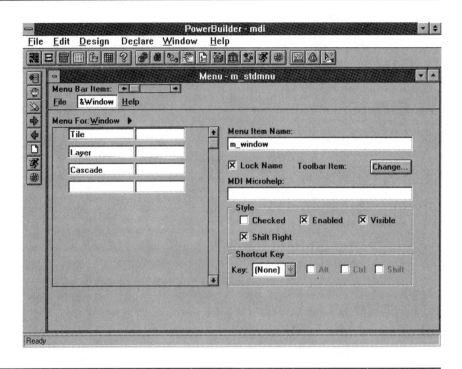

Figure 5.2   The ShiftToRight attribute in MenuItem.

be placed before the Window and Help items. The definition of
m_editmnu is shown in Figure 5.3.

Notice that even though the Edit item is shown last in Figure 5.3, it
will display before any items that are shifted to the right when executed, as shown in Figure 5.4.

ShiftToRight also applies to MenuItems within a menu bar item. For
example, assume the File MenuItem in m_stdmenu is defined with the
Remove, Close, and Exit menu items defined with their ShiftToRight set
to True, as shown in Figure 5.5.

ShiftToRight allows the creation of a Save As item to appear below
the Save option in m_editmnu. The Save As option is defined in
m_editmnu as shown in Figure 5.6.

When executed, the Save As option will appear after the Save option in the File Menu, as shown in Figure 5.7.

Although the ShiftToRight attribute is a great addition to Power-
Builder 4, there are still some limitations when inheriting menus in
PowerBuilder. First, ShiftToRight does not allow MenuItems to be in-

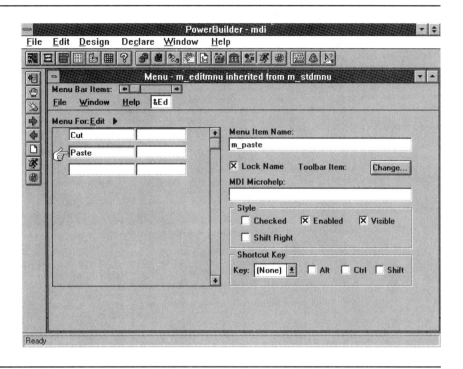

Figure 5.3   The definition of m_editmnu.

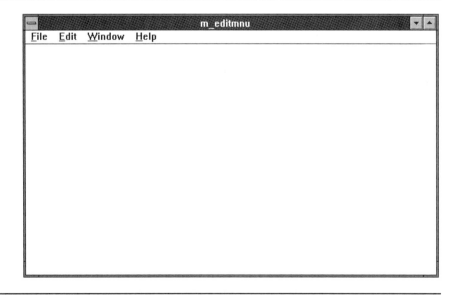

Figure 5.4   Edit item is shown first.

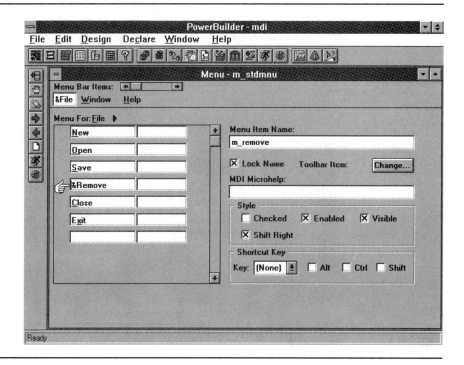

Figure 5.5   ShiftToRight as applied to MenuItems within a menu bar item.

serted between all MenuItems of an inherited menu. All new descendant MenuItems will be placed before all ancestor MenuItems with ShiftToRight set to True. In the previous example, it is not possible to create new MenuItems in m_editmnu between the Window and Help items. In addition to the limitations of ShiftToRight, the developer is unable to:

• Move or change the order of inherited MenuItems
• Delete an inherited MenuItem
• Insert MenuItems between two inherited items (other than before all shifted MenuItems)
• Dynamically add or subtract menu items

The Windows SDK does allow the developer to manipulate inherited menus using the **AppendMenu( )**, **InsertMenu( )**, and **ModifyMenu( )** functions. Because of PowerBuilder's limited functionality in this area, complex menu inheritance structures developed in PowerBuilder are not

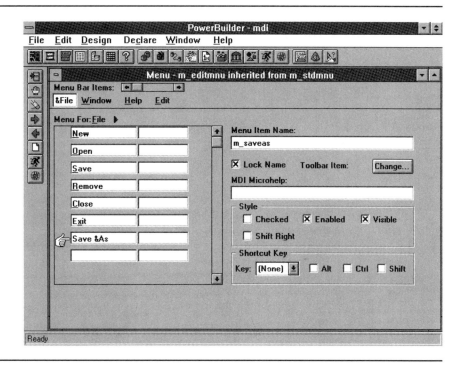

Figure 5.6   The Save As item defined.

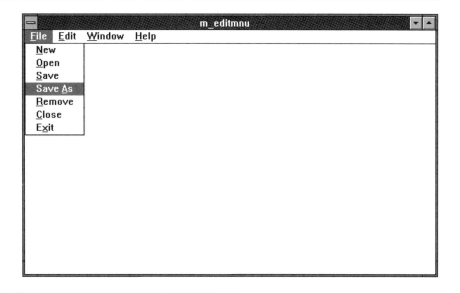

Figure 5.7   Save As option appears after the Save option.

particularly useful. Fortunately, most menus are simple in nature and complex menu inheritance structures are not needed. By creating a complete inheritance tree in advance, many of the MenuItems will not need to be manipulated programmatically.

When creating the inheritance structure for an application, it is good to decide if any Virtual Class menus (menus that will not be used but are only created to be inherited from) are needed . These menus can have the basic menu choices that need to be used by all different types of Windows. They should have MenuItems such as <u>N</u>ew, <u>O</u>pen, <u>S</u>ave, and <u>R</u>emove. After deciding on the Virtual Class menus, the developer can organize the inheritance tree such that each of the other menus inherit the base functionality from the ancestor.

An example of menu inheritance is shown in Figure 5.8. This tree illustrates the use of different layers of inherited menus. The first layer is the menu m_basemnu. Because PowerBuilder does not allow a menu to be saved without a MenuItem, it is saved with only the item Dummy (defined as invisible) in the MenuItem section. The menu m_basemnu contains all of the code for the menu functions **enableopen( )**, **enablenew( )**, **disableopen( )**, and **disablenew( )**. These four functions are used to enable and disable MenuItems based on the applica-

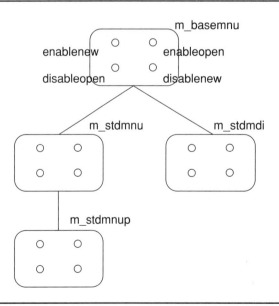

Figure 5.8   Menu Inheritance Example.

tion UserId. These four functions are discussed in the section covering menu functions. Having such functions in the base menu level allows the descendents to use these functions or override and extend them if necessary.

The next layer of inheritance, m_stdmnu, has most of the MenuItems needed for generic windows in an application. These MenuItems include <u>N</u>ew, <u>O</u>pen, <u>S</u>ave, <u>R</u>emove, and E<u>x</u>it. Another menu that inherits from the base menu, m_stdmdi, contains capabilities for the MDI screens within the application. This menu includes the code to open multiple MDI sheets and to manipulate the sheets using the **ArrangeSheet( )** function. A more detailed discussion of MDI applications is in Chapter 4.

The last layer of inheritance is the menu m_stdmnup. This menu, which is a descendant of the menu m_stdmnu, adds the capability to print within a window. A detailed discussion of printing within an application is contained in Chapter 10. Inheriting some menus from other menus allows the code that resides in the ancestor menu to be easily overridden and extended within the function script (as with other PowerBuilder objects).

MENU EVENTS, SCRIPTS, AND FUNCTIONS

The PowerBuilder Menu painter allows the developer to create PowerScript for both menu events and functions. Like other PowerBuilder objects, ancestor menu scripts can be extended or overridden. This section discusses the use of menu events and functions.

Menu Events

Like other PowerBuilder objects, menus have events associated with them. The two events associated with MenuItems are the clicked and selected events.

A clicked event is triggered for a MenuItem when the mouse button is released and both the enabled and visible attributes are True. An example of script that could be included in a clicked event is a checked or unchecked bitmap. Such a bitmap could be used when the MenuItem has a value of True or False. This would allow a user to see what state the MenuItem is in.

An example of using the clicked event is in the menu choice for an MDI section that indicates which sheet arrangement style has been chosen (i.e., Tile, Cascade, or Layered). The developer can either use the checked function or set the checked attribute to True or False (see Figure 5.9).

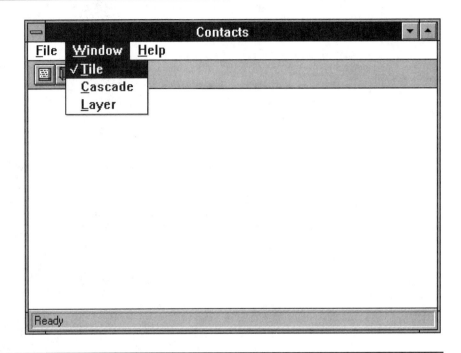

Figure 5.9   An example of checking menu items.

The code in the clicked event of the MenuItem Tile just described is:

```
mdi_frame.arrangesheets(Tile!)
this.check( )
parent.m_layer.uncheck( )
parent.m_cascade.uncheck( )
```

The other event associated with a MenuItem is the selected event. The selected event is triggered when the user highlights the MenuItem. This event is not used very often because most users do not associate the highlighting of a MenuItem with any action. However, the selected event can be used to show MicroHelp in an MDI application. An example of this is to use the **SetMicroHelp( )** function in the selected event of the Open MenuItem of menu m_stdmdi. The associated window is mdi_frame:

```
mdi_frame.SetMicroHelp("Open sheet")
```

Functions

Another way to maximize the use of menus is with functions. An example using menu functions is to restrict a user's options within an application by enabling and disabling menu options within a window. The first step in this example is to create four simple menu functions that are for public access and have a Boolean return type. These functions are **enableopen( )**, **enablenew( )**, **disableopen( )**, and **disablenew( )**. They are object functions for the menu m_stdmdi and contain the code to enable and disable the MenuItems in m_stdmdi based on the global GroupId that is set during the user's connection with the database.

The code within each of the functions is:

```
/*     Function - enableOpen     enable the "open" option. */
enable(m_file.m_open)
return true


/* Function - enableNew    enable the "New" option. */
enable(m_file.m_new)
return true


/*     Function - disableOpen    disable the "Open" option. */
disable(m_file.m_open)
return true


/*     Function - disableNew     disable the "New" option. */
disable(m_file.m_new)
return true
```

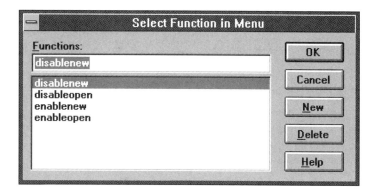

Figure 5.10   Object functions for the menu m_stdmdi.

Once the enable and disable menu functions have been created, the developer can call the window function **Security( )** in the open event of the window mdi_frame. **Security( )** checks the GroupId and either enables or disables the menu choices of the frame's menu based on its value:

```
/* Function - Security Enable or disable menu options according to
rights */

boolean bFailedOpen, bFailedNew

if G_GROUPID = "accounting" then
 bFailedOpen = m_stdmdi.disableOpen( )
 bFailedNew = m_stdmdi.disableNew( )
else
  m_stdmdi.enableopen( )
  m_stdmdi.enablenew( )
end if
if (not bFailedOpen) and (not bFailedNew) then
        /* to trap error*/
        MessageBox("Error","Security error",Exclamation!,OKCancel!,2)
        return false
end if
return true
```

Note: When referencing MenuItems within a script, make sure to fully qualify the reference (i.e., m_stdmdi.m_file.m_open.visible).

When referring to a window and its controls and attributes within a menu script, use the following notation:

Windowname

Windowname.attribute

Windowname.control.attribute

Rather than actually using the window name, use ParentWindow to refer to the window that the menu is associated with. For example, the following line of PowerScript will close the active window associated with the menu:

```
Close(ParentWindow)
```

Because a menu can be associated with many windows in an application, using ParentWindow provides a generic reference to the active window and greatly reduces the amount of code required to accommodate multiple windows which share a menu.

The amount of code in an application window can be simplified by using the **TriggerEvent** to call the event script associated with a MenuItem. In addition to reducing the amount of code, using **TriggerEvent** helps make code more manageable and easier to debug.

MENUS IN MDI APPLICATIONS

Menus can be easily added into MDI applications at the frame and sheet level. When designing an MDI application, the developer can set up the menus in two ways. The first method of menu design is to have only one menu in the frame and no menus associated with the sheets. The other method of design is to have a menu associated with the frame as well as with all of the sheets. A menu should always be associated with the frame window. If the frame does not have a menu associated with it, then the user can close all of the sheets without being able to close the application. In either method, the developer should associate a menu with the MDI frame window to avoid user confusion.

If an MDI application only has a menu associated with the frame and no menu associated for any menu sheets, all of the sheets or subapplications will utilize the frame's menu. The frame menu is actually acting as a menu for both the active sheet and the frame window. If the user closes all the sheets, then the frame menu provides a good way to close the application.

Consequently, a menu can be associated with each sheet. If the particular sheet has a corresponding menu, then the sheet menu becomes the frame's menu. An MDI application can have one or more sheets with corresponding menus and one sheet without a menu. In this case, the sheet without a menu will take the last active menu. The active menu could be the frame's menu or one of the other sheet's menu, depending on the last activated object. This can sometimes create problems for users because they are not sure which menu is associated with the sheet.

In the example in Figure 5.11 the frame has a menu called m_stdmdi and sheet1 has an associated menu called m_stdmnu. Since sheet2 does not have an associated menu, it uses the last active menu. Depending on which sheet was opened first, sheet2 will have either m_stdmdi or m_stdmnu.

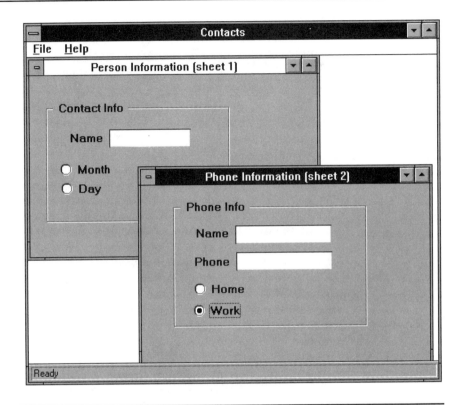

Figure 5.11   Sample MDI application with menus.

Note: When creating an MDI application, the developer should either provide one menu that will cover all sheets or associate a menu for each sheet.

Another function that PowerBuilder provides for MDI applications is the listing of open sheets within a menu. This is done in the **OpenSheet( )** function. **OpenSheet( )** takes a parameter specifying the number of the menu item (in the menu associated with the sheet) to which you want to append the names of the open sheets. If no value is provided, the list of open sheets will be displayed in the next-to-last menu item.

For example, the following script opens three MDI sheets and lists the name of the sheets under the first menu item:

```
string sWinName[] = {"sheet1", "sheet2", "sheet3"}
Window WinArray[]
integer i

For i = 1 to 3
      OpenSheet (WinArray [i], sWinName[i],mdi_frame,1)
Next
```

For simplicity, this script uses the hard-coded values of "sheet1," "sheet2," and "sheet3" to initialize the array sWinName[] and hard-codes the value 3 into the For...Next loop.

TOOLBARS

Toolbars represent a graphical, more user-friendly interface to application menus. They are generally used to provide the user a short-cut to specific functions and features that are used most often in an application, including the execution of external applications. Toolbars are created in the Menu painter by attaching bitmaps to a corresponding menu item. Because toolbar items are associated with menu items, a menu item must exist in order to have an item in the toolbar.

Table 5.1 describes some of the toolbar attributes useful to developers:

Table 5.1   Toolbar attributes

Attribute	Datatype	Uses
ToolbarItemDown	Boolean	Creates 3-D indention to show that item has been depressed
ToolBarItemName	String	Name of toolbar item bitmap or default picture name
ToolbarItemDownName	String	Name of the toolbar bitmap that is referenced when the toolbar is down
ToolbarItemOrder	Integer	The number of the item in the toolbar from 0–99
ToolbarItemSpace	Integer	An integer of the amount of space in front of toolbar item (in PB units)

Table 5.1   (*continued*)

Attribute	Datatype	Uses
ToolbarItemText	String	Value of text that is associated to the toolbar item
ToolbarItemVisible	Boolean	Sets the toolbar item to visible or invisible
ToolbarSheetTitle	String	Title of an MDI sheet toolbar when it is floating
ToolbarAlignment	Enumerated	Specifies where the toolbar is located in window
ToolbarHeight	Integer	Height of the toolbar when floating
ToolbarFrameTitle	String	Title of the toolbar that is created in an MDI floating toolbar

Toolbar attributes can be utilized within scripts to manipulate a toolbar's presentation to the user. An example using the **Toolbar ItemVisible** attribute follows. A window function **Security( )** will check the GroupId and disable the menu choice N̲ew as well as make the related toolbar item invisible.

```
/* Enable or disable menu options according to rights. */

boolean bCanOpen, bCanNew

if G_GROUPID = "accounting" then

m_stdmdi.disableNew( )
m_stdmdi.m_file.m_new.ToolbarItemVisible = False
end if
if (not bCanOpen) and (not bCanNew) then
     /* it makes no sense to be here if we can't do either of these */
          return false

end if
m_stdmdi.enablenew( )
m_stdmdi.m_file.m_new.ToolbarItemVisible = True
return true
```

Since toolbars are associated with menu items, it follows that the rules for toolbars are similar to the rules for menus. When an application's MDI frame has a toolbar and its sheets do not have a toolbar, each sheet will then utilize the frame's toolbar. In addition, when each sheet has a separate toolbar associated with it, the sheet's toolbar can be visible at the same time as the frame's toolbar. This is similar to PowerBuilder's implementation of the PowerBar. This capability allows the user of the application to click the right mouse button while positioned on a toolbar and invoke a popup window that allows the positioning of the sheet and/or frame toolbar to the top, bottom, left, right, or create a floating toolbar.

Figure 5.12 shows the frame mdi_frame and its sheet, sheet1, each with its own menu and toolbar. By clicking on either of the toolbars with the right mouse button, a popup window becomes visible to allow the user to modify the corresponding toolbar. Within the popup menu the user can also choose to disable either the frame toolbar or the sheet toolbar. If the developer chooses to open the sheet and not have the menu bar also visible, the toolbar function **Hide( )** can be used to make

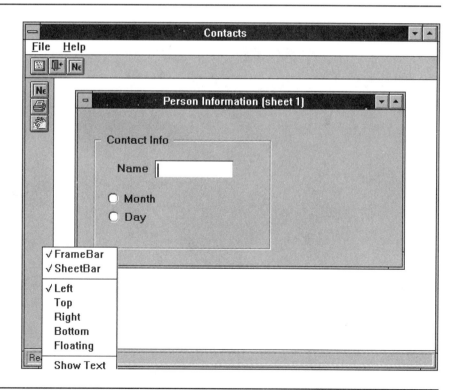

Figure 5.12   Frame and sheet, each with its own menu and toolbar.

the frame toolbar invisible. If the toolbar needs to be visible again, the **Show( )** function can be used.

As mentioned earlier, an MDI application can have one or more sheets with a corresponding menu and one sheet without a menu. Again, because toolbars are associated with menus, the sheet without a menu will take the last active menu and toolbar. This could be the frame's menu/toolbar or one of the other sheet's menu/toolbar, depending on the last activated object. The order in which you open the sheets determines what menu/toolbar a sheet without a menu will inherit.

Figure 5.13 shows the frame mdi_frame with a menu/toolbar associated with it and its sheet1 with a separate menu/toolbar. However, sheet2 does not have a menu/toolbar and will inherit the last open menu/toolbar when it is opened. In this case, the window sheet1 has been opened first and sheet2 inherits both the menu frame toolbar and the toolbar of sheet1. However, if sheet2 was opened first, it would have only inherited the frame's toolbar.

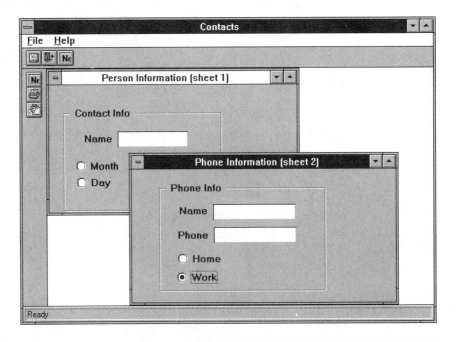

Figure 5.13   Mdi_frame with a menu toolbar.

Note: If there is a menu associated with a frame and a menu associated with a sheet, the sheet menu will replace the frame menu when opened. However, the sheet toolbar will not replace the frame toolbar when the sheet is opened. If the developer only requires the sheet toolbar to be visible, then hide the frame toolbar.

Many designers have a tendency to overuse toolbars. Toolbars should be designed and implemented on user requirements and not simply to add flash and pizzazz to an application. In addition, these functions should also have simple and easy-to-understand icons that should be symbolic to the majority of the users. The icons that appear in the toolbar should be 16 pixels × 15 pixels for good visual clarity. Unfortunately, PowerBuilder doesn't allow the user to change the size of the buttons associated with the menu items. Therefore, regular sized icon bitmaps don't appear very well in the toolbar.

INTEGRATING WITH INI FILE

Another useful function that can be integrated within menus is the ability to save user information into an initialization file. The developer can create MenuItems that will allow the user to save user preferences such as window position, window arrangement, toolbar position and items, and other user-specific items. PowerBuilder has three built-in functions designed to manipulate initialization files. The **ProfileString( )** and **ProfileInt( )** functions enable the developer to read from initialization files, and the **SetProfileString( )** function enables the developer to write to initialization files.

An example of this is to use **SetProfileString( )** in conjunction with the MenuItem S̲ave. This function writes the value of the fourth parameter, "sheet1" in this example, into the [LastSheet] section of WIN.INI. This would allow the developer to track the last unit of work that was saved by the user.

```
SetProfileString("win.ini","LastSheet","LastSheet1","sheet1")
```

This statement would produce the following line in WIN.INI:

```
[LastSheet]
LastSheet1=sheet1
```

This value could then be read using **ProfileString( )** to retrieve the last opened sheet in an MDI application. The **ProfileString( )** function will search for the WIN.INI file, open it, and retrieve the LastSheet entry for LastSheet1. If no value is supplied for this entry, the function will return the designated default (" "). This code is shown below:

```
string sLastFile
sLastFile = ProfileString("win.ini", "LastSheet", "LastSheet1", "")
```

The **ProfileInt( )** function works the same as the **ProfileString( )**, except it returns a numeric value instead of a character string and the default value must be numeric.

Another function the developer might want to create is a function to save the application workspace. The user can save the position of the frame and any sheets in an MDI application. This works similar to Windows' ability to save the user's workspace.

The example of this which follows, first saves the state (normal, minimized, or maximized), position, width, and height of the MDI frame into the WIN.INI variable MDIFrame (in section MyApp). After saving the frame, the sheet name and the same information given previously is saved for each open sheet. The WIN.INI variable name for the sheets is "sheet" followed by the number of the sheet (i.e., sheet1, sheet2, ...). This example uses instance variables to track the name of the sheets (*i_sOpenSheetNames*) and the actual sheet windows (*i_OpenSheets*). These variables were set as each sheet was opened. The code for this example is:

```
window currentsheet
string sWinState, sText
int i, iSheetNum

setPointer(hourGlass!)
/* first the frame */
/* figure out windowState */
choose case this.windowState
      case normal!
            sWinState = "0"
      case minimized!
            sWinState = "1"
      case maximized!
            sWinState = "2"
end choose
SetProfileString("win.ini","MyApp","MDIFrame",sWinState+&
      ","+string(this.x)+","+string(this.y)+","+string(this.width)+&
      ","+string(this.height))
```

```
/* now the sheets */
currentsheet = this.GetFirstSheet( )
DO WHILE IsValid(currentsheet)
        iSheetNum = iSheetNum + 1
        choose case currentsheet.windowState
               case normal!
                      sWinState = "0"
               case minimized!
                      sWinState = "1"
               case maximized!
                      sWinState = "2"
        end choose

SetProfileString("win.ini","MyApp","Sheet"+string(iSheetNum),&
      i_sOpenSheetNames[iSheetNum]+","+sWinState+","+&
      string(currentsheet.x)+","+string(currentsheet.y)+&
      ","+string(currentsheet.width)+&
      ","+string(currentsheet.height))

      currentsheet = this.GetNextSheet(currentsheet)
LOOP


/* now blank out any previous entries */
for i = iSheetNum+1 to 20 // arbitrary maximum
   if ProfileString("win.ini","MyApp","Sheet"+string(i),"") <> ""
then
       setProfileString("win.ini","MyApp","Sheet"+string(i),"")
   end if
next
w_mdi_frame.setMicroHelp("Workspace Saved.")
return true
```

The following shows how WIN.INI would look after saving the workspace in the previous example:

```
[MyApp]
MDIFrame=0,1029,449,1581,1060
Sheet1=w_sheet1,0,343,109,1353,500
Sheet2=w_sheet2,0,558,437,1353,500
Sheet3=w_sheet3,0,188,869,1354,500
```

Once the workspace has been saved, a corollary function will need to be written to read the information that was stored in the INI file. This function will restore the last state as well as the x, y, height, and width of the frame and each sheet.

```
/* Restore the user's workspace */

int i
string sSheetInfo
setPointer(hourGlass!)

/* first the sheets */
for i = 1 to 20                        //arbitrary maximum
      sSheetInfo = ProfileString("win.ini","MyApp","Sheet"+string(i),"")
      if sSheetInfo <> "" then
              i_sopensheetnames[i] = nextCSV(sSheetInfo)
              /* open the sheet - make the first menu opened its parent*/
              openSheet(i_openSheets[i],i_sopensheetnames[i],this,2,Original!)

              if not isValid(i_openSheets[i]) then
                      /* could not open - display message */
                      MessageBox("Open Sheet","Unable to open sheet saved"+&
                                       " in workspace. Re-save workspace.")
                      continue                // go to next saved sheet
              end if
              /* next parm is window state - 0 = normal 1 = min 2 = max */
              choose case nextCSV(sSheetInfo)
                    case "0" //normal
                          /* move and size it with following parms */
                      move(i_openSheets[i],integer(nextCSV(sSheetInfo)),&
                            integer(nextCSV(sSheetInfo)))
                      resize(i_openSheets[i],integer(nextCSV(sSheetInfo)),&
                            integer(nextCSV(sSheetInfo)))
                    case "1" //minimized
                          /* move and minimize it */
                          i_openSheets[i].WindowState = minimized!
                    case "2" //maximized
                          /* maximize it */
                          i_openSheets[i].WindowState = maximized!
              end choose
      else
          /* done with sheets */
          exit
      end if
next

i_inumopensheets = i -1
/* now the frame */
sSheetInfo = ProfileString("win.ini","MyApp","MDIFrame","")
if sSheetInfo <> "" then
      choose case nextCSV(sSheetInfo)
```

```
                    case "0" //normal
                        /* move and size it with following parms */
                        move(this,integer(nextCSV(sSheetInfo)),&
                            integer(nextCSV(sSheetInfo)))
                        resize(this,integer(nextCSV(sSheetInfo)),&
                            integer(nextCSV(sSheetInfo)))
                    case "1" //minimized
                        /* move and minimize it */
                        this.windowState = minimized!
                        move(this,integer(nextCSV(sSheetInfo)),&
                            integer(nextCSV(sSheetInfo)))
                    case "2" //maximized
                        /* maximize it */
                        this.windowState = maximized!
            end choose
    end if


/* setFocus to first menu */
if i_inumopensheets > 0 then
        setFocus(i_openSheets[1])
end if
w_mdi_frame.setMicroHelp("Workspace Restored.")
return true
```

The declaration and code of the window function **nextCSV**, used in the previous example for parsing comma-seperated strings, is shown in Figure 5.14.

```
/* This is used for parsing a parameter string separated by commas. */

Int iLen
string sTmp

iLen = pos(csvList,",")    // find end of this parm
if iLen = 0 then
      /* no comma - must be only parm */
      sTmp = csvList
      csvList = "" // clear it out
else
      /* remove the parm from the string */
      sTmp = Left(csvList,lng - 1) .    //don't want comma
      csvList = Right(csvList,len(csvList)-iLen)  //remove from string
end if


return tmp
```

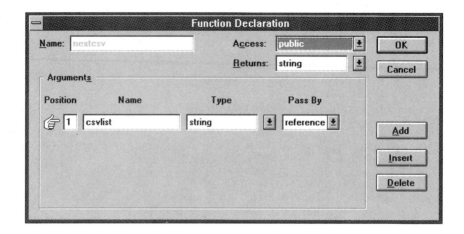

Figure 5.14   Nextcsv function Declaration.

ACCELERATOR AND SHORTCUT KEYS

Another way that the application designer can enhance the application is through the use of accelerator and shortcut keys. These offer the user the ability to do the same thing that is achieved with mouse movement by using the keyboard. PowerBuilder allows the developer to include these keys into the menus through the Menu painter. When developing menus for an application, it is considered good practice to include accelerator keys on all MenuItems. This allows the user to access any of the MenuItems with an Alt + Key. The accelerator key is denoted by the first letter of the MenuItem that is underlined. To create the accelerator key, the developer should include the ampersand (&) symbol in front of the MenuItem in the Menu painter.

In addition to accelerator keys the developer can use shortcut keys. These are a set of alternate keystrokes that can perform specific MenuItem tasks by using the Alt, Ctrl, or Shift keys in unison with an assigned keystroke. These items are denoted to the right of the appropriate MenuItem. These keystrokes are considered to be optional, but are of good use to users that have repetitive menu choices and prefer the keyboard for navigation. Windows has some conventions with regard to the shortcut keys, but the developer should create and adopt an application set of keystrokes.

MENUITEM ATTRIBUTES

The MenuItems that make up a menu have attributes and events associated with them. Both attributes and events allow the developer to further customize and manipulate the menus within the application.

The MenuID is a menu data type containing the identifying name of a menu (the name used to save the menu in the Menu painter). When you change the menu for a window from a script or display to a popup menu, use the MenuId attribute to identify the menu. Table 5.2 shows attributes of a MenuItem:

Note: The MenuItem name (prefix and suffix) can have up to 40 characters. If it exceeds this size, PowerBuilder uses only the first 40 characters.

When creating scripts to manipulate menu items, there are several PowerBuilder functions available that allow the developer to hide menu items, disable (grey), check, change menus, and change the text of menu items in a menu bar.

Table 5.2   Attributes of a MenuItem

Attribute	Type	Uses
Checked	Boolean	To illustrate that a MenuItem has been chosen
Enabled	Boolean	Allows user to choose the item, nongreyed
Item[ ]	Menu Array	Item[ ] is a string array containing the contents of a DropDownListBox or ListBox, or the items that appear under a MenuItem. Item is a static array and contains only the initial values that you assign to the ListBox. If you call the **AddItem( )**, **DeleteItem( )**, or **InsertItem( )** function to change the list during execution, the Item array does not reflect the changes.
ShortCut	Integer	Integer representation of the shortcut key
ParentWindow	Window	Name of the window object that owns the menu
Tag	String	Tagged name of a MenuItem
Text	String	Text for the MenuItem
Visible	Boolean	Make the item visible/invisible

One of the more popular functions is the **hide( )** function. This function can be used to hide any of the menu items that the developer does not want the user to see. This function can be used when the menu is inherited from another menu and an option is not used or does not apply to the particular descendant menu.

An example is when the MenuItem in the menu m_stdmnu does not need the inherited MenuItem O̲pen. The converse function of **hide( )** is the **show( )** function. The syntax for these functions are:

```
m_stdmnu.m_file.m_open hide( )
m_stdmnu.m_file.m_open show( )
```

The **enable( )** and **disable( )** functions are useful when the developer is maintaining security for an application. They allow the developer to grey out any of the MenuItems that cannot be used. This is helpful because it allows the user to see that the option is in the menu but cannot be accessed or used because of constraint within the application. It is also useful when the developer wants to only allow a user to use certain MenuItems during the flow of a unit of work.

An example of this is when the developer does not want the user to use the O̲pen MenuItem because of incorrect security privileges. In addition, the enable function can be used to restore the use of the MenuItem.

```
m_stdmnu.m_file.m_open.disable( )
m_stdmnu.m_file.m_open.enable( )
```

When the developer creates MenuItems with Boolean values, a checked bitmap can be associated with the appropriate MenuItems. This allows the user to see that a menu choice is invoked or not invoked. The checkmark can be associated either as a default in the menu painter or associated later via the check function.

An example is the checking of the Tile MenuItem in an MDI application to indicate that the sheets will be arranged in a tiled fashion.

```
m_stdmnu.m_file.m_tile.checked( )
m_stdmnu.m_file.m_tile.unchecked( )
```

Sometimes a developer will want to change from one menu to another during the flow of work in an application. This allows the developer to change menus without overriding and disabling another menu's choices. The **changemenu( )** function will handle the changing of the menu by using the Window attributes of MenuID and MenuName. Each of these is used by PowerBuilder to internally track the associated menu. PowerBuilder recommends that the developer not attempt to use these, but the attributes can be found and used for tracking.

For example, if the window mdi_ frame needed to utilize a different menu, the clicked event could change the menu by using **changemenu( )**:

```
mdi_frame.changemenu(m_stdmdi)
```

In addition to visually showing the check and uncheck bitmap, the developer can change the text in the MenuItem to reflect the state of the MenuItem. This gives the developer an option when dealing with MenuItems that do not easily work with the checked bitmap. This is done by using the Text attribute in the clicked event of the MenuItem.

An example of this would be the changing of the MenuItem in m_stdmnu from File—Open to File—Close when the MenuItem is clicked.

```
text = "Close"
```

DESIGN CONSIDERATIONS

One of the primary concerns of application design is the topic of standardization. The use of standards allows the user to manipulate each different application in a similar fashion and creates a cohesive flow for the application users to follow. In addition, standards can also reduce the time it takes for training on a new system as well as user satisfaction. Unfortunately, there is no one standard type of menu system look and feel. Some applications designers choose to implement IBM CUA standards and others create internal standards. However, most application designers choose to implement a menuing system that is similar to the current suite of Microsoft applications. Some examples would include the MS Word and MS Excel applications.

One of the first look and feel standards is the creation of a standard menu bar. The standard menu bar includes the use of File, Edit, View, Window, and Help within the menu bar. Another example of a menu standard is the use of shortcut keys. The shortcut key is denoted in a menu as the series of control keys that can be used to alternately choose a menu item. Additionally, PowerBuilder allows the application designer to create and utilize accelerator keys. These are the underlined letters within the menu bar or menu item that allow quick access to a MenuItem. Yet another standard is the use of three dots (ellipses) following a MenuItem choice. This indicates that a Window or popup Window will be invoked by clicking on this MenuItem. Menu standardization can be simplified through the use of inheritance. Inheritance allows the menu standards to be created once in the ancestor level and extended and overridden at the descendant level.

CHAPTER 6

Windows

This chapter discusses a critical object in the PowerBuilder development environment—the window object. The Window object is used in almost every PowerBuilder application. There are many different types of windows in PowerBuilder. Once the window type has been selected, the next important decision is the selection and placement of controls on the window.

This chapter discusses the following:

- Types of Windows
- Window Events
- PowerBuilder Variables
- Window Data Types
- Window Controls
- Window Attributes
- Window Paradigms

TYPES OF WINDOWS

PowerBuilder allows the developer to create several different types of windows. Each window type has a specific purpose, which may differ in functionality depending on the type of application interface used. The two basic types of application interfaces that PowerBuilder defines are the single document interface (SDI) and the multiple document interface (MDI). SDI allows the use of one set of screens; the MDI interface allows manipulation of multiple windows simultaneously. A complete definition of window types and their functionality can be found in Chapters 4 and 19.

The types of windows in PowerBuilder are:

- Main
- Popup
- Child
- Response
- MDI frame
- MDI frame with MicroHelp

They are selected on the Window Style screen in the Window painter, which is displayed by selecting Design/Window Style from the menu, as shown in Figure 6.1.

Main Window

The main window type is an independent window that is used as the anchor in an SDI interface application. A main window can have a title bar, a menu, and can be maximized or minimized. Any other type of window that is opened from a main window is subservient to the main window. Consequently, if a main window is minimized, the other windows associated with it are also minimized.

For example, use a main window with sales rep (employee) infor-

Figure 6.1   The Window Style screen.

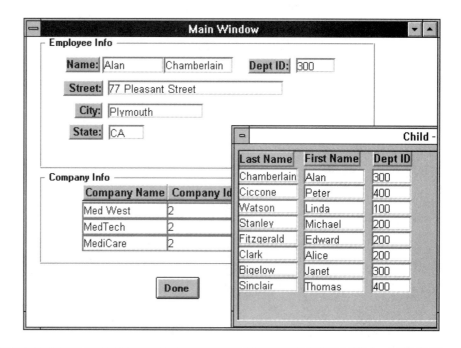

Figure 6.2   Main window and a child window.

mation and a child window with information about sales made by the employee (see Figure 6.2). If the main window is closed, the subservient window, Child—Sales, is also closed by the application.

This figure shows that the main window also controls the area that the child window can be seen in. When child windows are used in conjunction with main windows, they can be moved only within the area of the main window. That is, they cannot be moved outside the main window area. In addition, when a subservient window is minimized, it appears iconized inside the main window.

Popup Window

A popup window acts the same as a child window except its boundaries can extend beyond the boundaries of its parent window. Because popup windows are able to display outside the parent window area, they are sometimes used to display noneditable information or are displayed as a selection window. A popup window is subservient to its parent window and thus is minimized if the parent window is minimized. If only the popup window is minimized, however, it is shown iconized in the bottom of the Windows desktop, not in the parent window (as a child window is).

In Figure 6.3, a popup window is used to make a search list window called w_search for available customers. The window does not allow the user to make edits in w_search, but does allow selection of a name that is to be used to populate the parent window or to create a new user.

This example illustrates that popup windows are used as supporting windows because none of the fields are editable. Because popups are supporting windows, it is generally a good idea not to have any complex processing or functionality in them. Updating of tables should, for the most part, be done in either child or main windows. This maintains a logical unit of work and simplifies functionality.

Figure 6.3   A popup window.

It is important to note that if multiple popup windows are opened from a main window in PowerScript as displayed in the following PowerScript, each window becomes the parent of the next window opened.

In the open event of main window w_mainwindow:

```
Open(w_popupwindow1)
Open(w_popupwindow2)
Open(w_popupwindow3)
Open(w_popupwindow4)
```

For example, w_mainwindow is the parent of w_popupwindow1. When opening window w_popupwindow2, w_popupwindow1 has focus and therefore becomes the parent of w_popupwindow2. The same concept is true for the rest of the windows.

Child Window

A child window can be opened from a main or popup window. A child window does not have a menu.

As an example, take a main window, w_main, which is opened with a popup window, w_pop. The window w_pop, in turn, opens the child window w_child. Because the child window was opened by the popup window, it is subservient to it and must stay in the popup window's area. However, because the window w_pop is subservient to the main window, both the popup and child windows are subservient to the main window (see Figure 6.4).

This fairly simple example also shows nested window types in an application. As an application becomes large, it is recommended that the developer keep nested windows of different types to a minimum.

Response Window

The response window gives the user information and requires immediate response. Response windows are application modal and thus do not allow access to another window in the application until the user responds to this window. The user can, however, access other Windows applications before responding to this window.

Displaying MessageBox-like Response Windows If the developer wants to display a messagebox-like window when a control has been modified and the focus is changing, a response window can be used rather than a messagebox. A response window allows more flexibility and functionality than a messagebox. The first step would be to create a response

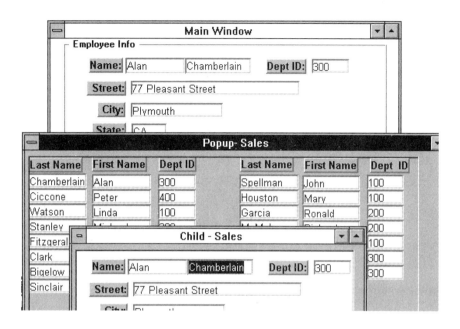

Figure 6.4   A main window with popup window and child window.

window with whatever message and command buttons are required. If different logic is required depending on which command button is pressed, the developer needs a way for the window to know which command button was pushed. One method of getting this functionality is to have the command buttons set global variables that can then be checked by the window. In the main window, the developer should create a user-defined event. In this event, the developer opens the response window and checks what the user did on the response window. If the focus is to remain on the control that has just been modified, the following lines should be added to the script in the user-defined event, somewhere after the open(responsewindow):

```
setfocus(parent)
setfocus(this)
```

This keeps the focus on the control that was just modified, rather than allowing focus to change to the control that was either tabbed to or mouse-clicked to. Finally, in the modified event of the control on the first window, the user-defined event should be posted by adding the following line to the script:

```
postevent(this,"whatever the developer has named the user-defined
event")
```

Unless a piece of information is required from the user or a special circumstance warrants, the developer should use messageboxes to communicate with the user. These windows are easier to create using the messagebox function.

MDI Frame/MDI Frame with MicroHelp Window

As the name implies, the MDI Frame is used with the MDI application interface. The MDI frame is the anchor window for the MDI application and any window type opened becomes subservient to it.

Refer to Chapter 4 for a detailed discussion of MDIs.

WINDOW EVENTS

The window object and its related controls have several associated events. These events allow the user to create script to perform functionality based on a user's actions. The window object has at least 28 different events predefined in PowerBuilder. The complete list of window events and descriptions can be found in the PowerBuilder Objects and Controls manual and online help. In addition to using PowerBuilder's standard control events, the developer can create custom user events.

Standard Events

When the developer creates a new window object, it has the following default events associated with it.

Window Event	*Description*
Activate	Occurs just before the window becomes active. When the activate event occurs, the first control in the tab order gets focused.
Clicked	The clicked event occurs when a user clicks on a window, control, or object or when the user selects it with the keyboard and presses ENTER.
Close	Occurs just before the window is removed from display to the user.

CloseQuery	Occurs when the window is removed from display.
Deactivate	Occurs when the window becomes inactive.
DoubleClicked	Occurs when the user double-clicks in a window.
DragDrop	Occurs when an object is dropped on a target object.
DragEnter	Occurs when an object is dragged to a target object.
DragLeave	Occurs when an object is dragged out of a target object.
DragWithin	Occurs when an object is dragged within a target object.
Hide	Occurs before a window is removed from view.
HotLinkAlarm	Occurs when a DDE server establishes a connection with PowerBuilder.
Key	Occurs when the insertion point is not a line edit and the user presses the Ctrl or Shift key.
MouseDown	Occurs when the mouse button is pressed on an empty part of the window.
MouseMove	Occurs whenever the mouse is moved in the window.
MouseUp	Occurs when the mouse button is released.
Open	Occurs before a window is created or displayed.
Other	Occurs when an event other than PowerBuilder occurs.
RButtonDown	Occurs when the right button is pressed.
RemoteExec	Occurs when the client application sends a command.
RemoteHotlinkStart	Occurs when a client wants to start a hotlink.
RemoteHotlinkStop	Occurs when a client wants to stop a hotlink.
RemoteRequest	Occurs when a client requests data from the server.
RemoteSend	Occurs when a client application sends data to PowerBuilder.
Resize	Occurs when a user or script opens a window or resizes a window or DataWindow control.

Show   Occurs after a window is opened but before it
                        is displayed.

SystemKey   Occurs when the insertion point is not a line
                        edit and the user presses the Alt or Alt+ key.

Timer   An event triggered by the timer function.

ToolbarMoved   An event triggered by moving the toolbar.

Examples of the open, resize, timer, and user-defined events can be found in Chapter 4, in the example about creating a clock in the MDI frame.

Open Event

The most common window event is the open event. The open event for a window is triggered when the window is opened and before it is displayed to the user. A common problem in creating windows is coding a large open script for a window that includes database connection, variable declarations, and array declarations. The script for the open event of the window should be kept to a minimum. Too much processing in the open event can be very inefficient. Everytime the window is opened all the code in the open event is executed. This gives the user a perception of a slow application.

Activate Event

Another key event associated with the window is the activate event. The activate event is also misused by placing a large amount of code in it. The activate event occurs before the window becomes active and the first control in the tab order receives focus. This event should contain script that deals with tab orders or other code that deals with object focus. It should not contain a lot of code pertaining to the window or database connections. A large amount of processing in this event can also affect the window's perceived performance.

CloseQuery Event

The closeQuery event occurs when a window is closed by the user. PowerBuilder must check the active windows to determine if the window can be closed. If the value in Message.ReturnValue is determined to be 1, the window cannot be closed. The developer can use this event to perform some processing or variable-checking before the window closes.

Another way to use the closeQuery event is to create two windows, where the first window, w_cmbo, opens a second window, w_grid, for example. The first window does not retrieve information until a command button in the second window is pressed. Figure 6.5 shows the main window w_cmbo and the popup window w_grid. The retrieve statement for the main window is executed from the w_grid window's button "Retrieve in w_cmbo" using the closeQuery event in w_grid.

The developer should first create a user event called getdata in window w_cmbo and map it to pbm_custom01. The code to retrieve the information into the window w_cmbo is placed in the user-defined event getdata. The code consists of the following:

```
//Script to retrieve information into w_cmbo from DB
dw_1.SetTransObject(sqlca)
dw_2.SetTransObject(sqlca)
dw_1.Retrieve ( )
dw_2.Retrieve ( )
```

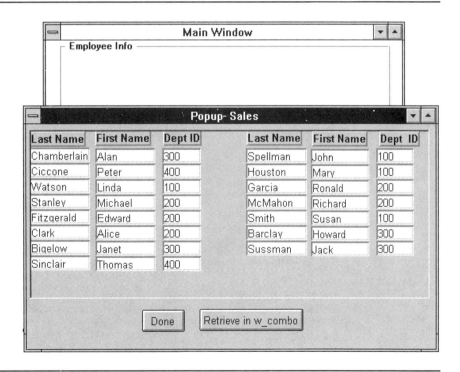

Figure 6.5   The main window with the popup window.

Next the developer places the following code in the clicked event of the "Retrieve in w_cmbo" button in window w_grid:

```
close(Parent)
```

This will cause the closeQuery event of w_grid to execute. This event will execute the getdata event of w_cmbo using the PostEvent function:

```
w_main.PostEvent("getdata")
```

Custom User Events

The developer can also create custom user events for a window or control by mapping to specific PowerBuilder events or choosing a custom-created event. The developer creates a custom event by choosing the <u>D</u>eclare, User <u>E</u>vent menu item. Custom user events can be used to call functions or trigger other events on controls in a window. The developer can map a custom user event to a predefined PowerBuilder event ID or to a custom ID for specialized uses.

Note: One cannot post events to the event queue for an application object. After the PostEvent is called, the return code must be checked to determine whether PostEvent succeeded and, based on the result, appropriate processing must be performed.

POWERBUILDER VARIABLES

Variable declaration is an important aspect of application design. When considering the use of variables, one has to think about memory conservation. To maximize memory efficiency, many things need to be considered. First is the type of data the variable is representing. Second is whether a variable needs to store positive and negative numbers. Third is the range of values that a variable needs to store. A final consideration is the scope of the variable.

PowerBuilder variables can be defined as local, instance, shared, or global in scope. All the previously-mentioned considerations are important when looking at an application as a whole. The proper use of variables can lead to efficient systems, especially in the Windows environment, where limited system resources are shared among different applications.

The first consideration when declaring a variable is the type of data the variable is representing. Examples include a name/description, quantity, identification number, date, loop/row counter, and error codes. For numeric data types, the developer has a great deal of control regarding the size and range of values for a variable. Because of this, the second consideration is whether a variable needs to store both positive and negative numbers. If it is known that a variable only needs to store positive numbers, memory can be saved by declaring the variable as unsigned, rather than signed. This is a very important concept that is often overlooked by developers. Following is the range of signed numbers for variables.

16-bit variable (Integer)—see Figure 6.6
Values range from $-32,768$ (-2^{15}) to $+32,767$ $((2^{15}) - 1)$

16-bit variable (Unsigned Integer)—see Figure 6.7
Values range from 0 to $+65,535$ $((2^{16}) - 1)$

32-bit variable (Long)—see Figure 6.8
Values range from $-2,127,483,648$ (-2^{31}) to $+2,127,483,647$ $((2^{31}) - 1)$

32-bit variable (Unsigned Long)—see Figure 6.9
Values range from 0 to $+4,294,967,295$ $((2^{32}) - 1)$

The third consideration is the range of values that the variable needs to store. For a 16-bit memory location, the range of signed (positive and negative) numbers that can be stored is $-32,768$ to $+32,767$. The same 16-bit variable defined as an unsigned (positive only) number can store anything in the range of 0 to 65,535. Thirty-two-bit signed variables can store values ranging from $-2,127,483,648$ to $+2,127,483,647$, while a 32-bit unsigned variable can store values ranging from 0 to $+4,294,967,295$. So, for example, an application that needs a variable to store numbers from 0 to 50,000 should use a 16-bit variable (unsigned integer) instead of a 32-bit variable. It is a common mistake for developers to declare a variable as a long when a 16-bit variable will suffice.

The fourth consideration is the scope of the variable. The developer must determine whether the variable is to be for private use within the script (local), private within the window (instance), private to instances of a window (shared), or global to the entire application (global). PowerBuilder allows the declaration of all four types of variables. The developer should minimize the use of global, shared, and instance variables, when possible. When a global variable is declared, it remains in memory until the application is terminated. When a shared or instance variable is declared, it remains in memory until the window for the variable is closed. Local variables are only in memory during the execution of the script in which the variable was declared, thus minimizing the overall application memory required.

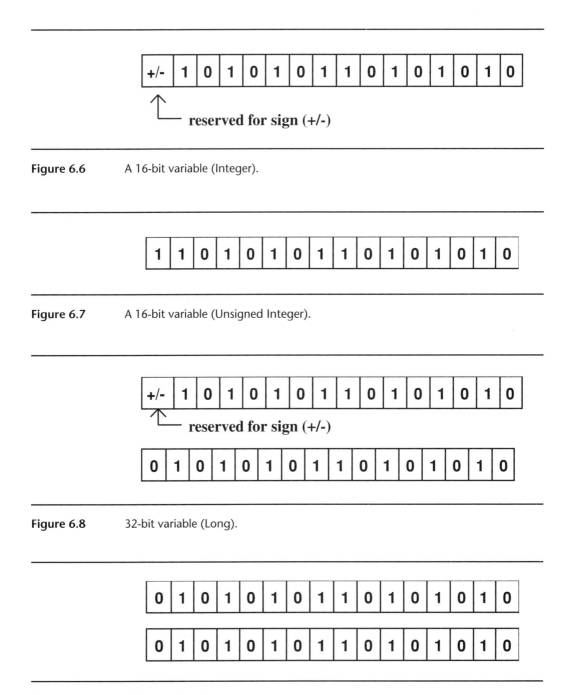

Figure 6.6   A 16-bit variable (Integer).

Figure 6.7   A 16-bit variable (Unsigned Integer).

Figure 6.8   32-bit variable (Long).

Figure 6.9   32-bit variable (Unsigned Long).

WINDOW DATA TYPES

Windows definitions are usually stored in a PowerBuilder library. When a window is run, a variable for the window is automatically generated. Other than being responsible for opening and closing the window, the developer does not need to act on the window to make it open.

At times, the developer needs to show the same window more than once on the screen at the same time, put all the visible windows in an array, and be able to manipulate them using an index. To do this, the developer must treat the window as a data type. Doing this allows the developer to create variables for and arrays of windows as would be done for integers or strings.

To understand how to use window data types, the developer should understand what really happens when a window is created in the Window painter. When a window is saved in the Window painter, PowerBuilder generates two entities with the same name as the window: a window data type and a global window variable. Internally, the window variable is declared as being of the window data type. If the developer declares a variable, the declaration would resemble the following:

```
w_window1   w_window1
```

where the "w_window1" on the left specifies the data type of the window and the "w_window1" on the right specifies the window variable.

This duplicate naming of the data type and variable provides a clever way for a new user to access the window through its variable part while ignoring the concept of data type. At the same time, the data type allows advanced users to create their own window variables. The data type also supports inheritance and other object-oriented features in PowerBuilder.

Another important concept to understand is how the open function works. The open function creates an instance of a window and places a reference to that window in the supplied variable. In the default format, open(w_window1), the data type of the window variable, not the name of the variable, determines which window is opened. Consider the following code:

```
w_window1   w_sheet
Open (w_sheet)
```

In this example, the open function determines the data type of the *w_sheet* variable, in this case, w_window1. It then opens an instance of w_window1 and assigns a reference to the *w_sheet* variable. Note that the *w_window1* global variable, which was part of the window definition, has not been set. In fact, variable *w_window1* still contains a NULL reference.

Extending this idea, the developer can open windows and place their references in an array. For example:

```
w_window1 WinArray[]
FOR i = 1 to 5
    Open (WinArray[i])
NEXT
```

This code creates five instances of window w_window1 and places them in WinArray. Creating multiple instances of the same window is not very interesting, so the example can be changed to create five different types of windows and place them in the same array:

```
Window          WinArray[]
FOR i = 1 to 5
    Open(WinArray[i],WinName[i])
NEXT
```

This example introduces two new features. First, notice that the type of WinArray has changed to "Window." Type Window is the system data type from which all user-defined windows are derived. In effect, variables of type Window can contain references to any window in the system. The other new feature is a second WinName argument in the Open function. In this form of Open, the data type of the window to be created is taken from the string supplied in the second argument and the resultant window reference is placed in the window variable in the first argument. In this example, an array of window data type names is supplied. As each window is opened, it is placed in the WinArray.

Using arrays can be a very powerful way to keep track of windows in an application, allowing the developer to access them and perform operations (such as open and close) on them as a group. There is further discussion of arrays and windows in Chapters 4 and 23.

WINDOW CONTROLS

When the developer creates a window, a number of window controls can be added to the window for functionality.

Table 6.1 contains some PowerBuilder window controls, their prefixes, and a description for each.

Unfortunately, window controls require the developer to code script to provide required functionality. Some of the most frequently used controls are the DropDownListBox, RadioButtons, and the SingleLineEdit.

Table 6.1   PowerBuilder window controls

Control Name	Prefix	Description
CheckBox	cbx_	Boolean
CommandButton	cb_	A button that allows a user to perform functionality
DataWindow	dw_	A window control that allows events to be associated with a DataWindow object
DropDownListBox	ddlb_	Drops down to show a list of choices for a field
EditMask	em_	A method of restricting data in a field
Graph	gr_	A graphical representation of the data in a window or datawindow
GroupBox	gb_	A line that surrounds controls and groups their functionality
Hscrollbar	hsb_	Allows the user to scroll horizontally
Line	ln_	A line in a window
ListBox	lb_	Allows multiple items to be shown
MultiLineEdit	mle_	Allows more than one line of information to be entered
Oval	oval_	An oval in a window
Picture	p_	A bitmap or graphic file
PictureButton	pb_	A bitmap or graphic file that contains script to perform functionality
RadioButton	rb_	Allows the user to choose an item
Rectangle	r_	A rectangle in a window
RoundRectangle	rr_	A round rectangle in a window
SingleLineEdit	sle_	Allows only a single line of data to be entered
StaticText	st_	Text used to label or describe the window
UserObject	uo_	A developer-created object that encapsulates coded functionality
Vscrollbar	vsb_	Allows the user to scroll vertically

DropDownListBox

The DropDownListBox (DDLB) allows the developer to show the user a series of choices for a particular field in a window. The DropDownListBox control combines the features of a SingleLineEdit and a ListBox (see the following explanations). There are two basic types of DDLBs—editable and noneditable.

Noneditable DDLB Noneditable DDLBs allow the developer to choose from a fixed set of choices for a field. They are denoted by having no space between the down arrow and the SLE. Because the user does not have the opportunity to enter an incorrect response for the field, the noneditable DDLB can be used as a type of data validation. They are typically used for items with difficult spellings or for code fields.

Sometimes it is necessary to blank out the text portion of a noneditable DDLB. This would be the case if the user selected an entry from this list and then realized this entry was not correct, nor were any of the other choices. An example of this would be to have a screen on which the saleperson's name was selected. If the user needed to clear the field, the DDLB functionality would not allow this. If a Clear function were added, the screen would look like the one in Figure 6.10.

In this example, the following code would be used in the command button **cb_clear**.

```
ddlb_1.Selectitem(0)
```

By changing the Allow Edit attribute of the DDLB, however, the user would be able to edit the entry in the DDLB. This could be done for people with a higher level of security, for example.

The following code in the command button **cb_clear** would provide this functionality.

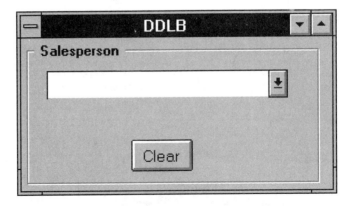

Figure 6.10   Using the **Clear** function to block out the text portion of the noneditable DDLB.

```
ddlb_1.allowedit = true
ddlb_1.visible = true
```

A complete listing of DDLB attributes and events is in the PowerBuilder *Objects and Controls* manual.

The DDLB also allows the user to perform a lookup on the DDLB values. When the lookup is performed, the text value in the DropDownListBox is used to find the first entry in the Items list. This could either be an exact match or a match of the text value with additional characters. For example, if the text value is abc and the list of items is:

ab

abcdefg

abc

the lookup would find abcdefg because it is the first entry that exactly matches the text value (even though it has additional characters).

In addition, hidden indexes in a DDLB can be used to perform functionality.

Editable DDLB The editable DDLB allows the user to type in data for a particular field. The developer can code script or call functions to vali-

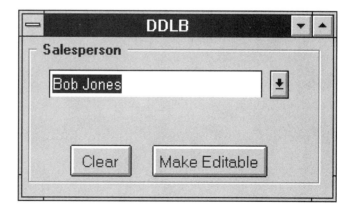

Figure 6.11   Changing the Allow Edit attribute in a noneditable DDLB.

date the entry. The editable DDLB is denoted by a space between the down arrow and the SLE.

ListBox

The ListBox allows the user to see a list of available choices. The ListBox differs from the DDLB in that it shows all of the user's choices at the same time.

An example of how to get the text from a list box would be to have a list of salespeople and allow the user to choose one. The chosen salesperson then fills the SLE sle_1 with the appropriate choice. This is demonstrated in Figure 6.12.

The following code is used to get the text for all of the selected items in the ListBox and then fill the SLE with the user's choice.

```
integer iCounter, iTotalNumberOfItems, j=1
string selected_items [ ]
// Get total number of items in ListBox
iTotalNumberOfItems = lb_1.TotalItems( )
// Loop through all items
For iCounter = 1 to iTotalNumberOfItems
```

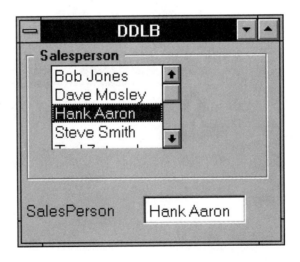

Figure 6.12   Getting text from a list box.

```
// Is the item selected?
  if lb_1.State(iCounter) = 1 then
    selected_items[j] = lb_1.Text(iCounter)
        sle_1.text = selected_items[j]
    j = j + 1
  end if
next
```

The **State( )** function is used in the loop to determine if an item was selected; the **Text( )** function is then used to get the text of the selected items. The **TotalSelected( )** and the **SelectedIndex( )** functions can also be used to make the previous function more efficient.

RadioButtons

RadioButtons are mutually exclusive objects. That is, in a given RadioButton, only one RadioButton can be active at a time. The exception to this is when group boxes are used with the RadioButtons. The group box frames several RadioButtons and segregates them as a unit. When an application requires that the user select a series of options and the developer chooses to use RadioButtons, it's a good idea to enclose each unique group of options (and corresponding RadioButtons) in a group box. This makes the choices clearer to the end user.

When a window has several RadioButtons that are not in a group box, the window acts as a group box and only allows one RadioButton to be active at a time; that is, unless the Automatic attribute for the RadioButton is False. This might be done for a RadioButton look with checkbox-like functionality. When the Automatic attribute is not checked, the developer must use scripts to control when the RadioButton is checked or not checked. When the Automatic attribute is False, multiple RadioButtons can be selected outside of a group. The Automatic attribute does not change how RadioButtons are processed inside a group box.

SingleLineEdit/ MultiLineEdit

The SingleLineEdit control allows the user to enter one line of information in a field. The MultiLineEdit allows the user to enter multiple lines of data in a field. Here is an example that allows the user to key over an entry in the SLE, instead of the default of inserting data. The MLE looks like the one in Figure 6.13.

The first step is to define a user event overtype for the SLE and map it

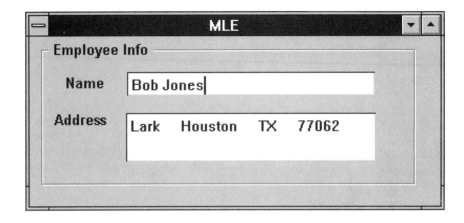

Figure 6.13   The MLF when a used keys over an entry in the SLE.

to the event id pbm_char. Next the developer defines a second user event delte and maps it to the PowerBuilder custom event id pbm_custom01.

The developer then places the following code in the overtype event of the SLE:

```
// the overtype event
PostEvent(this,"delte")
```

Next code the following in the delete user event.

```
// the delte event
Send (Handle (this),256,46,long(0,0))
```

The number 46 is the decimal equivalent of 2E hex which is the delete key. Sending this particular handle allows the field to be put into overtype mode.

MultiLineEdit Tab Stops Sometimes it is necessary to place tabs in an MLE to allow the data to line up properly. The following example defines tab stops in a MLE and places address information in it. This code places the tab stops in the MLE as shown in the Addresss field in Figure 6.13.

```
// Tab stops for MLE_1
// f1, f2, f3 fields that contain strings
```

```
string f1, f2, f3
// define first tabstop at position 5; define second tabstop 10
// positions after that.
mle_1.tabstop[1] = 5
mle_1.tabstop[2] = 10
f1 = "field1"
f2 = "field2"
f3 = "field3"
mle_1.text = f1 + " ~t " + f2 " " ~t " + f3
//Note: The ~t MUST have a blank space on each side and the t in ~t
//MUST be lowercase.
```

Window Control Array

When a window is created in PowerBuilder, an internal array that stores each of the different types and values for controls is created. The function in the following example accepts a window as an argument and resets controls on that window. It clears out the text attribute of MultiLineEdits, SingleLineEdits, and DropDownListBoxes on that window. It unchecks radiobuttons and checkboxes and it resets and puts a fresh row into one DataWindow control. It also retrieves data into another based on the name of the DataWindow control.

```
int tot, i
//window_arg is the window passed as an argument to this function (type
window)
tot = UpperBound(w_control.control)
FOR i = 1 to tot
 CHOOSE CASE Typeof(w_control.control[i])
    CASE singlelineedit!  //clear all text of all SLEs
         singlelineedit my_sle
         my_sle = w_control.control[i]
         my_sle.text = ""
    CASE multilineedit!   //clear text of all MLEs
         multilineedit my_mle
         my_mle = w_control.control[i]
         my_mle.text = ""
    CASE dropdownlistbox!   //clear text of all DDLBs
         dropdownlistbox my_ddlb
         my_ddlb = w_control.control[i]
         my_ddlb.SelectItem(0)
    CASE editmask!
         editmask my_em
         my_em = w_control.control[i]
         if my_em.maskdatatype = datemask! then
              my_em.text = "01/01/93"// set date to first of the year
```

```
                        else
                        if my_em.maskdatatype = numericmask! then
                              my_em.text = ".00"  // set numeric mask .00
                              else
                                    my_em.text = ""    // clear text of strings
                              end if
                        end if
            CASE datawindow!
                        datawindow my_dw
                        my_dw = w_control.control[i]
                        if my_dw.ClassName( ) = "dw_dataentry" then
//set up dw_dataentry for input
                              my_dw.Reset( )
                              my_dw.InsertRow(0)
                        elseif my_dw.ClassName( ) = "dw_getinfo" then
//retrieve info into dw_getinfo
                              my_dw.Retrieve( ) //assumes SetTransObject done
                        end if
            CASE radiobutton!   //uncheck all radiobuttons
                        radiobutton my_rb
                        my_rb = w_control.control[i]
                        my_rb.checked = False
            CASE chec kbox!   //uncheck all checkboxes
                        checkbox my_cbx
                        my_cbx = w_control.control[i]
                        my_cbx.checked = False
      END CHOOSE
NEXT
```

For more information about object class types in PowerBuilder, go to the Browse Class Hierarchy option of the Utilities menu in the Library painter.

Control Events

Most controls in the PowerBuilder environment have events associated with them. The only window controls that do not have events associated with them are the drawing objects (line, oval, rectangle, and round rectangle). PowerBuilder actually allows the developer to create custom user events for drawing objects, but does not allow the event scripts to be edited. The 11 standard events for window controls are:

Window Event	*Description*
Clicked	The clicked event occurs when a user clicks on a window, control, or object or when selected with the keyboard by pressing Enter

Constructor	Occurs before the open event of the window
Destructor	Occurs immediately after the close event of the window
DragDrop	Occurs when an object is dropped on a control
DragEnter	Occurs when an object is dragged into a control
DragLeave	Occurs when an object is dragged out of a control
DragWithin	Occurs when an object is dragged within a control
GetFocus	Occurs before a control receives focus
LoseFocus	Occurs before the control loses focus that is, becomes inactive
Other	Occurs when an event other than PowerBuilder occurs
RButtonDown	Occurs when the right mouse button is pressed

Control events are discussed in more detail throughout this book.

WINDOW ATTRIBUTES

In addition to events, each window object has a number of different attributes that the developer can change. A detailed discussion of window attributes can be found in the PowerBuilder *Objects and Controls* manual. Window attributes can be altered either with the Window painter or programmatically.

UnitsPerLine and LinesPerPage are examples of window attributes. These two window attributes can be set to control vertical window scrolling. The LinesPerPage attribute should be set to 10 to give 10 pagedowns to reach the bottom of the window. Setting LinesPerPage to anything other than 10 can yield undesired results. In terms of the UnitsPerLine attribute, consider the following equation for the page:

```
UnitsPerLine = (<WindowHeight> - LogicalPageHeight>)/100
```

The LogicalPageHeight is the number of PBUs that the developer needs to cover when doing one pagedown. Because the LinesPerPage attribute is being set to 10, this number would be calculated as follows:

```
<LogicalPageHeight> = <WindowHeight>/10
```

The following example shows how to control vertical window scrolling for a window that is 6000 PBUs deep.

```
<LogicalPageHeight> = 6000/10
                    = 600
```

```
UnitsPerLine        =(6000 - 600)/100
                    =5400/100
                    =54
```

In this case, LinesPerPage = 10 and UnitsPerLine = 54 would allow the developer to cover the entire depth of the 6000 PBU deep window.

Note: The reason that the logical page height is subtracted from the window height is that one page is already displayed on the screen, so 10 pagedowns have to cover the window height minus one page.

Horizontal Scrolling The same attributes used for vertical scrolling in a window are used to control horizontal scrolling. The logic is the same also. Given the previous example, ColumnsPerPage would be substituted for LinesPerPage, UnitsPerColumn for UnitsPerLine, <LogicalPageWidth> for <LogicalPageHeight>, and <WindowWidth> for <WindowHeight>.

Note: If the developer is controlling scrolling programmatically, he/she must always set the values for UnitsPerLine, LinesPerPage, and the like in the open event of the window. Setting these values in any other event has no effect.

To provide scrolling in a window using the PageUp and PageDown keys, the following code would be added in the window's open event:

```
int LogicalPageHeight, Max_Depth
Max_Depth = 3000     // Assumes that maximum depth to be covered
                     // by vertical scrolling of this window is 3000 PBUs.
                     // Change to whatever is appropriate.
This.LinesPerPage = 10
LogicalPageHeight = Max_Depth/10
This.UnitsPerLine = (Max_Depth - LogicalPageHeight) / 100
//In the Key event of the window, add:
int cur_win
cur_win = Handle(This)

if KeyDown(keyPageDown!) then
      Send(cur_win,277,3,0)
      Return
end if
```

```
if KeyDown(keyPageUp!) then
        Send(cur_win,277,2,0)
end if
```

WINDOW PARADIGMS

PowerBuilder applications are considered to be a subset of Windows applications. In Windows applications, there are some standard windows paradigms. These paradigms are based on the user's need to view information and the relationships of the underlying datasources. Some Windows/PowerBuilder paradigms include:

- Open Boxes
- Master/Detail
- List
- Form
- Dual Column
- Tab-folder

These paradigms are discussed in the sections of this chapter that follow.

Open Boxes

An open box is a specific dialog box that allows the user to select a single data object and send its key to another window to be acted on. An open box commonly presents a list (or lists) of rows in a DataWindow, from which the user can select a single row. An open box is always associated with another window, but not all windows have open boxes associated with them.

Most open boxes contain one or more open, new, and cancel command buttons. High volume open boxes, designed to display more than 200 choices, include search criteria field(s) which allow the user to specify the first few characters of a choice; only the rows that match the search pattern are displayed. (Instead of updating the list as the user keys search criteria characters, a **Refresh** button can be used for updating the list with current data.) Open boxes can contain more than one DataWindow, depending on how complex the data relationships are.

Standard Open Box In a standard open box, the user can select a row and press the **Open** button to load the associated window with the selected data object or press the **New** button to invoke the window with

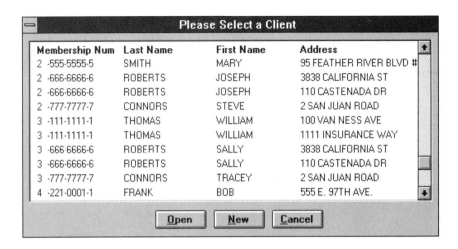

Membership Num	Last Name	First Name	Address
2 -555-5555-5	SMITH	MARY	95 FEATHER RIVER BLVD #
2 -666-6666-6	ROBERTS	JOSEPH	3838 CALIFORNIA ST
2 -666-6666-6	ROBERTS	JOSEPH	110 CASTENADA DR
2 -777-7777-7	CONNORS	STEVE	2 SAN JUAN ROAD
3 -111-1111-1	THOMAS	WILLIAM	100 VAN NESS AVE
3 -111-1111-1	THOMAS	WILLIAM	1111 INSURANCE WAY
3 -666-6666-6	ROBERTS	SALLY	3838 CALIFORNIA ST
3 -666-6666-6	ROBERTS	SALLY	110 CASTENADA DR
3 -777-7777-7	CONNORS	TRACEY	2 SAN JUAN ROAD
4 -221-0001-1	FRANK	BOB	555 E. 97TH AVE.

Figure 6.14   List of clients for selection in the standard open box.

a new, empty row. Figure 6.14 shows a list of clients from which one could be selected.

The Open box has the standard control menu and a descriptive title bar that can be used to invite the user to take action on a displayed object.

High Volume Open Box The high volume open box is similar to the standard open box except that a search criteria field is used to narrow the list of entries. A high volume open box should be used instead of a standard open box if the number of rows returned from the standard open box would be too large for performance or memory constraints (more than 200 rows is a good rule of thumb to use) and only one or two search criteria fields are necessary. Figure 6.15 shows an example in which the user can search on product description.

The tabular DataWindow in this open box narrows the selection set as the user keys each character into the search criteria field. If the DataWindow contains a large number of rows and the user must wait for the list to narrow after keying each character, the designer can remove this functionality and add a **Refresh** (or **Search**) button to the open box. In this scenario, the user would key data into the search criteria field and then press the **Search** button to narrow the list.

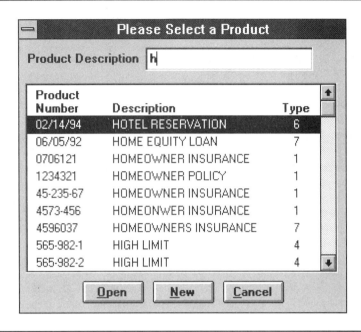

Figure 6.15   A high volume open box for product description selection.

Master/Detail

The master/detail model is designed for master/detail maintenance (implying a one-too-many relationship between two data entities). It extends the basic form functionality (see Figure 6.16) to include a list of detail records that can be opened or edited depending on required functionality. The master/detail window can be created with the detail portion of the window as either a pick list or editable.

This conversion has a descriptive title bar that clearly shows the data object retrieved. It also has a minimize button and a toolbar. It should also have a standard control menu and menu bar (with the File and Help menu items at a minimum). The DataWindow dw_main is display-only in this example, but it could be editable, if required.

List

The list model is designed for display/maintenance of multiple rows at the same time. Figure 6.17 shows a number of products displayed in a

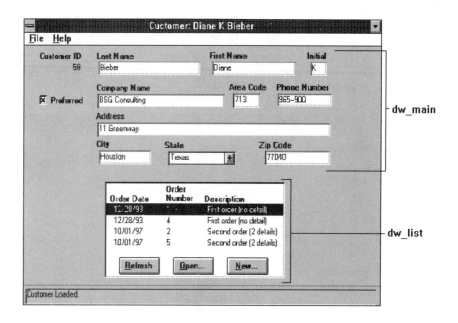

Figure 6.16   The master/detail model.

tabular DataWindow. The user is able to update any of the items in the screen while being able to see the other items.

This paradigm has a descriptive title bar that clearly shows the data object retrieved, a minimize button, and a toolbar. It should also contain a standard control menu and menu bar (with the File and Help menu items at a minimum). The tabular DataWindow is display-only in this example, but it could be editable, if required.

Form

The form model paradigm is designed for display/maintenance of a single record at a time. Figure 6.18 shows a single form that shows one product at a time.

This window has the standard control menu and a descriptive title bar clearly showing the data object that the user is currently viewing. It also has a minimize button and a basic menu bar.

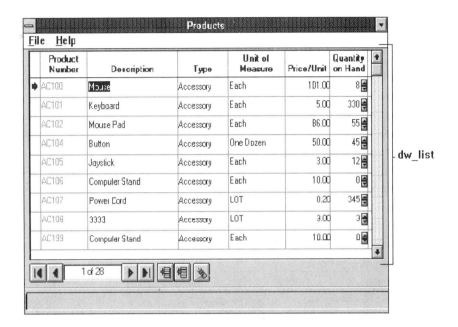

Figure 6.17   The list model showing a number of products displayed in a tabular DataWindow.

Dual Column

The dual column paradigm allows a user to select items from one column and add them to a second column. When the items are added to the second column, they are deleted from the first column.

Figure 6.19 shows a dual column window that allows values to be in both DataWindows. The user is able to add or subtract values from either side.

Tab-folder

This section will discuss different ways of implementing a tab-folder interface within PowerBuilder.

What is the Tab-folder Interface?   The tab-folder interface is a window interface designed after the tab-folder dividers used in traditional note-

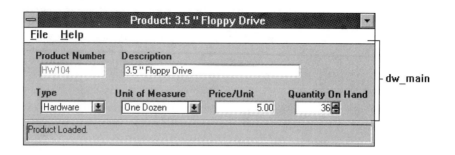

Figure 6.18   The form model paradigm.

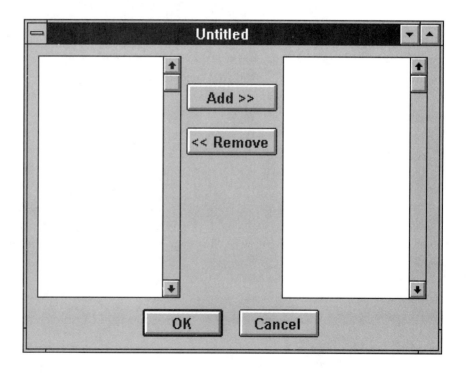

Figure 6.19   A dual column window.

books and binders. The Tab-folder interface has grown in popularity since some vendors have included the interface into their products. The tab-folder interface reduces the need for multiple windows in addition to providing a faster interface. The traditional graphical user interface (GUI) requires users to open multiple dialog boxes to access different information. With the tab-folder interface, multiple window controls can be grouped together and viewed by selecting a particular tab. In the example in Figure 6.20, to view detail auto, home, and life insurance information from a main insurance window that is already filled with data and controls, a new dialog box must be opened. With the tab-folder interface, each type of insurance and all the information associated with it can be grouped together and linked to different tabs within a single window.

Definitions: The following definitions are useful for understanding terms discussed in this section.

Tab—A tab is a single control that can be selected to view a logical grouping of information. By clicking a tab, the tab receives focus and the appropriate information gets presented.

Container—A container is an area on a window in which information is displayed.

Tier—A tier is a grouping of tabs. A tier can exist along any side of a container. Figure 6.20 shows a tier located along the top of the container. The Lotus Organizer interface shows tiers located along the right and left sides of the container.

Traditional Look and Feel (GUI) The diagram in Figure 6.21 shows that multiple windows are opened to access detail information about home, auto, and life insurance for a person.

The next section shows some different tab-folder interfaces. The interfaces are divided into single-tier and multi-tier tab-folder GUIs. Some of these interfaces are custom PowerBuilder interfaces and others are from third-party products.

Single-Tier Tab-folder Interface Figure 6.22 shows the GUI for a single-tier custom PowerBuilder tab-folder window. By selecting the different tabs along the top of the container, different information is presented within the container. This tab-folder GUI was developed in PowerBuilder.

Figure 6.23 shows the interface for a third-party tab-folder interface. This interface was developed by Lotus Corporation for their Lotus

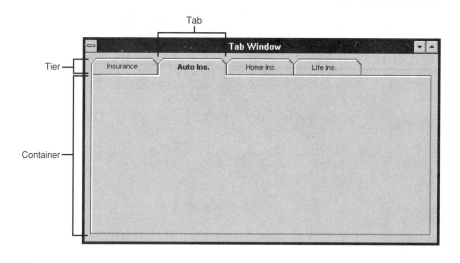

Figure 6.20   The tab-folder interface.

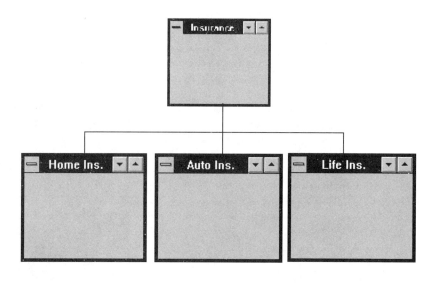

Figure 6.21   Multiple windows opened.

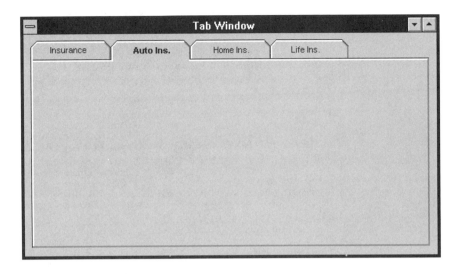

Figure 6.22   Single-tier custom PowerBuilder tab-folder window.

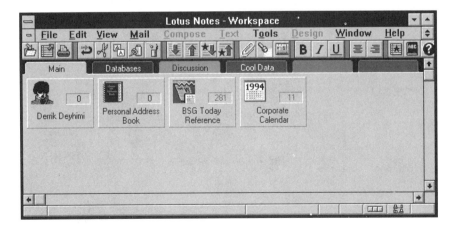

Figure 6.23   Third-party tab-folder interface.

Notes product. The main GUI difference in this tab-folder interface is the different colors for the unselected tabs.

The interface in Figure 6.24 was developed by Lotus Corporation for their Lotus Organizer product. This product, in addition to providing multicolor tabs, shows the tabs along the sides of the container. The selected tabs and every tab before them move from the right side of the container to the left side. This interface follows a more realistic tab-binder paradigm.

Multiple-Tier Tab-folder Interface Multi-tier tabs are a little different than single-tier tabs in that the different tiers are stacked on top of each other.

The Figure 6.25 shows a custom multi-tier tab-folder interface. In this drawing each tier has an additional tab associated with it. It is not

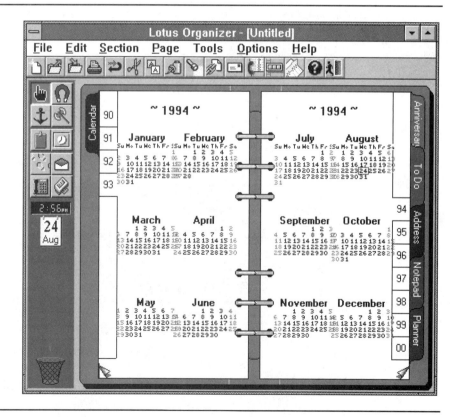

Figure 6.24   Lotus Corporation's interface with multicolor tabs along the sides.

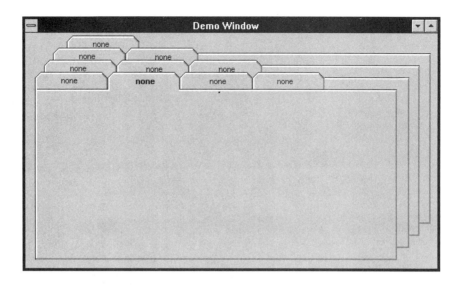

Figure 6.25   A custom multi-tier tab-folder interface.

a requirement of the multi-tier interface to produce this interface. When a tab from an upper tier is selected, different algorithms are used for bringing the selected tier to the front. The demo window in the figure uses a swapping algorithm for handling upper tier selections. Different vendors handle this process differently.

The third-party tab-folder interface in Figure 6.26 is from Microsoft Corporation's Word 6.0 product. This is an example of a third-party multi-tier tab interface.

In the next section the different design approaches associated with building a tab-folder interface within PowerBuilder will be discussed.

Tab-folder Interface in PowerBuilder When deciding to integrate a tab-folder GUI into PowerBuilder, one must first make the traditional build or buy decision. The following section discusses different options for developing a tab-folder interface. The features of a tab-folder control can include: multi-tier, keyboard maneuverability, GDI/resource/memory management, multiple tab colors, multiple tab sizes, application level and window level configuration, 3-D look and feel; finally, it must be reusable. There are many other things that must be looked at as part of tab-folder controls, but those previously mentioned are the major ones.

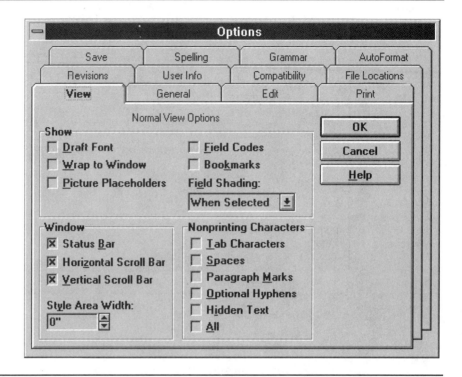

Figure 6.26   Microsoft's multi-tier tab interface.

Build Once the decision has been made to build tab-folders, another decision has to be made—that is to build tab-folder controls that can be reused across multiple windows and applications.

The Picture control solution (see Figure 6.27) will allow the developer to build a very simple and fast tab-folder interface for a window. The developer must realize that this solution is not the best solution, but it is the quickest one.

To implement this solution do the following:

1. Draw three bitmap files using a drawing tool such as Microsoft's PaintBrush. (see Figures 6.28–6.30)
2. Create a window in the PowerBuilder Window painter. (see Figure 6.31)
3. Place five Picture Object controls on the window and assign the unClickd.bmp file to the first four and the Container.bmp file to the fifth picture object (Figure 6.32).

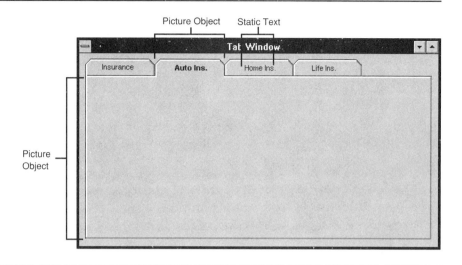

Figure 6.27   The Picture control solution.

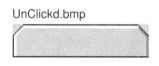

Figure 6.28   First bitmap file.

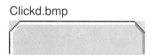

Figure 6.29   Second bitmap file.

Container.bmp

Figure 6.30   Third bitmap file.

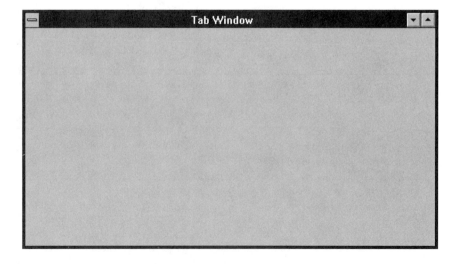

Figure 6.31   Creating a window.

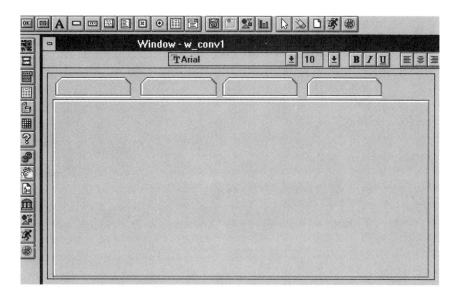

Figure 6.32   Five Picture Object controls.

4. Select a tab picture object and change the bitmap to the Clickd.bmp file. (see Figure 6.33)
5. Select the container picture object control and "send it to the back." (see Figure 6.34)
6. Align the tab controls and position them such that they barely cover the container. (see Figure 6.35)
7. Place four MultiLineEdit controls on the window and position them on top of the tabs. If necessary "bring the text to the front."

Hint: A MLE should be selected in order to support multiple lines of text.

---

8. Select appropriate verbiage for the four MLE controls and make the second text bold.
9. By now the "look" in Figure 6.38 has been created. What is remaining is the appropriate "feel." In the clicked event of the picture object the PictureName of the "clicked" tab must be changed to the Clickd.bmp and the previous tab must be changed to

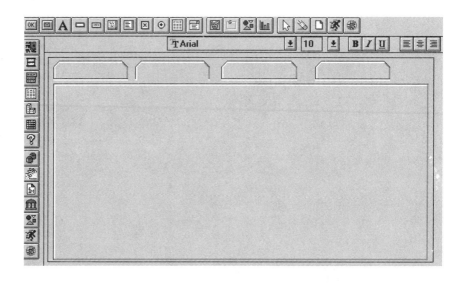

Figure 6.33   Select tab picture object and change bitmap.

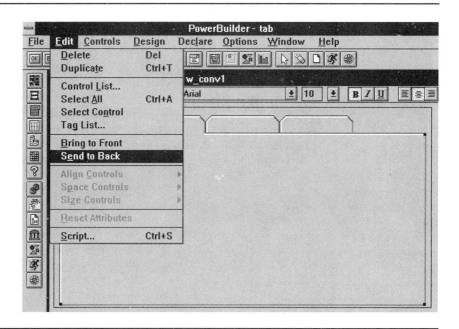

Figure 6.34   Select Container picture object control and "send it to the back."

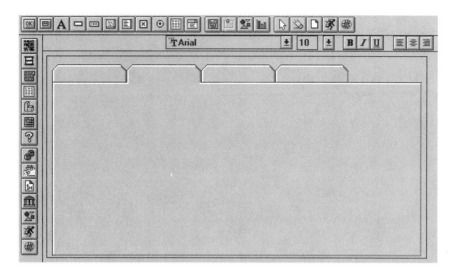

Figure 6.35   Align the tab controls.

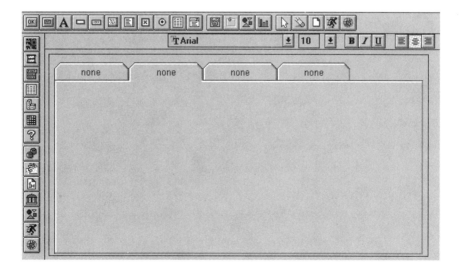

Figure 6.36   Place four MultiLineEdit controls.

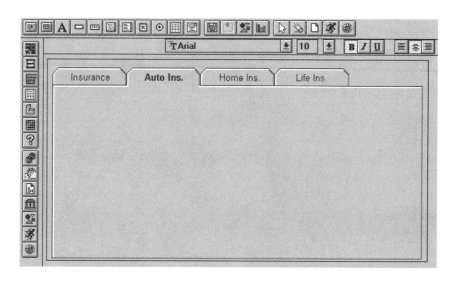

Figure 6.37   Select appropriate verbiage for MLE controls.

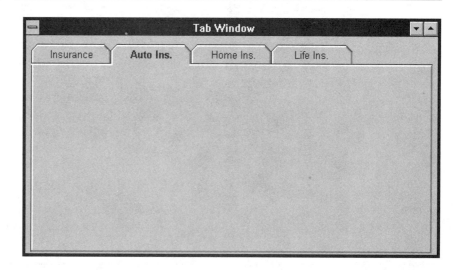

Figure 6.38   The final "look" of the Picture control solution.

UnClickd.bmp. In addition to the PictureName, the text for the "clicked" picture object must be made bold (weight = 700) and the previous text must be made normal/unbold (weight = 400).

Hint: To find out which picture object and static text were clicked last an instance structure could be kept and set each time a new tab is clicked.

---

10. Once the look and feel have been created, the detail information must be presented. Create a custom user object for each detail window (without border) and open it using the OpenUserObject function and pass it the X + n and Y + n coordinates of the container user object.

Hint: To prevent flickering when clicking across tabs, setredraw for the window to False and when all the processing is complete for that particular tab click, then setredraw for the window to True.

It is very important to build a generic tab-folder control such that it can be used by many developers and applications. In addition to the reuse, maintenance will be simple if the different applications inherit from a single tab-folder control. By inheriting the tab controls into an application any changes made to the tab controls will be reflected in different tab-windows for that application. There are two main approaches to building a tab-folder architecture. These two approaches will not be discussed in detail here. For a detailed discussion along with sample code please refer to Appendix D.

The tab-folder architecture shown in Figure 6.39 consists of a standard picture user object, a standard MultiLineEdit user object, two custom user objects, and a base window. The responsibility of the different controls is as follows:

Base Picture Tab UO (Standard UserObject)—Responsible for the processing of a single tab.

Base MLE Tab UO (Standard UserObject)—Responsible for the processing of the multiline edit.

Tab Tier Class (Custom UserObject)—Responsible for the processing of the tabs within a tier.

Customizable Tab Tier Class (Custom UserObject)—This is used for custom coding to the architecture per application.

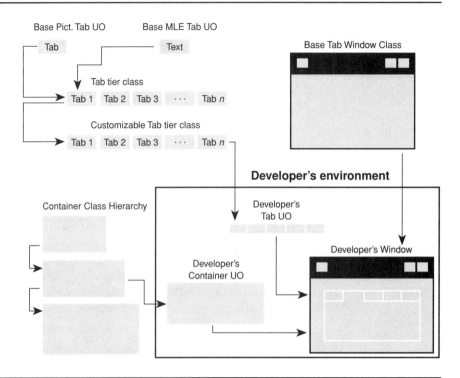

Figure 6.39   Tab-folder architecture using UserObjects.

Base Tab Window Class—Responsible for the processing of multiple tiers, sheet management, resource and memory management, and initialization.

The same functionality as just shown can be implemented using a DataWindow as the holder of the tabs and tiers. The main processing is done via the **dwGetObjectAtPointer**, **dwDescribe**, and **dwModify**. Again, a more detailed discussion of the different implementations of tab-folders in addition to the code to make it work is included in Appendix D.

Buy There are many tab control VBXs and DLLs that can be used as a VBX or external UserObject. There are also some class libraries/ODEs that support a tab-folder paradigm.

Note: For a more detailed discussion of tab-folders in addition to the code please refer to the Appendix E on tools and utilities.

CHAPTER 7

User Objects

PowerBuilder provides many mechanisms that enable developers to share code. Through the use of User Objects, PowerBuilder developers can develop reusable objects. Some of the more common objects of an application can be developed as User Objects and then shared throughout the application. An object placed on the appropriate window can be shared among one or more applications.

This chapter discusses the following aspects of User Objects:

- Types of User Objects
- Interfacing between windows and User Objects
- Dynamic User Objects
- Design considerations
- Third-party Controls (VBXs and DLLs)

TYPES OF USER OBJECTS

There are two main types of User Objects: visual and class. The visual User Object includes standard, custom, external, and VBX types. The class User Object includes standard and custom types.

Visual: Standard

Standard User Objects are used to extend the functionality of standard PowerBuilder objects. For example, if a CommandButton has certain functionality that is repeated in different places in an application, a standard CommandButton User Object can be created (see Figure 7.1).

To demonstrate, take an application that has two unrelated windows called w_window1 and w_window2. Each window has a close button that

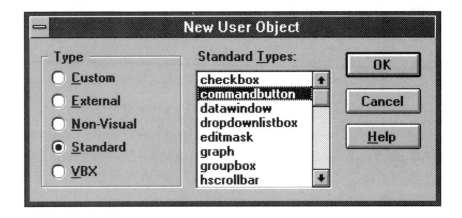

Figure 7.1   A standard CommandButton User Object.

closes the window. This can be done by creating a close CommandButton on each window or by having a single User Object CommandButton and placing it on each window. In the first case, the developer would have to write duplicate PowerScript in the clicked event of each CommandButton. In the case of creating a User Object, the developer would create the CommandButton User Object and place all the PowerScript within the User Object. Then, any window that needs the close functionality would add the User Object. This can be done as follows.

.   Create a window called w_window1 and w_window2, as shown in Figure 7.2.

Then create a CommandButton User Object, as shown in Figure 7.3.

Declare the following instance variable:

```
Window iwParent
```

In the Constructor event for the User Object, place the following PowerScript:

```
iwParent = Parent
```

In the Clicked event for the User Object, place the following PowerScript:

```
Close(iwParent)
```

Place the User Object on both (all) windows, as in Figure 7.5.

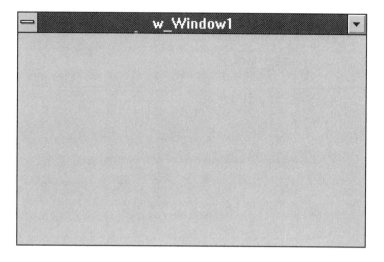

Figure 7.2   Created window.

Note: When a User Object is placed on a window, an inherited instance of the original User Object gets created. Looking more closely, the developer can see that the CommandButton (User Object on the window) is inherited from the original User Object (uo_close) (Figure 7.4).

This is a simple example, but it demonstrates how a standard User Object can extend the functionality of the base PowerBuilder objects. It also shows how sharing code can simplify both development and maintenance.

Figure 7.3   Created CommandButton User Object.

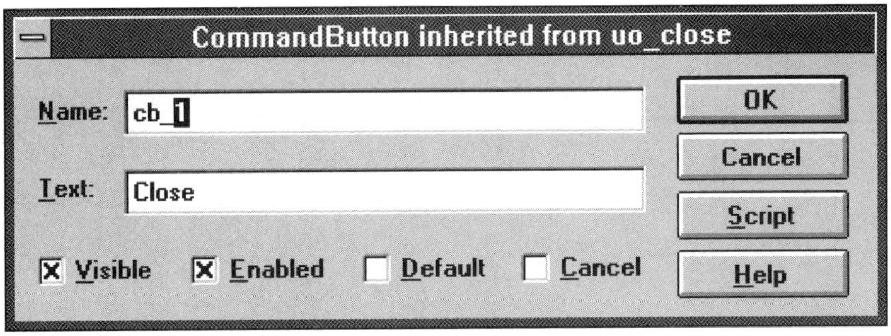

CommandButton inherited from uo_close

Name: cb_1

OK

Cancel

Text: Close

Script

X Visible   X Enabled   ☐ Default   ☐ Cancel

Help

Figure 7.4   CommandButton inherited from original User Object.

Note: This functionality could have been achieved using inheritance by placing the User Object CommandButton on a virtual window ancestor that both w_window1 and w_window2 were inherited from. This functionality could have also been achieved by creating a global function that contains all the code for closing a window, calling the function from the CommandButton.

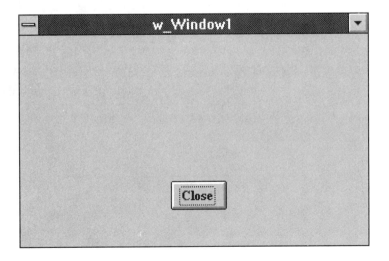

w_Window1

Close

Figure 7.5   User Object placed on the window.

Standard User Objects can be created with any of 16 standard PowerBuilder object classes:

CheckBox	ListBox
CommandButton	MultiLineEdit
DataWindow	Picture
DropDownListBox	PictureButton
EditMask	RadioButton
Graph	SingleLineEdit
GroupBox	StaticText
hScrollBar	vScrollBar

A standard User Object can be used to create many other types of objects. A few additional examples of standard User Objects follow.

ListBox(Directory Listing Object) This example shows how a ListBox User Object can be used to encapsulate some simple functionality for a DOS directory listing. Once this is done, the developer can simply drop the User Object on any window and that window is empowered with DOS directory listing capabilities. Here's how this User Object can be created.

The developer creates a ListBox standard User Object from the User Object painter and declares two instance variables for the filespec and filetype parameters of the **DirList( )** function.

```
UInt i_uiAllFiles = 16400
String i_sAllExtentions = "*.*"
```

Note: Within PowerBuilder, the **DirList** function has been prototyped as follows:

```
listboxname.DirList ( filespec, filetype {, statictext } )
```

filetype An integer representing the type of files you want to list in the ListBox:

0—Read/write files

1—Read-only files

2—Hidden files

4—System files

16—Subdirectories

32—Archive (modified) files

16384—Drives

32768—Exclude read/write files from the list

What's curious here is the recommended data type of integer. The last filetype option is 32768 and the largest positive integer value (16-bit data type) is 32767. Storing this field as an integer works, but it's quite confusing. If the developer would like to display only directory names in a ListBox, the following filetype parameter must be passed:

```
32768 + 16 = 32784
```

This value is stored in memory as –32752. What happens is that 32768 is stored as a negative 32768, so:

```
-32768 + 16 = 32752
```

Since this parameter does not need to store negative numbers, an unsigned integer data type could be used to make this less confusing. An unsigned integer data type still allocates only a 16-bit memory address, but it uses the 16th bit, which is reserved for the sign (+/–), for the positive number. So the largest value that can be stored in this address is 65535.

Place the following PowerScript in the constructor event:

```
this.DirList(i_sAllExtentions,i_uiAllFiles)
```

Place the following PowerScript in the double-clicked event:

```
String sItem
this.DirSelect(sItem)
this.DirList(sItem + i_sAllExtentions,i_uiAllFiles)
```

The last thing to do is to save the User Object and place it on the window (w_window1), as shown in Figure 7.6.

EditMask General purpose edit masks can be created for single line edits, such as a phone number edit mask. This edit mask can then be placed on any window to be used to input phone numbers. Edit masks both enforce data integrity and make input easier.

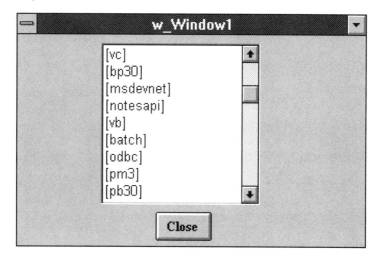

Figure 7.6   Placing the User Object on the window.

To create a phone number edit mask, the developer creates a standard Edit Mask User Object as shown in Figure 7.7. When the user double-clicks on the object, the Edit Mask window appears.

The Edit Mask window should be filled based on the window in Figure 7.8.

Then the User Object should be placed on the window as shown in Figure 7.9.

Then run the window by pressing Ctrl+W, and presto! It should look like the one in Figure 7.10.

DataWindow The standard User Object can also be used to create DataWindow control User Objects. This can be used for coding generic

Figure 7.7   Standard Edit Mask User Object.

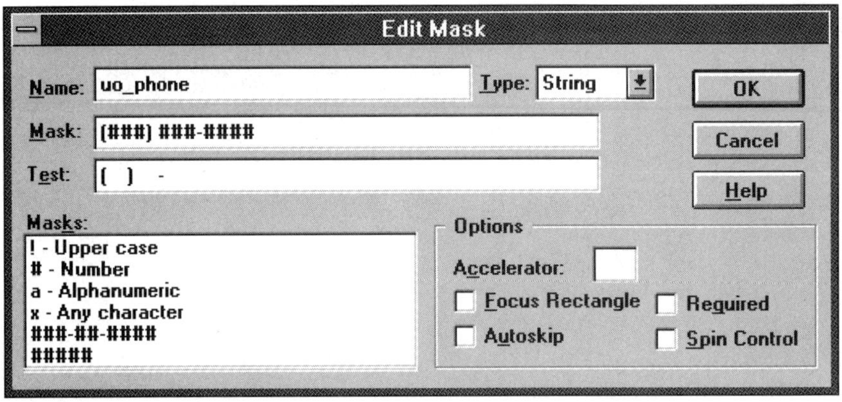

```
┌─────────────────────────────────────────────────────────────┐
│ ─                        Edit Mask                            │
├─────────────────────────────────────────────────────────────┤
│  Name: │ uo_phone                    │  Type: │ String  │▼│   ┌──────┐ │
│                                                           │  OK  │ │
│  Mask: │ (###) ###-####              │               └──────┘ │
│                                                         ┌──────┐ │
│  Test: │ (  )  -                     │                 │Cancel│ │
│                                                         └──────┘ │
│  Masks:                          ┌─Options──────────┐  ┌──────┐ │
│  ┌────────────────────────────┐  │                  │  │ Help │ │
│  │ ! - Upper case             │  │ Accelerator: □   │  └──────┘ │
│  │ # - Number                 │  │ □ Focus Rectangle  □ Required │
│  │ a - Alphanumeric           │  │ □ Autoskip  □ Spin Control    │
│  │ x - Any character          │  └──────────────────┘ │
│  │ ###-##-####                │                       │
│  │ #####                      │                       │
│  └────────────────────────────┘                       │
└─────────────────────────────────────────────────────────────┘
```

Figure 7.8   The filled Edit Mask window.

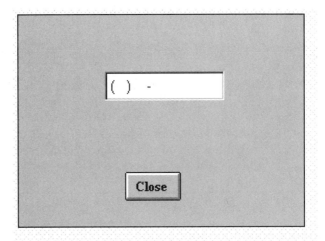

Figure 7.9   Place User Object on window.

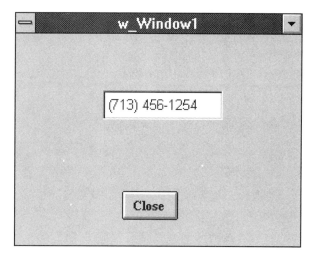

Figure 7.10   The completed window.

DataWindow-related functionality such as drag-and-drop, error check-ing, and DataWindow messages. To demonstrate this concept, an ex-ample of a standard DataWindow User Object is presented in the following discussion.

This example demonstrates how all field validation messages can be displayed on a window message line as opposed to a standard mes-sage box. Tag messages for each column are also be displayed on the message line. This functionality is generic for all editable DataWindows.

To do this, the developer first creates a standard DataWindow User Object and declares an instance variable of *type w_window* (w_window is the window from which w_window1 was inherited).

```
w_window i_wParent
```

Place the following PowerScript in the Constructor event of the User Object.

```
// Initialize the parent window to an instance variable, when the
// User Object is created. This is a generic method for determining the
// parent window of the User Object, at runtime.
i_wParent = parent
```

```
// Insert a blank row in the DataWindow User Object.
this.InsertRow(0)
```

Create a custom user event called Errormessage by selecting the Declare then User Events... menu options, as shown in Figure 7.11..

This window then displays the User Events window from which the custom event can be created, as shown in Figure 7.12.

The developer should place the following PowerScript logic in the ItemError event of the User Object:

```
// This line executes the PowerScript in the "errormessage" custom event.
TriggerEvent(this, "errormessage")

// Focus will then be set to this DataWindow
SetFocus(this)
```

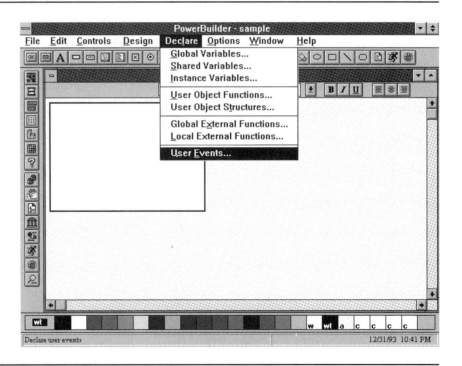

Figure 7.11   Creating the custom Errormessage user event.

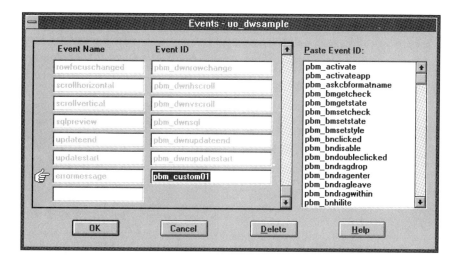

Figure 7.12   The User Events window.

```
// Supress the system error screen
SetActionCode(this,1)
```

Note: An ItemError event occurs when a field has been modified or loses focus and the current field does not pass the validation mask for its column.

Note: Here are some of the other action codes for the ItemError event:

0—(Default) Reject the data value and show a system error screen.

1—Reject the data value but do not show a system error screen.

2—Accept the data value.

3—Reject the data value but allow the focus to change.

Return to the w_window1 window and create the following functions:

f_DisplayErrMessage(string sErrMessage)

```
// When a validation error occurs, display the validation message
// on the message line.
st_message.text = sErrMessage
Beep(1)
```

f_DisplayTagMessage(string sMessage)

```
// Display the contents of sMessage string on the message line.
st_message.text = sMessage
```

In the Itemfocuschanged event, the following logic is coded:

```
String sMessage
// Retrieve the tag value for the current column.
sMessage = dwDescribe(this,GetColumnName(this)+".tag")

// If no tag value has been declared, PowerBuilder stores a "?" or a "!",
// then blank out the tag message variable.
if sMessage = "?" or sMessage = "!" then
      sMessage = ""
end if

// Call this function which should be declared in the parent window
// of the DataWindow User Object.
i_wParent.f_displayTagMessage(sMessage)
```

In the Errormessage custom event of the User Object, the following PowerScript is coded:

```
String sErrMessage

// Obtain the validation message for the current column.
sErrMessage = dwDescribe(this,GetColumnName(this)+".validationmsg")

// evaluate the message for embedded functions
sErrMessage = & dwDescribe(this,"evaluate("+sErrMessage+","&
+String(GetRow(this))+")")
If sErrMessage = "!" Then
      sErrMessage = "Field is invalid (no message supplied)."
End If

// Call the following function, in the parent window, and pass
// it the appropriate validation message.
i_wparent.f_displayErrMessage(sErrMessage)
```

Next, the developer creates a DataWindow object, with validation and tag values. Then the developer places the User Object on w_window1 and executes the window. Two things can be noticed. The first is that when each field gets focus, the tag message for that field gets displayed on the message line as shown in Figure 7.13. The second thing is that when a validation rule evaluates to False, the validation message displays on the message line and a beep sounds, indicating an error.

Note: When a validation error occurs, the developer can choose to change the color of the message text to red, to differentiate error messages from normal messages. This should be done in the **f_DisplayErrMessage** function of the w_window1 window. The following line of code can be used:

```
st_message.textColor = RGB(128,0,0)
```

Of course, if this is done, the **f_DisplayMessage** function must be changed to reset the message text color back to its original color.

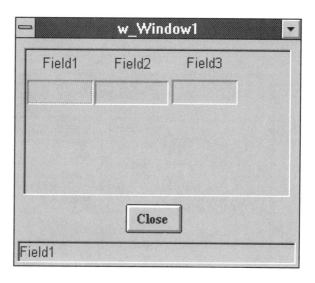

Figure 7.13   The executed window showing the tag message for Field1 on the message line.

Visual: Custom

Custom User Objects are meant to provide the developer with a level of flexibility above that of standard User Objects. With custom visual User Objects, the developer is not limited to the use of one PowerBuilder object. Rather, the developer can declare an object that includes multiple PowerBuilder objects. This allows creation of shared objects that are much more functional than those created as standard visual User Objects.

Note: Custom User Objects can be created not only with PowerBuilder objects but also with other standard or custom visual User Objects.

The following examples further clarify some uses of custom visual User Objects.

Directory Listing Object The example in Figure 7.14 is an extension of the ListBox example from the standard visual User Object section at the beginning of this chapter, showing a more powerful use of the directory listing object. The directory listing object in this example is given a more friendly interface. This object allows the user to find a file by selecting the appropriate directory paths. When the file is located, the user can perform specific processing on it. This is a generic object, which

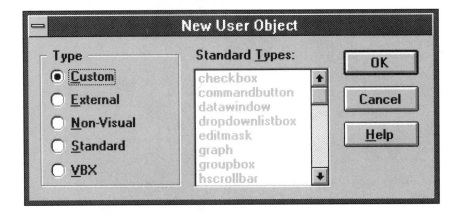

Figure 7.14   Custom User Object.

can be used on any window of an application by simply placing it on the window.

To create the custom User Object, the developer enters the custom User Object painter and creates the controls shown in Figure 7.15.

The developer places each of the objects shown in the figure on the User Object painter.

Note: This example uses the basic PowerBuilder objects, but each of the ListBoxes and DropDownListBoxes can be standard User Objects.

After the objects are placed on the User Object painter, the following PowerScript needs to be written in the User Object.

First declare the following User Object instance variables:

```
UInt i_uiFiles = 0     // Read/write files
UInt i_uiDirectories = 16 + 32768   // Only subdirectories
UInt i_uiDrives = 16384      // Drives
String i_sExtention = "*.*"  // All files
w_window i_wParent // Instance of the app. ancestor window
```

In the Constructor event of the User Object:

```
i_wParent = Parent
```

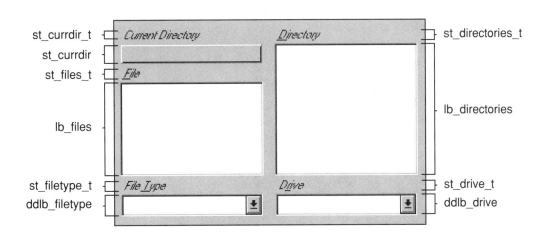

Figure 7.15   Controls that makeup the custom User Object.

Declare the following User Object external functions:

```
// change the directory to dirname
FUNCTION Int ChangeDir(String dirname) LIBRARY "pbdll.dll"
// get the current drive
FUNCTION String GetCurrDrive( ) LIBRARY "pbdll.dll"
```

These are two DLL functions that handle some of the application functionality. They are explained later in this example in conjunction with the C code for the DLL.

Place the following PowerScript in the Constructor event of ddlb_drive:

```
// list the drives in the ddlb
this.DirList (i_sExtention,i_uiDrives,st_currdir)
// select the current drive
this.SelectItem("[-"+GetCurrDrive( ),1)
```

In order to set the ddlb_drive field with the current drive, this function had to be created to retrieve the current drive. PowerBuilder does not provide a function to get this information. This is a custom DLL entry function, written in C.

```
/*******************************************************
     FUNCTION: LPSTR GetCurrDrive(void);
*******************************************************/
LPSTR FAR PASCAL GetCurrDrive(void)
{
     int idrive = 0;
     LPSTR lpszString = "z";
     char caDrive[] = {'a', 'b', 'c', 'd', 'e', 'f', 'g', 'h', 'i',
                       'j', 'k', 'l', 'm', 'n', 'o', 'p', 'q', 'r',
                       's', 't', 'u', 'v', 'w', 'x', 'y', 'z' };
     idrive = _getdrive( );
     caDrive[idrive] = '\0';
     lpszString = &caDrive[idrive - 1];
     return (LPSTR) lpszString;
}
```

Place the following PowerScript in the Selectionchanged event of ddlb_drive:

```
String sItem)
this.DirSelect(sItem)
lb_files.DirList (sItem+i_sExtention,i_uiFiles)
lb_directories.DirList(sItem,i_uiDirectories,st_currdir)
```

Place the following PowerScript in the Constructor event of lb_directories:

```
this.DirList(i_sExtention,i_uiDirectories,st_currdir)
```

Place the following PowerScript in the double-clicked event of lb_directories:

```
String sItem
this.DirSelect(sItem)

lb_files.DirList (sItem+i_sExtention,i_uiFiles)
If sItem = "..\" Then
        sItem = "sdfsdfdsf"
Else
        ChangeDir("..")
End If
this.DirList(sItem + i_sExtention,i_uiDirectories,st_currdir)
```

The following function has to be written to handle calling the PowerBuilder **DirList** function twice in a script. Because the **DirList** function actually changes the current directory to the directory selected, the current directory must be changed back to the previous position before executing the **DirList** function a second time.

```
/******************************************************
    FUNCTION: ChangeDir(const char *fname);
******************************************************/
int FAR PASCAL ChangeDir(const char *fname)
{
    return (int)_chdir(fname);
}
```

Place the following PowerScript in the Constructor event of lb_files:

```
this.DirList(i_sExtention,i_uiFiles)
```

Place the following PowerScript in the double-clicked event of lb_files:

```
String sPath
sPath = Trim( st_currdir.text)
If Not (Right(sPath,1) = "\") Then
      sPath = sPath + "\"
End If
i_wParent.f_ProcessFile( sPath + this.SelectedItem( ))
```

The **f_ProcessFile** function is a hook to the parent window. This function is for any processing that needs to be done on the selected file. For the purposes of this example, the function only displays the file in a message box. The prototype for this function looks like:

```
Int f_ProcessFile(String sPathFile)
```

The PowerScript in the function looks like:

```
MessageBox("File Processing for...", sPathFile)
Return 1
```

Place the following PowerScript in the Constructor event of ddlb_filetype:

```
this.SelectItem(1)
```

Place the following PowerScript in the Selectionchanged event of ddlb_filetype:

```
i_sExtention = Trim(Right(this.text,7))
lb_files.DirList (i_sextention,i_uiFiles)
```

The final step is to place the custom User Object on w_window1 and execute the window. The output should look like the one in Figure 7.16.

When the gator.ini file is double-clicked, the message box in Figure 7.17 appears.

Custom VCR Controls Figure 7.18 shows how a custom VCR control can be created to work with any DataWindow.

This custom VCR control can be developed and bound to any DataWindow at runtime simply by making one function call (see Figure 7.19). This VCR control can be developed as follows.

The following PowerScript logic should be placed in the different events of this custom User Object.

Declare the following two instance variables:

```
// variable indicating the total number of rows
UInt i_uiTotal
// variable pointing to the bound DataWindow control
DataWindow i_dwControl
```

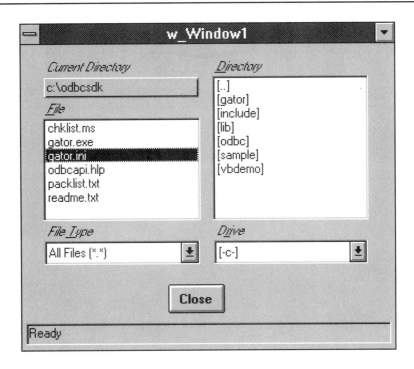

Figure 7.16   The executed window with the custom User Object.

Figure 7.17   The message box.

Figure 7.18   A custom VCR control.

In the Constructor event of the User Object, place the following PowerScript:

```
this.width = 1215
this.height = 165
```

Note: If the width and height of the User Object were to be set from an external object, it would be best to create two functions called:

f_SetWidth(Int iNewWidth)

f_SetHeight(Int iNewHeight)

The following five subroutines would be needed:

1. Private Subroutine **f_nextrow ( )**;

```
int iCurrent
iCurrent = Integer(st_current.text)
```

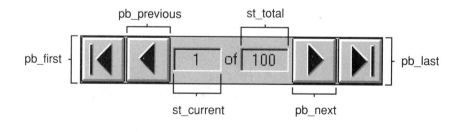

Figure 7.19   Controls used in a custom VCR control.

```
If iCurrent < Integer(st_Total.text) Then
        i_dwControl.ScrollToRow(iCurrent + 1)
        st_current.text = String(iCurrent + 1)
        SetFocus(i_dwControl)
End If
```

2.   Private Subroutine **f_previousrow ( )**;

```
int iCurrent
iCurrent = Integer(st_current.text)
If iCurrent > 1 Then
        i_dwControl.ScrollToRow(iCurrent - 1)
        st_current.text = String(iCurrent - 1)
        SetFocus(i_dwControl)
End If
```

3.   Private Subroutine **f_lastrow ( )**;

```
st_current.text = st_total.text
i_dwControl.ScrollToRow(i_uitotal)
SetFocus(i_dwControl)
```

4.   Private Subroutine **f_firstrow ( )**;

```
If i_uitotal > 0 Then
        st_current.text = "1"
        i_dwControl.ScrollToRow(1)
        SetFocus(i_dwControl)
End If
```

5.   Public Subroutine **f_init** (datawindow dwcontrol);

```
i_dwControl = dwControl
i_uiTotal = i_dwControl.RowCount( )
st_total.text = String(i_uiTotal)
```

These functions, except **f_init**, are called from the different PictureButtons within the VCR control.

The **f-FirstRow( )** function is called in the clicked event of the pb-first control. The **f-PreviousRow( )** function is called in the clicked event of the pb-previous control. The **f-NextRow( )** function is called in the clicked event of the pb-next control and the **f-LastRow( )** function is called in the clicked event of the pb-last control.

When the custom VCR User Object has been created, it can be placed on a window with a DataWindow. The last step is binding the two controls together. By calling the User Object's **f_init** function and passing it the DataWindow, the two controls will be bound at runtime. The **f_init** function must be called after the **Retrieve( )** function of the bound DataWindow control has been called. For example:

- dw_name is the name of the DataWindow to be bound
- uo_vcr is the name of the custom VCR User Object control

In the open event of the w_window1 window, the **f_init( )** function should be called after the **Retrieve( )** function.

```
dw_name.Retrieve( )
uo_vcr.f_init(dw_name)
```

Note: It is not necessary for the **f_init( )** function to be called from the open event. The only requirement is that it must be called after the **Retrieve( )** function of the bound DataWindow.

At this point, the window can be executed. The end result looks like Figure 7.20.

CommandButton with Colored Text At times, developers may want to change the text color of specific CommandButtons or PictureButtons. Unfortunately, PowerBuilder does not permit developers to alter the color of the standard CommandButtons or PictureButtons. Consequently, the developer will have to resort to other means to accomplish this task. Here are some options:

- Find out if there are any third-party VBXs that allow text color to be changed.
- Find out if there are any third-party DLLs that allow text color to be changed.
- Write your own VBX or DLL.
- Ask a friend to write a VBX or DLL for you.
- Use the VBX or DLL shipped with this book.
- Create a custom User Object to accomplish this task.

If the option to create a custom User Object is selected, this is how it can be done.

Use a custom User Object with a CommandButton (or Picture-Button) and a static text. Each time the CommandButton is pressed

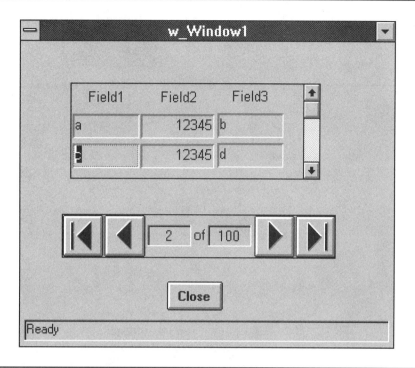

Figure 7.20   The executed window.

down, move the static text x positions to the right and y positions down. Each time the CommandButton is released (or pressed up), move the static text back to its original position. (see Figure 7.21)

When the button is pressed down, the st_text is moved x positions along the x-axis and y positions along the y-axis. The result looks like Figure 7.22.

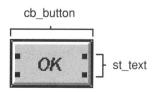

Figure 7.21   Using the CommandButton with static text.

Figure 7.22 Results of movement of the static t,ext.

Declare two instance variables to store the initial X and Y positions of st_text.

```
UInt i_uiX
UInt i_uiY
```

In the Constructor event of st_text, initialize the instance variables.

```
i_uiX = this.x
i_uiY = this.y
```

Declare two user events for cb_button shown in Figure 7.23.

The lbuttondown and lbuttonup user events trap the Windows message associated with pressing the left mouse button down (on cb_button) and then releasing the left button (on cb_button), respectively.

Place the following PowerScript in the lbuttondown event:

```
// moves the st_text 8 PowerBuilder units along the x-axis
st_text.x = st_text.x + 8

// moves the st_text 7 PowerBuilder units along the y-axis
st_text.y = st_text.y + 7
```

Place the following PowerScript in the lbuttonup event:

```
// reset the st_text back to its original X and Y coordinates
st_text.x = i_uiX
st_text.y = i_uiY
```

One more event has to be created. From the User Object painter create the Clickme custom event shown in Figure 7.24.

When this custom event has been created, the following PowerScript logic must be placed in the clicked event of cb_button:

```
// Trigger the clickme event of the parent, which is the User Object
// itself.
Parent.TriggerEvent("clickme")
```

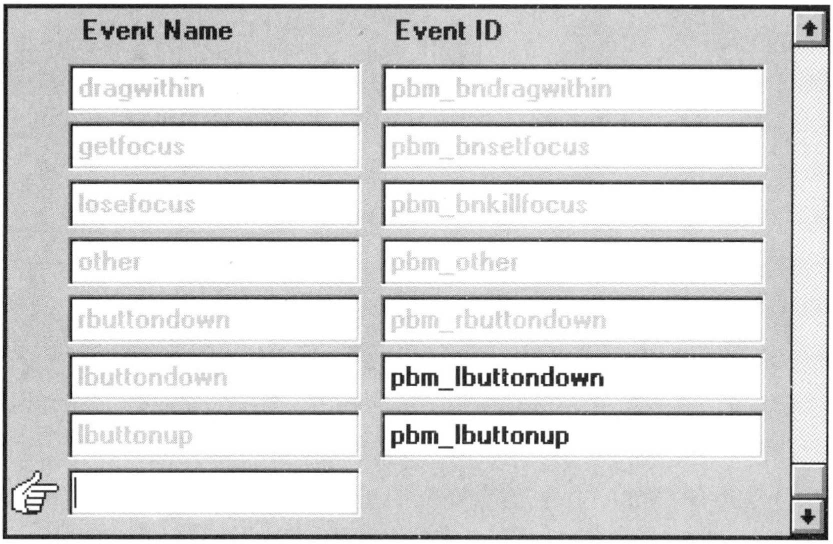

Figure 7.23   Declaring two user events.

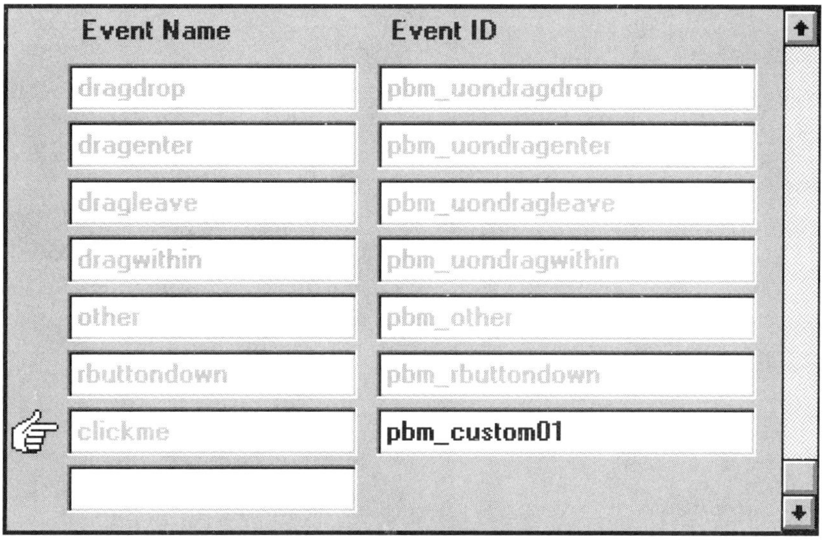

Figure 7.24   The Clickme custom event.

When the User Object is placed on the window, application-specific PowerScript can be placed in the Clickme event of the object, from the Window painter. For this example, the following code will be placed in the Clickme event:

```
MessageBox("Huh huh! Huh huh!","That's cool!")
```

Note: The Clickme event has to be created because events of each individual control, used to build the custom control, can't be accessed from within the instance of the User Object. In short, because there is not a clicked event for the User Object, one has to be simulated. In standard User Objects, the instance of the user object inherits all the events of the original object. In custom user objects, because there can be multiple controls, the individual events are not inherited. (For further explanation and illustrations, see the Standard and Custom User Object Class Hierarchy section later in this chapter.)

Upon execution the message box in Figure 7.25 is displayed.

Visual: External

The third type of visual User Object, the external User Object (see Figure 7.26), is one of PowerBuilder's hooks to the outside world. PowerBuilder developers can either write their own custom control DLL to be used as an external User Object or use DLLs that have been written by third-

---

Figure 7.25　　The message box.

party vendors. There are many third-party vendors that have written custom control DLLs, which can be used within PowerBuilder by creating an external User Object. One popular PowerBuilder third-party custom control DLL, the cpalette.dll, is provided by Blaise Computing, Inc. This DLL has a number of different class objects that can be declared as PowerBuilder external User Objects. This section discusses some of these object classes.

Following are some of the classes defined in the cpalette DLL.

Class	*Description*
cpButton	Similar to a CommandButton except the text can be different colors. The text also has a shadow.
cpCanvas	3-D background
cpCheckBox	3-D Checkbox with blue colors
cpMeter	Meter window that monitors progress (percent complete)
cpRadioButton	3-D Radiobutton with blue colors
cpStatic	3-D static text. This object has both a 3D background and text.

The cpalette DLL was very useful with previous versions of PowerBuilder in which 3-D controls were not an option. In PowerBuilder 3.0, most of the controls have 3-D options. There are some cpalette classes

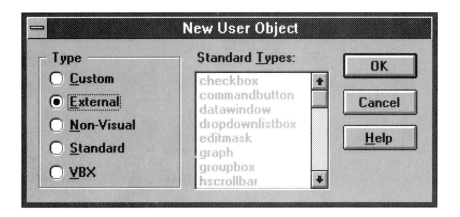

Figure 7.26   The external User Object.

that are still useful, however. These classes are discussed in more detail in the following sections.

cpCheckBox (see Figure 7.27) This is a simple 3-D Checkbox, except the check mark is a different color and it looks like a check mark rather than an X (see Figure 7.28).

This User Object has two PowerScript functions, **GetState( )** and **SetState(int)**.

The **GetState** function returns a zero (0) if the Checkbox is not clicked and a one (1) if it is checked. The **SetState** function sets the state of the checkbox to checked (1) or unchecked (0), programmatically. The only reason a developer would choose to use this User Object is if its look and feel are preferred to the standard PowerBuilder Checkbox.

cpMeter This User Object is a status meter bar (see Figure 7.29). It can be used as a popup window when specific application tasks take a while to complete. An example of such a task would be the startup process of an application. Usually, as part of the application startup process, a connection to the database has to be established, application security

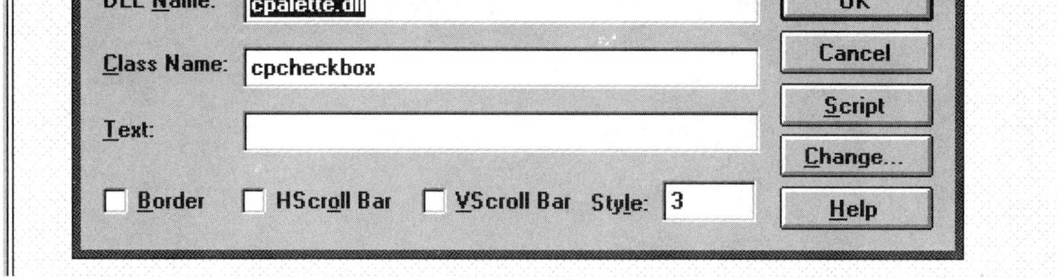

Figure 7.27   The cpCheckBox class.

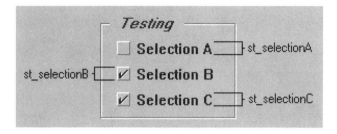

Figure 7.28   3-D CheckBox.

has to be checked, and static code table items are preloaded (for performance reasons). This process may require the user to sit idle. When a user has to sit idle for a long time, a status meter popup window can be displayed to give the user an idea of how the task is progressing. A typical status meter popup window looks like the one in Figure 7.30.

The meter User Object has one PowerScript function called **Set_Position**(int iPosition). The iPosition parameter is the value that

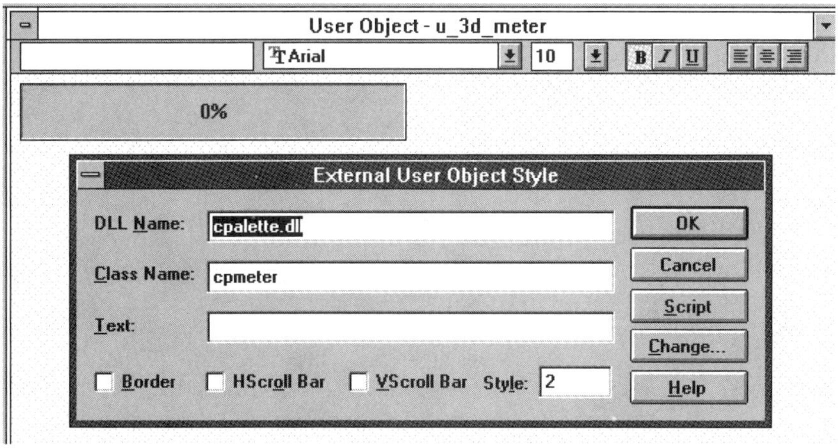

Figure 7.29   The cpMeter User Object.

Figure 7.30   A typical status meter popup window.

should be displayed on the meter bar. This requires numerous calls to the **Set_Position** function.

cpRadioButton (see Figure 7.31) The cpRadioButton displays the actual radiobutton in blue instead of the unchangeable black color of the PowerBuilder radiobutton.

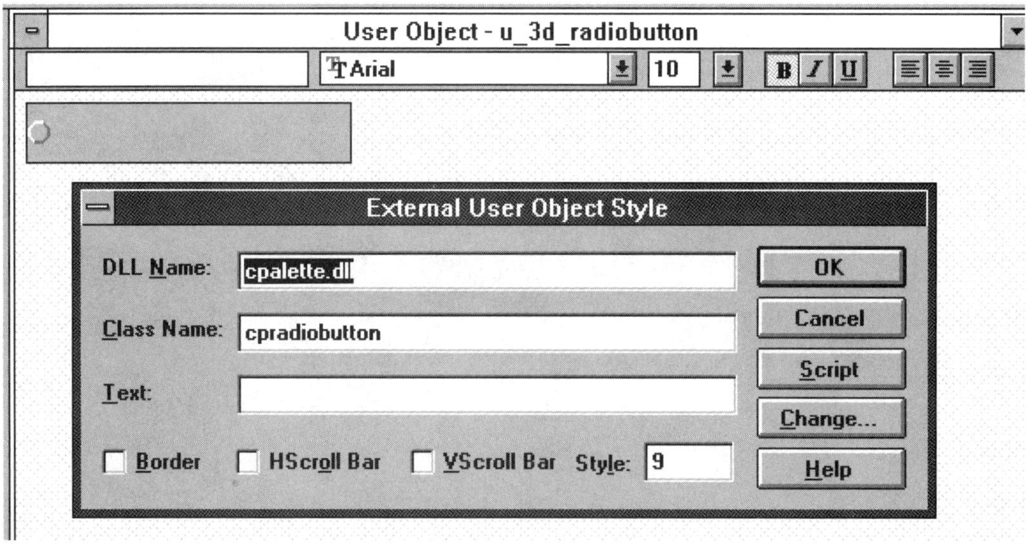

Figure 7.31   The cpRadioButton User Object.

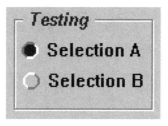

Figure 7.32   The RadioButton.

In conclusion, external User Objects are useful if there is an external DLL class of object that provides functionality that the PowerBuilder objects do not. External User Object DLLs can be developed by application developers, but most of the functionality needed is possible to achieve from within PowerBuilder.

Visual: VBX

VBX controls are designed and developed around Microsoft's Visual Basic Windows application development tool. Over the years, many third-party vendors have developed VBX controls to work with Visual Basic. Since VBX controls have become so popular and useful, application development tools such as PowerBuilder have created hooks so that developers can use VBX controls in their applications. From within PowerBuilder, VBX controls can be used by creating a VBX User Object, shown in Figure 7.33.

VBX controls work similarly to external User Objects, except that VBX controls declare *.vbx files instead of DLLs. It is useful to be familiar with as many third-party VBX controls as possible. Such familiarity may save developers many hours of having to develop objects and functionality that already exist as a VBX or DLL. For a list of third-party controls contact vendors like Microsoft and Powersoft.

This book will not get into VBX controls since Powersoft's support for VBX controls is limited and also since VBXs will soon become obsolete with the introduction of OCX controls. The authors of this book are looking forward to having OCX control support in PowerBuilder—maybe even in the next version?

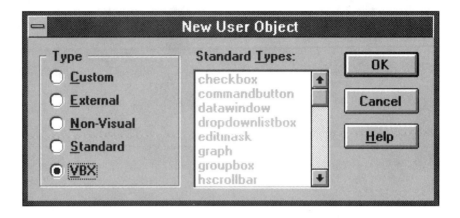

Figure 7.33   Creating a VBX User Object.

Class: Custom

Non-visual objects are objects with encapsulated functions, structures, and events that provide functionality to an application that is not visible to the user. (Refer to Figure 7.34) In an object-oriented environment, non-visual User Objects are similar to classes. Examples of different implementations of non-visual objects include:

- Playing wave files
- Print functionality
- Clipboard functionality
- Commandline functionality
- DDE functionality
- eMail functionality
- NOS functionality
- SystemResource functionality

Although this section discusses different implementations of nonvisual objects, they are not developed here. Many of these objects are explained in detail (with working code examples) in other chapters.

Multimedia Object A non-visual object can be created to implement much of the functionality available through the Windows multimedia API. The main Windows multimedia API is the mmsystem.dll (there

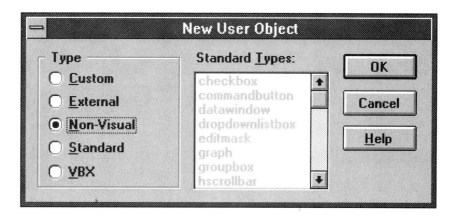

Figure 7.34   Highlighting the non-visual type of User Objects.

are others but this is the primary one). A non-visual User Object ancestor tree for handling many of the multimedia capabilities available using the mmsystem API might look like the one in Figure 7.35.

The u_MMBase User Object would have generic functions such as checking for the appropriate drivers, file i/o operations, and other generic functionality that would be common among the different multimedia objects.

One of the main functions in the u_MMAudio non-visual User Ob-

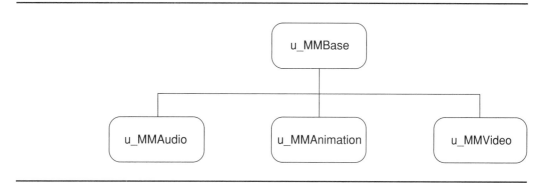

Figure 7.35   A non-visual User Object ancestor tree using the mmsystem API.

ject would be to play a wave file. A PowerBuilder non-visual object that plays a wave file can be created by doing the following.

Declare a local external function in the User Object.

```
Function Boolean SndPlaySound(String sWaveFile, Int iflags) &
                    Library "mmsystem.dll"
```

Declare a local PowerScript function called **Boolean f_PlayWave** (String sWavePathFile).

```
return SndPlaySound(sWavePathFile,0)
```

Simply calling the f_PlayWave(sWavePathFile) and passing it a wave file plays the sound on the wave file. This is just one example of a multimedia function. Many others can be written and included within non-visual User Objects.

Print Functionality Some of the functions that could be included in a User Object for doing all kinds of print i/o would be:

Member Functions	Description
f_dwPrint(DataWindow dwName, Integer iCount)	Print from 1 to N DataWindows.
f_Print(String sFilePathName,String sFileType, Integer iCount)	Print from 1 to N files of type (BMP or TXT).
f_getAvailablePrinters( )	Return an array of printer info structure. This function gets the name, drive map, and device map for each printer.
f_setDefaultPrinter( )	Pass the structure of the printer that needs to be set as default printer.
f_setPrintOrientation(Integer iStyle)	Dynamically change the orientation of a print setup from landscape to portrait and vice versa.

Clipboard Functionality A clipboard non-visual User Object would handle interfacing with the Windows clipboard IPC mechanism. Some of the functions that this User Object could contain would be:

Member Functions	Description
f_CaptureScreen	Get a snapshot of the screen.
f_ReadImage	Read an image from a file or database.
f_WriteClipboard	Write an image or text to the clipboard.
f_ReadClipboard	Read information that is stored in the clipboard.

Command Line Functionality A command line User Object could provide functionality to parse command line arguments. This User Object could have functions like **ARGV[]** and **ARGC** from the C programming language.

The equivalent PowerBuilder functions are:

f_ArgV(int iIndex)—This function returns the iIndexth command line argument.

The PowerScript for the **f-ArgV( )** function is:

```
Pointer pOldPointer

pOldPointer = SetPointer(hourGlass!)
String sParm

sParm = CommandParm( )
If s_parm = "" Then
        SetPointer(p_old_pointer)
        return ""
Else
        String  sParms[]
        Integer iPosition
        Integer iParmCounter = 1
        Integer iLength
        Do
                sParm = Trim(sParm)
                iLength = Len(sParm)
                iPosition = Pos(sParm," ")
                If iPosition = 0 Then
                        iPosition = iLength
                End If
                sParms[iParmCounter] =
Trim(Left(sParm,iPosition))
                sParm = Right(sParm,(iLength - iPosition))
                iParmCounter = iParmCounter + 1
        Loop Until (Len(sParm) < 1)
```

```
                    SetNull(sParms[iParmCounter])
                    If iIndex >= (iParmCounter) Then
                            SetPointer(pOldPointer)
                            return ""
                    Else
                            SetPointer(pOldPointer)
                            return sParms[(iIndex)]
                    End If
            End If
```

f_ArgC( )—Returns the number of the command line argument. The PowerScript for the **f-ArgC( )** function is:

```
Pointer pOldPointer

pOldPointer = SetPointer(hourGlass!)
String      sParm

sParm = CommandParm( )
If sParm = "" Then
    SetPointer(pOldPointer)
    return 0
Else
    Integer      iPosition
    Integer      iParmCounter = 0
    Integer      iLength
    Do
        sParm = Trim(sParm)
        iLength = Len(sParm)
        iPosition = Pos(sParm," ")
        If iPosition = 0 Then
                iPosition = iLength
        End If
        sParm = Right(sParm,(iLength - iPosition))
        iParmCounter = iParmCounter + 1
    Loop Until (Len(sParm) < 1)
    SetPointer(pOldPointer)
    Return iParmCounter
End If
```

DDE Functionality A DDE User Object could be set up as multiple inherited User Objects. For example, the shared functionality, such as connecting and disconnecting to the DDE server, could be encapsulated functions of the base class. Where specific DDE functionality is needed, separate DDE User Objects would be declared as descendants of the main DDE User Object (see Figure 7.36).

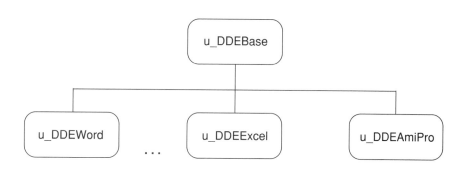

Figure 7.36   Separate DDE User Objects declared as descendants of the main DDE User Object.

The functionality in the descendants would include the specific functions needed to exchange data and execute commands on the DDE server.

eMail Functionality An eMail object could include functions to log in, validate an eMail address, display an address list, send mail, attach file(s), retrieve a count of new mail, and display mail (read or unread).

NOS Functionality A NOS User Object could include functions to get the network id, get the workstation id, get servers, get mapped drives, get mapped printers, and the like.

SystemResource Functionality A custom class User Object can be used to encapsulate system resource functionality. In this example the Windows SDK functions can be defined as local external functions and three PowerScript methods/functions can be written to retrieve GDI, memory, and resource values. What follows is an example of how system resources can be used in a sample About dialog box.

The About box in Figure 7.37 displays the percentage of free GDI, resources, and the amount of free memory. Most About box windows display a snapshot of the free resources from when the About box window was first opened. The About box window refreshes the values by using the timer event for the window. The window in the figure gets this information by using the System Resource User Object.

The Systeminfo User Object can be created by defining a custom class User Object. A custom class User Object is actually a non-visual object as shown in Figure 7.38.

The first thing that must be done is to declare two SDK local exter-

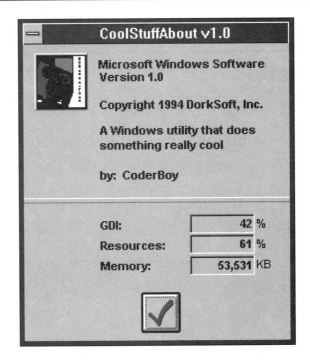

Figure 7.37   The About dialog box.

nal functions, one from the user library and the other from the kernel library, as shown in Figure 7.39.

The next thing that must be done is to declare two instance variables, as shown in Figure 7.40. These variables will be used as parameters for the **GetFreeSystemResources(...)** function. If the G_GDI is passed, then the percentage of free GDI resources is returned. If G_USER is passed into the function, then the percentage of free user resources is returned.

Next, the three User Object functions shown in Figure 7.41 must be declared. These are PowerScript functions that make calls to the system resource SDK function.

The **GetFreeMem** function returns the amount of free memory in kilobytes, as shown in Figure 7.42.

The **GetFreeUser** function returns the percentage of free user resources, as shown in Figure 7.43.

The **GetFreeGDI** function is the same as the **GetFreeUser** func-

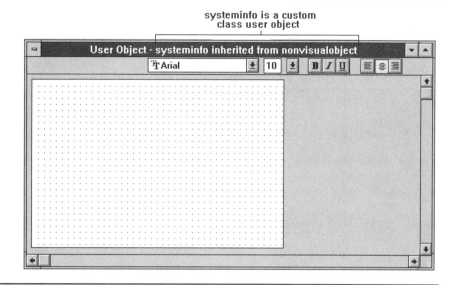

Figure 7.38   Defining a custom class User Object.

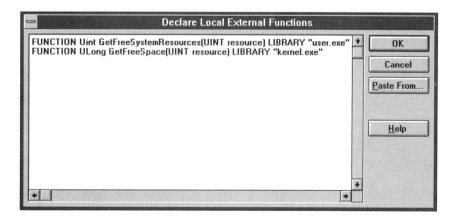

Figure 7.39   Declare two SDK local external functions.

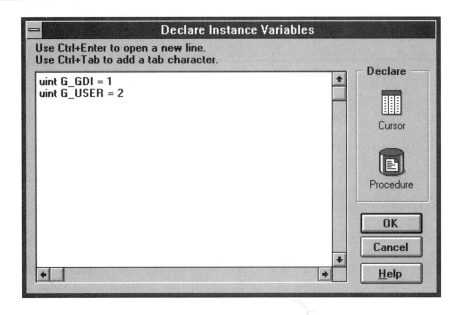

Figure 7.40 Declare two instance variables.

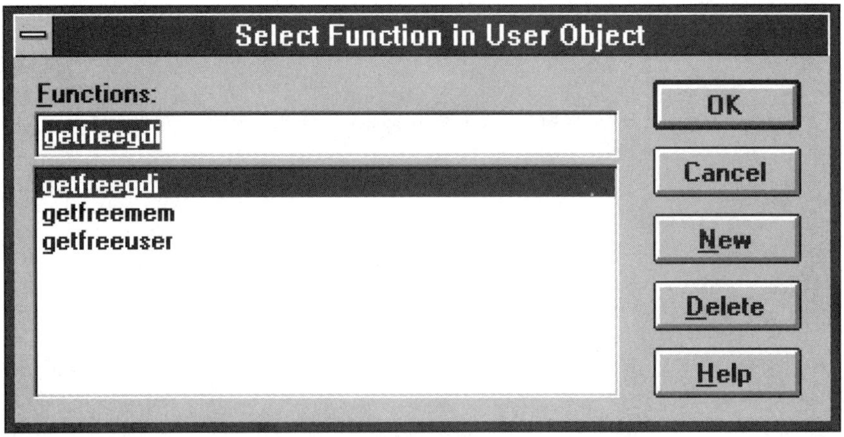

Figure 7.41 Declare three User Object functions.

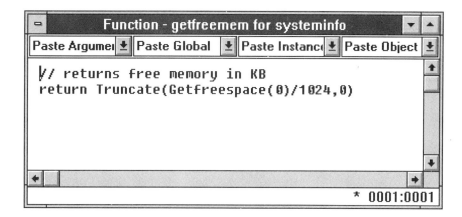

Figure 7.42   The **GetFreeMem** returns amount of free memory in kilobytes.

tion except the *G_GDI* variable is passed in as a parameter and it returns the percentage of free GDI resources.

In the About dialog-box window the following PowerScript must be added to reuse the Systeminfo User Object.

First, the following instance variable must be declared.

```
systeminfo sysinfo
```

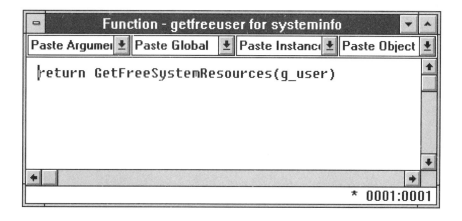

Figure 7.43   The **GetFreeUser** function returns percentage of free user resources.

The following PowerScript is in the Window Open event:

```
sysinfo = create systeminfo
Timer(.1)
```

The following PowerScript is in the Window Timer event:

```
timer(5)
st_memory.text = String(sysinfo.GetFreeMem( ),"#,###")
st_gd1.text = String(sysinfo.GetFreeGDI( ))
st_resources.text = String(sysinfo.GetFreeUser( ))
```

The About dialog-box example is an example of how a custom class User Object can be reused.

Class: Standard

The latest addition to the User Object family of types is the standard class User Object. The standard class User Object permits developers to build non-visual User Objects of the PowerBuilder non-visual datatypes shown in Figure 7.44.

A non-visual standard User Object of the class shown in the figure can be declared and then customized. Also, this version of PowerBuilder enables the developer to modify the default global variables, as shown in Figure 7.45.

With this new feature the developer can create any of the previously mentioned standard class User Objects. For example, the developer can add extra variables to the Default Message object to track additional error information. The developer can also create a standard Transaction Class User Object and define local external functions for DBMS RPCs.

To create the standard Transaction Class User Object do the following.

1. In the User Object painter, select New.
2. Select Standard from New User Object dialog.
3. Select transaction from select standard class type dialog.
4. Declare local external function.

```
function double spb8(ref double prm) rpcfunc subroutine
mypt(string prm) rpcfunc ALIAS FOR "pbdbms.put_line" subroutine
mygt(ref string prm, ref integer status) rpcfunc ALIAS FOR
                        "pbdbms.get_line"
```

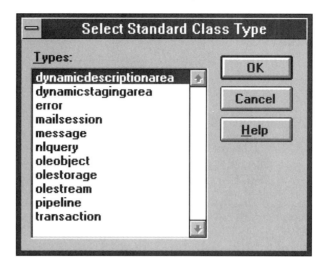

Figure 7.44   PowerBuilder non-visual datatypes of the standard class User Object type.

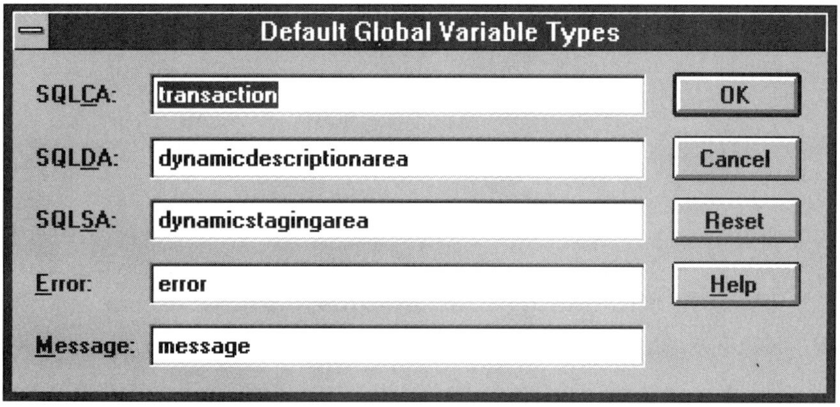

Figure 7.45   Modifying the default global variables.

5. Change global transaction data type to the name of the standard Transaction Class User Object, from the application painter.
6. From the PowerScript painter, code function in PowerScript.

```
int myresult=5
myresult=sqlca.spm8(myresult)
if sqlca.sqlcode <> 0 then
        messagebox("error", sqlca.sqlerrtext)
end if
```

Here is another example of the transaction User Object. Create a standard transaction class User Object with a function called **ODBCConnect( )**. The PowerScript for the function should look like:

```
this.dbms = "ODBC"
this.dbparm = "ConnectString='DSN=Powersoft Demo
DB;UID=dba;PWD=sql'"
testtrans trans
trans = this
connect using trans;
return this.SQLCode
```

This PowerScript is just an example, but all the processing for ODBC transaction processing can be located within this function. Also, the processing for obtaining the dbparm settings can also be handled from this User Object. Once the User Object has been created it can be saved as testtrans. In the application window event the following PowerScript can be created to connect to an ODBC data source using the developed function.

```
testtrans trans
trans = create testtrans
If trans.odbcconnect( ) = -1 Then
      // Error processing
End if
```

If the developer changes the global transaction SQLCA variable from transaction to testtrans then the following PowerScript can be substituted for the preceding Window PowerScript.

```
If SQLCA.odbcconnect( ) = -1 Then
// Error processing
End if
```

There are many other customizations that can be done not only to the standard transaction class User Object, but also to all the others.

INTERFACING BETWEEN WINDOWS AND USER OBJECTS

As mentioned throughout this book, it is very important to modularize code into objects so the objects can be reusable in other parts of the system (or other systems). When placing shared User Objects on windows, some form of communication between the window and the object must take place. Communication between a window and a User Object can be done by:

- Referencing the window generically
- Executing functions
- Adding User Objects to the window painter toolbar

Referencing the Window Generically

When developing generic User Objects, it is often necessary to reference the parent window on which the User Object will reside. There are a number of ways of referencing the parent window from a User Object.

- Hard-coding
- Passing the window name from the window (using this)
- Referencing the window from the constructor event (using the parent)

Hard-coding The simplest, but worst, method of referencing the parent window from a User Object is hard-coding the window name from the User Object. The main reason this is bad is because it requires developers either to use the User Object in windows having a standard name or to maintain multiple instances of the User Object.

For the developer who decides to hard-code the window name, here are three different implementations.

Method 1 Reference the hard-coded window name each time it's needed. For example, create a window called w_window1 with two standard User Objects, as shown in Figure 7.46.

From the User Object painter, place the following PowerScript in the clicked event of the uo_max button:

```
w_window1.WindowState = Maximized!
```

From the User Object painter, place the following PowerScript in the clicked event of the uo_restore button:

```
w_window1.WindowState = Normal!
```

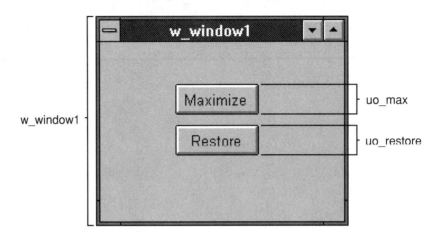

Figure 7.46   The created window w_window1 with two standard User Objects.

This works except when the developer decides to place the User Objects on another window. If the developer would like these User Objects on another window, the hard-coded window name has to be changed and each User Object has to be saved under another name. Too many copies of an object can lead to resource problems. This example only has one line of PowerScript behind each User Object, but if the User Object were more complex, the name of the window would be hard-coded in multiple places (events and functions) of the User Object. This would be a maintenance nightmare.

Method 2 The second method of referencing the parent window from a User Object is an extension of the first in that the window name is still hard-coded, but it's done in one location. The developer creates an instance variable of type Window. The instance variable is then initialized in the constructor event of the User Object.

Declare an instance variable:

```
Window i_wParent
```

In the constructor event of the User Object, initialize the instance variable:

```
i_wParent = w_window1
```

Throughout the events and functions of the User Object, the window can be referenced using the *i_wParent* variable. Although this second method is inefficient, at least it binds the window name to the instance variable in one place; this is certainly preferable to doing so in every function and event that the parent window needs to reference. This method is also a maintenance nightmare, however, because if any code needs to be added to the User Object, it must be added to all the copies of the User Objects that have been saved under another name.

Method 3 Although the third method still involves hard-coding the parentwindow name, all the other code is inherited. The developer initializes the parentwindow name using an init function that is called from the constructor event—Private function **f_init( )**.

```
i_wParent = w_window1
```

Call **f_init** function from constructor event, for example:

```
f_init( )
```

The big advantage of this method over the other hard-coded methods is, when other copies of the User Object are needed for other windows, a User Object can be inherited from the base uo_max User Object. The only code that would have to be placed in the inherited User Object would be an **f_init** function initializing the window's other window name. Although this is still not a preferred method of referencing the parent window, it is much better than the previous methods.

Passing the Window Name from the Window (Using this) Window names can be passed to the User Object in a more generic way than hard-coding using the reserved word, this. Similar to Method 3 just shown, a User Object function called **f_init** needs to be created—Public Function **f_init**(Window wParent)

```
i_wParent = wParent
```

This function is then called from the open event of the parent window of the User Object:

```
uo_max1.f_init(this)
```

Once **f_init** is called, the User Object can reference a generic instance variable. Thus, this User Object can be used in many different windows.

Referencing the Window from Constructor Event (Using parent) This method may be even more efficient because it does not require an **f_init** function to initialize the name of the parent window. The only line of code that must be added is in the constructor event of the User Object:

```
// initialize the User Object instance variable to the parent window
i_wParent = Parent
```

This is probably the most efficient of the strategies discussed in this section.

Executing Functions

Executing User Object functions from within a window is simple. For example, to execute an **f_init** function in uo_test, the following PowerScript must be written:

```
uo_test.f_init( )
```

Note: The **f_init** function must be declared as a public function if it is to be executed from a parent window.

By parsing through the Window control[] array, the different controls of a window can be referenced. The problem with this method is that if there is more than one User Object, it is difficult to know which one to execute. If, as part of the initialization of the window, a User Object **f_init** function must be executed in all windows, the control array can be used.

Adding User Objects to the Window Painter Toolbar

This is a simple but helpful option in the Window painter. Commonly used User Objects can be defined on the Window painter toolbar (PainterBar) as an icon. This is a quick way to place User Objects on a window, from the Window painter. The following must be done to add an icon to the Window PainterBar:

1. Click the right mouse button on the Window PainterBar.
2. Select Customize... from the popup menu, as shown in Figure 7.47.
3. Select the Custom RadioButton.
4. Drag-and-drop a toolbar icon from the selected palette on the current toolbar.
5. The window in Figure 7.48 appears.

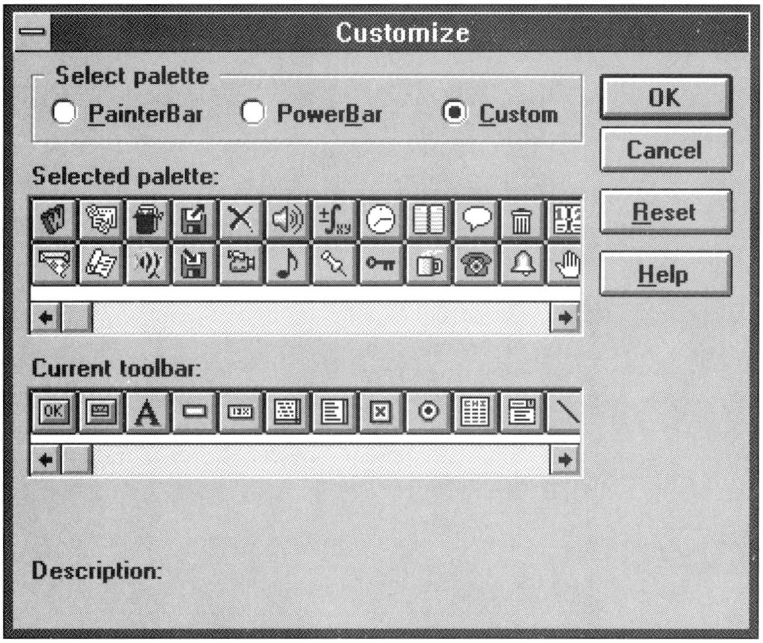

Figure 7.47   Select Customize... from the popup menu.

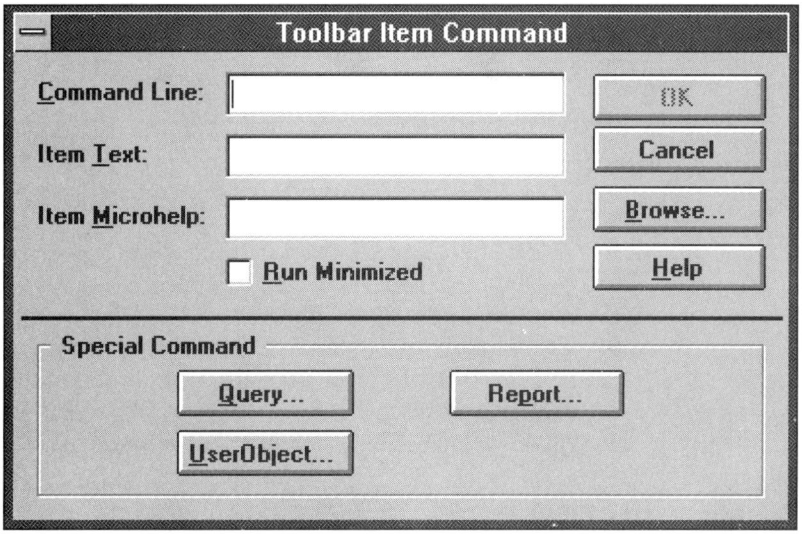

Figure 7.48   The Toolbar Item Command window.

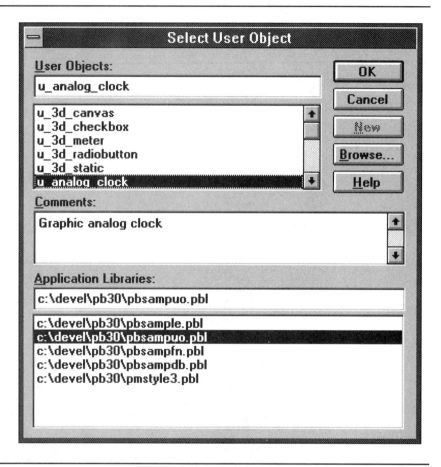

Figure 7.49   The Select User Object window.

6. Select the **User Object...** CommandButton
7. The window in Figure 7.49 appears.
8. Select a User Object, then press the OK button.
9. The window in Figure 7.50 appears.
10. Fill the Item Text and the Item Microhelp edit fields, then press the OK button.
11. The new User Object toolbar should be on the window PainterBar.

DYNAMIC USER OBJECTS

Powerbuilder User Objects can be opened dynamically on a given window. They can also be created, destroyed, moved, and hidden dynami-

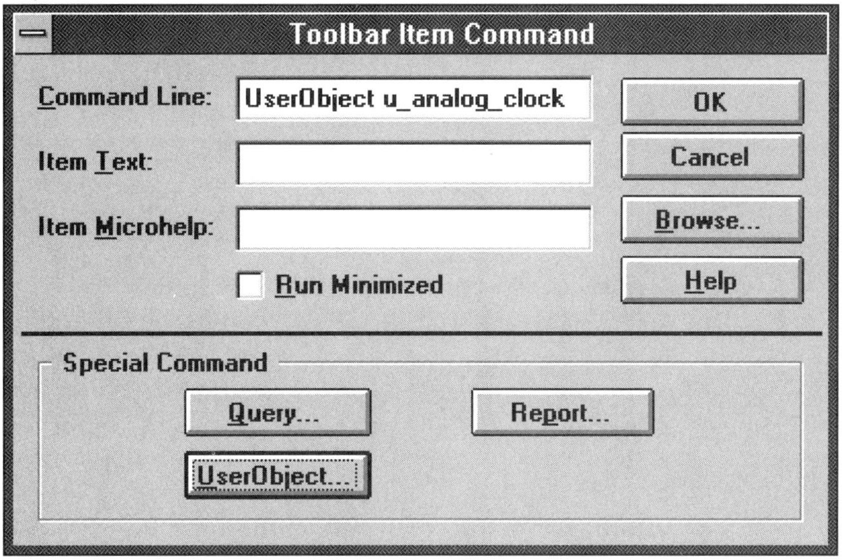

Figure 7.50 The Toolbar Item Command window.

cally. This makes PowerBuilder User Objects very powerful. Following is a list of functions that can make User Objects operate dynamically.

Function Name	Description
ClassName	Returns the PowerBuilder base class of an object. A base class could be a DataWindow, CommandButton, User Object, and so on. This function stores the result as a string.
CloseUserObject	Closes a User Object. In essence, this function destroys the instance of the User Object.
CloseUserObjectWithParm	Works the same as **CloseUserObject** except it also sets a parameter in the global message structure.
Drag	Starts or finishes the dragging of window control.
DraggedObject	Returns a reference to the object that is currently being dragged. Stores

	the result in a variable of type **DragObject**. This is a datatype that can store a reference to all PowerBuilder objects.
Move	Moves an object to another position within the current window.
OpenUserObject	Opens an instance of a User Object. This function basically instantiates a User Object within a window.
OpenUserObjectWithParm	Works the same as **OpenUserObject** except it also sets a parameter in the global message structure.
PointerX	Returns the number of PBUs an object is located from the left of the window.
PointerY	Returns the number of PBUs an object is located from the top of the window.
SetPosition	Specifies the position of a control in a front-to-back order.
TypeOf	Works the same as **ClassName** except it returns an enumerated datatype instead of a string.

The example in Figure 7.51 shows how to open, move, and close dynamic User Objects by simulating some features of the PowerBuilder Window painter.

The developer first creates standard User Objects for each of the nine controls in the toolbar (i.e., CommandButton, PictureButton, StaticText, SingleLineEdit, ListBox, CheckBox, RadioButton, DataWindow, DropDownListBox).

In the Window painter, create a new window and then declare an instance variable:

```
// reference each toolbar clicked by a number
Integer i_iType
```

In the clicked event of each of the toolbar controls, place the following PowerScript (with the exception of the number):

```
// the number 1 is for a CommandButton
i_iType = 1
```

Figure 7.51 Simulating some PowerBuilder window painter features to open, move, and close dynamic User Objects.

In the Dragleave event of the toolbar items, place the following PowerScript:

```
this.triggerevent(clicked!)
```

In the Dragdrop event of the window, place the following PowerScript:

```
Choose Case i_iType
    Case 1
        OpenUserObject(u_CommandButton, PointerX( ), &
                    PointerY( ))
        p_CommandButton.invert = True
        p_commandbutton.enabled = False
    Case 2
        OpenUserObject(u_PictureButton, PointerX( ), PointerY( ))
        p_PictureButton.invert = True
        p_picturebutton.enabled = False
```

```
Case 3
     OpenUserObject(u_StaticText, PointerX( ), PointerY( ))
     p_StaticText.invert = True
     p_statictext.enabled = False
Case 4
     OpenUserObject(u_SingleLineEdit, PointerX( ), PointerY( ))
     p_SingleLineEdit.invert = True
     p_singlelineedit.enabled = False
Case 5
     OpenUserObject(u_Listbox, PointerX( ), PointerY( ))
     p_Listbox.invert = True
     p_listbox.enabled = False
Case 6
     OpenUserObject(u_checkbox, PointerX( ), PointerY( ))
     p_CheckBox.invert = True
     p_checkbox.enabled = False
Case 7
     OpenUserObject(u_radiobutton, PointerX( ), PointerY( ))
     p_RadioButton.invert = True
     p_radiobutton.enabled = False
Case 8
     OpenUserObject(u_datawindow, PointerX( ), PointerY( ))
     p_DataWindow.invert = True
     p_datawindow.enabled = False
Case 9
     OpenUserObject(u_dropdownlistbox, PointerX( ), &
                PointerY( ))
     p_DropDownListBox.invert = True
     p_dropdownlistbox.enabled = False
Case else
     String sType
     DragObject      doObject
     doObject = DraggedObject( )
     Move(doObject,PointerX( ),PointerY( ))
     i_iType = 0
     sType ="~nMoved TypeOf = "
     Choose Case TypeOf(doObject)
          Case CommandButton!
               sType = sType + "CommandButton"
          Case PictureButton!
               sType = sType + "PictureButton"
          Case StaticText!
               sType = sType + "StaticText"
          Case SingleLineEdit!
               sType = sType + "SingleLineEdit"
          Case ListBox!
               sType = sType + "ListBox"
          Case CheckBox!
```

```
                                    sType = sType + "CheckBox"
                    Case RadioButton!
                            sType = sType + "RadioButton"
                    Case DataWindow!
                            sType = sType + "DataWindow"
                    Case DropDownListBox!
                            sType = sType + "DropDownListBox"
            End Choose
            sType = sType + "~nTo:~tX = "+String(PointerX( ))+&
                            "~tY = " + String(PointerY( ))
            MessageBox("Dynamic User Objects",sType)
End Choose
```

Figure 7.52 shows the result of dragging the CommandButton object from the toolbar onto the main section of the window.

The code to delete the object is located in the Dragdrop event of the p_Trash control.

```
Choose Case Typeof( DraggedObject( ))
    Case CommandButton!
            CloseUserObject(u_CommandButton)
            p_CommandButton.invert = False
            p_commandbutton.enabled = True
    Case PictureButton!
            CloseUserObject(u_PictureButton)
            p_PictureButton.invert = False
            p_picturebutton.enabled = True
    Case StaticText!
            CloseUserObject(u_StaticText)
            p_StaticText.invert = False
            p_statictext.enabled = True
    Case SingleLineEdit!
            CloseUserObject(u_SingleLineEdit)
            p_SingleLineEdit.invert = False
            p_singlelineedit.enabled = True
    Case ListBox!
            CloseUserObject(u_listbox)
            p_ListBox.invert = False
            p_listbox.enabled = True
    Case CheckBox!
            CloseUserObject(u_checkbox)
            p_CheckBox.invert = False
            p_checkbox.enabled = True
    Case RadioButton!
            CloseUserObject(u_radiobutton)
            p_RadioButton.invert = False
            p_radiobutton.enabled = True
```

Figure 7.52 The result of dragging the CommandButton object onto the main section of the window.

```
Case DataWindow!
        CloseUserObject(u_datawindow)
        p_DataWindow.invert = False
        p_datawindow.enabled = True
Case DropDownListBox!
        CloseUserObject(u_dropdownlistbox)
        p_DropDownListBox.invert = False
        p_dropdownlistbox.enabled = True
End Choose
```

DESIGN CONSIDERATIONS

PowerBuilder User Objects use many object-oriented techniques and concepts such as inheritance, polymorphism, encapsulation, and classes.

Inheritance and User Objects

PowerBuilder implements inheritance with User Objects in two ways:

- Object level
- Control level

Object Level User objects can be created at the object level by using the User Object painter. For example, if an application uses three different implementations of DataWindows, such as a master DataWindow, a detail DataWindow, and a standalone list DataWindow, an inheritance tree can be established that includes common modules in the highest ancestor. Though these DataWindows are different, they have some basic similarities. Error checking on the DBError event of the DataWindow, for example, would be similar on all three types of windows. Tag message-handling and validation message-handling would also be similar among the three DataWindows. When there are similarities among multiple User Objects, a User Object hierarchy can be created to share common modules, such as the one in Figure 7.53.

Much of the common functionality can be developed at the u_dw_ancestor level. The specific functions, events, structures, and variables that relate only to the lower-level inherited DataWindow User Objects, like u_dw_master, can be declared at the lower level. Inheritance in PowerBuilder can be multiple levels deep.

Note: When creating a standard User Object, all the encapsulated attributes, events, and functionality of the base PowerBuilder classes are inherited into the standard User Object. When creating custom User Objects, the events for the User Object are fixed and predetermined. They are not inherited from any base PowerBuilder class.

Control Level When a normal PowerBuilder control is placed on the surface of a window from the Window painter, the developer is, in essence, creating a local control that is inherited from the base classes built into PowerBuilder, as exemplified in Figure 7.54.

With User Objects, it works the same way: The User Object control that's placed on the window is actually inherited from the User Object that was created in the User Object painter.

Polymorphism and User Objects

Polymorphism (for definition and discussion, see Chapter 2) can be implemented using events and functions within User Objects.

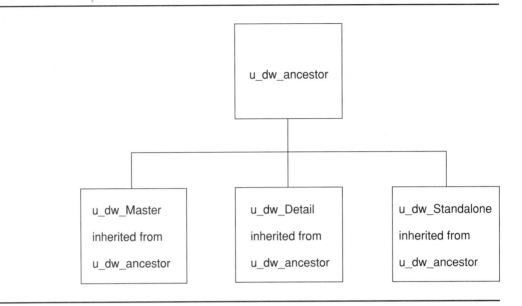

Figure 7.53   Sample User Object hierarchy.

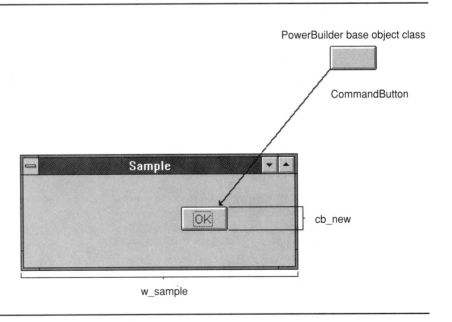

Figure 7.54   A local control inherited from the base classes.

Events In the previous standard DataWindow example, polymorphism could be implemented by placing generic code in the DBError event and extending the processing to handle more specific error-handling in the descendant events.

Functions Polymorphism can be implemented with functions in roughly the same way. The main difference is that functions cannot be extended; they can only be overridden. For example, a function **f_foo( )** is declared at different places in the hierarchy, but in this case is called from the ancestor object. The diagram below shows that the **f_foo( )** function has been declared in two places, in u_dw_ancestor and u_dw_master. The **f_foo( )** function is only called, however, from the u_dw_ancestor User Object.

In this example, when the u_dw_master User Object is placed on a window, upon execution, the function at the descendant level is executed and the function at the ancestor level is ignored. When either the u_dw_detail or u_dw_standalone User Objects are declared on a window, upon execution, only the **f_foo( )** function at the ancestor is executed.

The developer should take advantage of the power of polymorphism, both by way of events and functions, to enable reusable code and minimize duplicate code.

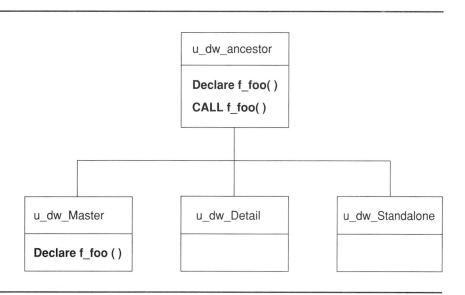

Figure 7.55   Declaring a function in multiple places in an object hierarchy.

Standard and Custom User Object Class Hierarchy Standard User Objects and custom User Objects have different inheritance structures. Standard User Objects are inherited from the basic PowerBuilder object classes; custom User Objects are inherited from the User Object class. Below are two diagrams that clarify this concept.

Standard User Object Class Hierarchy Standard User Objects inherit their attributes, events, and functions directly from a particular PowerBuilder object class. Inheriting directly from the base object class makes the User

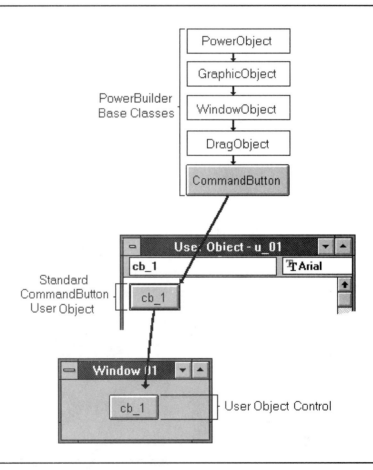

Figure 7.56   The hierarchy of the standard CommandButton User Object.

Object itself become an object of that particular object class, thus encapsulating all the attributes and events of that class. For example, the base object class that the standard CommandButton User Object is inherited from is the PowerBuilder CommandButton class. This causes the User Object to inherit all the events and attributes of a CommandButton. When the User Object is placed on a window, to the developer, it looks just like a CommandButton.

Note: Many of the functions that are particular to object classes are encapsulated into the PowerBuilder objects at the object base classes.

Custom User Object Class Hierarchy Custom User Objects, as opposed to standard User Objects, inherit their attributes and events from the User Object base class. Custom User Objects differ in this way because they can contain many different objects that are each inherited from a particular object class. Figure 7.57 shows a simple custom User Object with two command buttons. The diagram shows how the User Object itself is inherited from the User Object class, while the CommandButtons are each inherited from the CommandButton base class. When a custom User Object is placed on a window, it inherits only the events and attributes of the User Object, not those of each of the individual objects.

Encapsulation and User Objects

Some encapsulation is built into PowerBuilder, by default. PowerBuilder also has built-in flexibility to extend the default functionality using custom encapsulation. Custom encapsulation refers to the capability to extend the functionality of the base classes. For definition and further discussion of encapsulation, see Chapter 2.

Inherent Encapsulation Inherent encapsulation is a feature of PowerBuilder that is built into the painters and objects. All PowerBuilder objects have encapsulated events, attributes, and functions. Figure 7.58 shows an example of a PowerBuilder ListBox class declared on a window.

From the export file of this window, this section declares a global standard ListBox User Object called u_listbox that was inherited, by default, from the PowerBuilder ListBox base class.

```
global type u_listbox from ListBox
end type
```

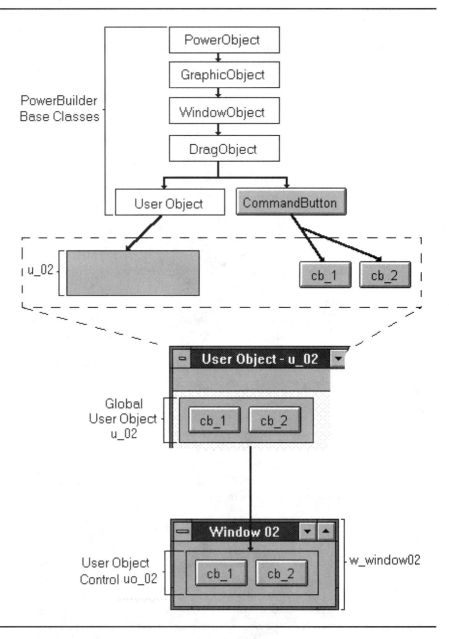

Figure 7.57 A simple custom User Object with two command buttons.

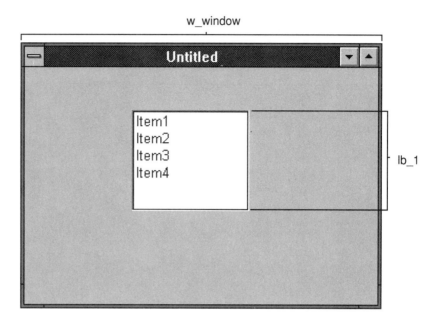

Figure 7.58   A PowerBuilder ListBox class declared on a window.

The following, which was declared as part of the object when the object was created, shows all the encapsulated attributes and events for the u_listbox User Object.

```
global type u_listbox from listbox
int Width=494
int Height=361
int TabOrder=1
boolean DragAuto=true
BorderStyle BorderStyle=StyleLowered!
boolean VScrollBar=true
long TextColor=33554432
int TextSize=-10
int Weight=400
string FaceName="Arial"
FontFamily FontFamily=Swiss!
FontPitch FontPitch=Variable!
end type
global u_listbox u_listbox
```

```
on rbuttondown;
     // place code for
     // this event here.
end on
on selectionchanged;
     // place code for
     // this event here.
end on
on constructor;
     // place code for
     // this event here.
end on
on destructor;
     // place code for
     // this event here.
end on
on doubleclicked;
     // place code for
     // this event here.
end on
on dragdrop;
     // place code for
     // this event here.
end on
on dragenter;
     // place code for
     // this event here.
end on
on dragleave;
     // place code for
     // this event here.
end on
on dragwithin;
     // place code for
     // this event here.
end on
on getfocus;
     // place code for
     // this event here.
end on
on losefocus;
     // place code for
     // this event here.
end on
on other;
     // place code for
     // this event here.
end on
```

When the User Object has been created, place it on the w_window window as shown in Figure 7.58. As the User Object is dropped on the window, a local ListBox, called lb_1, which is inherited from u_listbox, is defined.

```
type lb_1 from u_listbox within w_window
end type
```

The program listing on the bottom of this page shows all the descendant attributes and events for lb_1. Note that only the attributes that have been changed at the descendant level are visible in the export file. Because the User Object (lb_1) is, by default, inherited from the global User Object (u_listbox), all the events of the lb_1 are extended from the corresponding u_listbox events.

When an event is extended, the ancestor event is executed before the descendant event begins execution. PowerBuilder knows to call the ancestor script because it generates the following line of code:

```
on selectionchanged;
    // Calls the ancestor script
    call u_listbox::selectionchanged;
    // place descendant code here...
end on
```

Although the line of code to execute the ancestor event (call u_listbox::selectionchanged) is not visible from the painters, it can be seen when the window is exported.

```
type lb_1 from u_listbox within w_window
int X=572
int Y=237
end type

on selectionchanged;
    call u_listbox::selectionchanged;
    // place descendant code here...
end on
on constructor;
    call u_listbox::constructor;
    // place descendant code here...
end on
on destructor;
    call u_listbox::destructor;
    // place descendant code here...
end on
```

```
on doubleclicked;
     call u_listbox::doubleclicked;
     // place descendant code here...
end on
on dragdrop;
     call u_listbox::dragdrop;
     // place descendant code here...
end on
on dragenter;
     call u_listbox::dragenter;
     // place descendant code here...
end on
on dragleave;
     call u_listbox::dragleave;
     // place descendant code here...
end on
on dragwithin;
     call u_listbox::dragwithin;
     // place descendant code here...
end on
on getfocus;
     call u_listbox::getfocus;
     // place descendant code here...
end on
on losefocus;
     call u_listbox::losefocus;
     // place descendant code here...
end on
on other;
     call u_listbox::other;
     // place descendant code here...
end on
on rbuttondown;
     call u_listbox::rbuttondown;
     // place descendant code here...
end on
```

Custom Encapsulation The term custom encapsulation in User Objects merely refers to the flexibility of PowerBuilder in allowing developers to extend the functionality of the base classes. The base classes can be extended by declaring encapsulated events, public, private, or protected object-level functions (using PowerScript or external), and variables (local and shared). Both the standard and the custom events can be extended or overridden at any level of the visible ancestor tree. Again, all this flexibility demonstrates the tool's flexibility and object orientation.

Defining C++ Classes with User Objects

C++ developers often find it difficult to relate many of the object-oriented concepts from C++ to PowerBuilder. C++ developers will find the environment more familiar as they understand how PowerBuilder is structured. C++ developers should study some of the ways PowerBuilder implements inheritance, polymorphism, and encapsulation. The most obvious similarity between PowerBuilder and C++ is the way each defines classes.

As demonstrated throughout this chapter, PowerBuilder allows developers to develop totally customizable classes (objects) through its User Object painter. When a User Object is exported into an *.SRU file, it becomes clear how similar the object declarations are to C++ classes. Developers should also notice the capability to declare public, private, and protected functions. A developer should also look at the object class browser within the Library painter to see attributes and functions (methods) that are encapsulated in controls and objects. The object class browser, in addition to listing the ancestor structure for application objects, lists the internal ancestor structure for its object class inheritance hierarchy. As developers become familiar with the different types of User Objects (especially non-visual User Objects), these become very useful.

THIRD-PARTY CONTROLS (VBXs AND DLLs)

For a current list of third-party vendors and products, contact Microsoft and/or Powersoft.

CHAPTER 8

Functions

Functions are a key ingredient in any PowerBuilder application. PowerBuilder provides a great deal of flexibility with regard to functions, allowing them to be defined at either a global or object level, and allowing the linking of external functions written in C.

Note: External functions can be written in languages other than C (i.e., C++, COBOL). However, for the sake of this discussion, all references to external functions will assume the function is written in C.

This chapter discusses some of the issues concerning functions, such as:

- Types of functions
- Declaring external functions
- Parameter passing
- Design considerations

TYPES OF FUNCTIONS

Functions within PowerBuilder can be divided into two groups: built-in functions and user-defined functions.

Built-in Functions

Built-in functions are PowerScript functions used to obtain information about an object, to change or manipulate the attributes of an object, or to change the behavior of an object. Built-in functions include string manipulation functions, date manipulation functions, print functions, and DDE functions, among others. Each PowerBuilder object has a set of built-in functions. These functions are analogous to the set of member functions in a C++ class. For a complete list of built-in functions, the reader should refer to the PowerBuilder *Function Reference* manual.

User-defined Functions

In situations in which a built-in PowerBuilder function does not do the job or a specific task needs to be performed several times in an application, a user-defined function is needed. User-defined functions can be created using either PowerScript code or C code written as a DLL. In either case, the function may be global in scope or defined at the object level. If it is defined at the object level, it is only valid as long as the object for which it is defined exists.

Global Functions Global functions are not associated with any particular object and are public in scope, meaning that they can be called from anywhere within the application. Global functions can either be PowerScript code or C code.

Object-level Functions Object-level functions can be defined for windows, menus, and user objects. Unlike global functions, object-level functions can be defined with an access level of public, private, or protected. These terms are defined as:

- Public—can be called from anywhere within an application.
- Private—can only be called from events defined for the same object as the function. Private functions cannot be called from descendants of the object for which the function is defined.
- Protected—the same as private functions, with the exception that they can be called from descendants of the object for which the function was created.

Like built-in functions, object-level functions are analogous to member functions in a C++ class.

External Functions External functions allow developers to link C functions into a PowerBuilder application. This is a very powerful feature of PowerBuilder that makes it an open and extensible development tool. These C functions are stored in DLLs (using a "far pascal" declaration) that must be declared to the application before they can be called.

PowerBuilder 3.0 allows external functions to be either global or local in scope. Global external functions can be called from anywhere in the application; local external functions can only be called from events defined for the same object as the function.

Note: The pascal declaration is used by Windows because it is more efficient than the standard C function declaration. It causes the compiler to push parameters onto the stack from left to right, while normal C functions push parameters onto the stack from right to left. The pascal declaration gives responsibility for cleaning up the stack to the called function rather than to the calling function.

PowerBuilder provides a set of utility functions to use when making calls to external C functions. These functions, which handle communication between PowerBuilder and the Windows operating system, are:

Handle( )—returns the handle of a PowerBuilder object.

IntHigh( )—returns the high word of a long value returned from a C function.

IntLow( )—returns the low word of a long value returned from a C function.

Long( )—combines a low word and a high word into a long value.

It is often necessary to obtain the handle of a PowerBuilder window to pass to an external function. The following command button script, for example, maximizes the current PowerBuilder window by calling the PowerBuilder post function to post a message to the window's message queue:

```
/* maximize this window by posting the message to the window's message
queue */

post(handle(parent),274,61488,0)
```

This function is passed the handle of the current window (obtained using the **handle( )** function), the Windows message number (274 = WM_SYSCOMMAND), the integer value of the message (61488 = SC_MAXIMIZE), and the long value of the message (not necessary in this case). Windows message numbers can be obtained by referring to the Windows SDK documentation or by looking at the windows.h file that is part of the SDK. The following lines in the windows.h file define WM_SYSCOMMAND, SC_MINIMIZE, and SC_MAXIMIZE:

```
/****** WM_SYSCOMMAND support **********************/

#define WM_SYSCOMMAND   0x0112

#ifndef NOSYSCOMMANDS

/* System Menu Command Values */
#define SC_SIZE             0xF000
#define SC_MOVE             0xF010
#define SC_MINIMIZE         0xF020
#define SC_MAXIMIZE         0xF030
#define SC_NEXTWINDOW 0xF040
#define SC_PREVWINDOW       0xF050
#define SC_CLOSE            0xF060
#define SC_VSCROLL          0xF070
#define SC_HSCROLL          0xF080
#define SC_MOUSEMENU        0xF090
#define SC_KEYMENU          0xF100
#define SC_ARRANGE          0xF110
#define SC_RESTORE          0xF120
#define SC_TASKLIST         0xF130
#define SC_SCREENSAVE       0xF140
#define SC_HOTKEY           0xF150

/* Obsolete names */
#define SC_ICON             SC_MINIMIZE
#define SC_ZOOM             SC_MAXIMIZE

#endif /* NOSYSCOMMANDS */
```

Note that these values are listed in a hexadecimal format, and the developer should convert them to their decimal values before including them in a PowerScript function call.

The **IntHigh( )** and **IntLow( )** functions are used to analyze values returned from external function calls or Windows messages. For example, the following script is contained in a custom user event mapped to the pbm_syscommand event ID. This script uses **IntLow( )** to check the wordParm element of the PowerBuilder message structure. If this value is equal to the SC_CLOSE value of the WM_SYSCOMMAND message (61536), the window is closed.

```
/*****************************************************
** Trap event of user selecting control menu options. Specifically,
```

```
** the 'close' option, which is identified by the SC_CLOSE value of the
** WM_SYSCOMMAND message (61536).
*******************************************************/
uint uiWParm

/* Check for 'close' selection */
uiWParm = IntLow(message.wordParm )
if uiWParm = 61536 then
      close(this)
end if
```

DECLARING EXTERNAL FUNCTIONS

To declare an external function, select the Global External Functions...
option or the Local External Functions... option from the Declare menu
of an object painter or the PowerScript painter. If the external function
returns a value, the declaration syntax is:

```
FUNCTION rtndatatype functionname ( { REF }
    { datatype1 arg1, ..., datatypen argn } ) LIBRARY libname
```

For external functions that do not return a value (e.g., C functions
that have a return type of void), the declaration syntax is:

```
SUBROUTINE functionname ({REF}
    { datatype1 arg1 , ..., datatypen argn }) LIBRARY libname.
```

where,

> rtndatatype—the data type returned by the function.
>
> functionname—the name of the DLL function.
>
> datatype1, ... datatypen—the data types of arg1, ... argn (optional).
>
> arg1, ... argn—the names of arguments passed to the function
> (optional).
>
> libname—the name of the DLL that contains the function (string).
> This DLL must be in the DOS path during execution.

As an example, assume that the developer wants to add a function
to an application that checks to see if another application is currently
running. One way to do this is to call the Window's SDK function
GetModuleHandle( ). This function, which is located in the kernel.exe
file, returns an unsigned integer value of the application handle if it

exists. To declare this as a global function, one would add the line shown in Figure 8.1 to the list of global external functions.

Because this function is declared as a global external function, it can be called from anywhere within the application. To continue with this example, assume that the developer wants to open a DDE link with Microsoft Excel when a button in a PowerBuilder window is clicked. To determine if Microsoft Excel is running, the following script could be defined for the clicked event of the command button:

```
// Script to open a DDE link to Excel using the
// global external function GetModuleHandle to see
// if Excel is already open

integer iDDEhndl
uint uiHndl
string sAppname, sSheetname

sSheetname = dw_main.GetItemString(1,"sheetname")
// get handle of Excel application
sAppname = "excel.exe"
uiHndl = GetModuleHandle(sAppname)

// if handle is 0 start excel, else it is already running
if uiHndl = 0 then
```

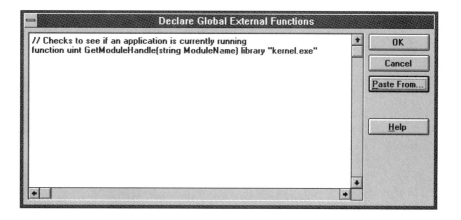

Figure 8.1   Declaring a global external function.

```
    run("c:\excel\excel.exe" + sSheetname)
end if

//Open DDE channel
iDDEhndl = OpenChannel ( "Excel", sSheetname )

// Other DDE functions...
...
...

// Close DDE channel
CloseChannel(iDDEhndl)
```

Refer to the Window's *SDK Programmer's Reference*, Volume 1: Overview for a listing of all Window's SDK functions.

PARAMETER PASSING

Parameter passing works in a similar fashion in PowerBuilder to the way it works in other programming languages. As with other programming languages, passing "by value" means that the function receives a copy of the argument and any changes made to it are not reflected in the original argument, while passing "by reference" means that the address of the argument is passed and any changes made to the argument within the function are reflected in the original argument. However, there are some differences in parameter passing between PowerScript functions and external functions.

PowerScript Functions PowerScript functions can be defined to accept parameters of any standard PowerBuilder data type. This includes the basic data types such as integers, longs, strings, and so forth. In addition, PowerBuilder objects such as windows, datawindows, and user objects can be passed to PowerScript functions either by reference or by value.

PowerBuilder also allows the passing of structures and arrays. This capability can be extended further by passing arrays of structures or structures of arrays. Combining arrays and structures allows large amounts of data to be passed to a function in a simple manner. To illustrate the passing of an array of structures, suppose structure st_person, which contains business contact information, is defined as shown in Figure 8.2.

The following code will define an array of type st_person, populate it by selecting data from the database, and pass it to a function that prints the list of names to a file (note that this code is shown as a single function for simplicity; in a real application it may be better to use more than one function):

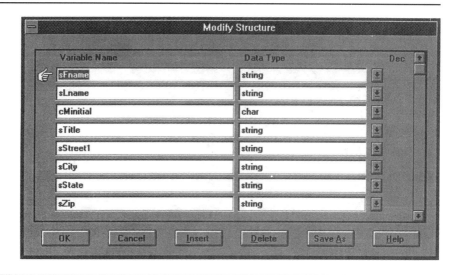

Figure 8.2   Definition of structure st_person.

```
/********************************************************
** This function declares an array of type st_person,
** populates it by selecting business contact data from
** the database, and passes it to a printing function.
********************************************************/
st_person st_contact[]
string sFname, sLname, sStreet, sCity, sState, sZip
int i = 1

// Declare the cursor to select contact data, and
// check for errors
declare get_person cursor for
SELECT first_name, last_name, street, city, state, zip
FROM contact
using SQLCA;
if SQLCA.SQLCode <>0 then
   MessageBox("Cursor Error", "Unable to declare cursor get_person")
   return
end if;

// Open cursor and check for errors
open get_person;
if SQLCA.SQLCode <>0 then
```

```
     MessageBox("Cursor Error", "Unable to open cursor get_person")
     return
end if;

// Fetch each row and load it into the array
DO WHILE SQLCA.SQLCode = 0
 fetch get_person into :sFname, :sLname, :sStreet, :sCity, :sState,
:sZip;
 st_contact[i].sFname = sFname;
 st_contact[i].sLname = sLname;
 st_contact[i].sStreet1 = sStreet;
 st_contact[i].sCity = sCity;
 st_contact[i].sState = sState;
 st_contact[i].sZip = sZip;
 i+=1
LOOP

// Close the cursor
close get_person;

// Call print function, passing the array and a
// count of the number of array elements
print_contacts("contacts.txt",st_contact[], i - 1)
```

The function **print_contacts( )** is defined as shown in Figure 8.3.
Notice the declaration of the second argument, people[]. It is declared as an array of type st_person, the structure described in Figure 8.2. The third argument, iNum_people, is used to represent the number of elements in the array. The code for **print_contacts( )** is:

```
/**************************************************
** This function takes a list of business contacts,
** passed in as the structure people[], and prints
** them to the passed file name.
**************************************************/
int i, iFnum

// Open the file
iFnum = FileOpen(sFname, LineMode!,Write!, LockWrite!, Replace!)
if iFnum = -1 then
   MessageBox("File Error", "Error opening Contacts file")
   return false
end if

// Go through each item in the passed array and print
// each structure element to the file
```

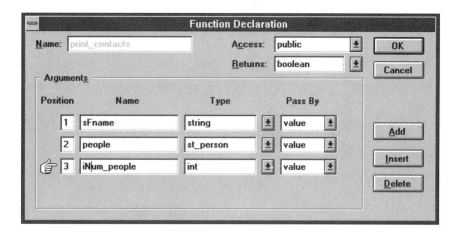

Figure 8.3   Declaration of function **print_contacts( )**.

```
FOR i=1 TO num_people
  FileWrite(iFnum, people[i].sFname + " " + people[i].sLname)
  FileWrite(iFnum, people[i].sStreet1)
  FileWrite(iFnum, people[i].sCity + ", " + people[i].sState + " " &
+ people[i].sZip)
  FileWrite(iFnum, " ")
NEXT

// Close the file
FileClose(iFnum)
return true
```

To show how a structure with array elements can be handled in functions, suppose there is a window that allows users to send an eMail message from a PowerBuilder conversation (this example is intended only to demonstrate the passing of a structure with array elements; Refer to Chapter 12 for a discussion of various eMail interfaces from PowerBuilder), as shown in Figure 8.4.

This window uses the structure st_email to store eMail log information. This structure keeps such items as message sender, message subject, date, a list of who the message was sent to (an array), and a list of who was listed in the cc: field of the message (an array). This structure is defined as shown in Figure 8.5.

The window function **load_struct( )** takes the data from the screen and loads it into a structure of type st_email. This function then calls a

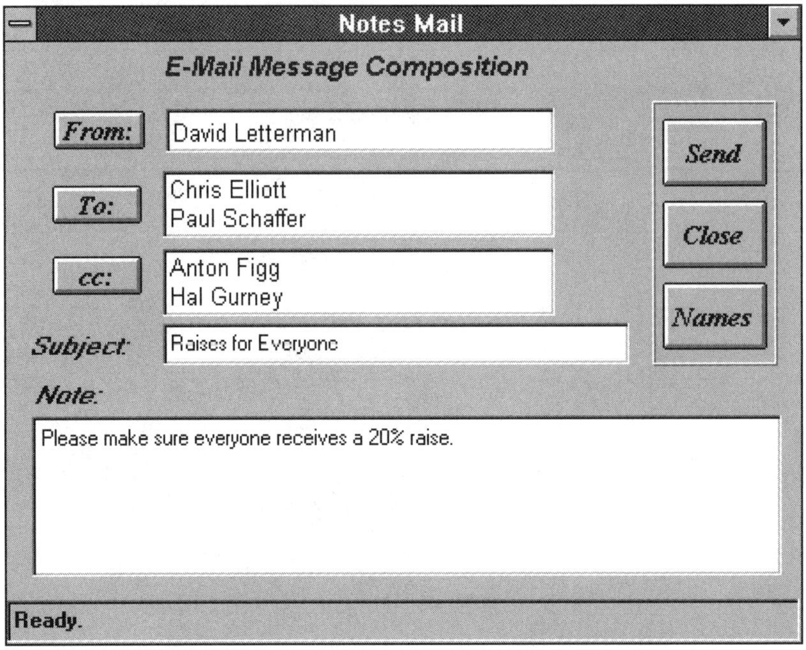

Figure 8.4   Sample PowerBuilder eMail interface.

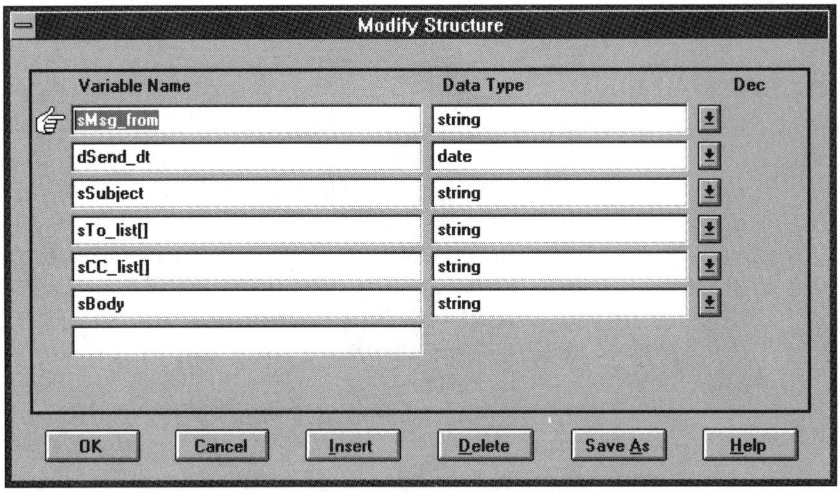

Figure 8.5   Definition of structure st_email.

custom DLL to send the message using the eMail API. After the message has been sent, the window function **log_email( )** writes information about the message to a log file. This function is called from the clicked event of the Send button:

```
/********************************************************
** This function takes the elements from the current screen,
** loads a structure of type st_email, calls a custom DLL
** to send an e-mail message, and calls a function to
** write information about the message to a log file.
********************************************************/
st_email msg_struct
integer i, iTotal_to, iTotal_cc, iRet

// Load the structure from the screen
msg_struct.sMsg_from = sle_from.text
msg_struct.dSend_dt = today( )
msg_struct.sSubject = sle_subject.text

// Add each item of the To: listbox to the array
FOR iTotal_to=1 TO lb_to.totalitems( )
     msg_struct.sTo_list[iTotal_to] = lb_to.text(iTotal_to)
NEXT

// Add each item of the cc: listbox to the array
FOR iTotal_cc=1 TO lb_cc.totalitems( )
     msg_struct.sCC_list[iTotal_cc] = lb_cc.text(iTotal_cc)
NEXT

msg_struct.sBody = mle_note.text
// Call the custom DLL that will take the structure and

// send an e-mail message based on its contents

iRet = SendMessage( msg_struct)
If iRet = 1 Then
  Beep(3)
  sle_message.text = "Mailed!"
Else
  sle_message.text = "Error."
End If

// Call function to log note information
log_email(i_logfile, msg_struct, iTotal_to - 1, iTotal_cc - 1)
```

The function **log_email( )** is defined as shown in Figure 8.6.
The arguments passed to **log_email** are the name of the log file, the

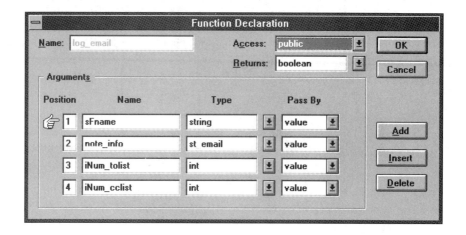

Figure 8.6   Definition of the function **log_email( )**.

structure containing all the information to be logged for a single message, the number of people the note was sent to, and the number of people who were on the cc: line of the note. The code for **log_email** is:

```
/**************************************************
** This function takes e-mail message information
** from the passed structure and prints log
** information to the passed file name.
**************************************************/
int i, iFnum

// Open the log file
iFnum = FileOpen(sFname, LineMode!,Write!, LockWrite!, Append!)
if iFnum = -1 then
    MessageBox("File Error", "Error opening Log file")
    return false
end if

// Take each element from the passed structure and
// print it to the log file

    FileWrite(iFnum, "From: " + note_info.sMsg_from)
    FileWrite(iFnum, "Date: " + string(note_info.dSend_dt))
    FileWrite(iFnum, "Subject: " + note_info.sSubject)
    FileWrite(iFnum, "To: ")
```

```
// Loop through the list of names on the to: line
   FOR i=1 TO iNum_tolist
       FileWrite(iFnum, " " + note_info.sTo_list[i])
   NEXT

   FileWrite(iFnum, "cc: ")
// Loop through the list of names on the cc: line
   FOR i=1 TO iNum_cclist
       FileWrite(iFnum, " " + note_info.sCC_list[i])
   NEXT

   FileWrite(iFnum, " ")

// Close the file
FileClose(iFnum)
return true
```

External Functions Like PowerBuilder functions, arguments can be passed from PowerBuilder to an external C function by value or by reference. The syntax for passing an argument by reference is *ref datatype arg*; the syntax for passing by value is *datatype arg*. All PowerBuilder datatypes, including structures, can be passed as arguments to a C function.

When passing items from PowerBuilder to external functions by reference, the argument passed must be a variable rather than a literal. This is because the function references the address of this variable, which does not exist in the case of a literal. To illustrate this, consider the function **foo( )**, which is defined as:

```
foo(ref string var1)
```

Calling function **foo** using PowerScript could normally be done in one of two methods:

1. foo("ha ha ha")
2. string mystring = "ha ha ha"
    foo(mystring)

In the first example, the pointer that is passed to **foo( )** is not pointing to the correct memory location because no memory is allocated (see Figure 8.7).

In the second example, mystring has been declared a string and memory has been allocated accordingly. When **foo( )** is called in this case, a pointer to the location of mystring in memory is passed, as shown in Figure 8.8.

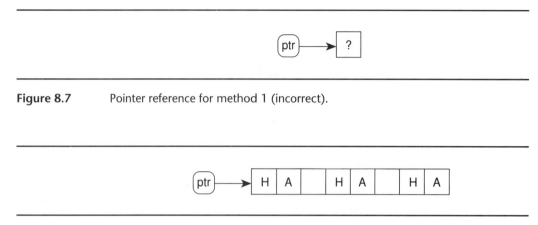

Figure 8.7   Pointer reference for method 1 (incorrect).

Figure 8.8   Pointer reference for method 2 (correct).

This illustrates that method 2 should be used to avoid memory allocation problems.

DESIGN CONSIDERATIONS

The concept of using functions as a method of segregating code into distinct modules is fairly straightforward. It is valid for both a nonobject-oriented environment and an object-oriented environment. What becomes more important in an object-oriented environment such as PowerBuilder is the scope of a function. With the ability to define object-level functions as public, private, and protected, it becomes important to know the purpose of a function so it can be defined in a way that increases developer productivity and application performance.

Global vs. Object Functions A well-designed object class hierarchy encapsulates any action to be performed on an object into object functions. These functions should only be called from events or functions defined within the same branch of the hierarchy tree. For example, consider the following object hierarchy, shown in Figure 8.9.

Functions defined for StdWindow can be called from any of the three objects in the hierarchy. However, functions defined for ReportWin should only be called from StdWindow, ReportWin, or any of ReportWin's descendants (if the function is not declared as private). Functions defined for ReportWin should not be called from QueryWin or any of its descendants.

Functions that need to be called from both ReportWin or QueryWin can either be defined for StdWindow or defined as global functions.

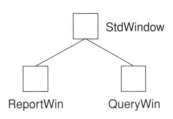

Figure 8.9   Sample window hierarchy.

Generally, functions that pertain to the object itself should be defined at the object level, while general-purpose functions should be defined as global functions. For example, functions that perform such tasks as initializing an object, enabling or disabling the controls of an object, or checking a user's rights to an object should be defined at the object level. On the other hand, functions that perform such tasks as setting up a transaction object and connecting to a database, returning values of global variables, or returning error messages should be global because they are used by objects of all types and do not pertain to any single object type.

Inheritance and Functions As stated earlier, object-level functions defined for ancestor classes may be extended or overridden by descendant classes. Ancestor functions are automatically overridden when the same function is defined for the descendant. The function declaration for the descendant must be identical to that of the ancestor; otherwise, the function will not be executed at the descendant level. (This is because polymorphism allows the definition of functions with the same name.)

Extending an ancestor function can be done by calling the function within the descendant function using the :: operator. Preceding the :: operator with the name of the ancestor object executes the ancestor function or event before continuing the descendant function. PowerBuilder also allows the use of the word "super" before the :: operator to execute the function or event of the **immediate** ancestor of the object. For example, in a master-detail conversation, it is more efficient to initialize a detail datawindow only if the master datawindow has been initialized without error. The following function, **initDWs( )**, calls the **initDWs( )** function of the ancestor before initializing the detail datawindow:

```
/********************************************************
** Extend to initialize the detail list datawindow.
********************************************************/
```

```
// initialize the master datawindow before the detail
if super::initDWs( ) then
        // Initialization code for detail datawindow
else
        return false
end if
```

As stated previously, inheritance should be used whenever possible to increase code reusability and maintainability.

Polymorphism and Functions Polymorphism (see Chapter 2) should be used to define functions that perform the same function, but either receive a different set of arguments or contain different code to accomplish the same function. A good example of using polymorphism is with the **enable( )** function. This function performs the same task, but will be different depending on the context in which it is called. Using the object hierarchy previously shown, the enable function defined for StdWindow might simply enable the window object. This function (accepting no arguments) would look like:

```
/*******************************************************
**     Enable this window.
*******************************************************/
this.enabled = true
return true
```

On the other hand, the enable function for ReportWin might enable a particular column on a datawindow. The code for this (accepting the arguments colname and taborder) is:

```
/*******************************************************
** Enable the argument column by setting the tabOrder to the argument
** value and changing the colors.
*******************************************************/
dwModify(this, ColName+".color=~""+DATA_COLOR+ "~" " + &
            ColName+".pointer=~"iBeam!~" " + &
            ColName+".TabSequence=" + string(tabOrder) + " " + &
            ColName+".Border=5" )
return true
```

Calling the enable function from an event or function defined for the window causes the first set of code to be executed; calling it from an event or function defined for the user object causes the second set of code to be executed.

PowerScript Functions vs. External Functions

Designers and developers of PowerBuilder applications need to consider how and when to use external functions instead of PowerScript functions.

External functions should be used for one of two reasons: (1) When a particular function cannot be done with PowerScript, or (2) when performance is an issue. Because PowerScript code is compiled into p-code that is interpreted at runtime, it is slower than C code. Therefore, any CPU-intensive processes are good candidates for C code.

In addition to developing custom DLLs, there are many third-party DLLs that can be used by PowerBuilder to provide a specific set of functionality. Examples include various graphics packages, eMail interfaces, and network operating system interfaces.

CHAPTER 9

Graphs and Reporting

The use of graphs and reports to present information to the user can be an effective and important part of a PowerBuilder application. Graphs and reports allow the user to view data in a meaningful fashion. This chapter discusses the following aspects related to graphs and reporting:

- Graphs
    - Parts of a graph
    - Overlays
    - Using graphs
    - Manipulating graphs
    - Drill Down graphs
    - 3-D graphs
- Reports
    - Report painter / PowerViewer
    - Printing reports
    - Saving reports
    - PowerMaker

GRAPHS

Parts of a Graph

PowerBuilder offers several types of graphs, including Area, Bar, Column, Line, Pie, and Scatter graphs. Each type of graph provides a different presentation of data to the user. A complete description of each type of graph and its particular use can be found in the *PowerBuilder User Guide*. PowerBuilder allows the developer to change the type of graph using the Graph Type dialog, shown in Figure 9.1.

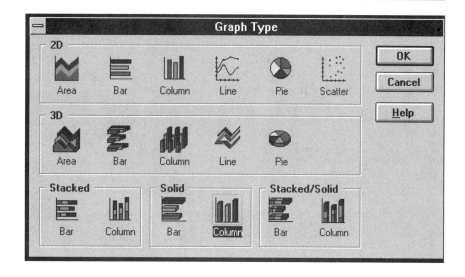

Figure 9.1   The Graph Type dialog box.

Although the presentation of the data differs, the parts of each graph type are the same. The parts of a PowerBuilder graph include:

- Category
- Value
- Series

Each of these parts is discussed in the following sections.

Category The Category represents a grouping of data points in a graph. The Category may contain a literal, an expression, or a column. When using a literal as the Category, all data is grouped into a single category and the value for the Category is displayed along the Category axis. When using a column as the Category, the data is displayed in the graph with each unique column value representing a category. Because the Bar and Column graphs change the orientation of the graph's axis, the Category is not always associated with the X axis.

In both the two-dimensional and three-dimensional graphs, the Category is associated with the X axis for Area, Line, and Column graphs and with the Y axis for Bar graphs. The Pie chart displays the Category as a colored portion or slice of the pie. When using code tables in a DataWindow graph, the **LookupDisplay( )** function can be used to dis-

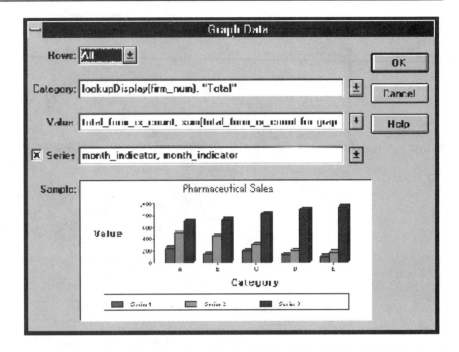

Figure 9.2   Defining multiple categories in a graph.

play the display values of a code table, rather than the data values. For example, **LookupDisplay( )** is used in Figure 9.2 to decode the value of firm_num, a DataWindow column that uses a code table. This function returns the display value of the code table and shows it, instead of the data value, on the graph.

Figure 9.2 also shows how multiple values can be designated in the Category section by separating the values with a comma. Each of the values then appears in the graph at the end of the Category section. A typical use for multiple values in the Category section is the creation of a Total category that sums the categories in the graph. Figure 9.2 defines the extra text entry "Total" in the Category section. This category corresponds to the sum (columnname for graph) entry in the Values section. The resulting graph in Figure 9.3 shows the total number of pharmaceuticals sold per month by hospitals.

Value The Value is the scale by which the category is measured in the graph. This component is associated with the Y axis in both 2-D and 3-

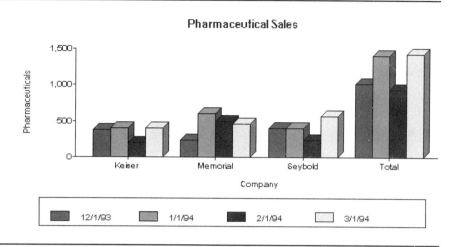

Figure 9.3   Total number of pharmaceuticals sold per month by hospitals.

D Area, Line, and Column graphs, and the X axis in the Bar graph. When the graph style is Pie, the data values are selected as a percentage of the total value amount.

Within the Value section of DataWindow graphs, a Dropdownlistbox shows all of the columns in the DataWindow as well as the aggregate functions **Count( )** and **Sum( )**. The function Count(columnname for graph) is for non-numeric columns and the function Sum(columnname for graph) is for numeric columns. This allows the developer to choose one of these items and see the values for the entire graph. In addition, the Value item can perform any type of arithmetic calculation by specifying the operation within the Sum function. For example, a sales of pharmaceuticals column could be divided by 2 using the function **Sum(rx_count/2 for graph)**.

Series The series component of the graph allows the developer to show information that relates to similar instances of categories. PowerBuilder automatically creates a legend with color-differentiated series components when the series checkbox is checked.

By indicating series components, the user is able to display each instance side-by-side. A series graph might show total sales by sales representative or sales by a specific billing date. The series value would be shown in the graph differently, depending on the type of graph and dimension chosen. The 2-D Area and Line graph series would be plotted in a different color on the same X and Y grid. In the 2-D Bar and Column graph, the series would be denoted by a different colored column in the Y and X axis, respectively.

When the 3-D graph is displayed, the series would be shown in the Z axis for the Area, Line, Column, and Bar graphs. If a series were specified, each item in the series would be graphed for each category. A Pie graph would show a different sized pie segment for each series.

An example of a series is similar classes of data but a different instance, such as Mercedes model numbers of 300, 500, or 700. Each model number would have its own datapoint, but they would be graphed on the same X and Y coordinates.

Overlays

Overlays can be used in a graph to illustrate a trend or call attention to a specific piece of information in a column or bar graph. The overlay functionality graphs a set of coordinates over an existing graph. The overlay can be defined as a set of information from a DataWindow column or as a specified type. The overlaid item is automatically added to the legend with an appropriate symbol to denote its values. The overlay syntax is specified by the developer in the series section.

One type of overlay allows the developer to overlay datapoints and add the points to the legend of a DataWindow graph. The column name that is used in the overlay syntax must be a column defined in the DataWindow. PowerBuilder selects the column and graphs the datapoints, then adds each of the datapoints associated with the column to the graph and the legend. This type of overlay is good for denoting data of special interest. The syntax for the addition of the column name is:

```
"@overlay~t" + columnName
```

The other type of overlay allows the developer to specify a secondary value item and label the associated datapoints with a value name. In the second type of overlay, the syntax is:

```
"@overlay~tValueName"
```

PowerBuilder automatically adds the value name to the legend and shows the overlay in a different color.

Figure 9.4 shows the definition of a DataWindow graph that shows the total sales by company and overlays the values for hardware sales by using the value name in the series section.

The resulting graph is shown in Figure 9.5.

In this example, the total hardware sales are overlaid to illustrate

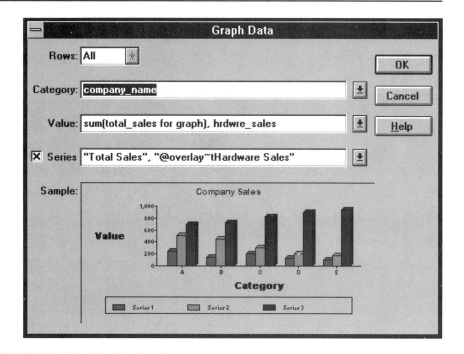

Figure 9.4   DataWindow graph showing total sales with overlay of hardware sales values using value name in the series section.

how much of the total sales pertains to hardware. The overlay is useful to show a trend or relevant detail on one graph.

Using Graphs

PowerBuilder graphs can be used within a DataWindow or Window object. This section discusses both types of graphs.

Graphs in the DataWindow The most frequent use of graphs is within a DataWindow. Because the graph is tied to the data in the database, it can change with the data, rather than being static. A DataWindow graph can either be created as a separate object within a DataWindow object or defined as the presentation style of a DataWindow.

Graph DataWindow Objects A graph object can be created and placed in an existing or new DataWindow by entering the chosen DataWindow and clicking the Graph icon (). In addition to the category, values,

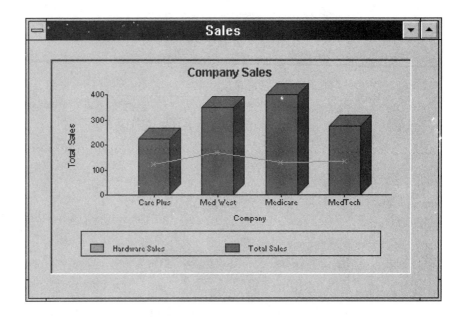

Figure 9.5 Resulting graph showing total sales and hardware sales.

and series parts of a graph discussed earlier in the chapter, DataWindow graphs (both graph DataWindow objects and graph presentation styles) allow the developer to specify the number of rows of data to use in the graph. The Rows value may contain one of the following:

All—Graphs all of the data that is retrieved into the DataWindow.

Page—Graphs all of the data that is retrieved into the displayed DataWindow by page.

Group—Graphs the data that has been retrieved into a DataWindow and grouped in a report.

Because the majority of application graphs use the All selection, PowerBuilder selects this as the default choice. For graph DataWindow objects, the Rows value can be modified by selecting the Data... option from the Graph Object's menu (displayed by selecting the graph object and clicking the right mouse button). However, for a DataWindow that uses a graph presentation style, the default value for Rows is All and cannot be changed.

The Data... option also allows the developer to specify the Category, Values, and Series values for the graph. For all DataWindow graphs, the Category and Series DDLBs contain a list of the columns defined in the DataWindow. The Values DDLB contains the same list of columns as well as the aggregate functions **Count( )** (for all non-numeric columns) and **Sum( )** (for all numeric columns).

Graph Presentation Style Rather than creating a graph object within a DataWindow, it is often desirable for an entire DataWindow to be represented as a graph. This is done by selecting the graph item when choosing a presentation style in the new DataWindow screen.

In this scenario, the graph can be resized by resizing the DataWindow control during execution. Like graph DataWindow objects, the developer defines the Rows, Category, Values, and Series values for the graph using the same methods and rules. The only difference is that the graph is saved as a DataWindow and not as an object within a DataWindow (as the DataWindow object graph is).

Graph Functions Graph functions allow the developer to do character manipulation or arithmetic on graph data. For DataWindow graphs, many of the same functions used with the DataWindow can be used with graphs. The following lists some of the functions that can be used with DataWindow graphs.

RowCount( )—Counts all of the rows that have been retrieved.

Sum( )—Calculates the sum of the items in the brackets.

Avg( )—Computes the average of the numbers in the brackets.

LookupDisplay( )—Uses the value from a DataWindow codes table to show the value's display value.

An example using the **LookupDisplay( )** function is shown in Figure 9.2.

Graphs in the Window Usually a graph is created within a DataWindow because it is easier to manipulate and it ties directly to the data in a database. However, graphs can also be created and manipulated within a window. Because the window graph does not directly tie to data in a database, the developer must create functions or scripts to create and populate the graph. Graphs can be created in a window by choosing the Graph icon on the toolbar. When the graph object has been added to the window, the data for the graph can be specified using the following PowerScript graph functions:

grAddCategory( )—Adds a category to the graph.

grAddData( )—Adds data to the graph. There are two function formats for grAdddata:

Non-Scatter graph—Adds a value to the end of the series identified in seriesnumber for the graph controlname. If categorylabel is specified, the category label identifies the tick mark on the category axis for this datapoint. If the category label has already been specified in a series in controlname, the data is added at the datapoint that corresponds to the existing category label.

For example, if the third category label specified in Series 1 is March and the developer adds data in Series 4 and specifies the category label March, the data is added at the datapoint 3 in Series 4.

Scatter Graph—Adds the x and y values of a data point to the end of the series identified in seriesnumber for the graph controlname.

grAddSeries( )—Adds a series to the graph and assigns it a number. The number, assigned sequentially beginning with 1, identifies the series within the graph.

grDeleteCategory( )—Deletes a category and its data values from a graph.

grDeleteData( )—Deletes a specific data value from a series of a graph.

grDeleteSeries( )—Deletes a series and its data values from a graph.

grImportClipboard( )—Copies the contents of the clipboard to a graph. The columns must be tab-separated in the clipboard.

grImportFile( )—Copies the contents of a file to a graph. The columns must be tab-separated in the file.

grImportString( )—Imports the contents of a string to a graph. The columns must be tab-separated in the string.

grInsertCategory( )—Inserts a category into a graph.

grInsertData( )—Inserts a data value into a series of a graph.

grModifyData( )—Changes a data value in a series of a graph. There are two formats of the **grModifyData( )** function, one for scatter graphs and one for non-scatter graphs.

grReset( )—Deletes data in a graph based on the value of the argument passed to the function. Valid arguments are:

All!—Delete all series, categories, and data

Category!—Delete all categories and data

Data!—Delete all data

Series!—Delete all series and data

grReset( ) can be used to clear the data in a graph before new data is added.

The graph in Figure 9.6 is created as follows.

The code behind the Graph button calls the window function **graph( )**, defined as Boolean. The code for this function uses the **grAddseries( )** function and the **grAddData( )** function to add the data about the series on the category line. The first line of the function resets all of the graphical data by using the function **grReset( )**.

```
// Code for graphing within a window
gr_1.grReset(all!)
// create the series

int iSeries, iRtn

this.setredraw(false)
```

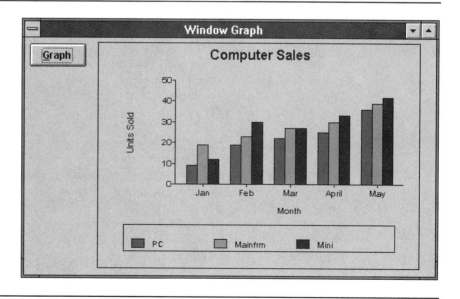

Figure 9.6   A window graph showing computer sales.

```
// Create the PC series
iSeries = gr_1.grAddSeries("PC")
iRtn = gr_1.grAddData(iSeries, 9, "Jan")
iRtn = gr_1.grAddData(iSeries, 19, "Feb")
iRtn = gr_1.grAddData(iSeries, 22, "Mar")
iRtn = gr_1.grAddData(iSeries, 25, "April")
iRtn = gr_1.grAddData(iSeries, 36, "May")

// Create the Mainframe series
iSeries = gr_1.grAddSeries("Mainfrm")
iRtn = gr_1.grAddData(iSeries, 19, "Jan")
iRtn = gr_1.grAddData(iSeries, 23, "Feb")
iRtn = gr_1.grAddData(iSeries, 27, "Mar")
iRtn = gr_1.grAddData(iSeries, 30, "April")
iRtn = gr_1.grAddData(iSeries, 39, "May")

// Create the Mini series
iSeries = gr_1.grAddSeries("Mini")
iRtn = gr_1.grAddData(iSeries, 12, "Jan")
iRtn = gr_1.grAddData(iSeries, 30, "Feb")
iRtn = gr_1.grAddData(iSeries, 27, "Mar")
iRtn = gr_1.grAddData(iSeries, 33, "April")
iRtn = gr_1.grAddData(iSeries, 42, "May")

this.setredraw(true)
return true
```

The script from the Graph button produces the graph in Figure 9.6. This graph illustrates the mainframe, mini, and PC sales for the months of January through May. Other functions or buttons could be added that would manipulate or alter the graphic values.

Manipulating Graphs

Once a graph has been created in either a window or DataWindow, its attributes can be altered programmatically. Attributes include both the graph's visual attributes and its data attributes. Visual attributes include the graph type, title, axis, and legend. Data attributes include such things as the number of categories and series in a graph, data values, and the style of a datapoint or series. This section discusses retrieving and modifying both the visual and data attributes of a graph.

Visual Attributes The developer can change the visual attributes of a graph in a window or DataWindow by simply specifying the graph attribute and the new value. The only difference between a window graph and a DataWindow graph is that changes to a window graph can be made directly, while changes to a DataWindow graph must be included within a **dwModify( )** statement.

PowerBuilder uses an internal object called grDispAttr to maintain the display attributes of the graph at runtime. This object is used for maintaining the display attributes of the title and legend graph components. Each of these components can be altered using the appropriate TitleDispAttr or LegendDispAttr values. The display attributes that can be changed include:

Attribute	*Description*
Alignment	Graph alignment
AutoSize	To turn the Autosize for the DataWindow on or off
BackColor	The background color of the graph
Escapement	The rotation of the text
FaceName	The font for the text
FillPattern	The object pattern to be filled with color
FontCharSet	The font character set for the text
FontFamily	Group of typefaces
FontPitch	Horizontal spacing of the text
Format	Value for the valid formatting
Italic	Italicize text
TextColor	Text color
TextSize	Text size
UnderLine	Underline text
Weight	Number to indicate the line thickness of the text

These attributes could be used, for example, to write a script for a button in a window that changes the title of a window graph to "Total Sales," changes the title to italic, changes the text of the legend to italic, and changes the size of the legend text to 20-point:

```
// Change the attributes of the title and legend for a window graph
gr_1.Title = "Total Sales"
gr_1.TitleDispAttr.Italic = TRUE
gr_1.LegendDispAttr.Italic = TRUE
gr_1.LegendDispAttr.TextSize = 20
```

If the graph were a DataWindow graph instead of a window graph, the same changes could be made by calling **dwModify( )**.

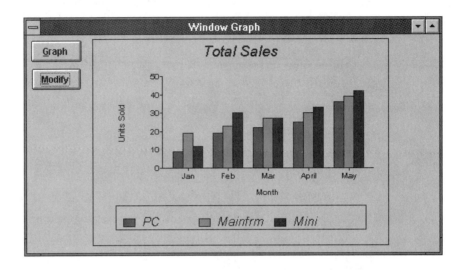

Figure 9.7 Modified window graph showing total sales.

With this code in the clicked event of the Modify button, the graph from the previous example looks like that in Figure 9.7 after the Modify button is clicked.

Note: In order to change the size of the text in either the title or legend, make sure the AutoSize attribute is disabled.

Unfortunately, when the graph is closed the changes are not saved in conjunction with the graph. If the changes that are made to the graph need to be made before the graph is shown to the user, a user-defined event can be created and mapped to the PowerBuilder event pbm_dwngraphcreate. An example illustrating the user-defined event can be found in the DrillDown Graph section later in the chapter.

Data Attributes PowerBuilder provides a set of functions for retrieving and modifying the data attributes of a graph. Many of the functions to modify a graph's data attributes were discussed earlier in the chapter. As with the visual attributes, retrieving the data attributes of a graph differs slightly between window graphs and DataWindow graphs. Window graph data attributes can be obtained directly, while DataWindow graph attributes are obtained using **dwDescribe( )**. The following functions are used to retrieve the data attributes of a window graph:

grCategoryCount( )—Returns the number of categories in a graph.

grCategoryName( )—Returns the name of the category and its internal number (integer).

grDataCount( )—Returns the number of datapoints in a series.

grDataStyle( )—Returns the color, fill pattern, or visual property of a datapoint.

grFindCategory( )—Returns the number of a category, given its name.

grFindSeries( )—Returns the number of a series, given its name.

grGetData( )—Returns the data value, given its series and position.

grSeriesCount( )—Returns the number of series in a graph.

grSeriesName( )—Returns the name of a series, given its number.

grSeriesStyle( )—Returns the color, fill pattern, or visual property of a specified series.

With DataWindow graphs, each time the DataWindow retrieves information from a database, the graph is destroyed and any changes that the developer made to the graph are lost. The developer can, however, place the data-access code in a user event that calls the appropriate function.

The PowerBuilder event id pbm_dwngraphcreate is triggered by a DataWindow control after it has created a graph and populated it with data, but before it has been displayed. The developer can create a user-defined event called pregraph and map it to the PowerBuilder event id called pbm_dwngraphcreate, as shown in Figure 9.8. A good use of this is to change the title of a graph before the graph is shown to the user. This is illustrated in the next example.

DrillDown Graphs

A DrillDown graph allows a user to click on specific data that needs to be seen in a more detailed (different) graph. The capability that allows the user to point and click within a graph is achieved by creating a clicked script in the DataWindow control or the window control.

This capability is enabled using the data attribute **grObject AtPointer( )** function. This function returns the object type that was clicked on as an **grObjectType** enumerated datatype. In addition to

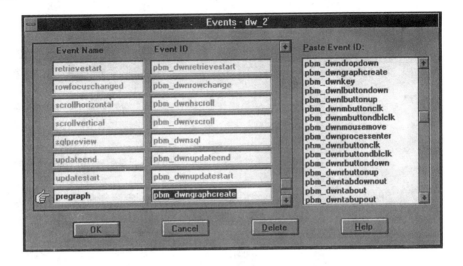

Figure 9.8   The pregraph custom event.

returning the object type, **grObjectAtPointer( )** also returns the series number and datapoint number that were clicked. These values are stored in function arguments passed by reference to **grObjectAt Pointer( )**.

Note: grObjectAtPointer( ) should be the first function called in the script for the clicked event for the graph control because decisions about the rest of the DrillDown can be determined from the values it returns.

The following example of a DrillDown graph shows the use of a user-defined event mapped to the PowerBuilder event pbm_dwngraphcreate, the use of the function **grObjectAtPointer( )**, and the altering of the other graphic data. In this example, the top graph in Figure 9.9 illustrates the sales of pharmaceuticals by company. When the user clicks on the column for one of the companies, the bottom graph fills with information about the choice (Care Plus in this example). In addition, the color and the title are set from gathering the information using the PowerBuilder GrFunctions.

First, create two graph DataWindows (dw_equipment and dw_company) with a SQL Select datasource. Next, create a window

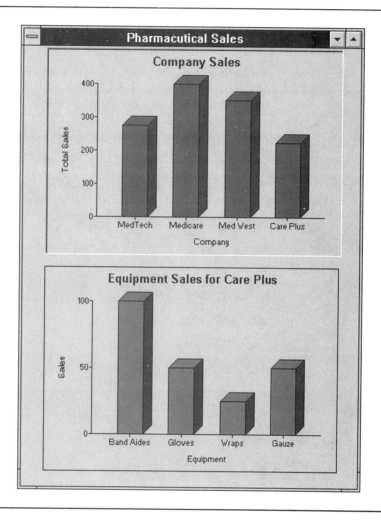

Figure 9.9   Example of a DrillDown graph.

(w_pharm) that includes both of the DataWindows. The first Data-
Window control, dw_1, should be visible and the second DataWindow,
dw_2, should initially be invisible. When the user clicks on one of the
columns in the first graph, the second DataWindow is filled with the
appropriate data related to the company that was clicked. The code for
the open event for window w_pharm is:

```
// Open script for pharmaceutical sales window w_pharm
```

```
dw_1.SetTransObject(sqlca)
dw_2.SetTransObject(sqlca)
dw_1.Retrieve ( )
```

This code assumes that SQLCA has been set up correctly and sets the transaction object for both dw_1 and dw_2 to it. After setting the transaction object, the data for the top DataWindow is retrieved and the company sales graph is displayed.

The code for the clicked event for the company DataWindow dw_1 calls **grObjectAtPointer( )** to gather the graph's name, series, and category. Next, the category is placed into a variable, *sCompany*, which is then used to retrieve the second DataWindow, dw_2. dw_2 is then displayed to the user using the **show( )** function:

```
/* Clicked script for dw_company */

grObjectType      ClickedObject

string  sCompany, grGraphName="gr_1", sSeriesName="Equipment"
int iRtn, iSeries, iCategory

/* Find out where the user clicked in the graph */
ClickedObject = this.grObjectAtPointer (grGraphName, iSeries, iCategory)

/* If user clicked on data or category, find out which one */
if ClickedObject = TypeData! or &
        ClickedObject = TypeCategory! then
        sCompany = this.grCategoryName (grGraphName, &
        iCategory)
        dw_2.dwModify (grGraphName + ".title=" + "'Equipment  Sales
for " + sCompany + "'")
        dw_2.Retrieve(sCompany)
        dw_2.Show( )
else
        MessageBox (Parent.Title, "Click on a company to display
detailed information")
end if
```

Finally, create a user-defined event (pregraph) for the DataWindow control dw_2 and map it to the PowerBuilder event id pbm_dwn graphcreate. This event fires before the graph is drawn on the screen, and will change the color of the series to purple before the graph is displayed to the user:

```
/* Pregraph script for dw_equipment */

string  sSeriesName
string  grGraphName = "gr_1"
int     iResult

/* Get the name of its series and set the color of that series to
purple. */

sSeriesName = grSeriesName (grGraphName, 1)
iResult = grSetSeriesStyle (grGraphName, sSeriesName, &
      Foreground!, Rgb (255, 0, 255) )
```

Using the GrFunctions, the series and style can be determined from the data and then altered programmatically using the GrSetfunctions.

3-D Graphs

In addition to the various types of two-dimensional graphs previously discussed, PowerBuilder also provides the capability to create 3-D graphs as both window and DataWindow graphs. When using 3-D graphs, the developer can alter the elevation, depth, rotation, and perspective of the graph. This is done by selecting the 3D View... option from the Graph Object's menu (displayed by selecting the graph object and clicking the right mouse button), as shown in Figure 9.10.

In addition to modifying a graph in the development environment, PowerBuilder 4 has added the following functions to programmatically modify a graph:

SetSeriesStyle( )—Sets the style and width for a series.

SeriesStyle( )—Returns the style and width of the line for a series.

DataStyle( )—Returns the style and width of the line for a series and datapoint.

SetDataStyle( )—Sets the style and width for the line for a series and datapoint.

SetDataPieExplode( )—Sets the percentage of explosion into the variable for the pie slice specified by a datapoint and series.

GetDataPieExplode( )—Returns the percentage of explosion for the pie slice specified by a series and datapoint.

As an example, A 3-D Pie graph can be used to show the allocation of employee salaries among different departments. This DataWindow

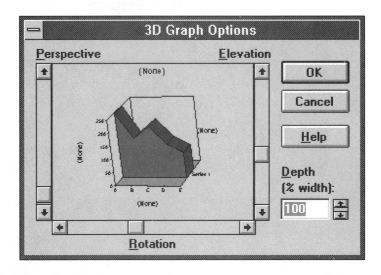

Figure 9.10   Selecting the 3D View... option.

graph indicates the percentage of the total salaries paid to employees broken down by each department, as shown in Figure 9.11.

From this graph, the user can double-click on one of the pie sections and display a second screen to alter the attributes of the graph (see Figure 9.13). This example will show how to change the attributes of

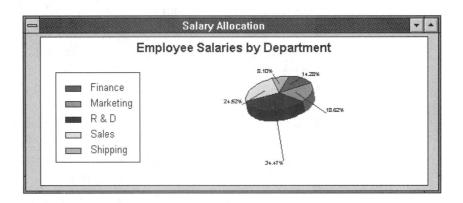

Figure 9.11   DataWindow graph showing employee salaries by department.

the graph and uses the new functions for getting and setting the pie explosion attributes of the graph.

First, create a structure called str_graphobjectatpoint to pass the needed information between windows. This is similar to the structure included with the PowerBuilder 4 example application, as seen in Figure 9.12.

Next, create a window called w_exp_grph and place a DataWindow control (dw_1) in it. The following code should be placed in the window's open event:

```
dw_1.settransobject(sqlca)
dw_1.retrieve( )
```

Next, add code to the double-clicked event of dw_1 to determine where the user clicked and open the window to allow the user to modify the graph's attributes:

```
// Determine where within the DataWindow the user clicked, populate
// the structure with the current graph attributes, and open the window
// to modify the attributes

int iSeries, iDatapoint
grobjecttype lgro_clickedtype
```

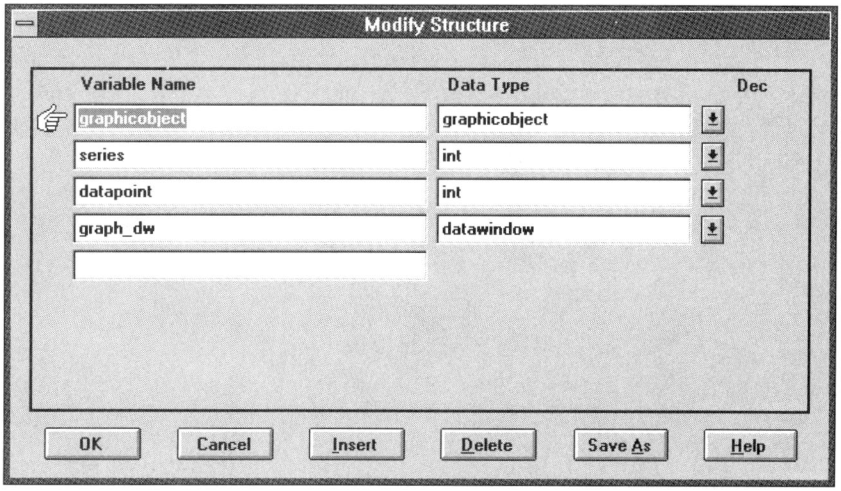

Figure 9.12   Definition of structure str_graphobjectatpoint.

```
int iGraphType
str_graphobjectatpoint lstr_graph

// Test for Pie (type 13) or Pie3d (type 17) graph types
iGraphType = Integer(dw_1.dwdescribe("gr_1.graphtype"))
If (iGraphType <> 13) and (iGraphType <> 17) Then Return

// Get the object, series, and datapoint that was double-clicked and
// pass this information in the lstr_graph structure and open the window
lgro_clickedtype = dw_1.grObjectAtPointer("gr_1",iSeries,iDatapoint)
If (iSeries > 0 and iDatapoint > 0) and &
    lgro_clickedtype = TypeData! Then
        lstr_graph.graphicobject = dw_1
        lstr_graph.graph_dw = dw_1
        lstr_graph.series = iSeries
        lstr_graph.datapoint = iDatapoint
        OpenWithParm(w_graph_attributes,lstr_graph)


End If
```

Next, create the w_graph_attributes window. This window allows the user to alter attributes of rotation, depth, elevation, and pie explosion percentage. This window includes four Edit Mask controls (em_rotation, em_depth, em_elevation, and em_explode), each with a range of -100 to 100. w_graph_attributes is shown in Figure 9.13.

After creating the four edit masks, create a user-defined event (ue_enchange) for each edit mask that maps to the PowerBuilder event id pbm_enchange. This event will be used to change the graph when the user changes one of the parameters in the edit mask. Before adding code to the ue_enchange event of each edit mask, create the following instance variables to store the graph's attributes:

object io_passed
graph igr_parm
datawindow i_dw
int i_iOriginalExplode
int i_iSeries
int i_iDatapoint
int i_iElevation
int i_iRotation
int i_iDepth

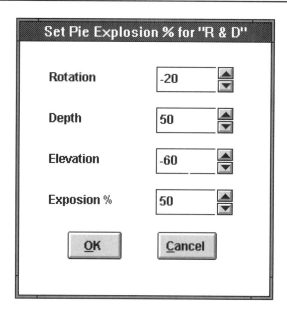

Figure 9.13   Display screen to alter attributes of the graph in Figure 9.11.

The open event of w_graph_attributes will take the parameter passed to it from the **OpenWithParm( )** function and assign values to the instance variables just listed:

```
graphicobject lgro_hold
grobjecttype lgrot_clickedtype
str_graphobjectatpoint1 lstr_graph
string sCategory

// Get the parameter passed to the window from the PB Message Object
// and assign values from the structure to the various instance variables
lstr_graph = Message.PowerObjectParm
lgro_hold = lstr_graph.graphicobject
i_iSeries = lstr_graph.series
i_iDatapoint = lstr_graph.datapoint
i_dw = lstr_graph.graph_dw

i_iElevation = Integer(i_dw.dwdescribe("gr_1.elevation"))
i_iDepth = Integer(i_dw.dwdescribe("gr_1.depth"))
i_iRotation = Integer(i_dw.dwdescribe("gr_1.rotation"))
```

```
// Determine the type of graph (DataWindow graph or window graph)
// and get the series, data point, and original explosion percentage.
If lgro_hold.TypeOf( ) = Graph! Then
        MessageBox("Graphs","Graph is not a datawindow", &
            Exclamation!,OKCancel!,2)
Elseif lgro_hold.TypeOf( ) = Datawindow! Then
        io_passed = Datawindow!
        i_dw.GetDataPieExplode("gr_1",i_iSeries,
            i_iDatapoint, & i_iOriginalExplode)
        sCategory = i_dw.categoryname("gr_1",i_iDatapoint)
End If


// Set the edit mask values to the original graph attributes and trigger
// the user-defined event ue_enchange to explode the pie graph
em_elevation.text = string(i_iElevation)
em_depth.text = string(i_iDepth)
em_rotation.text = string(i_iRotation)


If i_iOriginalExplode = 0 Then
        em_explode.text = "50"
        em_explode.triggerevent("ue_enchange")
Else
        em_explode.text = string(i_iOriginalExplode)
End If


//set window name to category
this.title = "Set Pie Explosion % for ~"" + sCategory + "~""
```

After creating the instance variables, add the following code to the ue_enchange event of em_explode:

```
// Code that tests to see if the graph is a datawindow and then
// set the variable to the value in the edit mask
If io_passed = Datawindow! Then
    i_dw.SetDataPieExplode("gr_1",i_iSeries,i_iDatapoint,&
    integer(em_explode.text))
End If
```

Add the following code to the ue_enchange event of em_elevation:

```
// Code for changing the graphs elevation
If io_passed = Datawindow! Then
        i_dw.dwmodify("gr_1.elevation =" +em_elevation.text)
End If
```

Add the following code to the ue_enchange event of em_depth:

```
// Code for changing the graph's depth
If io_passed = Datawindow! Then
    i_dw.dwmodify("gr_1.depth =" +em_depth.text)
End If
```

And finally, add the following code to the ue_enchange event of em_rotation:

```
If io_passed = Datawindow! Then
    i_dw.dwmodify("gr_1.rotation =" +em_rotation.text)
End If
```

Next, create **OK** and **Cancel** buttons. The **OK** button will close the parent window, while the **Cancel** button should ensure that the graph's attributes remain the same. The code for the clicked event of the **Cancel** button is:

```
If io_passed = Graph! Then
        igr_parm.SetDataPieExplode(i_iSeries,i_iDatapoint,&
                i_iOriginalExplode)
Elseif io_passed = Datawindow! Then
        i_dw.SetDataPieExplode("gr_1",i_iSeries,i_iDatapoint,&
                i_iOriginalExplode)
        i_dw.dwmodify("gr_1.elevation =" +string(i_iElevation))
        i_dw.dwmodify("gr_1.depth =" + string(i_iDepth))
        i_dw.dwmodify("gr_1.rotation =" + string(i_iRotation))
End If

Close (parent)
```

This example is now ready for execution. By double-clicking on one of the pie slices, the user is able to dynamically change the graph's attributes. This example illustrates some of PowerBuilder's 3D graph capabilities, including the use of some of the new PowerBuilder 4 graph functions.

REPORTS

Report Painter / PowerViewer

PowerViewer is designed to be used by an end-user for report creation. The PowerViewer user can create reports and graphs that the PowerBuilder developer can use in the creation of an application.

In addition, the PowerViewer documentation is simplified to allow nondevelopers to easily create usable reports for a PowerBuilder developer. The PowerViewer and the PowerBuilder development environment's reporting features are actually the same painter. Each of these painters allows the developer to create reports for an application. The reporting functionality in these tools creates a DataWindow, but does not allow the developer to insert and manipulate data from the Report painter.

Presentation Styles PowerBuilder's Report painter and PowerViewer allow the developer to show data using the Composite, Tabular, Grid, Freeform, Crosstab, N-Up, Label, and Graph formats. These formats are the same as those for DataWindows and are discussed in Chapter 3. However, this section does discuss the Crosstab report in greater detail.

Crosstab Reports The Crosstab style report allows the developer to create reports that present data in a spreadsheet-like grid. This type of report performs two-dimensional analysis of the data. The first dimension is the column, which displays data across the top of the graph. The second dimension is the row, which displays the data items down the report. Because the crosstab style is implemented as a grid DataWindow, the user can resize and reorder the columns at runtime.

Any cell of a Crosstab report can provide summary data, totals, or be a calculation based on the column values retrieved from the database. The crosstab style consists of the columns, rows, and values, as shown in Figure 9.14.

Each of these Crosstab report attributes is discussed in the following sections.

Columns When creating a Crosstab report, the developer specifies the columns to be used in the report in the Columns Dropdown listbox. Multiple columns may be selected by separating the entries with a comma (see Figure 9.15). If too many columns are included, however, the report expands beyond the screen and forces the user to use a scroll bar to view all of the data.

In addition to simply specifying the column name, the developer can use the **LookupDisplay( )** function. As mentioned earlier in this chapter, the **LookupDisplay( )** function displays the display value that is stored for a column in a DataWindow code table. Another way to specify columns is through a PowerScript function. For example, the **Month( )** function can be used to display only the month portion of a date:

```
Month(OrderDate)
```

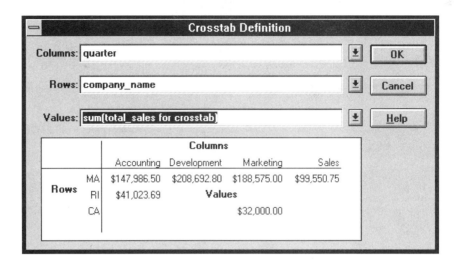

Figure 9.14   The Crosstab report style.

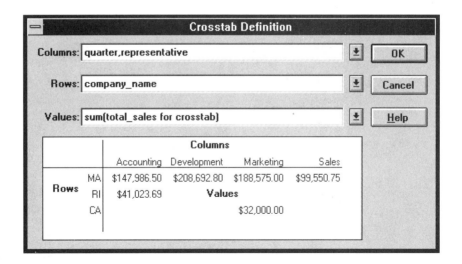

Figure 9.15   Selecting multiple columns when creating a Crosstab report.

The previous code will display the *OrderDate* variable as a numeric (1–12) for the month value (January to December).

If a Crosstab is created in the DataWindow painter, the developer can save initial values, validation expressions, and validation messages in the DataWindow using the Rows, Column Specifications MenuItem. If a Crosstab is created using PowerViewer or the Report painter, the developer can only view the columns and their type, as shown in Figure 9.16.

Rows When creating a Crosstab report, the developer should specify the rows to include in the report in the Rows DropDown listbox. (See Figure 9.14.) Like columns, multiple rows may be selected by separating the entries with a comma.

Values The Crosstab value is the data that is the intersection between the row and column. The value is an aggregate data value that summarizes the data for the row and column. By default, PowerBuilder fills the Dropdown listbox with the **count( )** of the column and row and a sum of the units for the Crosstab. The developer can also specify any other aggregate for the units in the Crosstab, if necessary.

Crosstab Summaries Another item that might be wanted in a report column is a total row or column. Aggregate values can be computed by columns or

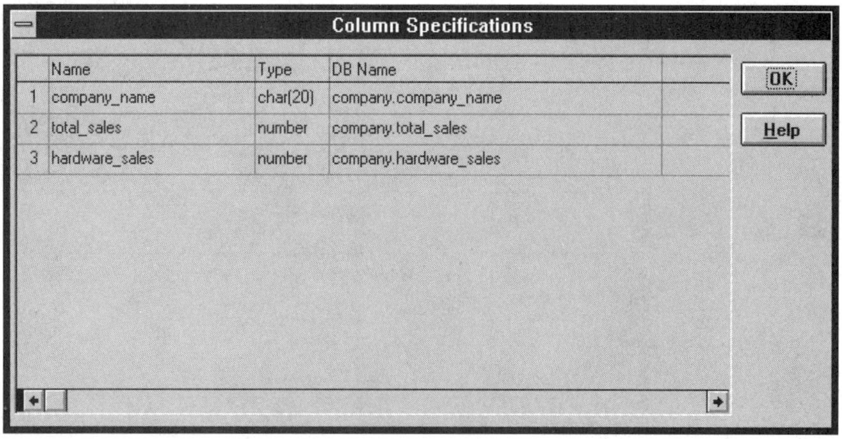

	Name	Type	DB Name
1	company_name	char(20)	company.company_name
2	total_sales	number	company.total_sales
3	hardware_sales	number	company.hardware_sales

Figure 9.16   The Column Specification dialog box.

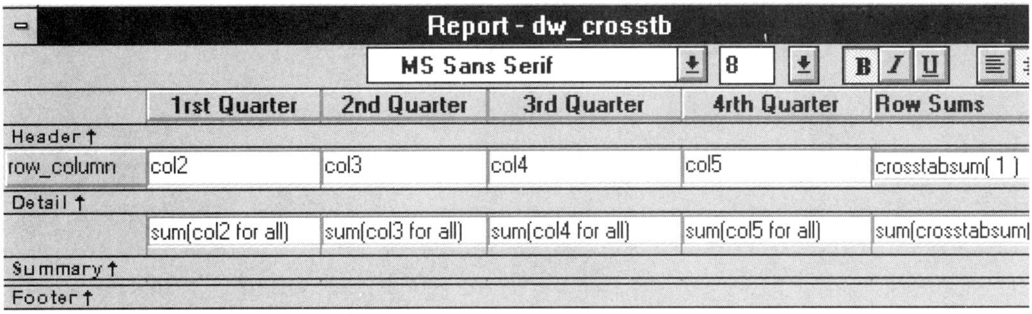
Report - dw_crosstb
MS Sans Serif
8
1rst Quarter
2nd Quarter
3rd Quarter
4rth Quarter
Row Sums
Header
row_column
col2
col3
col4
col5
crosstabsum(1)
Detail
sum(col2 for all)
sum(col3 for all)
sum(col4 for all)
sum(col5 for all)
sum(crosstabsum(
Summary
Footer

Figure 9.17 The summation of each of the columns and rows.

rows. For example, all of the values of a column can be summed together by creating a computed column or by using the summation.

In addition, a summary of the values for a row can be defined using the five predefined PowerBuilder crosstab aggregate functions. These functions are **CrosstabSum( )**, **CrosstabAvg( )**, **CrosstabCount( )**, **CrosstabMax( )**, and **CrosstabMin( )**. These functions perform the sum, average, count, max, and min, respectively, on rows that are selected.

Figure 9.17 illustrates the summation of each of the columns and rows.

Printing Reports

PowerBuilder allows the developer to provide print specifications in a report or DataWindow. In addition, PowerBuilder 4 offers some new printing capabilities.

When the developer chooses the Print Specifications... option under the Design menu, the screen in Figure 9.18 appears.

The document name specifies the name of the file when inserted into the print queue. In addition, if the user should be prompted with the Printer Setup dialog before the report prints, the checkbox at the bottom should be checked. PowerBuilder invokes the standard Windows Printer Setup dialog.

After the report's printing specifications have been defined, the report should be placed within a window. To allow the user to print the report, the developer should code the script to print all of the associated DataWindows that pertain to a report. The script should include the

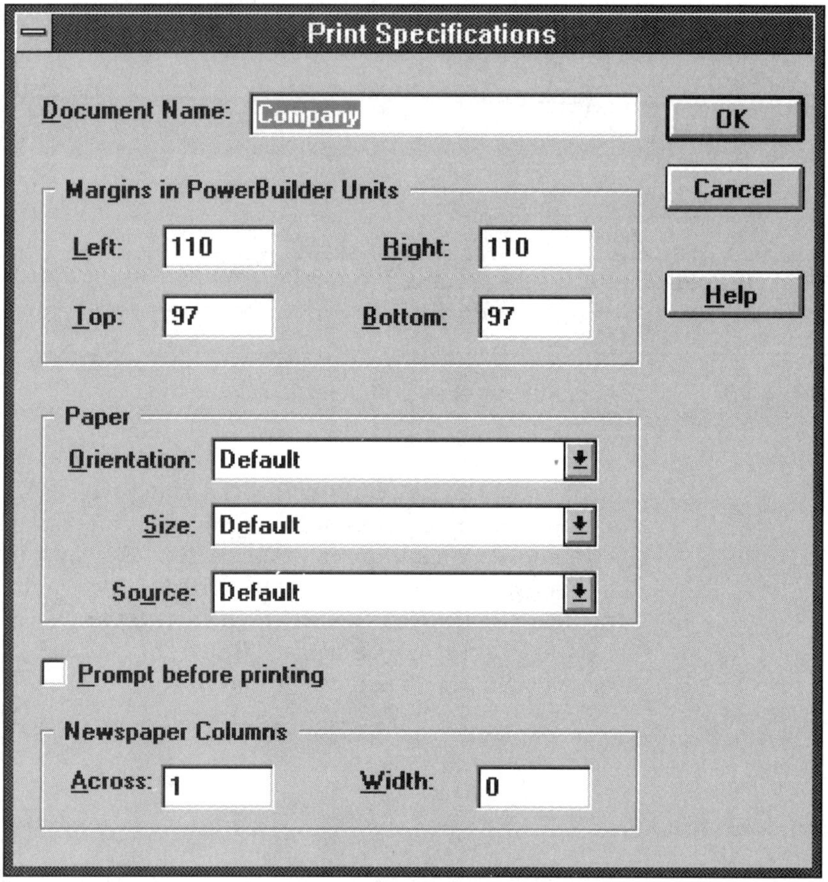

Figure 9.18 Choosing the Print Specifications... option.

PrintDataWindow( ) function that prints each of the DataWindows in the window. In addition, the **PrintOpen( )** function should be used to name the print job, including all of the DataWindows. The **PrintOpen( )** function defines a new blank page, specifies that all printing will be in the default font for the printer, and positions the cursor at the upper-left corner of the print area. If the developer specifies a name for the job, the name displays in the Windows 3.x Print Manager dialog box and in the Spooler dialog box.

For example, assume we want to print each of the two DataWindows in the window shown in Figure 9.19.

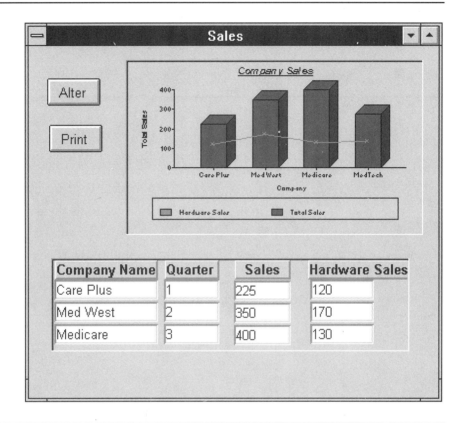

Figure 9.19   Printing two DataWindows.

To do this, place the following code in the print script for the window:

```
/* Print DataWindows dw_sales and dw_graph */
int iJob
iJob = PrintOpen("Sales Reports")

PrintDataWindow(iJob, dw_sales)
PrintDataWindow(iJob, dw_graph)
PrintClose(iJob)
```

The name of the print job is specified as "Sales Reports." This code prints the contents of the DataWindows dw_sales and dw_graph.

In addition to printing reports, PowerBuilder 4 has added the capability to print individual objects. This is done using the objectname. **Print( )** function.

The format of the **Print( )** function is

```
objectname.Print (printjobnumber,x,y {,width{,height}}}
```

where,

> objectname—the name of the object to print
>
> printjobnumber—the number the **PrintOpen** function assigns to the print job
>
> x—the X coordinate of the location to print the object
>
> y—the Y coordinate of the location to print the object
>
> width(optional)—the printed width of the object
>
> height(optional)—the printed height of the object

For example, to print the command button **cb_cancel** in its original size at location 200, 400:

```
int iJob
iJob = PrintOpen( )
cb_cancel.Print(iJob,200,400)
PrintClose(iJob)
```

In addition to printing individual objects, PowerBuilder 4 provides the **PrintScreen( )** function to print an entire screen. For example, the following code will print the current screen image in its original size at location 200, 400:

```
int iJob
iJob = PrintOpen( )
PrintScreen(iJob,200,400)
PrintClose(iJob)
```

Saving Reports

Another new PowerBuilder 4 feature is the Save Report As menu item located on the File menu in Print Preview in the Report painter. When this menu item is chosen, PowerBuilder saves the definition (source and object) and the data in the report to a file with the extension .PSR. Once the report is saved, it can be opened from File Manager, sent to other users, and opened from other applications. However, before the

.PSR file can be utilized from File Manager or other applications, it must be registered with the Powersoft 4.0 reports in the Windows registration database (REG.DAT) located in the Windows directory.

To open the report from File Manager, first associate the .PSR file with the Powersoft 4.0 Report (PM040.EXE). This can be done by selecting the Associate... option from the File menu in File Manager.

Note: To associate .PSR files with PowerBuilder or PowerViewer reports, use Browse on the Associate dialog and select the appropriate EXE file (PB040.EXE or PV040.EXE).

Reports saved as a .PSR file can be displayed in a DataWindow control by assigning the .PSR file name to the Dataobject attribute of the DataWindow control. For example, the following code will display the report file EXPENSE.PSR in the DataWindow control dw_1:

```
dw_1.dataobject=expense.psr
```

PowerMaker

PowerMaker, introduced with PowerBuilder 3.0, is an end-user tool designed to allow the user to manipulate a database, create forms, create queries, and create reports for use with a PowerBuilder application. Though designed as an end-user tool, PowerMaker users should have a basic understanding of SQL and some application-creation experience. This section covers:

- The PowerMaker environment
- The Database painter
- PowerMaker forms
- Queries
- Reports

The PowerMaker Environment The PowerMaker environment is very similar to the PowerBuilder development environment. PowerMaker allows the user to manipulate the development environment (e.g., with toolbars) in the same way as in PowerBuilder. The PowerMaker PowerPanel is shown in Figure 9.20.

PowerMaker allows the end-user to perform many of the same tasks as the PowerBuilder developer, but through an interface that is easier to understand. Each of the painters included in PowerMaker is similar,

Figure 9.20   The PowerMaker PowerPanel.

if not identical, to the painters in PowerBuilder, the only difference being fewer features available in PowerMaker.

The Database Painter The Database Painter allows the user to manipulate tables, insert data, create views, and create new tables in the same way as with PowerBuilder. Because the Database Painter itself is the same as in the PowerBuilder development environment, explanations of its use can be found in the PowerBuilder documentation.

PowerMaker Forms The PowerMaker environment offers the user a simple way to create and implement PowerBuilder windows, menus, and DataWindows by creating a new type of object called a Form. Whereas each object can be created separately in PowerBuilder, PowerMaker ties these objects together in a way that shields the user from the steps required to do this in the PowerBuilder development environment.

What Is PowerMaker Actually Doing? When the user creates a form, PowerMaker actually creates a DataWindow and an associated window of the same name. PowerMaker has a default application called Default that automatically creates the database link and allows the user to execute the application form in runtime. The end user, who does not see any of this happening, is able to create forms or executables of forms without ever seeing the complexity behind the process. In addition, PowerBuilder developers can create default forms or styles of forms for use by PowerMaker users.

When the user creates a PowerMaker executable, PowerMaker uses its default application, menu, and scripts to create an MDI application framework with the chosen forms included. The application creates the actual look and feel and functionality of the form that is shown to the user in the runtime mode in the Form painter.

Creating Forms The PowerMaker New Form dialog is shown in Figure 9.21.

The user has the choice of creating a form in one of the following formats:

- Master/Detail (One-to-Many)
- Master/Detail (Many-to-One)
- Freeform
- Grid

These formats are discussed in the following sections.

Master/Detail (One-to-Many) PowerMaker uses one of the Window paradigms discussed in Chapter 6 as a style for Form creation. The Master/Detail Form style ties one data entity to many associated entities.

The following example illustrates the creation of a simple Master/Detail style Form called f_open_purchase_orders. In the form, a single record for a vendor name is associated with many purchase order records.

When creation of a new form is selected in PowerMaker, the user is

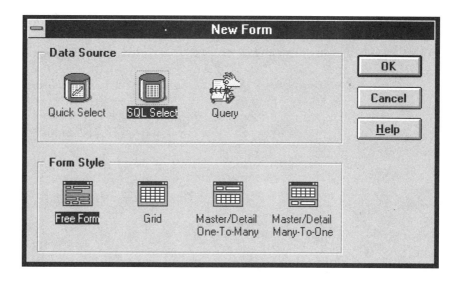

Figure 9.21   PowerMaker New Form dialog box.

led through the selection of tables, columns, and Where clause criteria. The top part of the form selects the company name, contact, and phone number from the table Vendor with the following SQL:

```
SELECT
vendor.id
vendor.name
vendor.contact
vendor.phone
FROM
vendor
```

The second part of the form selects the appropriate values from the tables and fields listed:

```
SELECT
purchase_order.number, purchase_order.product_id,
purchase_order.product, purchase_order.order_qty,
purchase_order.unit_price, purchase_order.total,
purchase_order.order_date
product.description
FROM purchase_order , product
WHERE purchase_order.product_id = product.id
```

After the user creates the form in the Form painter, PowerMaker actually creates two DataWindows (f_open_purchase_orders@1, f_open_purchase_orders@2) and one window (f_open_purchase_orders). The completed form is shown in Figure 9.22.

Because the created objects are basic PowerBuilder objects, they can be altered using either PowerMaker or PowerBuilder. Figure 9.23 shows the individual objects that make up the PowerMaker Form from within the PowerBuilder development environment.

Master/Detail (Many-to-One) The Master/Detail (Many-to-One) paradigm is exactly what the name describes— this style ties many records to one associated entity. This interface style might look like that in Figure 9.24.

This example shows many outstanding purchase orders for one vendor. Although the one-to-many style is most prevalent in developing simple applications, this style is sometimes useful.

FreeForm The Freeform style, which is the same as the freeform DataWindow presentation style, allows the user to select columns from a table and place them anywhere on the form. This style is generally used

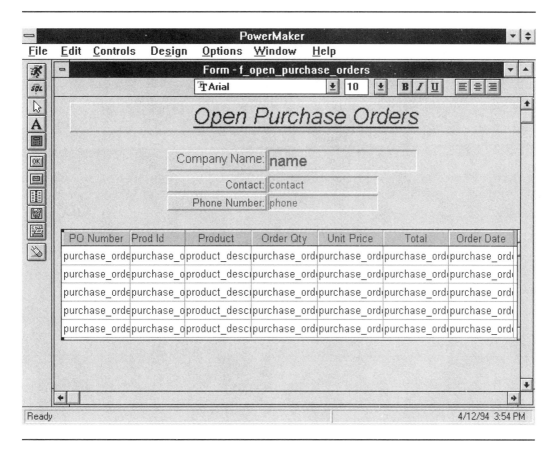

Figure 9.22   A simple Master/Detail Form.

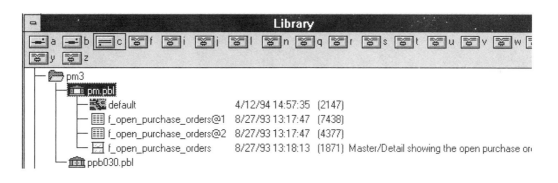

Figure 9.23   Individual objects that make up the PowerMaker Form.

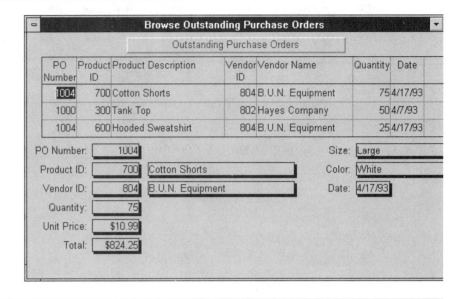

Figure 9.24   The Master/Detail (Many-to-One) interface style.

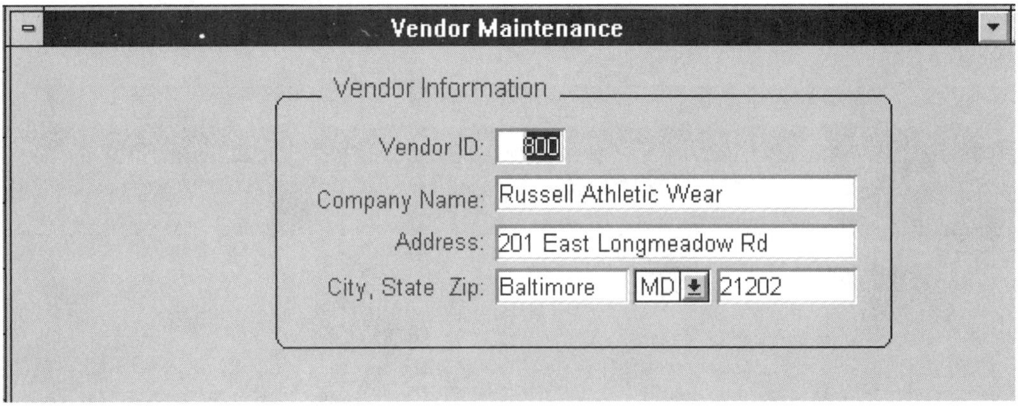

Vendor Maintenance

Vendor Information

Vendor ID: 800

Company Name: Russell Athletic Wear

Address: 201 East Longmeadow Rd

City, State Zip: Baltimore MD 21202

Figure 9.25   The Freeform style in PowerMaker.

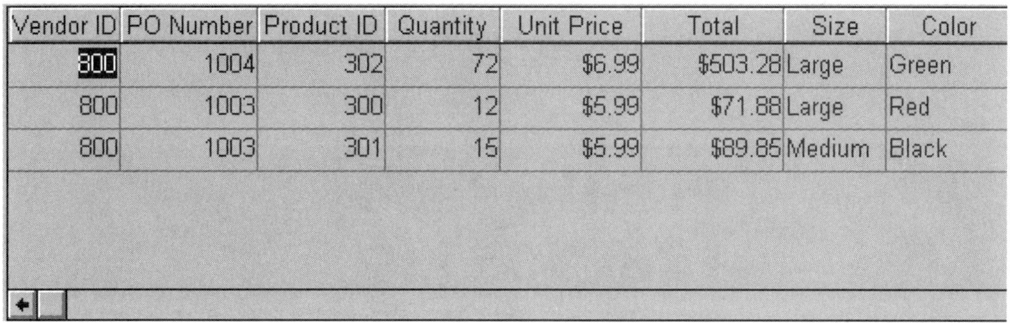

Vendor ID	PO Number	Product ID	Quantity	Unit Price	Total	Size	Color
800	1004	302	72	$6.99	$503.28	Large	Green
800	1003	300	12	$5.99	$71.88	Large	Red
800	1003	301	15	$5.99	$89.85	Medium	Black

Figure 9.26   Grid style Form in PowerMaker.

for maintenance screens or other data entry screens on which one record is accessed at a time. Figure 9.25 shows an example of the Freeform style.

This screen would be used for maintenance of a single vendor record.

Grid The Grid style Form is used to display many records simultaneously; it allows the user to update as many records as necessary on the same screen. Figure 9.26 shows a Grid style Form.

This screen would be used for maintenance of purchase order information for a particular vendor.

Queries PowerMaker also allows the user to create and save database queries as quick Selects. The Query Painter in PowerMaker is the same as in PowerBuilder.

Reports PowerViewer also allows the user to create and use reports in Forms. The Report painter in PowerViewer is the same as the Report Painter in PowerBuilder.

CHAPTER 10

Printing and
File/DOS I/O

This chapter is divided into two main sections: printing and file input/output (I/O). The first section covers different aspects of printing in PowerBuilder. The second section covers different aspects of writing and reading data to and from files in PowerBuilder. Some of the main topics covered in this chapter are:

- Printing:
  - How MS Windows printing works
  - Printing functions
  - Print area
  - Printing single DataWindows
  - Printing multiple DataWindows
  - Printing PowerBuilder objects
  - Printing graphs
  - PrintAll capabilities
  - Print Preview/Zoom
  - Print Dialog boxes
  - Changing MS Windows print settings
- File and DOS I/O:
  - File I/O functions
  - Reading files that exceed 32,766 bytes
  - Writing a file copy function
  - ImportFile function
  - Simulating the ImportFile function
  - Get DOS environment variables

- DOS Directory I/O
- Initialization (INI) Files

PRINTING

How MS Windows Printing Works

Most applications provide the capability for users to print information. Traditionally (in the non-Windows days), print functions had to deal with the varied and complex capabilities and requirements of many different applications. With Windows, applications do not print by interacting directly with the printer. Instead, the application sends output to a printer device context (see Figure 10.1). As such, developers need not worry about each printer's specific capabilities or requirements.

In support of printing, Windows applications first obtain information about the current printer. The printer model name, device driver, and printer port are obtained from the win.ini initialization file. This information is used to create a device context for the current printer. When the application sends output to a printer device context, Windows activates the print spooler to manage the print request.

Windows applications typically use six printer functions to control print jobs. In older versions of Windows, applications had to use printer escape sequences to communicate with the printer's device driver. (These escape sequences are available in the current version of Windows for backward compatibility.) Figure 10.2 shows that a current Windows application interfaces only with a standard print interface when printing. This interface then communicates with the printer drivers to translate the printer commands and print the data.

PowerBuilder implements its print capability by interfacing with

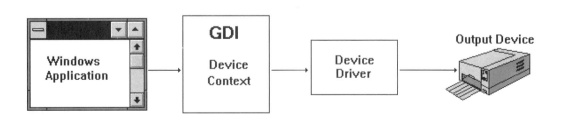

Figure 10.1   Windows applications send output to a printer device context.

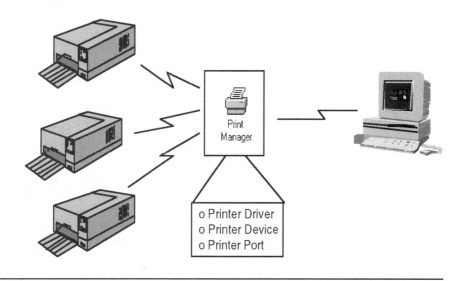

Figure 10.2   The Windows printer interface standard.

the standard Windows print interface. PowerBuilder makes life easy for developers by providing a standard set of print functions that can be called. Different methods for changing the current printer and/or settings are discussed in this chapter.

Many of a printer's settings can be changed by calling the **ExtDevice Mode( )** function in the printer driver. This function allows the developer to read and update printer settings. The **ExtDeviceMode( )** function puts setting information about the current printer into the tagDEVMODE structure. The following information can be returned from a printer's driver using the **ExtDeviceMode( )** function:

Item	*Description*
DeviceName	The name of the device the driver supports
SpecVersion	Version number of the structure
DriverVersion	Printer driver version number
Size	Size, in bytes, of the structure
DriverExtra	Size, in bytes, of the optional DriverData member for device specific data
Fields	Specifies which elements of the DEVMODE structure have been initialized

Orientation	Specifies the orientation of the paper (landscape or portrait)
PaperSize	Size of paper to print on
PaperLength	Paper length in tenths of a millimeter
PaperWidth	Paper width in tenths of a millimeter
Scale	Factor by which the printed output should be scaled
Copies	Number of copies printed
DefaultSource	Default bin from which the paper is fed
PrintQuality	Printer resolution
Color	If printer supports color or black/white output
Duplex	Duplex printing
YResolution	Y-resolution of the printer
TTOption	How TrueType should be printed

This list shows the many different printer attributes that can be changed manually or programmatically.

Printing Functions

PowerBuilder has the following print functions and events:

Print—Is a generic print function. It has five different formats: One format simply prints DataWindows; the other four print a string.

PrintOpen—Sets up a page for printing. This function returns a job id that can be used in most of the other PowerBuilder print functions.

PrintClose—Closes a print job. This is the last function called in a print session, unless the **PrintCancel** function is called first. This function sends the current page to the printer.

PrintStart Event—This is a DataWindow event. It is triggered when the contents of a DataWindow begin printing.

PrintEnd Event—This is a DataWindow event. It is triggered when the contents of a DataWindow have finished printing.

PrintCancel—The developer can cancel a job before it is closed by calling the **PrintCancel** function. This function sends the contents of the current page to the printer and cancels the print job.

PrintSetSpacing—This function sets the spacing of lines in a print job. The developer can specify a multiplier to be used to calculate the height of the cursor based on the current height of the characters. This function enables the developer to put the appropriate PowerScript in place to allow the user to print a document single-spaced, double-spaced, or even triple-spaced.

PrintDefineFont—This function allows the developer to put the appropriate PowerScript in place to define the fonts for a print job.

PrintSetup—This function opens the standard print setup dialog box.

PrintX—This function returns the X coordinate of the print cursor.

PrintY—This function returns the Y coordinate of the print cursor.

PrintSend—This function is similar to the Escape function in the Windows SDK. It allows the developer to send a printer escape sequence directly to a printer. Escape sequences are printer-specific.

PrintWidth—This function returns the width of a string in the current font of a specified print job number. The width is useful in determining the next print position.

PrintDataWindow—This function is used to print a DataWindow using the current print job number. This function is different from the DataWindow format of the print function. The print function simply sends the DataWindow printout to the default printer; it does not need a print job.

PrintText—Prints a string in the current font of the specified print job starting at specified X and Y coordinates. The last parameter of this function permits the developer to specify a different font than the one assigned to the print job. A different font can be set by calling the **PrintDefineFont** function.

PrintBitmap—This function, which prints a bitmap using a job number, starts printing at specified X and Y coordinates with specified height and width.

PrintLine—Prints a line starting at specified X and Y coordinates, ending at specified X and Y coordinates, with a parameter available to set the thickness of the line.

PrintOval—Prints an oval at the specified X and Y coordinates with parameters available for the width, height, and thickness.

PrintPage Event—This event is triggered before each print page of a DataWindow is formatted for printing. This event can be used in conjunction with the **SetActionCode** function, to force the printer to skip a page.

PrintPage—This function works similarly to the PrintPage Event. The event is specified for DataWindows whereas the **PrintPage**

function is used for print jobs. In order to skip a page, this function must be called.

PrintRect—This function is similar to the **PrintOval** function except it prints a rectangle.

PrintRoundRect—This function is similar to the **PrintRect** function except the rectangle that is printed has rounded corners.

These functions and events are used to manipulate printing. To skip a page, for example, the following code would be placed in the PrintPage event of a DataWindow: **SetActionCode**(1). If the developer does not want a page to be skipped, the following code is used: **SetActionCode**(0).

Print Area

In PowerBuilder, printing is defined in terms of the page area. The page area is analogous to the GDI Device Context when printing in native Windows. The print area is the physical page size less any margins. For example, if the page size is 8.5 by 11 inches, and the top, bottom, and side margins are all half an inch, the print area is 7.5 by 10 inches. All measurements in the print area are in 1/1000s of an inch. Figure 10.3 shows the relationship between the page and the print area; it also shows the coordinates for the print area in 1/1000s of an inch.

When printing, PowerBuilder uses a cursor to keep track of the print location. The cursor contains the X and Y coordinates of the upper-left corner of the location at which printing will begin. The **PrintX( )** and **PrintY( )** functions return the X and Y coordinates of the current print cursor. PowerBuilder updates the cursor (including tab position, if required) after each print operation. To position text, objects, lines, and pictures when creating complex reports, the developer specifies the cursor position as part of each print function call. All cursor parameters (including the print cursor) in the PowerBuilder print functions are measured in 1/1000s of an inch.

Printing Single DataWindows

Simple Case Printing a DataWindow is, in most cases, a simple process. The **Print( )** and **PrintDataWindow( )** functions provide the developer with a simple way of printing DataWindows. To print a DataWindow, the following code can be executed in the application:

```
dw_name.Print( )
```

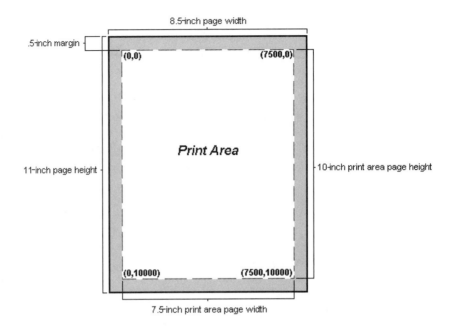

Figure 10.3   Defining the print area.

or

```
PrintDataWindow(printjobid, dw_name)
```

The first function **Print( )** should be used if the developer wants to display the standard Windows Print/Cancel dialog box when printing. The second function **PrintDataWindow( )** should be used if the developer wants to print the DataWindow as a print job.

Case of the Hidden DataWindow (First Method) If the developer wants to print a DataWindow in a format different from the way it displays on the screen, the process is a little more difficult. For example, a DataWindow is displayed in the format shown in Figure 10.4.

If the developer wants the user to be able to drag-and-drop a row onto the print icon and have its detail information printed as shown in Figure 10.5, the following must be done.

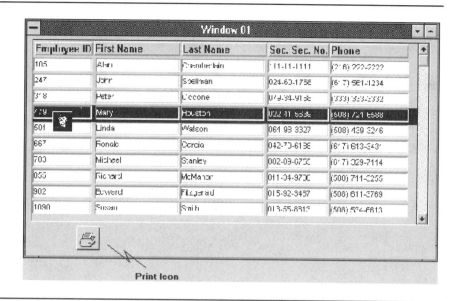

Figure 10.4   Sample DataWindow display format.

Figure 10.5   Sample DataWindow print format.

407

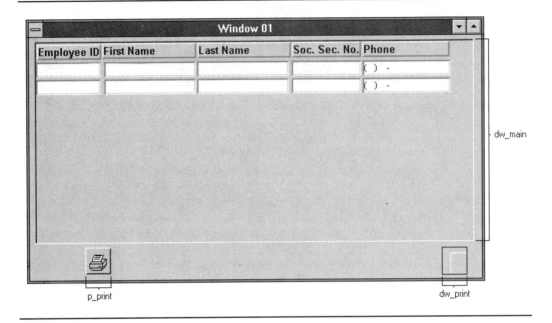

Figure 10.6   Controls in Figure 10.4 defined.

In Figure 10.6, the window has the following controls:

Controls	Purpose
dw_main	The main DataWindow. This is the DataWindow on which the user selects an employee to print.
p_print	This is a print control. The user can drag an employee from the main dw_main and drop it on p_print, for printing.
dw_print	This is the print DataWindow. This DataWindow is not visible to the user. When the user drops an employee on the p_print control, the detail information is retrieved into dw_print and then printed.

The dw_main control has the following lines of PowerScript: In the constructor event of dw_main:

```
if this.settransobject(SQLCA) = 1 then
        if this.retrieve( ) = -1 then
                error processing
```

```
                    Halt Close
            end if
else
            Halt Close
end if
```

In the clicked event of dw_main:

```
ULong ulRow
ulRow = this.GetClickedRow( )
if ulRow > 0 then
        i_iempid = this.GetItemNumber(ulRow,"empid")
        this.SelectRow(0,False)
        this.SelectRow(ulRow,True)
        this.Drag(Begin!)
end if
```

In the dragdrop event of p_print:

```
if dw_print.Retrieve(i_iEmpID) = -1 then
        // error processing
else if dw_print.Print( ) = -1 then
        // error processing
end if
```

In the constructor event of dw_print:

```
if this.settransobject(SQLCA) = -1 then
        // error processing
        Halt Close
end if
```

That's what it takes.

Case of the Hidden DataWindow (Second Method) Another approach to meeting the previously described requirement is to use shared result sets. This method is more efficient because it only submits one query to the database. This becomes an issue when retrieving large result sets from a database across the network. To use this second approach with shared DataWindows, the developer uses the following PowerScript:

In the constructor event of dw_main:

```
this.settransobject(SQLCA)
this.retrieve( )
this.dwShareData(dw_print)
```

In the dragdrop event for p_print:

```
dw_main.SetRedraw(False)
dw_print.SetFilter ("empid = " +String(i_iempid))
dw_print.Filter( )
if dw_print.Print( ) = -1 then
        // error processing
end if
dw_print.SetFilter("")
dw_print.Filter( )
dw_main.SetRedraw(True)
```

Note: Since the result sets are shared between dw_main and dw_print, when a filter is issued on dw_print both DataWindows are affected. In order to prevent the user from viewing the effects of the filter, the **SetRedraw** function can be used to prevent dw_main from being repainted.

Case of the Hidden DataWindow (Third Method) The third method uses pieces from each of the first two methods. This method retrieves data into both dw_main and dw_print, similar to the first method. The difference here is that all the data is returned from the start into both DataWindows using two retrieve function calls.

The following PowerScript is used in the open event of the window:

```
// Error processing needs to be done
dw_main.retrieve( )
dw_print.retrieve( )
```

Each time the user drags an employee from dw_main into the p_print control, the **SetFilter** and **Filter** functions are called for dw_print.

The following PowerScript is used in the dragdrop event of p_print:

```
dw_print.SetFilter ("empid = " +String(i_iempid))
dw_print.Filter( )
if dw_print.Print( ) = -1 then
        // error processing
end if
```

The advantage of this method over the first method is that the PowerScript in the dragdrop event of p_print does not do a retrieve every time. All the p_print control does is set the filter and print the resulting DataWindow.

Printing Multiple DataWindows

As with printing single DataWindows, when printing multiple Data-Windows, a hidden print DataWindow is necessary. The difference is the way multiple DataWindows are combined into one print DataWindow. Following are some examples that demonstrate multiple DataWindow printing techniques.

In this first example, a single record from the master grid DataWindow (see Figure 10.7) is combined with the record from the detail freeform DataWindow. The user selects the record from the master DataWindow and detail information about the selected record is displayed in the detail DataWindow. Then, the user can drag-and-drop the detail record on the print icon.

The controls in this example are shown in Figure 10.8.

Option 1 Create a hidden DataWindow and have the DataWindow join the master and detail tables and return the result set in a preformatted hidden print DataWindow. When the user drops the drag icon onto the print icon, the print icon executes the PowerScript in the dragdrop event of p_print:

```
if NOT dw_print.Retrieve(i_id) = -1 then
     if dw_print.Print( ) = -1 then
            // Error Processing
     end if
else
     // Error Processing
end if
```

Option 2 This second example prints the same two DataWindows without submitting an additional retrieve for printing. Because the print DataWindow needs to share data with the detail DataWindow, the **dwModify** function is used. The developer adds two dummy text fields to the hidden print DataWindow. Then, when the user drops the drag icon onto the print icon, the **GetItemString** function gets the selected person's first and last name from the master DataWindow. The **dwModify** function is used to set the values in the hidden print DataWindow. When this is done, the print DataWindow can be printed.

The PowerScript in the dragdrop event of p_print is:

```
Int iRow
iRow = dw_main.GetRow( )
dw_print.dwModify("dummy1.Text = '" + &
     dw_main.GetItemString(iRow,"fname") +"'")
```

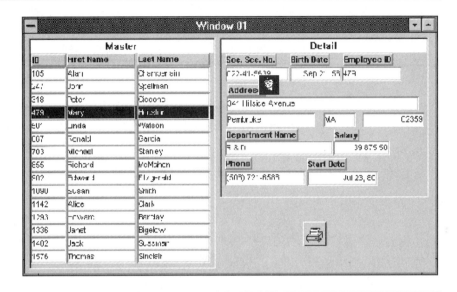

Figure 10.7 Printing the detail record using Drag-and-Drop.

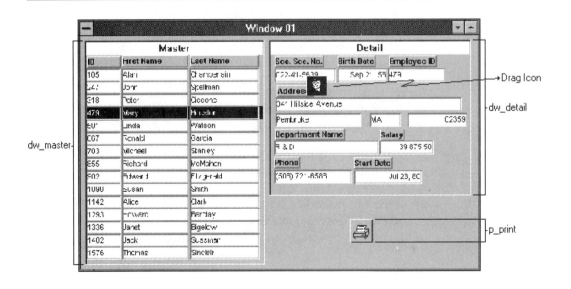

Figure 10.8 Controls defined in Figure 10.7.

```
dw_print.dwModify("dummy2.Text = '" +&
        dw_main.GetItemString(iRow,"lname") +"'")
if dw_print.Print( ) = -1 then
        // error processing
end if
```

Note: Using the dwModify Create and Destroy options in combination with the **SetRedraw** function, the hidden print DataWindow could be eliminated. Instead of the hidden print DataWindow, the detail DataWindow could be used. When the user drops the drag icon onto the print icon, the developer can do the following:

- Set redraw to False
- Dynamically create dummy1 and dummy2 text fields
- Set the dummy fields with the selected person's first and last name
- Print the detail DataWindow
- Dynamically destroy the dummy1 and dummy2 text fields
- Set redraw to True

This would eliminate the need for a hidden print DataWindow.

The previous example discusses the printing of two DataWindows when both DataWindows have only one record to print. The following example discusses the printing of two DataWindows where the detail DataWindow has multiple records to print.

In this example, header information is displayed about a customer in a Customer DataWindow and the customer's orders are listed in an Order DataWindow. The Select a Customer window is opened both when the window is first opened and when the user clicks the List-up button next to the Customer Number field. (see Figure 10.9)

The user can drag-and-drop the drag icon onto the print icon (from the Customer DataWindow) and the header information and the list of orders are printed. This example shows how a single record from one DataWindow is combined with multiple related records from another DataWindow and printed as one report. (see Figure 10.10)

This can be done using a temporary file and a hidden print DataWindow. The developer would place the following code in the dragdrop event of p_print:

```
Long lFileNo
String sTemp01 = "temp01.txt"
```

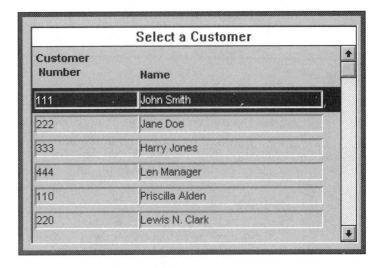

Figure 10.9   The select a customer window.

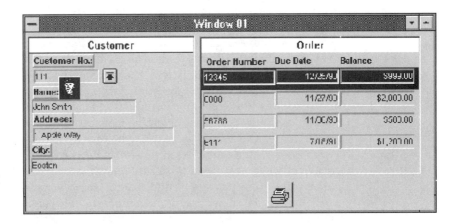

Figure 10.10   A single record from one DataWindow combined with multiple related records from another DataWindow and printed as one report.

```
// Clear the contents of the print DataWindow
dw_print.Reset( )

// Write the titles and data for the customer DataWindow to a temp file
// then import the file into the print DataWindow.
dw_customer.SaveAs(sTemp01,Text!,True)
dw_print.ImportFile(sTemp01)

// Write the titles and data for the order DataWindow to a temp file
// then import the file into the print DataWindow.
dw_order.SaveAs(sTemp01,Text!,True)
dw_print.ImportFile(sTemp01)

// Delete the temporary file
FileDelete(sTemp01)

// Print the print DataWindow
if dw_print.Print( ) = -1 then
      // error processing
end if
```

Note: If the developer wanted only certain fields in each DataWindow to be printed, he or she would have to programmatically get (using perhaps the **dwDescribe** or **GetItemString** function) the desired fields and write them to a temporary text file. The temporary file could then be imported into the print DataWindow.

In the next example in Figure 10.11, there are three DataWindows that need to be printed: the Customer DataWindow, the Order DataWindow, and the Order detail DataWindow. One record from the Customer DataWindow, one record from the Order DataWindow, and all the order details from the Order detail DataWindow are to be printed. In this case, the user drags and drops a particular order and all the items in that order are to be printed.

The developer puts the following code in the dragdrop event of p_print:

```
Long lFileNo
String sTemp01 = "temp01.txt"

// Clear the contents of the print DataWindow
dw_print.Reset( )
```

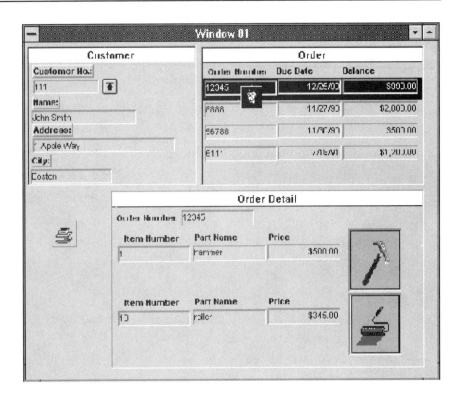

Figure 10.11   The Customer, Detail, and Order Detail DataWindows to be printed.

```
// Write the titles and data for the customer DataWindow to a temp file
// then import the file into the print DataWindow
dw_customer.SaveAs(sTemp01,Text!,True)
dw_print.ImportFile(sTemp01)

// Temporarily prevent the object from being repainted
dw_order.SetRedraw(False)

// Only display the selected order record
dw_order.SetFilter("order_number = " + String(i_iOrderNum))
dw_order.Filter( )

// Write the titles and data for the order DataWindow to the temp file
dw_order.SaveAs(sTemp01,Text!,True)
```

```
// Import the temp file into the print DataWindow
dw_print.ImportFile(sTemp01)

// Reset the filter
dw_order.SetFilter("")
dw_order.Filter( )

// Write the titles and data for the order_detail DataWindow to a temp
file
// then import the file into the print DataWindow.
dw_order_detail.SaveAs(sTemp01,Text!,True)
dw_print.ImportFile(sTemp01)

// Delete the temporary file
FileDelete(sTemp01)

// Allow the dw_order DataWindow to be repainted
dw_order.SetRedraw(True)

// Print the print DataWindow
if dw_print.Print( ) = -1 then
     // error processing
end if
```

Note: Using nested DataWindows with this version makes it easier to print multiple DataWindows.

Printing PowerBuilder Objects

Most PowerBuilder objects can be printed using PowerScript. Power-Builder also has functions that can print text and bitmaps. The printing of text functions can be useful if a developer would like to either print specific lines of text to the printer or manually print the entire contents of a window in a print job. If the developer were interested in printing data from the different non-DataWindow controls on a window, each data value could be obtained and printed in a print job or written to a temporary file and imported into a hidden, preformatted DataWindow.

With this version of PowerBuilder a couple of new print functions have been added to permit the developer and user to print objects. In previous versions of PowerBuilder only certain objects such as rectangles, circles, ovals, and some others could be printed. With this version and the addition of the two new functions the objects that can be printed have increased to include, among others, commandbuttons, singlelinedits, statictext and windows. The two new print functions are as follows. The first function is:

```
objectname.Print (printjobnumber, x, y{, width{, height}})
```

This function prints objectname using printjobnumber at x and y coordinates with specified width and height. If the coordinates are not specified, objectname is printed with its original coordinates. An example of the functions is:

```
int iJob
iJob = PrintOpen( )
cb_close.Print(iJob,500,1000)
PrintClose(Job)
```

The second new print function is called **PrintScreen( )**. This function does as its name dictates—it prints the screen using specified screen coordinates. Following is a prototype of the PrintScreen function.

```
PrintScreen (printjobnumber, x, y{, width{, height}})
```

The following PowerScript prints the current screen image in its original size at location 500, 1000:

```
int iJob
iJob = PrintOpen( )
PrintScreen(iJob,500,1000)
PrintClose(iJob)
```

Printing Graphs

When a graph is located in a DataWindow, printing it is the same as printing a DataWindow. The Print function can be called to print the DataWindow. Graphs can be created in four ways: as a user object, as a window control, as a control on a DataWindow, and as a graph DataWindow. PowerBuilder only supports printing of graphs that are controls on a DataWindow or graph DataWindow objects. There are functions that can export the data for the graph and subsequently print the data, but not the graph as an image.

PowerBuilder has the **grClipboard** function that can copy the image of a graph to the clipboard. When the image is in the clipboard, Windows SDK functions can be called to either print the image from the clipboard or just save it as a bitmap file and print it from PowerBuilder using the **PrintBitmap** function. A more detailed discussion of PowerBuilder graphs can be found in Chapter 9.

Print All Capabilities

When designing MDI applications, the developer may want a **Print All** function that prints all of the open sheets. This is similar to the **Close All** function discussed in Chapter 4. The MDI frame maintains a global array of open sheet handles. When the developer selects the **Print All** option from the menu, the following happens:

- A FOR loop is started that goes through the open sheet handle array.
- The first window is activated programmatically.
- The print event of the parentwindow is triggered (or a function in the parentwindow can be called) that handles printing for that particular window.
- This process continues until the upper bound of the array has been reached.

Print Preview/Zoom

PowerBuilder has a Print Preview and a Print Zoom option that allow a developer or user to preview what the output will look like. Following is an example.

Create a window that contains a DataWindow. Place a "zoom" commandbutton on the window that includes the following code as shown in Figure 10.12, in the clicked event.

```
String  sAttr, sValue

// store the datawindow attribute in a variable
sAttr = "datawindow.zoom"
// get the current value of the datawindow zoom attribute
sValue = dw_report.dwDescribe (sAttr)
// open a zoom window that displays zoom parameters
OpenWithParm (w_zoom, sValue)
// modify the zoom attribute of the datawindow with the value
// stored in message.stringparm
If message.stringparm <> "" Then
      dw_report.dwModify (sAttr + "=" + message.stringparm)
End If
```

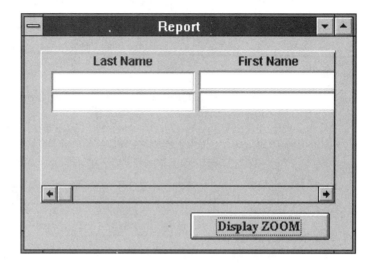

Figure 10.12   Sample window with zoom commandbutton.

The w_zoom window looks like that in Figure 10.13. A different magnification level should be selected and the OK command button must be clicked. Once the OK command button has been clicked, the zoom window is closed using the **CloseWithReturn(...)** function. The selected magnification must be passed as the second parameter of the **CloseWithReturn** function.

The output original Datawindow with 65 percent magnification looks like Figure 10.14.

Print Dialog Boxes

In most Windows applications, when users select the print option, a dialog box appears with some user options and a print button. Following are some Print dialog boxes from popular Windows applications:

The Print dialog box for Microsoft Word looks like Figure 10.15.

The Print dialog box for Lotus Organizer looks like Figure 10.16.

The Print dialog box for Microsoft Excel looks like Figure 10.17.

Dialog boxes can be created for PowerBuilder applications. A PowerBuilder print dialog box might look like the one in Figure 10.18.

When developing a common print dialog box for applications, it must

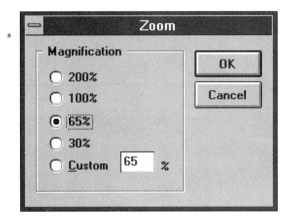

Figure 10.13   Window w_zoom.

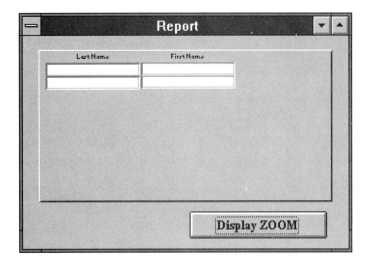

Figure 10.14   Sample window with 65 percent zoom setting.

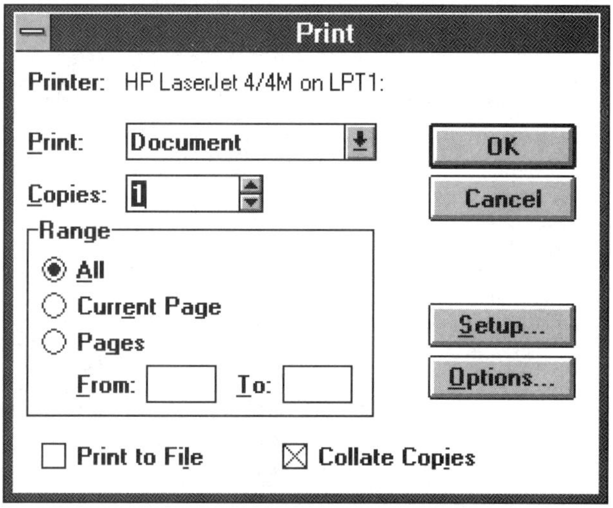

Figure 10.15   The print dialog box for Microsoft Word.

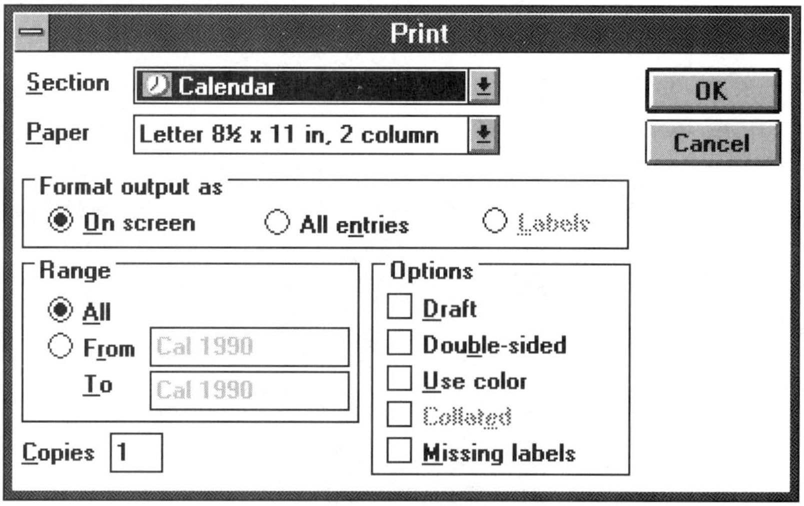

Figure 10.16   The print dialog box for Lotus Organizer.

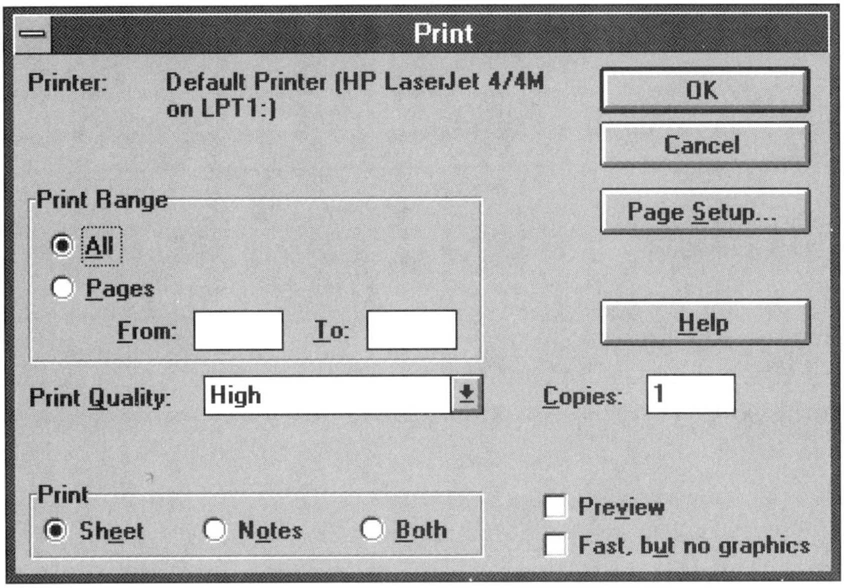

Figure 10.17   The print dialog box for Microsoft Excel.

be generic so the different modules of an application can use it. The following example describes how a common print dialog box can be developed. The application in this example can display various types of reports—some simple, some of medium complexity, and some complex. A simple report might be a window that contains DataWindows. A report of medium complexity might contain MultiLineEdits and ListBoxes. A complex report would have bitmaps and graph objects. Each of these types of reports could have hundreds of actual reports with different information on them. When designing this application, each report type could be a descendant window of a common report ancestor window, as shown in Figure 10.19.

To print each of the report types, different PowerScript logic would be executed. When the user selected the File/Print menu selection, the following process would take place.

A user-defined print event from the menu's ParentWindow (w_ReportAncestor) would be executed. The print event opens the common print dialog box and executes an initialization function within the common print dialog box window.

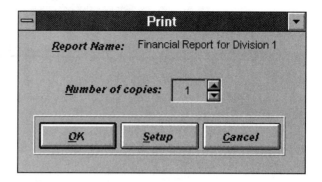

Figure 10.18   A PowerBuilder print dialog box.

```
Open(w_PrintDialogBox)
w_PrintDialogBox.f_init(this, this.title)
```

In the Print dialog box window, an instance variable of type report ancestor is declared as follows:

```
w_ReportAncestor i_wCaller
```

The **f_init(...)** function of the print dialog box has the following two parameters:

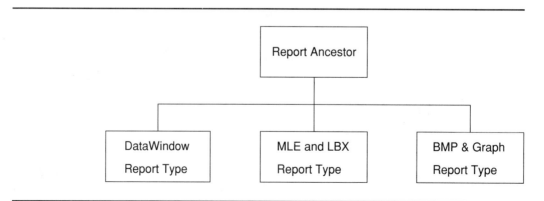

Figure 10.19   Sample reporting hierarchy.

```
f_init (ref window wCallerReport, string sReportName)

i_wCaller = wCallerReport

// set the report name to the report name static text in the dialog box
st_ReportName.text = sReportName
```

When the user clicks the OK command button, the following code is executed:

```
i_wCaller.f_PrintReport(Integer(em_NumberOfCopies.text))
close(parent)
```

In each of the report type windows there is an **f_PrintReport(...)** function that contains specific processing for that report type.

The print dialog in Figure 10.20 is a new dialog box that allows the user or developer to print all pages, a range of pages, only the current page, or only odd or even pages. The developer can also print multiple copies of the report, print to a file, and collate the copies. To access this

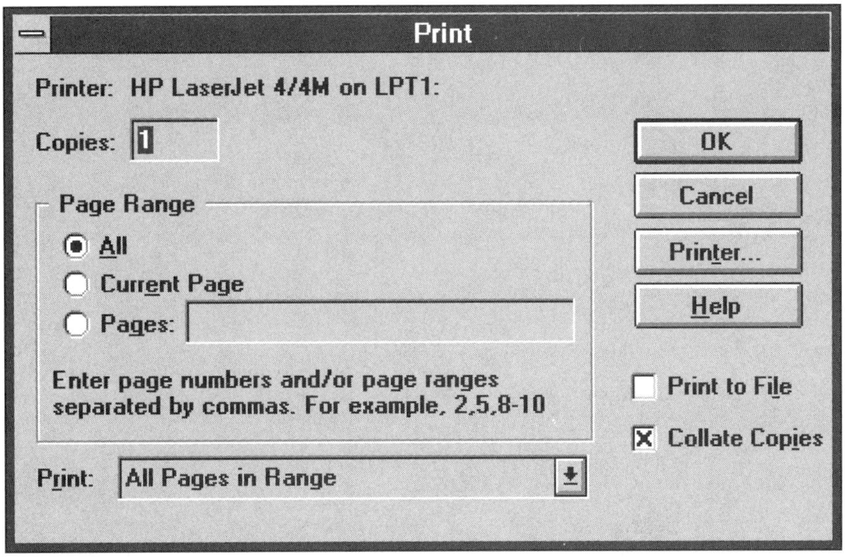

Figure 10.20   A print dialog box that allows the user to print all pages, as one choice.

dialog, select Print from the File menu in Preview. The developer can also use this dialog to change printers.

Changing MS Windows Print Settings

PowerBuilder has provided many DataWindow attributes to assist in the printing of DataWindows. The following DataWindow attributes change Windows printer settings for DataWindows. These attributes can be used in the DataWindow **dwDescribe(...)** function to get the value for the particular printer attribute. The attributes can also be used in a **dwModify(...)** function to set a printer setting to a new value.

dwDescribe/dwModify
Print Attributes

Print.Color

Print.Copies

Print.DocumentName

Print.Duplex

Print.Margin.Bottom

Print.Margin.Left

Print.Margin.Right

Print.Margin.Top

Print.Orientation

Print.Paper.Size

Print.Paper.Source

Print.Preview

Print.Preview.Rulers

Print.Preview.Zoom

Print.Prompt

Print.Quality

Print.Scale

There are times when a developer would like to retrieve information about a printer or print driver. This information can be used to programmatically handle printing in different ways and/or to display the information on a print dialog box. (see Figure 10.21)

These print attributes can enable PowerBuilder applications to interface with MS Windows print settings. These DataWindow settings

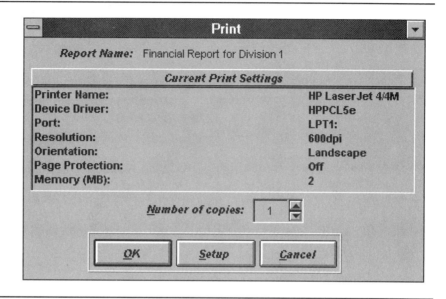

Figure 10.21   Displaying print attributes.

interface with print settings from the Windows SDK DEVMODE structure for a particular DataWindow.

FILE AND DOS I/O

PowerBuilder, like Windows, uses the MS-DOS file functions. When
interfacing with files, it is important to note that MS-DOS uses the
OEM character set, whereas Windows and PowerBuilder use the ANSI
character set. This is transparent to the PowerBuilder developer, however, because PowerBuilder handles it internally (calling Windows).
This is true also when using the low-level file functions in Windows.

Before any action on a file can be taken, the file must be opened.
PowerBuilder uses an integer value, called a file handle, to keep track
of the open files. Because only a limited number of files can be opened at
one time (determined by the FILES environment variable in DOS), files
should be closed as soon as possible after use.

This section discusses the file I/O functions available in
PowerBuilder and the DOS I/O functionality that can be accomplished
with PowerBuilder. Because the functionality of DOS and file I/O is
similar, the terms are used interchangeably in this chapter.

File I/O Functions

PowerBuilder has the following file I/O functions:

Functions	Description
FileOpen	Opens a DOS file and returns a file handle
FileClose	Closes a DOS file, using the file handle obtained from the **FileOpen** function
FileRead	Reads the contents of a file in LineMode or StreamModc
FileWrite	Writes data to a DOS file
FileSeek	Moves the file pointer to a particular character position
FileExists	Checks to see if a particular DOS file exists
FileDelete	Deletes a particular DOS file
FileLength	Determines the length of a DOS file in bytes

Reading Files That Exceed 32,766 Bytes

Because the PowerBuilder **FileRead** function can only read 32,766 characters at a time, a method of reading larger files is needed. The following code shows a way of reading files that are larger than 32,766 bytes.

```
// Function int f_FileRead(String sSource)
Int   iFileHandle, iLoops, i
Long    lFileLen, lBytesRead, lNewPos
Blob    b, bTot

SetPointer(HourGlass!)
lFileLen = FileLength (sSource)
if lFileLen > 32766 then
        if Mod(lFileLen, 32766) = 0 then
                iLoops = lFileLen/32766
        else
                iLoops = (lFileLen/32766) + 1
        end if
else
        iLoops = 1
end if

iFileHandle = FileOpen (sSource,streammode!,read!,Shared!)
FOR i = 1 to iLoops
     lBytesRead = FileRead(iFileHandle, b)
```

```
        bTot = bTot + b
        lNewPos = lNewPos + lBytesRead
        FileSeek(iFileHandle,lNewPos, FromBeginning!)
NEXT
FileClose(iFileHandle)
```

The **FileLength** function is used here to determine if the file exceeds 32K.

Writing a File Copy Function

The PowerScript that follows shows how to write a file copy function in PowerBuilder.

```
int f_copyFile(string sSource, string sDest)

Int  iSourceHandle, iDestHandle, iLoops, i
Long  lFileLen, lBytesRead, lNewPos
blob  b, bTot

SetPointer(HourGlass!)
// Check file length
lFileLen = FileLength (sSource)

// Determine the number of 32766 chars in the file
if lFileLen > 32766 then
        if Mod(lFileLen, 32766) = 0 then
                iLoops = lFileLen/32766
        else
                iLoops = (lFileLen/32766) + 1
        end if
else
        iLoops = 1
end if

// Open source and destination files
iSourceHandle = FileOpen (sSource,streammode!,read!,Shared!)
iDestHandle = FileOpen (sDest,streammode!,Write!,Shared!, Replace!)

// read through the source file
FOR i = 1 to iLoops
        // Read 32K buffer from source file
        lBytesRead = FileRead(iSourceHandle, b)
        // Write 32K buffer to destination file
        FileWrite(iDestHandle, b)
        // Point to next 32K buffer in destination file
```

```
            FileSeek(iDestHandle,32766 * i, FromBeginning!)
            // Calculate next 32K file position in source handle
            lNewPos = lNewPos + lBytesRead
            // Point to next 32K file position in source file
            FileSeek(iSourceHandle,lNewPos, FromBeginning!)
NEXT

// Close source and destination files
FileClose( iSourceHandle)
FileClose(iDestHandle)
return 1
```

This function copies a file from one location to another. It is similar to using a DOS copy command.

ImportFile Function

The **ImportFile** function is useful when importing text or .DBF files into DataWindows. When using the **ImportFile** function to import a tab-delimited file into a DataWindow, a separate column must be created for every tab column in the file. For example, to import the following file into a DataWindow, the DataWindow must be set up as an external DataWindow with six columns.

A DataWindow used to import such a text file could look like the one in Figure 10.22.

A window that looks like the one in Figure 10.23 could be created to display the imported file.

To do this, the following PowerScript would be placed in the clicked event of the **Import** command button.

```
dw_buffer.Reset( )
dw_buffer.ImportFile("sample.txt")
```

Table 10.1 External DataWindow with Six Columns

Division\Sales	Q1	Q2	Q3	Q4	Total
Division 1	$1,000	$2,500	$1,800	$3,000	$8,300
Division 2	$3,400	$4,000	$4,100	$2,900	$14,400
Division 3	$2,500	$2,000	$1,500	$3,600	$9,600
Division 4	$1,500	$1,500	$1,000	$700	$4,700
Division 5	$8,300	$5,000	$5,800	$7,700	$26,800
Total Sales	$16,700	$15,000	$14,200	$17,900	$63,800

DataWindow - d_buffer
Header
column1
column2
column3
column4
column5
column6
Detail
Summary
Footer

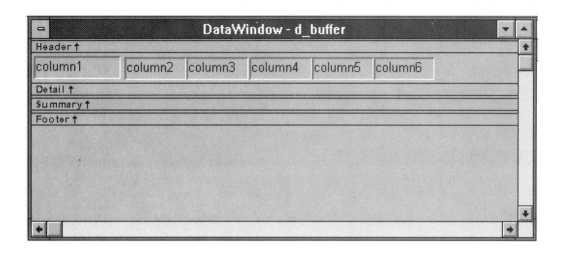

Figure 10.22 Sample DataWindow for importing a text file.

In an application that imports data from text files, if the column headings are constant but the data values keep changing, the developer can store the column headings in the header section of the DataWindow and import only the row headings and the data.

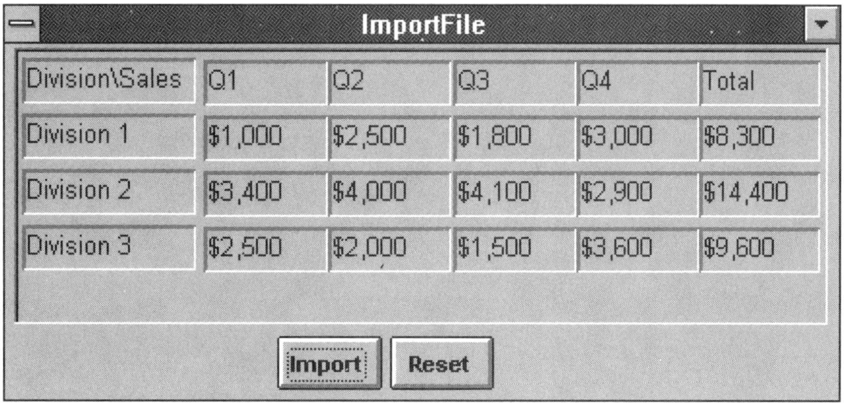

ImportFile
Division\Sales
Q1
Q2
Q3
Q4
Total
Division 1
$1,000
$2,500
$1,800
$3,000
$8,300
Division 2
$3,400
$4,000
$4,100
$2,900
$14,400
Division 3
$2,500
$2,000
$1,500
$3,600
$9,600
Import
Reset

Figure 10.23 Window displaying the imported text file.

Note: When trying to import large text files into a DataWindow, the
ImportFile function can be slow. It is much faster to import a tab-
delimited file into multiple DataWindow columns than a space-delim-
ited file into a single DataWindow column. The reason is that it requires
more than one space to align the columns of the file, but only one tab is
needed to separate columns.

Simulating the ImportFile Function

The following PowerScript, which uses standard PowerBuilder file I/O
functions, simulates the PowerBuilder **ImportFile** function:

```
// Function int f_ImportFile(DataWindow dwName, String sSource)

SetPointer(HourGlass!)
Integer iFNumSource
iFNumSource = FileOpen(sSource,LineMode!, Read!, Shared!)
if iFNumSource = -1 then
      return -10
else
      String sBuffer
      Integer iSourceRet, iCounter = 1
      Do While iSourceRet <> -100
            iSourceRet = FileRead(iFNumSource, sBuffer)
            if iSourceRet = -1 then
                  FileClose(iFNumSource)
                  return -12
            else
                  dwName.InsertRow(0)
                  dwName.SetItem(iCounter, 1, sBuffer)
            end if
            iCounter = iCounter + 1
      Loop
      iSourceRet = FileClose(iFNumSource)
      if iSourceRet = -1 then
            return -14
      end if
      return 1
end if
```

This function opens a text file and reads it into a single-column external DataWindow. The advantage of this function over the **ImportFile**
function is that with this function it does not matter if the source file has

tabs in the records. The disadvantage is that this method is slightly slower than the **ImportFile** function.

Get DOS Environment Variables

PowerBuilder does not provide a simple function call to retrieve a particular environment variable. The following custom and standard functions can be used as external PowerBuilder functions to enable a PowerBuilder application to retrieve DOS environment variables.

The following function, which can be used to retrieve any DOS environment variable, can be declared as an external function. The function should be declared in PowerBuilder as follows:

```
Function String PBGetEnv(String sEnvVar) Library "pbtools.dll"
/*******************************************************
     FUNCTION: PBGetEnv(const char *fname);
*******************************************************/
LPSTR FAR PASCAL PBGetEnv(LPSTR envvar)
{
     char FAR* lpszEnv;
     int icount;
     char FAR * string[1000];
     char FAR * var[1000];

     *var = NULL;
     // Return a pointer to the DOS environment
     lpszEnv = GetDOSEnvironment( );
     // while not end of environment
     while (*lpszEnv != '\0') {
          //ascii 61 is equal to "=". Point to one position after the "="
          icount = lstrlen(lpszEnv) - lstrlen(strchr(lpszEnv,61));
          icount++;
          // return the value into string.
          lstrcpyn((LPSTR) string,(LPCSTR) lpszEnv,icount);
          // null terminate the string
          string[icount] = '\0';
           // copy environment variable into var for the length of
           // envvar
          lstrcpyn((LPSTR) var,(LPCSTR)envvar,lstrlen(envvar)+1);
          var[lstrlen(envvar)] = '\0';
          // Compare the two strings, if they are equal
          // then return the value. Else try placing a space
          // after the variable.
          if (lstrcmpi((LPSTR) string,(LPCSTR) var) == 0)
                  return (LPSTR) lpszEnv + icount;
```

```
            else
                    lstrcat((LPSTR) var, " ");
                    if (lstrcmpi((LPSTR) string, (LPCSTR) var) == 0)
                            return (LPSTR) lpszEnv + icount;
            // move to the next environment variable
            lpszEnv += lstrlen(lpszEnv) + 1;
    }
    return (LPSTR) string;
}
```

The following SDK function copies the value of the Windir environment variable to the lpBuffer memory location. The Windir environment variable is the directory from which the win.com file is executed.

```
WORD GetWindowsDirectory(LPSTR lpBuffer, WORD nSize)
```

The sBuffer variable is passed from PowerBuilder by reference. When the function is called, the sBuffer variable holds the value of the Windir environment variable:

```
Function int GetWindowsDirectory(Ref String sBuffer, int iSize) Library
"kernel.exe"
```

The following SDK function copies the Windows system directory path to the lpBuffer memory location.

```
WORD GetSystemDirectory(LPSTR lpBuffer, WORD nSize)
```

The **GetSystemDirectory** function should be declared from PowerBuilder as an external function as follows:

```
Function int GetSystemDirectory(Ref String sBuffer, int iSize)
Library "kernel.exe"
```

The following PowerScript executes all three environment variable functions and stores them in three local variables:

```
String sWindowsDir, sSystemDir, sDOSPath
sWindowsDir = space(128)
sSystemDir = space(128)

GetWindowsDirectory(sWindowsDir, 128)
GetSystemDirectory(sSystemDir, 128)
sDOSPath = PBGetEnv("PATH")
```

Note: The **space( )** function should be used to preallocate memory into each variable used as a buffer for the **GetWindowsDirectory( )** and **GetSystemDirectory( )** functions. Because the buffer variables are passed by reference, the memory allocated for these variables must equal or be greater than the actual value stored in them by the two environment variable functions—**GetWindowsDirectory( )** and **GetSystemDirectory( )**.

DOS Directory I/O

Because PowerBuilder does not provide functions to create, remove, and change directories, the authors have created a set of DLL entry functions. They are included on the diskette that comes with this book. Because these functions do not exist in any standard MS Windows DLLs, they cannot be declared directly.

The **MakeDir( )** function shown here calls the C_**mkdir( )** function to create a DOS directory/subdirectory:

```
/******************************************************
FUNCTION: MakeDir(LPCSTR spszfname);
******************************************************/
int FAR PASCAL MakeDir(LPCSTR lpszfname)
{
return (int)_mkdir(lpszfname);
}
```

The external function declaration for this function would look like this:

```
FUNCTION int MakeDir(String sFileName) LIBRARY "pbtools.dll"
```

This next function corresponds to the DOS rd command:

```
/******************************************************
FUNCTION: RemoveDir(LPCSTR lpszfname);
******************************************************/
int FAR PASCAL RemoveDir(LPCSTR lpszfname)
{
return (int)_rmdir(lpszfname);
}
```

The external function declaration for this function would look like this:

```
FUNCTION int RemoveDir(String sFileName) LIBRARY "pbtools.dll"
```

This function is used to change directory:

```
/*****************************************************
FUNCTION: ChangeDir(LPCSTR lpszfname);
*****************************************************/
int FAR PASCAL ChangeDir(LPCSTR lpszfname)
{
return (int)_chdir(lpszfname);
}
```

The external function declaration for this function would look like this:

```
FUNCTION int ChangeDir(String sFileName) LIBRARY "pbtools.dll"
```

This function is used to delete a file. PowerBuilder has a **FileDelete** function, but if the file is a system, hidden, or read-only file then it can't be deleted by the **FileDelete** function from PowerBuilder. The following function will delete a file regardless of the DOS file attribute. This function is called **RemoveFile**.

```
/*****************************************************
FUNCTION: RemoveFile(LPSTR lpszFName);
*****************************************************/
int FAR PASCAL RemoveFile(LPSTR lpszFName)
{
        OFSTRUCT OpenBuff;
        _dos_setfileattr (lpszFName, _A_NORMAL);
        return OpenFile(lpszFName,&OpenBuff,OF_DELETE);
}
```

The external function declaration for this function should look like this:

```
FUNCTION int RemoveFile(String sFileName) LIBRARY "pbtools.dll"
```

This function is used to rename a directory:

```
/*****************************************************
FUNCTION: ReName(LPCSTR lpszoldname, LPCSTR lpsznewname);
*****************************************************/
int FAR PASCAL ReName(LPCSTR lpszoldname, LPCSTR
                      lpsznewname)
```

```
{
return (int)rename(lpszoldname, lpsznewname);
}
```

The external function declaration for this function should look like this:

```
FUNCTION int Rename(String sOldName, sNewName) LIBRARY
"pbtools.dll"
```

The **GetCurrDrive** function which follows was discussed in Chapter 7. Because PowerBuilder does not have a function that returns the current drive, this function was written as a DLL. It returns the letter of the current drive to PowerBuilder.

```
/*****************************************************
FUNCTION: GetCurrDrive(unsigned *drivename);
*****************************************************/
LPSTR FAR PASCAL GetCurrDrive(void)
{
    int idrive = 0;
    LPSTR string = "z";
    char drive[] = {'a', 'b', 'c', 'd', 'e', 'f', 'g', 'h', 'i',
                    'j', 'k', 'l', 'm', 'n', 'o', 'p', 'q', 'r',
                    's', 't', 'u', 'v', 'w', 'x', 'y', 'z' };
    idrive = _getdrive( );
    drive[idrive] = '\0';
    string = &drive[idrive - 1];
    return (LPSTR) string;
}
```

The external function declaration for this function would look like:

```
FUNCTION string GetCurrDrive( ) LIBRARY "pbtools.dll"
```

The following two functions are command line info functions. The two functions are called **f_argv(parmnumber)** and **f_argc( )**.

The **f_argv(parmnumber)** function retrieves the command line argument for the **parmnumber** commandline argument.

```
//*****************************************************
//   Purpose:    Return a specific command line parameter
//   Arguments:  Integer iParm
//*****************************************************
sSTR =      Trim(CommandParm( ))
```

```
IF sSTR = "" or iParm = 0 THEN
      return ""
ELSE
      String  sTmp
      Integer iPosition
      Integer iParmCounter = 0
      Integer iLength
      DO
              iLength = Len(sSTR)
              iPosition = Pos(sSTR," ")
              IF iPosition = 0 THEN
                      iPosition = iLength
                      sTmp = Left(sSTR,iPosition)
              ELSE
                      sTmp = Left(sSTR,iPosition - 1)
              END IF
              sSTR = Trim(Right(sSTR,(iLength - iPosition)))
              iParmCounter = iParmCounter + 1
      LOOP UNTIL iParm = iParmCounter
      if iParm > iParmCounter Then
              return ""
      end if
      return sTmp
END IF
```

This function can be called or the **CommandParm( )** function can be passed into the **f_strtok** function illustrated here. For example:

```
f_strtok(CommandParm( ), " ", n)
```

The **f_argc( )** function retrieves the number of command line parameters.

```
//******************************************************
//    Purpose: count the number of command line parameters
//******************************************************
String sParm
sParm = Trim(CommandParm( ))
IF sParm = "" THEN
      return 0
ELSE
      Integer   iPosition
      Integer   iParmCounter = 0
      Integer   iLength
      DO
              iLength = Len(sParm)
```

```
                iPosition = Pos(sParm," ")
                IF iPosition = 0 THEN
                        iPosition = iLength
                END IF
                sParm = Trim(Right(sParm,(iLength - iPosition)))
                iParmCounter = iParmCounter + 1
        LOOP UNTIL (Len(sParm) < 1)
        RETURN iParmCounter
END IF
```

The following function, called **f_strtok(...)**, is a string manipulation function that processes delimited strings.

```
//*******************************************************
//     Purpose:      Parse tokens from a string
//     Arguments:    String sSTR
//                   String sDelimit
//                   Integer iParm
//     Call Sample:
//             String sSTR = "XXYYZZ AABBCC"
//             String sString1, sString2
////             // returns XXYYZZ into sString1
//             sString1 = f_strtok(sSTR, " ", 1)
//             // returns AABBCC into sString2
//             sString2 = f_strtok(sSTR, " ", 2)
//*******************************************************
sSTR  =       Trim(sSTR)
IF sSTR = "" or iParm = 0 THEN
        return ""
ELSE
        String  sTmp
        Integer iPosition
        Integer iParmCounter = 0
        Integer iLength
        DO
                iLength = Len(sSTR)
                iPosition = Pos(sSTR,sDelimit)
                IF iPosition = 0 THEN
                        iPosition = iLength
                        sTmp = Left(sSTR,iPosition)
                ELSE
                        sTmp = Left(sSTR,iPosition - 1)
                END IF
                sSTR = Trim(Right(sSTR,(iLength - iPosition)))
                iParmCounter = iParmCounter + 1
        LOOP UNTIL iParm = iParmCounter
```

```
        if iParm > iParmCounter Then
                return ""
        end if
        return sTmp
END IF
```

These functions are an extension to the core PowerBuilder DOS/
File I/O functionality.

INITIALIZATION (.INI) FILES

Initialization (.INI) files are the standard means by which Windows
and Windows applications configure themselves, at runtime, according
to a user's needs and preferences. The two main benefits of using INI
files are that applications can be somewhat tailored for each user and
that application-level configuration can be performed without creating
an executable.

Discussion of initialization files can be divided into four topics:

- Standard initialization files
- Format of initialization files
- Initialization file usage
- Updating initialization files

Standard Initialization Files

The standard Windows and PowerBuilder initialization files are
CONTROL.INI, PROGMAN.INI, SYSTEM.INI, WIN.INI, and PB.INI.
The following list describes each of these files.

.INI File	*Description*
WIN.INI	This file contains entries that a user can set to alter the Windows environment according to personal preferences.
SYSTEM.INI	This file contains entries that a user can set to customize Windows to meet the system hardware needs.
CONTROL.INI	This file contains entries that describe the color schemes and patterns used in Windows and the settings for printers and installable drivers.
PROGMAN.INI	This file contains entries that define the content of program groups.

PB.INI — This file contains information about the PowerBuilder development environment.

application.INI — Application initialization files store configurable information about an application.

Format of Initialization Files

Initialization files are broken down into logical groups called sections. Each section is broken down into entries that are referred to as the key. Initialization file sections have the following format:

```
[section]
key=value
```

The section is the name of the section. The brackets around the section name are required. The left bracket must be in the leftmost column on the screen. The key is the name of the entry. The key can consist of any combination of letters and digits. For many entries, the key must be followed immediately by an equal sign. The value is the information an application uses. The value can be an integer, string, or a quoted string.

It is quite popular to store value as a Boolean. Booleans can be stored as True | False, Yes | No, On | Off, or 1 | 0.

It is a good idea to add comments to some initialization files so that users can understand each entry. To add a comment, place a semicolon at the beginning of each line of comment.

Note: There is a 64K limit for the size of initialization files. So, be frugal with your comments.

Initialization File Usage

Applications should create initialization files during installation or when the application cannot locate particular initialization files. When initialization files are created, default values should be assigned. Both Windows and PowerBuilder create their initialization files during installation. Some entries are added or changed when the user configures the application. Initialization files can be used for many different types of application-specific configurable parameters or user preferences.

User Preferences Initialization files can be used to store user-specific preferences. Examples of user preferences are window position, window arrangement, automated procedure settings, colors, toolbar position and items, default template, and default font, to name a few.

The user can save the default position of the main application groups. This is similar to Windows' ability to save a user's workspace. When the user exits Windows, the position of all the groups, icons, and other settings are saved to the PROGMAN.INI file.

```
[Settings]
AutoArrange=1
Window=4 26 635 434 2
Order=1 4 3 2
MinOnRun=1
```

Allowing applications to be configured based on each user's preferences is a desirable feature for most applications.

List Boxes Initialization files can also be used to store data for some of the application's list boxes. For example, some applications allow a user to search large lists of information by typing in key words. Storing the last two or more of the user's key words in a DropDownListBox is often desirable, as is saving these items. So, when the application is closed and reopened, the search DropDownListBox is filled. The search items can be stored in an initialization file, with each item separated from the other with a delimiter.

Doing this, for example, would allow a generic file editor that has been closed and reopened, to show the last five search items used in previous sessions, in a DropDownListBox, as shown in Figure 10.24.

When the application is closed, the last five items can be saved to an initialization file in either of the following formats. Method 1 has a format:

```
[SearchItems]
ItemCount=5
SearchItem1=item1
SearchItem2=item2
SearchItem3=item3
SearchItem4=item4
SearchItem5=item5
```

Method 2 has the following format:

```
[SearchItems]
Delimiter=";"
ItemCount=5
SearchItem1="item1;item2;item3;item4;item5"
```

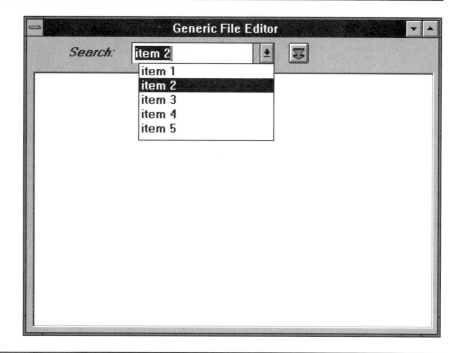

Figure 10.24   Displaying the last five search items using an initialization file.

The second method is a more efficient way of handling this case because, as search items increase, no additional reads are required to the initialization file.

Login Information Some applications require the user to log into an external system, such as a database or an eMail system. In these cases, most of the user's login information can be stored in an initialization file. The user's password or even the login id itself may have to be entered by the user for additional security. These settings can be stored in an initialization file to connect a user in a PowerBuilder application to a popular database.

Connecting to the PowerBuilder Demo Database, in Watcom, as the dba, the following information can be stored in an initialization file:

```
[PowerBuilder Demo DB]
DBMS=ODBC
Database=PowerBuilder Demo DB
```

```
DbParm=ConnectString='DSN=PowerBuilder Demo
     DB;UID=dba;PWD=sql'
```

This method stores both the user id and password in the initialization file. This may be acceptable for developers.

```
[PowerBuilder Demo DB]
DBMS=ODBC
Database=PowerBuilder Demo DB
DbParm=ConnectString='DSN=PowerBuilder Demo DB;'
```

When executing an application in production mode, the user should be required to input his or her password. Sometimes the user id may be required also. In the previous initialization file example, the user id and password have not been stored in an initialization file. That information will be collected during application startup and concatenated to the ConnectString retrieved from the initialization file.

System Settings When developing an application, there are some system-wide settings that need to be set. These system-wide settings are not necessarily user-specific. Thus, when developing client/server applications, some application-specific initialization files can be stored on the network rather than on each user's computer. A system-wide setting may enable or disable access to an eMail system, for example. In addition, all users may be denied access to the eMail system from the application if the eMail system is down. To do this in an application initialization file, the following entry can be made.

```
[email]
emailaccess=No
```

When the system comes back up, the initialization file setting can be changed to "Yes." In cases like this, it may be better to retrieve the setting from the .INI file each time the user wants to access eMail from the application. That makes the Emailaccess parameter more dynamic; when done this way, the users don't have to exit and restart the application every time the Emailaccess setting is changed. Application designers should think about which initialization file entries to make dynamic and which to make static based on the users' needs.

Note: One thing to remember is that a certain amount of performance degradation results if initialization file entries are read dynamically.

Many other system settings, such as application global variables, can be stored in initialization files. Doing this makes the application more configurable.

File Path Pointers Initialization files can also be used to store file path pointers. This is done in the Windows operating system for many things, such as, defining the location of the program manager group files. An example is:

```
[Groups]
Group1=C:\WINDOWS\MAIN.GRP
Group2=C:\WINDOWS\ACCESSOR.GRP
Group3=C:\WINDOWS\STARTUP.GRP
Group4=C:\WINDOWS\APPS.GRP
```

In PowerBuilder, there are also some file path pointer settings:

```
[application]
AppName=sample30
AppLib=c:\pb30\pbsample.pbl
DefLib=c:\pb30\pbsample.pbl
$c:\pb30\pbsample.pbl(sample30)=c:\pb30\pbsample.pbl;c:
\pb30\pbsampuo.pbl;c:\pb30\pbsampfn.pbl;c:\pb30\pbsampdb.
pbl;c:\pb30\pmstyle3.pbl;
```

These examples show how both the path and file name are stored. It is important to note that path names, which should not be hard-coded, can be stored in initialization files.

Windows searches for files in the following order: the user's current directory, the path pointed to by the *windir environment* variable, the Windows system directory, then the directories pointed to by the *path environment* variable, in order from left to right. As such, rather than storing file path names in the initialization files, the developer can design a system so that some files can be located in the Windows path.

The developer should study the Windows initialization file settings so that duplicate system information is not stored in application-specific initialization files.

Updating Initialization Files

To fully take advantage of initialization files, a mechanism must be in place to allow updates to the initialization files. Initialization files can be updated using three methods: manually opening the initialization file and modifying it, developing utilities that provide an interface for maintaining initialization files, and allowing applications to programmatically update the initialization file.

Manually Updating Initialization Files To be updated manually, an initialization file can be read into any text file editor. The SysEdit utility that comes with Windows allows the WIN.INI, SYSTEM.INI, AUTOEXEC.BAT, and CONFIG.SYS files to be updated. It is very important that a backup copy of the initialization file is created before any updates are made to it.

Programmatic Updates to Initialization Files Both PowerBuilder and the Windows SDK provide a set of functions that allows developers to programmatically maintain initialization files.

PowerBuilder Functions PowerBuilder provides three functions designed to manipulate initialization files. The **ProfileString** and **ProfileInt** functions enable the developer to programmatically read from initialization files; the **SetProfileString** function enables the developer to write to initialization files.

The **ProfileString** function provides read access to initialization file entries that are character strings. The two read functions have a default parameter that is used when the entry does not currently have a value specified for it. For example, to retrieve the DBMS value from the PB.INI:

```
PB.INI
[Database]
DBMS=ODBC
string s_database
s_database = &
      ProfileString("PB.INI", "Database", "DBMS", "ODBC")
```

The **ProfileString** function searches for the PB.INI file, opens it, and retrieves the DBMS entry. If no value is supplied for this entry, the function returns the designated default ("ODBC").

The **ProfileInt** function works the same as the **ProfileString** except it returns a numeric value instead of a character string. The other difference is that the default value must be a numeric value.

The **SetProfileString** function is used for writing to the initialization file. The fourth parameter to this function is the value the developer wants to write to the initialization file. This function writes the value in the fourth parameter into the specified key in the specified section of the specified initialization file. If the section or key is not found in the initialization file, the **SetProfileString** function creates them:

```
SetProfileString("INIFILE.INI","Section","Key","Value")
```

This statement produces the following line in the inifile.ini when either the section or key does not exist.

```
[Section]
Key=Value
```

PowerBuilder does not have a mechanism to delete sections or entries using its initialization file functions. In order to accomplish this, the Windows SDK's **WritePrivateProfileString** or **WriteProfileString** functions must be called. To delete entries using the **WritePrivate ProfileString** function, the following must be done. If the entry does not exist in the specified section, it is created. If the entry parameter is NULL, the entire section, including all entries within the section, is deleted. If the value parameter is NULL, the entry specified by the lpszEntry parameter is deleted.

The following is how the **WriteProfileString** function is declared in C:

```
BOOL WritePrivateProfileString(lpszSection, lpszEntry, lpszString,
lpszFilename)

LPCSTR lpszSection;          /* address of section   */
LPCSTR lpszEntry;            /* address of entry     */
LPCSTR lpszString;           /* address of string to add     */
LPCSTR lpszFilename;         /* address of initialization filename*/
```

The function can be declared in PowerBuilder, using the following PowerScript declaration:

```
FUNCTION int WritePrivateProfileString(string s_section, string
s_entry, string s_value, string s_filename) LIBRARY "kernel.exe"
```

Windows SDK Functions The PowerBuilder functions are actually calling the lower-level Windows SDK functions. The Windows SDK provides developers with six initialization file functions. These functions are described in the following list.

Function	*Description*
GetPrivateProfileInt	Returns an integer value in a section from a specified initialization file.
GetPrivateProfileString	Returns a character string in a section from a specified initialization file.

GetProfileInt	Returns an integer value in a section from the WIN.INI file.
GetProfileString	Returns a character string in a section from the WIN.INI file.
WritePrivateProfileString	Copies a character string to a specified initialization file or deletes one or more lines from a private initialization file.
WritcProfileString	Copies a character string to the WIN.INI file or deletes one or more lines from WIN.INI.

CHAPTER 11

Debugging

During the development of a PowerBuilder application, it is usually necessary to debug the application's script. There are a number of different tools for debugging PowerBuilder applications: the Debug painter, Runtime debugger, Database Trace debugger, and a number of third-party debugging tools. The Debug painter in PowerBuilder allows the developer to set breakpoints and step through the application code until problems are found and corrected. The Runtime debugger allows a developer to debug a PowerBuilder executable. The Database Trace debugger logs low-level database I/O transactions in detail. In addition to the PowerBuilder debugging facilities, there are a number of Windows debugging tools that can be used to assist in the debugging process.

This chapter discusses the following topics:

- Debug painter
- Runtime debug
- Trace debug
- Custom debug methods
- Third-party debug tools

DEBUG PAINTER

PowerBuilder allows the developer to run the application in debug mode using the Debug painter. The application runs until a breakpoint is reached; it then stops to allow the developer to view or change the variables in the script. PowerBuilder also allows the user to create watch lists.

When the Debug painter is opened, the Select Script window displays the names of the windows in the current application inside the Name

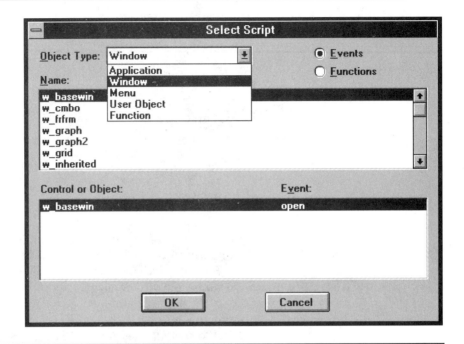

Figure 11.1   The Select Script window showing current application's windows.

box. (see Figure 11.1) A list of controls in the window that has scripts and the event that triggers each script display in the Objects box.

As shown in Figure 11.1, the user selects the appropriate type from the list in the DropDown listbox. After the type of script to debug has been chosen, PowerBuilder updates the lists in the Select Script window. If the user selects the Functions option, the function names display in the Name box and the Object box is blank.

Breakpoints

The most important feature of debugging in PowerBuilder is the use of breakpoints. The developer can place breakpoints in any of the objects' PowerScript code. The developer simply double-clicks at the appropriate line of code and a stop sign appears to denote the breakpoint. Removing breakpoints is accomplished by double-clicking on the stop sign.

Breakpoints can be placed on any line of code within an object except comment lines, blank lines, and variable declarations. PowerBuilder allows the developer to place a breakpoint at the first declaration statement or comment line in the open event of a window, however. This allows the debugger to enter the event and stop before it runs the code. The placing of a breakpoint at the first line of a declaration stops that code from starting for the object. In addition, the developer can place a breakpoint on the first line of a comment line in a function or event that contains no code (i.e., it only contains comment lines). This can be used to see if a particular event or function is actually being called.

Figure 11.2 shows a script run with the Debug painter. In this example, a breakpoint is placed in the open event of window secr002. When PowerBuilder encounters the breakpoint, it suspends the application before executing the statement shown with the stop sign.

When the application is stopped, the developer can view current values of the variables and attributes. In addition, the developer can edit the variables.

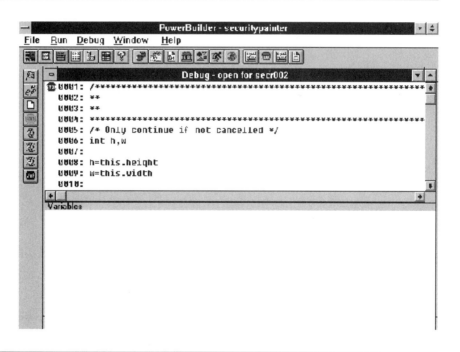

Figure 11.2   Breakpoint placed in the open event of Window secr002.

Note: The user should not set a stop in the Activate or Getfocus event because it can cause recursive event-triggering that hangs the debug session.

When breakpoints (also called stops) have been placed in a script, PowerBuilder saves the stop information in the PB.INI. In addition, the breakpoints can be enabled and disabled by highlighting them and clicking on the Enable or Disable buttons. This allows the user to save useful breakpoints but disable them when they are not needed.

Figure 11.3 illustrates that the window w_inherited has an enabled breakpoint in the first line of the open event and a disabled breakpoint in the second line of the object cb_1.

Watch List

Another important feature of the Debug painter is the creation of a Watch list. A Watch list can "watch" singular variables or groups of variables as the code is being stepped through. This saves the developer time.

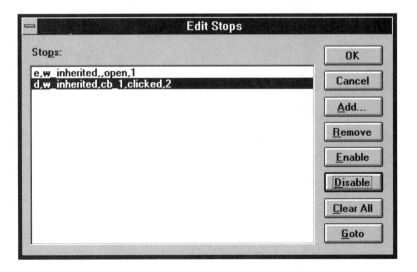

Figure 11.3   Window w_inherited showing enabled and disabled breakpoints.

To place variables in the Watch list, the developer selects the variable(s) and chooses the add icon. When the selected variable(s) have been added to the Watch list, PowerBuilder updates them as they change. Unfortunately, if the developer steps through the code too quickly, sometimes the Watch list is not updated correctly. To avoid this problem, the developer should press the Step icon in a measured fashion.

One good variable to choose as a watch variable is *sqlca* variable *sqlerrtext*. This variable can be found by the developer, but it requires stepping through a number of cascaded variable lists to find it. When the variable is found, adding it to the watch list saves valuable time.

In Figure 11.4, the variable *sqlerrtext* has been found in the cascaded variable list for global variables under Transaction *sqlca*. If it needs to be viewed more than once, the value is placed in the Watch variable section.

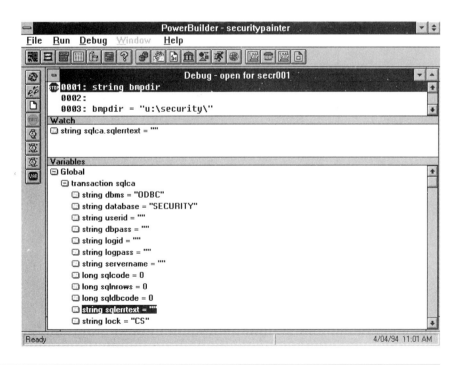

Figure 11.4   Finding the variable *sqlerrtext*.

Variables

When running an application in debug mode, the developer will want to track the variables. The global, shared, and local variables are shown in the Variable screen section. When the variable box has a + sign next to it, this denotes that there are variables that can be seen by double-clicking on the box. The debugger in PowerBuilder displays the first 128 characters of variables. If there are more than 128 characters, the string is followed by "more." To see the entire value, the developer double-clicks as though he or she were going to modify the variable. This allows scrolling through or modifying the entire string. The three main types of variables that are shown in the Debug painter are:

- Global
- Shared
- Local

The next three sections of this chapter discuss the debugging of these variable types.

Global The variables that are shown in this area are the global variables that are defined for the application. Figure 11.5 shows global variables of an application that is being run through the debugger.

The first three variables that are shown in the global section of the Debug painter are the PowerBuilder objects *sqlca*, *sqlda*, and *sqlsa*. Another variable shown in the list is the Windows Error variable—*error*. This variable contains the Windows error text and also the object, event, and line of the message. The next variable in the global list section is *message*. This variable contains the Windows message(s), information about the message(s), and the PowerBuilder message object. The variables shown after the standard PowerBuilder variables are the application-specific objects. Clicking on the plus sign causes a screen with detail information to display. In this example, the application-specific objects are window w_inherited and menu m_stdmnup.

Note: To locate instance variables at the window level, the developer must click on the appropriate window and look for the instance variables at the end of the list. If the instance variable was declared at an ancestor class window, then the parentwindow line within the window listing must be clicked to find the instance variable.

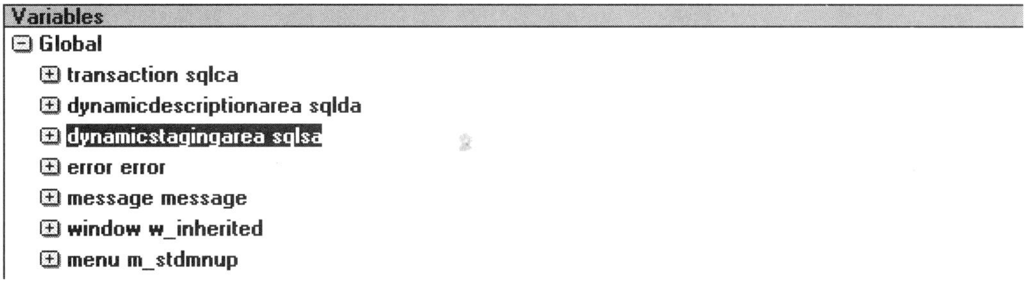

```
Variables
⊟ Global
   ⊞ transaction sqlca
   ⊞ dynamicdescriptionarea sqlda
   ⊞ dynamicstagingarea sqlsa
   ⊞ error error
   ⊞ message message
   ⊞ window w_inherited
   ⊞ menu m_stdmnup
```

Figure 11.5   Global variables of an application that is being run through the debugger.

Shared The shared area shows all of the variables that are shared by the windows and the application that is being stepped through.
Figure 11.6 shows the variables for the objects shown.

Local The local section shows the variables that are defined within the scope of an event or function. As the developer steps from one function/event to another, the scope of the local variables changes; therefore, it may be necessary to double-click on the local variables box again.

RUNTIME DEBUG

When an application's executable has been created, the developer can also run the executable with the PowerBuilder Runtime debug setting. This setting writes every executed line of code to a Trace file. Doing this is helpful to detect errors that occur in the executable, but not in the development environment. In addition, the Trace file allows the developer to view the order that scripts and functions are called. For each line executed, an entry is made in the Trace file. These entries show the

```
⊟ Shared
   ▢ For application mdi
   ▢ For window w_inherited
   ▢ For menu m_stdmnup
```

Figure 11.6   The shared variables.

creation and destruction of objects, and the execution of scripts and functions. They also show line-by-line use of the scripts in the functions and events.

A Trace file is created for the application executable by including the **/pbdebug** commandline switch when executing the application. Figure 11.7 shows an example of an application Trace file created for an application called MDI.EXE. The application includes a window with two DataWindows that retrieve information on a salesman (Employee Info) and the companies to which he has sold goods.

This application is run with the command switch **/pbdebug**, and the following MDI.DBG file is created. The file shows the creation and execution of each event and function for all of the window, menu, and user objects.

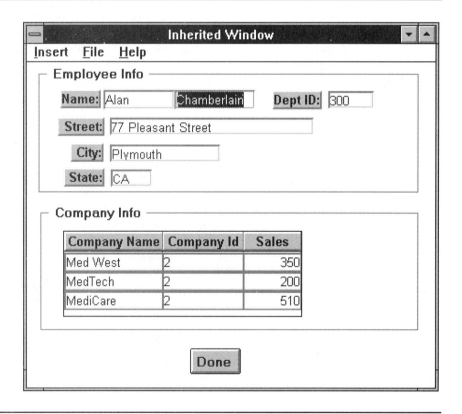

Figure 11.7   Two DataWindows in the created application Trace file.

Note: The output file will be created with the same name as the executable, but with a .DBG file extension.

```
Executing event script CREATE for class MDI, lib entry MDI
 Executing instruction at line 2
 Executing instruction at line 3
 Executing instruction at line 4
 Executing instruction at line 5
 Executing instruction at line 6
 Executing instruction at line 7
End event script CREATE for class MDI, lib entry MDI

Executing event script OPEN for class MDI, lib entry MDI
 Executing instruction at line 8
 Executing system function PROFILESTRING
 Executing instruction at line 11
 Executing system function SETPOINTER
 Executing instruction at line 13
 Executing system function PROFILESTRING
 Executing instruction at line 14
 Executing system function PROFILESTRING
 Executing instruction at line 15
 Executing system function PROFILESTRING
 Executing instruction at line 16
 Executing system function PROFILESTRING
 Executing instruction at line 17
 Executing system function PROFILESTRING
 Executing instruction at line 18
 Executing system function PROFILESTRING
 Executing instruction at line 19
 Executing system function PROFILESTRING
 Executing instruction at line 20
 Executing system function PROFILESTRING
 Executing instruction at line 22
 Executing instruction at line 0
 Executing system function OPEN
 Executing event script CREATE for class W_INHERITED, lib entry
W_INHERITED
   Executing instruction at line 3
   Executing event script CREATE for class W_BASEWIN, lib entry
W_BASEWIN
     Executing instruction at line 2
     Executing instruction at line 3
     Executing instruction at line 4
     Executing instruction at line 5
```

```
End event script CREATE for class W_BASEWIN, lib entry W_BASEWIN
Executing instruction at line 4
Executing event script CREATE for class M_STDMNUP, lib entry M_STDMNUP
 Executing instruction at line 2
 Executing instruction at line 3
 Executing instruction at line 9
 Executing instruction at line 5
 End event script DESTROY for class M_STDMNUP, lib entry M_STDMNUP
 Executing instruction at line 4
 Executing instruction at line 5
 Executing instruction at line 6
End event script DESTROY for class W_INHERITED, lib entry W_INHERITED
 Executing instruction at line 2
End event script CLICKED for class CB_1, lib entry W_INHERITED


Executing event script DESTROY for class MDI, lib entry MDI
 Executing instruction at line 2
 Executing instruction at line 3
 Executing instruction at line 4
End event script DESTROY for class MDI, lib entry MDI
```

This example is an excerpt from a five-page printout, indicating that debug files can become quite large. Despite their size, they are useful when problems occur in the executable that do not occur in the development environment.

TRACE DEBUG

The Trace debugger can be used to trace the interaction between the client and the database via the PowerBuilder database interface. To start the Trace debugger, the DBMS value in the transaction object must be preceded by the word "Trace." The transaction can be set-up to use trace within an application or from the database Preferences dialog box, as shown in Figure 11.8.

Once the Preferences database DBMS value has been set to use the Trace debugger, the developer can run the Database painter to begin generating log data. The Trace debugger writes low-level database interface I/O information to a pbtrace.log file located in the developer's Windows (windir) directory. When executing the Database painter, the message box in Figure 11.9 appears to show the location and name of the Trace file.

The first thing that happened is the Select Tables dialog box is displayed, as shown in Figure 11.10.

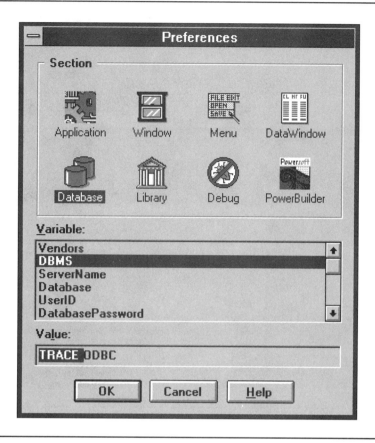

Figure 11.8 Setting the Trace debugger in the database Preferences dialog box.

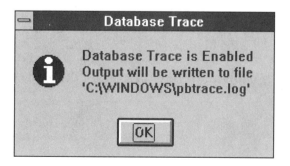

Figure 11.9 Message box showing the name and location of the Trace file.

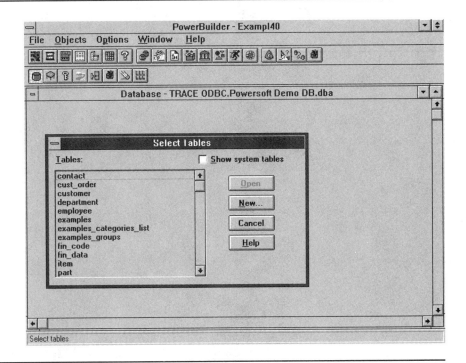

Figure 11.10   The Select Tables dialog box.

The Contact and Cust_order tables are selected, as shown in Figure 11.11.

Then, data within the Cust_order table is retrieved, as shown in Figure 11.12.

The due date for the first record is changed and the database is updated, as shown in Figure 11.13.

After these steps are completed, the developer can exit the Database painter and then review the pbtrace.log file.

Note: The trace utility must have the pbtra040.dll file in the developer's path to work.

The following listing shows the contents of the pbtrace.log file. It contains detail information associated with the steps taken in the Database painter, as shown in the previous figures.

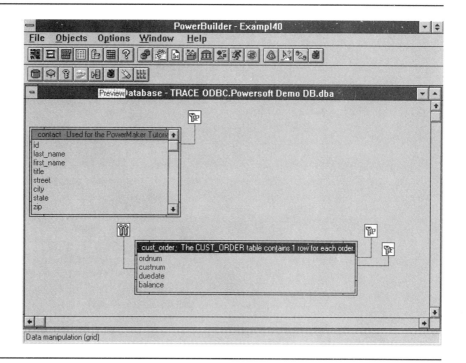

Figure 11.11   Selecting the Contact and cust_order tables.

```
DIALOG CONNECT TO TRACE ODBC:
USERID=dba
DATA=Powersoft Demo DB
DBPARM=ConnectString='DSN=Powersoft Demo DB;UID=dba;PWD=sql' (6152
MilliSeconds)
TABLE LIST: (275 MilliSeconds)
COLUMNS INFORMATION: TABLE=contact OWNER=dba (219 MilliSeconds)
PRIMARY KEY RETRIEVE: (110 MilliSeconds)
FOREIGN KEY RETRIEVE: (495 MilliSeconds)
COLUMNS INFORMATION: TABLE=cust_order OWNER=dba (165 MilliSeconds)
PRIMARY KEY RETRIEVE: (110 MilliSeconds)
FOREIGN KEY RETRIEVE: (330 MilliSeconds)
UNIQUE KEY CHECK: TABLE=cust_order OWNER=dba USER=dba (164 MilliSeconds)
YES, unique key found
PREPARE:
SELECT "ordnum", "custnum", "duedate", "balance" FROM "cust_order"
(55 MilliSeconds)
DESCRIBE: (0 MilliSeconds)
```

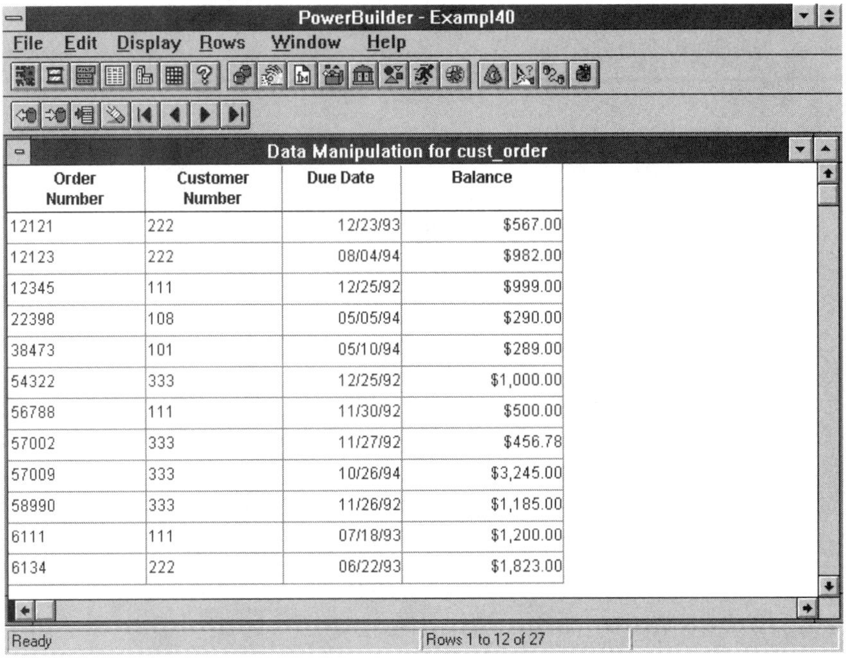

Order Number	Customer Number	Due Date	Balance
12121	222	12/23/93	$567.00
12123	222	08/04/94	$982.00
12345	111	12/25/92	$999.00
22398	108	05/05/94	$290.00
38473	101	05/10/94	$289.00
54322	333	12/25/92	$1,000.00
56788	111	11/30/92	$500.00
57002	333	11/27/92	$456.78
57009	333	10/26/94	$3,245.00
58990	333	11/26/92	$1,185.00
6111	111	07/18/93	$1,200.00
6134	222	06/22/93	$1,823.00

Figure 11.12 Retrieving data from the cust_order table.

```
name=ordnum,len=11,type=????
name=custnum,len=40,type=????
name=duedate,len=11,type=????
name=balance,len=40,type=FLOAT4
name=ordnum,len=11,type=CHAR
name=custnum,len=40,type=FLOAT
name=duedate,len=11,type=????
name=balance,len=40,type=FLOAT
EXECUTE: (0 MilliSeconds)
FETCH NEXT: (0 MilliSeconds)
    ordnum=12121        custnum=      duedate=12-23-1993 -1:00:00:000000
balance=
FETCH NEXT: (0 MilliSeconds)
    ordnum=12123        custnum=      duedate=08-04-1994 -1:00:00:000000
balance=
FETCH NEXT: (0 MilliSeconds)
    ordnum=12345        custnum=      duedate=12-25-1992 -1:00:00:000000
balance=
```

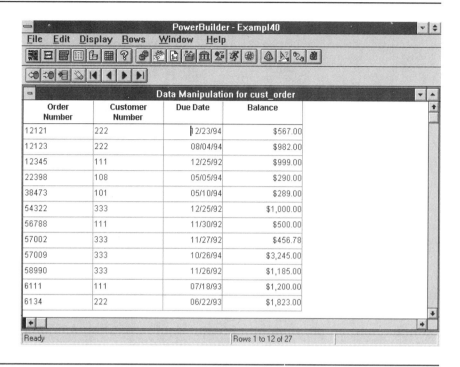

Figure 11.13   Due date for first record is changed and the database is updated.

```
FETCH NEXT: (0 MilliSeconds)
    ordnum=22398        custnum=      duedate=05-05-1994 -1:00:00:000000
balance=
FETCH NEXT: (0 MilliSeconds)
    ordnum=38473        custnum=      duedate=05-10-1994 -1:00:00:000000
balance=
FETCH NEXT: (0 MilliSeconds)
    ordnum=54322        custnum=      duedate=12-25-1992 -1:00:00:000000
balance=
FETCH NEXT: (0 MilliSeconds)
    ordnum=56788        custnum=      duedate=11-30-1992 -1:00:00:000000
balance=
FETCH NEXT: (55 MilliSeconds)
    ordnum=57002        custnum=      duedate=11-27-1992 -1:00:00:000000
balance=
FETCH NEXT: (0 MilliSeconds)
    ordnum=57009        custnum=      duedate=10-26-1994 -1:00:00:000000
balance=
```

```
FETCH NEXT: (55 MilliSeconds)
    ordnum=58990        custnum=      duedate=11-26-1992 -1:00:00:000000
balance=
FETCH NEXT: (55 MilliSeconds)
    ordnum=6111 custnum=      duedate=07-18-1993 -1:00:00:000000
balance=
FETCH NEXT: (0 MilliSeconds)
    ordnum=6134 custnum=      duedate=06-22-1993 -1:00:00:000000
balance=
FETCH NEXT: (0 MilliSeconds)
    ordnum=6167 custnum=      duedate=04-22-1994 -1:00:00:000000
balance=
FETCH NEXT: (0 MilliSeconds)
    ordnum=71637        custnum=      duedate=05-10-1994 -1:00:00:000000
balance=
FETCH NEXT: (55 MilliSeconds)
    ordnum=72211        custnum=      duedate=05-05-1994 -1:00:00:000000
balance=
FETCH NEXT: (0 MilliSeconds)
    ordnum=74321        custnum=      duedate=12-24-1993 -1:00:00:000000
balance=
FETCH NEXT: (0 MilliSeconds)
    ordnum=76901        custnum=      duedate=08-24-1994 -1:00:00:000000
balance=
FETCH NEXT: (0 MilliSeconds)
    ordnum=7777 custnum=      duedate=11-20-1992 -1:00:00:000000
balance=
FETCH NEXT: (0 MilliSeconds)
    ordnum=81111        custnum=      duedate=05-01-1994 -1:00:00:000000
balance=
FETCH NEXT: (0 MilliSeconds)
    ordnum=81112        custnum=      duedate=05-02-1994 -1:00:00:000000
balance=
FETCH NEXT: (0 MilliSeconds)
    ordnum=81724        custnum=      duedate=04-01-1994 -1:00:00:000000
balance=
FETCH NEXT: (0 MilliSeconds)
    ordnum=8888 custnum=      duedate=11-27-1992 -1:00:00:000000
balance=
FETCH NEXT: (55 MilliSeconds)
    ordnum=8892 custnum=      duedate=03-24-1992 -1:00:00:000000
balance=
FETCH NEXT: (0 MilliSeconds)
    ordnum=90000        custnum=      duedate=05-07-1994 -1:00:00:000000
balance=
FETCH NEXT: (0 MilliSeconds)
```

```
    ordnum=91102        custnum=      duedate=05-10-1994 -1:00:00:000000
balance=
FETCH NEXT: (0 MilliSeconds)
    ordnum=92822        custnum=      duedate=05-09-2004 -1:00:00:000000
balance=
FETCH NEXT: (0 MilliSeconds)
    ordnum=99001        custnum=      duedate=10-23-1994 -1:00:00:000000
balance=
FETCH NEXT: (0 MilliSeconds)
Error 1 (rc 100)
ROLLBACK: (0 MilliSeconds)
BEGIN TRANSACTION: (0 MilliSeconds)
PREPARE WITH BIND VARIABLES:
UPDATE "cust_order" SET "duedate" = ? WHERE "ordnum" = ? AND "custnum"
= ? AND "duedate" = ? AND "balance" = ? (0 MilliSeconds)
???? Length0 ID:1
VCHAR Length5 ID:2 *12121*
FLOAT Length0 ID:3
???? Length0 ID:4
FLOAT Length0 ID:5 (0 MilliSeconds)
EXECUTE: (55 MilliSeconds)
GET AFFECTED ROWS: (0 MilliSeconds)
^ 1 Rows Affected
COMMIT: (0 MilliSeconds)
DISCONNECT: (494 MilliSeconds)
SHUTDOWN DATABASE INTERFACE: (0 MilliSeconds)
```

The following pbtrace.log file is associated with the following select statement:

```
Select count(*) from contact;

DIALOG CONNECT TO TRACE ODBC:
USERID=dba
DATA=Powersoft Demo DB
DBPARM=ConnectString='DSN=Powersoft Demo DB;UID=dba;PWD=sql' (6317
MilliSeconds)
PREPARE:
select count(*) from contact (164 MilliSeconds)
PREPARE:
select count(*) from contact (0 MilliSeconds)
 DESCRIBE: (0 MilliSeconds)
name=count(*),len=40,type=????
GET EXTENDED ATTRIBUTES: TABLE=contact OWNER=dba (164 MilliSeconds)
 UNIQUE KEY CHECK: TABLE=contact OWNER=dba USER=dba (165 MilliSeconds)
```

```
YES, unique key found
PREPARE:
select count(*) from contact (0 MilliSeconds)
 DESCRIBE: (0 MilliSeconds)
name=count(*),len=40,type=????
name=count(*),len=40,type=FLOAT
 EXECUTE: (0 MilliSeconds)
 FETCH NEXT: (55 MilliSeconds)
     count(*)=
 FETCH NEXT: (0 MilliSeconds)
 Error 1 (rc 100)
 ROLLBACK: (0 MilliSeconds)
 CANCEL: (0 MilliSeconds)
 COMMIT: (0 MilliSeconds)
 DISCONNECT: (495 MilliSeconds)
  SHUTDOWN DATABASE INTERFACE: (0 MilliSeconds)
```

Note: If the developer is having any problems with a database from the PowerBuilder development environment or a PowerBuilder application, the developer must generate a pbtrace.log output file and send it to Powersoft to help them debug any database interface problems.

CUSTOM DEBUG METHODS

Writing Variables to a File

Another way to debug an application is to write variables to a file. To do this, the developer uses the **FileOpen**, **FileWrite**, and **FileClose** functions. These functions can be used in either the development environment in debug mode or in an executable.

Unfortunately, when an application is run from the Debug painter, it may not receive all of the Windows messages that are sent to it. Therefore, the application might run fine in the debug painter but bomb as an executable. When an application is run as an executable, the application receives all the Windows messages and other problems may become apparent. A way to isolate these problems is to write parameters or variable values to a file while the executable is running. This way, either the exact problem or the location of the problem can be determined.

An example of writing values to a file during debugging is placing the **FileOpen** and **FileWrite** script in a function called **custdebug** and referencing the function in a code segment. The function is defined as a Boolean with an argument called message of type string. The function **custdebug** would have the following code:

```
int FileNo
FileNo = FileOpen("custdebug.log", LineMode!, Write!, &
      LockWrite!, Append!)
FileWrite(FileNo, message)
FileClose(FileNo)
```

This function opens a debug file called Custdebug.log and writes the value, message, passed to it from the code segment.

Note: If the developer opens the debug file at the beginning of a program and does not close it until the end, the writes to the file may not get flushed to the disk and the file contents may be useless if the program blows up. The developer will want to open and close the debug file each time a write occurs so that the file content gets flushed to disk.

The code below shows the **custdebug** function being called in different places in the script. The following example will help detect the location of the problem. If the developer wants to write the contents of different variables within the script, he or she would simply pass the value into the **custdebug** function.

```
// Clicked script for dw_headcount
grObjectType ClickedObject
string s_company, grGraphName="gr_1", s_seriesname="Equipment"
int    ret, l_series, l_category
int    FileNo
string category_count
//     Find out where the user clicked in the graph
ClickedObject = this.grObjectAtPointer (grGraphName, l_series, &
                                   l_category)

If g_DEBUGMODE Then
     CustDebug("1")
End If

// If user clicked on data or a category, find out which one
if ClickedObject = TypeData! or &
     ClickedObject = TypeCategory! then
          If g_DEBUGMODE Then
               CustDebug("2")
```

```
                        End If
                        s_company = this.grCategoryName &
                        (grGraphName, l_category)
                        dw_2.dwModify (grGraphName + ".title=" + &
                                    "'s_company " + s_company + "'")
                        dw_2.Retrieve (s_company)
                        If g_DEBUGMODE Then
                              Write("3 ")
                        End if
                        dw_2.Show( )
            else
                  MessageBox (Parent.Title, "Click on a department to see
            employees")
            end if
```

In addition, for application debugging, the **custdebug** function can be created as an external function and called from any script in an application. Additional information about writing to files can be found in Chapter 10.

Messages

The developer can also create message boxes and beeps to denote a section of code that is being run. A message box can sometimes be useful in debugging to ascertain whether a loop is being executed properly or if a parameter is being set properly. The message box can be created as a function as in the file writing example and can be called where it is needed within the script to display a variable or parameter to the developer.

To create a message box use the preceding example. A function could be written to pass the name of the company to a function that creates a message box like the one in Figure 11.14.

The function's write code would be substituted with the following code to produce this message box.

```
//Function Write to create a messagebox

MessageBox("Company","Company Name is : " &
+ s_company,Exclamation!,OKCancel!,2)

return true
```

Unfortunately, a message box should not be used in conjunction with focus events of a window because a message box window causes PowerBuilder to become confused about which window should be get-

Figure 11.14   Created message box.

ting focus. In this case, a PowerBuilder beep function could be used to show whether a particular event is occurring. The event would generate an audible beep if the event is triggered.

THIRD-PARTY DEBUG TOOLS

Sometimes the PowerBuilder debugging facility does not provide all of the information needed to properly debug an application. The following MS Windows tools allow the developer to trap Windows messages that are sent from the PowerBuilder application. They also allow the developer to view memory allocations and debug dynamic link libraries (DDLs). Most of these tools are included in the MS Windows SDK.

Spy or WinView

Spy is a Windows application that allows a developer to view all Windows messages being sent to and from an application. Another useful tool, SPY DDE, allows the developer to view only DDE messages that are sent to and from an application.

HeapWalker

When the developer is creating an application, it is sometimes necessary to view the memory stack. HeapWalker is a Windows application that allows the developer to view the entire memory stack and the modules that are loaded in a machine's memory. HeapWalker is very helpful for finding memory allocation problems.

ADDRESS	HANDLE	SIZE	LOCK	FLG	HEAP	OWNER	TYPE
806E2120	2BEE	864		D		PBSYS030	Code 5
806E2480	2D66	10304		D		PBRTF030	Code 16
806E4CC0	2DFE	10784		D		PBRTF030	Code 8
806E76E0	340E	2016		D		PBDWE030	Code 42
806E7EC0	3496	5024		D		PBDWE030	Code 26
806E9260	34FE	6752		D		PBDWE030	Code 14
806EACC0	327E	12416		D		PBECT030	Code 6
806EDD40	32DE	3744		D		PBECT030	Code 2
806EEBE0	32D6	2912		D		PBPRT030	Code 2
806EF740	573E	2048		D		PB030	Code 1
806EFF40	2F76	11776		D		PBSYS030	Code 1
806F2D40	2AFE	4256		D		PBAPL030	Code 1
806F3DE0	3E2E	7776		D		PBCTL030	Code 1
806F5C40	4D3E	2368		D		PBFRM030	Code 1
806F6580	2CEE	10176		D		PBLIB030	Code 1
806F8D40	4E26	1600		D		PBMNU030	Code 1
806F9380	312E	8032		D		PBSCR030	Code 1
806FB2E0	4E0E	4256		D		PBWIN030	Code 1
806FC380	037E	288		D		DISPLAY	Resource Curso

Figure 11.15   Using HeapWalker to view the memory stack.

HeapWalker can, for example, show the PowerBuilder DLLs and their placement in the memory stack, as shown in Figure 11.15.

In the column headed Owner, the PowerBuilder DLLs are listed in the sequence they are loaded in memory. Their address, handle, and size are also shown. In this example, HeapWalker was invoked and then PowerBuilder was opened.

In addition to viewing the memory stack, HeapWalker also allows the user to sort the memory items, walk the stack, and discard and allocate segments of the memory.

Unload Utilities

There are a number of utilities that allow developers to view and unload or release modules loaded in memory. This is very useful for times when PowerBuilder causes a GPF and does not release all the PowerBuilder DLLs. There are a number of utilities that can do this; Figures 11.16 and 11.17 show two of them. Figure 11.16 is a utility called Microsoft Windows Process Status of Bogus Software.

Figure 11.17 is a utility called Unload Task or Library by Mike Sax.

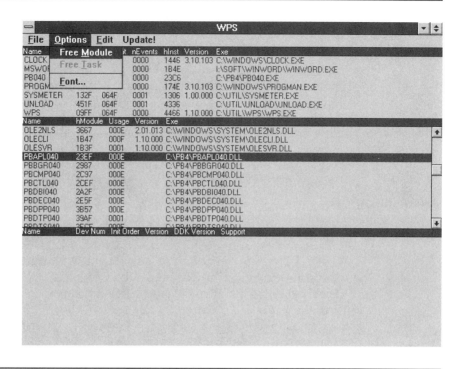

Figure 11.16   Microsoft Windows Process Status of Bogus Software utility.

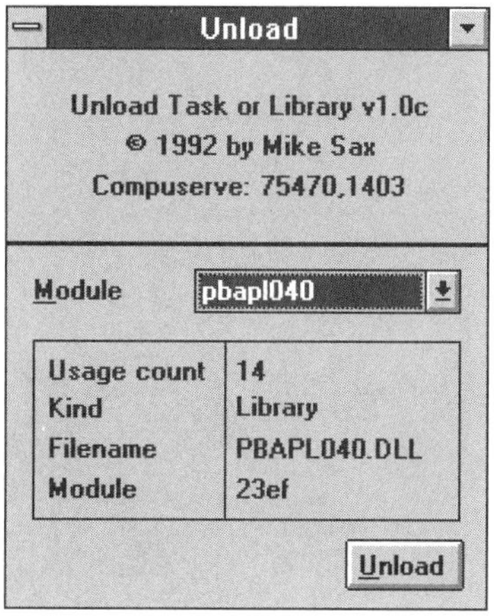

Figure 11.17   Unload Task utility.

CodeView

CodeView is a DOS-based debugger that allows the developer to debug C programs and DLLs. The CodeView environment has some similarities to the PowerBuilder debugger; for example, the use of breakpoints and watch variables. Unfortunately, the CodeView application is a character-based DOS program, not a Windows application. The CodeView application is discussed in detail in the *Professional Tools User's Guide* manual included with the Windows SDK documentation.

Windows Profiler

The Windows Profiler allows a developer to view statistics about an application's performance. Windows Profiler is a DOS-based source code debugger. This tool produces statistics that show the amount of time the application spends processing in the different functions. These statistics allow the developer to determine which functions can be optimized, thus increasing the speed of the entire application. Unfortunately, this tool is used in conjunction with source-level code and requires that the programmer write his or her own source-level breakpoints to be included in the compiled application executable. This tool is used by developers who write software made up of source code (not p-code like PowerBuilder). It is at too low a level for the corporate software developer.

PowerBuilder gives the developer ninety percent of what is needed for successful application debugging. Third-party debugging tools provide the rest. They should be explored for debugging such problems as memory stack errors.

PART III

Advanced Development Concepts

CHAPTER 12

eMail Interfaces

In the PowerBuilder environment, there are different levels at which eMail can be integrated into an application. These levels range from a straight DDE connection using a specific eMail system to using X.400 APIs to provide an interface capable of supporting a variety of different eMail systems. This chapter discusses the following topics related to eMail:

- Messaging standards
- PowerBuilder's DDE interface
- PowerBuilder's MAPI interface
- PowerBuilder Library for Lotus Notes
- eMail APIs

MESSAGING STANDARDS

MAPI and VIM

In the Windows environment, the two dominant eMail API standards available today are Microsoft's Messaging API (MAPI) and vendor independent messaging (VIM), a standard backed by such vendors as Lotus, Apple, Borland, IBM, and Novell.

There are two versions of MAPI—simple MAPI and Extended MAPI. PowerBuilder's MAPI interface is based on simple MAPI. Simple MAPI, which is included with the Windows SDK, provides basic eMail services. Simple MAPI is used in such products as Microsoft Mail and Windows for Workgroups. Extended MAPI provides developers a more robust API, giving them the capability to write low-level messaging services.

VIM is currently supported predominately by the two Lotus eMail systems: cc:Mail and Lotus Notes. Lotus has also developed a VIM interface to MAPI; this gives developers an interface to both VIM and MAPI eMail systems through the VIM interface.

Although the competition between MAPI and VIM has slowed the development of a single standard, vendors from both groups have come together to form an independent consortium called the X.400 API Association (Xapia). Xapia has developed a messaging standard known as the common mail call (CMC) interface. The CMC interface has the support of both Microsoft and Lotus and has a good chance to become the standard eMail interface.

X.400

The OSI standard for electronic message handling is X.400. It provides the specification for such things as message structure, message enveloping, and message transfer protocol. Using X.400 allows an eMail system to communicate with any other X.400-compatible system.

Communicating among different eMail systems using X.400 can be accomplished using an X.400 gateway that allows eMail to be translated from its native format to the format of its destination eMail system. For example, in an environment in which some users use MS Mail and others use Lotus Notes, an X.400 gateway can be added to allow eMail exchange between the two user groups (see Figure 12.1).

A true X.400 interface provides the most flexibility, but is complex

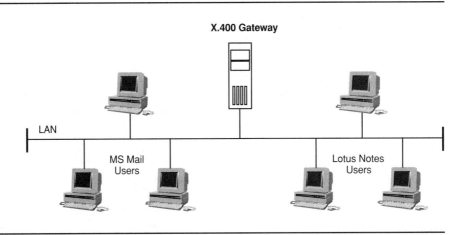

Figure 12.1   An X.400 gateway allows eMail exchange between different eMail systems, such as MS Mail and Lotus Notes.

to develop. Using a gateway allows the use of most eMail systems while eliminating the need to develop the X.400 interface. There are many third-party X.400 gateways available on the market, the most notable being the Retix OpenServer 400.

POWERBUILDER'S DDE INTERFACE

The simplest way to implement an eMail interface from PowerBuilder is using DDE to communicate directly with a specific eMail system. For example, to send Lotus Notes messages using a PowerBuilder interface, the developer could use a window like the one shown in Figure 12.2.

This window allows the user to enter a list of people in the To: field, a list of people in the cc: field, a subject, the message text, and a list of

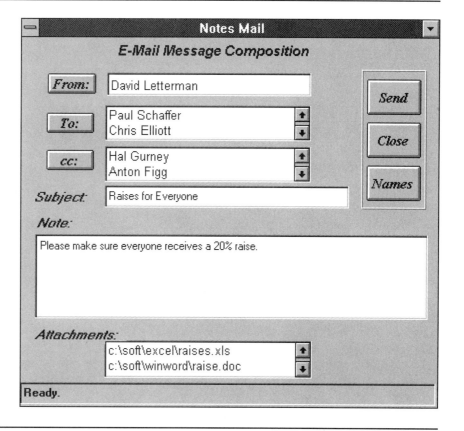

Figure 12.2   Using a PowerBuilder interface to send Lotus Notes messages.

attachments (as if they were in Lotus Notes). To send this using DDE, the following must be added to the open event of the window:

```
/*******************************************************
** Get the name of the Notes program from WIN.INI, and
** store it in the instance variable i_sMailExe
*******************************************************/

// Make sure Notes has been installed
if UPPER(ProfileString("Win.Ini","LotusMail", &
"Application",""))<>"NOTES" Then
      MessageBox("Error","Notes not installed.",StopSign!)
      Halt Close
end if

i_sMailExe = ProfileString("win.ini","LotusMail","Program","")
if i_sMailExe = "" then
      MessageBox("Error","Notes not installed.",StopSign!)
      Halt Close
end if
```

This script ensures that Notes has been installed and retrieves the fully qualified name of the Notes executable into the instance variable *i_sMailExe*.

To send the message, the developer adds the following script to the clicked event of the send command button, **cb_send**:

```
/*******************************************************
** Send message data from the window to Notes and send the message(s).
** i_sMailExe is an instance variable containing the name of the Notes
** executable
*******************************************************/

int iRtn, iHndl, iSendCnt, iAttachCnt
time tStartTime

SetPointer(HourGlass!)
// Open a channel with Notes
iHndl = OpenChannel("Notes","SendMail")

// If Notes not running, start it:
If iHndl < 1 then
Run(i_sMailExe, Minimized!)
      // Wait up to 2 minutes for Notes to load and the user to log on
      tStartTime = Now()
      Do
```

```
        Yield( )   //Yield control occasionally
        iHndl = OpenChannel("Notes","SendMail")
        if iHndl > 0 then Exit           // OK, Notes is active
      Loop Until SecondsAfter(tStartTime,Now( )) > 120 // Try again
If iHndl < 1 then
  Messagebox("Error","Cannot start Notes.",StopSign!)
  SetPointer(Arrow!)
  Return
 end if
end if


// Notes is active, so create a new message
iRtn=ExecRemote("NewMessage", iHndl)

// Should check return code each time. If iRtn <> 1 then the function
// did not succeed.

// Send the note to everyone in the To: list
FOR iSendCnt = 1 TO lb_to.totalitems( )
 iRtn=ExecRemote("To " + lb_to.item[iSendCnt], iHndl)
 sle_message.text = "Message sent to: " + lb_to.item[iSendCnt]
NEXT


// Send the note to everyone in the cc: list
FOR iSendCnt = 1 TO lb_cc.totalitems( )
 iRtn=ExecRemote("To " + lb_cc.item[iSendCnt], iHndl)
 sle_message.text = "Message sent to: " + lb_cc.item[iSendCnt]
NEXT


// Send the Subject and the message text
iRtn=ExecRemote("Subject "+ sle_subject.text, iHndl)
iRtn=ExecRemote("Text " + mle_note.text, iHndl)


// Add the attachments
FOR iAttachCnt = 1 TO lb_attach.totalitems( )
iRtn=ExecRemote("AttachFile " + lb_attach.item[iAttachCnt], iHndl)
NEXT


// Send the message and close the channel
iRtn=ExecRemote("Send",iHndl)
iRtn = CloseChannel(iHndl)
SetPointer(Arrow!)
```

This script sends the note to everyone in the To: and cc: fields and adds attachments listed in the Attachments: field.

Using DDE provides a fairly simple method of eMail integration with PowerBuilder. To provide this capability for multiple eMail systems, however, requires developing DDE code for each of the systems. For more information on DDE, see Chapter 14.

POWERBUILDER'S MAPI INTERFACE

PowerBuilder provides a set of objects specifically for dealing with simple MAPI. These objects include a system object (MailSession) and a set of functions, structures, and data types. These objects give the developer a way to interface with MAPI from PowerBuilder without writing directly to MAPI.

The PowerBuilder MailSession object has the following attributes:

- **SessionID**—Protected long containing the ID of the current mail session
- **MessageID[ ]**—String array of mail message IDs

Three PowerBuilder structures are defined specifically for use with MAPI. They are:

- **mailFileDescription**—A MAPI structure that identifies an attachment to a message. This structure has the following attributes:

Attribute	Data Type
FileName	String
PathName	String
FileType	mailFileType (enumerated)
Position	Unsigned Long

Note: If the position attribute is 1, the attachment is placed at the beginning of the note, preceded and followed by spaces. If position is greater than or equal to 0, the character at the location identified by position in the note is replaced with the attachment.

- **mailMessage**—A MAPI structure that describes a message. This structure has the following attributes:

Attribute	Data Type
ReceiptRequested	Boolean
MessageSent	Boolean

Unread	Boolean
Subject	String
NoteText	String
MessageType	String
DateReceived	String
ConversationID	String
Recipient[ ]	mailRecipient array
AttachmentFile[ ]	mailFileDescription array

- **mailRecipient**—A MAPI structure that identifies the sender or receiver of a message. This structure has the following attributes:

Attribute	*Data type*
Name	String
Address	String
mailRecipientType	mailRecipientType (enumerated)
EntryType	Protected blob

There are ten functions defined for the mailSession object. They are:

- **mailAddress(mailmessage)**—Used to address a message or display a list of valid mail addresses. **mailAddress( )** updates the mailRecipient array for the mail message. The mailRecipient structure contains information about recipients of a mail message.

   mailmessage is an optional parameter of the mailMessage datatype (see the previous discussion), that contains information about the message. If mailmessage is not entered, an address list is displayed.

   mailAddress( ) returns one of the following enumerated data types:
   - mailReturnSuccess!
   - mailReturnFailure!
   - mailReturnInsufficientMemory!
   - mailReturnUserAbort!
- **mailDeleteMessage(messageid)**—Used to delete the mail message identified by messageid.

   messageid is a string containing the ID of the message to be deleted. This ID can be obtained using the **mailGetMessages( )** function described next.

   mailDeleteMessage( ) returns one of the following enumerated data types:

- mailReturnSuccess!
- mailReturnFailure!
- mailReturnInsufficientMemory!
- mailReturnInvalidMessage!
- mailReturnUserAbort!
- **mailGetMessages(returnunreadonly)**—Used to populate the messageID array of the MailSession object with message IDs. The message IDs obtained using this function are used in other mail functions.

  returnunreadonly is an optional Boolean parameter denoting whether to populate the messageID array only with the IDs of un-read messages.

  mailGetMessages( ) returns one of the following enumerated data types:
  - mailReturnSuccess!
  - mailReturnFailure!
  - mailReturnInsufficientMemory!
  - mailReturnUserAbort!
  - mailReturnNoMessages!
- **mailHandle( )**—Used to obtain the handle of the MailSession object.
- **mailLogoff( )**—Used to terminate the current mail session.
  mailLogoff( ) returns one of the following enumerated data types:
  - mailReturnSuccess!
  - mailReturnFailure!
  - mailReturnInsufficientMemory!
- **mailLogon(userid, password, logonoption)**—Used to establish a new mail session or add the user to an existing mail session. userid and password are optional strings containing the mail system logon of the user. If these values are not entered, the user will be prompted by the mail system for this information.

  logonoption is an optional enumerated data type specifying one of the following logon options:
  - mailNewSession!
  - mailDownLoad!
  - mailNewSessionWithDownLoad!

  If logonoption is not entered, the user is added to the existing mail session and is not prompted to enter the User ID and password.

  mailLogon( ) returns one of the following enumerated data types:
  - mailReturnSuccess!
  - mailReturnFailure!
  - mailReturnLoginFailure!
  - mailReturnInsufficientMemory!
  - mailReturnTooManySessions!

- mailReturnUserAbort!
- **mailReadMessage(messageid, mailmessage, mailreadoption, mark)**—Used to open the mail message identified by messageid as specified in mailreadoption.

  messageid is a string containing the ID of the message to be read. The **mailGetMessages( )** function can be used to obtain the message ID.

  mailmessage is of the mailMessage datatype (discussed previously) containing information about the message.

  mailreadoption is an enumerated data type consisting of the following:
  - mailEntireMessage!
  - mailEnvelopeOnly!
  - mailBodyAsFile!
  - mailSuppressAttach!

  mark is a Boolean parameter denoting whether to mark the message as read. If it is True, the message will be marked as read.

  mailReadMessage( ) returns one of the following enumerated data types:
  - mailReturnSuccess!
  - mailReturnFailure!
  - mailReturnInsufficientMemory!

Note: To read an attachment, follow the call to mailReadMessage with statements that open and read the temporary file identified by the mailMessage.AttachmentFile.PathName attribute. Be sure to delete this temporary file when you no longer need it.

- **mailRecipientDetails(mailrecipient, allowupdates)**—Used to display details about **mailrecipient** using the recipient information window of the eMail system.

  mailrecipient is of the mailRecipient datatype, containing information about the recipient. mailrecipient must contain a recipient identifier returned by **mailAddress( )**, **mailResolveRecipient( )**, or **mailReadMessage( )**.

  allowupdates is an optional Boolean parameter that identifies whether the detail information can be modified. The default is False.

  mailRecipientDetails( ) returns one of the following enumerated data types:
  - mailReturnSuccess!
  - mailReturnFailure!
  - mailReturnInsufficientMemory!

- • mailUnknownReturnRecipient!
- • mailUnknownReturnUserAbort!
- • **mailResolveRecipient(recipientname, allowupdates)**—Used to resolve the name of **recipientname**.

  recipientname is of the mailRecipient datatype, containing information about the recipient.

  allowupdates is an optional Boolean parameter that identifies whether the recipient's name can be modified. The default is False.

  mailResolveRecipient( ) returns one of the following enumerated data types:
  - • mailReturnSuccess!
  - • mailReturnFailure!
  - • mailReturnInsufficientMemory!
  - • mailReturnUserAbort!
- • **mailSend(mailmessage)**—Used to send a mail message.

  mailmessage is an optional parameter of the mailMessage datatype, containing message information. If mailmessage is not entered, a Send Note dialog box is displayed for the user to enter the message.

  mailSend( ) returns one of the following enumerated data types:
  - • mailReturnSuccess!
  - • mailReturnFailure!
  - • mailReturnInsufficientMemory!
  - • mailReturnLogFailure!
  - • mailReturnUserAbort!
  - • mailReturnDiskFull!
  - • mailReturnTooManySessions!
  - • mailReturnTooManyFiles!
  - • mailReturnTooManyRecipients!
  - • mailReturnUnknownRecipient!
  - • mailReturnAttachmentNotFound!

PowerBuilder has also defined five enumerated data types specifically for use with MAPI:

1. **mailFileType**—Type of mail attachment. Valid values are:
   mailAttach!
   mailOLE!
   mailOLEStatic!
2. **mailLogonOption**—Type of logon. Valid values are:
   mailNewSession!
   mailDownLoad!
   mailNewSessionWithDownLoad!

3. **mailReadOption**—Portion of message to read. Valid values are:
    mailBodyAsFile!
    mailEntireMessage!
    mailEnvelopeOnly!
    mailSuppressAttach!
4. **mailRecipientType**—Type of message recipient. Valid values are:
    mailTo!

    mailCC!

    mailOriginator!

    mailBCC!
5. **mailReturnCode**—Return values from the **mailReadMessage** function. Valid values are:
    mailReturnAccessDenied!
    mailReturnAttachmentNotFound!
    mailReturnAttachmentOpenFailure!
    mailReturnAttachmentWriteFailure!
    mailReturnDiskFull!
    mailReturnFailure!
    mailReturnInsufficientMemory!
    mailReturnLoginFailure!
    mailReturnMessageInUse!
    mailReturnNoMessages!
    mailReturnSuccess!
    mailReturnTextTooLarge!
    mailReturnTooManyFiles!
    mailReturnTooManyRecipients!
    mailReturnTooManySessions!
    mailReturnUserAbort!

Take the previous example using DDE and do it using PowerBuilder's MAPI interface. Assume the same window completed as shown in Figure 12.3.

To send this using MAPI, the developer replaces the script cb_send with the following:

```
/******************************************************
** Obtain message information from the window and
** send the message(s) using MAPI
******************************************************/

mailSession        mSes
mailReturnCode     mRet
```

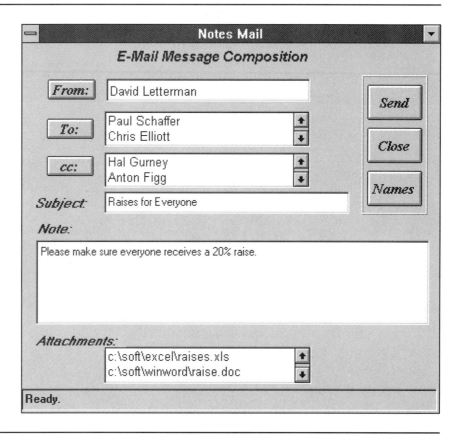

Figure 12.3 Using PowerBuilder's MAPI interface.

```
mailMessage        mMsg
int                iSendCnt, iAttachCnt

// Create a mail session.
mSes = create mailSession

// Log on to the session.
mRet = mSes.mailLogon ( mailNewSession! )

if mRet <> mailReturnSuccess! then
    DisplayMsg ("Mail Logon Error", "Unable to Log On to Mail System")
    Return
```

```
end if
// Populate the mailMessage structure with information about
// the message.
mMsg.Subject = sle_subject.text
mMsg.NoteText = mle_note.text

FOR iSendCnt = 1 TO lb_to.totalitems( )
 mMsg.Recipient[iSendCnt].name = lb_to.item[iSendCnt]
 sle_message.text = "Message sent to: " + lb_to.item[iSendCnt]
NEXT

// Send the note to everyone in the cc: list
FOR iSendCnt = 1 TO lb_cc.totalitems( )
 mMsg.Recipient[iSendCnt].name = lb_cc.item[iSendCnt]
 sle_message.text = "Message sent to: " + lb_cc.item[iSendCnt]
NEXT

// Add the attachments. Position of 1 puts the attachment at the
// beginning of the message
FOR iAttachCnt = 1 TO lb_attach.totalitems( )
 mMsg.AttachmentFile[iAttachCnt].FileName = lb_cc.item[iSendCnt]
 mMsg.AttachmentFile[iAttachCnt].FileType = mailAttach!
 mMsg.AttachmentFile[iAttachCnt].Position = 1
NEXT

// Send the mail.
mRet = mSes.mailSend ( mMsg )
if mRet <> mailReturnSuccess! then
      DisplayMsg ("Send Error", "Unable to send mail message" )
      return
end if

mSes.mailLogoff( )
destroy mSes
```

PowerBuilder's MAPI functionality also makes it easy to develop an interface for message management. For example, suppose the developer wants to provide the user the capability to list, read, and delete his/her messages. The PowerBuilder interface would look something like the one in Figure 12.4.

The open event contains the following script to read the list of messages for the user. This script retrieves the user's messages using the **mailGetMessages( )** function to populate the MessageID array of the mail session. The date, subject, recipients, and attachment files are then read from the mailMessage structure for each message:

```
/*******************************************************
** This script creates a mail session using the instance variable
** i_mSes. mailGetMessages( ) retrieves the list of message IDs into
** the MessageID array of i_mSes. The script then loops through each
** message, reading the envelope information and inserting a row into
** dw_msglist.
*******************************************************/


int            iMsgNbr, iIDcnt
long           lCurRow
mailReturnCode mRet
mailMessage    mMsg

// Create the mail session
i_mSes = CREATE MailSession
```

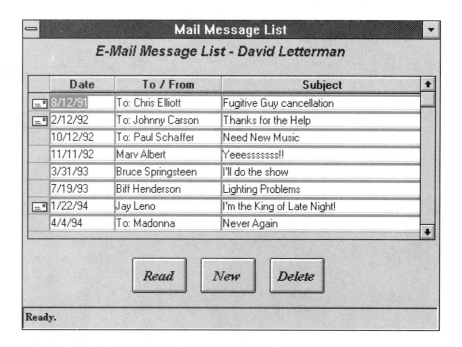

Figure 12.4   Interface for message management developed using PowerBuilder's MAPI.

```
// Log on to the session.
mRet = i_mSes.mailLogon ( mailNewSession! )

if mRet <> mailReturnSuccess! then
    DisplayMsg ("Mail Logon Error", "Unable to Log On to Mail System")
    Return
end if

// Call mailGetMessages to populate the MessageID attribute of
// the instance variable i_mSes of type mailSession

i_mSes.mailGetMessages(TRUE)

// Get the total number of messages
iMsgNbr = Upperbound(i_mSes.MessageID[ ])

// For each message, add a row to dw_msglist and use setItems
// to populate the messageID, message date, the first recipient, and
// the message subject. If the message has an attachment, set the
// attachment column to 1 to display the attachment bitmap
For iIDcnt = 1 to iMsgNbr
   lCurRow = dw_msglist.insertRow(0)
   mRet = i_mSes.mailReadMessage( i_mSes.MessageID[iIDcnt], mMsg, &
                    mailEnvelopeOnly!, True )

     if not(isNull(mMsg.AttachmentFile[1].FileName)) then
             dw_msglist.setItem(lCurRow,"attachment",1)
     end if
     dw_msglist.setItem(lCurRow,"messageID",i_mSes.
     MessageID[iIDcnt])
     dw_msglist.setItem(lCurRow,"person",mMsg.
     Recipient[1].name)
     dw_msglist.setItem(lCurRow,"send_date",date(mMsg.
     DateReceived))
     dw_msglist.setItem(lCurRow,"subject",mMsg.Subject)
Next
```

The clicked event of cb_read obtains the message ID of the current row and uses it to read the full text of the message:

```
/*******************************************************
** This script displays the message listed in the current row of
** dw_msglist. It assumes that the mail session i_mSes has been
** created and a successful logon has occurred.
*******************************************************/
```

```
int                  iRowNum, iRetVal
string               sMessageID
mailMessage          mMsg
mailReturnCode       mRet

// Get the row containing the selected row
iRowNum = dw_msglist.GetRow ( )

if iRowNum > 0 then

    // Obtain the mail Message ID to display
    sMessageID = dw_msglist.GetItemString ( iRowNum, 'MessageID' )

    // Reread this message to obtain entire contents (because
    // previously we read only the "envelope" and not the contents
    // of the message). Message information goes into mMsg
    mRet = i_mSes.mailReadMessage( sMessageID, mMsg, &
                    mailEntireMessage!, True )

    // Open the message display window and get the message text
    // from mMsg.NoteText
    ....
    ....
end if
```

The clicked event cb_delete obtains the message ID of the current row and deletes the message:

```
/*****************************************************
** This script deletes the message listed in the current row of
** dw_msglist. It assumes that the mail session i_mSes has been
** created and a successful logon has occurred.
*****************************************************/

string          sMsgID
int             iRowNum
mailReturnCode  mRet

iRowNum = dw_msglist.GetRow( )
if iRowNum > 0 then
    sMsgID = dw_msglist.GetItemString(iRowNum, "messageID")
    mRet = i_mSes.mailDeleteMessage(sMsgID)
end if
```

Using PowerBuilder's MAPI capabilities allows for the development of a PowerBuilder interface to any mail system that supports MAPI.

POWERBUILDER LIBRARY FOR LOTUS NOTES

Powersoft has recently released its Library for Lotus Notes product. This product provides PowerBuilder applications the ability to access not only SQL data, but also data stored in Lotus Notes databases. The PowerBuilder Library for Lotus Notes provides a set of PowerBuilder objects designed to automate the creation of a PowerBuilder interface to Lotus Notes. This interface can be developed using either the Notes simple messaging interface (SMI) or VIM.

In addition to the object libraries, the product provides a pre-built sample application and a set of utilities known as the PowerBuilder Library application for Lotus Notes (PLAN) toolkit. The PLAN toolkit provides an automated method of creating the various PowerBuilder objects used to access Notes data. The PLAN toolkit includes generators that create DataWindows in the form of encapsulated user objects that handle the interaction with the Notes API. These objects can then be added to a PowerBuilder application to provide a Notes interface with little additional code required.

To implement our previous example using the PowerBuilder Library for Lotus Notes instead of MAPI, do the following:

- Use the PLAN toolkit to create the application DataWindows and user objects. Use PLAN's View Generator to create the message list objects and the Form Generator to create the objects for reading an individual message. After generating the objects, go to the DataWindow painter and make any necessary changes. The DataWindow for the message list will eventually look the same as for the previous examples, as shown in Figure 12.5.
- Add the two new user objects to the window (controls dw_list and dw_msg) and create a window instance variable named *iui_db_handle* to store the handle to the Notes database. The two user objects are standard user objects containing the two respective DataWindow objects.
- Add the following PowerScript code to the open event of the window:

```
// Open the Notes database
if not f_database_open &
    ("c:\notes\mail\dletterm.nsf", iui_db_handle) then
    return
end if

// Assign database handle to DataWindow controls
dw_list.iui_db_handle = iui_db_handle
dw_msg.iui_db_handle = iui_db_handle
```

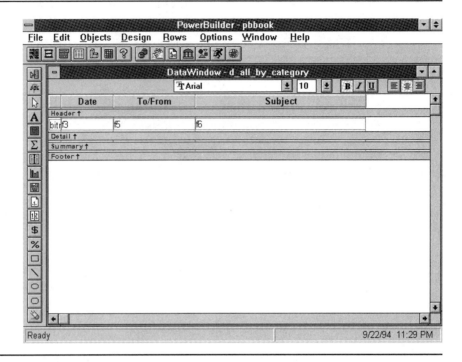

Figure 12.5 DataWindow for message list created using PowerBuilder Library for Lotus Notes.

```
// Initialize list object and retrieve data
dw_1.TriggerEvent("ue_init")
dw_1.TriggerEvent("ue_retrieve")
```

This script first calls **f_database_open( )**. This function is a PowerBuilder global function included with the PowerBuilder Library for Lotus Notes. The function calls the Notes API function to open the Notes database. The code for **f_database_open( )** is:

```
//////////////////////////////////////////////////////////////////////
///////
//
// Function: f_database_open
//
// Purpose:  Open a database.
//
// Scope:    Public
//
```

```
// Parameters: as_database_filename (STRING/Value) database file name
//             aui_db_handle        (UINT/Ref)  database handle
//
// Returns:   BOOLEAN, TRUE if successful, FALSE if fails
//
///////////////////////////////////////////////////////////////////
/////

INT li_api_error          // api error number

// Get the database handle
li_api_error = PB_NSFDbOpen(as_database_filename, aui_db_handle)
IF (li_api_error <> API_SUCCESS) THEN
        f_api_error(li_api_error)
  RETURN FALSE
END IF

RETURN TRUE
```

The ue_init and ue_retrieve events are user-defined events created
for the user objects generated by the PLAN toolkit generator. ue_init
creates the buffer used to transfer data from the Notes API .DLL to
PowerBuilder, while ue_retrieve retrieves data from the Notes database into the DataWindow. The important thing about this is
that this code is provided by the PowerBuilder Library for Lotus
Notes and doesn't need to be coded by the developer.

- Add the following code to the close event of the window:

```
f_database_close(iui_db_handle)
```

This closes the connection to the Notes database.

- Add the following code to the clicked event of cb_read to get the
  current row from dw_list and read the message by retrieving the
  message into dw_msg:

```
long ll_row
long ll_note_id

ll_row = this.getclickedrow( )
ll_note_id = this.getitemnumber(ll_row, "note_id")

dw_msg.iul_note_id = ll_note_id
dw_msg.TriggerEvent("ue_init")
dw_msg.TriggerEvent("ue_retrieve")
```

- Finally, add the following line to the clicked event of cb_delete. This single line of code will mark the document in the current row of dw_list for deletion and place a Trash can bitmap in the left-most column of the DataWindow:

```
dw_list.TriggerEvent("ue_document_delete")
```

As you can see, little code is required to implement a Notes interface from PowerBuilder using the PowerBuilder Library for Lotus Notes.

EMAIL APIS

Another way of providing an eMail interface from PowerBuilder is to write directly to a specific eMail API. Using its external function interface, PowerBuilder applications can interface with any eMail system that provides an API. For an example of how to use external functions, see Chapter 8.

Although writing to an API is more difficult than using DDE, PowerBuilder's MAPI interface, or the PowerBuilder Library for Lotus Notes, it provides the greatest amount of flexibility and gives the developer the capability to develop a more robust interface. As previously mentioned, writing directly to X.400 provides the most flexibility and is able to support the most eMail systems, but it is the most difficult interface to write.

In conclusion, some things to consider when deciding what type of eMail interface to write are the number of different systems that must be supported and the amount of functionality that is needed in the PowerBuilder application. For example, DDE may be suitable in a single-system Windows environment where the only requirement is to transparently send a message. However, in an environment where cc:Mail and Lotus Notes are both used, the best solution is more than likely to write directly to the VIM API. Finally, consider the case in which users of MS Mail, Lotus Notes, and Oracle Mail must exchange messages. In this case, the best solution may be to either write directly to X.400 or install an X.400 gateway and write to an API such as CMC. The point here is that there are many solutions to providing an eMail interface from PowerBuilder. The best answer varies depending on the requirements of the application.

CHAPTER 13

Open Repository CASE API (ORCA)

Client/server technology has been advancing at an increasing rate and will continue to do so in the years to come. This rate of advancement has moved us away from the single-vendor solution of the past into a more open environment. In the client/server arena, there are a number of technologies and many vendors, each providing a solution for different parts of a system. When developing mission-critical applications or products in this environment, one must insist on an open systems architecture. Powersoft has committed to an open architecture by releasing their client/server open development environment (CODE) initiative. This CODE initiative is Powersoft's way of allowing vendors to write interfaces between their products and PowerBuilder. This chapter discusses Powersoft's vision as it relates to their CODE initiative. Topics addressed in this chapter include:

- Powersoft's vision and the CODE initiative
- Open repository CASE API (ORCA)
      ORCA architecture
      ORCA features
      ORCA functions
      ORCA errors
      ORCA header file
      ORCA sample code

An example of ORCA code is provided.

POWERSOFT'S VISION AND THE CODE INITIATIVE

There are many factors to consider when choosing an application development tool. One must have defined the major technical and functional areas of the current product/application and also have foresight in envisioning the future direction of the product, given the different advances in technology. Powersoft's strategy is to focus on establishing PowerBuilder as the premier graphical client/server application development environment available in the marketplace—today and in the future. Powersoft has positioned PowerBuilder as an open development environment capable of tightly integrating with industry-leading, third-party software products. They decided it would be better to integrate with such products as project management tools, version control software, CASE tools, and the like, as opposed to writing their own packages to address these needs. This enables an organization to put together a "best of breed" client/server software solution and not be locked into what may be a less than optimal solution with a competing tool.

CASE companies such as LBMS Inc., Bachman Information Systems, Inc., and Popkin Software plan to or already have developed PowerBuilder CASE applications. These companies plan to integrate and resell PowerBuilder with their workbenches and thus provide complete development life cycle support. Powersoft also has agreements with other CASE/methodology vendors such as Chen & Associates, Ernst and Young, Intersolv, and LogicWorks.

Powersoft requests that all vendors publish application program interfaces (APIs) to their products and stop locking users into proprietary technologies. They reinforce their commitment to open computing with announcement of their client/server open development environment (CODE). CODE is essentially a standard API that allows PowerBuilder to interoperate with other vendors' products and tools. Network World has reported that Powersoft plans to establish relationships with vendors of version control systems, terminal-emulation products, object libraries, desktop applications, and desktop utility servers.

As part of Powersoft's CODE strategy, they have been able to give PowerBuilder users access to third-party source control/configuration management products such as Intersolv's PVCS and Legent Corp's Endevor. There will soon be a number of other version control vendors that will support PowerBuilder in its own development environment.

Some vendors try to do as much as possible, whether they are experts in all crafts. Similarly, some vendors want to sell you complete client/server development environments, even if they made their mark in only one area. Powersoft is not one of them. Since October 1992, Powersoft's CODE initiative has embraced a wide variety of strategic partners and products that complement PowerBuilder. DBMS magazine reports that about 30 vendors have jumped on PowerBuilder's bandwagon and the list grows each month.

OPEN REPOSITORY CASE API (ORCA)

As part of their CODE specification, Powersoft has publicly stated that they will peacefully coexist with the CASE world. Specifically, they will do whatever it takes to ensure their customers that state-of-the-art CASE solutions are available to augment the suite of PowerBuilder development tools. Some percentage of their customers, however, also require additional development life cycle tools that may never be offered by Powersoft or any other vendor. To address both of these requirements, Powersoft provides ORCA, an API that provides comprehensive access to all PowerBuilder library entities.

ORCA Architecture

The ORCA architecture provides vendors a standard method of interfacing with PowerBuilder. Figure 13.1 shows a variety of software products communicating with PowerBuilder using the ORCA API.

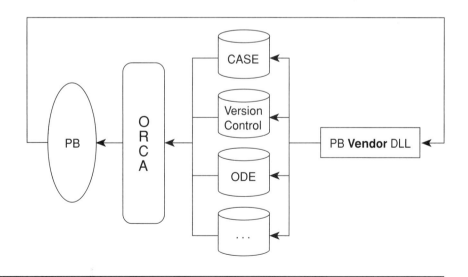

Figure 13.1   Software products communicate with PowerBuilder using the ORCA API.

If there is also a need to communicate from PowerBuilder back to the vendor's product, Powersoft or the vendor needs to write a vendor-specific DLL. This second interface is also shown in Figure 13.1.

ORCA Features

ORCA provides developers with many different features including session management, library management, compilation, executable construction, and object query. These features are made available through standard function calls which are listed and explained in the next section of this chapter.

Session Management All ORCA functions operate in the context of a session. Before any of the ORCA functions are called, a session handle must be obtained. A session handle in ORCA is like a file handle when opening a file. If processing is needed on the contents of a file, the file is opened and a file handle is obtained; the appropriate file functions are performed on the file and the file is closed. Using ORCA, the process is similar. If processing is needed on a set of PowerBuilder libraries, a session is opened. When the session handle is obtained, the ORCA library functions can be called. When all processing on the library is completed, the ORCA session is closed.

There are also several session service functions for setting the current library search path, setting the current application, and performing error handling. Before any setting of the current application occurs, the library search path must be set.

Library Management ORCA also has a set of library management functions that can be called. These functions allow libraries and library entities to be manipulated outside the context of a current application or library list. What this means is that a current application library search path does not have to be set for these library functions to work. The reason the library search path doesn't have to be set is because these functions act on the library as a whole and not its contents. Library functions can create libraries, delete libraries, and modify library comments. In addition, library entities can be copied, deleted, exported, and moved using these functions.

Compilation The ORCA compilation functions allow the developer to import and regenerate a single library entity or multiple library entities. All compilation must occur in the context of a current application and library list, so that all library references can be resolved.

Executable Construction These ORCA functions must also be performed in the context of a current application and library list. Application executable files and PowerBuilder dynamic libraries (PBDs) can be created using the ORCA executable construction functions. The authors recommend that the regeneration function be called before an executable or PowerBuilder dynamic library is created.

Object Query These ORCA functions allow for querying objects for object reference explosion and object hierarchy traversal. Object querying must occur in the context of a current application and library list.

ORCA Functions

ORCA functions are meant to be called from a custom DLL. The detail specifications of these functions and the PowerBuilder ORCA header file can be obtained by contacting Powersoft. The functions are:

PBORCA_SessionOpen	Establish an ORCA session. This call must be made before any other ORCA function calls. There are no overhead or resource issues related to keeping an ORCA session open. Therefore, once established, an ORCA session should be left open as long as it might be needed.
PBORCA_SessionClose	Terminate an ORCA session. This function frees any allocated resources related to the ORCA session. Because an ORCA session does not connect to anything, failure to execute this function does not result in any loss of data.
PBORCA_Session GetError	Get the current error for an ORCA session. This function should be called anytime another ORCA function call has resulted in an error. If there is no current error, " " is placed in the error buffer.
PBORCA_SessionSet LibraryList	Establish the library search path for an ORCA session. This function must be called prior to execution of any ORCA function that compiles objects, queries objects, or constructs executables. Certain library entry management

	functions and query functions can be called without setting the library list. Library names should be fully qualified, whenever possible.
PBORCA_SessionSet CurrentAppl	Establish the current application for an ORCA session. This function must be called after **PBORCA_SetLibraryList** and prior to execution of any ORCA function that compiles objects, queries objects, or constructs executables. The application library name should be fully qualified, whenever possible.
PBORCA_Library CommentModify	Modify the comment of a PowerBuilder library.
PBORCA_LibraryCreate	Create a new PowerBuilder library.
PBORCA_LibraryDelete	Delete a PowerBuilder library.
PBORCA_Library Directory	Explode the directory of a PowerBuilder library.
PBORCA_LibraryEntry Copy	Copy a PowerBuilder library entry from one library to another.
PBORCA_LibraryEntry Delete	Delete a PowerBuilder library entry.
PBORCA_LibraryEntry Export	Export the source for a PowerBuilder library entry.
PBORCA_LibraryEntry Information	Return information for a PowerBuilder library entry.
PBORCA_LibraryEntry Move	Move a PowerBuilder library entry from one library to another.
PBORCA_CompileEntry Import	Import the source for a PowerBuilder library entry and compile it.
PBORCA_CompileEntry ImportList	Import the source for a list of PowerBuilder library entries and compile them. All entries are imported first, have only their type definitions compiled, and then, assuming everything works, have the entire entry list fully compiled. This call can be used to import several interrelated objects— for example, a window, its menu, and

	perhaps a user object that it uses. Note that ancestor objects and user objects must be imported prior to any objects that are descended from them.
PBORCA_CompileEntry Regenerate	Compile a PowerBuilder library entry.
PBORCA_Executable Create	Create a PowerBuilder executable.
PBORCA_Executable PBDCreate	Create a PowerBuilder dynamic library (PBD).
PBORCA_ObjectQuery Hierarchy	Query a PowerBuilder object for other objects in its ancestor hierarchy.
PBORCA_ObjectQuery Reference	Query a PowerBuilder object for references to other objects.

These functions are all prototyped in the ORCA header file.

ORCA Errors

The standard PowerBuilder ORCA errors are:

Error Number	*Error Description*
-1	Invalid parameter list
-2	Duplicate operation
-3	Object not found
-4	Bad library name
-5	Library list is not set
-6	Library is not in the library list
-7	Library I/O error
-8	Object exists
-9	Invalid name
-10	Buffer size too small
-11	Compile error
-12	Link error
-13	Current application not set
-14	Object has no ancestor
-15	Object has no references

These error numbers are returned by the ORCA library management functions.

PowerBuilder ORCA Header File

The PowerBuilder ORCA header file is included on the diskette provided with this book. This file is needed to write programs that communicate with ORCA.

ORCA Sample Code

The diskette provided with this book includes a sample program that shows how to write to the ORCA API. This code shows how a number of the ORCA functions should be called. The code to import and export objects into PowerBuilder is included. The code to obtain a directory listing of objects within a PBL and the code to move and copy objects from within PBLs are also included. These code segments should be used for reference only; they should not be copied directly because they are simply examples of how some of the functions can be implemented.

CHAPTER 14

Interfacing with the Operating System

When developing PowerBuilder applications in most environments, it becomes important to interface with the operating environment and other applications. Although this chapter will emphasize the Windows operating environment, some additional operating systems that PowerBuilder supports will be discussed towards the chapter's end.

Windows application programming interfaces (APIs) and the Windows interprocess communication (IPC) mechanisms allow applications to communicate with the operating environment and other applications. This chapter covers the following:

- The Windows API
- Windows IPCs
    Messages

    Clipboard

    dynamic data exchange (DDE)

    object linking and embedding (OLE)
- Windows DLLs
- Cross Platform Issues
    Global Environment Object

    Apple Macintosh

    Windows NT

    UNIX (Posix/Motif)

THE WINDOWS API

An API is a set of all operating system service calls for a particular product. A set of APIs allows programmers or products to connect to a specified product or the Windows operating system. An API includes information about internal variables and ways to link into a package. Microsoft has released a set of Windows APIs known as the Microsoft Windows software development kit (SDK). The SDK has over 1,000 API Windows functions, divided into three groups: the Windows manager interface functions (User), the graphics device interface functions (GDI), and the system services interface functions (Kernel). The SDK enables programmers to interface with the Windows operating system with these APIs.

Making Windows API Calls

The GDI dynamic linked library (DLL) has export functions for handling the painting, drawing, plotting, printing, and color functions of Windows. The User DLL has export functions for everything in Windows that involves window creation, communication, hardware, and messaging. The Kernel DLL has export functions involving memory management, multitasking, and resources. The Kernel, GDI, and User DLLs handle most of the functionality of the Windows operating system. There are also device drivers in the Windows operating system that provide support for different levels of Windows functionality. Device drivers are responsible for exporting functions for Windows functionality, above and beyond what the Kernel, GDI, and User DLLs can provide.

Powersoft developed over 500 functions in PowerBuilder so that application developers do not have to call SDK functions to accomplish tasks. There are times, however, when application developers need to get information from the Windows operating system and PowerBuilder does not have the functions to accomplish that task. In this case, the application developer has to look for the function in the SDK. Most of the functions that PowerBuilder users need to call are in either the KERNEL.EXE, USER.EXE, or the GDI.EXE dynamic linked libraries (DLL).

The application developer should refer to the *Functions Manual* of the SDK to determine which functions are needed for certain tasks. When the SDK function has been located, the following questions have to be answered:

1. Can the parameters be passed from PowerBuilder using the appropriate data types?

2. Can PowerBuilder handle the function's return datatype?
3. Can the DLL that has the function be located?

If the answer to these questions is "yes," the developer can declare the function as an external function in the application.

External function syntax is as follows:

```
FUNCTION Return_Data_Type &
    FunctionName ( { REF } { Data_Type1 Arg1, ..., &
                            DataTypeN ArgN } ) &
        LIBRARY "Library Name"
```

If an external function does not return a value (for example, it has a void return type), the syntax for the external function declaration is:

```
SUBROUTINE
    FunctionName ({REF}{ DataType1 arg1 , ..., &
                        DataTypeN argn }) &
        LIBRARY "Library Name"
```

The following statement, for example, declares an external C function named *IsZoomed* that interfaces with the SDK and takes one argument (an integer called Handle):

```
Function Boolean IsZoomed(Int Handle) Library "User.EXE"
```

Windows Memory, GDI, and Resources on the Client

After Windows starts and protected mode is entered, several device drivers, font files, and OS libraries are loaded into memory. They are:

Library	Description
comm.drv	Serial communications
display.drv	Video display
fixedfon.fon	Fixed system fonts
fonts.fon	Proportional system font
keyboard.drv	Keyboard input
language.dll	Language-specified functions
mouse.drv	Mouse input
network.drv	Network drivers
sound.drv	Sound output

system.drv	Timer
taskman.exe	Task manager application
gdi.exe	Graphics device interface
krnl386.exe	Multitasking, memory, and resource management
user.exe	Window management

These libraries form the environment around which Windows operates. To most applications and libraries, Windows' Kernel, GDI, and User libraries represent the front-end to the operating system because these three files have most of the functions called by application or library code. Figure 14.1 shows the relationship between an application and the Windows DDLs.

Useful Windows Functions

Some of the SDK functions that are useful in developing PowerBuilder applications are:

GetActiveWindow

GetAsyncKeyState

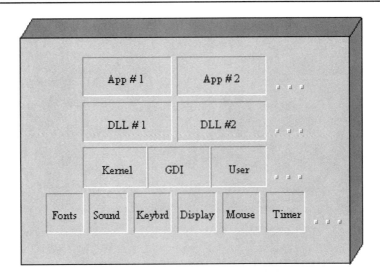

Figure 14.1   Relationship between an application and the Windows DDLs.

SetKeyBoardState

SwapMouseButton

GetBitmapDimension

SetBitmapDimension

GetCapture

SetCapture

GetCaretBlinkTime

SetCaretBlinkTime

GetCurrentPosition

GetCurrentPositionEx

GetCurrentTask

GetDC

ReleaseDC

GetDesktopWindow

GetTopWindow

GetWindow

GetDeviceCaps

GetDoubleClickTime

GetDriveType

GetFocus

SetFocus

GetFreeSpace

GetFreeSystemResources

EnableHardwareInput

GetKBCodePage

GetKeyboardType

GetKeyNameText

GetKeyState

GetModuleFileName

GetModuleHandle

GetModuleUsage

GetNextWindow

GetNumTasks

GetSystemDirectory

GetTempDrive

GetTickCount

GetTimerResolution

GetTopWindow

GetVersion

GetWindow

GetWindowDC

GetWindowOrg

GetWindowPlacement

SetWindowPlacement

GetWindowsDirectory

GetWindowTask

GetWinFlags

FatalExit

FatalAppExit

ExitWindows

ExitWindowsExec

DirectedYield

Syntax for declaring some of the Windows SDK functions listed is:

```
FUNCTION int GetWindowsDirectory(REF String swindir, int size) LIBRARY
"kernel.exe"
FUNCTION int GetSystemDirectory(REF String swindir, int size) LIBRARY
"kernel.exe"
FUNCTION int ExitWindows(ulong lng, uint lng1) LIBRARY "user.exe"
FUNCTION int SwapMouseButton(int lng1) LIBRARY "user.exe"
FUNCTION uint GetCaretBlinkTime( ) LIBRARY "user.exe"
FUNCTION uint SetCaretBlinkTime(uint blnk) LIBRARY "user.exe"
FUNCTION uint GetDoubleClickTime( ) LIBRARY "user.exe"
FUNCTION uint SetDoubleClickTime(uint blnk) LIBRARY "user.exe"
FUNCTION int GetDriveType( ) LIBRARY "user.exe"
FUNCTION ulong GetFreeSpace(uint lng1) LIBRARY "user.exe"
FUNCTION uint GetFreeSystemResources(uint lng) LIBRARY "user.exe"
FUNCTION int EnableHardwareInput(int fEnableInput) LIBRARY "user.exe"
FUNCTION int GetKBCodePage( ) LIBRARY "user.exe"
FUNCTION int GetKeyboardType(int fnKeybInfo) LIBRARY "user.exe"
FUNCTION int GetKeyNameText(LONG lParam, REF String lpszBuffer, int
cbMaxKey) LIBRARY "user.exe"
FUNCTION int GetKeyState(int vkey) LIBRARY "user.exe"
```

```
FUNCTION uint GetNumTasks( ) LIBRARY "user.exe"
FUNCTION int GetTempDrive(char chDriveLetter) LIBRARY "user.exe"
FUNCTION ulong GetTickCount( ) LIBRARY "user.exe"
FUNCTION ulong GetTimerResolution( ) LIBRARY "user.exe"
FUNCTION ulong GetVersion( ) LIBRARY "user.exe"
FUNCTION ulong GetWinFlags( ) LIBRARY "user.exe"
FUNCTION uint GetActiveWindow(uint hWnd) LIBRARY "user.exe"
FUNCTION uint GetModuleHandle(string ModName) LIBRARY "kernel.exe"
```

PowerBuilder's ability to interface with the operating system makes it a much stronger development tool.

WINDOWS IPCs

Windows IPC mechanisms are another way for applications to communicate with other applications. This section discusses IPC methods including messages, the clipboard, DDE, and OLE.

Messages

What Are Windows Messages? Windows messages are one of the four basic methods for an application to communicate with itself, other applications, and the Windows operating system. Messages, which are the input to an application, represent events to which an application may need to respond. They are basically a set of values that Windows sends to a window procedure, to provide input or request the window to carry out some action.

For example, an event occurs when the left mouse button or a key is pressed. When Windows detects this event, it notifies the appropriate application by sending messages to the application. A single message or a group of messages can be associated with an event. A message is a structure that has a message identifier and message parameters. The content of message parameters can differ depending on the message type.

Windows collects input messages in its message queue and then places them in one of its application message queues. The application then reads the message(s) and dispatches them to the appropriate window procedure. Windows sends some messages directly to a window procedure; when this happens it is said that Windows has **sent** a message. On the other hand, when Windows sends a message to an application message queue, it is said that Windows has **posted** a message. Figure 14.2 shows the relationship between the Windows message queues and each application's message queue.

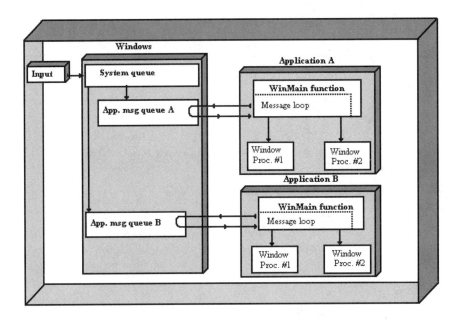

Figure 14.2   Relationship between Windows queues and each application's message queue.
Reprinted by permission from *Windows 3.1 Programming*, Charles Petzold, Microsoft Press,
1987–1992.

Figure 14.3 shows a test window with a single command button in
the center.

The code in Figure 14.4 is for the clicked event of the command
button.

At runtime, when the command button is clicked, Windows generates a series of messages that correspond to clicking the left mouse
button and sends them to the PowerBuilder application message queue.
The PowerBuilder application then reads the messages and sends them
to the window process, which executes the line of code in the clicked
event and causes the message box in Figure 14.5 to be displayed.

PowerBuilder Messages Mapped to Windows Messages   PowerBuilder
has its own set of messages. These messages are mapped to one or more
Windows messages. Refer to PowerBuilder documentation for a mapping of PowerBuilder's messages to Windows' messages.

Trapping a Windows Message   When a developer needs an application
to respond to a specific Windows message that PowerBuilder has not

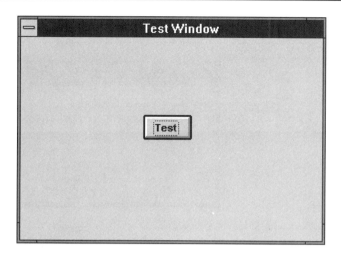

Figure 14.3   Test window with single command button.

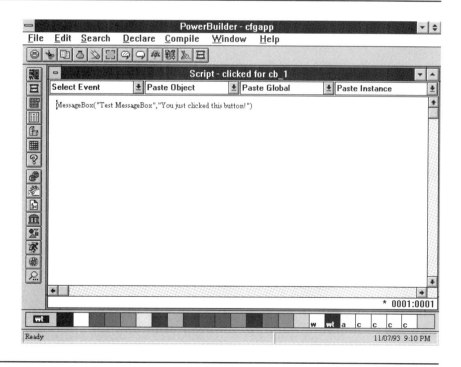

Figure 14.4   Code for the clicked event of the command button.

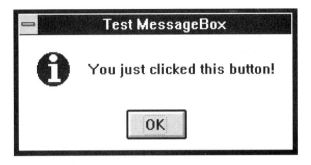

Figure 14.5 Message box displayed.

defined, the developer needs to trap the message. For example, when the user attempts to close the application using the control menu, a message box should appear asking the user to confirm his or her actions (closing the application). In order to accomplish this task, the developer needs to trap the appropriate Windows messages that are sent to the application. The developer must first study the Microsoft Windows SDK documentation on messages. This can be found in the *Programmer's Reference Volume 3: Messages, Structures, and Macros*. This book lists the different types of Windows messages, their purpose, and a detailed parameter listing. There are a number of different tools that can be used to determine which Windows messages are being generated. In the example that follows, SPY.EXE (a tool available from Microsoft) is used.

Using Spy, the Windows messages that are generated when the application is closed using the control menu can be determined. The message that is generated in this case is the WM_SYSCOMMAND. This can be determined by reviewing all the messages that are sent to the window and looking up what they mean (in the Messages section of the SDK documentation). The WM_SYSCOMMAND Windows message is generated when a user selects a command from the control menu or when a user selects the maximize button or the minimize button.

When the Windows message name is determined, the message number must be determined. This can be done using the third column in the Spy output window or opening the Windows header. The third column in the Spy window shows the message number of F060 (see Figure 14.6).

A more tedious method of determining the message number is looking at the Windows header file (the windows.h file is part of the MS Windows SDK). After opening the Windows header file, the developer

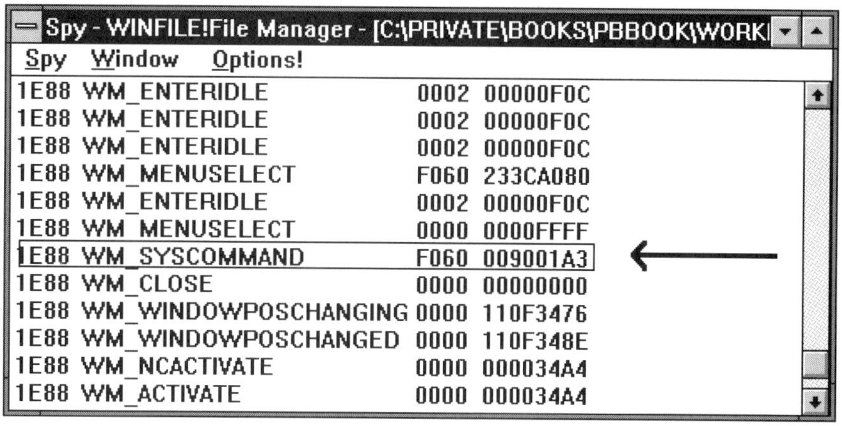

```
 ═ Spy - WINFILE!File Manager - [C:\PRIVATE\BOOKS\PBBOOK\WORK| ▼ ▲
  Spy   Window   Options!
 1E88 WM_ENTERIDLE            0002 00000F0C              ↑
 1E88 WM_ENTERIDLE            0002 00000F0C
 1E88 WM_ENTERIDLE            0002 00000F0C
 1E88 WM_MENUSELECT           F060 233CA080
 1E88 WM_ENTERIDLE            0002 00000F0C
 1E88 WM_MENUSELECT           0000 0000FFFF
 1E88 WM_SYSCOMMAND           F060 009001A3    ⟵────────
 1E88 WM_CLOSE                0000 00000000
 1E88 WM_WINDOWPOSCHANGING    0000 110F3476
 1E88 WM_WINDOWPOSCHANGED     0000 110F348E
 1E88 WM_NCACTIVATE           0000 000034A4
 1E88 WM_ACTIVATE             0000 000034A4              ↓
```

Figure 14.6   Spy output window.

must search for "#define WM_SYSCOMMAND" (see Figure 14.7). The search should locate the line:

```
define WM_SYSCOMMAND    0x0112"
```

When found, the developer must look for the appropriate system menu command value or parameter. As previously mentioned, the parameters for Windows messages are listed in the Messages section of the MS SDK documentation. Because the developer is interested in trapping the message when trying to close the application, the SC_CLOSE parameter option must be located. The SC_CLOSE parameter, of course, has message number 0xF060, the one found using Spy.

The next step is to convert the message number from hexadecimal to decimal. The decimal value of F060 is 61536. The Windows scientific calculator is a good tool for converting hexadecimal numbers to decimal numbers.

Finally, the developer must go to PowerBuilder and do several things. First, a user event must be declared. But before the developer attempts to declare the user event, the WM_SYSCOMMAND must be mapped to a PowerBuilder message. The PowerBuilder message name corresponding to WM.SYSCOMMAND is PBM_SYSCOMMAND. The developer should open the window for which the control menu close message needs to be trapped. When the correct window is opened, the Declare and User Events... menu items must be selected. The Events dialog box then opens.

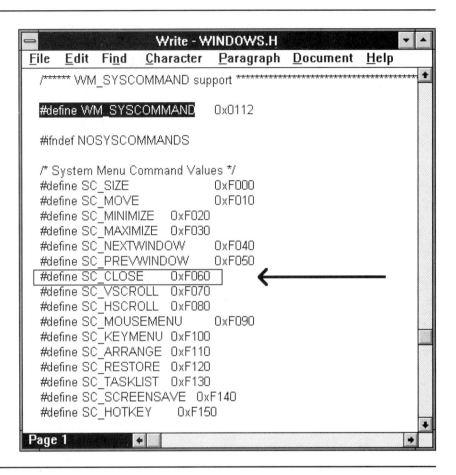

Figure 14.7   The Windows header file.

The developer can select any name for the event name and must choose the PBM_SYSCOMMAND as the event ID. When both the event name and ID have been selected, the developer should click the ⬚OK⬚ button. When this has been done, the developer can open the new event name from within the window and add the following PowerScript logic in the newly created event:

```
uint wParm

wParm = intLow(message.wordParm)
if wParm = 61536 then
```

```
        if ( MessageBox("Exit?",&
                        "You are about to close the application,~n" &
                        + "~tAre you sure?", Question!, YesNo!, 2) ) &
                        = 1 then
                Halt Close
        else
                message.processed = true
        end if
end if
```

When the application is running and the user tries to exit the application using the control menu, the message box in Figure 14.8 appears.

If this logic needs to be located in different windows in the application, the developer must think about the code reusability and inheritance discussions from previous chapters. The developer should either create a function and call the function from the application or the logic should be placed in the appropriate base class of the application architecture.

Note: The important point to note is that the message.wordParm variable must be trapped in the event mapped to the PBM_SYSCOMMAND. When this parameter is trapped, it can be passed to the function. If the message.wordParm is trapped in another event or another function, the value may be different. This is the nature of event-driven programming.

Custom EditMask If the developer wants to limit the user to entering only uppercase alphabetic characters in a SingleLineEdit, the developer

Figure 14.8   Message box appears when user tries to exit application.

must create a user-defined event for the SingleLineEdit. The user-defined event must be mapped to the PBM_CHAR PowerBuilder message, which maps to the WM_CHAR Windows message. The SLE style has a setting to require entry of only uppercase characters. To limit the user to entering alphabetic characters, the following PowerScript must be placed in the user-defined event of the SLE control:

```
uint uiMSG
uiMSG = intLow(message.wordParm)
if not ((uiMSG > 64 AND uiMSG < 123) OR uiMSG = 8) then
        beep(1)
        message.processed = true
end if
```

User-defined Messages The developer can also define application-level messages. These messages are different from the messages defined by Windows and PowerBuilder. Windows has made a range of messages available for developers to use without interfering with the messages generated by the operating system.

WM_USER is a constant used by applications to help define private messages. The WM_USER constant is used to distinguish between message values that are reserved for use by Windows and values that can be used by an application to send messages within a private window class. There are four ranges of message numbers:

Range	*Description*
0 through WM_USER - 1	Messages reserved for use by Windows
WM_USER through 0x7FFF	Integer messages for use by private window classes
0x8000 through 0xBFFF	Messages reserved for use by Windows
0xC000 through 0xFFFF	String messages reserved for applications

Message numbers in the first, third, and fourth ranges are not available to the PowerBuilder developer. Message numbers in the second range can be defined and used by an application to send messages within a private window class. These values cannot be used to define messages that are meaningful throughout an application, because some predefined window classes already define values in this range. For example, such predefined control classes as Button, Edit, Listbox, and

Comobox may use these values. Messages in this range should not be sent to other applications unless the applications have been designed to exchange messages and to attach the same meaning to the message numbers. The WM_USER constant message has the following value, which was obtained from the Windows header file:

```
#define WM_USER        0x0400
```

The decimal value of this message is 1024. This is the lower bound for private messages. The upper bound is 0x7FFF in hexadecimal, which is 524,287 in decimal. The predefined messages can be passed within applications using the **Send** or **Post** functions. Other useful functions for message-sending are the **Handle**, **IntHigh**, and **IntLow** functions.

Note: The Windows SDK manual states quite clearly in several places that no assumptions are to be made about the order of messages in the queue during a specified event. Message flow can be unpredictable at times, even though many of the problems have been fixed in Windows 3.1.

PowerBuilder Global Message Structure PowerBuilder, by default, declares a global message structure for all of its applications. When a Microsoft Windows 3.x event occurs that is not a PowerBuilder-defined event, PowerBuilder populates the Message object with information about the event. The Message object is a PowerBuilder-defined global object (like the default transaction object SQLCA and the Error object). This message structure is based on the Windows message structure.

Attributes of the PowerBuilder Message Structure The attributes of the Message object are described in Table 14.1. The first four attributes correspond to the first four attributes of the Microsoft Windows 3.x message structure.

Windows Message Structure Every message consists of four values: a handle that identifies the window, a message identifier, a 16-bit message-specified value, and a 32-bit message-specified value. These values are passed as individual parameters to the window procedure. The window procedure then examines the message identifier to determine what response to make and how to interpret the 16- and 32-bit values. The Windows message structure is defined in Table 14.2.

Table 14.1 Attributes of the Message Object

Attribute	Datatype	Description
Handle	UnsignedInteger	The handle of the event.
Number	UnsignedInteger	The number that identifies the event (this number comes from Windows).
WordParm	UnsignedInteger	The word parameter for the event (this parameter comes from Windows). The parameter's value and meaning are determined by the event.
LongParm	Long	The long parameter for the event (this number comes from Windows). The parameter's value and meaning are determined by the event.
Processed	Boolean	A Boolean value set in the script for the Other event: True—The program processed the event. False—(default) The default window procedure (DefWindowProc) will be called.
ReturnValue	Long	The value you want returned to Windows when Message.Processed is True. When Message.Processed is False, this attribute is ignored.
StringParm	String	A string or string variable.
DoubleParm	Double	A numeric or numeric variable.
PowerObjectParm	PowerObject	Any PowerBuilder object type including structures.

Table 14.2 Windows Message Structure

Attribute	Datatype	Description
hwnd	HWND	The handle to the window receiving the message.
message	UINT	The message identifier.
wParam	WPARAM	16 bits of additional message-specific information.
lParam	LPARAM	32 bits of additional message-specific information.
time	DWORD	The time the message occurred.
pt	POINT	Points to a structure that contains the x and y position of the mouse pointer.

Clipboard

Copying Text to and from the Clipboard Text can be copied to and from the clipboard using standard PowerBuilder clipboard functions. PowerBuilder in its current release only supports the exchange of textual data to and from the clipboard. Using MS Windows SDK functions, images (e.g., bitmap files) can be copied to and from the clipboard. The five major clipboard functions are:

Function Name	*Function Description*
Clipboard({string})	Returns the text contents of the clipboard. If the string parameter is specified, it replaces the contents of the clipboard with the value in string.
editname.Copy( )	Copies the selected text from the clipboard to the specified editname.
editname.Cut( )	Cuts the selected text from the clipboard to the specified editname.
editname.Paste( )	Pastes the selected text from the clipboard to the specified editname.
dwname.ImportClipboard(...)	Similar to the **ImportFile** and **ImportString** functions except that it copies data from the clipboard to the specified DataWindow.

These functions are simple to use. For a detail explanation of each, please refer to the PowerBuilder online help or the *Functions* reference manual.

Simulating the Alt+PrintScrn Functionality The following function copies an image in the active window into the clipboard for other applications to use or so it can be printed. Just as this function can be used to copy images to the clipboard, a similar function can be written to copy the contents of the clipboard to a file, an OLE Blob field, a picture object, or a Blob variable.

```
/*******************************************************
    FUNCTION: CopyToClip(HWND hWnd)
    PURPOSE: Simulates the Alt+PrintScrn Functionality.
```

```
The developer can pass a handle of the active window,
and it will be copied to the clipboard.
******************************************************/

int FAR PASCAL CopyToClip(HWND hWnd)
{
RECT tagRect;
int iWidth, iHeight;
HDC hdcSourceDC, hdcDestDC;
HGDIOBJ bhandle, dhandle = NULL;

GetWindowRect(hWnd, &tagRect);
iWidth = tagRect.right - tagRect.left;
iHeight = tagRect.bottom - tagRect.top;
hdcSourceDC = CreateDC ("DISPLAY", 0,0,0);
hdcDestDC = CreateCompatibleDC (hdcSourceDC);
bhandle = CreateCompatibleBitmap (hdcSourceDC, iWidth, iHeight);
SelectObject (hdcDestDC, bhandle);
BitBlt (hdcDestDC, 0,0, iWidth, iHeight, hdcSourceDC, tagRect.left,
tagRect.top, SRCCOPY);
OpenClipboard (hWnd);
EmptyClipboard ( );
SetClipboardData (CF_BITMAP, bhandle);
CloseClipboard( );
DeleteDC(hdcDestDC);
ReleaseDC(dhandle, hdcSourceDC);
return 1;
}
```

PrintScreen

This statement prints the current screen image in its original size at
location 500, 1000:

```
integer Job

Job = PrintOpen( )
PrintScreen(Job, 500,1000)
PrintClose(Job)
```

DDE (Dynamic Data Exchange)

MS Windows, through the use of another IPC method called dynamic
data exchange (DDE), allows an application to transfer data. DDE is a
message protocol that developers can use for exchanging data between
Windows applications.

Note: Windows does not support sharing Global Memory handles directly. Because of expanded memory considerations as well as compatibility with other versions of Windows, it is not recommended that Global Memory handles be dereferenced using the **GlobalUnlock** function. DDE is the only Windows mechanism that supports passing of Global Memory handles between applications.

MS Windows/PowerBuilder DDE Messages Because DDE is a message-based protocol, it employs no special Windows functions or libraries. All DDE transactions are performed by passing certain defined DDE messages between the client and server windows (see Figure 14.9). A description of these messages follows.

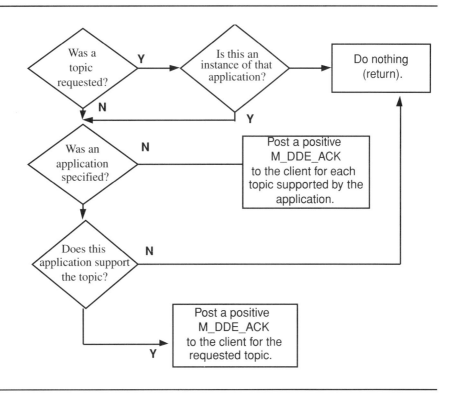

Figure 14.9   DDE message flow.

WM_DDE_ACK—This message notifies the application of the receipt and processing of (acknowledges) most of the other messages.

WM_DDE_ADVISE—The listener on the server end that responds to a DDE client's request to start a hot link or permanent data link.

WM_DDE_DATA—This message is fired off on the client when the DDE server has sent new data to the client.

WM_DDE_EXECUTE—This message is fired off on the DDE server when the server receives a request to execute a command from the client.

WM_DDE_INITIATE—This server message is fired off when the client requests a conversation be started/initiated on the server.

WM_DDE_POKE—This server message is fired off when a remote or client application has sent data.

WM_DDE_REQUEST—This server message is fired off when a remote or client application has requested data.

WM_DDE_TERMINATE—This message is fired off when a request has been made by either the client or server to terminate a conversation.

WM_DDE_UNADVISE—The listener on the server end that responds to a DDE client's request to stop a hot link or permanent data link.

PowerBuilder DDE Functions/Attributes Though DDE is a message-based protocol, PowerBuilder does have certain functions to make things simpler for the developer. These functions could be used for something as simple as calling the Windows SendMessage or PostMessage and passing the appropriate message(s). Here is a list of PowerBuilder DDE client functions and how they map to specific Windows messages.

OpenChannel—Open a channel to a DDE server application.

CloseChannel—Close a channel to a DDE server application.

ExecRemote—Request a specific command to be executed on the DDE server application.

GetDataDDE—Get the new data from a server application using a hot link channel.

GetDataDDEOrigin—Get the origin of the data that has arrived from a server application using a hot link channel.

GetRemote—Request data from a server application.

RespondRemote—Send an acknowledgment to the server application.

SetRemote—Request the server application to set one of its values to a specific value.

StartHotLink—Initiate a hot link to a server application.

StopHotLink—Terminate a hot link channel with the DDE server application.

Following is a list of DDE Server functions and their descriptions.

StartServerDDE—Cause a PowerBuilder application to start acting as a DDE server.

StopServerDDE—Cause a PowerBuilder application to stop acting as a DDE server.

GetCommandDDE—Get the command that the client application has sent.

GetCommandDDEOrigin—Get the client that sent the command.

GetDataDDE—Get the data the client has sent.

GetDataDDEOrigin—Get the client that sent the data.

RespondRemote—Send acknowledgment to the client.

SetDataDDE—Send data to the client application.

Examples of these functions are shown throughout this section.

DDE to MS Word and MS Excel There are times when an application may want to establish a DDE link to a word processor or spreadsheet simply to take advantage of the specific features of each. The developer can establish a DDE link to Word, pass it some information, and be able to display a form or newsletter with formatting and presentation only a word processor could do. The same thing can be done with a spreadsheet. The application may want to pass certain financial information to a spreadsheet and have the spreadsheet perform all the necessary financial calculations. An example of how a DDE link can be made to MS Word (a word processor) or MS Excel (a spreadsheet) follows.

Maximizing Word and Excel There are times when an external application needs to be called using the PowerBuilder **Run( )** function. Simply calling the **Run( )** function does not always yield the same results.

For example, assume an application needs to start MS Word when the user presses the Word Processing icon. If MS Word is not already running, it needs to be invoked using the PowerBuilder **Run( )** function. If, however, an instance of MS Word is already running, it needs to be opened and maximized for the user. If the developer chooses to use the run command, a new instance of MS Word will be opened, even if an instance of MS Word is already opened. The developer wants to build the intelligence into the application such that if an instance of MS Word is already running when the user clicks the word processing button, the instance is opened and maximized; otherwise, MS Word is started. To accomplish this, the developer must declare the following local external function (unless it will be called from other windows); as shown in Figure 14.10.

The developer also must place a picture button on a window (see Figure 14.11) or add the functionality to a toolbar.

In the clicked event, pb_winword, the following PowerScript is needed:

```
string ModuleName
uint hWnd
// This function checks to see if other instances of this application
// are running
hWnd = GetModuleHandle("winword.exe")
if hWnd = 0 then
        Run("winword.exe", Maximized!)
else
        hWnd = OpenChannel("WinWord","System")
```

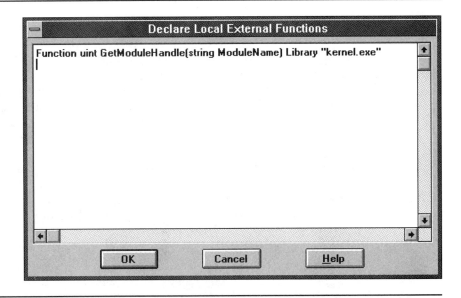

Figure 14.10   Declare local external function.

pb_WinWord

Figure 14.11   Placing a picture button on a window.

```
        ExecRemote("[AppMaximize]",hWnd)
        CloseChannel(hWnd)
end if
```

To do the same thing with MS Excel, the following PowerScript would be placed in the pb_Excel PictureButton:

```
string ModuleName
uint hWnd
hWnd = GetModuleHandle("excel.exe")
If hWnd = 0 Then
        Run("i:\soft\excel\excel.exe", Maximized!)
Else
        hWnd = OpenChannel("Excel","System")
        ExecRemote("[App.Maximize]",hWnd)
        CloseChannel(hWnd)
end if
```

An MS Excel picture button would be used instead of the MS Word picture button, as shown in Figure 14.12..

Passing Data from PowerBuilder to MS Word In this example, data is sent from a PowerBuilder application to MS Word. The user enters name and address data into the fields of the following window and clicks the

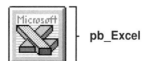

pb_Excel

Figure 14.12   The MS Excel picture button.

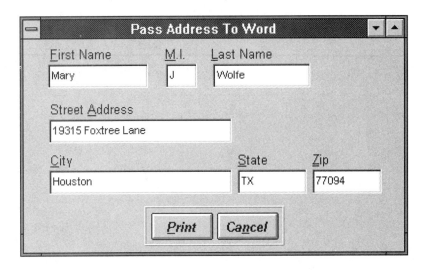

Figure 14.13 Data transferred to MS Word.

Print button. This transfers the entered data to a predefined standard form in MS Word for printing, as shown in Figure 14.13.

```
String sFname, sMI, sLname, sStAddress, sCity, sState, sZip
Integer iDDEHandle

sFname = dw_main.GetItemString(1,"Fname")
sMI = dw_main.GetItemString(1,"MI")
sLname = dw_main.GetItemString(1,"Lname")
sStAddress = dw_main.GetItemString(1,"StAddress")
sCity = dw_main.GetItemString(1,"City")
sState = dw_main.GetItemString(1,"State")
sZip = dw_main.GetItemString(1,"Zip")

if f_StartWord( ) then
        iDDEHandle = OpenChannel("WinWord", "System")
        // open document and send data to it
        ExecRemote("[FileOpen.Name = ~"form.doc~"]", iDDEHandle)

        // Send the data to Word, and set it to the appropriate bookmark.
        SetRemote("Fname",sFname, iDDEHandle)
        SetRemote("MI",sMI, iDDEHandle)
```

```
        SetRemote("Lname",sLname, iDDEHandle)
        SetRemote("StAddress",sStAddress, iDDEHandle)
        SetRemote("City",sCity, iDDEHandle)
        SetRemote("State",sState, iDDEHandle)
        SetRemote("Zip",sZip, iDDEHandle)

        ExecRemote("[FilePrint]",DDEHandle)
end if
```

The form in MS Word could look like that in Figure 14.14.

The appropriate bookmarks are selected in MS Word by clicking on the Insert/Bookmark menu items. The dialog box in Figure 14.15 appears.

Bookmarks are used as a reference to actual locations in a Word document. From PowerBuilder, bookmark names can be used by the **SetRemote** function to set values.

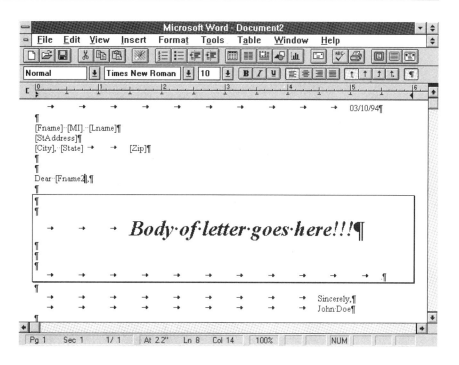

Figure 14.14　　The form of the data in MS Word.

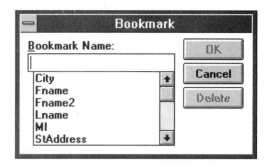

Figure 14.15   The Bookmark dialog box.

DDE Client/Server Two applications participating in dynamic data exchange are said to be engaged in a DDE conversation. The application that initiates the request is the client and the application that responds to the request is the server. The terms client and server are not used in the same way here as in a discussion about client/server architecture, where a workstation (client) makes requests of the database or file server(s). Although they mean different things in these different discussions, they are similar in theory. Figures 14.16 and 14.17 show the similarity in that the client requests data/information from the server and the server responds. The major difference is that, with DDE, the client and server relationship is happening on one workstation. With client/server architecture, the client and server are on different workstations and can be thousands of miles apart.

The DDE conversation takes place between two windows, one for each of the applications that are exchanging data. The windows may be the main window of the application; a window associated with a specific document, as in an MDI application; or a hidden window, whose only purpose is to process DDE messages.

Note: A pair of client and server windows can never be involved in more than one DDE conversation at any given time.

OLE (Object Linking and Embedding)

"Object Technology will empower information departments to deliver more flexible, higher quality systems, and will reduce the

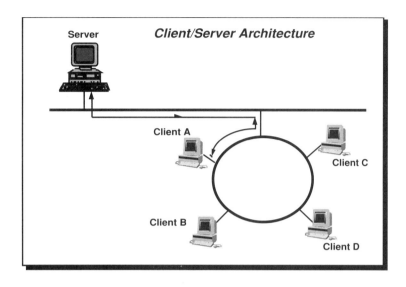

Figure 14.16   Client/server architecture.

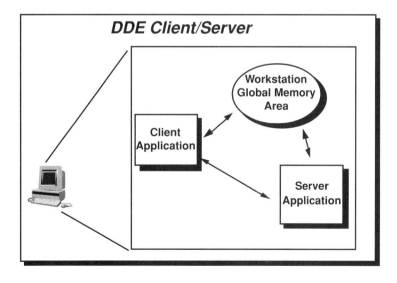

Figure 14.17   DDE client/server.

time and resources required for system programming, implementation and maintenance. Corporations can receive the benefits of Microsoft object technology today through applications and development tools supporting Object Linking and Embedding (OLE), a breakthrough in object-enabling system software. Software components based on OLE are revolutionizing the software industry." - Microsoft

OLE is another one of MS Windows' IPC methods. PowerBuilder, in its previous releases, only supported OLE 1.0. OLE has come a long way with the OLE 2.0 specification and PowerBuilder 4 includes support for OLE 2.0 by implementing OLE container applications and OLE automation.

A new type of control has been added to the Window painter which allows the developer to place an OLE 2.0 object on a PowerBuilder window. New PowerScript functions have been added to let the developer manipulate the control at runtime. Other PowerScript functions have been added to support OLE 2.0 automation. This means that the developer can automate OLE 2.0 servers from within PowerBuilder. For example, the developer can merge data from PowerBuilder into Microsoft Word using WordBasic language from PowerBuilder.

This section includes the following topics:

- Microsoft OLE 2.0 features
- PowerBuilder OLE 2.0 functions
- PowerBuilder OLE 2.0 control attributes
- PowerBuilder OLE 2.0 container application support
- PowerBuilder OLE 2.0 sample code

Microsoft OLE 2.0 Features The primary feature of OLE that allows software components to be connected is called the OLE component object model (COM). There are many additional OLE features, however, that directly benefit both users and corporate developers. Some of the major features of OLE follow.

OLE Component Object Model COM provides all of the interface standards and handles all intercomponent communication that allows software components to be integrated. Because it is a binary standard, OLE software components can be written in any language and be supplied by any software vendor, yet still be seamlessly integrated within a single application.

OLE Automation Automation allows applications to expose command sets that operate within and across applications. For example, a user can invoke a command from a word processing program that sorts a range of cells in a spreadsheet created by a different application.

OLE Controls OLE controls are OLE-enabled software components that can be purchased to extend and enhance an application's functionality. OLE controls can be used in custom or off-the-shelf OLE-enabled applications.

OLE Drag-and-Drop Users can drag objects from one application to be autonomously upgraded without affecting the operation of the component-based solution.

OLE Documents OLE documents are a form of compound documents which can incorporate data created in any OLE-enabled application. For instance, an OLE-enabled word processor can accept tables and charts from an OLE-enabled spreadsheet. OLE documents allow users to convey their ideas more effectively by incorporating any type of information into their documents. In addition to incorporating static information like charts and tables, OLE documents can also incorporate live data such as sound, video, and animation. OLE documents also make users more productive by improving the process of creating compound documents. The following are features specific to OLE Documents:

OLE object linking and embedding—Through object linking, applications can be linked to data objects within other applications. For example, a spreadsheet table can be linked into multiple custom business reports; as changes are made to this table within the spreadsheet application, all report documents are automatically updated. Object embedding is the ability to embed an object within another document without maintaining a link to the object's data source. In both object linking and object embedding, applications supplying objects are called OLE servers, while applications containing objects are called OLE containers. An application can be both an OLE container and an OLE server.

OLE visual editing—Visual editing allows users to create rich, compound documents easily, incorporating text, graphics, sound, video, and other diverse object types. Instead of switching between applications to create parts of the compound document, users can work within the context of their document. As the user begins to edit an object that originated in another application, such as a spreadsheet or graphic, the menus and tools of the container application automatically change to the menu and tools of that object's native (server) application. The user can then edit the object in the context of the document, without worrying about activating and switching to another application.

Nested object support—Objects can be nested in multiple layers within other objects. Users can directly manipulate objects nested within other objects and establish links to nested objects.

Object conversion—Objects can be converted to different types so that different applications can be used with the same object. For example, an object created with one brand of spreadsheet can be converted so that it can be interpreted by a different spreadsheet application for editing.

Optimized object storage—Objects remain on disk until needed and are not loaded into memory each time the container application is opened. Also, OLE has complete transacted object storage, supporting commits and rollbacks of objects to disk. This ensures that data integrity is maintained as objects are stored in the file system.

PowerBuilder OLE 2.0 Functions

OLE 2.0 Control Functions

InsertFile—Inserts a new object into the OLE control with a default template.

InsertClass—Inserts a new object of a certain class. Some classes include "Excel.Sheet" or "Excel.Chart" or "Word.Document."

InsertObject—Prompts the user with the standard InsertObject dialog and inserts an object based on the selection.

LinkTo—Links an OLE control with a file or a portion of a file.

Activate—Activates the object in the control. It will activate it in place when InPlace! is specified. If OffSite! is specified, the object becomes active in the server application.

Save—Saves the object in the control to the storage from which it was loaded or to the storage which was specified by a previous **SaveAs**.

SaveAs—Saves the object in the control to a specified storage file.

Open—Opens the file specified and loads the object into the control. The file is "owned" by the control.

Clear—Releases the object in the control and deletes references to it without updating the storage.

Copy—Copies the contents of the control to the Clipboard.

Cut—Copies the contents of the control to the Clipboard and clears the control.

Paste—Pastes the contents of the Clipboard into the control.

PasteLink—Pastes a link to the contents of the Clipboard into the control.

PasteSpecial—Presents the users with a dialog allowing them to select **Paste** or **PasteLink**.

DoVerb—Executes the verb specified for the control.

Drag—Puts the control in drag mode.

OLE 2.0 Automation Functions

ConnectToObject—(Format 1) Opens a specified file and connects to the application associated with it.

(Format 2) Opens a specified file and connects to the object using the specified class name.

(Format 3) Connects to the currently active object of the specified class name.

ConnectToNewObject—Creates a new instance of the class specified and connects to it.

DisconnectObject—Releases any object previously connected to the control.

PowerBuilder OLE 2.0 Control Attributes The attributes that are new to the OLE control are listed in Table 14.3.

PowerBuilder OLE 2.0 Container Application Support In the Window painter the developer can link or embed objects. The developer can select OLE 2.0 from the Control menu bar item in the Window painter (see Figure 14.18) or can use the OLE 2.0 icon on the toolbar.

When the developer places an OLE 2.0 control on a window, he or she will be prompted with the standard Insert Object dialog (shown in Figure 14.19) which allows the developer to embed an object, embed a file, or link to a file. If the developer does not want to assign an object to the control, the cancel button should be selected. Using new PowerScript functions, the developer will be able to assign objects at runtime. These functions are discussed later in the chapter.

If the Create New radiobutton is chosen, the developer can select from a list of applications which are registered as OLE 2.0 servers. If the developer selects one, the application will be started with a new instance of the application's object and the developer will be able to use the application as desired. For example, if the developer chooses Microsoft Excel worksheet, an image of the object will appear in the OLE 2.0 control on the window when the developer exits the application. (see Figure 14.20)

Table 14.3   Attributes New to OLE Control

Attribute	Datatype	Description
Activation	omActivation	Specifies how the OLE object will be activated.
ClassLongName	String	The long name for the server application associated with the OLE object in the control.
ClassShortName	String	The short name for the server application associated with the OLE object in the control.
ContentsAllowed	omContentsAllowed	Specifies whether the OLE object in the control must be embedded or linked or whether either method is allowed.
DisplayName	String	User-readable name for the OLE control. This name is displayed in OLE dialog boxes and windows, that show the object's name. If this value is not specified, the name of the control (such as ole_1) is used for DisplayName.
DisplayType	omDisplayType	Specifies how the OLE object will be displayed in the control. The control can display the actual contents or an icon to represent the object.
DocFileName	String	The name of an OLE storage file or a data file of the server application that has been opened for the control.
IsDragTarget	Boolean	Specifies whether an OLE object can be dropped on the control.
LinkItem	String	The name of an item within the server application's data file to which the control is linked.
LinkUpdateOptions	omLinkUpdateOptions	Specifies how a linked object in the control will be updated. If automatic, the link will be updated when the object is opened and whenever the object changes in the server application. If manual, the link will not be updated.

Table 14.3 (*continued*)

Attribute	Datatype	Description
Object	omObject	The link information that connects the control to the server's data.
ObjectData	Blob	If the object is embedded, the object itself is stored as a Blob in the ObjectData attribute.
ParentStorage	OMStorage	Specifies the parent storage.

Once the OK button is selected, the OLE server application is opened and the developer can type in new data. As the data is being typed into each cell, the corresponding OLE control is automatically updated.

When the data has been updated, the update menu selection can also be selected (see Figure 14.21).

If the Create from File radiobutton is selected, the developer will then be prompted for a file name. Once the developer selects a file, the

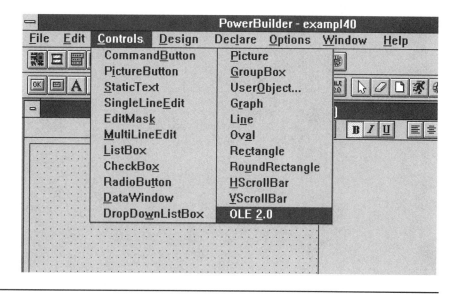

Figure 14.18 Selecting OLE 2.0 from the Controls menu bar item.

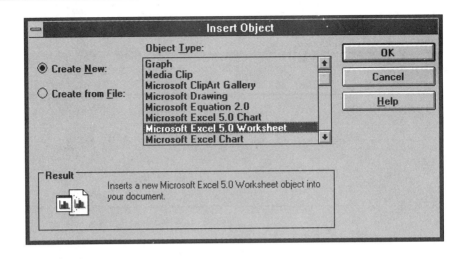

Figure 14.19   Insert Object dialog box.

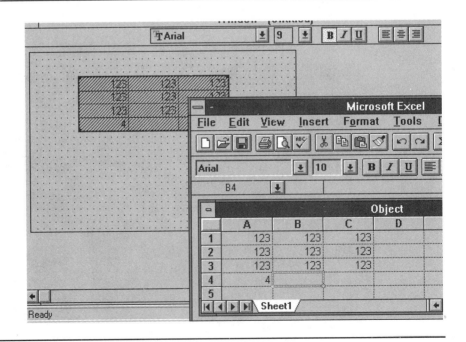

Figure 14.20   Excel OLE object placed on the PowerBuilder window.

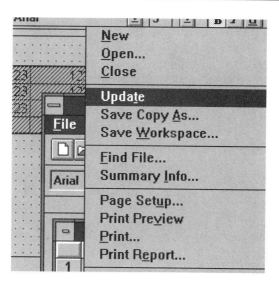

Figure 14.21   Update menu selection.

application which is associated with that file's extension in the Windows Registration Editor will be started and that file will be active. For instance, if the developer chooses README.DOC, Microsoft Word will be started and the file README.DOC will be opened and active. After the developer exits the application, the object will be embedded into the OLE 2.0 control. The contents of the file will be copied into the developer's object.

If the developer wants to have this OLE 2.0 control linked to the original file, thereby sharing the data, the link checkbox must be checked (see Figure 14.22).

The following PowerScript functions allow the developer to **Insert** or **Link** to objects at runtime. Details of these functions are available in the PowerBuilder documentation.

InsertObject( )

InsertClass(string class)

InsertFile(string filename)

LinkTo(string filename)

Saving Embedded or Linked Objects Embedded or linked objects can be saved as files, as Blobs, or as OLE Storages. To save objects as files or

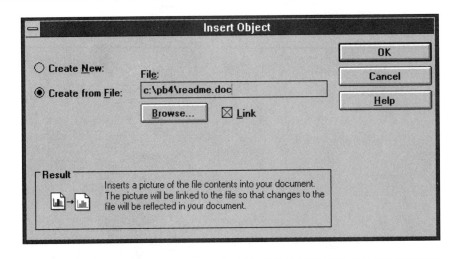

Figure 14.22   Checking the Link checkbox.

OLE Storages, the developer can use the **SaveAs** function. To save the object as a Blob, the developer can use the OLE 2.0 control attribute of ObjectData which is of type Blob. For example:

```
blob myblob
myblob = ole_1.ObjectData
```

PowerScript Automation Facilities New PowerScript functions provide the ability to write scripts to automate OLE 2.0 server applications and OLE 2.0 controls.

A dynamic object type, OLEObject, is available in PowerBuilder 4 to support OLE 2.0. For this object type, the compiler will accept attribute names, function names, and parameter lists which are not already defined for the object.

The following code shows automation of an OLE 2.0 server application from PowerBuilder:

```
OLEObject MyOLEObject
MyOLEObject = Create OLEObject
MyOLEObject.ConnectToNewObject("excel.application")
MyOLEObject.application.visible = true
MyOLEObject.application.cells(1,1).value = 14
Destroy MyOLEObject
```

If the developer wants to use automation for an OLE 2.0 control, a simple call to the server's methods prefacing it with the Object attribute of the OLE 2.0 control will do. Note, the developer does not need to do any of the steps previously listed.

```
OLE_1.object.application.cells(1,1).value = 14
```

Note, OLE_1 is an OLE 2.0 control.

PowerBuilder OLE 2.0 Sample Code

Loading a file:

```
string ls_path,ls_filename
GetFileOpenName("select file to open",ls_path,ls_filename)
If ls_filename ="" Then return
ole_1.insertfile(ls_path)
st_type.text = ole_1.classlongname
```

Loading an object:

```
ole_1.insertobject( )
st_type.text = ole_1.classlongname
```

Paste Special:

```
int li_rc
li_rc = ole_1.pastespecial( )
If li_rc <> 0 Then return -1
st_type.text = ole_1.classlongname
```

Paste:

```
int li_rc
li_rc = ole_1.paste( )
If li_rc <> 0 Then return -1
st_type.text = ole_1.classlongname
```

Activate in place:

```
ole_1.activate(inplace!)
```

Activate off site:

```
ole_1.activate(offsite!)
```

Copy:

```
int li_rc
li_rc = ole_1.copy( )
If li_rc <> 0 Then return -1
```

Updating a table called "ole" from an OLE control, a static text and a MultiLineEdit would be as follows:

```
blob lb_object
lb_object = ole_1.objectdata
INSERT INTO "ole"( "id", "object", "description" )
VALUES ( :sle_title.text,' ', :mle_desc.text );
if SQLCA.SQLCode = -1 then
     MessageBox("SQL error",SQLCA.SQLErrText,Information!)
     return -1
end if
UpdateBlob "ole" set "object" = :lb_object
     where "id" = :sle_title.text;
if SQLCA.SQLCode = -1 then
     MessageBox("SQL error",SQLCA.SQLErrText,Information!)
     return -1
end if
commit;
```

Retrieving into an OLE control from a database table called "ole" would be:

```
string ls_index
blob ole_blob
SELECT "ole"."id", "ole"."description"
     INTO :sle_title.text, :mle_desc.text
     FROM "ole"
     WHERE "ole"."id" = :ls_index ;
if SQLCA.SQLCode = -1 then
     MessageBox("SQL error",SQLCA.SQLErrText,Information!)
end if
selectblob "object" into :ole_blob from "ole"
       where "id" = :ls_title;
if SQLCA.SQLCode <> 0 then
       MessageBox("SQL error",SQLCA.SQLErrText,Information!)
end if
ole_1.objectdata = ole_blob
st_type.text = ole_1.classlongname
```

WINDOWS DLLs

A DLL is a special library that allows applications to share code and resources. A DLL is an executable module with export functions that the application calls to do certain tasks. DLLs are linked to an application at runtime. This allows code and resources to be shared by the PowerBuilder application and the Windows environment. A DLL's main purpose is to provide a library of callable functions or resources. A DLL needs to be loaded into memory in order to call its functions. It remains in memory until the last application referencing the DLL has been unloaded from memory. DLLs have many uses, some of which are registering and storing global window classes, writing device drivers, housing large quantities of resources (e.g., bitmaps, icons, dialogs), and providing a library of instantly usable debugged code.

Why Write Your Own DLLs

PowerBuilder provides built-in capabilities to handle most of the functionality typical in Windows application development. There are times when a developer needs to build certain functionality into an application that is above and beyond the inherent capabilities of PowerBuilder. This functionality can range from using a DLL to interface with other vendors' APIs, to doing complicated mathematical calculations in computation-intensive applications (which are better compiled in C or Assembler). When this type of functionality is needed, the developer must write a DLL.

DLLs and Applications

The Windows environment works with two fundamental program units: applications (.EXE executable files) and DLLs (.DLL, .DRV, .EXE, and .FON files). Both applications and DLLs are referred to as loadable or executable modules. Applications are different from DLLs in that applications can have multiple copies or instances executed. Each copy of an application is kept track of and referenced by an instance handle. The reason for this is that Windows shares code and resource segments; the data segment of an application is the only thing that is unique; that is what is referenced by the instance handle.

DLLs, on the other hand, are loaded into memory once and have only a single instance handle. When an application is loaded into memory, it is given its own stack in local memory. A DLL module does not have its own stack; it uses the stack of the task that called it.

When an application is executed, it is actively processing messages, creating windows, interacting with the user, and generating output. In contrast, a DLL library function is passive. It serves only as a function that can be called by an active application to perform some operation. With very few exceptions, DLL modules are as passive as any other library function.

When an application or a DLL is first loaded into memory, Windows creates a data structure known as a Module database. A Module database, like all other program segments (i.e., code, data, and resources), is stored in the global heap. A Module database has information found in the New-style .EXE header of applications and DLLs. This header has a wealth of information regarding all the program's exported functions, resources, and other unique unchangeable information. Under Windows, a Module database is kept track of with a module handle.

DLLs have different file extensions, depending on whether they're font resources (.FON), device drivers (.DRV), or operating system files (.EXE). All operate on the same basic principle, but there are some differences between each DLL type. Device-driver DLLs are always loaded into the lower portion of DOS conventional memory and their segments are marked as fixed and page-locked so that memory can't move or be paged to disk. This is because device-driver code interfaces with interrupts and must always be in the same position in memory each time it's called. Font DLLs also have some unique properties. Font DLLs do not have any code or data segments, only resource segments that contain fonts. Only font DLLs can house resource segments. If a developer wrote a DLL to house resources such as icons and bitmaps, it would have to have at least one code segment holding the DLL's entry point (LibEntry) and exit point (WEP).

A DLL's Assembly-language-defined entry point is called when it is first loaded into memory. The first piece in a DLL, which is an optional piece, is the **LibEntry( )**. The LibEntry, when included, can initialize the DLL's local heap, link in C startup code, and make a call to **LibMain( )**. The main initialization for DLLs is usually done in the **LibMain( )** call. When the initialization is complete, control is passed back to Windows and the DLL is ready to be accessed. The DLL is idle until a Windows module calls one of its exports or until it is unloaded from memory. When a DLL is unloaded from memory, its **WEP( )** is called by Windows for any final cleanup of memory. The **WEP( )** is often referred to as the DLL's exit procedure (see Figure 14.23).

How to Write a DLL

DLLs are generally written in the C programming language, thus a C compiler is needed. The C examples in this section and throughout the

INITIALIZATION

    LibEntry( )   *optional*

    LibMain

INSTANCE

    Code

    Data

    Resources

TERMINATION

    WEP( )

Figure 14.23   Components of a DLL file.

book were written and compiled in Microsoft's Visual C++, but most C/ C++ compilers such as the Borland C++ compiler version 3.1 or above, the MS C/C++ compiler version 7.0, and the MS Quick C compiler should work with minimal modification (see Note which follows). As described in the previous section, a DLL has an initialization procedure **LibMain( )** and an exit procedure **WEP ( )**. The remaining portions of the DLL have all the DLL's functions. These export functions can be called directly from PowerBuilder or other C modules. A DLL has a number of different files. In writing a simple DLL, a developer may need a module definition file, a source file, a make file, and some header files, for example:

Files	*Description*
sample.def	module definition file
sample.c	C source file
sample.h	header file
sample.mak	make file

Note: Different things need to be considered when writing DLLs using different compilers. Here are a few pointers (no pun intended) for the developer. Using Visual C++ for this is really easy. The functions should be written in a .c file with **FAR PASCAL _export** function attributes/ calling conventions. The compiler and linker handle everything from there if you specify the appropriate project template. This assumes that no initialization or cleanup is needed.

If the compiler is Borland C++ 3.1 or above, the developer needs to add a **LibMain** and a **WEP** function to the .c file, as explained previously. **LibMain** allows for any global initialization such as grabbing the DLL's instance handle. This is required if the developer needs to get a resource. An explanation of LibMain and WEP was given previously, but because most simple DLLs don't do anything special in their LibMain and WEP functions, Microsoft decided to add default LibMain and WEP functions in their Visual C++ product.

If the compiler used is Microsoft C/C++ 7.0 or earlier versions of Quick C for Windows, the developer must make sure to link with the LIBENTRY.LIB library. The documentation explains this fairly well; basically it adds some code to initialize the DLL's data segment. The older compiler versions also require that there be an EXPORT section in the .DEF file.

Basically, the simplest way to write a DLL is to get an existing DLL from the SAMPLES that come with the compiler, and compile and link it. Examining the output gives an understanding of what is needed. Then all the developer needs to do is to modify it.

Module Definition File The Module definition file is used to establish certain unchangeable program-wide characteristics. These include giving the module a name, declaring heap and stack sizes, exporting functions, and establishing attributes for code and data segments. The Module definition file greatly affects the organization and structure of a completed module.

The Module definition file, Module database, and .EXE header have much in common. Each of these structures has program-wide information. For example, when a program is compiled and linked, information from the Module definition file is placed near the beginning of the module's binary image. This block of memory, which is present for every application and DLL, is referred to as the New-style .EXE header. Like the .DEF file, it contains module-wide information that can be shared between program instances. When a program is loaded into memory by Windows, it creates a global heap entry called a Module database, which contains much of the information found in the .EXE header.

The format of a Module definition file for DLLs is:

```
LIBRARY    Sample
DESCRIPTION   'Sample - Sample DLL'
```

```
EXETYPE   WINDOWS
STUB      'WINSTUB.EXE'
CODE MOVEABLE DISCARDABLE
DATA MOVEABLE SINGLE
HEAPSIZE 0
EXPORTS
WEP          @1    RESIDENTNAME
Sample   @2
```

Source File The source file contains the **LibMain** and **WEP** functions as well as all the exported functions. A source file looks like this:

```
#include <windows.h>

/*******************************************************
      FUNCTION: LibMain(HINSTANCE, WORD, WORD, LPSTR)
      PURPOSE: Called by the initialization function for a DLL.
          Required by Windows.
      COMMENTS:
          This function is called by the entry routine found in
          LIBENTRY.LIB.
          It is responsible for initializing the DLL. Because this DLL
          requires no initialization, it simply returns a 1.
*******************************************************/
int FAR PASCAL LibMain(HINSTANCE hInst, WORD wDataSeg,
               WORD cbHeapSize, LPSTR lpszCmdLine)
{
      if (cbHeapSize !=0)
              UnlockData(0); /* The entry function called LocalInit( ) */
                         /* Because this call locked the DataSegment, */
                          /* UnlockData(0) is required to unlock it. */
              return 1;    /* 1 => successful, 0 => unsuccessful */
}
/*******************************************************
      FUNCTION: Sample(int)
      PURPOSE: Sample Export Function for this example.
      COMMENTS:
          The export function sample( ) is listed.
*******************************************************/
int FAR PASCAL _export Sample(int nParameter)
{
      Return nParameter++;
}
/*******************************************************
      FUNCTION: WEP(int)
      PURPOSE: Called by Windows and required by Windows.
      COMMENTS:
           This function processes messages sent to the DLL from Windows.
```

```
                    It is used to properly close the DLL. It simply returns a 1.
**********************************************************/
int FAR PASCAL WEP(int nParameter)
{
      /* This functions is necessary but all it does
              is return a 1 regardless of the message sent to it */
      if (nParameter == WEP_SYSTEM_EXIT)
      {
              return 1;
      }
      else if (nParameter == WEP_FREE_DLL)
      {
              return 1;
      }
      else
      {
              return 1;
      }
}
```

The **sample( )** export function does not have any application functionality. It is used mainly to show the structure of an export function. If more export functions need to be added to the DLL, both the Module definition file and the source file reflect the changes for the new function. In PowerBuilder, the sample function should be declared as shown in Figure 14.24.

Note: From the PowerBuilder documentation:

```
FUNCTION [returntype] MyFunction( [ [ref] datatype MyArg [, ...] ] ) )
LIBRARY "mylib.dll"
```

The C counterpart must be declared as **FAR PASCAL**.

Passing values back from an external DLL call can be done using one of two methods:

1. Pass the result back with a return.

```
From the C DLL:

      LPSTR FAR PASCAL _export f_foo(void)
      {
```

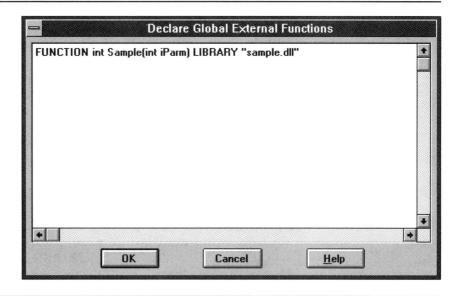

Figure 14.24 Sample function.

```
return "Hello";
}
```

From PowerBuilder:
```
FUNCTION string f_foo( ) LIBRARY "mydll.dll"

String sSTR

sSTR = f_foo( )
// process sSTR
```

2. Use the parameter list and pass a variable by reference. When the external function is being declared in the PowerBuilder External Functions dialog, the Ref modifier must be used on the parameter's type. For example:

From the C DLL:
```
void FAR PASCAL _export f_foo(LPSTR lpszSTR)
{
strcpy(lpszSTR, "Hello");
}
```

```
From PowerBuilder:

     SUBROUTINE f_foo(ref string sSTR) LIBRARY
         "mydll.dll"

     String sSTR
     sSTR = Space(10);
     f_foo(sSTR)
     // process sSTR
```

This method allows the C function to update a string variable called *sSTR* that should be declared in the PowerScript code. Without the Ref modifier, PowerBuilder ignores any changes made to the pointer or value it passes to the external function. It is **very** important when passing strings by reference that sufficient space is allocated for the return buffer **before** the external call is made. If space is not pre-allocated, a General Protection fault occurs in PBSHARE.DLL. This is why the PowerBuilder **Space(...)** function was used in the previous example.

It is important to note the following concerning the *sSTR* variable, as shown in Figure 14.25.

PowerBuilder and C SDK Datatype Mapping Appendix C of the *Power-Script Language Reference* has a list of supported and unsupported datatypes and their mappings between PowerBuilder and the Windows SDK. The most common ones are:

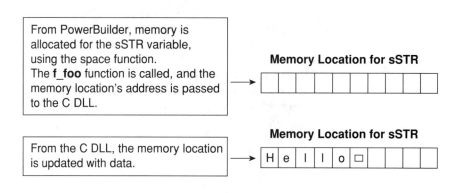

Figure 14.25   Update of the *sSTR* variable.

PowerBuilder	C Windows SDK
string	LPSTR
integer	int
uint	UINT
word	UINT
long	long
ulong	DWORD/ULONG
uint	HANDLE
char	BYTE
Boolean	BOOL

When using this chart, it is important to remember that while PowerBuilder is not case-sensitive, C is.

CROSS PLATFORM ISSUES

PowerBuilder in its v4 release has opened the product to additional operating systems. Some of those operating systems include Macintosh, Windows NT, and UNIX.

Global Environment Object

Table 14.4 lists and describes the PowerBuilder Environment object.

For example, if a developer is running PowerBuilder Enterprise 4.0 under Windows 3.1 on an Intel 486 computer with Super VGA, the Environment object would include the following values:

Attribute	Value
CPUType	i486!
OSFixesRevision	0
OSMajorRevision	3
OSMinorRevision	10 (that is, Windows 3.10)
PBFixesRevision	0
PBMajorRevision	4
PBMinorRevision	0
NumberOfColors	16
ScreenHeight	800

Table 14.4

Attribute	Datatype	Description
CPUType	CPUTypes	The CPU.
OSFixesRevision	Integer	The maintenance version of the operating system.
OSMajorRevision	Integer	The major version of the operating system.
OSMinorRevision	Integer	The point release of the operating system.
PBFixesRevision	Integer	The maintenance version of PowerBuilder.
PBMajorRevision	Integer	The major version of PowerBuilder.
PBMinorRevision	Integer	The point release of PowerBuilder.
NumberOfColors	Long	Number of colors on the screen.
ScreenHeight	Long	Height of the screen in pixels.
ScreenWidth	Long	Width of the screen in pixels.
OSType	OSTypes	Operating system or environment.
PBType	PBTypes	Version of PowerBuilder product (for example, Enterprise or Desktop).

ScreenWidth	600
OSType	Windows!
PBType	Enterprise!

Apple Macintosh

PowerBuilder 4 on the Apple Macintosh (MAC) will have a direct interface to Oracle and Sybase. Using ODBC, it can interface with WATCOM, Q+E and PageAhead. PowerBuilder will handle most keyboard mapping. There is support for Apple events. There will be an easy move from PowerBuilder on the PC to PowerBuilder on the MAC. There is separate support for preference variables.

Some other MAC features include:

- PowerScript functions that return platform
- Undo
- Alias support
- Shared bitmap formats
- Window to specify SIZE resource
- Version Control (Apple's Source Server)

- Multiple developer environment
- Support for native graphics types

Here are some Do's and Don'ts on the MAC environment.

Do's
1. Understand keyboard and mouse differences:
   - MAC has reserved accelerator keys (i.e., Command-? for help and Command-Q for Quit).
   - MAC mouse has only one button.
   - MAC applications share the same desktop.
2. Learn how MAC and Windows handle the user interface.
3. Use TrueType fonts:
   - Windows system font will be converted to Chicago on the MAC. Chicago is larger than the Windows system font; leave space in the window so the text can expand and still fit.
   - Use TrueType when not using Windows system font.
4. Be careful when mapping keys:
   - Map quick keys to command keys and not the Ctrl key on the MAC; be careful not to use reserved command keys.
   - Not all MAC keyboards have function keys; map to a command key combination.
   - Function keys should be optional.
5. Be aware that windows are not clipped by a frame:
   - All MAC windows share the master window.
   - Windows can be moved outside a frame window.
   - Screen size (# of pixels) varies with display size.

Don'ts
1. Don't force the 3-D look for controls.
2. Don't place controls in MDI frames.
3. Don't rely on tabbing:
   - Tabbing can be done between edit fields but not controls.
4. Don't use minimize:
   - MAC windows can be zoomed up and down, but not minimized.
5. Don't rely on focus:
   - MAC applications always require a mouse; do not write scripts dependent on GetFocus and LoseFocus events.
6. Don't use DDE:
   - MAC applications do not support DDE.
7. Don't use Windows APIcalls:
   - All PB events are supported; however, using the Other event to call an external API will fail.

- Don't use user events to communicate with external API's.
- Don't depend on Windows message IDs.

8. Don't use VBX controls.

Windows NT

PowerBuilder on Windows NT will essentially operate as it did on Windows 3.1. PowerBuilder requires NT version 3.5 or later.

Note: Can't call 16-bit DLLs (NT limitation).

UNIX (Posix/Motif)

Powersoft has announced that PowerBuilder will support the Sun Solaris 2.3, HP/UX, IBM AIX (RS/6000), and DEC OSF/1 (Alpha) flavors of UNIX. The visual interface for each of these operating systems will be based on Motif.

CHAPTER 15

Network Considerations

One of the beauties of client/server systems is that they can be run on top of a wide variety of networks using many different communication protocols to communicate between clients and servers. This capability allows data to be distributed throughout a network on different machines using different operating systems, providing a great deal of scalability and flexibility in client/server systems.

In the simplest type of PowerBuilder application, PowerBuilder communicates with a single database using either a direct database interface or ODBC. However, things are not always this simple. In many cases, PowerBuilder must retrieve data from a variety of data sources, including those on mainframes in both relational and nonrelational formats.

This chapter is not intended to discuss the basic concepts of LANs and WANs, but rather to discuss some of the network and communication issues encountered when developing PowerBuilder applications. The following topics are discussed:

- The OSI Model
- Supporting multiple protocols
- Interfacing with a network operating system (NOS)
- Middleware

THE OSI MODEL

To accommodate the wide range of network architectures used in client/server systems, the Open Systems Interconnect (OSI) model was developed by the International Standards Organization (ISO). The OSI model is a seven-layer structure designed to break down the communication of data from the hardware to the user interface. Each of the seven OSI

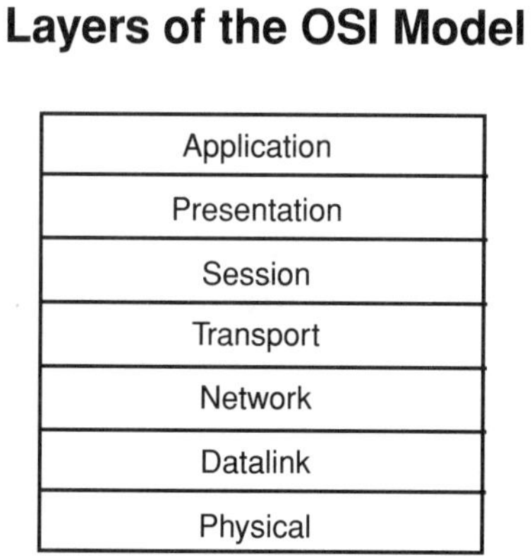

Layers of the OSI Model

Application
Presentation
Session
Transport
Network
Datalink
Physical

Figure 15.1   Seven layers of the OSI model.

layers provides services to the layer immediately above it in the model. All data communication products fall into one or more of the OSI layers, depending on the roles they play. The seven layers of the OSI model are shown in Figure 15.1.

Application Layer The application layer is the layer to which an application directly communicates. The network operating system (NOS) and its applications make themselves available to the user at this layer.

Presentation Layer The presentation layer supplies an application with the information it needs to read and understand the data it receives. This layer resolves differences between data representation from one computer to another. An example of this is the translation of data from the ASCII character set on PCs to the EBCDIC character set on mainframes.

Session Layer The session layer establishes and maintains communication between applications. The layer gets its name from the communication session that it establishes and terminates. Coordination is required if one system is slower than the other or if packet transfer is not orderly. This layer adds the beginning and the ending brackets plus information about the communication protocol that is being used and sends the message to the transport layer.

Transport Layer The transport layer controls the flow of data between applications, handling transmission errors, and ensuring reliable data delivery. Reliable in this instance means that delivery is either confirmed or denied. If the product operating at the transport layer determines that delivery has failed, it notifies the layers above so that the application can handle the failure.

Network Layer The network layer breaks data into packets and directs these packets to their intended destination. The size of each packet is determined by the cable access method or by the operating system. In sending the packets, the network layer is also responsible for matching names and addresses of destinations on the network. At the receiving end, the network layer is responsible for reassembling the data packets into complete messages. Routing software, for example, operates at the network level.

Datalink Layer The datalink layer consists of the specific protocols for accessing a network and creating packets. In a multiprotocol setting, the datalink layer is responsible for directing packets to the appropriate network adapter or protocol stack.

Physical Layer The physical layer is the lowest level of connectivity. It defines the physical and electrical characteristics of the connections that make up the network. The physical layer consists of the actual hardware used to connect computers on a network and transfer data. Standards are well defined at this layer and include IEEE 802.3 (Ethernet) and 802.5 (Token Ring).

SUPPORTING MULTIPLE PROTOCOLS

PC clients often must support more than one protocol type. In many cases, the NOS requires one type of protocol, while communications with a database server or remote host require another type of protocol. For example, an application may need to communicate with a UNIX database server through TCP/IP, the de facto industry standard for communication with UNIX servers. Therefore, to communicate with both the NOS and the database server, a client workstation must be able to support at least two protocol stacks, the NOS stack, and TCP/IP.

The key to supporting multiple protocols is device-driver standards. The two prominent standards are Novell's open datalink interface (ODI) and Microsoft/3Com's network driver interface specification (NDIS). Each of these standards establishes a layer of software between the NIC (network interface card) driver and the network protocol. This software is responsible for directing data packets to the appropriate protocol stack or adapter. Figure 15.2 shows where ODI and NDIS fit into the OSI model in a typical NetWare and TCP/IP environment.

Considering the example in Figure 15.2, assume the user must also

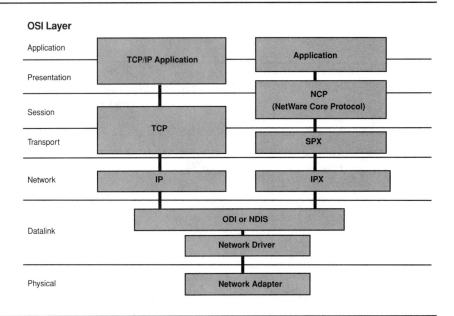

OSI Layer

Figure 15.2   Multiprotocol support with ODI/NDIS.

communicate with an IBM mainframe using the LU6.2 protocol. This can be done using IBM's LAN Support. LAN Support is a set of drivers that, like ODI, allows a single network adapter to support multiple protocol stacks. LAN Support is used in combination with ODI to allow a client to communicate with an IBM mainframe, a UNIX server, and a NOS. Figure 15.3 shows where the ODI/NDIS and LAN Support drivers fit into the OSI model.

As the diagram indicates, the NOS-specific protocols exist at layers above the ODI or NDIS drivers. Because of this, and the fact that the major NOSs (NetWare, LAN Manager, and VINES) all support either ODI or NDIS, any of the major NOSs can be used without significant impact to the technical architecture. This provides an open solution that allows the use of any of the major NOSs.

INTERFACING WITH A NETWORK OPERATING SYSTEM (NOS)

Applications sometimes have the need to access such data as network login IDs, node IDs, network printers, server names, and the like. To obtain this data, the application must interface with the NOS at some level.

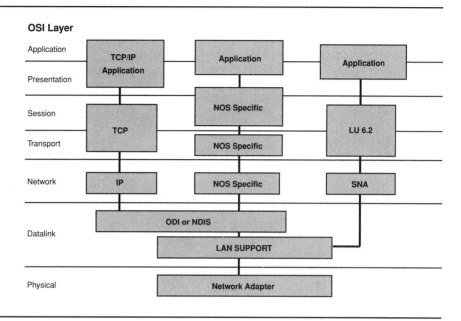

OSI Layer

Figure 15.3   Multiprotocol support using LAN Support.

In a NetWare environment, interfacing with the NOS can be done using the NetWare C API. The NetWare API is a set of functions that provides information on such things as network file servers, diagnostics, and connection information. These functions can be used in a PowerBuilder application by declaring them as either global or object-level external functions (see Chapter 8).

The following example shows the use of the NetWare API. This example logs a user into a NetWare network and maps a drive used for storing user reports.

```
/********************************************************
** This function logs the user into the network and maps a drive.
** The user name and password are global variables previously set at
** login time. The directory and drive letter of the new drive mapping
** are read from the user's application INI file — MYAPP.INI. If there
** are no values in MYAPP.INI, the report is put in the user's root
** directory and the letter R is assigned as the new drive mapping.
********************************************************
string sRptPath, sRptDrive
int iRtn
```

```
if LoginToFileServer(name, 1, password) <> 0 then
     DisplayMsg("Network Login Error", "The login to NetWare " &
  + "failed. Please contact the system administrator. ")
     return false
end if


sRptPath = ProfileString ( "MYAPP.INI, "REPORTS", "DIRECTORY", "C:\" )
sRptDrive = ProfileString ( "MYAPP.INI, "REPORTS", "DRIVE", "R" )

// Map a network drive that corresponds to the user's report directory
iRtn = MapDrive(0, 255, sRptPath, 1, 0, sRptDrive)
if iRtn <> 0 then
     DisplayMsg("Drive Mapping Error", "Drive mapping for the " &
  + "reports directory " + sRptPath + " failed with return code " &
  + string(iRtn) + ". Please contact the system administrator. ")
     return false
end if
```

The PowerBuilder external function declarations for the **LoginTo FileServer( )** and **MapDrive( )** functions are:

```
/* NetWare interface DLL functions */

function int LoginToFileServer(ref string username, int objtype, ref
string password) library "nwconn.dll"

function int MapDrive(int ConnectionID, int baseDriveNumber, ref string
directoryPath, int flag, int SearchOrder, ref string DriveLetter)
library "nwdir.dll"
```

The PowerBuilder Library for NetWare can also be used to provide NetWare network information to a PowerBuilder application. This product was developed by Powersoft to provide a simple interface from a PowerBuilder application to the NetWare API. The PowerBuilder Library for NetWare contains a set of functions and structures designed to shield developers from some of the complexities of dealing with low-level NetWare API functions. It also contains a sample application that developers can use to further reduce the amount of code required to interface with NetWare. For more information on the PowerBuilder Library for NetWare, contact Powersoft.

There are also APIs for other network environments. For example, many of the TCP/IP products provide an API that can be used for such tasks as FTP file transfers, remote logins, or obtaining IP addresses.

MIDDLEWARE

Middleware refers to a type of software used to provide a seamless method of network communication and data access across multiple platforms using different protocols. As distributed computing continues to grow, applications are evolving from the traditional two-tier "client/database server" architecture to a 3-tier services-based architecture. Middleware serves as the glue that allows the variety of platforms and protocols that make up this type of architecture to work together as a single system.

Middleware is designed to decrease development time by eliminating the need for developers to know the specifics of a network protocol or database interface. Because middleware supports a large variety of network types and protocols, the need to choose a single protocol on which to run an application is also eliminated.

In its most basic form, middleware works by translating client requests into the appropriate protocol and sending the requests to a server. In the case of data access, middleware also translates data requests and data to/from the client and the appropriate database server. This translation adds another layer to the normal client/server communication model. The tradeoff when using middleware is the flexibility and reduced development time compared to the performance degradation caused by the required protocol and data translation.

There are many middleware products currently on the market. The most prominent form of middleware available today is Microsoft's ODBC. ODBC provides a standard data access method to a large number of data sources. Refer to Chapter 16 for a detailed discussion of ODBC.

This section provides an overview of the two types of middleware architectures: remote procedure calls (RPCs) and message-passing. In addition to RPCs and message-passing, this section also discusses the two emerging standards in the area of middleware and distributed computing: DCE and CORBA. Finally, this section discusses database gateways and transaction processing (TP) monitors. Database gateways and TP monitors take advantage of middleware to provide distributed data access and other capabilities to client/server applications.

RPCs and Message-passing

In traditional, non-client/server applications, all process-to-process communication is handled within the confines of a single machine. In this environment, all data and the programs that access it are kept together, as shown in Figure 15.4.

In today's client/server applications, however, data is usually sepa-

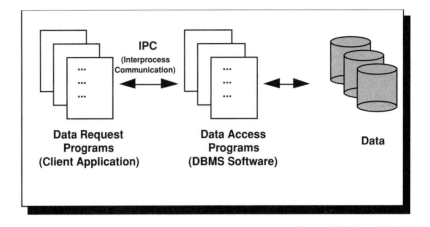

Figure 15.4 Process-to-process communication in traditional, non-client/server applications.

rated from the machine running the application that accesses it. RPCs and message-passing systems provide the two methods of communicating in this type of distributed environment.

RPCs function the same way as a normal function call; the only difference is that the function is executed on a different machine from which the function is called. For example, when retrieving data using an RPC, the function call is made on the machine requesting the data and the function is executed on the "remote" machine. Retrieved data is then sent from the server to the requesting client, as shown in Figure 15.5.

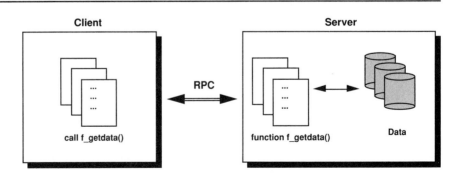

Figure 15.5 Using an RPC to send retrieved data from server to client.

RPCs provide a direct synchronous connection between two machines. Although some RPCs support asynchronous communication, the majority of RPCs are designed to support synchronous communication only.

Like RPCs, message-passing provides a way of communicating between different machines in a network. However, instead of one machine calling a procedure located on another machine, message-passing systems communicate by placing messages into an application's message queue.

An example of a message-passing system is shown in Figure 15.6. When retrieving data in a message-passing system, the application requesting the data places a "data request" message into its outbound queue. This message is then sent to the inbound queue of the receiving application. The receiving application then answers the request by placing the requested data in its outbound queue in the form of a message. This message is then sent to the requesting application's inbound queue, where the requesting application retrieves the data.

Message-passing systems are considered to be more flexible than RPCs. Rather than relying on the existence of a direct connection between two machines, a message-passing system asynchronously moves a message through the network until it reaches its final destination.

One drawback to message-passing systems is that the lack of a direct connection makes it less reliable than RPCs. A common use of message-passing systems is electronic mail systems.

The previous examples represent a simplistic view of how RPCs and message-passing systems work. The implementation of RPC and message-passing systems varies depending on the specific product being used. For more details, refer to the documentation of the RPC or message-passing product.

There are many third-party tools available that allow developers to easily build applications that use an RPC or message-passing architecture. These tools shield developers from the underlying network protocols, requiring development of only the business functionality. Many of these tools also provide a program generator that provides the developer a way of using underlying communication protocols such as TCP/IP, IPX/SPX, and LU 6.2 without having to know the details of each protocol, as shown in Figure 15.7.

Another benefit of this type of architecture is that because the application interfaces with the RPC or message API and not the network, any changes to the underlying network do not impact the application.

Data can be retrieved for a PowerBuilder application using both RPC and message-passing APIs. Like other third-party DLLs, the functions of the API are linked to a PowerBuilder application by declaring external functions.

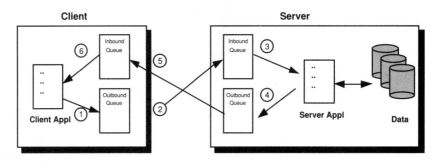

① The requesting application puts "get data" message in its outbound queue.

② The message is sent to the inbound queue of the server application.

③ The server application processes the message.

④ The server application retrieves the data and puts the "data message" into its outbound queue.

⑤ The message is sent to the inbound queue of the client application.

⑥ The client application retrieves the "data message" from its inbound queue.

Figure 15.6 Message-passing system to communicate between different machines in a network.

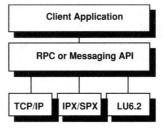

Figure 15.7 Building an application with underlying communication protocols using an RPC or message-passing architecture.

DCE and CORBA

In an effort to establish a standard for the development of client/server applications in a distributed heterogeneous environment, the Open Software Foundation (OSF) has developed the distributed computing environment (DCE) standard. The DCE standard addresses such areas as data representation, naming services, and security services, among others. Included in the DCE standard is a specification for an RPC mechanism (DCE has yet to adopt a messaging standard). Although DCE is still relatively new and has not yet been widely adopted, it is anticipated to become the standard for distributed computing. Many vendors, including IBM, Hewlett Packard, Open Environment Corporation, and Digital Equipment Corporation, have developed (or are in the process of developing) DCE products.

Along these same lines, another effort is under way to address the growing acceptance of object technology into mainstream computing. This effort involves a large group of vendors who are attempting to develop a standard specification for supporting multivendor, distributed object-oriented systems. This effort has resulted in the formation of the Object Management Group (OMG), a nonprofit international corporation comprised of over 300 vendors, developers, and users.

OMG has developed the object management architecture (OMA) to provide a foundation for the development of distributed object-oriented systems. At the heart of the OMA is the object request broker (ORB). An ORB is the mechanism by which application objects interface with service objects to transparently send and receive messages in a distributed environment. Application objects in this case refer to application-specific objects as well as objects common to multiple applications; service objects refer to the set of objects designed to provide various services to application objects such as communication, data access, printing, and the like.

To provide a standard interface between objects, OMG has developed the common object request broker architecture (CORBA) as its ORB standard. CORBA is a specification providing a standard for how objects make requests and receive responses using ORBs in a distributed environment across multiple platforms. Although many vendors, including IBM, Hewlett Packard, Digital Equipment Corporation, and AT&T Corporation, have already developed CORBA-compliant products, CORBA has yet to be widely implemented. It is expected that the CORBA 2 standard will lead to greater acceptance and wider use of the CORBA standard.

The development of standards such as DCE and CORBA should help developers quickly produce object-oriented systems capable of running in a distributed heterogeneous environment using a variety of protocols.

DRDA

Distributed relational database architecture (DRDA) is IBM's solution for communication among distributed databases. Access to DRDA databases is accomplished using IBM's distributed database connection services/2 (DDCS/2). DDCS/2 provides an API that allows applications to access any DRDA-compliant database, including DB2/MVS, SQL/DS, DB2/2, and OS/2 database manager (DBM), among others.

Although PowerBuilder does support such DRDA-compliant databases as DB2/2 and OS/2 DBM, it currently does not provide an interface to all DRDA-compliant databases. For example, there is currently no direct PowerBuilder interface to DB2/MVS. The reason for this is that although the DDCS/2 API provides the necessary interface to any DRDA database, the SQL dialect and system tables of each database is different. At this time, PowerBuilder is only able to support the SQL dialect and system tables of DB2/2, DB2/6000, and OS/2 DBM.

DRDA provides a good solution in an all-IBM environment; for example, a distributed environment with DB2/MVS running on a mainframe, DB2/6000 on an RS/6000 running AIX, and DB2/2 running under OS/2. However, even with such vendors as Oracle, Sybase, and Informix providing DRDA support in their products, it has yet to be widely accepted as a complete solution in a multivendor environment.

Database Gateways

Database gateways are often used in situations where a direct database interface is not possible or efficient. Many gateways on the market today are designed to provide access to mainframe-based data sources in a client/server environment. PowerBuilder currently provides a direct interface to many database gateway products, including Micro Decisionware's (MDI) Database Gateway for DB2, Sybase's Net-Gateway for DB2, and Oracle's Transparent and Procedural gateway products.

Database gateways allow a client application to transparently retrieve data from a variety of data sources through a single interface. For example, the MDI DB2 gateway provides access not only to DB2, but also to other mainframe data sources (relational and nonrelational) such as SQL/DS, VSAM, IMS, and IDMS, among others. Figure 15.8 shows the generic network topology when using a gateway to access mainframe data sources.

As this figure shows, access to any mainframe data source is accomplished using a single interface from the client application to the database gateway. All required data sources are then accessed transparently from the gateway.

While a gateway provides transparent access to distributed data

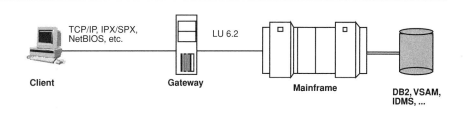

Figure 15.8   Generic network topology when using a gateway to access mainframe data sources.

sources, it does so at the cost of performance. Part of the performance impact of using a gateway arises from the fact that the gateway must translate the data from its native format to the format used by the gateway and finally to the format used by the client. The gateway must also perform any protocol translation required between the gateway environment and the environment of the data source. When dealing with mainframe data sources, this usually involves translation to/from the protocol used between the gateway protocol and an SNA protocol such as LU 6.2. In addition, because the gateway adds another layer between the client and the data source, network delay and latency can also slow performance.

Most of the major RDBMS vendors (including Oracle, Sybase, and Informix) have gateway products available as extensions to their particular RDBMS. These gateways provide access to both mainframe data sources and data from other server databases.

TP Monitors

Like database gateways, transaction processing (TP) monitors can be used to provide transparent access to a variety of data sources. However, TP monitors are generally used to increase performance in high-volume OLTP applications. TP monitors provide a way of increasing system performance by managing processes in a way that makes efficient use of system resources. For client/server database applications, a TP monitor can be used to manage the number of connections to a database and control access to distributed data sources. For example, database applications without a TP monitor require at least one database connection per user process. These connections remain active throughout the entire user session, as shown in Figure 15.9.

This type of architecture is adequate in most small- to medium-scale applications. However, in a large-scale OLTP application, the sys-

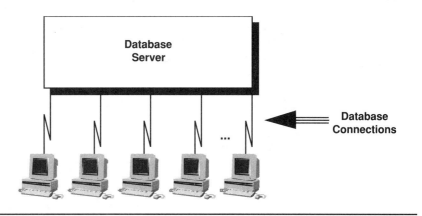

Figure 15.9   Active database connections.

tem resources required to manage each user connection can drastically impact system performance.

With a TP monitor, database connections are managed such that a database connection is established only when necessary, as shown in Figure 15.10. Because the number of connections is reduced, the database is capable of supporting many more users.

A TP monitor can act as a transaction manager, scheduling and controlling transactions in such a manner that does not overload the system. TP monitors can also provide load balancing across multiple processors.

In addition to performance benefits, a TP monitor also provides the capability to access multiple data sources using a single API. Much like a database gateway, a TP monitor can serve as a single interface from an application to data distributed across multiple heterogeneous databases and servers. This capability provides a level of data abstraction such that data can be distributed across multiple DBMSs and servers. Distributed data access services provided by the TP monitor are generally executed from the machine on which the TP monitor resides.

While a TP monitor can increase the performance of large-scale applications, there are some disadvantages to using one. First, the services provided by a TP monitor are developed in a 3-GL such as C and/ or COBOL. This usually requires a significant development effort and increases application maintenance responsibilities.

Second, a TP monitor adds some performance overhead. It is, therefore, important to make sure the performance gains outweigh the overhead of using the TP monitor. In applications with few users and low transaction volumes, performance may actually degrade because of a TP monitor.

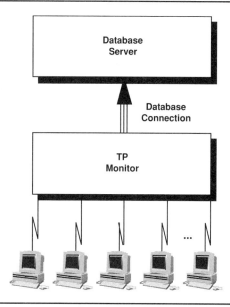

Figure 15.10   Using a TP monitor to manage database connections.

For these reasons, a TP monitor should only be used for large-scale applications with many users and a high volume of transactions.

In the IBM world, CICS is the most prominent TP monitor. In the past, CICS has only existed in mainframe environments. However, CICS has recently been ported to different platforms, including AIX.

The three leading UNIX TP monitors are USL's Tuxedo, Transarc's Encina, and NCR's Top End. Of these, only Encina is DCE-based. Also, Transarc has recently released EncinaBuilder, a product designed to provide a seamless integration between PowerBuilder and Transarc's Encina for Windows product. EncinaBuilder allows PowerBuilder developers to develop Encina client applications within the PowerBuilder development environment. EncinaBuilder does this by generating a set of user objects and DataWindows that represent different Encina application services. The Encina services can then be invoked from the PowerBuilder application via RPCs.

Many DBMS products are also XA (X/Open's standard interface between TP monitors and databases) compliant, meaning that the DBMS can interface directly with any TP monitor that is also XA compliant.

With direct interfaces to middleware products such as EncinaBuilder, PowerBuilder becomes a much more viable tool for developing large-scale applications in a multi-tier distributed environment.

PART IV

Database Connectivity

CHAPTER 16

Open Database Connectivity (ODBC)

On November 14, 1991, Microsoft Corporation introduced open database connectivity (ODBC), a database connectivity API that allows applications to communicate with different DBMSs (see Figure 16.1).

ODBC is based on the SQL Access Group's call level interface (CLI) specification, which uses SQL to access database environments. ODBC supports access to both SQL and non-SQL data. The ODBC layer provides a transparent mechanism for applications to communicate with different DBMSs. Traditionally, applications could only connect to different DBMSs by interfacing with each DBMS's proprietary CLI. Though the method of communicating with a DBMS's CLI has some advantages (performance is better, for example), it typically binds applications to a specific DBMS's CLI. Binding applications to specific DBMS CLIs makes switching from one DBMS to another difficult. With ODBC, switching from one DBMS to another requires little or no program modification.

This chapter discusses some of the following topics:

- Advantages of ODBC
- Disadvantages of ODBC
- ODBC architecture
- ODBC SQL processing
- ODBC conformance levels
- INI File settings
- Connecting to ODBC from PowerBuilder
- Setting up ODBC on the client
- Runtime ODBC modules
- Other ODBC-like standards

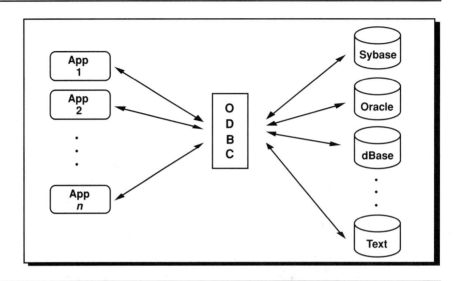

Figure 16.1   ODBC allows applications to communicate with different DBMSs.

ADVANTAGES OF ODBC

The many advantages of ODBC include:

- Developers and independent software vendors (ISVs) use a single set of function calls in all applications to access multiple DBMSs. The burden of writing code for a particular database is gone, as is the need to update code for new releases of DBMSs.
- DBMS vendors have a more streamlined way to provide end-user connections to their data. By writing a single driver that supports ODBC, the database vendor can in a sense "plug into" an ODBC "socket" created by the front-end ISV.
- Customers gain transparent access to many data sources, accessing multiple databases with equal ease from their front-end application.
- Because many front-ends can be used, ODBC offers the potential for a wider selection of applications to give users access to the database they need.

DISADVANTAGES OF ODBC

There are two major drawbacks of ODBC. They are:

- Performance can be slow because an additional layer has been added between the DBMS and the client.

> **Note:** There are different schools of thought when it comes to ODBC performance. Many developers do not consider performance to be a problem. There have been comparisons of ODBC and DB-Lib; some test results show that OBDC yielded faster performance than DB-Lib. On the other hand, there are developers who claim that ODBC is having a hard time living up to its reputation when it comes to functionality, performance, or stability.

- Specific features of a DBMS may not always be used because ODBC does not support features of all DBMSs. This may limit a developer's use of DBMS's functionality.

ODBC ARCHITECTURE

Figure 16.2 shows single- and multi-tier driver architecture. In both cases, the application interacts with the ODBC Driver Manager (ODBC.INI). The Driver Manager fields application calls to the particular DBMS. It sits on top of one or more other drivers. It loads and unloads drivers from memory, performs status checking, and manages multiple connections between applications and data sources. Single-tier drivers sit directly above the data source and process calls directly to the DBMS. Multi-tier drivers process the function calls and send the SQL request to the server for processing.

In both cases, the Driver Manager processes the application's function calls and sends them to the appropriate loadable driver. Some driv-

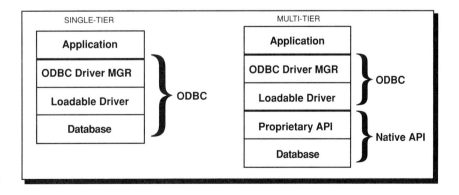

Figure 16.2   Single-tier vs. multi-tier driver architecture.

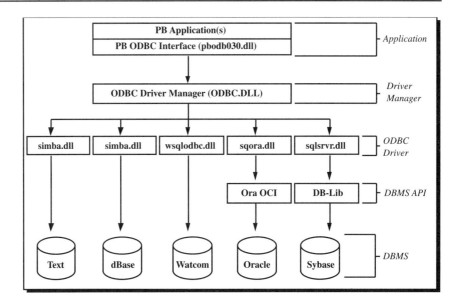

Figure 16.3   Examples of different single- and multi-tier DBMS ODBC drivers.

ers map the ODBC function calls to a library of proprietary DBMS APIs; others send the request directly to the DBMS. Figure 16.3 shows examples of different single- and multi-tier DBMS ODBC drivers.

ODBC SQL PROCESSING

In order to truly understand how ODBC works, it is best to learn how ODBC executes a SQL query and returns the result set. When a SQL query is to be executed, the following occurs.

Memory for the ODBC environment is allocated and pointed to by an environment handle. Only one environment handle per application is possible. When an environment handle has been created, a connection handle is obtained. This handle points to a memory location containing information about a particular connection. There can be multiple connection handles for each environment handle. A lower-level handle is then created. This third type of handle, which is called a statement handle, is used for processing a query within a connection. There can be multiple statement handles for each connection. Figure 16.4 shows this process.

Figure 16.4 shows the relationship between the different ODBC handles. The flow within the Process SQL / Retrieve Results box is detailed in Figure 16.5.

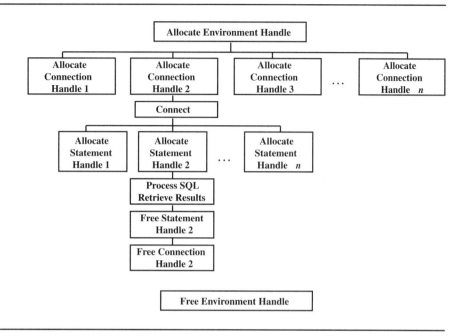

Figure 16.4   The process involved when ODBC executes a SQL query.

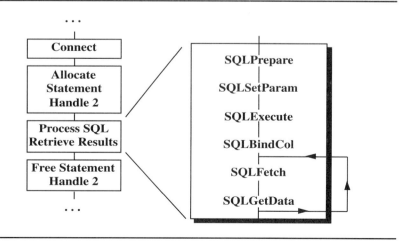

Figure 16.5   The flow within the Process SQL/Retrieve Results box.

This figure shows the ODBC functions called to process a SQL query and retrieve the results.

ODBC CONFORMANCE LEVELS

SQL Access Group (SAG) is a consortium of vendors with a mission to provide a standard for the language of relational databases—SQL. Despite the efforts of SAG, vendors have produced variants in their implementation of SQL. ODBC is structured around the work of SAG. A conformance level establishes the amount of interoperability that a driver has with its corresponding data source. ODBC defines conformance levels for drivers in two areas: the ODBC API and the ODBC SQL grammar (which includes the ODBC SQL data types). Conformance levels help both application and driver developers to establish standard sets of functionality.

API Conformance Levels

The ODBC API defines a set of core functions that correspond to the functions in the X/Open and SQL Access Group Call Level Interface specification. ODBC also defines two extended sets of functionality, Level 1 and Level 2. API calls at each level are closely tied to the class of ODBC functions supported by the DBMS's ODBC driver, which is closely tied to the functional capability of the data source. The following summarizes the functionality included in each conformance level.

Core API

- Allocate and free environment, connection, and statement handles.
- Connect to data sources. Use multiple statement handles on a connection.
- Prepare and execute SQL statements. Execute SQL statements immediately.
- Assign storage for parameters in a SQL statement and result columns.
- Retrieve data from a result set. Retrieve information about a result set.
- Commit or roll back transactions.
- Retrieve error information.

This functionality can be implemented using the following functions.

Core Functions

SQLAllocConnect—Obtains a connection handle.

SQLAllocEnv—Obtains an environment handle. One environment handle is used for one or more connections.

SQLAllocStmt—Allocates a statement handle.

SQLBindCol—Assigns storage for a result column and specifies the datatype.

SQLCancel—Cancels a SQL statement.

SQLColAttributes—Describes attributes of a column in the result set.

SQLConnect—Connects to a specific driver by data source name, user ID, and password.

SQLDescribeCol—Describes a column in the result set.

SQLDisconnect—Closes the connection.

SQLError—Returns additional error or status information.

SQLExecDirect—Executes a statement.

SQLExecute—Executes a prepared statement.

SQLFetch—Returns a result row.

SQLFreeConnect—Releases the connection handle.

SQLFreeEnv—Releases the environment handle.

SQLFreeStmt—Ends statement processing and closes the associated cursor, discards pending results, and, optionally, frees all resources associated with the statement handle.

SQLGetCursorName—Returns the cursor name associated with a statement handle.

SQLNumResultCols—Returns the number of columns in the result set.

SQLPrepare—Prepares a SQL statement for later execution.

SQLRowCount—Returns the number of rows affected by an insert, update, or delete request.

SQLSetCursorName—Specifies a cursor name.

SQLSetParam—Assigns storage for a parameter in a SQL statement.

SQLTransact—Commits or rolls back a transaction.

Level 1 API

- Meet the core API functionality conformance level.
- Connect to data sources with driver-specific dialog boxes.
- Set and inquire about values of statement and connection options.
- Send part or all of a parameter value (useful for long data).
- Retrieve all or part of a result column value (useful for long data).
- Retrieve catalog information (columns, special columns, statistics, and tables).

- Retrieve information about driver and data source capabilities, such as supported datatypes.
- Supports both scalar functions and ODBC functions.

This functionality can be implemented using the following functions.

Level 1 Functions

SQLColumns—Returns the list of column names in specified tables.

SQLDriverConnect—Connects to a specific driver by connection string or requests that the Driver Manager and driver display connection dialogs for the user.

SQLGetConnectOption—Returns the value of a connection option.

SQLGetData—Returns part or all of one column of one row of a result set. (Useful for long data values.)

SQLGetFunctions—Returns supported driver functions.

SQLGetInfo—Returns information about a specific driver and data source.

SQLGetStmtOption—Returns the value of a statement option.

SQLGetTypeInfo—Returns information about supported datatypes.

SQLParamData—Returns the storage value assigned to a parameter for which data will be sent at execution time. (Useful for long data values.)

SQLPutData—Send part or all of a data value for a parameter. (Useful for long data values.)

SQLSetConnectOption—Sets the transaction isolation level for a particular connection. (A more detailed discussion of this function follows).

SQLSetStmtOption—Sets a statement option.

SQLSpecialColumns—Retrieves information about the optimal set of columns that uniquely identifies a row in a specified table and the columns that are automatically updated when any value in the row is updated by a transaction.

SQLStatistics—Retrieves statistics about a single table and the list of indexes associated with the table.

SQLTables—Returns the list of table names stored in a specific data source.

Level 2 API

- Meet the core and level 1 API functionality conformance level.
- Browse available connections and list available data sources.

- Send arrays of parameter values. Retrieve arrays of result column values.
- Retrieve the number of parameters and describe individual parameters.
- Use a scrollable cursor.
- Retrieve the native form of an SQL statement.
- Retrieve catalog information (privileges, keys, and procedures).
- Call translation DLL.

This functionality can be implemented using the following functions.

Level 2 Functions

SQLBrowseConnect—Returns successive levels of connection attributes and valid attribute values. When a value has been specified for each connection attribute, it connects to the data source.

SQLColumnPrivileges—Returns a list of columns and associated privileges for one or more tables.

SQLDataSources—Returns a list of available data sources.

SQLDescribeParam—Returns the description for a specific parameter in a statement.

SQLExtendedFetch—Returns multiple result rows.

SQLForeignKeys—Returns a list of column names that comprise foreign keys, if they exist for a specified table.

SQLMoreResults—Determines whether there are more result sets available and, if so, initializes processing for the next result set.

SQLNativeSql—Returns the text of a SQL statement as translated by the driver.

SQLNumParams—Returns the number of parameters in a statement.

SQLParamOptions—Specifies the use of multiple values for parameters.

SQLPrimaryKeys—Returns the list of column name(s) that comprise the primary key for a table.

SQLProcedureColumns—Returns the list of input and output parameters as well as the columns that make up the result set for the specified procedures.

SQLProcedures—Returns the list of procedure names stored in a specific data source.

SQLSetPos—Positions a cursor within a fetched block of data.

SQLSetScrollOptions—Sets options that control cursor behavior.

SQLTablePrivileges—Returns a list of tables and the privileges associated with each table.

SQL Conformance Levels

ODBC defines a core grammar that corresponds to the X/Open and SQL Access Group CAE draft specification (1991). ODBC also defines a minimum grammar, to meet a basic level of ODBC conformance, and an extended grammar, to provide for common DBMS extensions to SQL. The following sections summarize the grammar included in each conformance level.

Minimum SQL Grammar

- Data definition language (DDL): CREATE TABLE and DROP TABLE.
- Data manipulation language (DML): simple SELECT, INSERT, UPDATE, SEARCHED, and DELETE SEARCHED.
- Expressions: simple (such as A > B + C).
- Datatypes: CHAR.

Core SQL Grammar

- Minimum SQL grammar.
- DDL: ALTER TABLE, CREATE INDEX, DROP INDEX, CREATE VIEW, DROP VIEW, GRANT, and REVOKE.
- DML: full SELECT, positioned UPDATE, and positioned DELETE.
- Expressions: sub-query, set functions such as SUM and MIN.
- Datatypes: VARCHAR, DECIMAL, NUMERIC, SMALLINT, INTEGER, REAL, FLOAT, DOUBLE PRECISION.

Extended SQL Grammar

- Minimum and core SQL grammar.
- DML: outer joins.
- Expressions: scalar functions such as SUBSTRING and ABS; date, time, and timestamp literals.
- Datatypes: LONG VARCHAR, BIT, TINYINT, BIGINT, BINARY, VARBINARY, LONG VARBINARY, DATE, TIME, TIMESTAMP.
- Batch SQL statements.
- Procedure calls.

Although a DBMS does not support all three levels, it is ideal if your DBMS conforms to all three levels. Both API and SQL conformance should be a consideration when selecting a DBMS.

Sample C ODBC Example:

This example shows how ODBC functions can be used in a C program to retrieve data from a Watcom data source. In the following example (using Visual C++), an application executes a static SELECT statement to return a result set of employee names. It then calls **SQLBindCol** to bind the column of data to local storage locations. Finally, the application fetches each row of data with **SQLFetch** and displays each employee's name.

```c
#include "windows.h"
#include "sql.h"
#include "sqlext.h"

#define MAXVAL 25

UCHAR * server = (UCHAR*) "PowerBuilder Sample DB";
UCHAR * uid = (UCHAR*)"dba";
UCHAR * pwd = (UCHAR*) "sql";

HENV henv;
HDBC hdbc;
HSTMT hstmt;

RETCODE rc;

SDWORD datalen;
UCHAR * data;
UCHAR select[] = "Select name from customer";
HDC hdc;
int i = 1;

// Create an environment handle
rc = SQLAllocEnv(&henv);
if (rc == SQL_SUCCESS) {
        // Allocate a connection handle
        rc = SQLAllocConnect(henv, &hdbc);
        if (rc == SQL_SUCCESS) {
                // Connect to data source
                rc = SQLConnect(hdbc, (UCHAR *) "PowerBuilder Demo DB",
                                       SQL_NTS, (UCHAR *) "dba",
                        SQL_NTS, (UCHAR *) "sql", SQL_NTS);
                if (rc == SQL_CONNECT || rc == SQL_SUCCESS_WITH_INFO) {
                        // Create a statement handle
                        rc = SQLAllocStmt(hdbc, &hstmt);
                        if (rc == SQL_SUCCESS) {
```

```
                                              // Prepare and execute the SQL
                                              SQLExecDirect(hstmt,select,SQL_NTS);
                                              datalen = MAXVAL;
                                              data = (UCHAR *) malloc(MAXVAL);
                                              // Bind local variables with data
                                              SQLBindCol(hstmt, 1, SQL_C_CHAR,data,
                                                         MAXVAL,&datalen);
                                              do {
                                                   // Fetch next row
                                                   rc = SQLFetch(hstmt);
                                                   // the output for each row is
                                                   // stored in "data" process
                                                   // accordingly.
                                              } while (rc == SQL_SUCCESS || rc ==
                                                   SQL_SUCCESS_WITH_INFO);
                                    }
                          }
                }
      }
// Release statement handle
SQLFreeStmt(hstmt, SQL_DROP);
// Disconnect from data source
SQLDisconnect(hdbc);
// Release connection handle
SQLFreeConnect(hdbc);
// Release environment handle
SQLFreeEnv(henv);
```

The previous code segment is an example of static SQL execution. In this case the retrieval columns are known. If the developer is interested in writing a code segment that executes and displays the results of ad-hoc queries, some additional functions must be called. There are a couple of items that need to be determined in an ad-hoc query situation. The first thing is the type of query (select, update, insert, delete, or a DDL statement) and the second thing is the number of columns to be returned, for a SELECT statement. The following code segment is an alternative in determining the above information:

```
// determine the number of result columns
SQLNumResultsCol(hstmt, &rColumnCount);
// if the number of result columns is equal to zero then the statement
// is not a SELECT statement
if (resColumnsCount == 0)
{
        // determine the number of affected rows
```

```
                    SQLRowCount(hstmt, &rCount);
                    // if the number of affected rows is greater than zero then
                    // the statement is either an UPDATE, INSERT or
                    // DELETE statement
                    if (rCount > 0)
                    {
                            // the statement requested is either an INSERT,
                            // UPDATE, or DELETE
                    }
                    // if the number of affected rows is less than zero then
                    // the statement is some type of DDL statement
                    else
                    {
                            // the statement requested is a DDL statement
                    }
            }
            // if the number of result columns is greater than zero then
            // the statement is a SELECT statement
            else
            {
                    for (i = 0; i < resColumnCount; i++)
                    {
                            // for each type of result column the column type,
                            // name and length needs to be determined.
                            // this information is needed to allocate memory
                            // and to bind the data with result variables.
                            SQLDescribeCol(hstmt, i + 1, ColumnName,
                                (SWORD)sizeof(ColumnName),
                                &ColumnNameLength, &ColumnType,
                                &ColumnLength[i], &Scale, &Nullable);

                            // bind columns
                    }
                    // process the rest of display code...
            }
```

.INI FILE SETTINGS

ODBC Driver Manager Initialization File (ODBC.INI)

The ODBC.INI file is the main ODBC initialization file (see Figure 16.6). The ODBC Driver Manager uses this file to get the detail information about a unique data source name to connect to the DBMS. This file includes all the ODBC DBMSs and their corresponding drivers, DBMS ODBC driver and data source name mappings, and detail information about a data source.

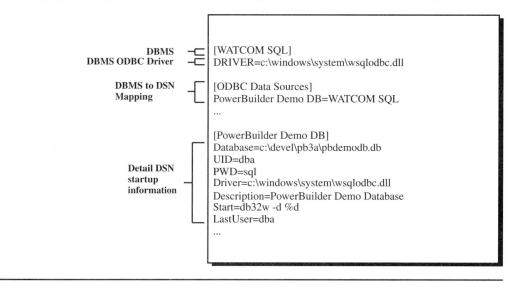

Figure 16.6   The ODBC.INI file.

ODBC Installation Initialization File (ODBCINST.INI)

This file (see Figure 16.7) is mainly used by ODBC installation programs to install different ODBC drivers. When troubleshooting, this INI file can also be looked at to verify driver information for the installed data sources.

PowerBuilder ODBC Configuration File (PBODB040.INI)

PowerBuilder takes advantage of extended capabilities of ODBC drivers and navigates around shortcomings by utilizing PBODB040.INI file entries in the data source, DBMS driver, or DBMS section. If no sections exist for a particular connection, PowerBuilder runs as an ODBC-compliant client and extensions that might be available cannot not be used.

The search algorithm for the entries is:

```
IF section and entry are present for current datasource
THEN use entry value
ELSE IF section corresponding to DBMS_Name Driver_Name exists
THEN use entry value if it exists
ELSE IF section corresponding to DBMS_Name exists
THEN use entry value if it exists
```

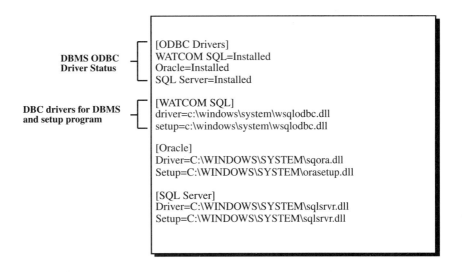

Figure 16.7   The ODBC installation initialization file.

If PowerBuilder searches for SQL syntax and no entry is found with respect to this search criteria, PowerBuilder searches the syntax section that corresponds to the current data source's SQL grammar conformance level.

If the developer wants to override the more general settings of DBMS_Driver or DBMS_Name, a data-source-specific section would have to be created.

The PBODB040.INI file also has a debugging option for ODBC connections. If the PBTrace entry of the PBCONNECTOPTIONS section is set to ON, all ODBC interface calls are written to the file pointed to by the PBTraceFile entry of PBCONNECTOPTIONS section:

```
[PBCONNECTOPTIONS]
PBTrace='ON'
PBTraceFile='c:\PBSQL.LOG'
```

CONNECTING TO ODBC FROM POWERBUILDER

With ODBC, an application connects to the data source by specifying the data source name and any additional information needed to complete the connection.

The following list shows the database variables in the PowerBuilder initialization file (PB.INI). These parameters can be set by either editing the PB.INI file or using the preferences icon on the power panel.

Vendor—ODBC

DBMS—ODBC

LogID—Developer's log ID (used only if the ODBC SQL driver CONNECT call is not supported)

UserID—Developer's user ID (optional; use with caution because it overrides the connection's UserName attribute returned by the ODBC SQLGetInfo call)

AutoCommit—True; data updates cannot be rolled back
—False (default); data updates can be rolled back if the back-end data source supports transaction processing

Lock—Lock value

DBParm—PowerBuilder uses the DBParm variable for a connect string

The lock variable is used for ODBC transaction isolation levels. When the developer sets the Lock parameter to either RV (Uncommitted read), RC (Committed read), RR (Repeatable read), TS (Serializable transactions), or TV (Transaction versioning), PowerBuilder internally makes a call to SQLSetConnectOption and sets the isolation level. Following is an example of connecting to a Watcom SQL local database through ODBC, using the default SQLCA transaction object.

```
SQLCA.DBMS = sDBMS
SQLCA.dbparm =
    "ConnectString='DSN=" + sDataSourceName + ";UID=" &
        + sUserId + ";PWD=" + sPassword + "'"
connect;
if sqlca.sqlcode = -1 then
        MessageBox ("Error Connecting to Database", sqlca.sqlerrtext)
        // error proccessing code
end if
```

Note that there is no hard-coding in this case. Hard-coding should be avoided, especially with the transaction object parameters. Most of the parameters can be stored in initialization files, encrypted files, security tables, or entered at runtime. If the transaction object were filled with hard-coded values from the script, each time a new user is added, the database name is changed, or passwords are changed, the code would have to be modified. It is better to have configurable parameters and user-specific parameters separate from the code.

DBParm Settings

The DBParm parameter has many attributes that can be set, either in the preferences or in the application script, using the transaction object shown in the previous sample code.

The developer can set asynchronous operations, delimited SQL syntax, scrolling and locking options for cursors, the list of displayed tables, and the PowerBuilder catalog owner using the DBParm parameter.

Asynchronous Operations PowerBuilder supports synchronous and asynchronous operations. In this context, asynchronous means occurring at any time without regard to the main flow of a program; synchronous means occurring at a particular time as a direct result of the execution of a particular machine instruction. In PowerBuilder, the asynchronous option in preferences is set to a value of one. In the transaction object, the following must be entered:

```
TransactionObject.DBPARM="Async=1"
```

This would be used, for example, when retrieving multiple non-dependent DataWindows and not wanting to wait for the results of one to issue the next query.

DBGetTime When the asynchronous option is set, the developer can specify the number of seconds that PowerBuilder should wait for an ODBC driver response to a SQLExecuteDirect statement, when a Retrieve is executed with a Retrieve Row event. The DBParm DBGetTime parameter can be set to the number of seconds. The default value is zero, which waits indefinitely.

DelimitIdentifier This option allows the developer to determine whether identifiers will be delimited in SQL syntax. If the developer does not want SQL syntax to be delimited, for example, when importing SQL, the DBParm variable should be set to no. The default value for the DelimitIdentifier is yes. To set the delimit identifier in PowerScript using the default transaction object, the following syntax must be used:

```
SQLCA.DBParm = "delimitidentifiers=No"
```

Other DBParm Settings   There are a few other DBParm options that can be set to control scrolling and the locking of cursors, displaying table listings, and options to override settings in the PBODB040.INI file.

SETTING UP ODBC ON THE CLIENT

To execute ODBC applications, the ODBC administrator and drivers need to be installed and data sources need to be configured. The ODBC installation kit adds an ODBC Administrator icon to the Windows Control Panel. Before data can be accessed from an application, a data source must be created.

The main purpose of the ODBC Administrator is to create and manage data sources. Each data source is identified by a unique name. To add a new data source for a Watcom database, for example, the following steps are followed. From the ODBC Administrator, the Watcom ODBC driver is selected and the "Add New Name" button is clicked, as shown in Figure 16.8.

This brings up the screen in Figure 16.9.

A unique data source name must be given, as must a database file. When the two fields are entered, clicking the OK button installs the data source (see Figure 16.10).

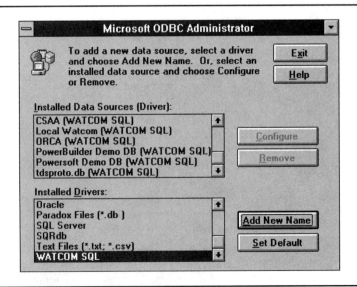

Figure 16.8   Selecting the Watcom ODBC driver and the "Add New Name button" from the ODBC Administrator.

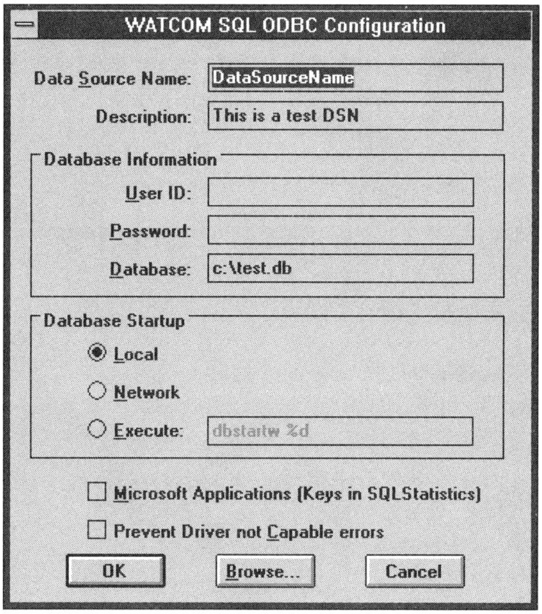

Figure 16.9   The Watcom SQL ODBC Configuration screen.

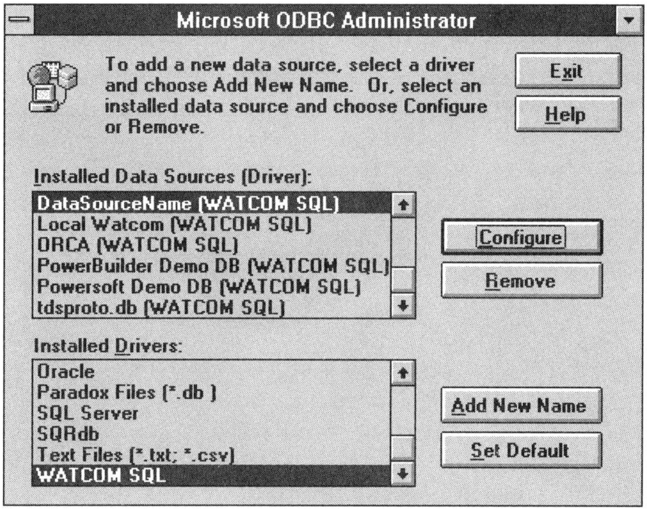

Figure 16.10   The installed data source.

When the data source is defined, the program makes the following changes to the ODBC.INI file:

```
[WATCOM SQL]
DRIVER=c:\windows\system\wsqlodbc.dll

[ODBC Data Sources]
PowerBuilder Demo DB=WATCOM SQL
DataSourceName=WATCOM SQL

[PowerBuilder Demo DB]
Database=c:\devel\pb3a\pbdemodb.db
UID=dba
PWD=sql
Driver=c:\windows\system\wsqlodbc.dll
Description=PowerBuilder Demo Database
Start=db32w -d %d
LastUser=dba


[DataSourceName]
Driver=c:\windows\system\wsqlodbc.dll
Description=This is a test DSN
Database=c:\test.db
Start=dbstartw %d
```

This process could have also been done from the configure ODBC menu option of the Database painter, an ODBC Administrator painter, or programatically at install or runtime.

The following PowerScript function is an example of creating an ODBC data source for a Watcom database:

```
int f_IsValidDSN(string sDSN, string sUID, string sPWD,
          string sDescription, string sDatabase)
```

The PowerScript for this function is:

```
String sODBCINI = "odbc.ini"
String sDriver = "wsqlodbc.dll"
String sStartup = "db32w %d"
String sDSType = "Watcom SQL"
String sODBCDS = "ODBC Data Sources"

If FileExists (sODBCINI) Then
    Integer iFNum
    If NOT Trim( ProfileString (sODBCINI,sDSType,"Driver","")) = "" Then
```

```
   If Trim ( ProfileString (sODBCINI, sODBCDS,sDSN,"")) = "" Then
      SetProfileString (sODBCINI,"ODBC Data Sources",sDSN,sDSType)
      SetProfileString (sODBCINI,sDSN,"Driver",sDriver)
      SetProfileString (sODBCINI,sDSN,"UID",sUID)
      SetProfileString (sODBCINI,sDSN,"PWD",sPWD)
      SetProfileString (sODBCINI,sDSN,"Description",sDescription)
      SetProfileString (sODBCINI,sDSN,"Database",sDatabase)
      SetProfileString (sODBCINI,sDSN,"Start",sStartup)
   Else
    return 100
   End If
 Else
    return -1
 End If
Else
   return -1
End If
return 1
```

The **f_IsValidDSN(...)** function can be called at the start of an application to verify that an ODBC data source has been set up; if it hasn't, one can be set up in the program.

The **f_IsValidDSN(...)** function is a simple process of verifying the existence of an ODBC data source. The following functions are ODBC Installer (ODBCINST.DLL) API calls that can be used in an application to setup an ODBC application.

SQLConfigDataSource—Adds, modifies, or deletes data sources.

SQLGetAvailableDrivers—Reads the "[ODBC Drivers]" section of the ODBC.INF file and returns the descriptions of the drivers that the user may install.

SQLGetInstalledDrivers—Reads the "[ODBC Drivers]" section of the ODBC.INF file and returns the descriptions of the installed drivers.

SQLInstallDriver—Adds information about the driver to the ODBCINST.INI file and returns the path of the target directory for the installation.

SQLInstallDriverManager—Returns the path of the target directory for the installation. The caller must actually copy the driver manager's files to the target directory.

SQLRemoveDefaultDataSource—Removes the default data source specification section from the ODBC.INI file. It also removes the default driver specification section from the ODBCINST.INI file.

SQLRemoveDSNFromIni—Removes a data source from the ODBC.INI file.

SQLWriteDSNToIni—Adds a data source to the ODBC.INI file.

RUNTIME ODBC MODULES

In addition to the application EXE, PBDs, custom DLLs, INI files, and PB runtime DLLs (found on the DDK diskettes), the following ODBC files are needed:

PBODB040.DLL

ODBC.DLL

ODBCINST.INI

ODBC.INI

DBMS ODBC driver (for Watcom is WSQLODBC.DLL)

These files are included with PowerBuilder.

OTHER ODBC-LIKE STANDARDS

There are different companies and/or groups of companies that have other data access standards similar to ODBC. Just a few of the different standards are:

QELIB—Q+E Software, Inc. is the creator of QELIB. Q+E is working on both an ODBC and an IDAPI interface.

IDAPI—Borland, IBM, Novell, and WordPerfect have created a data access initiative called IDAPI.

Oracle GLUE—Oracle Corporation's data access layer that allows applications to communicate with different DBMSs.

Each of these provides a generic method of data access. ODBC, however, is more widely accepted than these standards are.

CHAPTER 17

WATCOM SQL

WATCOM SQL, which is an ANSI SQL 89 compliant relational data-base, comes packaged with the PowerBuilder development environment. WATCOM SQL can run as either a local PC database or on a network file server accessible to many users. This chapter discusses the following topics related to WATCOM SQL:

- Database architecture and features
- Connecting to WATCOM SQL from PowerBuilder
- The PowerBuilder System tables
- Data types
- SQL extensions
- Locking
- Backup and recovery

Note: This chapter discusses the database architecture and features of the WATCOM SQL version 3.2b only. Although most of the material in this chapter is true for both versions of WATCOM SQL (version 3.2b and 4), refer to Powersoft documentation for specific information on WATCOM SQL version 4.

DATABASE ARCHITECTURE AND FEATURES

Database Architecture

The WATCOM SQL database engine runs as a single process, using a relatively small amount of system memory. A WATCOM SQL database is made up of one or more database files and a single transaction log

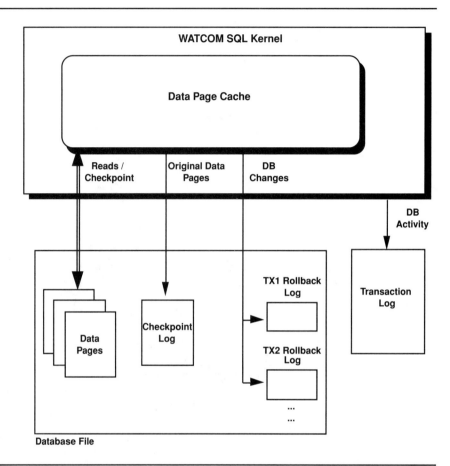

Figure 17.1 The WATCOM SQL architecture.

file. WATCOM also uses checkpoint logs and rollback logs to provide recovery from system errors. Figure 17.1 shows the WATCOM SQL architecture.

WATCOM SQL reads data in the form of pages from a database file into the data page cache in memory. When a particular data page is changed, the original page is first copied to the checkpoint log. For performance reasons, updated pages are not immediately copied back to the database file but remain in memory in the data page cache.

Data pages are copied to disk when either the data page cache becomes full or a checkpoint occurs. A checkpoint occurs in the following instances:

- A **Checkpoint** command is issued explicitly.
- The server is idle for a long enough period of time to write all updated data pages to disk.
- A transaction is committed and no transaction log is being used.
- The database engine is shut down.
- The amount of time since the last checkpoint is greater than the value contained in the CHECKPOINT_TIME configuration parameter.
- The estimated time to perform a recovery is greater than the value in the RECOVERY_TIME configuration parameter.

When a checkpoint occurs, all updated pages in the page cache are copied to disk and the checkpoint log is cleared.

WATCOM SQL maintains a rollback log for each transaction. This log contains any changes to the database made in the given transaction. Rollback logs are used only for recovery purposes.

Each WATCOM SQL database can also have a transaction log. The transaction log maintains information for all activity performed against a database. Without a transaction log, a checkpoint is issued every time a **Commit** command is executed. This slows performance because the updated data pages are copied to disk after each transaction. It is recommended that a transaction log be used for both performance and recovery purposes. The transaction log is discussed further in the Backup and Recovery section at the end of this chapter.

The WATCOM SQL Optimizer

WATCOM SQL uses a cost-based query optimizer to improve performance of database queries. The optimizer attempts to pick the best execution path for a query based on a guess of the percentage of rows returned using different operators. For example, WATCOM SQL might assume that the following operators return the percentage of rows shown in Table 17.1.

Table 17.1   Operators and Percentage of Rows Returned

Operator	% Rows Returned
=	5
<>	95
<, <=, >, >=	25

Each of the other operators, such as, LIKE, BETWEEN, and EX-ISTS, also has arbitrary values for the estimated percentage of rows returned from a query.

When a query is executed, estimates for each possible execution path are derived and the quickest estimated execution path is used. The estimates are based on such things as the size of the tables, indexes, and the query's Where clause.

Developers can include their own estimate within a query by putting the criteria in parenthesis and adding the estimated percentage of rows returned to the Where clause. For example, if it is estimated that sales commissions over $10,000 occur only in 3 percent of sales (rather than the default estimate of 25 percent), the developer could write the SELECT statement like this.

```
SELECT cust_id, sales_date
FROM sales
WHERE ( commission >= 10000, 3);
```

This capability provides developers a way to override the default estimates of WATCOM SQL and choose a more efficient query execution path.

Triggers and Stored Procedures

Version 3.2b of WATCOM SQL does not support triggers and stored procedures, although they are supported in version 4.

Database Security

WATCOM SQL allows the creation of users and groups, each of which can have either CONNECT, RESOURCE, or DBA privileges. CON-NECT privilege is the lowest level of rights and only allows users/groups to connect to the database and perform data manipulation language (DML) commands, if they have that privilege also. RESOURCE privilege allows users/groups to create tables and views. DBA privilege is the highest level of rights and allows users/groups to do anything with the database.

Like other databases, SELECT, INSERT, UPDATE, and DELETE privileges can be granted to users/groups to allow various DML commands to be performed against a table or view. UPDATE privilege can be given to the entire table or only to specific columns within a table. WATCOM SQL also allows WITH GRANT OPTION to be specified, to allow users/groups to grant the same privilege to other users. For example, to grant user BMarley the UPDATE privilege to the Songs table and allow him to give other users the privilege to update the Songs table, the grant command would look like:

```
GRANT UPDATE ON songs to BMARLEY
WITH GRANT OPTION;
```

Database privileges can be revoked using the **Revoke** command.

CONNECTING TO WATCOM SQL FROM POWERBUILDER

Creating a Data Source

Connecting to a WATCOM SQL database from PowerBuilder first requires the configuration of a WATCOM SQL ODBC data source. This can be done from the Database painter by selecting the Configure ODBC... option from the File menu. This displays the Configure ODBC window, which looks like the one in Figure 17.2.

To create a new WATCOM SQL database, the developer clicks the **Create...** button. This displays the WATCOM SQL ODBC Configuration window, as shown in Figure 17.3.

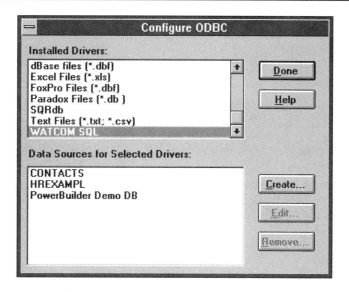

Figure 17.2   The Configure ODBC window.

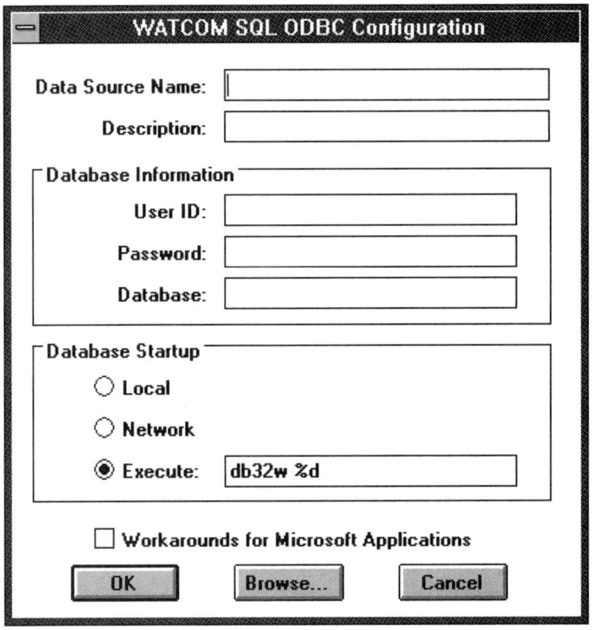

Figure 17.3   The WATCOM SQL Configuration window.

The fields on the screen are:

Field	*Description*
Data Source Name	A short name of the data source. This value becomes the name of the database profile.
Description	A description of the data source [optional].
User ID	Database User ID [optional].
Password	Database Password [optional].
Database	The file name of the data source. This should be the fully qualified name of the data source file (e.g., C:\PB3\MYNEWDB.DB).

The Database Startup group box has three options for starting a WATCOM SQL database: Local, Network, and Execute. The default option of Execute with the value db32w %d should be suitable for most users. However, some hard drives do not allow WATCOM SQL to use its default fast I/O routines. To determine if this situation exists, start the database. If the DOS prompt appears and the system must be rebooted, this is most likely the problem. To correct the problem, change the value to db32w -d %d. This option uses DOS I/O instead of the WATCOM SQL fast I/O.

Connecting to the Data Source

When the data source has been created, the user can connect from both the development environment and from within an application. To connect from the development environment, the developer either sets the correct attributes in the PowerBuilder preferences or creates a database profile. Database profiles should be created when switching between different data sources. This prevents the developer from having to enter connection information every time the data source is changed. To create a database profile, the developer selects the Setup... option from the Connect option of the File menu, as shown in Figure 17.4.

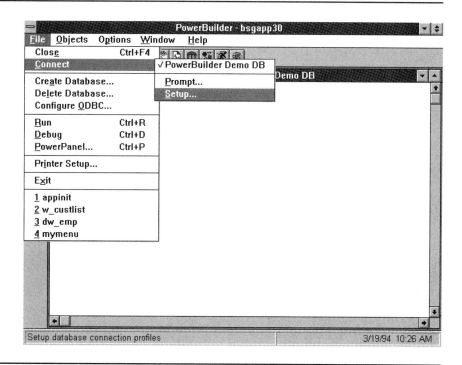

Figure 17.4   To create a database profile, select the Setup . . . option.

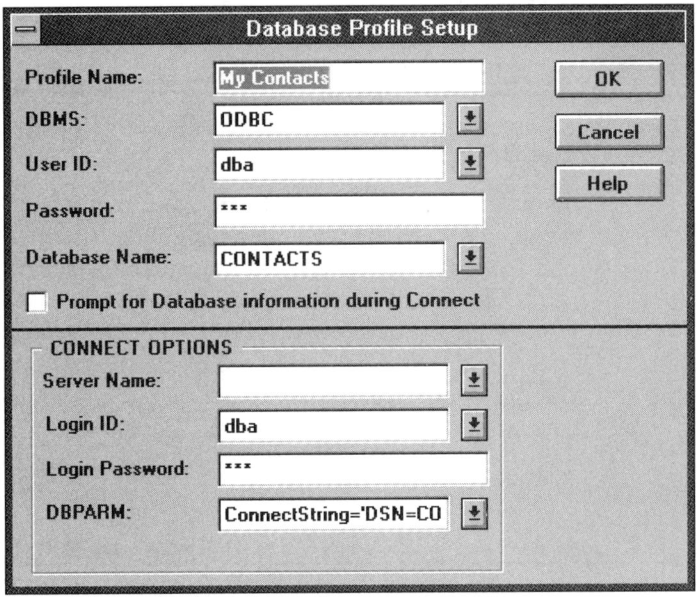

Figure 17.5   The Database Profile Setup window.

This displays the Database Profile window, from which a profile can be created or modified. To create a new profile for the data source CONTACTS.DB, the developer would complete the Database Profile Setup window as shown in Figure 17.5.

This creates a profile, which is shown in the Connect list in the Database painter (see Figure 17.6).

Switching between data sources can now be done by simply selecting a menu option. Note that database profiles can be established for any data source, not just WATCOM SQL or ODBC data sources.

To connect from an application, a transaction object needs to be created (unless using SQLCA). The attributes of the transaction object should be set according to those in Table 17.2.

Note: If the ODBC SQL driver CONNECT call is supported, PowerBuilder uses the value in DBParm to connect to the database. Otherwise it uses the DSN value of the connect string along with the LogID and LogPassword values to connect using the ODBC SQL CONNECT call.

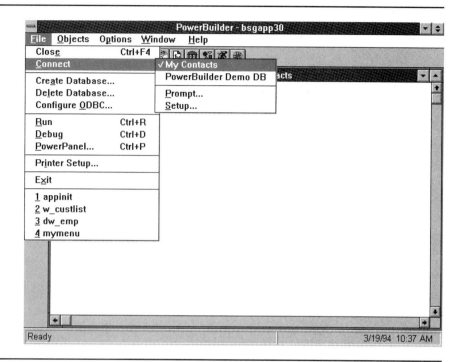

Figure 17.6   Profile in the <u>C</u>onnect list in the Database pointer.

Table 17.2   Transaction Objects Attributes and their Values

Attribute	Value
Vendor	ODBC
DBMS	ODBC
LogID	Database Login ID
UserID	Database User ID
AutoCommit	True—Updates cannot be rolled back
	False (default)—Updates can be rolled back (if the DBMS supports transaction processing)
LogPassword	Database Login Password

Lock	Lock Value:
	    RU—uncommitted read
	    RC—committed read
	    RR—repeatable read
	    TS—serializable transactions
	    TV—transaction versioning

Table 17.2   (*continued*)

Attribute	Value
DBParm	ConnectString = 'DSN = ODBC datasource name, UID = userID, PWD = password, any other required datasource-specific parameters'

When using ODBC, parameters can be set in DBParm to specify the following.

Asynchronous Operation This allows the setting of asynchronous operation. Although most ODBC data sources do not allow asynchronous operation, PowerBuilder does allow it. To change from the default of synchronous operation to asynchronous operation, the developer adds the following to the DBParm parameter of the transaction object:

```
transobj.DBParm="Async = 1"
```

When using asynchronous operation, PowerBuilder waits for an ODBC driver response to be set using the dbgettime parameter. For example, to set the operation mode to asynchronous and the wait time from the default time of 0 to 10 seconds, the developer adds the following to the DBParm parameter of the transaction object:

```
transobj.DBParm="Async=1,dbgettime=10"
```

Identifier Delimiters in SQL Syntax This allows the delimit identifiers feature to be turned on/off. To change from the default value of Yes to No, the developer adds the following to the DBParm parameter of the transaction object:

```
transobj.DBParm="delimitidentifiers=No"
```

This parameter would be used when importing SQL into PowerBuilder objects, for example, to obviate the need to use delimiters.

Cursor Scrolling and Locking Options This allows the setting of cursor scrolling and locking options for those databases that support these features. The options available for scrolling are:

Forward—The cursor acts as a forward-only cursor.

Keyset—The ODBC driver keeps the key for every row retrieved.

Dynamic—The cursor is keyset-driven to a certain point, after which it is dynamic.

The locking options are:

Lock—The cursor uses intent-to-update locks.

Opt—The cursor uses optimistic concurrency control, comparing timestamps.

Opt Value—The cursor uses optimistic concurrency control, comparing values.

To set the scrolling option to Forward and locking option to Opt, for example, the developer would add the following to the DBParm parameter of the transaction object:

```
transobj.DBParm="CursorScroll='Forward', CursorLock='Opt'"
```

Tables Displayed in the Database Painter This allows the developer to restrict the list of tables displayed in the Database painter. This value, which is used only in the development environment, is set using the TableCriteria attribute. The TableCriteria attribute can be used to restrict the table list based on table name, owner, and/or table qualifier criteria. For example, to restrict the list of tables to those beginning with EMP and owned by user DRM, the developer would set TableCriteria as follows:

```
TableCriteria = 'EMP%, DRM'
```

Note: To keep the table list from displaying altogether, set the TableDir attribute to 0.

The PowerBuilder Catalog Owner This allows the developer to set the owner of the PowerBuilder catalog tables. Setting this value overrides what is in the PBODB040.INI file. This value is set using the PBCatalogOwner attribute. For example, to set the catalog owner to DRM, the developer would add the following to the DBParm parameter of the transaction object:

```
transobj.DBParm-"PBCatalogOwner='DRM'"
```

So, to set the attributes of the SQLCA transaction object to connect to a WATCOM SQL data source named Mydata with the User ID "syslogin" and the password "bigdog", the developer executes the following script:

```
SQLCA.DBMS = "ODBC"
SQLCA.LogID = "syslogin"
SQLCA.LogPass = "bigdog"
SQLCA.UserID = "sysusr"
SQLCA.DBParm = "ConnectString = 'DSN=mydata, UID=sysusr, PWD = bigdog'"
```

This sets up SQLCA with all the data necessary to connect a WATCOM SQL data source. When this has been done, each DataWindow should be set to use SQLCA by calling the **SetTrans( )** or **SetTransObject( )** functions.

THE POWERBUILDER SYSTEM TABLES

The following tables listed in Table 17.3 are used by PowerBuilder to store extended table and column information. These tables are created the first time someone connects to the database from the PowerBuilder Database painter. Data stored in these tables is used by the DataWindow painter when referencing a table or view in the SELECT statement of a DataWindow.

Table 17.3   PowerBuilder Tables

Information	Table Name	Description
Table level	PBCATTBL	Default fonts for columns in a table or view.
Column level	PBCATCOL	Formats, validation rules, headers, labels, case, initial value, and justification for particular columns.
Display format	PBCATFMT	Column formatting (output) information. Some formats are defined automatically when this table is created. The developer can create additional formats.
Validation rules	PBCATVLD	Column validation (input) information. The developer can define all the validation rules.
Edit styles	PBCATEDT	Column edit style information. The developer can define edit styles.

Note: It is important that the owner of a database be the first to connect to the database using PowerBuilder. This enables all of the users of the database to access it.

DATATYPES

WATCOM SQL supports the following datatypes:

BINARY [(size)]—Binary data of length size. Default length of 1; maximum length of 32,767.

CHAR/VARCHAR [(size)]—Character data in length *size*. Default length of 1; maximum length of 32,767.

DATE—Calendar date. Year values range from 0001 to 9999. Time value is allowed but Powersoft (Watcom) does not recommend its use (TIMESTAMP should be used instead). Fixed length of 4 bytes.

DECIMAL/NUMERIC [(precision[,scale])]—Decimal number of precision digits and scale number of digits after the decimal point. Variable length is computed as:

```
2 + int((before + 1)/2) + int((after + 1)/2)
```

where before and after are the number of significant digits before and after the decimal point. Default values of precision = 30; scale = 6.

DOUBLE—Double precision floating-point number. Fixed length of 8 bytes; values range from 2.22507385850720160e–308 to 1.79769313486231560e+308.

FLOAT/REAL—Single precision floating-point number. Fixed length of 4 bytes; values range from 1.175494351e–38 to 3.402823466e+38.

INTEGER/INT—Signed integer. Fixed length of 4 bytes; maximum value of 2,147,483,647.

LONG BINARY—Variable length binary data; maximum size of 2 gigabytes.

LONG VARCHAR—Variable length character data; maximum size of 2 gigabytes.

SMALLINT—Signed integer. Fixed length of 2 bytes; maximum value of 32,767.

TIME—Time of day, of hour, minute, second, and fraction of a second. Fixed length of 8 bytes. When using ODBC, the developer should not use Time datatypes in the Where clause of a SELECT statement because it is extremely difficult to get the intended results, that is, a match.

TIMESTAMP—Point in time containing year, month, day, hour, minute, second, and fraction of a second. Fixed length of 8 bytes.

SQL EXTENSIONS

While WATCOM SQL does conform to the ANSI SQL89 level 2 and IBM SAA standards, it does have some extensions designed to increase its power and flexibility to developers. Many of these features are defined in the ANSI SQL92 and IBM DB2 specifications. Some of these extensions are:

- Date Operations—WATCOM SQL supports the following date operations:

    date + integer—Adds a specified number of days to a date.

    date – integer—Subtracts a specified number of days from a date.

    date – date—Returns the number of days between two dates.

    date + time—Creates a timestamp from a date and a time.

    (In addition, many date and time functions are supported by WATCOM SQL. Refer to the WATCOM SQL documentation for a list of these functions.)
- Automatic Joins—This allows joins to automatically occur based on foreign key relationships. This prevents developers from having to add the join to the Where clause.
- Multi-table Updates—Multiple tables can be updated with a single **Update** command. This is also true for views.
- Subqueries within a Column List—Instead of having to appear after an operator in a Where clause, a subquery can appear in the column list of a SELECT statement.
- Arbitrary Movement of a Cursor Pointer—When using cursors, the cursor position can be moved arbitrarily using the FETCH statement.
- Declarative Referential Integrity—Primary and foreign keys can be defined in CREATE TABLE and ALTER TABLE statements.
- Enhanced ALTER TABLE Statement—Datatype can be changed, columns can be added, modified, deleted, or renamed using the ALTER TABLE statement.

WATCOM SQL also supports many datatype conversions that are extensions to the ANSI SQL standard.

LOCKING

WATCOM SQL uses row-level locking to handle concurrent access by multiple database users. There are three types of locks in WATCOM SQL:

Read Locks—Read locks are used whenever a transaction reads a row. Because read locks are nonexclusive, multiple transactions can have Read locks on the same row. Read locks cannot be put on rows write-locked by another transaction, and Write locks cannot be put on rows read-locked by another transaction.

Write Locks—Write locks are used whenever a row is inserted, updated, or deleted. Because Write locks are exclusive, no other transaction can put a Write lock on a row that is read- or write-locked by another transaction.

Phantom Locks—Phantom locks are Read locks acquired by transactions with an isolation level of 3. Isolation levels are discussed in the next section.

Isolation Levels

Isolation levels refer to the degree that operations in one transaction are visible to other concurrent transactions. Isolation levels are used to handle the three types of inconsistencies that can occur when a database is accessed by multiple users:

Dirty Reads—Dirty reads refer to a transaction reading a row after another transaction has modified the row, but before the row has been committed. If the data is later rolled back, a dirty read has occurred.

Nonrepeatable Reads—Nonrepeatable reads occur when a transaction reads a row that is later modified and committed by another transaction. Reading the row again returns the updated row rather than the original row.

Phantom Rows—Phantom rows occur when a transaction reads a set of rows that is later modified and committed by another transaction. Retrieving the set of rows again returns a different result set.

WATCOM SQL supports four isolation levels, numbered 0 to 3:

- **Level 0**—Allows dirty reads, nonrepeatable reads, and phantom rows to occur.
- **Level 1**—Only allows nonrepeatable reads and phantom rows to occur.
- **Level 2**—Only allows phantom rows to occur.
- **Level 3**—Does not allow dirty reads, nonrepeatable reads, or phantom rows to occur.

The isolation level that should be used depends on the type of transactions occurring against a database. For highly concurrent applications in which rows are retrieved for a long period of time, a lower isolation level is best. This allows other transactions to access the same rows. For applications with little concurrency that do not "hold" rows for a long period of time, a higher isolation level can be used.

For ODBC data sources, the isolation level can be set using the Lock parameter of the transaction object.

BACKUP AND RECOVERY

Backup

WATCOM SQL provides utilities for doing either a full database or an incremental backup. Full database backups involve backing up only the database file(s); incremental backups involve an initial backup of the database file(s), backing up only the transaction logs thereafter.

A recommended approach to backups is to back up the database file(s) weekly and the transaction log daily, as shown in Figure 17.7.

If a large amount of database activity results in a large transaction log file, full database backups may be needed more frequently.

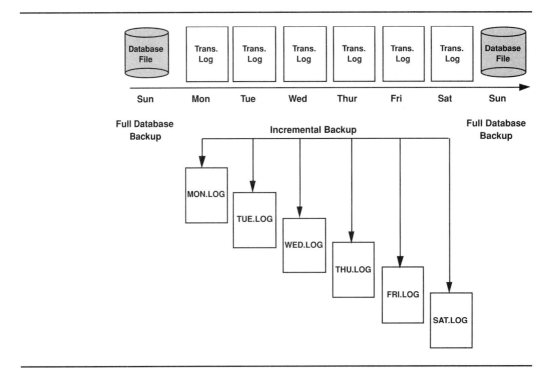

Figure 17.7   Backup of database file weekly and transaction log daily.

Note: It is a good idea to check the database file(s) for corruption using the DBVALIDW utility before backing up the database.

To back up the database, the DBBACKW utility is run:

```
DBBACKW [flags]directory
```

For example, to back up the running database CONTACTS to the user's root directory, DBBACKW is run as follows:

```
DBBACKW -c dba,sql C:\
```

If the database is not running, the backup command is:

```
DBBACKW -c dba,sql,C:\PB3\CONTACTS -s "db32w %d" C:\
```

Notice that the database name must be given with the user ID and password in the -c switch. This value is substituted for the %d parameter in the **db32w** command used to start the database. This command is used to start the database, make a backup, and shut down the database. The results are displayed in a manner similar to that in Figure 17.8.

When doing incremental backups, only the transaction log needs to be backed up. This can be done by adding the -t switch to the DBBACKW command. To back up only the log file, for example, to back up the transaction log for the running database CONTACTS to the user's root directory, DBBACKW is run as follows:

```
DBBACKW.EXE -c dba,sql -t C:\
```

If the database is not running, the backup command is:

```
DBBACKW -c dba,sql,C:\PB3\CONTACTS -s "db32w %d" -t C:\
```

After the log file has been backed up, it can be deleted. This helps control its size. A transaction log file can be erased using the DBERASE utility.

When recovering a database that has been backed up incrementally, the database file must be restored first, followed by each transaction log **in the correct order**. For more information on the options available for the DBBACKW utility, refer to WATCOM SQL documentation.

To ensure that all transactions and data are backed up, it is recommended that backups be done when the database is offline. Online backups can also be done using the DBBACKW utility. Using DBBACKW when a database is offline is equivalent to doing a file copy of the database file(s).

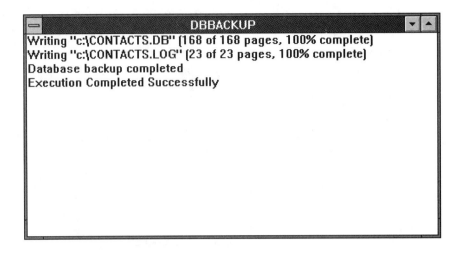

Figure 17.8   The results of using the **DBBACKW** command.

At least two backups of a database should be kept at all times. This allows for recovery when a system failure occurs while doing a backup. Backup files can be kept on any storage media, including floppy disks, tape, or another hard drive. If network backups are done on a regular basis, backups can be stored on a network drive. This is a good practice because it ensures that the files are being backed up and one group (e.g., LAN Administrator) keeps control of the files. It is also good practice to store backups at an offsite location in case of such disasters as fire and flood.

Recovery

The method used for WATCOM SQL database recovery depends on the type of error that has occurred. System failures, such as power outages, in which the database and transaction files are still intact, are corrected automatically by WATCOM SQL when the database is restarted. In this case, all committed transactions are intact and any pending transactions are rolled back. WATCOM SQL's automatic recovery involves three steps:

1. Using the checkpoint log to restore all pages to the most recent checkpoint.
2. Using the transaction log to apply any pending changes after the

last checkpoint. This step is executed only when using a transaction log.

3. Using the rollback log to roll back any uncommitted transactions.

In situations in which media failure has occurred or a file is corrupted, the recovery action to take depends on which files need to be recovered. If, for example, both the database and transaction log files are no longer usable, the following steps must be taken to completely restore the database:

1. Restore the database file(s) from the most recent full database backup.
2. Restore, in the correct order, each transaction log created after the most recent database backup was made. To apply the transaction log to the database, start the database with the -a switch. For example, to restore transaction logs MON.LOG, TUE.LOG, and the current transaction log CONTACTS.LOG against the database CONTACTS, the following commands would be executed:

```
db32w CONTACTS.DB -a MON.LOG
db32w CONTACTS.DB -a TUE.LOG
db32w CONTACTS.DB -a CONTACTS.LOG
```

3. Start the database.

If the transaction log is usable, but the database file(s) is not, the following steps should be taken:

1. Backup the transaction log.
2. Restore the database file(s) from the most recent full database backup.
3. Restore, in the correct order, each transaction log created after the most recent database backup was made. To apply the transaction log to the database, start the database with the -a switch. For example, to restore transaction logs MON.LOG, TUE.LOG, and the current transaction log CONTACTS.LOG against the database CONTACTS, the following commands would be executed:

```
db32w CONTACTS.DB -a MON.LOG
db32w CONTACTS.DB -a TUE.LOG
db32w CONTACTS.DB -a CONTACTS.LOG
```

4. Start the database.

Notice that the only difference in recovering from the loss of a database file as opposed to the loss of both a database file and the transaction log is that if the log exists, it should be backed up first. This needs to be done because the transaction log is the only existing record of any database changes.

If the database files are usable, but the transaction log is not, do the following:

1. Backup the database file.
2. Start the database with the -f switch. This starts the database without a transaction log.

```
db32w CONTACTS.DB -f
```

This creates a new transaction log.

It is best to keep database files and transaction log files on separate devices, if possible. If there is more than one disk controller, keeping database and log files on disks controlled by different controllers can reduce problems. Disk mirroring should also be used, if possible, to provide a second copy of files in the case of media failure.

As previously mentioned in the Database Architecture section, WATCOM SQL uses three different type of logs: the checkpoint log, the rollback log, and the transaction log. Each log is used to provide a different level of recovery.

CHAPTER 18

Other Databases

PowerBuilder provides connectivity to a variety of databases. Combining native database interfaces with ODBC (see Chapter 16) makes PowerBuilder able to communicate with just about any database on the market today. These databases range from small Xbase systems to large server database systems. This chapter focuses on three of the more popular server databases:

- Oracle
- SQL Server (Microsoft and Sybase)
- Informix

These databases were chosen over the many others simply because of their large market share.

While it is beyond the scope of this book to discuss the many features of each of these databases, this chapter focuses specifically on the areas relevant to a PowerBuilder developer. These areas include:

- Database architecture and features
- Connecting from PowerBuilder
- The PowerBuilder System tables
- Datatypes

ORACLE

PowerBuilder supports both Oracle version 6 and 7. This section discusses Oracle7 only. (specifically version 7.0)

Database Architecture and Features

Database Architecture   Oracle7 employs a multiprocess architecture comprised of memory structures, system and user processes, and disk structures. The system global area (SGA) is a shared memory area containing data and control information for a single Oracle instance. An Oracle instance is defined as the SGA plus the set of Oracle background processes discussed later in this section. Figure 18.1 illustrates the Oracle7 architecture.

There are two types of processes in an Oracle instance—user processes and system processes. User processes, which are spawned from application programs such as PowerBuilder, communicate with a server

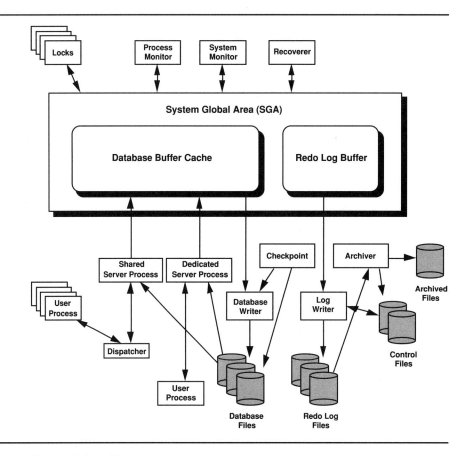

Figure 18.1   The Oracle7 architecture. *(This figure is reprinted with premission from the Oracle7™ Server Concepts Manual.)*

process through the Oracle program interface. System processes are responsible for the overall operation of the database. System processes are divided into server processes and background processes.

Server processes are created by Oracle to handle requests from user processes. Server processes may either be dedicated or shared. Dedicated server processes operate in a one-to-one relationship with a user process; shared server processes are used in a multithreaded architecture to provide a set of server processes available to be shared among all user processes. Shared server processes can communicate directly with user process or can use the dispatcher process to communicate indirectly with a user process.

The Oracle7 background processes are a set of system processes used for such tasks as disk I/O and user process cleanup. The background processes are:

- **Database Writer (DBWR)**—Writes modified data pages from the SGA's Database Buffer Cache to disk.
- **Log Writer (LGWR)**—Writes pages from the SGA's Redo Log Buffer to disk.
- **Checkpoint (CKPT)**—An optional process that signals the DBWR process when a checkpoint occurs and writes a checkpoint record to all data files and control files. If CKPT is not used, LGWR handles this task.
- **Recoverer (RECO)**—Resolves pending distributed transactions.
- **System Monitor (SMON)**—Performs instance recovery.
- **Process Monitor (PMON)**—Performs user-process recovery.
- **Archiver (ARCH)**—Archives Redo log files.
- **Locks (LCKn)**—Handles interinstance locking in parallel server systems. n ranges from 0 to 9.
- **Dispatcher (Dnnn)**—Routes user-process requests to a shared server process in a multithreaded architecture.

During processing, database pages are read from disk into the Database Buffer Cache of the SGA. As the data changes, the original data is copied into rollback segment records in the SGA, and the Oracle server process for the current user process writes the activity to the Redo log buffer.

Meanwhile, the DBWR and LGWR are periodically copying data from the Database Cache Buffer and Redo Log Buffers to disk. This process continues until either a COMMIT or ROLLBACK is executed for the current transaction. When a COMMIT is issued, the following occurs:

- A system change number (SCN) is generated for the transaction.
- LGWR copies data from the Redo Log Buffers into a Redo log file.

The SCN is also written, indicating that the transaction has been committed.
- All locks on the affected rows are released.
- The transaction is marked complete.

When a transaction is rolled back, the following occurs:

- All changes are undone using the rollback segments.
- All locks on the affected rows are released.
- The transaction is ended.

For more information, refer to the Oracle7 system documentation.

PL/SQL PL/SQL is Oracle's Procedural Language extension to SQL. All Oracle7 triggers and stored procedures are written in PL/SQL. PL/SQL combines SQL with procedural constructs such as IF THEN statements and looping. For information on PL/SQL, refer to the Oracle documentation.

SQL Optimization Oracle7 supports both cost-based and rules-based SQL optimization. A cost-based optimizer uses statistics in the data dictionary to determine the execution path of a SQL statement; a rules-based optimizer uses a predefined ranking of access paths to determine the access path of a SQL statement. A rules-based optimizer allows developers to structure a SQL statement in a way that takes advantage of a more efficient execution path.

Triggers and Stored Procedures Oracle supports the use of triggers and stored procedures. Oracle triggers can be divided into four trigger types, each of which may have three trigger events associated with it (INSERT, UPDATE, and DELETE). The four trigger types are:

1. BEFORE statement—Executes the trigger once, before the triggering statement is executed.
2. AFTER statement—Executes the trigger once, after the triggering statement has been executed.
3. BEFORE row—Executes the trigger once for each row affected by the triggering statement, before the triggering statement is executed.
4. AFTER row—Executes the trigger once for each row affected by the triggering statement, after the triggering statement is executed.

Prior to PowerBuilder 4, Oracle stored procedures could not be used as a DataWindow data source because, unlike other vendors' implementations, Oracle's stored procedures are not designed to return result sets. However, PowerBuilder 4 includes a built-in method of returning the result set of an Oracle stored procedure into a DataWindow.

PowerBuilder 4 obtains the result set by using a modified version of the Oracle7 system package DBMS_OUTPUT. This package, named PBDBMS, uses the **Put_Line( )** function to store the text of the SQL Select statement. After the complete SQL statement has been stored into a buffer, the procedure is executed. After execution, PowerBuilder will execute the package function **Get_Line( )** to retrieve the SQL statement text from the buffer and execute the query to return the results into the DataWindow.

Using this approach requires the developer to modify stored procedure code to add the **Put_Line ( )** function calls. It will also be slower than a standard SQL Select statement because of the time required to obtain the SQL statement text before actually executing the query. Also, this approach prevents the use of bind variables or cached statements and cannot be used in embedded SQL (only as a DataWindow data source). While this method is clearly not the most desirable way to obtain result sets, it does the job of providing a solution to one of the most glaring problems of past PowerBuilder/Oracle applications.

PowerBuilder 4 has also improved the support of remote stored procedures. Support for Oracle PL/SQL tables and parameters defined as input and output has been added to PowerBuilder 4. In addition, stored procedures may be referenced using Object.Function notation, which provides better performance and allows the use of overloaded procedures. This notation may be used for referencing stored procedures in other databases in addition to Oracle.

An Oracle7 stored procedure can be executed via embedded SQL from PowerBuilder in one of two methods. The first method requires the PowerBuilder DECLARE statement to assign a logical name to the stored procedure. This logical name is then used in the EXECUTE statement to execute the procedure. For example, to execute the stored procedure my_proc from PowerBuilder using the SQLCA transaction object, the script would look like this:

```
DECLARE proc1 PROCEDURE FOR my_proc USING SQLCA;

EXECUTE proc1;
```

The second method involves embedding the stored procedure call in a PL/SQL block. PL/SQL blocks start with a BEGIN statement and end with an END statement. The PL/SQL block can be copied to a PowerBuilder string variable. The string variable can then be used in the **Execute**

Immediate command to execute the stored procedure. For example, the script to call the stored procedure my_proc using a PL/SQL block would look like this:

```
string s_plsql

s_plsql = "BEGIN MY_PROC; END"
EXECUTE IMMEDIATE :s_plsql USING SQLCA;
```

Bind Variables and Statement Caching PowerBuilder 4 has also enhanced its support of bind variables and SQL statement caching. Because of Oracle's support of these two features, the changes made in PowerBuilder 4 have a direct impact on PowerBuilder/Oracle applications.

Prior to version 4, PowerBuilder supported bind variables only in the Select statement of DataWindows. Version 4 adds support for bind variables in DataWindow updates as well as embedded SQL. This not only can improve performance, but also allows PowerBuilder to use strings longer than 255 characters in an Update or Insert statement. PowerBuilder's support of bind variables applies not only to Oracle, but to any DBMS that supports bind variables. The use of bind variables can be controlled using DBParm parameter DisableBind, described later in the chapter.

Caching SQL statements can improve performance by reusing SQL statements that have already been parsed, executed, and described. PowerBuilder provides support for statement caching in both DataWindow-generated SQL and embedded SQL. When a statement is cached, it is parsed, optimized, and described once and cached for future use (the cursor and the result set description are retained). The benefits of caching are realized in situations where the same statement is executed frequently and variable binding is supported. A cached statement will only be used if the syntax of the cached statement exactly matches the new statement. The use of bind variables will greatly increase the chance of this happening. Caching will be of little value when using a DBMS that does not support bind variables. As with bind variables, PowerBuilder's support of statement caching applies not only to Oracle, but to any DBMS that supports it. The setting of the SQL cache size can be controlled using the DBParm parameter SQLCache, described later in the chapter.

Sequences A sequence is a special Oracle7 database object used to automatically generate sequential numbers. This feature is extremely useful in multi-user environments using system-generated sequential values. Multiple sequences can exist in a database. When referencing a sequence in a Select statement, developers can retrieve either the current value of the sequence or increment the sequence and use the new value. For example, the following script retrieves the current value from the sequence object employee_num:

```
SELECT employee_num.CURRVAL from dual;
```

To increment the sequence and use the new value, the script would be:

```
SELECT employee_num.NEXTVAL from dual;
```

Note: "dual" is a special Oracle table that has a single row and column and is used to guarantee a known result.

Using sequences eliminates the need for developers to programmatically determine sequential values.

SELECT FOR UPDATE In order to lock selected rows, Oracle supports the For Update clause in Select statements. All rows selected with the For Update clause are locked until a COMMIT or ROLLBACK is issued. To avoid data contention problems, rows selected with the For Update clause should only be held for short periods of time.

Connecting to Oracle from PowerBuilder

PowerBuilder communicates with an Oracle7 database using Power-Builder's PBORA040.dll in conjunction with Oracle's ORA7WIN.dll and COREWIN.dll. These DLLs then communicate with Oracle's SQL*Net, which accesses data using the underlying network protocol.

SQL*Net is designed to provide a common interface for Oracle applications so that the underlying network is transparent to the application. SQL*Net supports most of the available network and transport layer protocols, including TCP/IP and IPX/SPX among many others. Although the SQL*Net software must be obtained Oracle Corporation, the Oracle Windows API is available on the Powersoft Bulletin Board (BBS). It can be obtained by downloading ORACLE.ZIP or ORA7DLL.ZIP from the main BBS conference.

The connection from PowerBuilder to an Oracle7 database running on a UNIX server in a TCP/IP environment would look something like that in Figure 18.2.

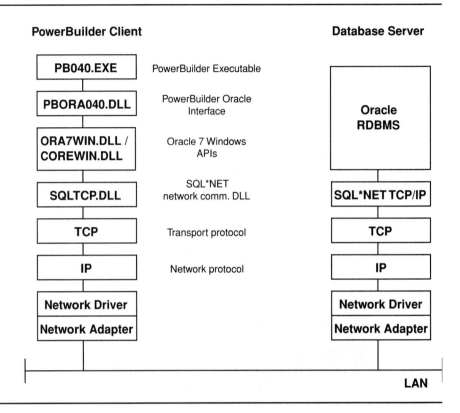

PowerBuilder Client

PB040.EXE	PowerBuilder Executable
PBORA040.DLL	PowerBuilder Oracle Interface
ORA7WIN.DLL / COREWIN.DLL	Oracle 7 Windows APIs
SQLTCP.DLL	SQL*NET network comm. DLL
TCP	Transport protocol
IP	Network protocol
Network Driver	
Network Adapter	

Database Server

Oracle RDBMS

SQL*NET TCP/IP

TCP

IP

Network Driver

Network Adapter

LAN

Figure 18.2   The connection from PowerBuilder to an Oracle7 database in a TCP/IP environment.

The same connection in an IPX/SPX environment would look like the one in Figure 18.3.

Notice that the only difference between these two examples is the underlying transport/network protocols and the SQL*Net driver used on both the client and the server.

The SQL*Net driver is dependent on the network protocol being used. The following list shows the SQL*Net DLL required for some of the more common network protocols:

Network Protocol	*SQL*Net Driver*
TCP/IP	SQLTCP.DLL
IPX/SPX	SQLSPX.DLL
Named Pipes	SQLNMP.DLL

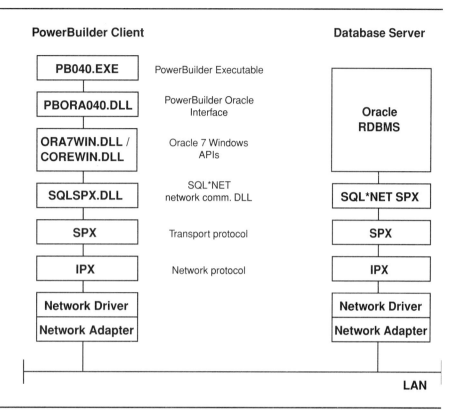

Figure 18.3   Connection from PowerBuilder to an Oracle7 database in an IPX/SPX environment.

NetBIOS	SQLNTB.DLL
Vines	SQLVIN.DLL

Many problems in connecting to Oracle occur for one of the following reasons.

The Oracle configuration is not set up correctly. Installing SQL*Net should handle setting up the client Oracle environment. However, there are some things that should be checked when a problem occurs:

• Make sure ORA7WIN.DLL and COREWIN.DLL are in the DOS path.
• The CONFIG environment variable is set to the full path of the CONFIG.ORA file. This can be done by adding the following line to

the AUTOEXEC.BAT (assuming CONFIG.ORA is in the ORAWIN directory):

```
SET CONFIG=C:\ORAWIN\CONFIG.ORA
```

• The SQL*Net driver is loaded before starting Windows.

There is an invalid connect string. The connect string specifies the network protocol, database server name, and possibly a database name. The connect string is used by the Oracle APIs to establish a database connection. The connect string has the following format:

```
@identifer:LogicalServerName:DatabaseName
```

where identifier is a one-letter abbreviation for the network protocol. Valid identifiers are:

T—TCP/IP, SQLTCP
X—Novell, SQLSPX
P—Named Pipes, SQLNMP
B—NetBIOS, SQLNTB
V—Vines, SQLVIN

LogicalServerName is the logical name of the database server, and DatabaseName is the name of the database. DatabaseName is optional; it is needed only if more than one database is running on a single server. For example, the connect string to connect to an Oracle database DB1 running on server ARUBA using IPX/SPX would be:

```
@X:ARUBA:DB1
```

Note: A default connect string can be stored in CONFIG.ORA using the LOCAL parameter. This prevents a developer from having to enter the connect string when connecting to a database.

Transaction Object Attributes The attributes necessary to use a transaction object to connect to Oracle7 are:

Attribute	*Value*
DBMS	OR7
Servername	Server Connect String

LogID   Server Login ID
LogPass   Server Login Password

Note that a database parameter (if necessary at all) is not required because it is part of the connect string. Note also that AutoCommit is not supported by Oracle.

When using Oracle7, the DBParm attribute of a transaction object can be used to:

- **Set the blocking factor**—The blocking factor refers to the number of rows fetched from a database at one time. Because of Oracle's array processing capabilities, multiple rows can be returned from the server in a single fetch. Oracle recommends a blocking factor of 100 (the default), although any value from 1 to 500 may be used. To set the blocking factor to 150, for example, the following would be added to the DBParm parameter of the transaction object:

  ```
  transobj.DBParm="BLOCK=150"
  ```

- **Specify Date, Time, and DateTime formats**—PowerBuilder can either use its own format or the Oracle format to handle these data-types. The default format is the Oracle format. To change the format of all three of these data types to the PowerBuilder format, the following would be added to the DBParm parameter of the transaction object:

  ```
  transobj.DBParm="Date=PB_date_format,
  Time=PB_time_format, DateTime=PB_datetime_format"
  ```

- **Disable Binding**—Input parameters to a Select statement are, by default, bound using the Oracle Call interface (OCI). This binding can be disabled by setting the DisableBind attribute of DBParm to 1:

  ```
  transobj.DBParm="DisableBind=1"
  ```

- **Specify Mixed Case**—Oracle can be made case-sensitive by setting the MixedCase attribute of DBParm to 1:

  ```
  transobj.DBParm="MixedCase=1"
  ```

- **Set SQL Cache Size**—To set the SQL cache size, set SQLCache to a value that is less than the maximum number of cursors that can be opened on the client. To determine this number, use the following formula.

```
transobj.DBParm="SQLCache=n"
```

where *n* is <= open_cursors - 5 - declare_cursor_space.

open–cursors—The server setting for the number of cursors that a process may have open.

5—The number of reserved cursors. Five cursors should be reserved for use by the PowerBuilder Oracle interface.

declare_cursor_space—The maximum number of cursors that you expect to open from within the PowerBuilder environment per connection.

The PowerBuilder System Tables

Table 18.1 shows the tables that are used by PowerBuilder to store extended table and column information. To ensure that these tables have the correct owner, the first user to connect to an Oracle database should log in as the Oracle user SYSTEM. Data stored in these tables is used by the DataWindow painter when referencing a table or view in the Select statement of a DataWindow.

To ensure that developers have the proper access to these tables, the first user should be the Oracle7 SYSTEM user.

Table 18.1   PowerBuilder System Tables

Information	Table Name	Description
Table level	SYSTEM.PBCATTBL	Default fonts for columns in a table or view.
Column level	SYSTEM.PBCATCOL	Formats, validation rules, headers, labels, case, initial value, and justification for particular columns.
Display format	SYSTEM.PBCATFMT	Column formatting (output) information. Some formats are defined automatically when this table is created. The developer can create additional formats.
Validation rules	SYSTEM.PBCATVLD	Column validation (input) information. The developer defines all the validation rules.
Edit styles	SYSTEM.PBCATEDT	Column edit style information. The developer can define the edit styles.

Datatypes

Oracle7 supports the following data types:

CHAR (*size*)—Fixed-length character data of length *size*. Maximum length of 255.

VARCHAR2 (*size*)—Variable-length character data of length *size*. Maximum length of 2,000 bytes.

DATE—Date and time data. Values range from January 1, 4712 B.C. to December 31, 4712 A.D. Default format of DD-MON-YY. Fixed length of 7 bytes.

NUMBER(*p,s*)—Variable-length numeric data. Maximum precision *p* and/or scale *s* is 38. Maximum length is 21 bytes.

LONG—Variable-length character data. Maximum length of 2 gigabytes.

RAW (*size*)—Variable-length raw binary data of length *size*. Maximum length of 2,000 bytes.

LONG RAW—Variable-length raw binary data. Maximum length of 2 gigabytes.

ROWID—Binary data representing a row address. Fixed length of 6 bytes.

MLSLABEL—Variable-length binary data representing OS labels. Size ranges from 2 to 5 bytes.

Of these datatypes, PowerBuilder supports all except the ROWID and MLSLABEL types. These types are used internally by Oracle. When data is selected or updated, PowerBuilder automatically converts between Oracle datatypes and corresponding PowerBuilder datatypes.

SQL SERVER

PowerBuilder provides an interface to both the Microsoft and Sybase versions of SQL Server. While these systems may differ somewhat in their features and implementation, the interface from PowerBuilder is basically the same. This section discusses the PowerBuilder interface along with some of the differences among Microsoft SQL Server for OS/2, Microsoft SQL Server for Windows NT, and Sybase SQL Server.

Database Architecture

While Oracle employs a multiprocess architecture, all versions of SQL Server use a single-process, multithreaded architecture. In this type of architecture, all database tasks, including user connections, are handled as threads of a single process. This has the advantage of being able to switch among tasks more quickly because everything is handled in a single process. Handling everything in one process also means that the architecture does not have to rely on the underlying operating system to perform many of its tasks. This architecture is generally considered more efficient than a multiprocess architecture because of the cost involved in managing multiple processes in the multiprocess architecture.

This architecture does have some disadvantages, however. First, because each user connection uses a single thread, all user requests in a single user connection must be handled by that thread. The inability to distribute the requests of a single user connection among multiple threads can slow performance. In addition, because everything is done in a single process, any problems in a thread of the process have a greater probability of impacting the DBMS engine.

The SQL Server architecture is shown in Figure 18.4.

The SQL Server kernel performs many of the tasks generally performed by the operating system—for example, task switching and caching. As previously mentioned, this makes SQL Server more efficient because it does not have to go to the operating system for these services. Each task shown in Figure 18.4 (Task 1 through n) can either be a SQL Server system task or a user database connection.

SQL Server uses multiple databases in its operation. These databases are divided into system databases and user databases. The SQL Server system databases are the Master, Model, and Temporary databases. The Master database is used to maintain system-related information such as logins, devices, and lock information. The Model database provides a template from which all new databases are created. Any modifications to the Model database are reflected in all databases created after the time of modification. The Temporary database is used by the system for such things as sorting or grouping a result set. The Temporary database can also be used by developers as a temporary storage location.

User databases are all non-system databases used in an application. User databases are created from the Master database and contain a subset of the system tables from the Master database.

During execution, a SQL Server user must connect to a single database. All SQL is then executed against that database. As data is requested, data is read from disk into the data cache. The date cache contains both data pages and log pages. As data changes, transactions are written to the transaction log (the Syslogs System table) for the current database. This process continues until a checkpoint occurs. A checkpoint is performed either by the server automatically, after a preset time interval has expired, or explicitly by the database owner (DBO).

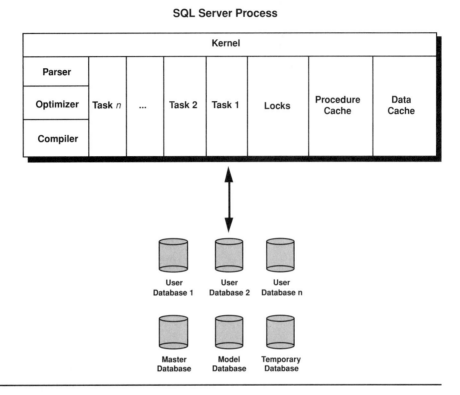

Figure 18.4   The SQL Server architecture.

When a checkpoint occurs, the following events are executed:

- All transactions updating the database are frozen.
- Transaction log pages are written to the database file.
- All modified data pages are written to the database file.
- A checkpoint record is written to the transaction log.
- All frozen transactions are allowed to continue.

For more information, refer to SQL Server system documentation.

TRANSACT-SQL TRANSACT-SQL is SQL Server's extension to SQL. TRANSACT-SQL is compatible with both ANSI SQL and IBM's SAA SQL standards. All SQL Server triggers and stored procedures are written in TRANSACT-SQL. TRANSACT-SQL combines SQL with procedural constructs such as IF THEN statements and looping.

For more information on TRANSACT-SQL, refer to SQL Server documentation.

SQL Optimization SQL Server supports only cost-based SQL optimization. A cost-based optimizer uses statistics in the data dictionary to determine the execution path of a SQL statement.

Triggers and Stored Procedures SQL Server supports the use of triggers and stored procedures. As previously mentioned, all SQL Server triggers and stored procedures are written in TRANSACT-SQL. SQL Server triggers are executed only once for each triggering statement (Insert, Update, or Delete), not once for each row affected by the triggering statement.

PowerBuilder supports SQL Server stored procedures and triggers. Executing a SQL Server stored procedure from PowerBuilder requires the PowerBuilder Declare statement to assign a logical name to the stored procedure. This logical name is then used in the Execute statement to execute the procedure. For example, to execute the stored procedure my_proc from PowerBuilder using the SQLCA transaction object, the script would look like this:

```
DECLARE proc1 PROCEDURE FOR my_proc USING SQLCA;

EXECUTE proc1;
```

If the stored procedure required two arguments, the Execute statement would look like this:

```
DECLARE proc1 PROCEDURE FOR my_proc USING SQLCA;

EXECUTE proc1 (:arg1, :arg2);
```

Result sets from a stored procedure are handled much like a cursor in that the Fetch command is used to obtain each row of the result set. Because SQL Server stored procedures return result sets, they can be used as a data source for a DataWindow object.

SQL Server NT vs. SQL Server OS/2 Because of its increased capacity and scalability over OS/2, Windows NT provides a much more robust operating platform for SQL Server. The biggest advantage in terms of scalability is NT's support of symmetric multiprocessing (SMP). Currently, OS/2 only supports a single Intel processor; Windows NT supports multiprocessor architectures made up of either Intel or RISC processors.

SQL Server NT has been designed to take advantage of the Windows NT operating system to provide a more powerful and better performing DBMS than its OS/2 counterpart. SQL Server NT supports up to 2 gigabytes of cache and over 400 terabytes of disk space. In addition, the maximum number of users is increased from 255 in SQL Server OS/2 to 32,768 in SQL Server NT.

Both SQL Server OS/2 and SQL Server NT use a multithreaded architecture. However, the way these threads are handled is different. Because OS/2 limits the number of threads a single process can use, SQL Server is forced to simulate its threads using its own nonpreemptive scheduler. These simulated threads are managed by a single "worker" thread. Because this worker thread must manage every user connection, the performance of SQL Server OS/2 decreases rapidly as the number of users increase.

SQL Server NT, on the other hand, uses a pool of worker threads, each of which can be allocated to a single user connection. If all worker threads are busy when a user request is made, a new thread is created for the new request. This continues until the maximum thread limit is reached. As the number of user requests decrease, threads are eliminated to increase available memory.

These are just some of the differences between SQL Server OS/2 and SQL Server NT. For more information, refer to the system documentation for each product.

Sybase System 10 Sybase System 10 is a set of products that includes Sybase's SQL Server. Enhancements in the System 10 SQL Server include support of cursors and declarative referential integrity.

The System 10 line of products includes:

- **Replication Server**—Used for replicating data across databases in a distributed environment.
- **Navigation Server**—Used in a symmetric multiprocessing (SMP) or massively parallel processing (MPP) environment.
- **Control Servers**—A set of products for managing and controlling a distributed environment. These products include SA Companion for administration, SQL Monitor for monitoring and tuning, Configurator for capacity planning, Audit Server for auditing, and Backup Server for backups.
- **OmniSQL Gateway**—Provides transparent access to SQL Server, Oracle, and DB2 databases.

Connecting to SQL Server from PowerBuilder

PowerBuilder communicates with all versions of SQL Server using its PBSYB040.DLL in conjunction with W3DBLIB.DLL. However, the version of W3DBLIB.DLL used to connect to a Microsoft SQL Server database is different from the version with Sybase SQL Server. The correct version of this DLL should be obtained from the appropriate vendor. For Sybase System 10, PowerBuilder 4 also adds the interface to Sybase's CTLIB. Although W3DBLIB.DLL can still be used to communicate with a Sybase database, the CTLIB interface allows the developer to take advantage of all the features provided by System 10.

PowerBuilder applications send all data requests to PowerBuilder's SQL Server interface file, PBSYB040.DLL. PBSYB040.DLL then passes the request to the SQL Server DB-Library (or CTLIB) programs located in W3DBLIB.DLL (or CTLIB). When the request passes from PowerBuilder to the W3DBLIB library, PowerBuilder waits for a response while the SQL Server programs process the request.

W3DBLIB uses the network protocol and the values defined in the WIN.INI file to determine which communication files it uses to communicate with SQL Server.

The following examples show the files used for communicating from PowerBuilder to the three different versions of SQL Server. First, the connection from PowerBuilder to the SQL Server for NT database using IPX/SPX is shown in Figure 18.5.

In this example, W3DBLIB.DLL communicates with SQL Server using Microsoft's NetLib DLL. In this case, the following lines should be added to the WIN.INI file:

```
[SQLServer]
myserver=DBMSSPX3
```

where myserver is the server name.

Figure 18.6 shows the connection from PowerBuilder to a Sybase SQL Server database running on a UNIX server in a TCP/IP environment.

In this example, W3DBLIB.DLL communicates with SQL Server using Novell's LAN Workplace TCP/IP driver, WDBNOVTC.DLL. In this case, the following lines should be added to the WIN.INI file:

```
[SQLServer]
myself=WDBNOVTC, 128.6.222.180,2025
```

where myserver is the server name, 128.6.222.180 is the IP address of the database server, and 2025 is the server listening port used by Sybase.

The communication DLL used by W3DBLIB.DLL can vary depending on which vendor's TCP/IP package is used. The DLL files for various TCP/IP vendors are:

WDBHPTCP.DLL—HP Arpa Services

WDBNOVTC.DLL—Novell LAN Workplace

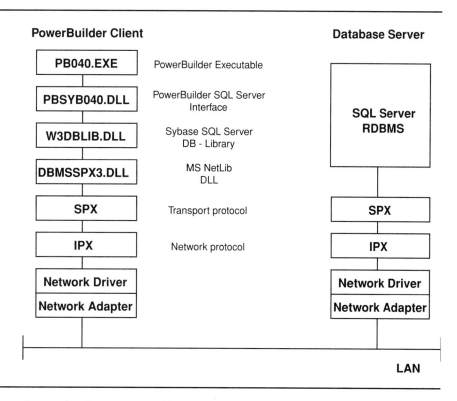

Figure 18.5   Connection from PowerBuilder to SQL Server for NT database using IPX/SPX.

WDBFTPTC.DLL—FTP Software, Inc

WDBWOLTC.DLL—Wollongong Group, Inc

Figure 18.7 shows the connection from PowerBuilder to a SQL Server for OS/2 database using Named Pipes.

In this example, W3DBLIB.DLL communicates with SQL Server using the Named Pipes protocol. In this case, the following lines should be added to the WIN.INI file:

```
[SQLServer]
DSQUERY=DBNMP3
```

Many problems involved with connecting to SQL Server have to do with mismatched communication files or bad versions of the various DLLs used for data access. It is important to know the network environ-

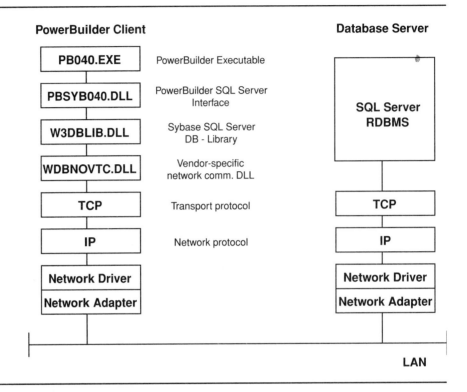

Figure 18.6   Connection from PowerBuilder to a Sybase SQL Server database in a TCP/IP environment.

ment and to make sure the correct version of the many programs involved is used.

Transaction Object Attributes The attributes necessary to use a transaction object to connect to any SQL Server database are:

Attribute	*Value*
DBMS	Sybase
Servername	Database server name
LogID	Server Login ID
LogPass	Server Login Password
Database	Name of the database to which the transaction is connecting

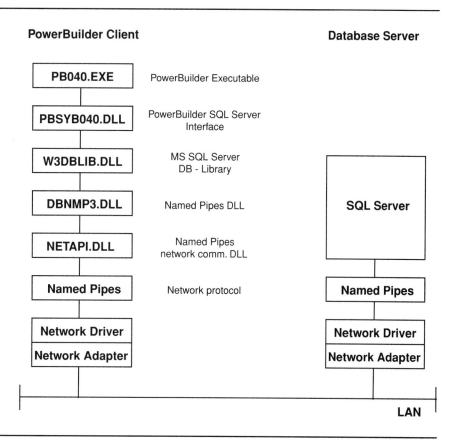

Figure 18.7   Connection from PowerBuilder to an SQL Server for OS/2 database.

AutoCommit   Commits after each Insert, Update, or Delete if
                  True (= 1)

When using SQL Server, parameters can be set in DBParm to specify
the following:

• **Release 4.2**—When using SQL Server version 4.2 or later, the release attribute should be set to 4.2. To do this, the developer adds
  the following to the DBParm parameter of the transaction object:

```
transobj.DBParm="Release='4.2'"
```

- **Asynchronous Operation**—To change from the default of synchronous operation to asynchronous operation, the developer adds the following to the DBParm parameter of the transaction object:

    ```
    transobj.DBParm="Async = 1"
    ```

    When using asynchronous operation, the time DB-Library waits for a SQL Server response can be set using the dbgettime parameter. For example, to set the operation mode to asynchronous and the wait time from the default time of 0 to 10 seconds, the developer adds the following to the DBParm parameter of the transaction object:

    ```
    transobj.DBParm="Async = 1, dbgettime = 10"
    ```

- **Cursor Scrolling and Locking Options**—The options available for scrolling are:

    Forward—The cursor acts as a forward-only cursor.

    Keyset—The ODBC driver keeps the key for every row retrieved.

    Dynamic—The cursor is keyset-driven to a certain point, after which it is dynamic.

    The locking options are:

    Lock—The cursor uses intent-to-update locks.

    Opt—The cursor uses optimistic concurrency control, comparing timestamps.

    Opt Value—The cursor uses optimistic concurrency control, comparing values.

    When setting these options, the release attribute should be set to 4.2. For example, to set the scrolling option to Forward and the locking option to Opt, the developer adds the following to the DBParm parameter of the transaction object:

    ```
    transobj.DBParm="Release='4.2', CursorScroll='Forward',
    CursorLock='Opt'"
    ```

- **AppName and Host**—The setting of an application name and host server allows the use of the SQL Server tools to view database users. To set the application name to "myapp" and the host name to "MAUI," the developer adds the following to the DBParm parameter of the transaction object:

    ```
    transobj.DBParm="Appname='myapp', Host='Maui'"
    ```

The PowerBuilder System Tables

The tables listed in Table 18.2 are used by PowerBuilder to store extended table and column information. These tables are created the first time the database owner connects to the database from the PowerBuilder Database painter. Data stored in these tables is used by the DataWindow painter when referencing a table or view in the Select statement of a DataWindow.

Table 18.2   PowerBuilder System Tables

Information	Table Name	Description
Table level	DBO.PBCATTBL	Default fonts for columns in a table or view.
Column level	DBO.PBCATCOL	Formats, validation rules, headers, labels, case, initial value, and justification for particular columns.
Display format	DBO.PBCATFMT	Column formatting (output) information. Some formats are defined automatically when this table is created. The developer can create additional formats.
Validation rules	DBO.PBCATVLD	Column validation (input) information. The developer defines all the validation rules.
Edit styles	DBO.PBCATEDT	Column edit style information. The developer can define the edit styles.

To ensure that developers have the proper access to these tables, the first user should be a user with DBA privileges.

Datatypes

Microsoft SQL Server for OS/2 supports the following datatypes:

BINARY (*size*)—Binary data of length *size*. Maximum length of 255.

VARBINARY (*size*)—Variable-length binary data of length *size*. Maximum length of 255.

CHAR (*size*)—Fixed-length character data of length *size*. Maximum length of 255.

VARCHAR (*size*)—Variable-length character data of length size. Maximum length of 255.

DATETIME—Date and time data. Fixed length of 8 bytes.

INT—Integer value ranging from -2^{31} to $2^{31} -1$ ($-2,147,438,648$ and $2,147,483,647$). Fixed length of 4 bytes.

SMALLINT—Integer value ranging from $-32,768$ to $32,767$. Fixed length of 2 bytes.

TINYINT—Positive integer value ranging from 0 to 255. Fixed length of 1 byte.

FLOAT—Floating-point number. Range and precision are machine-dependent. Fixed length of 8 bytes.

BIT—Binary digit, either 0 or 1. Fixed length of 1 byte, with 8 bit datatypes per byte.

MONEY—Money data. Fixed length of 8 bytes, with values ranging from $-922,337,203,685,447.5808$ to $922,337,203,685,447.5807$.

TEXT—Large text data. Minimum length of 2K bytes; maximum length of 2 gigabytes.

IMAGE—Large binary data. Minimum length of 2K bytes; maximum length of 2 gigabytes.

TIMESTAMP—Used exclusively to maintain timestamps for browse mode.

Both Sybase SQL Server and Microsoft SQL Server NT support the following datatypes:

BINARY (*size*)—Binary data of length *size*. Maximum length of 255.

VARBINARY (*size*)—Variable-length binary data of length *size*. Maximum length of 255.

CHAR (*size*)—Fixed-length character data of length *size*. Maximum length of 255.

VARCHAR (*size*)—Variable-length character data of length *size*. Maximum length of 255.

DATETIME—Date and time data. Fixed length of 8 bytes. Values are any date greater than January 1, 1753.

SMALLDATETIME—Date and time data. Fixed length of 4 bytes. Values are any date from January 1, 1900 to June 6, 2079.

INT—Integer value ranging from -2^{31} to $2^{31}-1$ ($-2,147,438,648$ and $2,147,483,647$). Fixed length of 4 bytes.

SMALLINT—Integer value ranging from $-32,768$ to $32,767$. Fixed length of 2 bytes.

TINYINT—Positive integer value ranging from 0 to 255. Fixed length of 1 byte.

FLOAT—Floating-point number. Range and precision are machine-dependent. Fixed length of 8 bytes.

BIT—Binary digit, either 0 or 1. Fixed length of 1 byte, with 8 bit datatypes per byte.

MONEY—Money data. Fixed length of 8 bytes, with values ranging from –922,337,203,685,447.5808 to 922,337,203,685,447.5807.

SMALLMONEY—Money data. Fixed length of 4 bytes, with values ranging from –214,748.3649 to 214,748.3648.

TEXT—Large text data. Minimum length of 2K bytes; maximum length of 2 gigabytes.

IMAGE—Large binary data. Minimum length of 2K bytes; maximum length of 2 gigabytes.

TIMESTAMP—Used exclusively to maintain timestamps for browse mode.

Of these datatypes, PowerBuilder supports all except TIMESTAMP. This type is used internally by SQL Server. When data is selected or updated, PowerBuilder automatically converts between SQL Server datatypes and corresponding PowerBuilder datatypes.

INFORMIX

PowerBuilder supports the following Informix database products:

- INFORMIX-Local v4.1
- INFORMIX-SE v4.1 and 5.x
- INFORMIX-OnLine v4.1 and 5.x

Of these products, INFORMIX-OnLine v5.x provides the greatest amount of functionality and is the best suited for high-volume OLTP applications. For these reasons, this section discusses only INFORMIX-OnLine v5.x.

Database Architecture and Features

Database Architecture Like Oracle7, the INFORMIX-OnLine architecture is a multiprocess architecture composed of a shared memory area, system and user processes, and disk structures. Currently, INFORMIX-OnLine runs on NetWare, Windows NT, and most UNIX platforms. The OnLine architecture is shown in Figure 18.8.

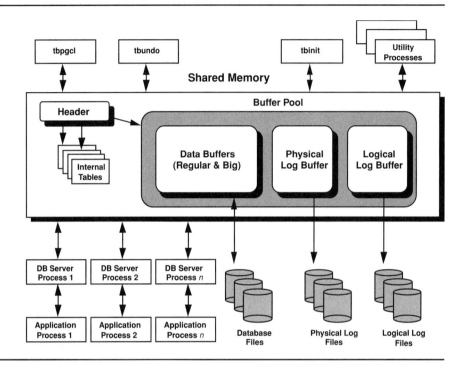

Figure 18.8   The INFORMIX-OnLine architecture.

As shown in this figure, the OnLine shared memory area is divided into three areas: the header, the OnLine internal tables, and the buffer pool. The header has pointers to all the other shared memory structures (i.e., the internal tables and buffer pool). The OnLine internal tables are used to track shared memory resources. The buffer pool is composed of four types of buffers:

Regular buffers—Used to store data pages from disk. Each regular buffer is the size of one page (page sizes are platform-dependent).

Big buffers—Used to increase the performance of large disk reads/ writes. Big buffers are the size of eight pages. One big buffer exists for every 100 regular buffers.

Physical log buffers—Used to store Before images of data pages. Physical log buffers are written to Physical log files when a checkpoint occurs.

Logical log buffers—Used to track database changes. Logical log buffers are written to Logical log files when a checkpoint occurs.

OnLine user processes are divided into three types:

Daemon processes—Used to perform system-wide tasks. The three daemon processes are:

- **tbinit**—The main OnLine daemon, responsible for disk and memory initialization.
- **tbundo**—Performs cleanup of "hanging" processes.
- **tbpgcl**—"Page cleaner" daemon. Used to write pages from shared memory to disk.

Utility processes—Used to perform utility tasks such as database monitoring and tape archiving.

Database server processes—Used to manage database access. Database server processes are used in a one-to-one relationship with parent application processes to provide a database connection. When a database connection is requested, an application process and database server process are created; the application process serves as a parent to the database server process.

During processing, database pages are read from disk into the Shared Memory buffer pool. As the data changes, the original data is copied into the Physical log buffer and the activity is written to the Logical log buffer. This process continues until a checkpoint occurs. A checkpoint is caused by any one of the following events:

- A preset time interval has expired.
- The physical log becomes 75 percent full.
- OnLine detects that the next Logical log file to become current contains the most recent checkpoint record.
- A checkpoint is forced explicitly by the DBA.

When a checkpoint occurs, the following events are executed:

- The contents of the Physical log buffer are copied to the Physical log file.
- All modified data pages in the buffer pool are written to disk.
- A checkpoint record is written to the Logical log buffer.
- The Physical log file is logically emptied (the contents can be overwritten).
- The contents of the Logical log buffer are copied to the Logical log file.

For more information, refer to the INFORMIX-OnLine system documentation.

SPL SPL is Informix's stored procedure language (SPL) extension to SQL. All OnLine stored procedures are written in SPL. SPL combines SQL with procedural constructs such as IF THEN statements and looping. For more information on SPL, refer to the Informix documentation.

SQL Optimization OnLine supports both cost-based and syntax-based SQL optimization. A cost-based optimizer uses statistics in the data dictionary to determine the execution path of a SQL statement; a syntax-based optimizer allows a developer to structure the SQL code in a way to take advantage of a faster execution path. OnLine also allows the optimization level to be set explicitly to high or low. Setting the optimization level to high (the default) causes the server to examine and select the best of all possible optimization strategies. This can slow performance because of the increased time to choose the execution path. Setting the optimization level is done using the Set Optimization statement.

Triggers and Stored Procedures OnLine supports the use of triggers and stored procedures. OnLine triggers can be executed once before or after (using the Before or After clause) the triggering statement, or once for each row affected by the triggering statement (using the For Each Row clause).

As previously mentioned, OnLine stored procedures are written in Informix's SPL. PowerBuilder supports OnLine stored procedures. Executing an OnLine stored procedure from PowerBuilder requires the PowerBuilder Declare statement to assign a logical name to the stored procedure. This logical name is then used in the Execute statement to execute the procedure. For example, to execute the stored procedure my_proc from PowerBuilder using the SQLCA transaction object, the script would look like this:

```
DECLARE proc1 PROCEDURE FOR my_proc USING SQLCA;

EXECUTE proc1;
```

If the stored procedure required two arguments, the Execute statement would look like this:

```
DECLARE proc1 PROCEDURE FOR my_proc USING SQLCA;

EXECUTE proc1 (:arg1, :arg2);
```

Result sets from a stored procedure are handled much like a cursor in that the **Fetch** command is used to obtain each row of the result set.

Because OnLine stored procedures return result sets, they can be used as a data source for a DataWindow object.

INFORMIX-OnLine Dynamic Server, v6.0 INFORMIX-OnLine Dynamic Server is Informix's latest database server product. It employs a true multithreaded architecture designed to take advantage of both single-processor and SMP systems. As mentioned earlier in this chapter, a multithreaded architecture can provide better performance than a multiprocess architecture. OnLine Dynamic Server is based on Informix's dynamic scalable architecture (DSA) and is intended to provide a scalable, high-performing parallel database architecture. For more information on the INFORMIX-OnLine Dynamic Server architecture, refer to Informix documentation.

While the architecture of OnLine Dynamic Server is different from other Informix database servers, the PowerBuilder interface is unchanged. The following sections address PowerBuilder's connectivity to all of the mentioned Informix database servers, including OnLine Dynamic Server.

Connecting to Informix From PowerBuilder

PowerBuilder communicates with an Informix OnLine database using its PBINF040.DLL in conjunction with Informix's LDLLSQLW.DLL. LDLLSQLW.DLL then communicates with Informix's I-NET driver, which is loaded as a terminate-and-stay-resident (TSR) program (rather than as a DLL). The connection from PowerBuilder to an OnLine database running on a UNIX server in a TCP/IP environment would look something like the one shown in Figure 18.9.

Because it is executed as a TSR rather than a DLL, the connection to an OnLine database is done outside of Windows. The connection occurs when I-NET is loaded. I-NET is loaded by executing the following command:

```
REMSQL -h hostname -u username -s servicename -p password
```

where hostname is the name of the host, username is the user ID, servicename is the name of the client's Informix service, and password is the user password.

Note: Although Informix requires only one environment variable, INFORMIXDIR, the following environment variables can be used to store connection parameters:

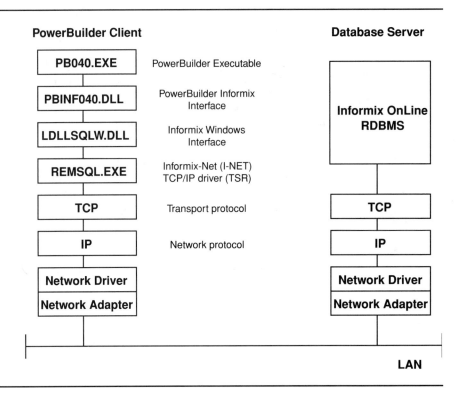

Figure 18.9   Connection from PowerBuilder to an OnLine database in a TCP/IP environment.

SQLUSER = username
SQLHOST = hostname
SQLSERVICE = servicename
SQLPASS = password

When REMSQL is executed, I-NET is loaded, unabling PowerBuilder to communicate with an OnLine database. I-NET provides the connection using one of the following network drivers:

- PC-NFS from Sun Microsystem, Inc.
- PC/TCP from FTP Software, Inc.
- Pathway Access from Wollongong Group, Inc.
- StarGROUP from AT&T.
- IPX/SPX from Novell, Inc.

The first four network drivers listed are used when TCP/IP is the network protocol; the last item is used when IPX/SPX is the network protocol.

Transaction Object Attributes The attributes necessary for a transaction object to connect to Informix OnLine are:

Attribute	*Value*
DBMS	INFORMIX
Database	Name of the database to which the transaction is connecting
LockValues	Used to set the isolation level for record locking. The valid values are: Dirty Read Committed Read Cursor Stability Repeatable Read
SQLReturnData	The serial number of the row is stored in this variable after an Insert statement executes

Note that a server name and user ID/password are not required. This is because this information has already been given when loading I-NET. Note also that AutoCommit has no effect in an Informix database.

When using Informix, the DBParm attribute of a transaction object can be used to set the Scroll parameter. A scroll cursor allows the fetching of rows from the active result set in any sequence. To specify a scroll cursor, the developer adds the following to the DBParm parameter of the transaction object:

```
transobj.DBParm="scroll="
```

The PowerBuilder System Tables

The tables listed in Table 18.3 are used by PowerBuilder to store extended table and column information. These tables are created the first time the database owner connects to the database from the PowerBuilder Database painter. Data stored in these tables is used by the DataWindow painter when referencing a table or view in the Select statement of a DataWindow.

To ensure that developers have the proper access to these tables, the first user to access them should have DBA privileges.

Table 18.3   PowerBuilder System Tables

Information	Table Name	Description
Table level	INFORMIX.PBCATTBL	Default fonts for columns in a table or view.
Column level	INFORMIX.PBCATCOL	Formats, validation rules, headers, labels, case, initial value, and justification for particular columns.
Display format	INFORMIX.PBCATFMT	Column formatting (output) information. Some formats are defined automatically when this table is created. The developer can create additional formats.
Validation rules	INFORMIX.PBCATVLD	Column validation (input) information. The developer defines all the validation rules.
Edit styles	INFORMIX.PBCATEDT	Column edit style information. The developer can define the edit styles.

Datatypes

Informix OnLine supports the following datatypes:

BYTE—Binary data. Theoretical limit of 2^{31} bytes. The actual limit is determined by available disk storage.

CHARACTER/CHAR (*size*)—Fixed-length character data of length *size*. Maximum length of 32,767.

VARCHAR (*m,r*)—Variable-length character data with a maximum length of *m*. *r* is the minimum amount of space reserved for the column.

DATE—Calendar date stored as an integer equal to the number of days since 12/31/1899. Fixed length of 4 bytes.

DATETIME—Calendar date and time of day. The number of bytes required for storage can be determined using the following formula:

```
total # of digits for all fields/2 + 1
```

DECIMAL/DEC/NUMERIC (*p,s*)—Decimal floating-point number up to a maximum of 32 significant digits, where *p* is the precision and *s* is the scale. The number of bytes required for storage can be determined using the following formula:

```
precision/2 + 1
```

INTEGER/INT—Integer value ranging from -2^{31} to $2^{31}-1$ ($-2,147,483,647$ to $2,147,483,647$). Fixed length of 4 bytes.

INTERVAL—Span of time value in either a year-month format or a day-time format. The number of bytes required for storage can be determined using the following formula:

```
total # of digits for all fields/2 + 1
```

SMALLINT—Integer value ranging from $-32,767$ to $32,767$. Fixed length of 2 bytes.

FLOAT/DOUBLE PRECISION (*n*)—Double-precision floating-point number with up to 16 significant digits. The range is machine-dependent. *n* is used to specify the precision.

SMALLFLOAT/REAL—Single-precision floating-point number with approximately eight significant digits. The range is machine-dependent. SMALLFLOAT TYPES usually require 4 bytes.

SERIAL (*n*)—Sequential integer assigned automatically by OnLine when a row is inserted. Only one serial column is allowed per table. Maximum number is $2,147,483,647$. Fixed length of 4 bytes.

MONEY (*p,s*)—Money data. Stores fixed-point numbers up to a maximum of 32 significant digits, where *p* is the precision and *s* is the scale. The number of bytes required for storage can be determined using the following formula:

```
precision/2 + 1
```

TEXT—Large text data. Theoretical limit of 2^{31} bytes. The actual limit is determined by available disk storage.

PowerBuilder supports all the datatypes just listed. When data is selected or updated, PowerBuilder automatically converts between Informix datatypes and corresponding PowerBuilder datatypes.

PART V

Administration

CHAPTER **19**

Project Standards and Naming Conventions

Programming standards can be one of the most important parts of building and maintaining an application. They should be created and implemented before development begins. Standards allow teams of developers, even large teams, to create applications that are easily maintained. This chapter discusses the following topics:

- Programming standards
- Naming conventions
- Window type standards
- Error handling

Most programming standards are based on common sense. Still, if a project begins without them, they should be determined and retrofitted. A little perseverance in this area pays off grandly when system modification or maintenance is needed.

When creating a large mission-critical application, the creation and use of programming standards is imperative. Although not one of the most exciting aspects of application design, overlooking standards can be financially draining and time-consuming. Regardless of the conventions that are used, standards should be enforced and documented. Two types of standards are needed—programming standards and naming conventions. Both client and server standards should be addressed.

PROGRAMMING STANDARDS

In a multideveloper environment, programming standards become the thread of similarity among the developers. Standards also provide new developers an easier transition into the development environment and thus increase project team productivity. In the PowerBuilder environment, programming standards should address the following areas:

- Hard-coded references
- Code modularization
- Encapsulation
- Comments
- Function visibility

Each of these types of standards is discussed in the following sections.

Hard-coded References

One of the most important programming standards is to avoid the use of hard-coded references. In order to maximize the use of the object-oriented principles of polymorphism and overloading, the developer should code with generic references. The PowerBuilder keywords used to reference objects generically are given in Table 19.1.

Using the references of This, Parent, and ParentWindow, the developer can create reusable generic script in windows, menus, and user objects. These references allow the script to determine and use the correct object, even if the name of the object changes.

This The generic reference of This is most commonly used by Power-Builder to create an implied reference for object attributes. This can be illustrated by exporting a simple window, sheet1, from an MDI application and viewing the Create and Destroy sections of the resulting .SRW file. The example illustrates how PowerBuilder creates all of the objects (e.g., command buttons, radiobuttons) by referring to each of the window's controls as This.controlname instead of using the hard-coded window name (sheet1).

Table 19.1 PowerBuilder Keywords to Reference Objects

Convention	Type of Script	Object Type
This	Window, User Object, Control	Reference that indicates the object or control
Parent	MenuItem, Window, User Object	Object that contains the control
ParentWindow	MenuItem	Window that is associated with the MenuItem at runtime.

```
on sheet1.create
if this.MenuName = "m_stdmdi" then this.MenuID = create m_stdmdi
this.cb_1=create cb_1
this.rb_2=create rb_2
this.rb_1=create rb_1
this.sle_1=create sle_1
this.st_1=create st_1
this.gb_1=create gb_1
this.Control[]={ this.cb_1,&
this.rb_2,&
this.rb_1,&
this.sle_1,&
this.st_1,&
this.gb_1}
end on


on sheet1.destroy
if IsValid(MenuID) then destroy(MenuID)
destroy(this.cb_1)
destroy(this.rb_2)
destroy(this.rb_1)
destroy(this.sle_1)
destroy(this.st_1)
destroy(this.gb_1)
end on
```

Another example using This in a script is shown in the window function **titlebar( )**. This function sets the specific string Windowtitle to the name of the person in the instance variables *i_first_name*, *i_middle_name*, and *i_last_name*. The window function **titlebar( )** can be placed in a virtual class window for use by descendant windows. Because the script uses This as a window reference, it allows the variable *windowtitle* to be used with any window.

```
/* Set the title bar with some descriptive information about this
customer.*/

this.windowtitle = i_first_name + " " + i_middle_initial + " " &
+ i_last_name
return true
```

Parent The keyword Parent can be used by window controls, user objects, or menu items. Using Parent in the script of a window control refers to the window that contains the control. Using Parent in the script of a user object control refers to the user object. Using Parent with menu items refers to the menu item for which the script is written.

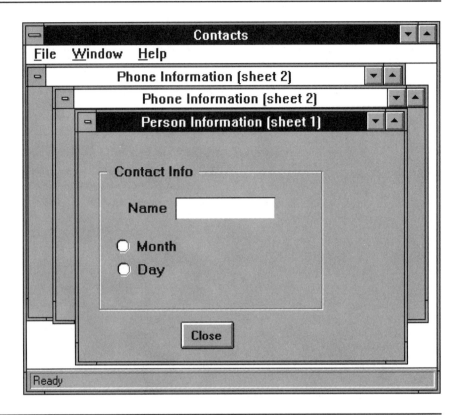

Figure 19.1 How parent can be used in a window control.

Figure 19.1 shows how Parent can be used in a window control. This example uses a command button, **cb_close**, to close the active sheet in an MDI application. Using Parent allows the same command button to be used for closing any of the MDI sheets:

```
Close(Parent)
```

Now take this example a step further. Assume **cb_close** is a standard user object rather than a window control. Replacing the clicked event of the user object with the **hide( )** function causes the button itself to be hidden, rather than the window that has the user object control:

```
Parent.Hide( )
```

Because Parent is being used in the script of a user object control, it hides the related object **(cb_close)**, not the related window (sheet1).

The third use of Parent is within MenuItem scripts. In this case, Parent refers to the MenuItem for which the script is written. An example is a script to disable the menu item File in a sub-MenuItem script Disable:

```
Parent.Disable( )
```

The menu would look like the one in Figure 19.2.

ParentWindow The keyword ParentWindow is not used as frequently as Parent or This, but it can be used in MenuItem scripts. For example, ParentWindow is used in the following script of the menu item File, Close. The script closes the window that is associated with the menu at runtime. This reference allows the menu to be used with any window.

```
Close(parentWindow)
```

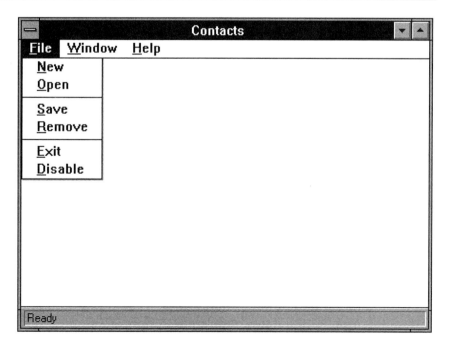

Figure 19.2 The menu when Parent is used within MenuItem scripts.

Code Modularization

Another important programming standard is modularization of code. Whenever possible, common or frequently used code should be broken into separate modules that can be used throughout the application. Modularization combined with the identification of common application functionality can yield code reusability, which results in simplified debugging and maintenance. Such application functions as displaying messages and error handling are good candidates for modularization because they are generally done throughout an application. An example of modularization follows. **Applicationinit( )**, a function executed at login time, sets a global variable to a value in an APPLICATION.INI file. This is achieved with the PowerBuilder function **ProfileString( )**. This functionality is broken into three functions in order to modularize certain code segments that may be used repeatedly in the application.

Because, in this example, **ProfileString ( )** is a function that is used throughout the application, it can be modularized by creating a new function, **appProfile( )**. **AppProfile( )** calls **ProfileString( )** and passes it the section and key values the **ProfileString( )** requires. This puts the calls to **ProfileString( )** in a single location and, because these values are not hard-coded in the call to **ProfileString( )**, provides greater flexibility. **AppProfile( )** is defined as shown in Figure 19.3.

The **appProfile** function is used to hide the name of the APPLICATION.INI file.

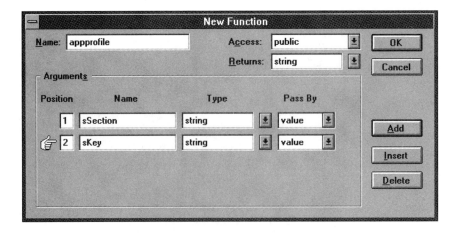

Figure 19.3 The **AppProfile( )** function definition.

```
/* Return the value associated with the argument section and key in
MYAPP.INI. If none exists, return an emptystring. */

return ProfileString("myapp.ini",sSection,sKey,"")
```

When this function is called, it takes the value from the MYAPP.INI file in the passed section and key. Assume MYAPP.INI looks like this:

```
[Servers]
dev_server=devserv
cert_server=testserv
prod_server=corpserv1

[Preferences]
ReportDir=c:\rpts\
ReportName=myrpt.txt
```

A second function, **setDBServer( )**, is created to take the value from MYAPP.INI and assign it to the global variable *g_dbServer* (see Figure 19.4). This value is used in the application to set up different transaction objects. With this code in a separate function, *g_dbServer* is set in a single place rather than having the same code in a number of places throughout the application.

```
/*Set the global variable value*/

g_dbServer = sAvalue
return g_dbServer
```

The final step in this example is to create the function **applicationinit( )** (see Figure 19.5). This function sets the global variable for the default database server name. Getting the server name from the .INI file and setting it equal to a global variable, the developer is able to set up the necessary transaction objects for connecting to either a development, certification, or production database server.

```
/*Function to initialize the global variable g_dbServer */
setPointer(hourGlass!)

/* System User value */
setDBServer(appProfile("Servers","dev_server"))

return true
```

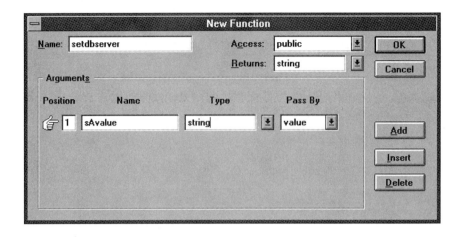

Figure 19.4   The **setDBServer( )** function definition.

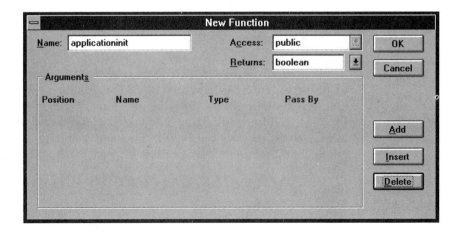

Figure 19.5   The **applicationinit( )** function.

This clearly shows how code can be modularized instead of putting it all into one larger function.

Encapsulation

Another programming technique that should be incorporated into programming standards is encapsulation (see Chapter 2). Encapsulation is used both to hide complexity from other developers and to simplify code maintenance. By encapsulating code into functions that reference nonlocal variables instead of calling them directly, changes can be made in the one function only, instead of having to change code throughout an application.

Note: Developers should avoid referencing nonlocal variables directly; a function should be called to get the value.

Comments

Many developers preach about the merits of well-commented code. Unfortunately, while frequently preached, it is often not practiced. The rules for commenting PowerScript (or any other 4GL) are no different from those for any other programming language. Developers should use a small section at the top of a script to explain the functionality of the script, noting when the code was written (and modified). If a script is complex or calls other functions, it is a good idea to briefly describe what is going on in the script. Comments should be written to help those who may have to maintain the code. They are not intended to be a narrative of the script.

PowerBuilder gives the developer the choice of using the C++ standard of the double slash //

```
// Comments
```

or the C standard of

```
/* comment */.
```

Either set of characters is acceptable to set off comments.

Function Visibility

The visibility of object-level functions in PowerScript can be controlled by designating one of the following access levels:

Access Level	*Description*
Private	Visible to window instances in the class but not descendants.
Protected	Visible to instances and descendants.
Public	Visible to any code.

The Function painter defaults the access level to public. The use of private and public access allows the developer to create truly encapsulated scripts. Tightening the access ensures that the function can never be inadvertently called from another script. The use of the public access is different from the use of a global function because the function is bound to the object and is accessible only as long as the object has been instantiated. (For a further discussion of this subject, see Chapter 8.)

NAMING CONVENTIONS

Naming conventions, which are often overlooked because they do not seem to be important, do not become an issue until they are not implemented. A lack of naming conventions causes developers to spend more of their valuable time trying to debug and maintain application code. Naming conventions should be addressed for objects, variables, datatypes, controls, and database objects.

Objects

The naming convention for objects is fairly straightforward. It mimics PowerBuilder's own naming scheme by designating the first letter(s) as the type of object that is being created as shown in Table 19.1.

Figure 19.6 shows objects in pbbook.pbl named using this convention.

A second approach is to use an application-specific three- or four-letter prefix for each object. Because the PowerBuilder Library painter shows a different icon for each type of object, this method allows the developer to see which objects are associated with each other.

```
[application abbreviation][object number] _ [type of object][type
number]
```

In Figure 19.7, all of the windows, menus, and datawindows in test.pbl are named with the application abbreviation (eprm), followed by the number of the associated object and type of DataWindow (ob), and its corresponding number.

Table 19.1   Naming Convention for Objects

Convention	Object Type
a_	Application
w_	Window
m_	Menu
u_	User Object
d_	Datawindow
st_	Structure
q_	Query
f_	Function

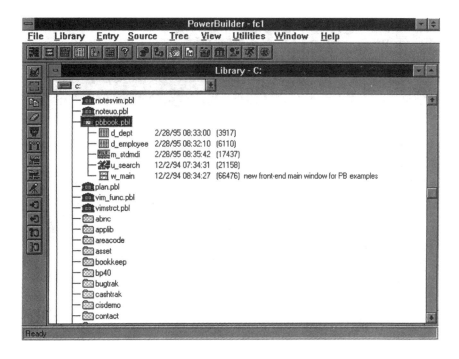

Figure 19.6   Objects in pbbook.pbl.

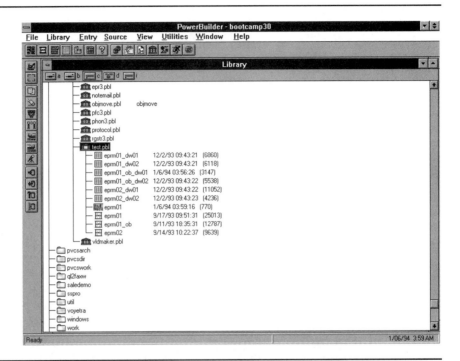

Figure 19.7   Objects named using an application-specific abbreviation.

Table 19.2   Abbreviations for Naming Variables

Convention	Object Type	Description
l_	Local	Declared in a script and exists as long as the script is being processed. No other script can access this variable.
i_	Instance	Declared at the object level and can only be accessed by a single instance of the window.
s_	Shared	Declared at the object level and can only be accessed by scripts within any instance of the object.
g_	Global	Declared at the application level and is accessed by all objects (windows, functions, menus, etc.)

Table 19.3   Abbreviations for Variable Datatypes

Convention	Object Type
_bl	Blob
_b	Boolean
_c	Character
_d	Date
_dt	DateTime
_dec	Decimal
_dbl	Double
_i	Integer
_l	Long
_r	Real
_s	String
_t	Time
_ui	UnSignedInteger
_ul	UnsignedLong

Variables

The abbreviations in Table 19.2 are widely used for naming variables.

Datatypes

The abbreviations listed in Table 19.3 are widely used to designate the datatype of a variable.

The following illustrates the combination of abbreviations used for the variable type and datatype for a variable, Var:

```
Local:
      Integer
            l_iVar
```

```
        UnsignedLong
                l_ulVar
        String
                l_sVar
Shared:
        Integer
                s_iVar
        UnsignedLong
                s_ulVar
        UnsignedInt
                s_uiVar
Instance:
        Integer
                i_iVar
        UnsignedLong
                i_ulVar
        UnsignedInt
                i_uiVar
Global:
        Integer
                g_iVar
        UnsignedLong
                g_ulVar
        UnsignedInt
                g_uiVar
```

In order to distinguish variable names from the datatype abbreviation, the use of underscores or capitalization is recommended.

Controls

PowerBuilder controls also follow a naming convention. This naming convention consists of a prefix representing the control type, followed by an underscore and the number of the control within the object. The numeric portion of the name should be changed by the developer to represent a name that has some meaning to the function of the control. The prefixes used by PowerBuilder for some of the more popular control types are shown in Table 19.4.

For example, the default names assigned to command buttons that open and close a window are cb_1 and cb_2. These names should be changed to something more descriptive such as cb_open and cb_close.

The name assigned to DataWindow controls should also be changed from dw_1 and dw_2 to something more descriptive—dw_master and dw_detail in a master/detail relationship window, for example.

Table 19.4   Control Type Prefixes

Convention	Object Type
cb_	CommandButton
pb_	PictureButton
sle_	SingleLineEdit
st_	Static Text
mle_	Multi-line Edit
lb_	List Box
dw_	DataWindow
ddlb_	DropDownListBox
em_	EditMask
rb_	RadioButton
cbx_	CheckBox

Database Objects

Some form of naming convention should be developed for database objects. Here again, the actual standard used is not as important as simply having a standard in place. A suggested approach for the naming of database objects is given in the following list.

Object	Convention
Database	[application abbreviation]
Tables	[application abbreviation]_tablename
Views	[application abbreviation]_viewname
Indexes	tablename_ndx#
Stored Procedures	sp_[application abbreviation]_spname
Insert Trigger	ins_[table_name]
Update Trigger	upd_[table_name]
Delete Trigger	del_[table_name]
Reports	rpt_[application abbreviation]_rptname

WINDOW TYPE STANDARDS

When developing an application, one of the key decisions is whether the application will adhere to Windows standards or other standards. If the application is to adhere to Windows standards, there are some window types that allow developers to create an application that is consistent with other Windows applications. Each of the PowerBuilder window types (i.e., Main, Response, Child, and Popup) has a specific use in an application. They should adhere to a set of standards depending on the type of application being created—MDI (see Chapter 4) or SDI (single-document interface).

SDI

The SDI, which interfaces with one instance of a document at a time, uses PowerBuilder Window types as follows:

Main—The main window is a standalone window that is considered to be the base of an SDI application. It is thus considered the parent window; all other windows in the application should be subordinate to it. The main window should have a title bar and a menu associated with it. It should be able to be minimized and maximized and the icon should appear in the MS Windows desktop.

Child—The child window is always subordinate to the parent window. It is closed when the associated parent window is closed. The child window is similar to the MDI sheet, with the parent as the main window. The child window usually does not have a menu, but can have a title bar. It can be minimized but displays as an icon inside the parent window.

Popup—Popup windows, although not used frequently, can have a title bar and a menu. They can be minimized and maximized and the icon appears in the MS Windows desktop.

Response—The response window is application-modal and provides the user with information. This type of window cannot be minimized and does not have a menu. The response menu can be used for messages, printing, or opening files.

Note: If a parent window is not explicitly named for a Child or Popup window, the last active Main window becomes the parent window.

MDI

The MDI application, which interfaces with multiple instances or sheets at the same time, uses PowerBuilder Window types as follows:

MDI Frame (with MicroHelp)—The MDI frame window is the base window for an MDI application. The MDI frame is the parent window for the other sheet windows, even though they are really Main window types. Because the MDI frame is the parent window, when the frame is closed all of the related sheets are closed. The MDI frame window should have a menu/toolbar associated with it and each sheet's menu passes through the frame's menu. For further explanation, see Chapter 5.

Main—The main window is used primarily in MDI as the sheet for the main frame. The sheet is always the child of the frame; it is only seen within the frame. Each of the sheet windows should have a title bar and a menu associated with it. The sheets should be able to be minimized and maximized, but are iconized within the frame window. Any open sheets are closed when the MDI frame window is closed.

Child—The child window is always subordinate to the parent window and is closed when the associated parent window is closed. In an MDI application, the sheet (main), which is the parent window, closes any child windows if the sheet closes.

Popup—In MDI applications, the use of popup windows is replaced by the functionality of the sheet (main) window.

Response—MDI applications use response windows the same way as SDI applications. The response window is application-modal and provides the user with information pertaining to a particular sheet. The response window is not usually invoked directly from the MDI frame. This type of window cannot be minimized and does not have a menu. The response menu can be used for messages, printing, or opening files.

A further discussion of MDI applications is in Chapter 4.

ERROR HANDLING

Error handling is critical in any application, and some level of error handling must exist in every application. It is the opinion of the authors that the more error-handling logic built into an application, the more solid that application will be. Detected errors may be of many different levels of severity. Actions taken when an error is encountered can range from informational messages, warning messages, or serious error messages, to doing some critical secondary processing. For example, if an application is trying to connect to a server and the server is down, the developer could either give the user a message, try a few more times, or just try to connect to another server. There are many choices a developer has for handling different error situations. A common misconception is that error handling is not necessary in all situations. This opinion is incorrect and can cause developers, end users, and support personnel many headaches if it is followed. The most important point here is that the developer should have as much error-handling code in the application as possible.

Error handling is critical in all parts of an application, but is especially important when interfacing with external pieces of an application. External pieces of an application can be database servers, file servers, other applications, external libraries, and/or application programming interfaces (APIs), for example. Following are some examples of error handling for external pieces of an application.

Database Error Handling

PowerBuilder has powerful built-in capabilities for handling errors from transaction activities. PowerBuilder has functions, events, and structures specifically for handling database errors. The PowerBuilder transaction object, through which all database communication takes place, has three error-trapping attributes. These attributes are SQLCode, SQLDBCode, and SQLErrText. The two latter attributes are useful because they store the particular database vendor's error code and message, respectively. SQLCode, on the other hand, is a PowerBuilder generic error attribute. Its value can be either 0—which yields a successful transaction, 100, which means no result set was returned from the database for that particular transaction—or –1, which means that an error occurred. To determine which error occurred, the developer can either use the vendor entries in the transaction object or use the **DBErrorCode** and **DBErrorMessage** functions that PowerBuilder provides. These functions also return vendor-specific information.

Note: The **DBErrorMessage** and **DBErrorCode** functions can only be called from the DBError event of the DataWindow control. When doing this, the developer can suppress the vendor-specific messages that get automatically displayed by setting the action code in the DBError event to 1 (by using the **SetActionCode** function).

Example: Handling Deadlocks in SQL Server In Microsoft's SQL Server for OS/2 and Sybase's SQL Server for UNIX, problems with deadlocks have occurred. The infamous database error number 1205 has frustrated many DBAs and developers. A deadlock occurs when two users each have a lock on a separate object, and each user wants to acquire an additional lock on the other user's object. When this happens, the first user is waiting for the second to let go of the lock, but the second user won't let it go until the lock on the first user's object is freed.

SQL Server detects this situation and chooses one of the users. SQL Server rolls back that user's transaction, notifies the application of this action with message number 1205, and allows the users' processes to move forward. The first user's process is canceled, and a nonfriendly and wordy message is displayed on the user's computer. The developer can trap the deadlock (1205) error number from within PowerBuilder. The developer can then choose to either display the error message, suppress the error message, or send the SQL through again. In the "dberror" event of the DataWindow, the developer should use the following logic to trap the deadlock error and resend the SQL.

```
SetActionCode(this,1)
If dbErrorCode(this) = 1205 Then
    // Code to resend the SQL
Else
    MessageBox("DB Error","Error Code="+dbErrorCode(dw_main)+&
                "~nError Message="+dbErrorMessage(dw_main))
End If
```

This is a simple, graceful, and user-friendly solution to handling a deadlock.

Dynamic Load-balancing of Database Servers Error handling can be a very powerful feature if used effectively. Dynamic load-balancing routines can be written to manage multiple databases from within Power-Builder. If multiple database servers are available to an application at startup, the system can connect the user to the one that is least busy. With good error-handling routines, if a database server fails when a user issues a query, the system can, transparently, connect the user to a different server and execute the query again.

System Error Handling

PowerBuilder has objects and events to handle system errors at runtime. If a serious error occurs when executing an application (failure loading a dynamic library for one of the application external functions, for example), the application is halted abnormally and a very unfriendly message is displayed to the user. (Windows sends the message to PowerBuilder and PowerBuilder displays it.) A way to avoid issuing an unfriendly message is to use PowerBuilder's system event and error structure to trap the system errors and do some custom processing.

Within the application object, PowerBuilder has defined a SystemError event. When an execution error occurs, PowerBuilder automatically triggers this event. If this event has a script, PowerBuilder executes the script and does not display a message box. From within the SystemError event, the developer can access the data within the message structure. The message structure includes the following information:

Number—An integer identifying the PowerBuilder error.

Text—A string containing the text of the error message.

WindowMenu—A string containing the name of the Window or Menu object in which the error occurred.

Object—A string containing the name of the object in which the error occurred. If the error occurred in a window or menu, Object will be the same as WindowMenu.

ObjectEvent—A string containing the event for which the error occurred.

Line—An integer identifying the line on the script at which the error occurred.

The structure allows a developer to trap any of the PowerBuilder errors, using the error structure from within the SystemError event, and then provide custom processing.

A script written in the SystemError event to handle errors can be tested using the **SignalError** function. This function simply causes a SystemError event at the application level. Powersoft has made available a list of Execution error numbers. These error numbers, in addition to any others that the developer comes up with, can be trapped from within the SystemError event. The published execution error messages are:

Number	*Description*
1	Divide by zero
2	Null object reference
3	Array boundary exceeded
4	Enumerated value is out of range for function
5	Negative value encountered in function
6	Invalid DataWindow row/column specified
7	Unresolved external when linking reference
8	Reference of array with NULL subscript
9	DLL function not found in current application

10	Unsupported argument type in DLL function
12	DataWindow column type does not match GetItem type
13	Unresolved attribute reference
14	Error opening DLL library for external function
15	Error calling external function
16	Maximum string size exceeded
17	DataWindow referenced in DataWindow object does not exist
50	Application reference could not be resolved
51	Failure loading dynamic library

A developer might want to trap two of the error numbers and display a more friendly message to the user. The following script is an example of the code that could be added to the SystemError event of the application object:

```
Choose Case error.number
Case 3
    MessageBox("Oooops","The application accidentally burped, "&
                         +"please call the application "&
                         +"administrator.~nSee you soon!")
Case 14
    MessageBox("Don't worry","The application has some minor "&
                         +"problems. We are currently hunting "&
                         +"down the developer.")

End Choose

Halt
```

The developer may also choose to write the additional information provided by the error structure (e.g., the error text, window or menu name, object/control name, object event name, and line number) into an error log. Such a log could be used as an audit trail for the person responsible for fixing the problem.

Error Checking Dynamic Data Exchange (DDE) with Other Applications

When establishing a link to a DDE server application, it is important to do extensive error checking. Obviously, if an error occurs while trying to connect (open a channel) to the DDE server, the other DDE commands should not be executed. For example, when an **OpenChannel(...)** function is called, the **ExecRemote**, **GetRemote**, or any other DDE handle-dependent functions should not be called if an error occurs. Code for this is:

```
int i_Handle, i_Ret
i_Handle = OpenChannel(...)
If i_Handle > 0 Then
    i_Ret = ExecRemote(...,iHandle)
    If i_Ret > 0 Then
        //...other DDE processing
    Else
        return iRet
    End If
Else
    return gi_ERROR
End If
```

If a DDE channel is not established at first, the user may want to try again until a connection is established. Code for this is:

```
Boolean b_Continue = TRUE
i_Handle = OpenChannel(...)
Do While bContinue
    b_Continue = FALSE
    If i_Handle > 0 Then
        ExecRemote(...,i_Handle)
        If i_Ret > 0 Then
            //...other DDE processing
        Else
            return i_Ret
        End If
    Else
        If MessageBox("DDE Error","Try "+&
                "Again?",Question!,YesNo!,2) = 1 Then
            b_Continue = TRUE
        End If
    End If
Loop
```

There are many other ways error handling can be used with DDE. The preceding coding examples show two ways of taking advantage of PowerBuilder's error-handling capabilities.

Error Handling when Calling Dynamic Linked Libraries (DLLs)

When calling DLLs or any other external library function, it is critical to do error checking. When calling published APIs, it is important to study the return codes for each function and handle the errors accordingly. Error handling in this situation can be done by logging the errors in detail, so that the person responsible for correcting them can detect exactly what went wrong.

Nested Error Handling

There are many different ways to handle error messages programmatically. One method is by nesting the code within the error-handling logic. This coding example shows how nested error handling can be accomplished.

```
If Not Function( ) Then
    If Not Function2( ) Then
        If Not Function3( ) Then
            return success
        Else
            return error
        End If
    Else
        return error
    End If
Else
    return error
End If
```

ImportFile Error Messages

The ImportFile function in PowerBuilder can be used to demonstrate how error messages can be displayed. To do this, the developer should write a function (**f_ImportFileMsg(l_error)**) that returns, as a string, the text of the error message:

```
Choose Case l_error
Case -3
    return "Invalid argument"
Case -4
    return "Invalid input"
Case -5
    return "Could not open the file"
Case -6
    return "Could not close the file"
Case -7
    return "Error reading the text"
Case -8
    return "Not a .TXT file"
Case Else
```

```
    return ""
End Choose
```

A function like **f_ImportFileMsg** can reduce duplicate code in an application. The following code demonstrates how the **f_ImportFileMsg** function can be used:

```
Long l_error

l_error = dw_1.ImportFile("textfile.TXT")
If l_error < 0 Then
     MessageBox("ImportFile Error",f_ImportFileMsg(l_error))
End If
```

The **f_ImportFileMsg** can be created in an ancestor window so that all descendant windows have access to it. This way, every time the ImportFile function is called, the developer simply calls the **f_ImportFileMsg** function to handle the error messages.

Location of Error Logs

When an error occurs, the support person must be able to locate the exact line at which the error occurred. Sometimes this is difficult, but as much information as possible should be given to the person responsible for resolving the error. One option is to display detail information (including information similar to that provided within the error object) about a particular error to the user. However, this information may be somewhat cryptic (unfriendly) to the user. Writing this information to an error log is often a better alternative. Such an error log can be a file on the user's computer or on the network. Other options include printing to the closest printer or updating an application-specific error log table in the database.

A key thing to remember when designing an error log mechanism is how to handle errors in the mechanism itself. For example, if an error log is being written to a file on a network drive and the drive suddenly becomes full, the error-handling mechanism must be able to detect this and act accordingly. The best way to approach this is to have some type of contingency plan in place for error logging.

Error Actions

It is often a good idea to centralize error processing by calling a series of generic error functions. There can be error functions for writing detail information in a log file, displaying error or warning messages, or returning message numbers, for example. It is often a good idea to use a generic error-display function. Such a function can be used to display all application errors, regardless of where the message text comes from.

Another issue concerns the storage of messages. Error messages should be stored in a central location rather than hard-coded in application code. This simplifies maintenance as well as provides a method for accessing all possible error messages from a single location.

Messages are usually stored in a file or in a database. Storing messages in a database involves a risk because if an application cannot connect to the database, the error message stating that cannot be retrieved. The performance sacrifice of storing error messages in a centralized location can be minimized by loading the error messages into memory at login time. Although this increases the amount of time it takes to log in, it eliminates the delay of retrieving a message every time it is needed.

Action functions are an important aspect of error handling. One can divide application error messages into categories based on their level of severity. It makes sense to have one category for each type of action to be taken. For example, a group of errors for which you would want someone paged immediately could be grouped together in one category. This way, when different actions take place, a specific category of error occurs. Types of error action functions that can be performed include dialing a pager number, leaving a voice mail, sending an eMail message, writing to an error log, broadcasting a system-wide message, shutting down the system, and displaying an error message, to name a few. All of these can be handled programmatically.

There are a number of ways to accomplish proper error handling. However it is done, the important thing is that error handling is done throughout the application.

CHAPTER **20**

Creating an Executable

The final step in putting together an application is the creation of an executable file. This involves both the creation of the .EXE file and the building of any PowerBuilder Dynamic Library files (.PBDs) required by the application. This is also the point at which the binding of all external resources (bitmaps, icons, cursors, etc.) occurs.

This chapter discusses the following topics related to building an application executable:

- What happens when building the .EXE
- Using .PBDs
- The library search path
- Resource files
- Optimizing .PBLs
- Building the .EXE file

This chapter gives the developer a good understanding of issues and techniques related to the creation of executables within the PowerBuilder environment.

WHAT HAPPENS WHEN BUILDING THE .EXE

When building the executable code for an application, compiled Power-Builder objects can be either part of the .EXE file itself or part of a .PBD file. A PowerBuilder Resource (.PBR) file is used to include any dynamically referenced objects or any objects not automatically included by PowerBuilder into the .EXE file or a .PBD file.

When building the .EXE, PowerBuilder copies all referenced compiled objects from the .PBLs listed in the library search path of the application that are **not** declared to be .PBDs. By default, the .EXE is created in the directory where the .PBL containing the application object is located. This location can be changed by selecting a different directory when building the executable. The .EXE contains the following:

- A Windows bootstrap routine
- Compiled code for all referenced objects in the .PBLs listed in the library search path of the application
- All external resources listed in the .PBR file of the .EXE

In addition, most compilers translate programs into machine code such that the computer can execute them directly. PowerBuilder executables are compiled into p-code. P-code produces much smaller programs than machine code, but the computer cannot execute them directly. Instead, programs compiled into p-code are executed by a runtime interpreter, which is a small program incorporated into the executable file. Programs compiled into p-code are slower than programs compiled to machine-code.

USING .PBDS

.PBDs function in much the same way as Windows .DLL files; that is, they allow the dynamic linking of code into an application at runtime. A .PBD contains compiled PowerBuilder objects plus any resources specified in a .PBR file. Like an .EXE, the compiled objects in a .PBD are copied from the .PBLs listed in the library search path of the application. At runtime, PowerBuilder loads the entire .EXE file into memory, but loads individual objects from a .PBD only as they are needed.

The capability to distribute objects among the .EXE and .PBDs provides some flexibility with regard to memory usage and other performance considerations. For example, in a simple application, performance could be increased by including all objects and resources within the .EXE and not using any .PBDs. This results in a larger .EXE file, but means that all objects are loaded into memory when the application begins, thus eliminating the need to load objects into memory from a .PBD throughout the execution of the application. Obviously, performance is going to depend on such things as the configuration of the client workstation and network and the size of the .EXE file. As a general guideline, Powersoft recommends that an .EXE file be no larger than 1.5 megabytes and that a .PBL be smaller than 800K and contain no more than 60 objects.

For most medium- to large-scale applications, Powersoft and the authors recommend that .PBDs be used. In addition to the benefits of dynamic linking, .PBDs reduce the size of the .EXE file and allow an application to be broken down into smaller, more manageable parts. The authors have found it best to group objects into .PBLs (and .PBDs) based on their functionality. This allows objects often used together to exist in a common file, which makes bug fixes and upgrades easier to manage and distribute. This is true because changes made to an object in a .PBD require only the rebuilding of the .PBD file, not the complete rebuilding of the .EXE (Rebuilding the .EXE usually takes more time and resources.) When the change is made and the .PBD is rebuilt, only this file needs to be delivered to users. .PBDs can also be shared among different applications, providing code reusability.

Note: Because global variables and external function calls in an application object can change, including the application object in a .PBD can reduce the number of times an .EXE needs to be rebuilt.

THE LIBRARY SEARCH PATH

The library search path of an application is very important and often overlooked when building a PowerBuilder application. It is important because it dictates the path that PowerBuilder follows when searching for objects during execution. When retrieving an object, PowerBuilder first looks in the .EXE file. If the object is not found there, PowerBuilder searches each .PBD in the order they are listed in the library search path of the application. As such, the order of the .PBLs in the library search path becomes a significant factor in application performance. To enhance performance, the .PBLs containing the most often used objects should be put at the top of the library search list. The authors also recommend that .PBLs containing ancestor objects be listed before .PBLs containing descendant objects.

RESOURCE FILES

Resources such as bitmaps, compressed bitmaps, icons, and cursors can be included as part of the .EXE file or as part of any application .PBD. Including these files prevents developers and system administrators from having to distribute these files separately. To specify which files are included as part of an .EXE or .PBD, create an ASCII file (usually with a .PBR extension) with each resource listed on a separate line. For example, the .PBR file to include the two bitmaps INSERT.BMP and DELETE.BMP would look like:

```
C:\BMP\INSERT.BMP
C:\BMP\DELETE.BMP
```

One important thing to note is that the way the resource is referenced in the .PBR file is the exact way it must be referenced throughout the application. In the previous example, the resource listed as C:\BMP\INSERT.BMP must be referenced as C:\BMP\INSERT.BMP in the application.

Note: A good way to avoid problems and confusion when creating the .PBR file is to keep all resource files in a single directory. This directory can then be used by developers when referencing resources.

PowerBuilder DataWindow objects can also be included in the .PBR file. To specify the DataWindow, list the name of its .PBL followed by the name of the DataWindow in parenthesis:

```
C:\PB\COMMON.PBL(d_clock)
```

Note: To dynamically change the DataWindow object of a DataWindow control, the DataWindow object must exist in either a .PBD or .PBR file.

After creating the .PBR file, it can be linked to the .EXE by specifying it in the Create Executable window, as shown in Figure 20.1.

Different resource files can be specified for the .EXE and any application .PBDs. To link a .PBR file to a .PBD, specify it when building the .PBD file, as shown in Figure 20.2.

Note: To avoid having to rebuild the .EXE file to accommodate a change in a .PBR file, bind the .PBR file to a .PBD rather than the .EXE. When done this way, a change in the .PBR file is treated the same as a change to an object of the .PBD. Only the .PBD file to which the .PBR file is bound needs to be rebuilt.

OPTIMIZING .PBLS

.PBLs are linked lists containing both source code and compiled code for each of the PowerBuilder object types. During the course of develop-

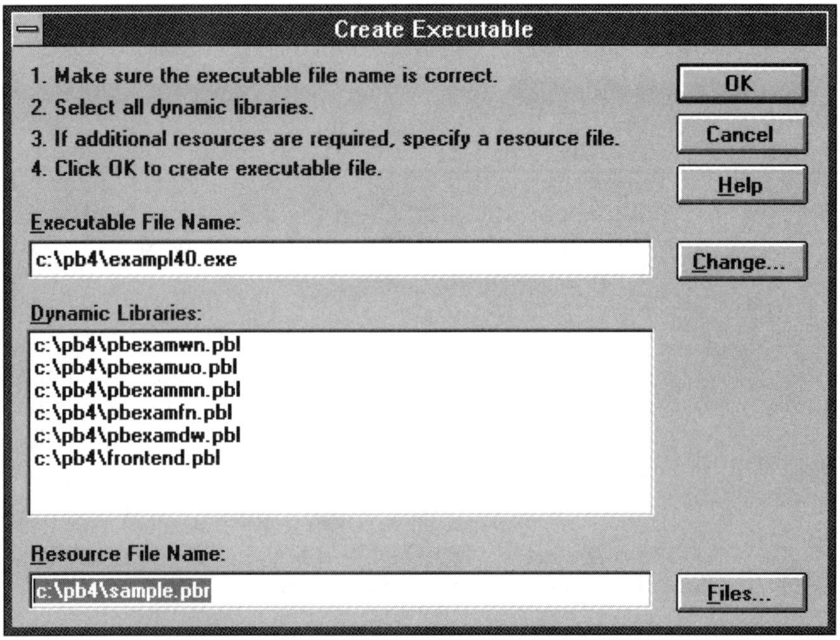

Figure 20.1 The Create Executable window.

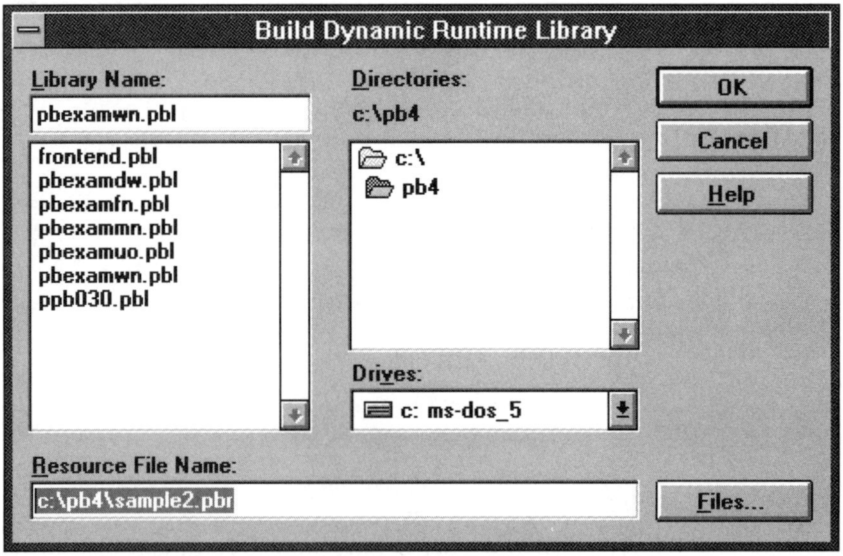

Figure 20.2 Linking a .PBR file to a .PBD.

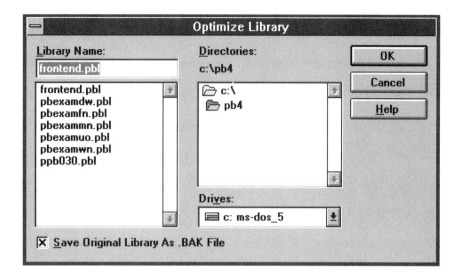

Figure 20.3   Selecting the Optimize option from the Library menu.

ment, as objects are created, modified, and deleted, the storage of object data and indexes can become inefficient and disorganized. One example of this is when an object is deleted from a .PBL. What actually happens when a developer deletes an object is that references to the object are removed from the .PBL, but the code for the object still exists.

Optimizing cleans up .PBL by removing code for any deleted objects and reorganizing object storage and indexes within the .PBL. Optimizing should be done at regular intervals throughout the development cycle and immediately before building an executable. To optimize a .PBL, select the Optimize option from the Library menu in the Library painter, as shown in Figure 20.3.

BUILDING THE .EXE FILE

The time it takes to build the .EXE can be reduced by increasing the amount of memory on the machine where the build is being done. The larger the application, the more memory is needed. If a great deal of disk activity occurs while building the .EXE or it is taking a particularly long time to build the .EXE, consider adding more memory to the machine. Based on the author's experience, the following method works best for creating .EXEs:

1. Copy all .PBLs to your hard disk.

    This speeds up the building of the .EXE by eliminating network delays. In addition, make sure to modify the library search path to point to the .PBLs on the local disk.
2. Regenerate all objects twice.

    This resolves any pointer inconsistencies between objects. Such inconsistencies can exist between objects that reference each other—for example, ancestor and descendant objects in an application using inheritance.
3. Optimize all .PBLs.
4. Build all .PBDs, specifying .PBRs, if necessary.
5. Create the .EXE, specifying a .PBR, if necessary.

PowerBuilder executables can be created using either the Create Executable window shown in Figure 20.1 or the Project Painter. The Project Painter, introduced in PowerBuilder 4 coordinates all aspects of building an executable and allows information about the executable such as the filename, PBDs to create, and resources to be saved in a project object for later use. The Project Painter can also work with version control software to control which version of a PowerBuilder object is used when building an executable. Using the Project Painter can simplify the process of creating an executable for any application of significant size.

In conclusion, an executable PowerBuilder application will usually be a combination of an .EXE file and one or more .PBD files. This method allows objects to be distributed among different files, providing a degree of modularity, flexibility, and tuning capability. The size and nature of an application should be determined before deciding the best method of distributing PowerBuilder objects and external resources among the .EXE and .PBDs. These decisions can affect the performance and maintainability of the application.

CHAPTER 21

Testing PowerBuilder Applications

This chapter provides a testing methodology for PowerBuilder client/server applications. The development of increasingly complex PowerBuilder client/server applications is bringing to light the need for more effective software testing and quality assurance (QA). Among the client/server challenges that we face are new graphical user interfaces (GUIs), which replace traditional character-based, non-modal interfaces; a wider variety of development tools and platforms; multi-user systems across heterogeneous networks; multiprocessor systems connected through highly layered communications protocols; distributed processing on a central database; and concurrent processing on client workstations. When confronted with applications testing, developers must meet the challenges of test design for adequate testing coverage, a central testing repository, and management and control of the testing process. Some new testing tools are appearing on the market to assist in this effort, but overall, the problem being faced in testing requires an entirely new approach to the testing process. This chapter covers the following topics:

- Testing relative to the System Development Life Cycle (SDLC)
- Application test stages
    Unit test
    Integration test
    External interface test
    Security/Error test
    System test
    Performance test

> Documentation test
> User acceptance test
- Testing tools
- A Stress/Performance test approach

Sample testing forms are also provided at the end of the chapter.

TESTING RELATIVE TO THE SYSTEM DEVELOPMENT LIFE CYCLE (SDLC)

The testing effort is as important as the System Development Life Cycle (SDLC). That's why the testing effort must be fully integrated with the entire SDLC. Testing parallels the design and development process. It is not isolated in one phase of development as a step that occurs after programming.

Testing has its own life cycle. Figure 21.1 shows the System Development Life Cycle (SDLC) relative to the phases of the Systems Testing Life Cycle (STLC). Systems testing begins when the system requirements document is delivered and continues for the life of the system.

The STLC phases are as follows:

- **Planning**—The test planning phase begins when the system requirements document is delivered. This phase establishes the test strategy.

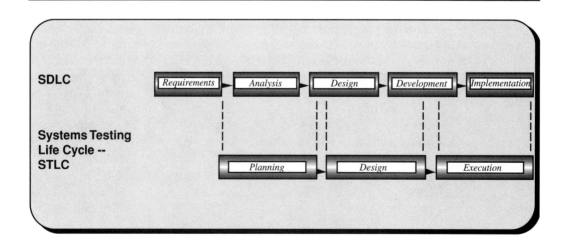

Figure 21.1   Integration of testing with SDLC. Reprinted by permission from *Testing Client/Server Applications*, Patricia Goglia, QED, 1993.

- **Design**—The test design phase overlaps with the planning phase. It begins in the design phase of the SDLC, after the systems test objectives and approaches are defined.
- **Execution**—The testing execution phase begins when programming of individual code modules has been completed. Both the SDLC and STLC design phases have been completed at this point.

At times, testing can be addressed during the design and even in the later stages of the system requirements phase. To ensure that an application can be adequately tested, the designer of a client/server PowerBuilder system should take into account the complexities of testing across multiple platforms, the variety of communications protocols used, and the mixture of development tools being used. Other characteristics peculiar to the way client/server has been implemented should also be considered.

Additional considerations that have not changed with the introduction of client/server, but that are essential to a successful testing effort, are avoiding the last minute crunch to get an application tested, the scheduling of adequate resources, the development of test data that fully exercises all business scenarios (before the application is released), and managing the integration of the different testing phases (to avoid schedule dependencies).

Taking all of this into account and dividing systems testing into phases, with the planning and design phases beginning well before programming starts, achieves several goals:

- Adequate time is allocated for planning, design, and documenting test criteria and results.
- Sufficient lead time and knowledge are available to write or acquire testing tools.
- Test conditions are designed from the system requirements document, not the program specifications or the code itself.

This last item is a key goal: The test conditions are designed early in the SDLC. They can be used as examples in design reviews. Users can use them to verify that the requirements definition is complete and software developers can use them to verify that the design supports the identified requirements.

APPLICATION TEST STAGES

The testing of an application in its entirety is referred to as the application test. The application test includes a number of different stages. Throughout this chapter, the terms "application test" and "test" are used

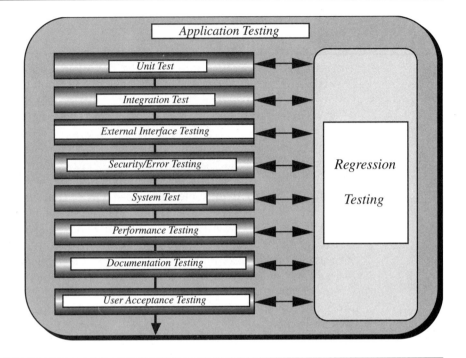

Figure 21.2 Relationship of the application test stages.

interchangeably. Figure 21.2 shows how the different application test stages relate to each other. The first stage of testing is the unit test which is performed by the developer as each module is completed. As additional modules are successfully unit tested, the integration test stage can begin. This stage tests the different modules of the system working together. Because the integration test is often done only with internal pieces of the system, an external interface test needs to be done. The external interface test is done to test the links of the PowerBuilder application with the different external pieces of the system such as eMail, fax, and imaging. This stage is also used to test the interface between the new application and existing applications.

The next phase of testing includes the security and the error handling of the system. These two pieces are considered a separate stage in the testing process because of their importance and scope. The next stage is the system test. The system test is the first time the application is tested as a whole—a unit. When system testing has been completed (or in its later stages), performance testing and stress testing are done. In this phase, the performance of the system and each individual module is examined to make sure everything is running at optimal speed. The performance testing stage applies not only to the PowerBuilder application on the client side, but also to the servers, specifically the DBMS.

At this point, documentation testing is done. This testing stage checks for appropriate online and hard-copy documentation. It also examines the user-friendliness of the system. The less friendly the system is, the more documentation is required. Alternatively, the system is modified to provide a more friendly interface.

The last stage of testing is the user acceptance test. During this testing stage, the end users of the system test it to make sure it meets their requirements and that the data/information presented is correct. The user-acceptance testing stage is used to get sign-off (final system approval) from the user group(s).

During the testing process, if any modifications are made to pieces of the system that have already been tested, a regression test must be done. The regression test stage of the STLC can occur at any time during the testing process. Regression testing, as Figure 21.2 shows, may be necessary during any or all of the testing stages.

The different stages of application testing are discussed in detail in the sections of this chapter that follow.

Unit Testing

In the client/server world, a unit is defined as a logical unit of work. Test cases for all logical units should be developed based on all functional and performance requirements. Design documentation provides a good framework to begin building unit test cases. Critical units should be developed and tested first. When a test unit has been developed, additional test cases can be added and testing can begin. Additional White and Black box test cases should be added to the test plan during the design and development phases, as they arise.

Unit testing is an iterative process that is not complete until all test cases have been tested with perfect results. Although one cannot be absolutely certain that software will never fail, one can determine when sufficient testing has been completed using statistical methods. Numerous units undergo unit testing in parallel. Identifying units that closely interact helps determine scheduling dependencies. Unit testing should be managed closely to facilitate integration testing.

White box testing uses knowledge of the internal design of the unit to develop test cases. White box testing is generally done for the following:

- **Interfaces:** Ensure information properly flows into and out of the unit.
- **Logical paths:** Ensure all logical paths, including error trapping, are tested.
- **Local data structures:** Ensure data stored temporarily maintains its integrity.
- **Boundary conditions:** Ensure proper operation at boundaries established to limit or restrict processing.

Black box testing, which assumes no knowledge of the internal design of a unit, focuses on testing functional and performance requirements.

In both White and Black box testing, test cases should be documented with a set of expected results. Because a unit is not a standalone program, drivers and/or stubs need to be created. Drivers emulate the higher-level program structures that invoke a unit. Stubs emulate any subroutines that are invoked by a unit. The creation of drivers and stubs represents overhead and thus should be managed judiciously.

Integration Test

Integration testing is a systematic technique for combining unit-tested modules and building the program structure according to system design, while at the same time conducting tests to uncover errors associated with combining these units. String testing methods are used to combine tested units together into the system structure. String testing combines units that have directly related inputs and outputs. After successful testing of the interfaces between two related units, a third is added and tested, then a fourth, and so on. This iterative approach creates clusters of related units that are then integrated into the entire system structure.

Volume and stress tests of integrated units are done with simulated inputs and environmental conditions. Integration testing should be limited to internal interfaces only. If external interfaces are necessary for data inputs or environmental conditions, these should be carefully simulated in order to adequately control the testing environment.

The proper approach and timing of integration testing depends both on the kind of system being built and the nature of the development project. Enhancements to existing systems and entirely new systems have very different requirements related to integration testing. In addition, very large systems generally have several relatively large components that can be built and integrated separately before being combined into a full system.

The two main types of integration testing that help dictate when to perform integration testing are nonincremental and incremental.

- **Nonincremental**—All units are combined at once and the entire system is tested as a whole. This is usually referred to as the Big Bang approach.
- **Incremental**—Units are linked together and tested in small segments or clusters. After all interfaces and functional tests are passed for the tested segments, new units are added. The test cases, test scripts, control drivers, and test stubs are modified, and all interfaces and functional tests are done again. This iterative process is repeated until all units are combined. Incremental testing can be conducted in parallel with unit testing and development, as soon as some related units are successfully unit tested.

Nonincremental integration testing is typically done on small or simple systems or simple enhancement projects.

External Interface Test

External interface testing is done to ensure the interfaces to other systems are functioning properly. Some applications interface with other applications using DDE, OLE, Clipboard and/or Windows messages. There are also times when other applications are simply executed from within the application. Other major areas that must be included in the external interface test are external interfaces that extend beyond the user's workstation, that is, when there are applications running on remote servers or other workstations. These include links between applications—to make sure the two applications connect without timing out (for DDE, timeout is an issue) and to test the time it takes for one application to connect to the other. Other areas that must be tested vary based on the specific external application interfaces.

Security/Error Test

Because it is best to isolate security and error checking in separate modules in a PowerBuilder system, special attention should be given to the security and error-checking modules, when testing. That is why they are placed as a separate testing phase in the STLC. Security testing is done to ensure that the system is protected from improper penetration. Error testing is done for a number of reasons:

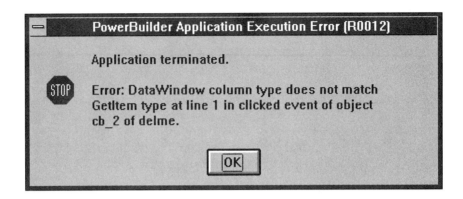

Figure 21.3 An unacceptable error message.

Error Messages Must Read Properly It is important that the error messages display a descriptive, friendly message. The error message in Figure 21.3, for example, should not be considered acceptable.

A message such as the one shown in Figure 21.4 should be substituted for this unfriendly message. Any detail information about the error needed by the application administrator to resolve the problem can and should be written to a log file.

Error messages can include more specific information than the preceding one, but should be friendly to the user. During the error-testing

Figure 21.4 An acceptable error message.

process, all the error messages are reviewed to ensure they read properly and are aligned correctly.

Error Messages Must Display when a Particular Error Occurs The next thing that must be tested is that the correct message is displayed when a particular error occurs.

Error Logs Must Be Generated Properly Sometimes developers choose to create error logs or dumps when an error occurs. Error logs should specifically detail the exact nature of the error encountered. Details that would be helpful to the application administrator, who must understand and then fix the problem, should be shown on the error log.

Error Actions Must Work Correctly When an error occurs, many different things could happen: A message may be displayed for the user, an error log created or updated, an eMail message sent to the appropriate support person automatically, or a support person immediately paged or called. Depending on the severity of the error, different combinations of these responses can occur. In any case, the appropriate tests must be done to ensure that all the error actions work as planned.

System Test

The system test is executed after integration testing is completed and before acceptance testing begins. System testing is critical because the entire system is tested and reviewed as an entity. The client workstation, the LAN, the WAN, the gateway(s), the file server, the DBMS server, and all the other external pieces that make up the system/application are tested for the intended functionality. This stage of testing is to ensure not only that the system functions correctly but also that the system functions based on the requirements given by the users of the system. The functional requirements are tested before the system is handed over to the user for acceptance testing, to detect any obvious problems that could cause embarrassment to the development team.

Performance Test

Performance testing is a runtime test of an entire integrated system. During this stage, a series of stress tests can also be done. Many different pieces of the system need to be tested for performance and stress.

Each piece of a system typically has its own unique tools for testing or monitoring activity. The network, for example, has LAN analyzers/protolyzers that can be used to monitor data, stress, usage, and the like.

The DBMS engine has different tools for monitoring activity within the engine during testing.

To monitor performance of a system, it is useful to simulate the absolute maximum number of users that could potentially be using the system at one time. This can be done using a workstation for each potential user and running through the application manually or automatically using a recording tool. If the number of workstations or people to execute the application are not available for testing, simulation applications must be written to assist in the process. To simulate 40 users with only eight workstations, for example, five instances of the simulation application should run on each of the eight workstations.

To test performance in a PowerBuilder application, a number of things can be done. Major parts of the system where performance could be an issue should be identified. Some of those areas can be:

- The login process
- Security verification
- Window creation and display
- Retrieving data
- Updating data
- Interfacing with external modules (e.g., eMail, MS Word, fax, etc.)
- Printing

A timestamp function must be written to be called from the different parts of the system to monitor performance.

PowerScript for an **f_timestamp(String sMSG)** function is as follows:

```
integer iFileHandle

iFileHandle = FileOpen(g_sLogFile, LineMode!, Write!)
// perform error checking
FileWrite(iFileHandle, sMSG + "~t" + String(Today( )) + "-" + &
                    String(Now( )))
// perform error checking
FileClose(iFileHandle)
// perform error checking
```

In the event in which the **Retrieve( )** function is called, the **f_time stamp( )** function should be called before and after the call, like this:

```
f_timestamp("Start Retrieve dw_Persons")
dw_persons.Retrieve( )
f_timestamp("End Retrieve dw_Persons")
```

When this program has been executed a few times, an Error log file that the tester has created can be used to analyze performance statistics. The tester can modify the **f_timestamp** to gather other information such as the system resources, memory, and GDI count. This is done by calling the Windows SDK **GetFreeSystemResources** function. Alternatively, or in addition, the **GetFreeSpace** function can be called for other memory information.

For an example of a stress and performance test plan, see the test plan provided towards the end of this chapter.

Documentation Test

This may seem to be a trivial test stage, but it is not. This test determines the user-friendliness of written documentation and online help provided to the user to facilitate system operation. To do this test, random users who do not have any experience with the application can be selected. They should be asked to use the system and see if the interface is intuitive enough for them to be productive. If they have difficulty, they should refer to the online and written documentation to figure out how to use the application. An assessment of their ease and success with the documentation should be done. Parts they have difficulty with should be changed.

User-acceptance Test

User-acceptance testing is the validation of all system requirements. Normally, it is performed by the users in their environment. If it is not practical to have end users perform this function, as with packaged software, it can be tested in-house in an internal application environment, or **alpha** and **beta** testing can be substituted for user-acceptance testing. (Alpha testing is conducted by a user at the developer's site; Beta testing is conducted by users at their site.) User-acceptance testing is usually the final test performed.

A user-acceptance, Alpha, or Beta test plan should be created. Ease of use and functionality of all aspects of the system should be tested. The users should systematically execute the tests and the results should be documented.

Regression Testing

Application testing is both progressive and regressive. The progressive phase introduces and tests new functions, uncovering problems in or related to recently added modules. The regressive phase concerns the effects of recently introduced changes to a module on all the previously integrated (and tested) code. Problems arise when errors made in incorporating new functions have an effect on previously tested functions. Regression testing is particularly important in software maintenance, where it is not uncommon for bug fixes in one module to disrupt seemingly unrelated functions. The process of regression testing often uncovers new functional problems as well. Regression testing is impossible unless there are detail records of past testing and all software maintenance efforts are structured. When performing regression testing, attention should be focused on a system's critical modules.

Regression testing can be done at any level (unit, integration, or system). What makes a test a regression test is that changes, or new modules or functions, have been introduced to previously tested areas. Groups of regression tests can either be run periodically or after a change is made.

The integration test plan is invaluable during software maintenance when regression tests are necessary. A detailed history of all the tests, bugs found and fixed, and expected and actual results reduces the amount of effort for regression testing and also enhances the overall quality of a change or correction. The following is an effective approach to regression testing that can be used during production as well as for long-term maintenance:

- Identify both a comprehensive set of regression tests for the entire system and two kinds of subsets for every module. The first subset for each module is a collection of tests for newly introduced units or functions; the other is a sample set from the full set of regression tests for the system, selected with this module's functionality in mind. Selection of these subsets should be based on the complexity of the individual areas being tested and on the success history of the test cases themselves. Keep in mind that regression problems often stem from rare business cases that are overlooked in functional testing.
- Run the comprehensive regression bucket periodically.
- Run the subsets after every change is made.

It is important to remember that new test cases may be needed when system maintenance adds functionality to a system.

TESTING TOOLS

Automated Testing Tool(s) for Unit Testing

Using an automated testing tool, even if the developers/testers have experience with the tool, actually increases the amount of time it takes to test a unit. Therefore, in initial unit testing, there is no time savings in using a testing tool. One can test a unit against the requirements documentation manually in much less time than it would take to "capture" a test script of a finished unit that has already been manually checked, and then execute and debug the test script to capture all the actual results. Any time savings would not be recognized until later in integration and regression testing.

For reasons noted later, however, the authors recommend use of automated testing tools at this stage if the selected automated test tool will also be used for integration and system testing. If this is the case, the unit test scripts should be written with later testing phase needs in mind.

Automated Testing Tool(s) for Integration and System Testing

This is where the benefits of automated testing tools can be recognized. The accuracy and efficiency of having a tool execute a long series of test steps and record the actual results is where the time savings with testing tools can be realized. However, testing the integration of a number of units by using an automated testing tool is obviously only effective if those units have test scripts developed. Of course, the scripts that were used for unit testing cannot be used for integration testing, only parts of them can. In addition, if it becomes necessary to test a unit that had to be modified as the result of integration testing, the old unit test scripts can be re-executed. Therefore, using a testing tool in integration and system testing has benefits, but if you don't have complete unit test scripts, the time savings start slipping away.

Time Savings

As mentioned in the previous paragraph, the accuracy and efficiency of having an automated test tool execute long series of test steps and record the actual results is where the benefits of testing tools can be experienced. Manual testers get tired, bored, and don't execute tests exactly the same way each time. Therefore, the quality of testing in any development effort is significantly enhanced by the use of testing tools. This is most dramatic in regression testing. For example, say a developer developed an order entry system with the assumption that "unit of measure" is dozen. Later, the company changes its policy to a new unit of measure (eaches). The question is: What is the system impact? The developer makes the necessary database changes and programming changes, but now there are approximately 20 different windows and reports that use unit of measure. The dream is to have a repository of test scripts that take the developer/tester all the way through unit tests and on through to system tests. Only then would the developer/tester feel comfortable that the impact of that change has been fully tested.

Implementing a Testing Tool

It is important to capitalize on any and all time savings and quality enhancements by testing with an automated tool. The problem is that developers get frustrated with having to develop the system and then, in addition, having to develop all the test scripts. This frustration can be avoided by including test script development in the project plan/schedule. Note that as soon as the testing tool learning curve is climbed by developers, the hard work is done. The inclusion of the testing tool in subsequent testing phases and projects has less and less impact on project time.

One way to get started using testing tools is to take the following steps:

- Staff a development effort with consideration of rolling some of the developers (the ones that usually roll off the project early) into a testing team.
- Test all conversations to the requirements manually.
- Give the tested conversations to the testing team. They then develop the complete conversation unit test scripts, begin putting together the required test data, and begin developing the integration and system test plans and associated test scripts.

Having done this, the test team has familiarity with the project and the relevant business needs. In addition, test scripts tend to depersonalize testing and thus avoid the pride of authorship problems that may sometimes result in testers going easy on their own code.

The testing team wraps up after full testing and implementation of the system. They produce as their final deliverable the regression testing approach, complete with a repository of test scripts from unit to full system test.

This or a similar approach takes advantage of automated testing tools while minimizing the investment in time and resources. The obvious benefit is that a group of people develop a new set of skills, not only in testing in general, but also with an automated testing tool(s).

Table 21.1 gives a list of some of the testing tools in the market.

SAMPLE STRESS/PERFORMANCE TEST PLAN

This test plan was originally written for a real-world PowerBuilder development project for a real business.

Stress tests attempt to determine the performance thresholds for an application. Performance tests emulate a production environment

Table 21.1   Testing Tools

Tool Name	Company Name	Attribute	Operating System
TestPro for Windows	Sterling Software	cp, tg, te, co, sc	Windows
Auto Tester	Auto Tester, Inc.	cp, tg, rt	Windows
Soft Test	Bender and Associates	rq, tg, cm	DOS
TestRunner	Mercury Interactive	cp, ni	Windows
WinRunner	Mercury Interactive	cp	Windows
SQA: Robot	SW Quality Automation	cp, tg, el	Windows
SQL: Manager	SW Quality Automation	tm, er, el	Windows
Automated Test Facility	Softbridge, Inc.	cp	Windows
MS Test for Windows	Microsoft	cp	Windows
Ferret	Tiburon Systems	cp, tg, co, sc, el	OS Independent
BattleMap	McCabe and Associates	cm	UNIX
BattlePlan	McCabe and Associates	cc	UNIX
VISTA	Veritas	cc	UNIX
Hindsight	ASA	cc	UNIX

LEGEND:

cp—capture/playback

cc—code coverage

el—error logging

te—test execution

cm—complexity

rq—requirements

sc—scripting

tg—test generation

rt—requirements tagging

ni—nonintrusive

tm—test management

er—error tracking

co—compare

(before the new application is put into production) to ascertain if the performance of the new system will be acceptable. The information collected from these tests will help reduce the risk associated with implementing the new application.

Stress Test

The stress test will help avoid unforeseen performance problems in the existing LAN architecture that could occur when the new application goes into production. The goal of this test will be to quantify the incremental impact of the new application on the LAN architecture. The stress test will attempt to define performance thresholds for application usage on the current LAN. The following stress points will be measured:

- DBMS server usage
- Network horizontal and vertical ring traffic
- Network bridging traffic
- File server performance
- Workstation performance

Approach The stress test will focus on creating stress on the network by systematically increasing the load placed on the network. To accomplish this, application simulation programs will be used to collect most of the stress test statistics. Because application simulation programs are executed on workstations, this approach generates network traffic beyond the normal network load—the steady-state load. An attempt must be made to quantify the incremental load placed on the network.

The application simulation approach simplifies setup and execution of the stress test. Using it should achieve more uniformity in the results across test cycles. The application simulation program uses carefully selected excerpts of code from different parts of the real application. They are executed in a loop to simulate rapid and concurrent use of the new system.

To the extent possible, all times will be collected and recorded electronically. The application simulator will have the following features:

- A times interface to allow for execution synchronization across machines
- Programmatic collection of runtime statistics (to the extent possible)
- A process to write workstation execution statistics to a flat file

For the stress test cycles, the variability of workstation configuration should be eliminated. This will allow for collection of results that are more directly correlated to the tested stress points.

Note: Some stress test cycles may need to be conducted outside of normal business hours. Some way to generate a steady-state load on the network will be needed, if this is done.

High-level Test Conditions The variables that will be manipulated to stress the application are:

- Number of workstations simulating application usage
- Number of database connections
- Number of concurrent database accesses

By increasing the values of these three conditions, measurable increases in overall network traffic should occur.

Test Cycles For the stress test, a test cycle defines the number of times the application simulation program will need to be executed to collect the desired information. This stress test has the following test cycles as shown in Table 21.2.

Note: In the event that a test cycle fails to execute because a performance threshold has been met, the test cycle will be re-executed up to five times. If the test cycle cannot be passed, the test cycle will be re-executed using staggered execution times. The remaining test cycles will be executed to the extent possible. All configuration changes will be documented on a cycle-by-cycle basis.

The approach for increasing the number of database connections will be to execute multiple instances of the application simulation program. The application simulation program will be designed to maintain database connections until the entire cycle is completed.

Monitored Variables The variables collected from each test cycle in the stress test will include those in Table 21.3.

Performance Test

The performance test will measure user-perceived and actual performance of the new system. This test will help establish user expectations and will help drive future workstation purchase decisions. Performance will be measured by varying workstation configurations and recording

Table 21.2   Stress Test Test Cycles

Cycle Number	Workstations	Database Connections	Maximum Concurrent Active Connections	Number of Executions
1	1	1	1	5
2	1	3	1	5
3	1	5	1	5
4	3	11	3	1
5	3	13	3	1
6	3	15	3	1
7	5	21	5	1
8	5	23	5	1
9	5	25	5	5
10	7	31	7	1
11	7	33	7	1
12	7	35	7	1
13	9	41	9	1
14	9	43	9	1
15	9	45	9	1
16	10	46	10	1
17	10	48	10	1
18	10	50	10	5
19	10	75	10	1
20	10	100	10	1

the variations in execution times within the application. The impact of increasing the number of users will also be evaluated.

Approach The application performance test will test the application's performance from the user's perspective. This test will collect statistics as users proceed through the application. In addition, this test will take workstation configuration variations into consideration. Unlike the stress test, the application performance test will be executed using the actual (not simulation) application. To collect the most significant results, the application must be configured as it would be in production. The only exception will be minor modifications made to programmatically collect the required performance statistics (through file I/O).

Table 21.3   Variables from Each Test Cycle

Monitored Variable	Variable Tests...	Collection Source	Calculation Method
Workstation Throughput (Kb/sec)	Workstation Configuration	Application Simulator	Aggregate data throughput to workstation (Kb) divided by total test cycle execution time
Server CPU Usage (%)	DBMS Server Configuration	Stored procedure executed at the end of each cycle	CPU utilization divided by total test cycle execution time
Server I/O Usage (%)	DBMS Server Configuration	Stored procedure executed at the end of each cycle	CPU I/O divided by total test cycle execution time
Server Packets (Packets/sec)	DBMS Server Configuration	Stored procedure executed at the end of each cycle	Total packets (received + sent) divided by total test cycle execution time
Disk Device Utilization (%)	DBMS Server Configuration	LAN Administration	N/A
Network Interface Utilization (%)	DBMS Server Configuration	LAN Administration	N/A
Backbone Utilization (%)	LAN Architecture: Utility Ring	LAN Administration	Bandwidth utilization as a percent of theoretical maximum (4Mbps)
Bridge Utilization (%)	LAN Architecture: Bridge Utilization	LAN Administration	Packets per second as a percent of theoretical maximum (14,000pps)
Horizontal Ring Utilization (%)	LAN Architecture: Workstation Ring	LAN Administration	Bandwidth utilization as a percent of theoretical maximum (16Mbps)

Table 21.3   *(continued)*

Monitored Variable	Variable Tests...	Collection Source	Calculation Method
Server CPU Usage (%)	File Server Configuration:	LAN Administration	CPU utilization divided by total test cycle execution time
Server I/O Usage (%)	File Server Configuration:	LAN Administration	CPU I/O divided by total test cycle execution time
Server Packets (Packets/sec)	File Server Configuration:	LAN Administration	Total packet (received + sent) divided by total test cycle execution time
Disk Device Utilization (%)	File Server Configuration: OS/2	LAN Administration	N/A
Network Interface Utilization (%)	File Server Configuration: OS/2	LAN Administration	N/A
Server Response Time	File Server	LAN Administration	Periodic snapshots of server response time
Server Response Time	DBMS Server	LAN Administration	Periodic snapshots of server response time

High-level Test Conditions   The variables that will be manipulated in this test are:

- Number of workstations using the application
- Workstation configuration variations

Test Cycles   For the performance test, a test cycle is defined by the number of times the execution script is run. These test cycles vary the workstation configuration and the number of concurrent workstations using the application. The planned test cycles are shown in Table 21.4.

Table 21.4   Test Cycles for Performance Test

Cycle Number	Workstations	Workstation Configuration	No. of Executions
1	1	High	5
2	1	Medium	5
3	1	Low	5
4	3	High	5
5	3	Medium	5
6	3	Low	5
7	5	Mixed	5
8	7	Mixed	5
9	10	Mixed	5

Monitored Variables The results from this portion of the test will be determined from the information in Table 21.5 collected from each application performance test cycle.

Stress Test Execution Script

Application Simulation Program The stress test application simulation program will attempt to simulate the stress the new application will put on the LAN, the network, the database server, and the DBMS. The application will be designed as follows.

Application General Flow

1. The application will start execution when the workstation time is equal to or greater than the execution time SingleLineEdit.
2. The application will establish one connection.
3. The application will execute stored procedures against the database and record the time.
4. There will be some application input parameters. The following parameters must be entered on the front-end screen before execution can commence:

```
Workstation:    CPQ386-33m
RAM:            12
Loop Counter:   Max # of times to execute loop
DB ID:          DEYHID01
Cycle #:        01
```

Table 21.5   Information from Each Application Performance Test Cycle

Monitored Variable	Variable Tests...	Collection Source	Calculation Method
Workstation Throughput (Kb/sec)	Workstation Configuration	Application modification	Aggregate data throughput to workstation (Kb) divided by total test cycle execution time
Workstation User Resource Usage (%)	User resource space used by the application	Application modification (call to Windows SDK)	N/A
Workstation GDI Resources (%)	GDI resources used by the application	Application modification (call to Windows SDK)	N/A
Workstation Memory (%)	Amount of global memory used by the application	Application modification (call to Windows SDK)	N/A

```
Workstation #:    01
Execution #:      01
Instance:         01
Time:             Execution time
```

5. The application front-end screen will look like the one in Figure 21.5.

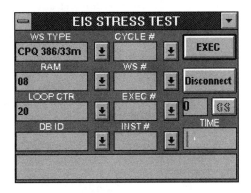

Figure 21.5   The application front-end screen in a stress test simulation.

	DATABASE ID :	DEYHID01	
WORKSTATION :	CPQ386-33M	**WORKSTATION # :**	1
RAM :	12	**INSTANCE :**	1
DATE :	date|time	**COUNTER :**	10

Loop Counter	Task	Start Time	End Time
01	RUNRATES	starttime	endtime
01	RUNRATES	starttime	endtime
01	RUNRATES	starttime	endtime
...	...	...	...
01	RUNRATES	starttime	endtime

Figure 21.6   Output file of application simulation.

Application Output The application simulation program will create an output file for each application in a test directory called:

```
outXXYY.txt    where
XX = Workstation number   and
YY = Instance
```

Each file will look like the one in Figure 21.6.

SAMPLE TESTING FORMS

Here is a multipart unit testing form the authors have found useful.

APPLICATION NAME **CONVERSATION UNIT TEST**

Created By:
Date: 11/02/93 05:43 PM
Modified By:
Date: 11/03/93 07:32 PM

Status:

Conversation:

Developer:

Reviewer:

Date Performed:

Tested by:

Date:

Approved by:

Date:

Components Developed:

Name	Type

Reused Components:

Name	Type

Note to Tester:

Windows Used:

Main Window	PB Component Names

SECTION 1—STANDARDS:

Test/Expected results *Open Boxes*	Actual Results	Initials	Data
Background is white			
Title should read "Please Select a [Object Name]"			

Test/Expected results *Windows*	Actual Results	Initials	Date
Background is white			
System menu			
Menu bar			
Minimize button			
Message line			

Test/Expected results *Scrolling DataWindows*	Actual Results	Initials	Date
Background is white			
Vertical scroll bar			

Test/Expected results *Non-Scrolling DataWindows*	Actual Results	Initials	Date
Background is white			
Fields are white with no border			

Test/Expected results *Group Boxes*	Actual Results	Initials	Date
Dark blue background with black border			
Heading text is white			

Test/Expected results *Buttons*	Actual Results	Initials	Date
Text is 13pt MS Sans Serif			
Text is black and bold			
Buttons are aligned and spaced evenly			

Test/Expected results *Background Text/Labels*	Actual Results	Initials	Data
Text is 13pt MS Sans Serif—**bold**			
Text is black (background should be the color of the datawindow)			
No border			
Left positioned above and one character to the left of its entry field if associated w/ a field on a freeform-based datawindow; centered if associated w/ a column of a tabular or grid datawindow			

Test/Expected results	Actual Results	Initials	Date
Non-Editable Fields			
Text is 13pt MS Sans Serif			
Text is blue (background should be the color of the datawindow)			
No border			
Left positioned for alphanumeric; Right positioned for numeric or fields validated to be numbers only			

Test/Expected results	Actual Results	Initials	Date
Editable Fields			
Text is 13pt MS Sans Serif			
Text is black on white background			
Use black border			
Left positioned for alphanumeric; Right positioned for numeric or fields validated to be numbers only			

Test/Expected results	Actual Results	Initials	Date
DropDownListBoxes			
Text is 13pt MS Sans Serif			
Text is black on white background			
No border			
Uneditable and use vertical scroll bar when all options aren't visible			

Test/Expected results	Actual Results	Initials	Date
Boolean or Single-Character Flag Fields			
Text is 13pt MS Sans Serif—**bold**			
Text is black on white			
No border			
Checkbox with values of Y = ON and N = OFF, and left justify			

Test/Expected results	Actual Results	Initials	Date
Mutually Exclusive Options			
Text is 13pt MS Sans Serif—**bold**			
Text is dark blue on white			
No border			
Radiobuttons and left justify			

Errors Found/Comments:

Sign-Off Initials/Date:

SECTION 2—FUNCTIONALITY:

Part 1—Menu Options:

Test/Expected Results— Menu Option	Actual Results	Initials	Date
File/ New/ Business Associate—Clears out Business Associate Window and puts user in New mode			
File/ New/ BA Address—Inserts new row into dw_all_addresses			

Test/Expected Results—Menu Option	Actual Results	Initials	Date
File/ New/ BA Contact—Inserts new row into dw_all_contacts			
File/ Open—Clears out Business Associate Window and puts user in Open mode			
File/ Save—Saves changes to the database			
File/ Remove/ BA Deactivate—Sets current date into Deactivated Date column and saves changes to the database			
File/ Remove/ BA Address—Removes currently selected address			
File/ Remove/ BA Contact—Removes currently selected contact			
File/ Exit—Close Business Associate Window			
Help/ Context—Displays help specific to the conversation			
Help/ General—Displays help specific to the conversation			
Help/ Index—Displays the help index for ABC			
Help/ About—Displays the System About box			

Part 2—Controls:

Test/Expected Results—Controls	Actual Results	Initials	Date

Errors Found/Comments:

Sign-Off Initials/Date:

SECTION 3—PROCESSING

Part 1—Error Processing—Validation/Required Fields

For required-fields testing, required columns should be left blank in the Data Entered section to ensure correct error messages are given. Each required field should be tested separately.

Description	Data Entered	Expected Error Message	Date/Initials
BA class is required	**dw_main** BA Number: 13 BA Class: BA Type: Corporate BA Name: A NEW BA	"Please select a BA class"	
Social Security number must be 9 digits	**dw_main** BA Number: 13 BA Class: Vendor BA Type: Corporate BA Name: A NEW BA SSN: 12345678	"Please enter a 9-digit social security number with no delimiters"	

Errors Found/Comments:

Sign-Off Initials/Date:

Part 2—Normal Processing

1. Data Retrieval—If fields are formatted differently for different conditions during data retrieval, each case must be tested separately.

Table Data	Expected Data Displayed on Window	Expected Formatting—Tab Orders, Menu Options, etc.	Date/Initials

Errors Found/Comments:

Sign-Off Initials/Date:

2. Data Update—Creating, modifying, and deleting a retrieved record should be tested separately.

Data Entered	Expected Database Results	Expected Formatting—Tab Orders, Menu Options, etc. after update	Date/Initials
New Record:			
Modified Record:			

Errors Found/Comments:

Sign-Off Initials/Date:

Part 3—Special Processing

Description	Data Entered	Expected Result	Date/Initials

Errors Found/Comments:

Sign-Off Initials/Date:

CHAPTER 22

PowerBuilder Software Migration

When building applications, whether corporate systems or packaged software, the integrity of the code as it evolves from development to production is important. Because of the many components in a client/server environment, software migration is an important issue. This chapter explains a software migration life cycle, especially as it pertains to PowerBuilder. It is important to note that the life cycle/methodology discussed in this chapter is one option. The developer must select a software management methodology that best suits his or her needs. In addition, the tools mentioned in this chapter are not the only ones available. Again, the developer must select the appropriate tool(s) that matches his or her specific requirements. The following topics are discussed in this chapter:

- Software development life cycle
- File types and locations
- Directory structure
- Client/server PowerBuilder job duties
- Version control interface
- Migration forms

SOFTWARE DEVELOPMENT LIFE CYCLE

Software migration is a process in which individual code modules are saved (to document iterations of effort) and provide a framework from which a release can be assembled from all of its component parts. The software migration process begins after programs have been successfully unit tested. Because programs in production occasionally require maintenance, it doesn't end until code is no longer used. At every stage in between, programmers must use the latest version of the code.

As an application is developed, it evolves. Each new version has more features and functionality. Before a software product becomes a fully released version, it goes through different stages of development and testing. A software package may go through various stages of release. At each stage, a controlled migration must occur.

When an application (especially a software package) has been system tested, it typically migrates from the Alpha to the Beta testing stage, then to different release stages. PowerBuilder itself usually goes through a number of different release stages, which Powersoft calls candidates, then on to final release, which Powersoft calls the Gold Disk. Alpha and Beta are when the product is made available to a select few for review and testing. All the stages prior to the Gold Disk stage are usually not available to the general user community.

Each stage of development, testing, and release may be iterative. Normally, the developer checks out the object into his or her local development directory. When the code changes are completed and tested, the developer submits the code to the object manager for review. When the object manager has tested the module(s), he or she checks the code into a shared area. After the modifications are complete for this phase/release/version of the software, the code is submitted for system test. After system testing is successful, the code is moved into a staging area and the user test area. When the users have signed off on the system, the application is moved to the production environment. This process is called the software migration life cycle (see Figure 22.1).

As depicted in Figure 22.2, during the alpha stage of development, a number of iterations and/or steps must occur before a product is available as an alpha release. The steps may include migration from a developer's local work area, obtaining the object manager's approval, system testing, user testing, and finally release.

Since a number of developers generally work on different pieces of an application concurrently, it is imperative that each is always working on the newest version of the program. The common phraseology used in version control is check in/check out. Before working on a particular program, a developer must check it out to his or her own work area. Ideally, this work area is a separate drive on the development network, but it can also be a local drive on the developer's workstation. When the developer has finished creating or fixing the code and has tested it, he or she checks it in. While a programmer has a piece of code checked out, no other programmer can work on it. A software management tool that helps manage versions of each type of program is vital.

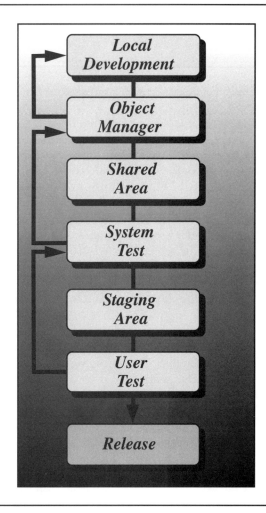

Figure 22.1 The software migration life cycle.

Applications in production and released software packages may go through a number of releases as depicted in Figure 22.3.

Typically, when a version number changes to the next whole number, major changes have been made to the application.

Putting all of the steps and iterations of software migration together, the process looks something like that in Figure 22.4.

Success is guaranteed only through diligent tracking of each component in an application or software package.

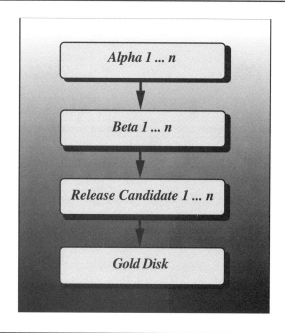

Figure 22.2   Alpha stage of development.

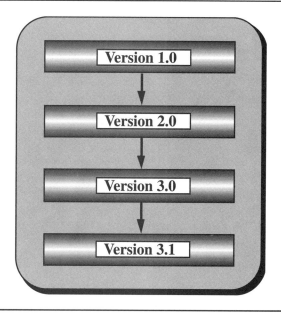

Figure 22.3   Number of releases.

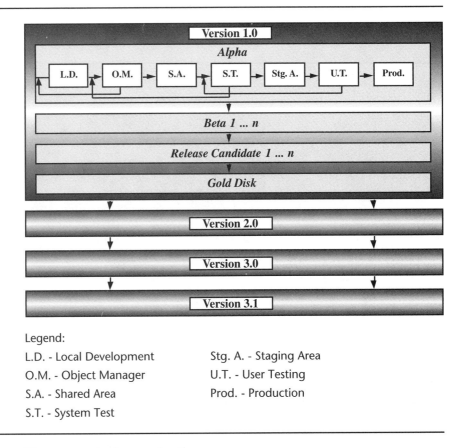

Figure 22.4   The process of software migration.

FILE TYPES AND LOCATIONS

When building a client/server application many different types of files are involved. These files can be located on individual workstations, file servers, and/or database servers. The person responsible for software migration/version control must be very familiar with all the different files that are needed and where they reside. Following is a list of some different file types that may be part of a PowerBuilder application.

File Type	Description
PBL	PowerBuilder Library
PBD	PowerBuilder Dynamic Library
DLL	Dynamic Linked Library

SQL	Query, Table Schema script
DOC	Application Documentation, Migration Form, Design Spec
C	C Source program
H	C Header file
DEF	C Module Definition file
RES	C Resource file
PBR	PowerBuilder Resource file
EXE	Executable
TXT	Text file
INI	Windows or Application Initialization file
HLP	Help file
PRJ	Help project file
MAK	C Make file
RTF	Rich Text Format file (for help file creation)
LIB	Windows/DOS Static Library
A	UNIX Static Library
AWK	UNIX AWK Script file
BMP	Bitmap
ICO	Icon
BAT	Batch file

These file types, and possibly many more depending on the particular environment, must be managed with release or configuration control software. They must be managed such that if a previous file from a certain version were needed, it could be easily retrieved.

A number of version control software products communicate with PowerBuilder. These products have different mechanisms to help a developer manage files that are located on different servers or platforms. Being able to do this from a single server addresses the most complex release management issue. This is depicted in Figure 22.5.

DIRECTORY STRUCTURE

Before application development or any work is done as part of the application development process, it is important to set up a directory structure that supports not only the current application development effort, but also the entire application environment. This would take into ac-

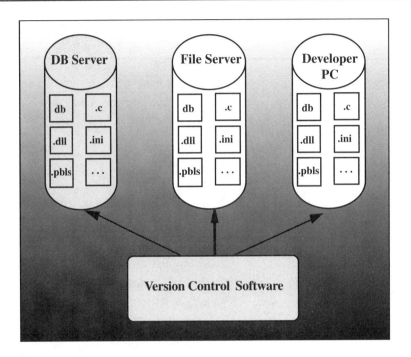

Figure 22.5   Cross-platform software version control.

count a set of common modules that all applications can share, common modules shared by one or more applications, and other applications themselves (see Figure 22.6).

Having a standard directory structure in place prior to beginning a development effort makes code management easier. This way, developers spend a minimal amount of time looking for a specific piece of code. When it is time to create the application executable, all files (of similar type) that are included in it reside in the same place. Only production-ready code is compiled into the executable.

Figure 22.6 and Table 22.1 that follows represent the way a PowerBuilder directory structure might be organized. This structure should be altered depending on the number of servers and applications involved. If a particular environment has a large number of other types of files, a subdirectory should be created for each.

If multiple applications are being developed on the same server, there should be an entire \dev structure under a directory name denoting the application as shown in the previous directory structure diagram. In

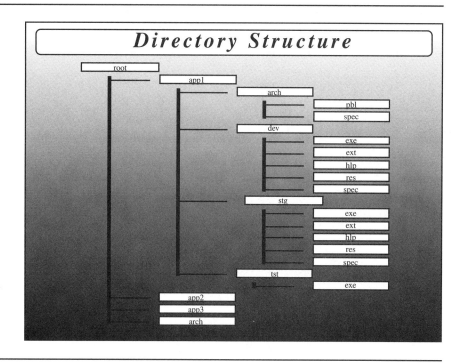

Figure 22.6   The directory structure.

Table 22.1   Organization of Directory Structure

Location	Extension	Nature	Description
\DEV\	N/A	N/A	Source directory (contains no files)
\DEV\EXT	C, H, RC, RES	External	Used to store files used to create external objects (e.g., DLLs)
DEV\PBL	PBL	Libraries	Used to store PBL-related files used by the application
\DEV\RES	BMP, ICO, PBR	Resources	Used to store application resources
\DEV\HLP	HLP	Help	Used to store application help files
\DEV\SPEC	DOC	Specifications	Used to store files related to specifications (e.g., pre- and post-design documents)
\DEV\EXE	EXE, PBD, DLL	Executable	Used to store files necessary to execute the application

addition, under \app1, there should be the following directories parallel to the ..\dev directory:

> **..\tst**—a testing area, where unit testing is done. Only the executables should be here.
>
> **..\stg**—a staging area, where unit-tested software is a frozen copy of the ..\dev directory, for later system testing.
>
> **..\arch**—where common modules for the application are stored.

Note: There should be both an \arch directory under the root directory to store common modules for all applications and an arch directory under the specific \app directory for more application-specific common modules.

AN EXAMPLE OF A TYPICAL SOFTWARE MANAGEMENT ENVIRONMENT

The following setup provides for multiple layers of security within an application development cycle. There are a number of logical roles in this scenario, as follows:

> Version Control Manager—The version control manager is responsible for the integrity of the version control repository. The version control manager typically interfaces with the object manager to store and release source from the version control repository. The only person that has access to the version control repository is the version control manager.
>
> Object Manager—The object manager is responsible for the integrity of all the code that is on the application server. The object manager interfaces with both the version control manager and each application lead.
>
> Application Lead—The application lead is responsible for the integrity of the code for an application module. The application lead is responsible for interfacing with the object manager and all the developers for the particular application module under the responsibility of the lead.
>
> Developer—The developer is responsible for the pieces of code that are assigned to him/her. The developer is responsible for interfacing with the application lead.

Figure 22.7 shows the interaction between all the different people within a multiple application software development environment.

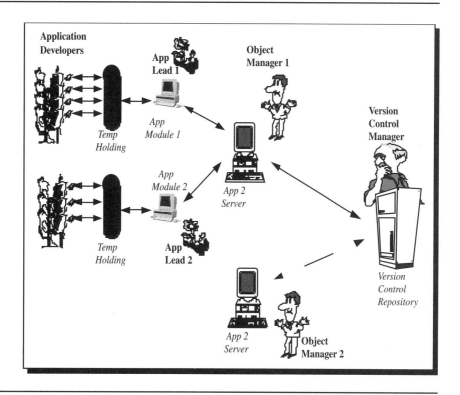

Figure 22.7   Interaction between the different roles in the multi-application software development environment.

The different source code locations are:

Version Control Repository—The repository holds all the source code.

Application Server—This is where the version control manager places the code recently taken from the repository.

Application Module Directory Tree—This is where the code for each application module, that needs to be modified, resides.

Temporary Holding Area—In order to prevent the developer from having write access to the application module directory tree, the temporary holding area can be created. When the developer is ready to check in some code he/she checks it into the holding area and the application lead immediately moves it into the application module directory tree.

Table 22.2   Levels of Access

	Version Control Repository	Application Server	Application Module directory tree	Temporary holding area	Developers hard disk
Version Control Manager	W	W	R	R	N
Object Manager	R	W	W	W	N
Application Lead	N	R	W	W	N
Application Developer	N	N	R	W	W

* R—Read Access; W—Write Access; N—No Access

Table 22.2 shows who has what level of access to each server or directory tree.

This configuration is only a suggestion. There are a number of different alternatives for setting up a software management environment.

VERSION CONTROL IN POWERBUILDER

PowerBuilder has version control capabilities that can be used in different ways. The first method is the standard library check-in\check-out process. This process is simplistic, but it works. The second method is to use an external vendor's version control product. Such vendor products include PVCS, Endeavor, and CCC.

Default Version Control

The default version control capabilities of PowerBuilder include check-in and check-out functionality. The toolbar that performs these operations is available from the Library painter (see Figure 22.8).

Figure 22.8   Toolbar for check-in/check-out

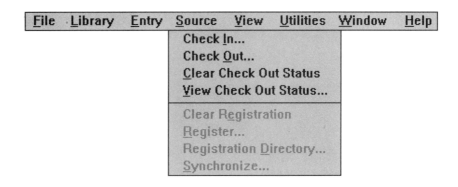

Figure 22.9   Toolbar showing default version control capabilities of PowerBuilder.

Version control functionality is also available from the Source menu, as shown in Figure 22.9.

When the developer attempts to check out an object for the first time, PowerBuilder prompts with the dialog box shown in Figure 22.10.

PowerBuilder keeps track of checkout based on the user ID parameter entered here. The developer should key in his or her user ID and click the OK button, as shown in Figure 22.11.

When this is done, PowerBuilder modifies the user preferences as shown in Figure 22.12.

After the user ID information is entered, PowerBuilder prompts with a dialog box (see Figure 22.13) for the destination library, usually the developer's local library.

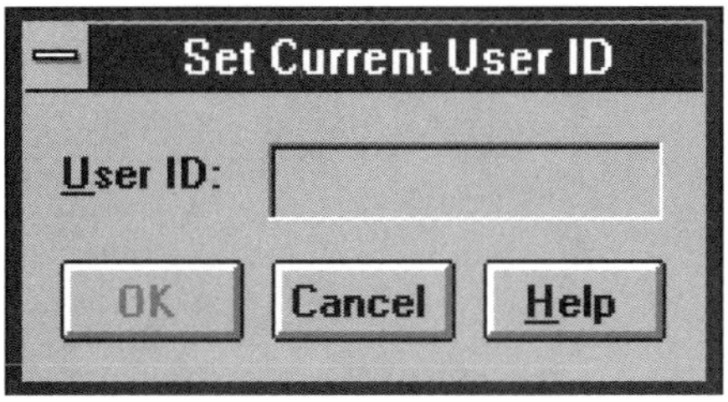

Figure 22.10   Dialog box for User ID.

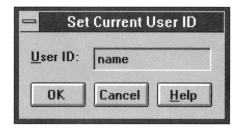

Figure 22.11 Developer enters ID.

Figure 22.12 Modified user preferences.

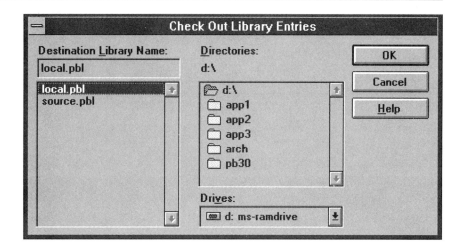

Figure 22.13   Dialog box for the destination library.

This is the extent of PowerBuilder's version control capabilities. The default process is deficient, especially for larger development projects. Consequently, Powersoft has provided a mechanism for vendors to be able to link their version control software to PowerBuilder. The next section discusses how PowerBuilder's architecture is set up for communication to and from version control software.

External Version Control Software

When a vendor's version control product has been installed, the Source-Vendor entry in the preferences dialog must be set (e.g., to PVCS for PVCS) (see Figure 22.14).

Figure 22.15 shows how PowerBuilder communicates with a version control software product. From PowerBuilder, a vendor-specific DLL has to be written to link the check-in and check-out process directly with the vendor's repository. This figure also shows that the version control software has to communicate through the PowerBuilder open repository case API (ORCA) to provide information to PowerBuilder.

When the third-party version control software is installed on the workstation and the link to PowerBuilder has been established, the menu items that had been grayed out become available (see Figure 22.16).

Note that before developers can check objects in and out, the Power-Builder objects must be registered (see menu in Figure 22.16).

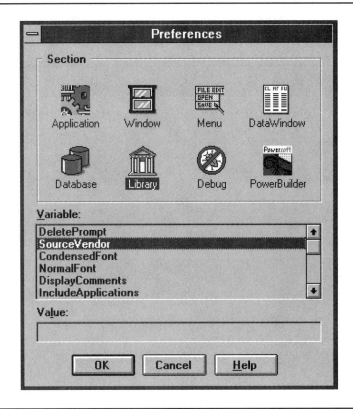

Figure 22.14 The SourceVendor entry in the Preferences dialog box.

Following is a list of some more popular version control products. They are not necessarily PowerBuilder-enabled, but more and more are releasing links to PowerBuilder everyday.

Company Name	*Product Name*
Atria Software, Inc.	ClearCase
Burton Systems	TLIB
Computer Associates International Inc.	CA-PAN/LCM
Computer Associates International Inc.	CA-Librarian
Computer Associates International Inc.	CA-PANVALET
ILSE	DRTS

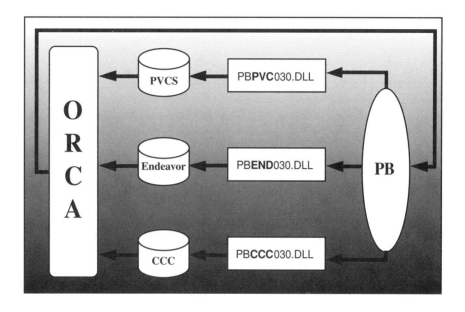

Figure 22.15 PowerBuilder communicates with a version control software product through ORCA.

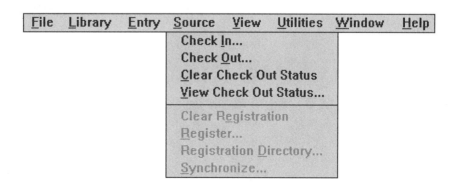

Figure 22.16 The available menu items when using version control software.

IBM	CMVC
Intersolv, Inc.	PVCS
Intersolv, Inc.	Configuration Builder
Mortice Kern Systems, Inc.	MKS RCS
Object Technology International, Inc.	ENVY/Developer
OneTree Software	SourceSafe
Opus Software, Inc.	Opus Make
Softool Corporation	CCC/Life Cycle Manager
Software Maintenance & Development Systems Inc.	Aide-De-Camp
SunPro	TeamWare
TeamOne Systems, Inc.	TeamTools
TransWare Enterprises, Inc.	Source Manager

To give the reader a feel for using a third-party product, some procedures that could be used by users of PVCS are included. They are:

PVCS Procedures

Creating Initial Source Files When a task or process has been assigned to the programmer, he or she should inform the PVCS administrator, providing the following information:

The programmer's name.

The name of the program file, including extension (e.g., rass1002.pco).

A short description of the purpose and/or function of the program.

Upon receiving this information, the PVCS administrator creates the initial archive file. Then the programmer can check the file in and out, as necessary.

Source Migration When a developer thinks that a program is functioning according to requirements, he or she is permitted to "promote" the source code to "test" status. In test status, the program is further tested against other called and/or calling procedures. This environment uses its own data set and looks at system-wide functionality. A UNIX script file can be created to simplify this process. It would be called as follows:

```
promote <filename.ext>
```

Upon successful completion of system-wide testing, a program is promoted by the code administrator through the following levels using PVCS:

Simulation Test: Programs are tested in a realistic setting.

Acceptance Test: Programs are tested by a select group of users.

Retrieving a Source File To shield developers from the PVCS syntax for retrieving source code files, a UNIX script file simplifies the process. To check out a program, use the following command:

```
checkout <filename.ext>
```

PVCS retrieves the file and places it in the directory from which the retrieval script was invoked. All files should be retrieved into your development subdirectory.

Returning a Source File Upon completion of a program or at the end of the day, source files are to be archived back to PVCS. A UNIX script file simplifies this process. To return a program, use the following command:

```
checkin <filename.ext>
```

When you check a program in, PVCS places it in the version manager archive directory. The most recent read-only version of the file is maintained in the /development/ras/ref subdirectory. Files in this location can be used for viewing, printing, or compiling.

WARNING: *Making copies of these files, modifying the copies, and then attempting to check them in will result in a PVCS error. You must use the **checkout** command to retrieve a writeable source file. See Retrieving a Source File for more information.*

MIGRATION FORMS

It is critical to have a well-documented process for migration from one development/testing stage to the next. The project team can develop some standard migration forms or use products such as Lotus Notes, in setting up a migration database. A simple migration form might look like this:

CODE MIGRATION REQUEST FORM

Requested By _____ Date Requested _____

Reason for Change

_____

_____

Application: __Batch, __Contract, __Corp., __Credit, __Discount, __EBB, __Noms, __Plmaps, __Rates, __Sched

Mgr. Approval _____ Explain SQL Required :　　Y/N　　　Entry

Type: (PB, SQR, etc.) _____

636 SE Notify _____ Curr to:　UnitTest Y/N,　UserAccep Y/N,　Prod Y/N.

SQR MIGRATIONS

Program Name	Source Directory on LAN	Destination Server (Production/Development)			Program Type *	
		Development	SystemTest	Prod	Report	Update

*Report programs should only read from the database. Programs that change the database are Updates.

New SQR Program Migration (this section only required for new SQR programs)

　Program Name: _____

　Description: _____

Input Parameters:

Description / Prompt	Type	Required

POWERBUILDER OBJECT MIGRATIONS

Object Name	Type	Source PBL	Destination PBL (Prod/Enhancement)		
			Development	System Test	Production

ADMINISTRATOR USE ONLY

Completed By _____ Date Completed _____

CHAPTER 23

Performance Considerations

In even the simplest client/server application, there are many different elements that work together to make up the application system, as shown in Figure 23.1.

As this figure shows, these elements include the client workstation, network architecture, database design, and the application itself. Each of these elements has an impact on overall application performance and should be addressed individually to provide the best possible performance.

While briefly discussing other performance-related issues of client/server applications, this chapter focuses primarily on the performance issues regarding the design and development of a PowerBuilder application. Application performance refers to both actual performance and perceived performance. Perceived performance is the user's view of application performance, which may be better than actual performance. Other topics discussed in this chapter include:

- Client configuration
- Network architecture
- Database design
- PowerBuilder application design issues
- PowerBuilder application development

CLIENT CONFIGURATION

There are many things on the client workstation that can be done to increase application performance including:

- Increasing workstation memory. Memory is often the limiting factor in Windows, largely because of the capability to run many applications simultaneously.
- Because Windows does not use expanded memory, using extended memory can increase application performance.
- Loading as many programs as possible in high memory. Loading programs in high memory leaves more of the 640K base memory available for DOS applications. Items that should be loaded in high memory include device drivers, network drivers, and any terminiate-and-stay-resident (TSR) programs.
- Using a disk-caching program, such as SMARTDRV.EXE, and allocating as much memory as possible. This can provide a big performance improvement in Windows.
- Not using a wallpaper as the background in Windows. To save memory, use a color or pattern rather than a wallpaper for a background.
- Configuring Windows to use a permanent swap file, which increases Windows performance because it is stored in contiguous blocks on the hard disk. To create a swap file, click the Virtual Memory button of the 386 Enhanced window from the Windows Control Panel, as shown in Figure 23.2.

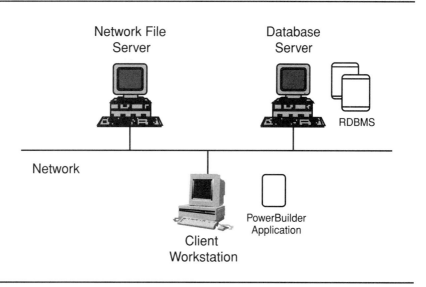

Figure 23.1   A typical client/server application.

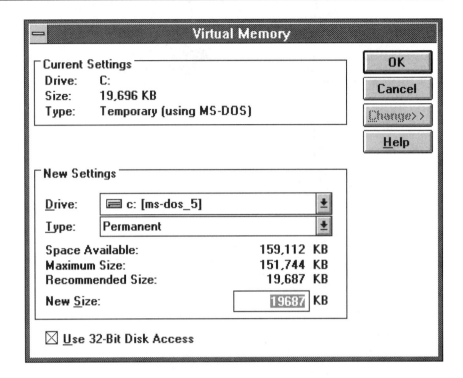

Figure 23.2   Configuring Windows virtual memory.

Note: The space available for creating a permanent swap file is only as large as the largest contiguous block available on the hard disk. A permanent swap file cannot be created if Stacker is running.

- If using a temporary swap file, not storing it on a network drive. The network delays and contention with other users can significantly decrease performance.
- Regularly defragmenting the hard drive.

In addition, the developer should refer to DOS and Windows documentation in an effort to completely understand the effect of each item in the CONFIG.SYS, AUTOEXEC.BAT, WIN.INI, and SYSTEM.INI files on performance.

NETWORK ARCHITECTURE

The network architecture of an application includes such items as the network type (e.g., Ethernet, Token Ring, ArcNet), the network operating system (e.g., NetWare, VINES, LAN Manager), and the protocols used to communicate between different systems (e.g., TCP/IP, IPX/SPX, NetBIOS, SNA).

Today's systems can run on many combinations of network type, network operating system, and protocols. While network performance tuning differs among the various combinations, there are some general areas that, regardless of the combination of network type, NOS, and protocol, should be looked at when addressing network performance. They include:

- **Number of Peak Users**—When designing a network, the architect needs to know the approximate number of peak users in order to make such decisions as the required bandwidth, the access media (e.g., fiber optic, coaxial cable, twisted pair), the number of segments or rings, and the number of servers required. The number of peak users should be considered for the entire network as well as for each network segment or ring.
- **Type of Applications**—In order to estimate the type, frequency, and volume of data the network must support, the network designer needs to know the type(s) of applications that will be run on it. For example, an imaging system usually requires more network resources than a word processing application.
- **Placement of Network File Servers**—Users accessing a network file server are impacted by the number of **hops** between the user workstation and the server. Hops refers to the number of bridges, switches, and so forth, that lie between the network segment or ring of the user's workstation and the network segment or ring of the server. For example, consider the following Ethernet network architecture in Figure 23.3.

  In this network, all communications between the client and network server must go across two routers to get from Segment A to Segment C. This obviously slows performance. If possible, frequently accessed servers should be on the same segment or ring as the client(s), as shown in Figure 23.4.

  While it is not always possible to have the client and server on the same network segment or ring, analysis should be done when designing the network architecture to minimize the number of hops between user workstations and servers.
- **Network Packet Size**—The packet size is the size of each data

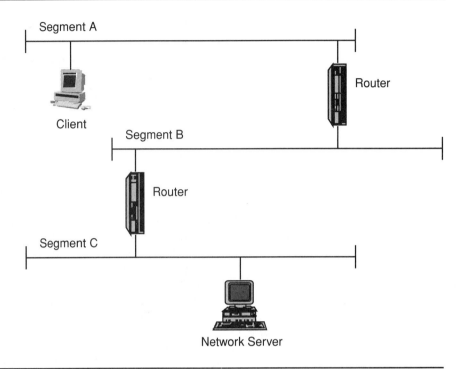

Figure 23.3 A network architecture requiring two "hops" from client to server.

packet sent across the network. The smaller the packet size, the more packets that must be sent across the network. Having a large number of packets can adversely affect performance. On the other hand, packets that are too large may clutter a network with only a few users or processes running. Refer to NOS documentation for recommended packet size.

DATABASE DESIGN

There are many things at the database level that can be done to increase system performance. These range from design decisions to tuning the database when the application goes into production. Design time considerations include:

- Number of concurrent users
- Number of database connections per user

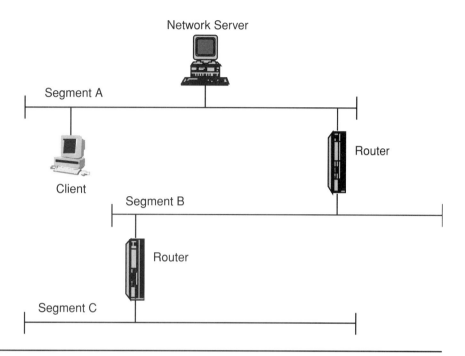

Figure 23.4 Minimizing the number of "hops" between client and server by placing both on the same network segment.

- The types of transactions to be performed (query versus update)
- Proper database sizing
- Choosing the proper platform
- Normalization of the data model

Things that can be done as a function of RDBMS and application tuning include:

- Proper use of indexes
- Optimization of the SQL
- Tweaking the RDBMS configuration parameters
- Data distribution

While the methods of dealing with these issues differ among the different RDBMS products, each of them exists for most systems and thus should be addressed when considering performance.

POWERBUILDER APPLICATION DESIGN ISSUES

Before beginning to develop a PowerBuilder application, there are many design decisions that need to be made. In addition to improving the productivity during the development cycle, these design decisions can impact application performance. This section addresses some of the design issues that should be considered before starting development.

Partitioning Application Components

A client/server application may consist of many pieces of code distributed among the various components of the architecture. For example, a single PowerBuilder application can consist of PowerScript and C code on the client side, along with triggers, stored procedures, and other 3GL code on the server side. Because using the correct type of code can have a positive effect on performance, the developer must decide certain things that are discussed in the following sections.

When to Use Database Triggers

Most relational databases support the use of triggers. A trigger is a set of code performed automatically by the database in response to a specific database action. Although triggers are implemented differently by the different RDBMS vendors (see Chapter 18 for a detailed description of how triggers are implemented in different RDBMSs), they may be fired in response to an INSERT, UPDATE, or DELETE SQL statement performed against the database.

Because of this, triggers should be used whenever a specific action must be performed in response to changes made to the database. It is much more efficient to use triggers for this purpose, rather than performing such a function at the client workstation. Performing this action at the client workstation requires another call to the database, thus increasing network traffic and decreasing performance. The SQL that makes up a trigger can usually be optimized, which results in more efficient execution of the SQL than if it were submitted from the client.

Note: In databases that support declarative referential integrity, it is best to enforce referential integrity declaratively rather than through triggers.

When to Use Stored Procedures

Although not all relational databases support stored procedures, taking advantage of them in those databases that do can significantly impact application design and performance. A stored procedure, like a trigger, is a collection of SQL code. However, unlike a trigger, a stored procedure is not executed automatically based on database activity. A stored procedure must be called explicitly from within an application, trigger, or another procedure.

Stored procedures should be used as a method for executing commonly used SQL (or vendor-specific SQL extensions) within a database. Although a stored procedure is nothing more than SQL, there are advantages to using stored procedures instead of SQL scripts. Because stored procedures are stored in a compiled form, their performance is generally better than that of native SQL. Stored procedures can also provide a level of application security in that a user allowed to execute a procedure does not need access to the data the procedure uses.

As mentioned previously, stored procedures, in most cases, can be used to increase performance over standard SQL queries. Figure 23.5 illustrates the performance advantage of stored procedures over standard SQL queries in Microsoft's SQL Server.

The fewer the steps, obviously, the better the performance.

When to Perform Validation

The time and location of data validation is another design issue that should be considered by developers. Should data be validated as it is entered or at save time? Should validation occur on the client or at the server using a trigger or stored procedure?

The answers to these questions depend on the type of validation being done and whether database access is required to validate the data. Validating such things as the format of the data entered in a field or the length of the data entered should be done on the client as the user attempts to leave the field, usually through the edit mask or validation code defined for the column in the DataWindow painter. The reason for doing this type of validation immediately is that it is more friendly to the users to be presented with a problem as they attempt to leave a field rather than notifying them of the problem after they have spent time entering data in all of the fields on the screen.

To reduce the number of database queries, any validation that requires database access should be done at save time. Doing this for many fields as the user attempts to leave each one can greatly reduce performance.

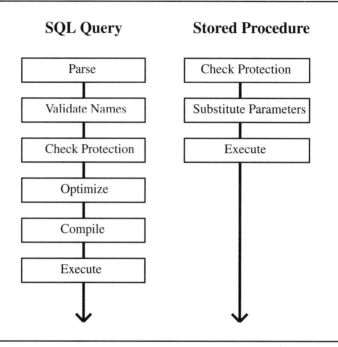

Figure 23.5 Execution of a SQL query vs. a stored procedure.

Whether to perform validation on the client or server is a decision that should be made based on the nature of the validation code. If the validation code requires a great deal of processing or involves some complicated SQL, it is usually best to perform the validation on the server. As previously mentioned, this code can be optimized to improve performance. Note that when performing validation on the server, it is important that the PowerBuilder application handle the return code of the trigger or stored procedure and display an appropriate message to the user.

PowerScript Functions vs. External Functions

As mentioned in the discussion of functions in Chapter 8, external C functions can be used to improve the performance of a PowerBuilder application. This is because PowerScript code is compiled into p-code that is interpreted at runtime, which executes more slowly than C code. Any CPU-intensive processes should be considered for development in C rather than PowerScript.

One EXE vs. Several EXEs

Performance can be increased for a large application by breaking it into a series of smaller EXEs, rather than having one large one. The application should be divided into portions (EXEs) that can run in a standalone mode, independent of the other parts of the application.

For example, an application with functions for both the Marketing division and the R and D division of a company could more than likely be divided into two smaller EXEs, one for each division. Because PowerBuilder EXEs can be kept relatively small by using PBD and PBR files, this problem should not occur frequently.

Building PBLs into Both the EXE and PBDs

For the best performance, all PBLs should be bound into the executable. If the application is too large for a single executable, performance can also be increased by doing one of two things: creating an executable with all application PBLs in their respective PBDs or creating an executable with some PBLs in the executable and some as PBDs. The advantage in creating one executable with all PBLs as PBDs is that the executable is small and the memory usage is minimal. If this is done, however, it is critical to place the objects in PBLs with respect to usage. This is because the opening and closing of application PBDs can net a performance decrease. If the developer ignores the placement of objects in PBLs with respect to usage, he or she may end up with the following type of situation: The application executes the command to open window1, but because the controls on window1 are inherited from objects that physically reside in different PBDs, each PBD must be opened for window1 to be displayed. Figure 23.6 shows the problem; for window1 to be opened, PBD1, PBD2, and PBD3 also need to be opened.

To improve performance, it is better to combine objects used together in one PBD. In this example, objects A, E, and F should be placed in the same PBD, as shown in Figure 23.7.

This way, only PBD1 has to be opened to open the window.

Sometimes it is best to combine some of the application PBLs with the executable and compile some into PBDs. The objects in the application that are used most often should be bound into the executable; less frequently accessed objects can be compiled into PBDs.

Distribution of Application Components

In a client/server environment, there are many places to store application components. Client components can be stored on either the user workstation or a network file server. Server components can reside on

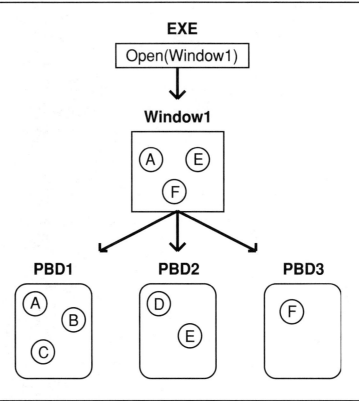

Figure 23.6   Opening Window1 requires the opening of 3PBDs, slowing performance.

either a database server or another application server. Application components include the following:

- PowerBuilder runtime DLLs (including the PowerBuilder interface to the RDBMS)
- PowerBuilder application dynamic libraries (.PBDs)
- Additional application DLLs
- Any external client-side software packages (e.g., a word processor, spreadsheet, or reporting tools)
- Additional server-side application programs

Two things that should be considered when determining where to store application components are application maintenance and performance. In general, although storing components on a server accessible

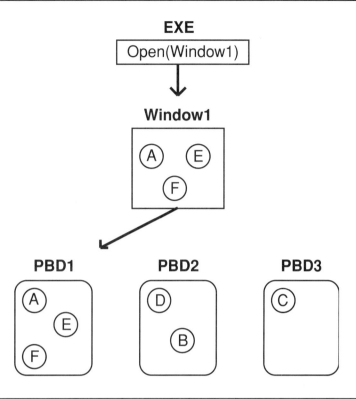

Figure 23.7   Improving performance by grouping objects used together into a single .PBD.

to many users may decrease maintenance efforts, it will usually hinder performance because files have to be transferred across the network from the server to the target machine.

Another issue is the medium on which the components are to be stored. Options include hard disk, tape, and optical disk. The storage medium has an impact on system performance. In most cases, hard disk access is faster than optical disk, which is faster than tape.

Yet another issue is the amount of storage space available on the target machine. Obviously, if a workstation or server lacks the disk space to store application components, the components will have to be kept on another server.

The approach to distributing application components should be to provide a system in which maintenance is reduced as much as possible without decreasing performance to an unacceptable level. For example, if a particular PowerBuilder application is to be updated every month, it may be easier (from a maintenance perspective) to store the application libraries on a network file server rather than try to maintain releases of the application on each user's workstation.

Note: When placing applications on users' hard drives for performance reasons, a software distribution mechanism should be in place to simplify maintenance. Software distribution can be handled either with third-party tools or manually. One approach to manual software distribution is for the workstation, at startup, to check the date of its application executable against the one on the network. If the date of the network executable is different from the date of the workstation executable, a new application executable and associated files should get copied to the client workstation. This is a simple example of a mechanism that simplifies maintenance. There are many different ways they can be implemented so that the users experience optimal performance while the application administrators do not have to deal with frequent manual copying of software to each user's workstation.

It is difficult to recommend a single solution for the distribution of application components. Solutions vary according to such things as client and server storage capacity, network traffic, and concurrent users of an application. For the client, storing components on the user workstation may improve performance, but this also uses more disk space and increases required configuration management. On the server side, if the load on the database server is too much, for example, moving one or more server application programs to another server can help. But while this reduces the load on the database server, it will certainly increase network traffic and can thus decrease overall performance.

Preloading Windows

Preloading application windows refers to the loading of application windows into the memory of the client workstation at application login time. At login time, if a window is preloaded, it is opened and then hidden. Any calls to open the window result in the display of the hidden window rather than the reopening of the window, which is slower. When a preloaded window is closed, it is actually hidden instead of closed. Preloading windows slows the login procedure, but provides faster access to the window at any point after login. This increases overall application performance if a window is opened and closed many times throughout an application.

The price of preloading a window is sacrificing available memory on the client workstation, because the window remains resident in memory even after it is "closed." The number of windows that can be preloaded is limited by the amount of available memory on the client workstation and depends on the size of the windows.

The windows that are to be preloaded can either be determined at development time and built into the application or determined dynamically based on a user profile. For example, system administrators may use screen 1 much more often than they use screen 2, while clerks use screen 2 more than screen 1. Without dynamic preloading, if screen 1 were preloaded, all users would incur the longer login caused by the preloading of screen 1. For users who do not regularly access this screen and therefore do not benefit from the performance gain of preloading, this is inefficient. With dynamic preloading, the system could be configured to preload screen 1 only for system administrators and screen 2 only for clerks.

In either case, in order to obtain the greatest benefit of preloading, it should be done only with windows that are opened and closed frequently in a user session.

Without preloading, all windows are opened each time they are displayed. This can be slow and inefficient, depending on such things as the size of the window and the number of database requests made when opening a window.

Choosing PowerBuilder Controls

Understanding the set of PowerBuilder controls and their intended use can keep developers from writing unnecessary code that can decrease performance and lead to inconsistency among application components.

PowerBuilder controls are an extended set of the standard Windows controls. Each control has a set of built-in capabilities that allow the user to interface with an application by either entering data, initiating an action, or choosing an option. Each control placed on a window uses part of the Windows User Heap. The Windows User Heap is a 64K region of memory used by Windows to store handles, controls, resources, and other objects used by Windows applications.

There is no limit to the number of controls that can be placed on a window. However, the time required to open a window increases as the number of controls on the window increases. Powersoft recommends that the number of controls (visible and hidden) on a single window be less than 20.

Note: It is important to remember that each user object counts as the number of controls that make up the user object; they are not viewed as a single control.

DataWindows In addition to all the advantages the DataWindow object provides a developer with regard to database access and validation, it can also enhance performance. This is because a DataWindow control is treated as a single control by Windows, rather than multiple standard controls. Assume, for example, the developer wants to enter the ID, first name, last name, status, and salary of an employee. Doing this without using a DataWindow would require the placement of 12 controls onto the window, as shown in Figure 23.8.

When this window is opened, each of the 12 controls must be painted separately. Doing this with a DataWindow results in only a single control, the DataWindow control, on the window, as shown in Figure 23.9.

The DataWindow can be treated as a single control because it is

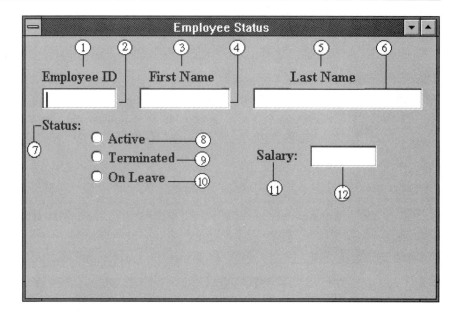

Figure 23.8   A window with 12 controls.

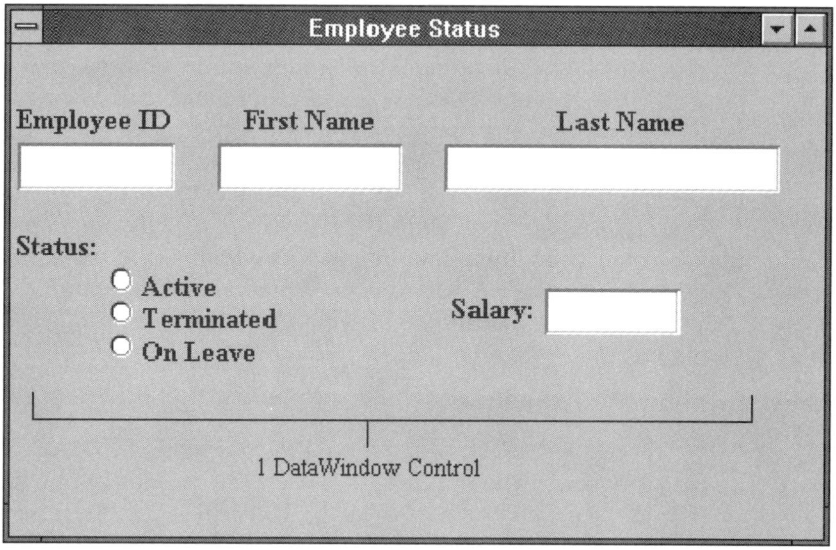

Figure 23.9   Using a DataWindow, the same window now has only one control.

managed by PowerBuilder rather than by Windows. Treating the DataWindow as a single control reduces the amount of the Windows User Heap required because only one control needs to be painted when the window is opened. This results in better performance. Regardless of how many items are placed within a DataWindow, it is still treated as only one control by Windows. Therefore, the more complex the DataWindow, the greater the performance gain of using the DataWindow control instead of standard controls.

DataWindows vs. DropDownListBoxes Developers are often faced with the question of whether to use a DataWindow or DropDownListBox to list a set of options available to the user. The answer to this question depends on the data in the list. If the data is static and does not reside in a database, it is more efficient and easier for the developer to use a DropDownListBox window control. The values can then be hard-coded into the control with no other changes required to display the set of values.

If the data is being retrieved from the database, however, it is more efficient to use a DataWindow. Without using a DataWindow, the developer would have to write the code to retrieve the data from the database and add the retrieved data to the DropDownListBox control.

Static vs. Dynamic Interfaces

A static interface is an interface that remains unchanged during the execution of an application. Most simple applications have a static interface.

A dynamic interface, on the other hand, is an interface that can change at runtime. A dynamic interface can be implemented in PowerBuilder by such measures as hiding and displaying controls, dynamically creating objects, changing the DataWindow object of a DataWindow control, changing pictures on a PictureButton or Picture object, or enabling and disabling controls on a window. While application requirements may dictate a dynamic interface, keep in mind that the more dynamic the interface, the worse an application will perform.

Inheritance and Performance

Many people mistakenly believe that while inheritance provides many benefits in the development of PowerBuilder applications, it does this at the expense of performance. Not only is this an incorrect assumption, but also it can be just the opposite. If implemented correctly, inheritance can actually increase performance. The best way to show this is through an example. Suppose the following inheritance hierarchy in Figure 23.10 is in place.

The shaded boxes are virtual classes while the Product, Order, and Customer windows are actual application windows. Using this hierarchy, all three windows share code in the StdMaint and StdWindow classes, while the Order and Customer windows share code in the MastDet, StdMaint, and StdWindow classes. When opening the Customer window for the first time, PowerBuilder does the following:

1. Searches the library search list for Customer.
2. Sees that Customer is inherited from MastDet. Searches for MastDet.
3. Sees that MastDet is inherited from StdMaint. Searches for StdMaint.
4. Sees that StdMaint is inherited from StdWindow. Searches for StdWindow.
5. Loads StdWindow.
6. Searches for and loads objects contained within StdWindow.
7. Loads StdMaint.
8. Searches for and loads objects contained within StdMaint.
9. Loads MastDet.
10. Searches for and loads objects contained within MastDet.
11. Loads Customer.
12. Searches for and loads all objects within Customer.
13. Executes the open event of Customer.

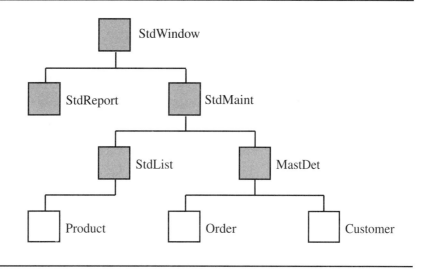

Figure 23.10   Sample object hierarchy.

When Customer has been loaded into memory, loading Order is done much more quickly because the code contained in the virtual classes is already resident in memory and thus doesn't need to be loaded. To open Order with Customer open, PowerBuilder:

1. Searches the library search list for Order.
2. Sees that Order is inherited from MastDet, which is already resident in memory.
3. Loads Order.
4. Searches for and loads all objects within Order.
5. Executes the open event of Order.

Because much of the code used by the application windows is contained in the virtual classes, the size of the application windows is smaller than it would be without using inheritance. This makes the opening of the application windows much faster. Refer to Appendix E for a more detailed discussion of PowerBuilder Inheritance and Performance.

POWERBUILDER APPLICATION DEVELOPMENT

Many things can be done by developers to increase application performance. Performance of a PowerBuilder application can be divided into three areas: object creation, script execution, and data retrieval. Developers can do specific things in each of these areas to increase performance. This section lists some of the things developers should be aware of when developing PowerBuilder applications.

Scope of Variables and Functions

Variables and functions should be declared only in the scope for which they are needed. Global variables remain in memory throughout the execution of the application, while local, instance, and shared variables remain in memory only as long as the object(s) for which they are defined exist. Thus, global variables and functions should only be used when necessary. Global functions are slower than object-level functions.

Managing PowerBuilder Libraries

Although there is no physical limitation on the size of a PBL, Powersoft recommends that PBLs be less than 800K in size. A PBL file is nothing more than a linked list of objects. Knowing this, it is easy to see why a large PBL could decrease performance. The larger the PBL, the more time PowerBuilder may require to access an object at runtime. It also takes longer to open or save an object in the development environment with a large PBL.

Powersoft also recommends that the number of objects in a single PBL be limited to approximately 50. This is primarily to simplify the use of the Library painter in the development environment. While it is important to keep PBLs from becoming too large or cluttered, using a large number of smaller PBLs can also negatively impact performance. This is because each new library must be added to the library search list of the application. Increasing the number of libraries in the search list can decrease performance by forcing PowerBuilder to search through more files in order to access an object.

The library search path of an application plays an important role in the performance of an application. It is important because it dictates the path that PowerBuilder follows when searching for objects during execution. When retrieving an object, PowerBuilder first looks in the .EXE file. If the object is not found in the .EXE file, PowerBuilder searches each .PBD in the order it is listed in the library search path of the application. This makes the order of the .PBLs in the library search path a significant factor in application performance. To achieve better performance, put the .PBLs containing the most often used objects at the top of the library search list. It is also recommended that .PBLs containing ancestor objects be listed before .PBLs containing descendant objects.

PowerBuilder libraries should be optimized often and regenerated before creating an .EXE. Optimizing the library removes any unused space in the .PBL. Unused space in a .PBL increases as objects are updated and deleted during the development cycle. Regenerating the objects in a .PBL cleans up any pointer references among the objects in the .PBL that may have been corrupted during development. For more information, refer to Chapter 20.

PowerScript Coding Considerations

Restrict Function Calls in Loop Control Statements Although it may reduce the number of lines of code, putting a call to a function that returns a constant value in a loop control statement can greatly reduce performance. The degree to which performance is reduced depends on the function called and the number of times the loop is executed. For example, when initializing the elements of an array, instead of the following:

```
// This function initializes the passed array

integer iArray_cnt

FOR iArray_cnt = myArray.UpperBound( ) TO 1 STEP -1
    myArray[iArray_cnt] = iArray_cnt * .05
NEXT
```

load the value returned by the function into a variable and use the variable within the loop as follows:

```
// This function initializes the passed array

integer iArray_cnt, iArray_len

iArray_len = myArray.UpperBound( )

FOR iArray_cnt = iArray_len TO 1 STEP -1
    myArray[iArray_cnt] = iArray_cnt * .05
NEXT
```

Use Object-level Functions In addition to the benefits of object-level functions with regard to data encapsulation, object-level functions also improve performance when compared to global functions.

When the call is made to a global function, it is located by searching through the .EXE file and all application .PBD files until it is found.

When the function has been located, it is executed and removed from memory. This process is repeated each time the function is called.

Object-level functions, on the other hand, are loaded into memory at the same time as the parent object is. When a call is made to the function, execution is much faster because it is already in memory.

Minimize the Use of UpperBound( ) and LowerBound( ) Because the **UpperBound** and **LowerBound** functions are relatively slow, try to minimize the number of times they must be called. One way to do this is to store the return values of these functions in variables and reference these variables throughout the application.

Use Compound Commands for dwDescribe and dwModify Take advantage of PowerBuilder's ability to pass multiple commands to the **dwDescribe( )** and **dwModify( )** functions. This improves performance by reducing the number of function calls and by reducing the number of calls made to Windows to repaint the screen.

Use SetRedraw( ) When making several changes to controls within a window, use the **SetRedraw( )** function to turn off screen painting until all the changes have been made. Leaving redraw on while making changes slows performance and causes the screen to flicker as the changes are being made. It is important that **SetRedraw( )** be called after the changes have been made—to turn drawing back on again. The following example shows how to use **SetRedraw( )** when disabling all the columns in a DataWindow:

```
/****************************************************
** Disable all of the columns in this datawindow by setting tab
** order to zero and visually representing it as disabled.
****************************************************/
string sObjects, sAnObject, sObjType

setPointer(hourGlass!)
setRedraw(this,false)
sObjects = dwDescribe(this,"datawindow.objects")

// the nextParm function returns the next value in the tab
// delimited string returned from the line above

sAnObject = nextParm(sObjects)
do while sAnObject <> ""
        if left(sAnObject,4) <> "obj_" then
```

```
                    /* only deal with named objects */
                    if dwDescribe(this,sAnObject+".type") = "column" then
                          this.disable(sAnObject)
                     end if
        end if
        sAnObject = nextParm(sObjects)
loop
setRedraw(this,true)
return true
```

Note: In certain instances, turning redraw on again by calling **setRedraw(this,true)** may not cause the screen to be repainted. In these situations, force the redraw by sending the WM_PAINT message to the window.

Use Static Arrays instead of Dynamic Arrays While dynamic arrays provide a great deal of flexibility to a developer, this flexibility is at the cost of performance. Performance decreases when the dynamic array is created and each time the array must grow to accommodate new data elements. This performance decrease occurs because of the way PowerBuilder handles the growth of an array. When a dynamic array needs to grow, the following events occur:

1. PowerBuilder requests additional memory from Windows.
2. Windows allocates the new memory. The amount of memory allocated is the size of the existing array plus the size of the next array element.
3. The existing array is copied to the new memory location.
4. PowerBuilder releases the old memory back to Windows.

Performing this sequence of events each time the dynamic array grows has obvious performance implications. One approach to reduce the number of times these steps need to be performed is to start from the last element of an array and work back towards the beginning. For example, when initializing the elements of a dynamic array, looping from the last element to the first is more efficient than the traditional looping from first to last:

```
// This function initializes the passed array

integer iArray_cnt
```

```
FOR iArray_cnt = iArray_len TO 1 STEP -1
    myArray[iArray_cnt] = iArray_cnt * .05

NEXT
```

With static arrays, the amount of memory required is known when the array is declared and can be allocated at this time, with no additional overhead required.

Pass Arguments to Functions by Reference Passing arguments by reference is more efficient than passing by value. This is because passing an argument by value causes a copy of the argument to be made for use by the function. This increases the amount of memory used as well as increases the time to execute the function. When passing by reference, on the other hand, a pointer to the argument is passed and no additional memory is required to execute the function.

No Long-running Events in Open and Activate Events Because a window is not displayed until the open and activate events have completed execution, try to limit the amount of code in these events. When putting a large amount of code in these events cannot be avoided, provide a mechanism such as a message line or changing cursor to improve perceived performance.

Posting a User-defined Event to Perform Retrieval Posting to a user-defined event to perform long-running tasks such as data retrieval can improve perceived performance. This is because posting to a user-defined event allows processing to continue before the process is complete.

RetrieveRow Decreases Performance Any code (even a comment) in the RetrieveRow event of a DataWindow decreases performance. This is because PowerBuilder performs a Yield after each row returned to the DataWindow.

Limit Code in ItemChanged and ItemFocusChanged Events Too much code in ItemChanged or ItemFocusChanged events causes delays in moving from column to column within a DataWindow.

Limit Code in a Clicked Event if a Double-clicked Event Exists In situations where there are both a clicked and a double-clicked event, too much code in the clicked event may keep a second click from being registered. This effectively prevents the code in the double-clicked event from being triggered.

Don't Use the Other Event The Other event is designed to handle a Windows event that does not correspond with a PowerBuilder event. It is a holdover from previous versions of PowerBuilder and should not be used. Instead of using this type of event, create a user-defined event or use the PowerBuilder message object to handle Windows events.

Database Connectivity Considerations

Use SetTransObject( ) instead of SetTrans( ) To minimize the number of times an application connects to the database, use **SetTransObject( )** rather than **SetTrans( )**. Using **SetTrans( )**, the application connects to the database, performs an action, and disconnects from the database *for each database transaction*. This decreases performance because of the added time to connect to the database.

Using **SetTransObject( )** makes the developer responsible for connecting to the database from within a script. This allows multiple database transactions to be performed during a single connection with the database. With **SetTransObject( )**, developers are also responsible for committing or rolling back any data as well as explicitly disconnecting from the database.

The following example shows how a master and detail DataWindow can be updated within a single database connection using **SetTrans Object( )**:

```
/****************************************************
** Update our datawindows—maintain transaction appropriately.
** Update transaction from bottom up—from child to parent to
** ensure the integrity of the data. This assumes that myTrans has
** already been created and set up correctly.
****************************************************/

dw_master.SetTransObject(myTrans)
dw_detail.SetTransObject(myTrans)

connect using myTrans;

if dw_detail.update( ) = 1 then
     if dw_master.update( ) = 1 then
          dw_detail.dwResetUpdate( )
          dw_master.dwResetUpdate( )
          disconnect using myTrans;
          return true
     end if
end if
```

```
// Error in update. This will be handled by the DataWindow
disconnect using myTrans;
return false
```

Using Retrieve As Needed Retrieve As Needed provides the ability to bring a result set from the server to the client only as the rows are needed for displaying in a DataWindow. For example, if a DataWindow control is sized to show only three rows at a time, Retrieve As Needed initially brings back only enough data from the server to show the first three rows. As the user pages down through the data, PowerBuilder continues to return data from the server to display in the DataWindow. The user may or may not continue to page down until all the data in the result set has been returned to the client. The diagram in Figure 23.11 illustrates how Retrieve As Needed differs from traditional data retrieval.

PowerBuilder implements Retrieve As Needed by opening a cursor and maintaining it as rows are retrieved from the server. When data is needed on the client, PowerBuilder simply fetches enough rows from the server (in two-page increments) to update the display of the DataWindow (see Figure 23.12).

Retrieve As Needed must be used properly to achieve performance gains. If the user is going to page through a large percentage of the result

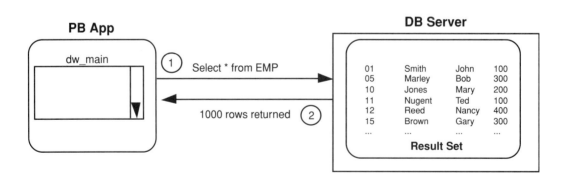

(1) dw_main.Retrieve() sends query to server

(2) Server sends entire result set to client buffer

Figure 23.11   Data retrieval without Retrieve As Needed.

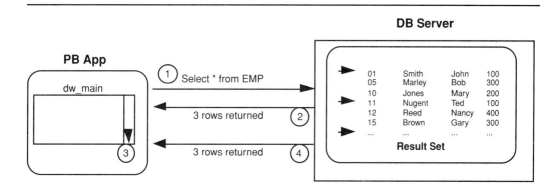

1. dw_main.Retrieve() opens a cursor and fetches the first three rows from the server.

2. Server only sends the first three rows to the client buffer.

3. User pages down in dw_main causing the client to fetch the next three rows from the server.

4. Server sends the next three rows to the client. The new rows are added to the client buffer.

Figure 23.12   Data retrieval with Retrieve As Needed.

set, Retrieve As Needed decreases perceived performance because data retrieval is being done each time the user scrolls. In this situation, Retrieve As Needed should not be used. However, if a large result set is being retrieved and the user will usually not page through the result set, Retrieve As Needed can provide a significant gain in perceived performance.

Preloading Data The preloading of data refers to the loading of database values into the memory of the client workstation at application login time. This can reduce the number of database queries and thus improve application performance. Preloading data slows the login procedure, but provides faster data access at any point after login. The price that is paid for preloading is available memory on the client workstation. Data preloading should be determined on a per-application basis.

The amount of data that can be preloaded is limited to the amount of available memory on the client workstation. The preloading of data is accomplished by retrieving data from the database at application login time and storing these values in a global array. After the data is loaded into the array, all subsequent requests for this data access the array rather than the database. This reduces network traffic and increases performance.

There are some drawbacks to preloading data, however. With the data stored in memory, any changes made to the data in the database are not reflected immediately to the user. Because the data is read from the database at login time only, the user would have to exit the system and log in again to see any changes. For this reason, if the data is fairly dynamic and the user needs to see updates in a relatively short time frame, preloading this data should not be done. If, however, the data is accessed in a read-only mode or is fairly static, preloading should be considered as a way to increase performance. As previously mentioned, preloading data slows the login procedure, but increases overall performance if the data is referenced many times throughout an application.

Analysis should be done to determine what data should be preloaded. Codes tables are a good candidate for data preloading, because this data is usually fairly static and used many times throughout an application. Without preloading, data that is referenced multiple times throughout an application requires a separate database query for each reference.

Minimize Number of Connections The number of connections to a database can impact performance on both the client and database server. All databases have a limit on the number of concurrent connections allowed. While this value varies among different platforms and RDBMS products, each connection consumes server resources. On the client side, each connection requires a separate PowerBuilder transaction object.

Commit Often Because committing changes to the database removes any pending locks and frees server resources, a commit statement should be issued as often as possible within the logical unit of work.

Tune SQL Statements Tuning the SQL sent to the server reduces the time and resources the server needs to process the statement. Most databases have either a rule-based or cost-based optimizer that allows developers to structure a SQL statement in a way that achieves the best performance. It is important for developers to know how these optimizers work in order to take advantage of them. For example, Oracle7 provides a rule-based optimizer that chooses an execution plan based on a ranking of access paths. The access paths are ranked by Oracle7 as follows:

Rank	*Access Path*
1	Single row ROWID
2	Single row by cluster join
3	Single row by hash cluster key with unique or primary key
4	Single row by unique or primary key
5	Cluster join
6	Hash cluster key
7	Indexed cluster key
8	Composite key
9	Single-column indexes
10	Bounded range search on indexed columns
11	Unbounded range search on indexed columns
12	Sort-merge join
13	MAX or MIN of indexed columns
14	ORDER BY on indexed columns
15	Full table scan

When the Oracle engine receives a query and is using its rules-based optimizer, the execution path chosen depends on the rank of all the valid access paths of the query.

CHAPTER 24

The Data Pipeline

The Data Pipeline object, introduced in PowerBuilder 4, allows the transfer of data between tables in a database. Data may be transferred between tables in the same database or among tables in different databases—including databases from different DBMSs.

The Data Pipeline is a very powerful feature that has many potential uses. In the development environment, it provides an easy way of making a local copy of data for a developer to use during development. In a production environment, the Data Pipeline can be used to simplify any data distribution or synchronization of data among different databases in a distributed environment. While these functions can be performed without the Data Pipeline, using it eases the job of the developer and data administrator.

This chapter discusses the following:

- Creating a Data Pipeline object
- Data Pipeline object attributes, events, and functions
- Executing a Data Pipeline

CREATING A DATA PIPELINE OBJECT

Data Pipeline objects are created using the Data Pipeline painter. For example, assume we want to transfer data from the employee table in the Powersoft Demo DB to the Contacts database.

Note: Although both of the databases in this example are local WATCOM databases, the source and destination database could be any database supported by PowerBuilder.

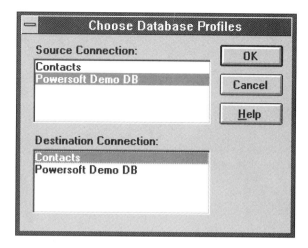

Figure 24.1   Choosing source and destination database profiles.

When creating a new pipeline object, the developer is prompted for the source and destination database profiles, as shown in Figure 24.1. Once the source and destination profile is chosen, a table listing from the source database profile is displayed, as shown in Figure 24.2.

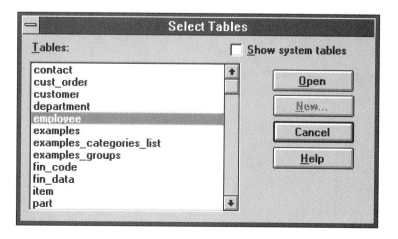

Figure 24.2   The Select Tables dialog box.

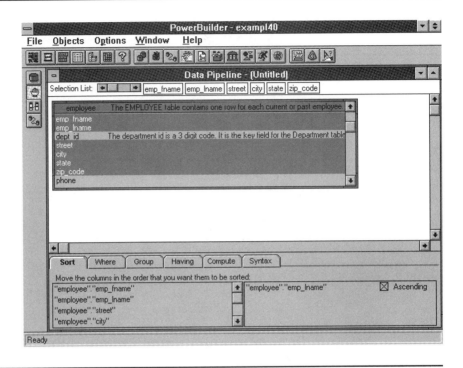

Figure 24.3 The SQL painter for the query.

The Select Tables dialog works the same way as for other PowerBuilder functions, allowing the developer to select one or more tables to be used in building the query. For this example, only the employee table is required. After the table(s) selection is made, the query is built using the PowerBuilder SQL painter. For this example, select the employee name and address and sort the results by the employee's last name. The SQL painter for this query is shown in Figure 24.3.

After building the query, return to the Data Pipeline workspace by clicking the Data Pipeline icon on the painter toolbar. The Data Pipeline workspace is shown in Figure 24.4.

The Data Pipeline painter contains the following fields.

Table

This field is the name the table will have in the destination database. The default is the name of the source table, but this may be changed.

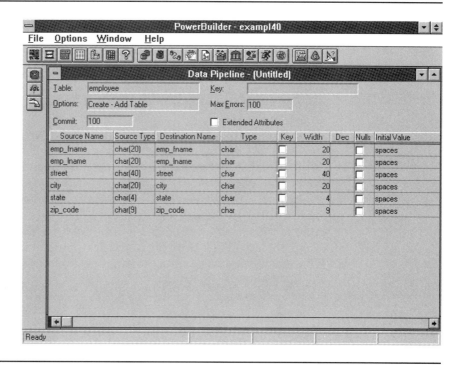

Figure 24.4   The Data Pipeline workspace.

Option

This field designates the data transfer method. Choices are:

- **Create - Add Table**—Creates a new table in the destination database and copies data from the source table to the newly created table. If the destination table already exists, an error will occur.
- **Replace - Drop/Add Table**—Drops and recreates the table in the destination database and copies data from the source table to the newly created table. No error will occur if the destination table already exists.

  When using either the Create - Add Table or Replace - Drop/Add Table options, the table definition of the destination table can be modified. All modifications must follow the rules of the destination database. Also, if a value is entered in the Key field, a key column must be specified for the destination table (and vice versa). PowerBuilder will create a primary key or index (whichever is supported by that DBMS) for the table in the destination database.

- **Refresh - Delete/Insert**—Adds data to the destination table by first deleting all data from the table and then copying data from the source table to the destination table. When using this option, the destination table must exist.
- **Append - Insert**—Appends data from the source table to the destination table. No data is deleted from the destination table before inserting the source data. When using this option, the destination table must exist.
  When using either the Refresh - Delete/Insert or Append - Insert options, the destination table must exist, but can be any table in the destination database. Also, only the Commit and Max Errors fields can be changed.
- **Update - Update/Insert**—Updates data in the destination table using data from the source table. Any new rows from the source table are inserted into the destination table, while rows from the source table that already exist in the destination table are updated. When using this option, the destination table must exist and the Key field must be specified.

Commit

Specifies the number of rows copied to the destination database before the changes are committed. The default value for this field is 100; that means 100 rows will be copied to the destination table before a Commit statement is issued. If Commit is 0, PowerBuilder issues a Commit only after all rows have been read. In this case, either all changes are made to the destination database or no changes are made. If Commit is less than 100, PowerBuilder uses it as the blocking factor. For example, if the commit field is 10, 10 rows will be read and then written at once.

Key

This is the name of the primary key for the table in the destination database. When using the Create - Add Table or Replace - Drop/Add options, PowerBuilder will create the primary key using the name specified in this field.

Max Errors

This is the maximum number of errors allowed before stopping the pipeline. The default value for this field is 100 which means that when the 100th error occurs during a pipeline execution, the pipeline is stopped. All pipeline errors are displayed in a DataWindow that allows the user to manually correct the errors and update the destination database with the corrected values. Correcting pipeline errors is discussed later in the chapter.

Extended Attributes

This allows any extended attributes (validation rules, edit masks, or display formats) to be copied from the source table to the destination table. Columns in the source table with extended attributes should have the extended attributes copied to the new table in order to use them in the destination table.

Column Definition

This defines the name and type of each column from the source table along with the following information for each column in the destination table:

- **Destination Name**—Name of the column in the destination table.
- **Type**—Datatype of the column in the destination table.
- **Key**—Specifies if the column is a key column in the destination table.
- **Width**—Specifies the precision of the column.
- **Dec**—Specifies the scale of the column.
- **Nulls**—Specifies whether the column allows Nulls.
- **Initial Value**—Specifies the initial value of the column.

PowerBuilder obtains the initial column information from the Select statement used to retrieve data from the source database. When using the Create - Add Table or Replace - Drop/Add Table options, this information may be changed. However, when using any of the other options, the column information may not be changed.

Once the column information has been entered, save the Data Pipeline object by selecting the Save As... option from the File menu and giving the object a name (p_example in our example).

EXECUTING A DATA PIPELINE

Data Pipelines can be executed within the development environment or added to an application and executed at runtime. This section discusses the execution of a Data Pipeline in both environments.

Using Pipelines in the Development Environment

To execute a pipeline within the development environment, simply click the Execute Pipeline icon from the Data Pipeline painter (⬛) as shown in Figure 24.5 or select the Execute option from the Options menu.

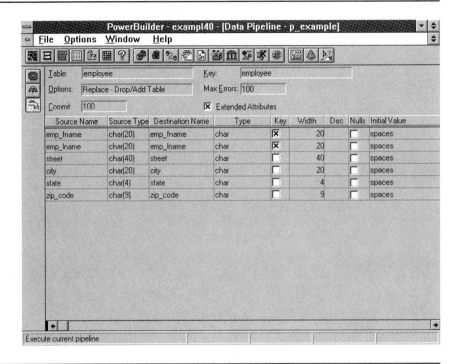

The table in the figure contains the following data:

Source Name	Source Type	Destination Name	Type	Key	Width	Dec	Nulls	Initial Value
emp_fname	char(20)	emp_fname	char	☒	20		☐	spaces
emp_lname	char(20)	emp_lname	char	☒	20		☐	spaces
street	char(40)	street	char	☐	40		☐	spaces
city	char(20)	city	char	☐	20		☐	spaces
state	char(4)	state	char	☐	4		☐	spaces
zip_code	char(9)	zip_code	char	☐	9		☐	spaces

Figure 24.5   Executing a Data Pipeline.

During pipeline execution, the number of rows read, the number of rows written, the elapsed time, and the number of errors will be displayed in MicroHelp.

Note: To change the source or destination database of a pipeline object, select the Source Connect or Destination Connect option from the File menu and choose the new database.

Errors encountered when executing a pipeline from the development environment are displayed in a special Error DataWindow. The Error DataWindow displays the name of the table in the destination database in which the errors occurred and the option that was selected in the Data Pipeline painter. The Error DataWindow also displays each error message and the values in the row in which each error occurred.

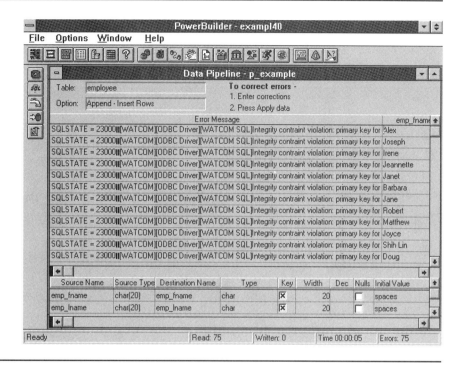

Figure 24.6   The Error DataWindow.

Errors may be corrected by changing the values in the Error DataWindow and clicking the Update Database icon (⌷). When correcting errors, PowerBuilder will update the database and display any remaining errors in the Error DataWindow. For example, in the previous example, change the option to Append - Insert Rows. Because data is already in the destination table, a duplicate key error will occur for each row. When executing the pipeline, the Error DataWindow will be displayed as shown in Figure 24.6.

When all errors have been corrected, the user is returned to the Data Pipeline Design dialog. The user may also return to the Design dialog without correcting the errors by clicking the Design icon (⌷).

Note: Pipeline errors may be printed or saved to a file by selecting the Print or Save As... options from the File menu.

Using Pipelines in an Application

Using a Data Pipeline in an application requires the creation of the Data Pipeline object as well as the creation of a standard nonvisual user object of the Pipeline type. Using the previous example, create a Pipeline user object as shown in Figure 24.7.

This will create a nonvisual user object inherited from the PowerBuilder Pipeline object (see Figure 24.8). This user object has special attributes, events, and functions associated with it. The attributes, events, and functions of the Pipeline user object type are described in the next section.

After saving the new user object (named p_pipe_example), it can be created dynamically within the application. For example, assume there is a window designed to use the Data Pipeline object created earlier in the chapter. This window contains a DataWindow for the employee table of the PowerBuilder Demo database, a DataWindow for the employee table in the Contacts database, and a DataWindow to be used as the Error DataWindow for the pipeline. In addition to these controls, the window also contains static text controls to show the number of rows read, written, and in error, and a set of command buttons. This window is shown in Figure 24.9.

The open event of the window will call a function to set up and

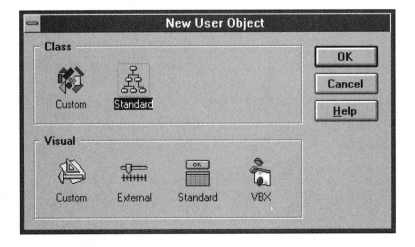

Figure 24.7   Creating a Pipeline user object.

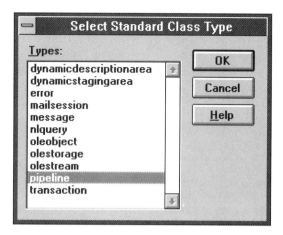

Figure 24.8   A nonvisual user object created from PowerBuilder Pipeline object.

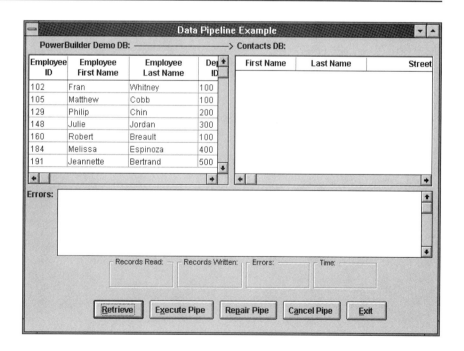

Figure 24.9   Sample window for executing a Data Pipeline in an application.

connect the source and destination transaction objects and create the instance variable i_pipe, of type p_pipe_example. i_pipe will be used throughout the application to refer to the Data Pipeline nonvisual user object. The first thing done after i_pipe is created is to set its Dataobject attribute to p_example, the Data Pipeline object created earlier in the chapter. The code for the window open event is:

```
setpointer (hourglass!)

//function to connect to source & destination transactions to the
//database
connect_dbs( )

//create an instance variable of our pipeline user object type and
//set its dataobject attribute to the pipeline object p_example
//(this is where our non-visual user object is created)

i_pipe = create p_pipe_example
i_pipe.dataobject = "p_example"
```

The window function **connect_dbs( )** reads connection information from EXAMPLE.INI and creates a separate Transaction object for the source and destination transactions. After connecting to each database, the **setTransObject( )** function is called for the two main application DataWindows:

```
//create source and destination transactions and connect to each database

//i_source will be the source transaction
i_source = create transaction

i_source.DBMS     = ProfileString("example.ini","sqlca","dbms","")
i_source.database = ProfileString("example.ini","sqlca","database","")
i_source.userid   = ProfileString("example.ini","sqlca","userid","")
i_source.dbpass   = ProfileString("example.ini","sqlca","dbpass","")
i_source.logid    = ProfileString("example.ini","sqlca","logid","")
i_source.logpass  = ProfileString("example.ini","sqlca","logpass","")
i_source.servername = ProfileString("example.ini","sqlca","servername","")
i_source.dbparm   = ProfileString("example.ini","sqlca","dbparm","")

connect using i_source;
If i_source.sqlcode <> 0 then
        Messagebox("Source Connect Err",i_source.sqlerrtext)
```

```
        Return
End If


//i_dest will be the destination transaction
i_dest = create transaction

i_dest.DBMS      = ProfileString("example.ini","contacts","dbms","")
i_dest.database = ProfileString("example.ini","contacts","database","")
i_dest.userid    = ProfileString("example.ini","contacts","userid","")
i_dest.dbpass    = ProfileString("example.ini","contacts","dbpass","")
i_dest.logid     = ProfileString("example.ini","contacts","logid","")
i_dest.logpass   = ProfileString("example.ini","contacts","logpass","")
i_dest.servername = ProfileString("example.ini","contacts","servername","")
i_dest.dbparm    = ProfileString("example.ini","contacts","dbparm","")


connect using i_dest;
If i_dest.sqlcode <> 0 then
        Messagebox("Destination Connect Err",i_dest.sqlerrtext)
        Return
End If


//Set the transaction objects of the two DataWindows to the new
//transactions
dw_employee_demo.setTransObject(i_source)
dw_employee_contacts.setTransObject(i_dest)
```

The [sqlca] and [contacts] sections of EXAMPLE.INI are:

```
[sqlca]
dbms=ODBC
database=
userid=dba
dbpass=sql
logid=
logpass=
servername=
DbParm=ConnectString='DSN=Powersoft Demo DB;UID=dba;PWD=sql'

[contacts]
dbms=ODBC
database=
userid=dba
dbpass=sql
```

```
logid=
logpass=
servername=
DbParm=ConnectString='DSN=Contacts;UID=dba;PWD=sql'
```

Initially, there will be no data in the employee table of the Contacts database, and the window will look like Figure 24.9 after the <u>R</u>etrieve button is clicked. When the E<u>x</u>ecute button is clicked, the pipeline is executed as shown in the clicked event of the button:

```
//This script will execute the pipeline data transfer of the employee
//table from the PowerBuilder Demo DB to the Contacts DB
int     iRtn
long    lStartTime, lEndTime

//get the starting time of the transfer
lStartTime = Cpu ( )

//execute the pipeline, passing dw_1 as the Error DataWindow
iRtn = i_pipe.start (i_source, i_dest, dw_1)

//get ending time
lEndTime = Cpu ( )

//display the transfer time along with the number of rows read, written,
//and in error (using the pipeline object attributes)
st_time.text = string((lEndTime - lStartTime)/1000,"##0.0")
st_read.text = string(i_pipe.RowsRead)
st_written.text = string(i_pipe.RowsWritten)
st_inerror.text = string(i_pipe.RowsInError)

//retrieve from Contacts employee table to show changes
dw_employee_contacts.SetRedraw(false)
dw_employee_contacts.retrieve( )
dw_employee_contacts.SetRedraw(true)
```

This example assumes that the Data Pipeline object is using the Replace - Drop/Add Table option in which the data is deleted from the destination database before the pipeline is executed. The results of executing the pipeline are shown in Figure 24.10.

If we changed the option of the Data Pipeline object from Replace - Drop/Add Table to Append - Insert and executed the pipeline again, we would receive a duplicate key error for each row. Each row that contains an error (in this case all rows) would be displayed in the Error DataWindow, as shown in Figure 24.11.

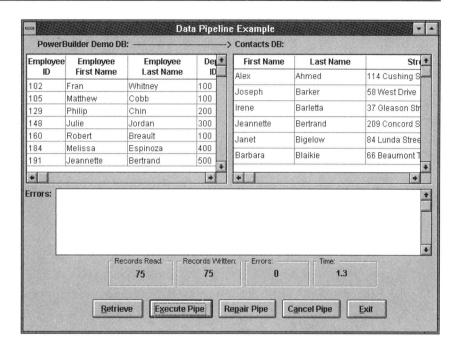

Figure 24.10   Data Pipeline execution result.

At this point, there is freedom to make any corrections within the Error DataWindow and update the destination database by clicking the Repair Pipe button. If one were to change the key value (last name + first name) of the first two rows and click the Repair Pipe button, the two corrected rows would be copied to the destination database and the window would look like the one in Figure 24.12.

Notice that the Records Read, Records Written, and Error values have changed from the original pipeline execution to correspond to the two corrected records. The code for the Repair Pipe button is:

```
//This script will take any changes to the error datawindow (Dw_1) and
//try to commit them to the destination database
long    lStartTime, lEndTime

//get time for a total elapsed time
lStartTime = Cpu ( )
```

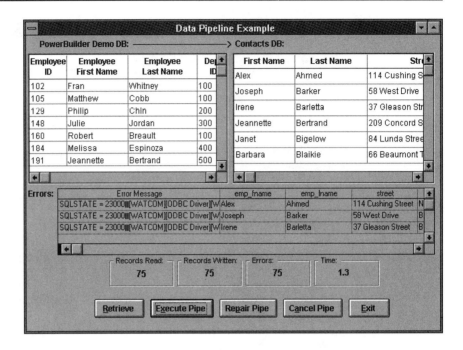

Figure 24.11 The Error DataWindow.

```
//execute the pipeline repair function
i_pipe.repair (i_dest)

//get ending time
lEndTime = Cpu ( )
st_time.text = string((lEndTime - lStartTime)/1000,"##0.0")

st_read.text = string(i_pipe.RowsRead)
st_written.text = string(i_pipe.RowsWritten)
st_inerror.text = string(i_pipe.RowsInError)

//update the Contacts DataWindow in case some errors were corrected.
dw_employee_contacts.retrieve( )
```

The previous examples show how Data Pipelines can be used from the PowerBuilder development environment as well as within a PowerBuilder application.

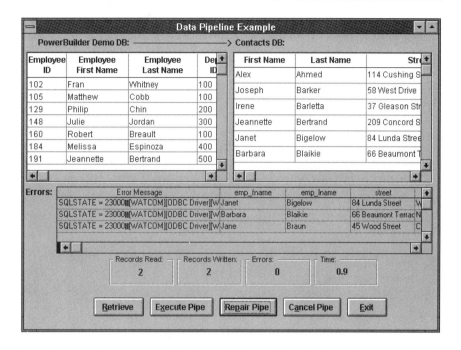

Figure 24.12   The Data Pipeline window after the two currected rows are copied to the destination database.

DATA PIPELINE OBJECT ATTRIBUTES, EVENTS, AND FUNCTIONS

This section lists the attributes, events, and functions associated with a Data Pipeline object. Note that these are associated with the nonvisual Data Pipeline user object and not the Data Pipeline object itself. The relationship between the Data Pipeline user object and the actual Data Pipeline object is the same as the relationship between a DataWindow control and a DataWindow object.

Data Pipeline objects have the following attributes:

- **RowsRead**—Long value containing the number of rows read by the pipeline.
- **RowsWritten**—Long value containing the number of rows written by the pipeline.
- **RowsInError**—Long value containing the number of rows the pipeline found in error. Possible errors include duplicate keys in the

destination table, Null values copied into a column that does not allow Nulls, or an invalid datatype.

- **DataObject**—String value containing the name of the pipeline object.
- **Syntax**—String value containing the syntax of the pipeline object.

The following events are associated with Data Pipeline objects:

- **PipeEnd**—Fired when the **Start( )** or **Repair( )** functions have completed.
- **PipeMeter**—Fired after each block of rows is read or written during a pipeline execution. The size of each block is determined by the Commit setting specified when creating the Data Pipeline object.
- **PipeStart**—Fired when the **Start( )** or **Repair( )** function is started.

The following functions exist for Data Pipeline objects:

- **Start( )**—Executes a defined Data Pipeline object. The format of the **Start( )** function is:

```
pipelineobject.Start (sourcetransaction, destinationtransaction,
errordatawindow {,arg1, arg2,..., argn })
```

where:

> ***pipelineobject***—The name of the pipeline object to be executed.
>
> ***sourcetransaction***—The name of the Source transaction object.
>
> ***destinationtransaction***—The name of the Destination transaction object.
>
> ***errordatawindow***—The DataWindow control containing the pipeline Error DataWindow.
>
> ***argn***(optional)—Retrieval arguments defined in the Select painter.

The **Start( )** function returns a 1 if successful and a -1 if an error occurs.

- **Repair( )**—Executes a defined Data Pipeline object to update the destination database with corrections contained in the pipeline's Error DataWindow. The format of the **Repair( )** function is:

```
pipelineobject.Repair (destinationtransaction)
```

where:

> ***pipelineobject***—The name of the pipeline object to be repaired.
>
> ***destinationtransaction***—The name of the Destination transaction object.

The **Repair( )** function returns a 1 if successful and a -1 if an error occurs.

- **Cancel( )**—Stops the execution of a Data Pipeline object. This function should only be called when a Data Pipeline is being executed or repaired. The format of the **Cancel( )** function is:

```
pipelineobject.Cancel ( )
```

where:

> *pipelineobject*—The name of the pipeline object to be canceled.

The **Cancel( )** function returns a 1 if successful and a -1 if an error occurs.

In conclusion, the Data Pipeline object provides a simple way of transferring data between tables in the same database or among different databases in a distributed data environment. This is a very powerful feature that may be used within the PowerBuilder development environment or within an application by using the PowerBuilder nonvisual pipeline user object. This user object type encapsulates the attributes, events, and functions necessary to dynamically transfer data among databases from a PowerBuilder application.

APPENDIX A

Creating Windows Help Files

Creating and maintaining help is a topic that is often overlooked in the design and development of PowerBuilder applications. Before starting, the developer should decide the type of help that will be provided and how the help files will be created. This appendix covers:

- Definitions
- Types of help
- Creating help with Windows SDK
- Creating help with third-party products

DEFINITIONS

Good help files include the use of popups, jumptext, and hotspots.

Popups are windows similar to PowerBuilder popup windows: When the user clicks on a word, a window with additional information about the word is displayed. Popups are usually denoted by a word that is green in color and has a single dashed underline.

Another help item is the jumptext. Jumptext allows the user to click on a word and go directly to the help topic that addresses the key word. Jumptext is usually denoted by a word that is green in color and has a single solid underline.

Hotspots are used in help in conjunction with bitmaps to denote areas of interest to the user. When the user moves the mouse over the bitmap, the pointer changes to a hand. That denotes the ability to access additional information on the area or item that has been hotspotted. A hotspot is usually denoted by a different color or symbol in the bitmap file; the hotspot can be a jumptext, a popup, or a macro. Hotspots are created using the SHED.EXE application that is included with the MS Windows SDK.

TYPES OF HELP

Through the use of the Microsoft Help compiler, developers can create help files that are either context-sensitive or application-specific. Help files can be created and used by developers during the creation of a system or by end users doing their job.

Context-sensitive Help

PowerBuilder itself is an example of context-sensitive help. PowerBuilder allows the user to highlight a keyword and press Shift-F1 to access the appropriate help file. The advantages of context-sensitive help are that it is user-friendly and screen-specific.

To create context-sensitive help, the developer must code keywords or text strings for the particular screens or functions to pass to the help engine. The help files must, in turn, be indexed on the specific keywords or phrases. Unfortunately, context-sensitive help is time-consuming to create and maintain. If the application requires help for each function or screen, however, context-sensitive help is the recommended approach. In addition, if funding allows for the required project time and maintenance, context-sensitive help is recommended. Unfortunately, most departmental and project budgets do not allow for additional time to create and maintain help systems.

On the screen shown in Figure A.1 the function **Retrieve( )** is highlighted and the corresponding context-sensitive help file is shown.

PowerBuilder first checks the highlighted word to see if there are any matching files in the USR030.HLP file. If no matches are found, the user is passed to the PowerBuilder .HLP file, where the appropriate help text is found.

Application-specific Help

Application-specific help allows a user to search for specific functionality or information about the application. Application-specific help is not quite as user-friendly as context-sensitive help, but it is much easier to create and maintain. Because application-specific help is not tied directly to particular screens and columns, it is a logical choice for projects that have a limited budget. The developer can create a set of help files that use popups or hotspots for descriptions of specific functionality in an application. An example would be to show a bitmap representation

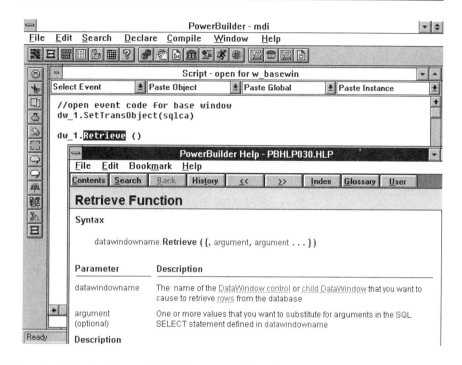

Figure A.1   The **Retrieve( )** and the context-sensitive help file.

of a screen and related columns in a help file and have hotspots that the user can click for a description of each column.

User Help

The most obvious reason to create help is to assist the end user with a PowerBuilder application. To do this, the developer should create a text file that contains the help text and a project file that contains the build information. The formats are as follows:

```
<Project Name>.RTF
<Project Name>.HPJ
```

When both of these files have been created, the Windows Help compiler is used to create the <Project Name>.HLP file. PowerBuilder allows the developer to use the PowerScript function **ShowHelp( )** to access the help file.

Developer Help

Another reason to create help files is for the use of a development team that has a number of user-defined functions or complex reusable objects. For developers to access application-specific help, the text and project files should have the following format:

```
<Function Name>.RTF
<PBUSR030>.HPJ
```

The .RTF file must have a topic index with the title of index_user_help inserted at the beginning of the first topic. When the User button in the PowerBuilder help is chosen (see Figure A.2), the help engine searches for the file PBUSR030.HLP. Next the engine searches the PBUSR030 file for the phrase index_user_help, to determine the first screen to be displayed.

CREATING HELP WITH WINDOWS SDK

One method of help file creation is to use a text editor and the Microsoft Help compiler included in the Windows SDK. To create a compiled .HLP file, the developer must first create three different types of files:

- Text
- Project
- Graphic

Text File

The text file should contain the help text. The text file is created using a text editor or word processor (e.g., Microsoft Word). The file is then saved in the .RTF (Rich Text) format. Help topics as well as the specific Windows Help Compiler context must be in the text file.

The following example shows the creation of a new help topic that

Figure A.2   The User button in PowerBuilder Help.

has a title and context string of "Contents." The first line of script defines the text color to be blue. A bitmap file, start.bmp, is included.

```
\deff0
{\colorbl
\red0\green0\blue255:}
#{\footnote Contents}
${\footnote Contents}
K{\footnote Contents}
+{\footnote Contents}
The following Help Topics are available:
Introduction
Function Reference
Process Diagrams

\{bml start.bmp\}
\par
\page
```

The first two lines of the example show the \deff statement, which specifies the color of the help text. The colors of the help file must also be defined with the \colortbl statement followed by the specific amount of each primary color to be used (red, green, and blue). The next statements, starting with \footnote, denote the beginning of a topic followed by a context string denoted by the (#) symbol, the topic title denoted by the ($) symbol, the keyword denoted by the (K), and the browse sequence denoted by the (+) symbol. Next, the text for the help file is included with the ID_ listing for the jump to the appropriate topic. Last, the \par statement is used to denote the end of the paragraph and the \page statement, to denote the end of the topic. The text file must include a specific set of commands and syntax to create the help file with the needed components. This simple example illustrates the difficulty in creating help files; the process is neither intuitive nor quick and easy. Later in this chapter, the use of third-party help tools and the simplicity they offer the developer are discussed. The complete list of help statements and syntax for the MS Help Compiler can be found in the *Microsoft Programmer's Reference Volume 4: Resources and MS Professional Tools User's Guide*.

Project File

The next step in help file creation is to create a project file that contains all of the names of the files (with extensions) for the text and graphics to be included in the help file. The project file, which is specified with the .HPJ extension, is made up of several sections that are differentiated by brackets. They are:

Section	*Description*
[OPTIONS] optional section	A section to include any build options (e.g., compress = True)
[FILES]	Specifies the text file with the topics
[BUILDTAGS] optional section	Specifies the tags for files to be built
[CONFIG]	Specifies the nonstandard menus or other features
[BITMAPS]	Specifies any bitmaps to be included
[MAP] optional section	Specifies the context strings with context numbers
[ALIAS] optional section	Assigns different context strings to the same topic name
[WINDOWS] optional only if no secondary windows	Specifies the characteristics of the primary help window
[BAGGAGE] optional only if no secondary windows	Specifies any additional files that are to be placed within the help file

The complete list of help statements and project file section descriptions is in the *Microsoft Programmer's Reference Volume 4: Resources and MS Professional Tools User's Guide*.

An example of a simple project file is:

```
[OPTIONS]
COMPRESS = TRUE
ERRORLOG = ERRORLG.TXT

[FILES]
APPLCN.RTF
```

This project file specifies that a compressed help file be created and forces the error messages to be written to a file named ERRORLG.TXT. This keeps the help file small. The help file is made up of the file APPLCN.RTF.

When the project file and text files have been created, the developer compiles the .HPJ file at the DOS command line with the Windows 3.x Help Compiler HC.EXE. File PBUSR030.HLP is generated. When the new file is copied to the PowerBuilder application directory, the user can access the application help.

Graphic File

The developer may want to include graphic files in the help file. A graphic file is included in the text file by specifying the file with the prefix of BMR or BML. The BML statement inserts the bitmap at the left margin; BMR inserts the bitmap at the right margin. The MS Windows help engine requires that the graphic file be in one of the following formats:

- Windows bitmap (.BMP)
- Multiple Resolution Bitmap (.MRB)
- Segmented Graphics Bitmap (.SGB)
- Placeable Windows Metafile (.WMF)

The graphic file can be a simple bitmap file or a hypergraphic file (usually .SGB format) that has been edited to include hotspots. The bitmap file can be edited with the MS SHED.EXE file to create the appropriate jumps, popups, or macro references to other items in the help file. When the graphic file has been created, the standard bitmap reference codes (BMC, BML, or BMR) are used to include it in the text file.

Hotspots on a hypergraphic work are like standard textual links in an RTF file. Hotspots must reference valid context strings for a help project. The Help compiler displays a warning if a hotspot references a nonexistent context string.

An example of creating a BMP file with a hotspot is shown in Figure A.3.

In this example, a bitmap called BSGLOGO.BMP is loaded into the hotspot editor. The hotspot is created by designating the appropriate area and clicking on the right mouse button. This allows the developer to place the correct ID_ context string and specify the type of jump that should be included in the file. When the file has been hotspotted, it is included in the help file creation like any other graphic file.

Creating Help with Third-party Products

Because creating help files with the Windows SDK is cumbersome, several third-party products have been introduced. Some of these products are shown in Table A.1.

Help creation tools answer a variety of needs. Some of the more advanced tools allow the creation of computer-based training (CBT) exercises that allow the user to step through a sample system or view video of the system. Other products simplify creation of MS Windows help files for inclusion with a PowerBuilder application. The majority of the help products allow the developer to create the help text using a

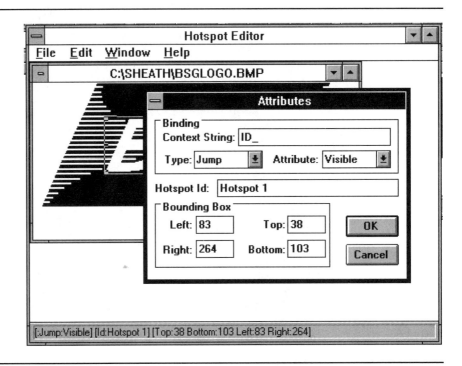

Figure A.3   Creating a .BMP tile with a hotspot.

Table A.1   Third-party Products for Creating Help Files

Name	Company	Description
Doc-to-Help	Wextec Systems Inc.	Provides the capability of creating MS Windows help for applications with the use of a word processor and the MS SDK.
Help Breeze	Solutionsoft Corporation	Provides the capability of creating MS Windows help for applications with the use of a word processor and the MS SDK. In addition, offers the capability to incorporate slide shows and animation.
Universal Help	Softronics	Provides the capability of authoring simultaneous Windows and OS/2 source files. Offers standard features (jumptext, popups, and graphics).
RoboHelp	Blue Sky	Provides the capability of creating MS Windows help for applications with MS Word and the MS SDK.
Quest	Allen Communication	Creates CBT training applications for DOS-based systems.
WinCALIS	Humanities Computing Facilities	Supports multiple languages and multimedia access. Provides lesson plan creation and a video interface.

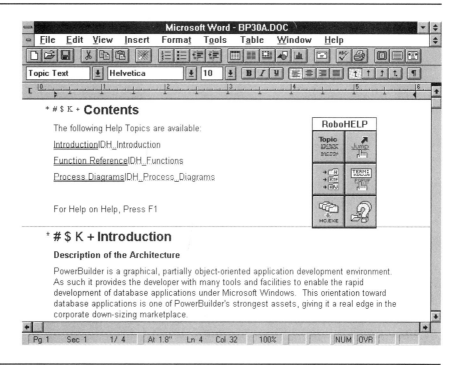

Figure A.4   Creating a text file using the windows SDK method with RoboHELP.

word processor, using a specially created template. Toolbars allow the developer to select particular features and the correct Windows SDK syntax is placed in the file for the user. This allows the developer to concentrate on creating the help files and not learning the Window SDK syntax. The authors recommend any of the third-party help creation products over using the Windows SDK method.

Take an example of a simple third-party product—RoboHelp by Blue Sky software. The templates for Robohelp are automatically loaded into Word and the application is activated when the Robohelp help template is selected. The application allows the developer to create all of the necessary files and also has a floating toolbar for the addition of topics, popups, hotspots, file creation, and for help file compilation.

The example in Figure A.4 shows creation of the same text file created earlier in this chapter using the Windows SDK method.

Robohelp works in the Word application to add the correct SDK syntax to the text file. To create jumptext, popups, or macros, the developer simply chooses the appropriate menu item or toolbar selection.

APPENDIX B

PB.INI Settings

This appendix discusses the PB.INI file, describing the different sections in the file and some of the variables within each section.

Note: The PB.INI file used by PowerBuilder is located using the INITPATH variable in the PowerBuilder section of WIN.INI. Power-Builder 4 has added the variable INITPATH040 to allow the execution of PowerBuilder 3.0 and 4.0 without having to change the value of INITPATH. If INITPATH040 does not exist in WIN.INI, PowerBuilder will use the value for INITPATH to locate PB.INI.

Like other Windows .INI files, the PB.INI file serves as a place to store all settings and preferences that pertain to the PowerBuilder environment. The format of PB.INI is the same as that of other Windows .INI files. This format looks like the following:

```
[section_name]
Variable=Value
```

While the number of sections and set of variables for each section will differ among developers, Table B.1 describes each of the default sections found in PB.INI and mentions some of the variables in each section of interest to developers. Variables new to PowerBuilder 4 are shown in bold in the Variable column, while default values are shown in bold in the description column.

[PB]

This section contains settings related to the PowerBuilder environment as a whole. Included in this section are values for fonts used in the Library painter, Application painter, and MicroHelp, settings to enable compiler warnings and database warnings, and settings for the toolbar used in the development environment.

[APPLICATION]

The Application section contains settings for a user's PowerBuilder applications, including the default application name (**AppName**), the .PBL in which the default application is stored (**AppLib**), the default .PBL where application objects will be stored (**DefLib**), and a library search path for each of the user's PowerBuilder applications. In the list of applications, each application begins with a dollar sign ($) followed by the application .PBL and name, an equal sign, and the application's

Table B.1   PB.INI Default Sections and Some Variables

Variable	Value	Description
CompilerWarnings	0/1	0 - Do not display script compiler warnings **1** - Display script compiler warnings
DatabaseWarnings	0/1	0 - Do not display database warnings **1** - Display database warnings
FontName	*fontname*	Name of font family for Application painter, Library painter, and MicroHelp text (default **MS Sans Serif**)
Layer	0/1	0 - Cascade windows as they are opened **1** - Layer windows as they are opened
PowerPanel	0/1	0 - Use PowerBar mode **1** - Use PowerPanel mode
SharedIni	*Filename*	Name of an .INI file shared among many users (located on a network drive)
ToolbarFontHeight	*n*	Height of Toolbar text (default **6**)
ToolbarFontName	*fontname*	Name of font family for Toolbar text (default **Small Fonts**)
WatchMem	0/1	**0** - Display date/time information in MicroHelp 1 - Display memory allocation information instead of date/time in MicroHelp

library search list. A sample Application section with two defined applications (Exampl40 and EmpMaint) follows.

```
[Application]
DefLib=c:\pb4\pbbook.pbl
AppLib=c:\pb4\pbexamwn.pbl
AppName=Exampl40
$c:\pb4\pbexamwn.pbl(Exampl40)=c:\pb4\pbexamwn.pbl;c:\pb4\pbexamuo
.pbl;c:\pb4\pbexammn.pbl;c:\pb4\pbexamfn.pbl;c:\pb4\pbexamdw.pbl;c:\pb
4\frontend.pbl;
$c:\pb4\drmlocal(EmpMaint)=c:\pb4\drmlocal.pbl; c:\pb4\common.pbl;
```

[WINDOW]

This section contains settings related to the Window painter, including default control names (e.g., cb_ for CommandButton controls), grid settings, and whether to show object status, as shown in Table B.2.

[MENU]

This section contains only one setting—the prefix for MenuItem names, as shown in Table B.3.

[DATABASE]

This section contains settings related to the Database painter, including the current database connection parameters, colors used for various items in the Database painter, and items related to the table list displayed by PowerBuilder (see Table B.4).

Table B.2   Window Painter Settings

Variable	Value	Description
CommandButton	String	Default prefix for new CommandButton controls (default **cb_**). Values in PB.INI for all controls
Default3D	0/1	**0** - Do not display controls in 3D by default **1** - Display controls in 3D by default
Status	0/1	**0** - Do not display Selected Object Status **1** - Display Selected Object Status window

Table B.3   Prefix for MenuItem Names

Variable	Value	Description
Prefix	String	Default prefix for new MenuItems controls (default **m_**)

Table B.4   Settings Related to Database Painter

Variable	Value	Description
AutoCommit	True/False (Note: Was 0/1 in PB 3.0)	True—Turn off normal recoverable transaction processing **False**—Normal recoverable transaction processing
AutoQuote	0/1	0—Do not automatically add quotes 1—Automatically add quotes to Where clause expressions in the Select and Query painter
Database	String	Default database name
DatabasePassword	String	Database password
DBMS	String	Default database vendor name
DBParm	String	DBMS-specific parameters
HideComments	0/1	**0**—Show table and column comments in Database painter 1—Do not show comments
LogId	String	Default database logon ID
LogPassword	String	Default database logon password
PrimaryKeyLineColor	RGB	Color of line from table to primary key icon Database painter (default **Blue**). Also varies for ForeignKeyLineColor and IndexKeyLine
Prompt	0/1	**0**—Do not prompt when connecting to database 1—Prompt user when connecting to database
ServerName	String	Default database server name
ShowRefInt	0/1	0—Do not show referential integrity (primarykey, foreign key) lines in Database painter 1—Show referential integrity lines in Database painter
StayConnected	0/1	0—Maintain database connection only until you exit the Database painter 1—Maintain database connection until you exit PowerBuilder
TableDir	0/1	0—Do not display table list when entering Database painter 1—Display table list when entering Database painter
TableListCache	Number	The amount of time that must pass before the table listing in the Database painter is refreshed

Table B.4   *(continued)*

Variable	Value	Description
TerminatorCharacter	Character	Character used to terminate an SQL statement in the DBA painter
UserID	String	Database user ID
Vendors	String	Comma-separated list of database vendors, beginning with the default vendor name

[DATAWINDOW]

This section contains settings related to DataWindow painter, including default data sources and presentation styles, default values for the color and border style of new columns and text for each presentation style (see Table B.5).

Table B.5   Settings Related to DataWindow Painter

Variable	Value	Description
DefaultFileOrLib	0/1/2	**0**—Display only .PSR files from the current .PBL **1**—Display only .PSR files from the current directory **2**—Display .PSR files from the current .PBL and the current directory
Preview_RetainData	0/1	**0**—Do not retain data (retrieve data for each preview) **1**—Keep data in temporary file between design and preview toggles (do not retrieve data for each preview)
PreviewOnNew	0/1	**0**—Go to the DataWindow painter after selecting a data source **1**—Preview a new DataWindow immediately after selecting a data source
PreviewRetrieve	0/1	**0**—Do not automatically retrieve data when previewing (user must initiate retrieval) **1**—Retrieve data automatically when previewing

Table B.5   (*continued*)

Variable	Value	Description
PrintOnNew	Yes/No	**Yes**—Preview DataWindow after creation No—Do not preview DataWindow after creation
PrintPreviewZoom	Number	Zoom percentage for the print preview window (default 100)
Status	0/1	**0**—Do not display Selected Object Status window 1—Display Selected Object Status window
stored_procedure_build	0/1	0—Prompt user to build result set 1—Use stored procedure to build result set

[LIBRARY]

This section contains settings related to the Library painter, including the display characteristics of objects in the Library painter, object reporting parameters, and objects to include when using the object browser (see Table B.6).

Table B.6   Settings Related to the Library Painter

Variable	Value	Description
DisplayComments	0/1	0—Do not display library or library entry comments 1—Display library and library entry comments
DisplayDates	0/1	0—Do not display the last modification date library entries 1—Display the last modification date for library entries
IncludeApplications	0/1	0—Do not include application objects when browsing 1—Include application objects when browsing (Note: a variable exists for all object types)
SaveBackupsOnOptimize	0/1	0—Do not create backup .PBL before optimizing 1—Create backup .PBL before optimizing

Table B.6 (*continued*)

Variable	Value	Description
SourceVendor	String	ID of source control vendor (i.e., PVCS)
UserID	String	ID used for check-in/check-out
WindowAttributes	0/1	0—Do not include window attributes in developer reports **1**—Include window attributes in developer reports (Note: MenuAttributes does the same for menus)
WindowPicture	0/1	0—Do not include window images in developer reports **1**—Include window images in developer reports

[DEBUG]

This section contains settings related to the PowerBuilder Debugger, including settings to display the Variable and Watch windows and the list of stops (see Table B.7).

[SQL PAINTER]

This section contains settings related to the SQL painter, including whether to show table and column comments as well as which tab item is enabled in the SQL Toolbox.

Table B.7 Settings Related to the PowerBuilder Debugger

Variable	Value	Description
VariablesWindow	0/1	**0**—Do not show the Variables window 1—Show the Variables window
WatchWindow	0/1	**0**—Do not show the Watch window 1—Show the Watch window
Stop*n*	Parm List	One line describing each stop defined to the debugger. Each line contains the state (enabled/disabled), object name, control name, event name, and line number within the script (e.g., e,w_m_employee,cb_update, clicked,4)

Table B.8	Settings Related to the Script Painter	
Variable	*Value*	*Description*
FontName	*fontname*	Name of the font family used in the Power painter, DBA notepad, and File Editor (default **System**)
TabWidth	Number	Number of spaces between tab stops (default 3)

[SCRIPT]

This section contains settings related to the Script painter, including the DBA notepad and the File Editor (see Table B.8).

[DBMS_PROFILES]

This section contains a listing of all defined database profiles and two variables: *Current*, which stores the current profile name, and *Profiles*, which lists all defined profiles. A sample DBMS_PROFILES section is:

```
[DBMS_PROFILES]
CURRENT=Powersoft Demo DB
PROFILES='Powersoft Demo DB', 'SQL Server DB1', 'MDI - CONTACTDB'
```

For each defined profile, a section containing connection information will exist in PB.INI. For example, for the profile 'Powersoft Demo DB' previously defined, the following section will exist in PB.INI:

```
[Profile Powersoft Demo DB]
DBMS=ODBC
Database=Powersoft Demo DB
UserId=dba
DatabasePassword=
LogPassword=
ServerName=
LogId=
Lock=
DbParm=ConnectString='DSN=Powersoft Demo DB;UID=dba;PWD=sql'
Prompt=0
```

This appendix has defined each major section of the PB.INI file and described some of the variables in each section that are of interest to developers.

APPENDIX C

PowerBuilder Development Environment Library Description

This appendix provides a brief description of the DLLs that make up the PowerBuilder Enterprise Edition Development Environment.

DLL File	Description
CPALLETE	Windows Control Pallete custom control DLL
EWAPI100	English Wizard API version
PBAPL040	PowerBuilder Application painter
PBBGR040	PowerBuilder Business Graphics DLL
PBCMP040	PowerBuilder Compiler
PBCTL040	PowerBuilder Custom controls
PBDBI040	DB Interface DLL
PBDEC040	DECIMAL DLL
PBDPP040	PowerBuilder Data Pipeline painter
PBDTP040	PowerBuilder Database painter
PBDTS040	PowerBuilder Painters' shared routines
PBDWD040	PowerBuilder Drawing routines
PBDWE040	PowerBuilder DataWindow routines
PBDWP040	Powersoft DataWindow painter

PBDWT040	Powersoft DataWindow painter for test
PBECT040	PowerBuilder SUPER Edit
PBFRM040	PowerBuilder Form painter
PBGEN040	A PowerBuilder Linked List Library used to store the generated application modules
PBIDBF40	DataWindow Import DBASE II and III file
PBITXT04	DataWindow Import Text file
PBLBM040.DLL	PowerBuilder 4 LBMS interface
PBLIB040	PowerBuilder Library painter
PBLMI040	PowerBuilder Library Manager
PBMNU040	PowerBuilder Menu painter
PBNDV040	PowerBuilder Endeavor interface
PBODB040	ODBC DLL
PBODBM40	PB Master
PBORC040	PowerBuilder Open Repository Case API
PBOUI040	PowerBuilder OLE 2.0 User interface
PBPRT040	PowerBuilder print services
PBRTE040	RUNTIME DLL
PBRTF040	PowerBuilder runtime functions
PBSCR040	PowerBuilder Script painter
PBSHR040	PowerBuilder utilities
PBSQL040	PowerBuilder SQL painter
PBSTR040	PowerBuilder Structure painter
PBSYS040	PowerBuilder Main DLL
PBTAB040	PowerBuilder Tab control
PBTRA040	TRACE DLL
PBTYP040	Partially encrypted, export file, source code for some PowerBuilder, dialog boxes and painters
PBUDO040	PowerBuilder UDO painter
PBVBX040	PowerBuilder VBX Support DLL
PBWIN040	PowerBuilder Window painter

Note: If you aren't a geek, skip the rest of this appendix. A couple of PowerBuilder's DLLs are not really DLLs. They are stored in a similar structure (linked list) as the PowerBuilder library (PBL). The two DLLs are PBTYP040.DLL and PBGEN040.DLL. The PBGEN040.DLL file includes the source code for the application generation objects. The authors guess that the PBTYP040.DLL includes the source code for portions of PowerBuilder itself. Yes, we think that parts of PowerBuilder were written in PowerScript. Powersoft has stored most of the source code in an encrypted format, but towards the end of the file some source code exists for 10 windows and 6 menus. Figure C.1 is an example of some of the PowerBuilder modules and the associated exported PowerScript.

```
forward
global type w_pbstyle_zoom from Window
end type
type cb_cancel from commandbutton within w_pbstyle_zoom
end type
type cb_ok from commandbutton within w_pbstyle_zoom
end type
type st_1 from statictext within w_pbstyle_zoom
end type
type sle_custom from singlelineedit within w_pbstyle_zoom
end type
type rb_custom from radiobutton within w_pbstyle_zoom
end type
type rb_25 from radiobutton within w_pbstyle_zoom
end type
type rb_75 from radiobutton within w_pbstyle_zoom
```

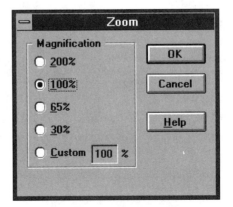

Figure C.1   Some PowerBuilder modules and associated exported PowerScript.

```
end type
type rb_100 from radiobutton within w_pbstyle_zoom
end type
type rb_200 from radiobutton within w_pbstyle_zoom
end type
type gb_1 from groupbox within w_pbstyle_zoom
end type
end forward

global type w_pbstyle_zoom from Window
int X=860
int Y=337
int Width=1212
int Height=801
boolean TitleBar=true
string Title="Zoom"
long BackColor=12632256
boolean ControlMenu=true
boolean Resizable=true
WindowType WindowType=response!
cb_cancel cb_cancel
cb_ok cb_ok
st_1 st_1
sle_custom sle_custom
rb_custom rb_custom
rb_25 rb_25
rb_75 rb_75
rb_100 rb_100
rb_200 rb_200
gb_1 gb_1
end type
global w_pbstyle_zoom w_pbstyle_zoom

on w_pbstyle_zoom.create
this.cb_cancel=create cb_cancel
this.cb_ok=create cb_ok
this.st_1=create st_1
this.sle_custom=create sle_custom
this.rb_custom=create rb_custom
this.rb_25=create rb_25
this.rb_75=create rb_75
this.rb_100=create rb_100
this.rb_200=create rb_200
this.gb_1=create gb_1
this.Control[]={ this.cb_cancel,&this.cb_ok,&
this.st_1,&
this.sle custom.&
```

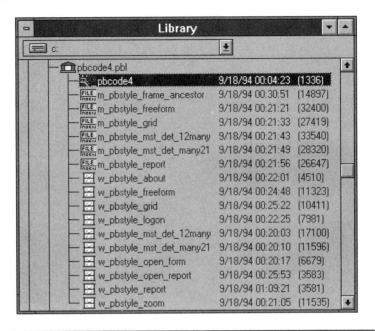

Figure C.2 Objects imported into PowerBuilder.

The previous source code, in addition to others, was retrieved from PBTYPE040.DLL.

The objects in Figure C.2 have been extracted from the PBTYP040.DLL and imported into PowerBuilder. The rest of the file was encrypted and could not be extracted.

Tools and Utilities

This appendix briefly discusses some tools and utilities available with this book. The executables are located on the attached diskette. In the case of the tab-folder class libraries, the PowerBuilder libraries will be available with the diskette. What follows is a description of each of these tools and utilities:

- DLLViewer—PBEXEHDR.EXE
- BMPViewer—BMPVIEWR.EXE, BMPVIEWR.PBL
- ASCIIUtil—ASCIIUTIL.EXE
- Tab-folder controls
- DLL function calls

Everything needed to run these tools and utilities is included on the diskette.

Although not discussed in this chapter, the diskette also contains the following:

ORCA source code for import/export (ORCA.C)

.INI File Update Utility (INICHG.EXE)

Application Loading Utility (DROPIT.EXE)

File Find Utility (PATHSCAN.EXE)

For more information on all of the tools and utilities provided on the diskette, refer to the README.TXT file located in the root directory of the diskette. Also, help documents can be found in the HELP directory on the diskette.

DLLVIEWER

This utility is used to view header information on files, specifically DLL files. This utility is basically a GUI interface to the MS Windows Exehdr program. The following functionality related to a DLL file is available:

- DLL file can be viewed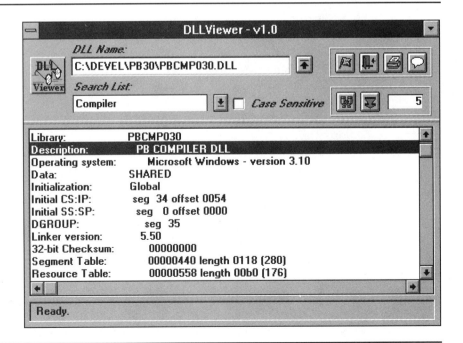
- DLL file can be printed
- Searches can be done on specific items in the DLL file and the user can scroll to each found item

The DLLViewer interface looks like Figure D.1.

BMPVIEWER

The BMPViewer utility is used to view bitmap files. The left portion of the screen allows the user to navigate through the directory structure to look for BMP files; the right side of the window displays the bitmap.

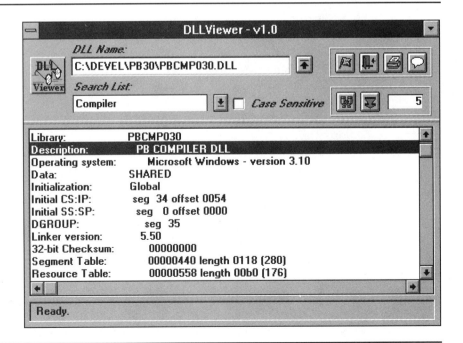

Figure D.1   The DLLViewer interface.

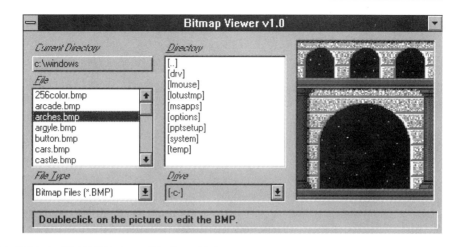

Figure D.2   The BMPViewer utility user interface.

To edit a BMP file, the user double-clicks on the picture and the program executes PaintBrush, displaying the selected bitmap for editing. Figure D.2 shows the BMPViewer utility user interface.

ASCIIUTIL

ASCIIUtil converts ASCII characters to Character and vice versa. The user interface looks like Figure D.3.

Figure D.3   The ASCII Utility user interface.

POWERBUILDER TAB-FOLDER CLASS LIBRARY

Overview

This section discusses the details of a tab-folder class library. A tab-folder class library can be used across multiple windows or even applications. A tab-folder class library should provide not only the standard single-tier tab functionality, but also some additional features. What follows is a discussion of some of the features of a tab-folder class library.

Features

The tab-folder class library in this section has many different features. Before listing some of its features, it is important to note that PowerBuilder's implementation of some of the more popular object-oriented concepts were taken advantage of when developing this library. Some of the object-oriented concepts are polymorphism, inheritance, data-hiding, and encapsulation. Some of the tab-folder specific features include:

- **Detail sheet management**—This tab-folder library manages its sheets or the grouping of controls associated with a tab as a user object. This way the detail controls do not have to all be placed on the window when it is first opened. When the window is opened, the default sheet is opened dynamically at runtime; as each additional tab is selected, the detail sheet associated with the tab is opened, again dynamically at runtime. If a user clicks on a previous tab, then the detail sheet is given focus. In order to prevent many detail sheets to be opened and kept open at the same time, an initialization file option is provided. This option allows the developer to select the maximum number of open sheets per individual window. Once this number is selected, as any additional sheets beyond the specified number are opened, the first sheet is closed based on a FIFO (first in, first out) basis.
- **Dynamic sheet instantiation**—When a tab is selected, a predefined sheet is opened dynamically, at runtime. This is an option within the tab-folder architecture discussed in this section. The other option is to have a group of controls on a window that are associated with a tab and are shown or hidden as a tab is selected.
- **Resource management**—This option is integrated within the sheet management functionality of the tab-folder libraries. When a sheet is opened, the system resources are checked against the predefined system resource allowance; if enough resources are available, the sheet is opened.

- **Single- and multiple-tier management**—This provides the functionality of having multiple tiers of tabs within a window.
- **Keyboard functionality**—Keyboard functionality is built into the tab-folder libraries.
- **Smart Commit**—This option permits the management of transactions across tabs.

Overall Architecture

The overall architecture (see Figure D.4) consists of a single picture and MultiLineEdit user object, a custom user object, a user object ancestor for the controls, a window ancestor, and a 3-D container. On the attached diskette the following PBLs are included:

BSGApp.PBL—Contains the application object

BSGTab.PBL—Contains the tab class objects

BSGLocal.PBL—Contains a sample application

PowerBuilder Modules

Figure D.5 shows the contents of the BSGTab.PBL.
Following is an explanation of each of the objects in the BSGTab.PBL.

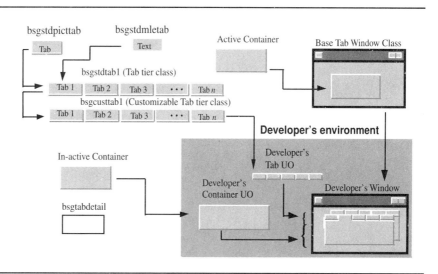

Figure D.4   Overall architect use of Tab-folder class library.

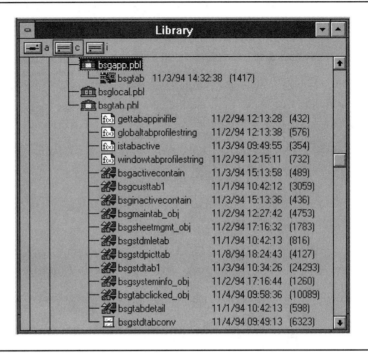

Figure D.5   The contents of the BSGTab.PBL.

gettabappinifile—Returns the application initialization file.

windowtabprofilestring—Returns tab data from the window initialization file.

globaltabprofilestring—Returns tab data from the global initialization file.

istabactive—Returns True if the window is a tab-folder window and False if it's not.

bsgactivecontain—This is the 3-D picture object for the active container.

bsginactivecontain—This is the 3-D picture object for the inactive container.

bsgtabdetail—This is the base sheet user object ancestor. This is the ancestor user object from which the user object containing the controls associated with a tab will be inherited.

bsgstdmletab—This is a standard MultiLineEdit user object. This user object is used to display text for the tabs.

bsgstdpicttab—This is a standard picture user object. This user object is used to display the 3-D look (BMP or RLE) of a single tab.

bsgcustpicttab—This is the inherited custom layer for the bsgstdpicttab control. Enhancements to the tab can be made at this layer.

bsgstdtab1—This is a custom user object. This user object will contain a single tier of tabs. It will include bsgcustpicttabs and bsgstdmletabs.

bsgcusttab1—This is the inherited custom layer for the bsgstdtab1 control. Enhancements to the tier can be made at this layer.

bsgmaintab_obj—This custom class (nonvisual) object maintains the tab configuration structure and all its methods. This object must be instantiated at the bsgstdconv window level.

bsgsheetmgmt_obj—This custom class (nonvisual) object contains the methods for sheet management. Sheet management includes, among other things, the opening, closing, and displaying of controls associated with a tab. This object must be instantiated at the bsgstdconv window level.

bsgsysteminfo_obj—This custom class (nonvisual) user object includes the methods for accessing the system resource data. Based on a comparison of the current system resources and those specified for a window the architecture can determine if enough resources are available to open a sheet. This object must be instantiated at the bsgstdconv window level.

bsgtabclicked_obj—This custom class (nonvisual) object contains all the multi-tier functionality. This object must be instantiated at the bsgstdconv window level.

bsgstdtabconv—This is the base window that contains some functions and the instantiated objects for tab processing.

bsgcusttabconv—This is the customizable window layer. This is the window from which all the application windows can be inherited. If the developer would like to add the tab-folder functionality to another window and ignore the bsgstdtabconv and the bsgcusttabconv windows, all he or she has to do is instantiate the nonvisual user objects at the new window ancestor and create the few functions that are in bsgstdtabconv.

DLL FUNCTION CALLS

This section briefly discusses the DLL functions in the PBTools.DLL Windows dynamic library available with this book. These DLL functions are as follows.

Rename

The following function renames a DOS file: **<u>C DLL Function</u>**

```
int FAR PASCAL Rename(const char *oldname, const char *newname)
```

The PowerBuilder Declaration is:

```
FUNCTION int Rename(string sOldName, string sNewName) Library
"PBTools.DLL"
```

DelFile

The following function deletes a DOS file, even if the file is a read-only file: **<u>C DLL Function</u>**

```
int FAR PASCAL DelFile(const char *fname)
```

The PowerBuilder Declaration is:

```
FUNCTION int DelFile(string sFileName) Library "PBTools.DLL"
```

ChangeDir

The following function changes the current directory to *sDirName*: **<u>C DLL Function</u>**

```
int FAR PASCAL ChangeDir(const char *dirname)
```

The PowerBuilder Declaration is:

```
FUNCTION int ChangeDir(string sDirName) Library "PBTools.DLL"
```

MakeDir

The following function creates a directory called *sDirName*: **<u>C DLL Function</u>**

```
int FAR PASCAL MakeDir(const char *dirname)
```

The PowerBuilder Declaration is:

```
FUNCTION int MakeDir(string sDirName) Library "PBTools.DLL"
```

RemoveDir

The following function removes the directory called *sDirName*: **C DLL Function**

```
int FAR PASCAL RemoveDir(const char *dirname)
```

The PowerBuilder Declaration is:

```
FUNCTION int RemoveDir(string sDirName) Library "PBTools.DLL"
```

PBGetEnv

The following function returns the value of the *sEnvName* environment variable: **C DLL Function**

```
LPSTR FAR PASCAL PBGetEnv(LPSTR envvar)
```

The PowerBuilder Declaration is:

```
FUNCTION string PBGetEnv(string sEnvName) Library "PBTools.DLL"
```

PBGetEnvVar

The following function returns a tab-delimited string of all the environment variables: **C DLL Function**

```
LPSTR FAR PASCAL PBGetEnvVar(void)
```

The PowerBuilder Declaration is:

```
FUNCTION string PBGetEnvVar( ) Library "PBTools.DLL"
```

GetCurrDrive

The following function returns the current drive: **C DLL Function**

```
LPSTR FAR PASCAL GetCurrDrive(void)
```

The PowerBuilder Declaration is:

```
FUNCTION String GetCurrDrive( ) Library "PBTools.DLL"
```

PowerBuilder Inheritance and Performance

The following was taken from a white paper written by Eric Reed of BSG. Eric is a Technical Director at BSG who has been working with PowerBuilder since its introduction in 1991 and has extensive experience in the development of client/server application architectures, including BSG's BluePrint Object Development Environment (ODE) for PowerBuilder.

Unfortunately, the topic of inheritance and performance is too often discussed *after* an application has been developed. The proper time to discuss inheritance implications is during the design phase of a development project.

Inheritance in its pure form is indeed a powerful tool in building applications. However, there is a performance implication to consider when using the object-oriented features of PowerBuilder. This section attempts to dispel any misconceptions that are currently held about inheritance and its effect on system performance.

THE MYTH

Inheritance has its benefits, but performance suffers terribly and is, therefore, not worth it (also known as: somebody said you should never have more than three levels in an inheritance tree).

THE REALITY

Inheritance has major benefits, and, in a system of any size, an intelligent inheritance hierarchy can actually *improve* performance as well as the memory efficiency of an application system. It is the authors' opinion that any limiting of inheritance to an arbitrary number of levels is founded on a misunderstanding of the real-world application of this powerful concept.

Okay, you say. That sounds interesting, but why is the general public's perception that of the myth, and how do we prove the reality? Well, read on...

THE TEST CASE (THAT SUPPORTS THE MYTH)

The first thing that someone confronted with this question usually does is produce a quick case to test the inheritance vs. performance theory. That seems easy, so they usually create a couple of windows with inheritance characteristics similar to those in Figure E.1.

WinF1 and WinI1 are functionally equivalent (the exact functionality is irrelevant to this test, as the windows' performance will be measured relative to one another). The only difference between the two windows is the use of inheritance. WinF1 is a flat implementation — no inheritance is used. WinI1 is the same functional window, but inherited from one or two (or how ever many) ancestors. The visual components and functionality of

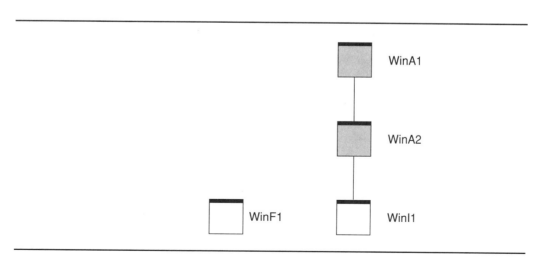

Figure E.1   Created windows with inheritance characteristics.

WinI1 are distributed throughout the ancestors and WinI1 itself, so that the tester can get a feel for a "real" inheritance situation.

Now, the tester, stopwatch in hand, opens the two windows in an application. WinF1 opens in 4 seconds, and... whoa, WinI1 takes 6 seconds to open! The actual times here are arbitrary. What is important is that the tester sees that the exact same window (functionally, that is) takes longer to open if it is inherited than it does if it is not.

The tester thinks, "Inheritance carries a major performance price. Maybe it's not worth it."

Hmmm....tough to argue with, and, in fact, in this case, inheritance has cost a price in performance. However, **this case is _not_ representative of an inheritance hierarchy in a real application system**. But, before we get into that, let's take a look at why this case behaved this way.

Here are the steps (more or less) that PowerBuilder went through to open these two test windows:

WinF1	*WinI1*
- open is issued on WinF1	- open is issued on WinI1
- PB searches libraries for object WinF1	- PB searches libraries for object WinI1
- PB sees that WinF1 is not inherited	- PB sees that WinI1 is inherited from WinA2
- PB loads object WinF1	- PB searches libraries for object WinA2
- PB searches for and loads objects within WinF1	- PB sees that WinA2 is inherited from WinA1
- PB executes the WinF1 open event	- PB searches libraries for object WinA1
- PB displays WinF1	- PB loads object WinA1
	- PB searches for and loads objects within WinA1
	- PB loads object WinA2
	- PB searches for and loads objects within WinA2
	- PB loads object WinI1
	- PB searches for and loads objects within WinI1
	- PB executes the WinI1 open event
	- PB displays WinI1

Okay, no wonder. PowerBuilder has to search for and load more objects in the inherited window. This is, obviously, going to take more time. Notice, however, that it won't take three times as long to open WinI1 even though it looks like PowerBuilder has to do three times the work. This is because the total size of WinI1, WinA2, and WinA1 together is equal to the size of WinF1. That is, if WinF1 were 50k in size, the size of WinI1 plus the size of WinA2 plus the size of WinA1 would also equal 50k (or be extremely close to it). So, the amount of information being loaded when we open the two windows is roughly equivalent. It is just coming from three different places when we load WinI1. Therefore, the actual load time of the objects is roughly equivalent. The difference when loading WinI1 is the search and load time on the two additional windows. Still, it does take longer to load WinI1. So the tester thinks "maybe inheritance *isn't* worth" it ....let's stop right there.

Let's say, just for the sake of argument, that this case *were* representative of a real-world implementation (which it is not). Saying that inheritance "is not worth it" implies a cost/benefit decision. However, all our test case shows is the cost. It does not deal with the benefits of inheritance, which are found in development and, more important, maintenance of applications. It is very possible (we would even say probable) that the performance costs experienced in the above example might be significantly outweighed by the benefits of faster delivery, higher quality, and easier maintainability of the system. If you discarded the use of inheritance based on the above test, the next logical step would be to discard PowerBuilder as well. After all, the system will run much faster if we code the whole thing in C. But, why stop there, let's code it in Assembler; then it'll really scream...

Of course, this is ridiculous. People choose PowerBuilder because they feel that the benefits of the tool (the ability to develop a real system in less than a year) outweigh the cost (i.e., slower execution than the same program written in C or Assembler). The point here is that the attainment of sheer maximum performance cannot be the only criterion by which we measure the choice of implementation approach.

But, as we said earlier, this test case is flawed. It does not represent the use of inheritance in a real application system. And the performance costs are not as great as this test would indicate. In fact, there might even be some situations in which inheritance *improves* system performance.

THE ACTUAL CASE (THAT PROVES REALITY)

The flaw in the above test case is that the inheritance tree is not a tree at all. It's a log. It has no branches; it's just a straight-line inheritance structure. If, in fact, this was the way inheritance were used, there would be no benefit to it. With only one window inheriting from both WinA1 and WinA2, there is no leverage of reusable code, no development benefits, and no maintenance benefits.

In an actual application system, an inheritance hierarchy would look more like that in Figure E.2.

The shaded windows are virtual classes. In other words, they are not windows in the application system at all; they are architectural components that implement common functionality for a particular class of window. In this example, we have several virtual classes, from StdWin (a common ancestor for all windows in our system) all the way down to specific process models like SList (a single list style window) and MDEdit (a master/detail style window), and so on.

The nonshaded windows are the actual windows in the application system. In this example, we have three normal windows, Prod (Product Maintenance), Order (Order Maintenance), and Cust (Customer Maintenance). Actually, that's a pretty trivial system, but, it is good enough to prove our point.

As you can see, this tree *is* a tree (well, an upside-down tree). It has a number of branches and the leaves, the actual application system windows, share some set of common ancestors. This is where the benefits of inheritance come into play. All things common to all windows are defined in StdWin. They only have to be defined (and tested) once

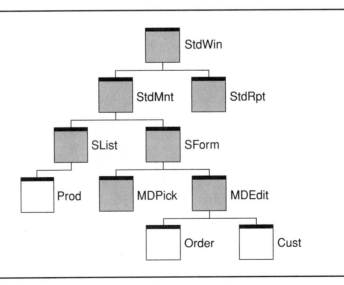

Figure E.2   An inheritance hierarchy in an actual application system.

and, if they must change, they can be changed once. The benefits of inheritance are realized — higher productivity, higher quality and consistency, and reduced testing and maintenance. Each subsequent virtual class implements functionality that is common to a more and more specific class of window.

In other words, the most generic functionality is at the root of the tree. As you go down the branches, the functionality defined in the virtual classes gets more and more specific to a particular class of window, until, finally, the most specific functionality (the business logic) is in the leaves — the actual application system windows. An important point that may be overlooked here is that *only* the specific logic is within these "leaf" windows. They do not have to replicate code or attributes that are common to one of the defined classes of windows. All of this is inherited. This makes our application system windows much smaller and simpler than they would be without the inheritance hierarchy.

Now, let's implement our test case with this real-world inheritance tree. Let's take the Order Maintenance window (Order) and compare it to one developed without the benefit of inheritance (Order2). The inheritance characteristics of the two windows would look like Figure E.3.

Again, Order and Order2 are functionally equivalent, and, their exact functionality is irrelevant to this test because they will be measured relative to one another. The only difference between them is the

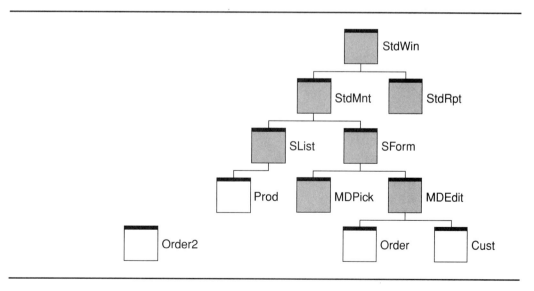

Figure E.3   Comparison of inheritance characteristics of two windows.

use of inheritance (or lack thereof). Order inherits attributes and functionality from several ancestors that define these features as they apply to general classes of windows; Order2 contains all the same attributes and functionality as Order, but completely within itself.

Now if we rerun the test, the results will be similar. Order2 will open a bit faster than Order because of the extra work PowerBuilder performs to locate and load the additional windows. The actual steps aren't important, but it is clear that they are similar to the ones in the first test case. For the sake of simplicity, let's say that it took 8 seconds to open Order2 and 10 seconds to open Order. So, "where's the beef?" you say. Well, we're only dealing with a single window here. Real systems have more than one window, and Windows is a graphical, *windowing* environment. Systems properly designed for this environment are meant to have multiple windows open at once. This capability promotes fast task switching for the user and GUI functionality like drag and drop between different portions of the system.

Now let's add a noninherited version of the Customer Maintenance window (Cust2) to our picture as shown in Figure E.4.

Now, let's rerun the first part of our test — open Order2 and Order. They take 8 and 10 seconds, respectively (as they did before). And, simulating a user working with multiple windows in a large system, let's open Cust2 as well. It also takes 8 seconds to open (for simplicity, assume the

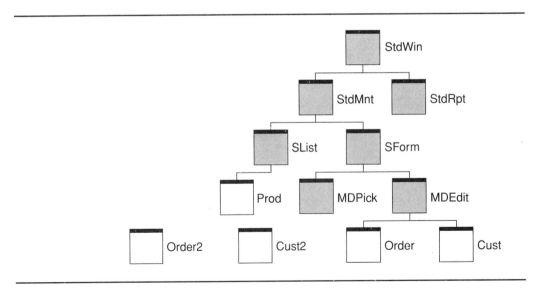

Figure E.4   The addition of the Customer Maintenance window.

Cust windows are exactly the same size as the Order windows). Finally, open Cust. Whoa...it opens in 3 seconds! Significantly *faster* than the noninherited version of the same window. How can this be?

We just saw how it takes longer to search for and load inherited windows than noninherited ones. Well, let's take a look at the steps PowerBuilder goes through to open Cust and Cust2 after Order and Order2 are already open:

Cust2	*Cust*
- open is issued on Cust2	- open is issued on Cust
- PB searches libraries for object Cust2	- PB searches libraries for object Cust
- PB see that Cust2 is not inherited	- PB sees that Cust is inherited from MDEdit and it is already in memory (because Order is loaded)
- PB loads object Cust2	- PB loads object Cust
- PB searches for and loads objects within Cust2	- PB searches for and loads objects within Cust
- PB executes the Cust2 open event	- PB executes the Cust open event
- PB displays Cust2	- PB displays Cust

So now the steps in the process are roughly equivalent for the two windows because all of the ancestor windows were already loaded in memory (they were loaded when we opened Order). So, if the number of steps were roughly equivalent, why did Cust open so much faster than Cust2? Remember that the size of Cust2 is roughly equivalent to the sum of the sizes of Cust and all of its ancestors. And remember that Cust contains *only* the logic specific to it. Therefore, while Cust2 is still 100k in size, Cust is only about 20k in size (again these numbers are for comparison purposes only). So, opening Cust2 involved loading 100k but opening Cust involves loading just 20k. The other 80k is already in memory, because it is shared with Order.

This leads to the heart of the performance-related advantages of inheritance. Because Order and Cust actually physically *share* about 80% of their content, this model is much more memory-efficient than the flat model of Order2 and Cust2. When both Order2 and Cust2 are loaded in an application, they take up 200k of memory. However, when both Order and Cust are loaded in an application, they take only 120k of memory. This too can impact performance, because when Windows runs out of physical memory, it begins to swap to the hard disk, which is significantly slower than doing just about anything in memory. The inheritance model makes more efficient use of physical memory and allows the user to load a lot more windows before swapping, when major performance degradation begins.

Now, consider the impact in a more representative system — one with more than two windows. Opening another window with common ancestors, only loads that which is different and not already in memory. If there were another MDEdit type window in our system, and we opened it as well, all three would take 140k of memory. Compare this to the flat implementation in which three similar windows would occupy 300k of memory. The larger the system, the more significant the memory efficiency becomes.

THE REAL WORLD

BSG Consulting's BluePrint Object Development Environment can be used as a further, and even more applicable, real-world example. BluePrint implements several class hierarchies similar to the example above for windows, datawindows, and other objects. This structure has proven to be invaluable in a great many application systems built for many companies. It has provided a common framework for systems in these companies and has allowed very fast reaction to changes in PowerBuilder internals between maintenance releases.

Some of these companies, upon having performance problems with their systems, have attempted to determine if BluePrint, or its use of inheritance, was adversely affecting the performance of their systems. One site went to the effort to cut the number of levels of inheritance in half (from 6-8 down to 3-4 levels). No perceptible benefit in performance was achieved as a result of this effort. However, a great deal of benefit in system maintenance was lost. This company has since re-instated all levels of inheritance in their system.

The authors feel that this test has not only proven that the impact of inheritance on performance in large systems may be negligible, but also that the increased memory efficiency may actually improve performance in most cases. Powersoft has stated that PowerBuilder 2.0 contains a bug that makes inherited windows take longer to open than they should. The fact that removing up to three or four levels of inheritance did not increase performance perceptibly, further proves that the benefits of inheritance far outweigh the costs. Powersoft has fixed this bug, as well as made other general performance improvements, in their soon to be released 3.0 version.

Very large, complex systems (those with hundreds or thousands of windows, many of which are large and complex) built with PowerBuilder using inheritance may be slow. Based on the data presented here and the results of real world efforts to eliminate inheritance like the one above, however, the authors have concluded that this has more to do with the fact that a system is large and complex than it does with inheritance. Based on the facts presented here, complex systems built without the benefit of an inheritance environment like BluePrint would certainly take much more memory and performance would be worse.

MORAL

We've seen how inheritance, when used properly in a real-world application system will probably have a positive impact on performance. And, overall, the memory efficiency of the system is greatly improved. This, in turn, increases performance even more.

In short, this performance and memory efficiency, together with the far-reaching development and maintenance benefits of inheritance, more than justify the proper implementation of this very powerful object-oriented concept.

Suggested
Additional Readings

Books/Manuals:

All Power Builder 3.0 documentation (Powersoft Corporation)

Informix-OnLine Database Server Administrator's Guide (version 5.0) - Informix Software, Inc. Copyright 1981–1991

Microsoft SQL Server for Windows NT Administrator's Guide (copyright 1992–1993 Microsoft Corporation)

Oracle7 Server Concepts Manual - Oracle Corporation

Oracle7 Server Administrator's Guide - Oracle Corporation

PowerBuilder Advanced DataWindow course material (Powersoft Corporation)

White Papers:

Microsoft SQL Server for Windows NT: An Overview of Technical Enhancements - Microsoft Corporation (Copyright 1993 Microsoft Corporation)

Index